AFRICAN HISTORICAL DICTIONARIES
Edited by Jon Woronoff

1. *Cameroon,* by Victor T. LeVine and Roger P. Nye. 1974. *Out of print. See No. 48.*
2. *The Congo,* 2nd ed., by Virginia Thompson and Richard Adloff. 1984. *Out of print. See No. 69.*
3. *Swaziland,* by John J. Grotpeter. 1975.
4. *The Gambia,* 2nd ed., by Harry A. Galley. 1987.
5. *Botswana,* by Richard P. Stevens. 1975. *Out of print. See No. 70.*
6. *Somalia,* by Margaret F. Castagno. 1975.
7. *Benin (Dahomey),* 2nd ed., by Samuel Decalo. 1987. *Out of print. See No. 61.*
8. *Burundi,* by Warren Weinstein. 1976. *Out of print. See No. 73.*
9. *Togo,* 3rd ed., by Samuel Decalo. 1996.
10. *Lesotho,* by Gordon Haliburton. 1977.
11. *Mall,* 3rd ed., by Pascal James Imperato. 1996.
12. *Sierra Leone,* by Cyril Patrick Foray. 1977.
13. *Chad,* 3rd ed., by Samuel Decalo. 1997.
14. *Upper Volta,* by Daniel Miles McFarland. 1978.
15. *Tanzania,* by Laura S. Kurtz. 1978.
16. *Guinea,* 3rd ed., by Thomas O'Toole with Ibrahima Bah-Lalya. 1995.
17. *Sudan,* by John Voll. 1978. *Out of print. See No. 53.*
18. *Rhodesia/Zimbabwe,* by R. Kent Rasmussen. 1979. *Out of print See No. 46.*
19. *Zambia,* 2nd ed., by John J. Grotpeter, Brian V. Siegel, and James R. Fletcher. 1998.
20. *Niger,* 3rd ed., by Samuel Decalo. 1997.
21. *Equatorial Guinea,* 3rd ed., by Max Liniger-Goumaz. 1999.
22. *Guinea-Bissau,* 3rd ed., by Richard Lobban and Peter Mendy. 1996.
23. *Senegal,* by Lucie G. Colvin. 1981. *Out of print. See No.* 65.
24. *Morocco,* by William Spencer. 1980. *Out of print. See No. 71.*
25. *Malawi,* by Cynthia A. Crosby. 1980. *Out of print. See No. 54.*
26. *Angola,* by Phyllis Martin. 1980. *Out of print. See No. 52.*
27. *The Central African Republic,* by Pierre Kalck. 1980. *Out of print. See No. 51.*

28. *Algeria,* by Alf Andrew Heggoy. 1981. *Out of print. See No. 66.*
29. *Kenya,* by Bethwell A. Ogot. 1981. *Out of print. See No. 77.*
30. *Gabon,* by David E. Gardinier. 1981. *Out of print. See No. 58.*
31. *Mauritania,* by Alfred G. Gerteiny. 1981. *Out of print. See No. 68.*
32. *Ethiopia,* by Chris Prouty and Eugene Rosenfeld. 1981. *Out of print. See No.* 56.
33. *Libya,* 3rd ed., by Ronald Bruce St John. 1998.
34. *Mauritius,* by Lindsay Rivire. 1982. *Out of print. See No.* 49.
35. *Western Sahara,* by Tony Hedges. 1982. *Out of print. See No. 55.*
36. *Egypt,* by Joan Wucher King. 1984. *Out of print. See No. 67.*
37. *South Africa,* by Christopher Saunders. 1983.
38. *Liberia,* by D. Elwood Dunn and Svend E. Holsoe. 1985.
39. *Ghana,* by Daniel Miles McFarland. 1985. *Out of print. See No.* 63.
40. *Nigeria,* 2nd ed., by Anthony Oyewole and John Lucas. 2000.
41. *Côte d'Ivoire (The Ivory Coast),* 2nd ed., by Robert J. Mundt. 1995.
42. *Cape Verde,* 2nd ed., by Richard Lobban and Marilyn Halter. 1988. *Out of print. See No.* 62.
43. *Zaire,* by F. Scott Bobb. 1988. *Out of print. See No. 76.*
44. *Botswana,* 2nd ed., by Fred Morton, Andrew Murray, and Jeff Ramsay. 1989. *Out of print. See No. 70.*
45. *Tunisia,* 2nd ed., by Kenneth J. Perkins. 1997
46. *Zimbabwe,* 3rd ed., by Steven C. Rubert and R. Kent Rasmussen. 1998.
47. *Mozambique,* by Mario Azevedo. 1991.
48. *Cameroon,* 2nd ed., by Mark W. DeLancey and H. Mbella Mokeba. 1990.
49. *Mauritius,* 2nd ed., by Sydney Selvon. 1991.
50. *Madagascar,* by Maureen Covell. 1995.
51. *The Central African Republic,* 2nd ed., by Pierre Kalck; translated by Thomas O'Toole. 1992.
52. *Angola,* 2nd ed., by Susan H. Broadhead. 1992.
53. *Sudan,* 2nd ed., by Carolyn Fluehr-Lobban, Richard A. Lobban, Jr., and John Obert Voll. 1992.
54. *Malawi,* 2nd ed., by Cynthia A. Crosby. 1993.
55. *Western Sahara,* 2nd ed., by Anthony Pazzanita and Tony Hedges. 1994.
56. *Ethiopia and Eritrea,* 2nd ed., by Chris Prouty and Eugene Rosenfeld. 1994.
57. *Namibia,* by John J. Grotpeter. 1994.
58. *Gabon,* 2nd ed., by David Gardinier. 1994.

59. *Comoro Islands,* by Martin Ottenheimer and Harriet Ottenheimer. 1994.
60. *Rwanda,* by Learthen Dorsey. 1994.
61. *Benin,* 3rd ed., by Samuel Decalo. 1995.
62. *Republic of Cape Verde,* 3rd ed., by Richard Lobban and Marlene Lopes. 1995.
63. *Ghana,* 2nd ed., by David Owusu-Ansah and Daniel Miles McFarland. 1995.
64. *Uganda,* by M. Louise Pirouet. 1995.
65. *Senegal,* 2nd ed., by Andrew F. Clark and Lucie Colvin Phillips. 1994.
66. *Algeria,* 2nd ed., by Phillip Chiviges Naylor and Alf Andrew Heggoy. 1994.
67. *Egypt,* 2nd ed., by Arthur Goldschmidt, Jr. 1994.
68. *Mauritania,* 2nd ed., by Anthony G. Pazzanita. 1996.
69. *Congo,* 3rd ed., by Samuel Decalo, Virginia Thompson, and Richard Adloff. 1996.
70. *Botswana,* 3rd ed., by Jeff Ramsay, Barry Morton, and Fred Morton. 1996.
71. *Morocco,* 2nd ed., by Thomas K. Park. 1996.
72. *Tanzania,* 2nd ed., by Thomas P. Ofcansky and Rodger Yeager. 1997.
73. *Burundi,* 2nd ed., by Ellen K. Eggers. 1997.
74. *Burkina Faso,* 2nd ed., by Daniel Miles McFarland and Lawrence Rupley. 1998.
75. *Eritrea,* by Tom Killion. 1998.
76. *Democratic Republic of Congo (Zaire),* by F. Scott Bobb. 1998. (Revised edition of *Historical Dictionary of Zaire,* No. 43)
77. *Kenya,* 2nd ed., by Thomas P. Ofcansky and Robert M. Maxon. 1999.

Historical Dictionary of Nigeria

Second Edition

Anthony Oyewole and John Lucas

African Historical Dictionaries, No. 40

The Scarecrow Press, Inc.
Lanham, Maryland, and London
2000

SCARECROW PRESS, INC.

Published in the United States of America
by Scarecrow Press, Inc.
4720 Boston Way
Lanham, Maryland 20706
http://www.scarecrowpress.com

4 Pleydell Gardens, Folkestone
Kent CT20 2DN, England

British Library Cataloguing in Publication Information Available

Library of Congress Cataloging-in-Publication Data

Oyewole, A.
Historical dictionary of Nigeria / Anthony Oyewole and John Lucas.—2nd ed.
p. cm. — (African historical dictionaries ; no. 40)
Includes bibliographical references.
ISBN 0-8108-3262-3 (alk. paper)
1. Nigeria—History—Dictionaries. I. Lucas, John, 1963- II. Title. III. Series.

DT515.15 .O94 2000
966.9′003—dc21 00-021921

∞™ The paper used in this publication meets the minimum requirements of American National Standard for Information Sciences—Permanence of Paper for Printed Library Materials, ANSI/NISO Z39.48-1992.
Manufactured in the United States of America.

To my wife, Mary
and
my children: Adebayo, Ayodele, and Adenike

—Anthony Oyewole

To my wife, Kate
and
our children: Peter and Joe

—John Lucas

Contents

Editor's Foreword

Africa's most populous country, one of the largest in size, with a talented and energetic population, Nigeria seemed destined to lead and conceivably dominate much of the continent. Yet, perhaps because it is so large and heavily populated, and its peoples are so diverse and ebullient, this has not happened. Nigeria is still trying to find itself, to define a suitable political structure and organize its economy. The progress has been very uneven and the setbacks many.

Nigeria's path is not easy to follow. Politically, the country passed through several democratic phases crudely interrupted by military coups and regimes with the military in charge more often than civilians. Even administratively, regions and states have been divided or created to meet ethnic and other demands. The approach to economics has varied considerably, although avoiding the extremes of state capitalism and socialism, if not corruption, ultimately depending excessively on a fickle resource: oil. Finally, with the restoration of a democratic regime, and attempt to revive the economy, Nigeria is making (another) new start. Let us hope this one succeeds.

To get a handle on what Nigeria was, is, and can be, it is extremely useful to have a guide to its many political parties, ethnic groups, civilian and military leaders as well as its cultural heritage, economic endowment and much more. That is the purpose of this *Historical Dictionary of Nigeria*, which should help newcomers—and specialists—get their bearings in an exceptionally variegated and often confusing nation. While the individual entries are designed to clarify just one aspect or another, together they give a rather complete view of the situation. This is rounded out with a chronology, introduction and bibliography that provides access to other sources of information.

This second edition of the *Historical Dictionary of Nigeria* has two authors. The first, Dr. Anthony Oyewole, was also the author of the first edition. He knows the country very well, having lived and filled major teaching positions there, including most recently Reader in the Department of

Political Science at the Obafemi Awolowo University in Ile-Ife. He was ably assisted by John Lucas who is professor of political science at Pierce College, and has a particular interest in Northern Nigeria. This revised and expanded volume should be a notable contribution toward facilitating the study of Nigeria as it enters a new phase.

Jon Woronoff
Series Editor

Nigeria

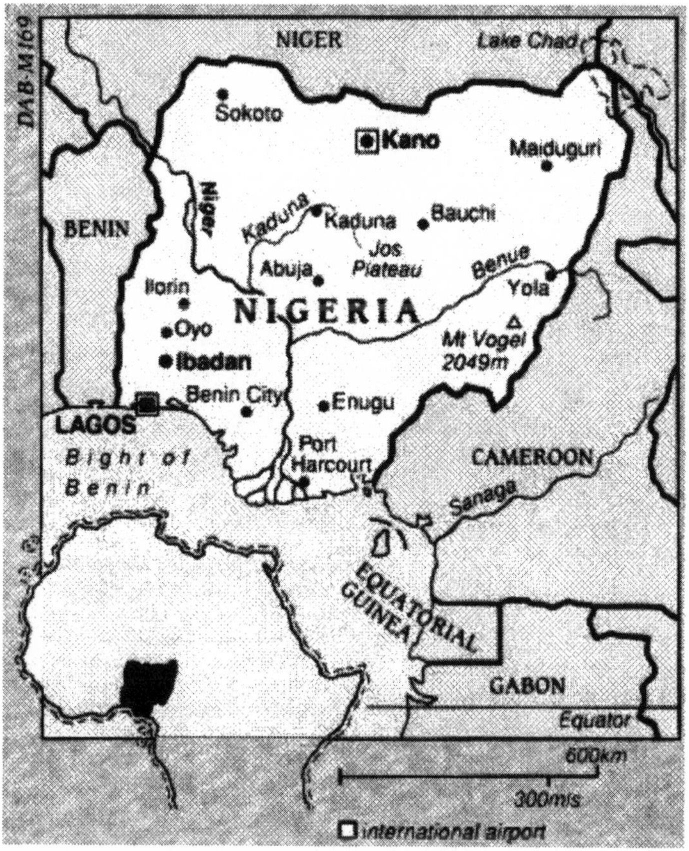
DAB-M169
NIGER
Lake Chad
Sokoto
Kano
Maiduguri
Niger
Kaduna
Kaduna
Bauchi
BENIN
Jos
Plateau
Benue
Abuja
Ilorin
Yola
NIGERIA
Oyo
Mt Vogel
2049m
Ibadan
Benin City
Enugu
LAGOS
Port
Harcourt
Bight of
Benin
CAMEROON
Sanaga
EQUATORIAL
GUINEA
GABON
Equator
600km
300mls
international airport

Abbreviations and Acronyms

ABN	Association for Better Nigeria
ABU	Ahmadu Bello University
ACB	African Continental Bank
ACSTWU	African Civil Servants and Technical Workers' Union
AD	Allaince for Democracy
ADP	Agricultural Development Project
AFCA	Armed Forces Consultative Assembly
AFRC	Armed Forces Ruling Council
AG	Action Group Party
ANTUF	All-Nigeria Trade Union Federation
APP	All People's Party
AWAM	Association of West African Merchants
BCGA	British Cotton Growing Association
BDPP	Benin Delta Peoples Party
BYM	Bornu Youth Movement
CAC	Christ Apostolic Church
CBE	Commander, Order of the British Empire
CBN	Central Bank of Nigeria
CD	Campaign for Democracy
CDC	Constitution Drafting Committee
CENPETO	Centre for the Propagation of Religious and Ethnic Tolerance
CLO	Civil Liberty Organization
CMB	Commodity Marketing Boards
CMG	Companion, Order of St. Michael and St. George
CMS	Church Missionary Society
COLA	Cost of Living Allowance
COR	Calabar-Ogoja-Rivers State
CWTC	Central Water Transportation Company
DO	District Officer
DNPC	Democratic Party of Nigeria and Cameroons
ECA	United Nations Economic Commission for Africa

ECN	Electricity Corporation of Nigeria
ECOMOG	ECOWAS Monitoring Group
ECOWAS	Economic Community of West African States
ESIALA	Eastern States Interim Assets and Liabilities Agency
FAO	Food and Agricultural Organisation
FBS	Federal Broadcasting Service
FCC	Federal Capital City
FCT	Federal Capital Territory
FCTA	Federal Capital Territory Authority
FEC	Federal Executive Council
FEDECO	Federal Electoral Commission
FESTAC	African Festival of Arts and Culture
FIIR	Federal Institute of Industrial Research
FRCN	Federal Radio Corporation of Nigeria
GCE	General Certificate of Education
GCE A	Level General Certificate of Education, Advanced Level
G.C.M.G.	Knight Grand Cross, Order of St. Michael and St. George
GCON	Grand Commander of the Order of the Niger
GDP	Gross Domestic Product
GNPP	Great Nigerian People's Party
HND	Higher National Diploma
ICFTU	International Confederation of Free Trade Unions
ICJ	International Court of Justice
ICRC	International Committee of the Red Cross
IITA	International Institute of Tropical Agriculture
IMF	International Monetary Fund
ING	Interim National Government
INPFL	Independent National Patriotic Front of Liberia
ITP	Ilorin Talaka Parapo
ITT	International Telephones and Telegraphs
IULC	Independent United Labour Congress
JAC	Joint Action Committee
JAMB	Joint Admissions and Matriculation Board
JPC	Joint Planning Committee
KBE	Knight Commander, Order of the British Empire
KCMG	Knight Commander, Order of St. Michael and St. George
KNC	Kamerun National Congress
LYM	Lagos Youth Movement
MBPP	Middle Belt Peoples Party
MDF	Mid-West Democratic Front

MOSOP	Movement for the Survival of the Ogoni People
MPC	Mid-West People's Congress
MPP	Mid-West People's Party
MZL	Middle Zone League
NA	Native Authority
NAB	Nigerian Agricultural Bank
NAC	National African Company
NADECO	National Democratic Coalition
NALDA	National Agricultural Land Development Authority
NANS	National Association of Nigerian Students
NAP	Nigeria Advance Party
NBC	Nigerian Broadcasting Corporation
NCNC	National Council of Nigeria and the Cameroons
NCNC	National Council of Nigerian Citizens
NCTUN	National Council of Trade Unions of Nigeria
NDA	Nigerian Defence Academy
NDC	Niger Delta Congress
NDE	National Directorate of Employment
NDSC	National Defence and Security Council
NEC	National Economic Council
NEC	National Electoral Commission
NEC	National Executive Council
NEPA	National Electric Power Authority
NEPC	Nigerian Export Promotion Council
NEPU	Northern Element Progressive Union
NERFUND	National Economic Reconstruction Fund
NET	Nigerian External Telecommunications Limited
NICO	National Insurance Corporation of Nigeria
NIIA	Nigerian Institute of International Affairs
NIP	National Independence Party
NIPC	National Investment and Properties Company Limited
NISER	Nigerian Institute of Social and Economic Research
NLC	Nigerian Labour Congress
NNA	Nigerian National Alliance
NNDP	Nigerian National Democratic Party
NNFL	Nigerian National Federation of Labour
NNOC	Nigerian National Oil Corporation
NNPC	Nigerian National Petroleum Corporation
NPA	Nigerian Ports Authority
NPC	Northern People's Congress

NPF	Northern Progressive Front
NPFL	National Patriotic Front of Liberia
NPN	National Party of Nigeria
NPP	Nigerian People's Party
NPPC	Nigerian Printing and Publishing Company
NRC	National Republican Convention
NSO	Nigerian Security Organization
NTA	National Television Authority
NTUC	Nigerian Trade Union Congress
NUC	National Universities Commission
NUNS	National Union of Nigerian Students
NUPENG	National Union of Petroleum and Gas Workers
NUT	Nigerian Union of Teachers
NYC	Nigerian Youth Congress
NYM	Nigerian Youth Movement
NYSC	National Youth Service Corps
OAU	Organization of African Unity
OBE	Officer, Order of the British Empire
OFN	Operation Feed the Nation
OFR	Order of the Federal Republic of Nigeria
OIC	Organization of Islamic Conference
OMPADEC	Oil Mineral Producing Areas Development Commission
OND	Ordinary National Diploma
OPEC	Organization of Petroleum Exporting Countries
PDP	People's Democratic Party
PPA	Progressive Parties Alliance
PRC	Provisional Ruling Council
PRP	People's Redemption Party
PWD	Public Works Department
QPM	Queen's Police Medal
RAF	Royal Air Force
RNC	Royal Niger Company
RWU	Railway Workers Union
SAN	Senior Advocate of Nigeria
SAP	Structural Adjustment Program
SDP	Social Democratic Party
SMC	Supreme Military Council
SPC	Southern People's Congress
SUM	Sudan United Mission
SWAFP	Socialist Workers and Farmers Party

TAC	Technical Aid Corps
TCPC	Technical Committee on Privatisation and Commercialisation
TUC	Trade Union Congress
TUC(N)	Trade Union Congress of Nigeria
UAC	United African Company
ULC	United Labor Congress
UMBC	United Middle Belt Congress
UNESCO	United Nations Educational, Scientific, and Cultural Organization
UNIA	Universal Negro Improvement Association
UNIP	United National Independence Party
UPE	Universal Primary Education
UPGA	United Progressive Grand Alliance
UPN	Unity Party of Nigeria
UPP	United People's Party
VISTA	Visiting Scientists Teaching Abroad
WAAC	West African Airways Corporation
WAEC	West African Examination Council
WAFF	West African Frontier Force
WAISER	West African Institute of Social and Economic Research
WAPCB	West African Produce Control Board
WASU	West African Student Union
WHO	World Health Organization
WNBS	Western Nigeria Broadcasting Service
WNDC	Western Nigeria Development Corporation
WNTV	Western Nigeria Television Service

Chronology

800	The Sefawa dynasty of Kanem-Bornu was founded by Saef Ben Dhu Yasan.
999	The Bagoda dynasty was founded in Kano.
1000–1100	Islamic faith and ideas began to come into the Kanem-Bornu area.
1200–1300	The Seven Hausa States were founded.
1472	The first Portuguese traders, Ruy Sequira and Fernando Gomez, sailed to the Bight of Benin.
1485	Benin City received a visit from João Alfonso d'Aveiro, a Portuguese explorer.
1562	The first British ship, captained by Sir John Hawkins, carried slaves from the west coast of Africa to Haiti.
1788	The African Association was formed to explore trade possibilities in the interior of Africa.
1795	Mungo Park started his first expedition to trace the course of the Niger River.
1796	Mungo Park became the first European to discover the eastern course of the Niger River.
1804	The Muslim holy war (jihad) of Usman dan Fodio began in Gobir and spread to other Hausa States.
1805	Mungo Park, together with his men, died at the rapids at Bussa.
1807	British Parliament abolished the slave trade in England.
1830	Richard Lander discovered the mouth of the Niger, thereby opening legitimate trade in the hinterland.
1841	The Anglican Church sent its first missionaries to Nigeria.
1842	Methodist missionaries reached Badagry.
1846	Presbyterian missionaries were the first group of missionaries to land in Calabar.

1849	John Beecroft was appointed British consul for the Bights of Benin and Biafra, thus opening up the first diplomatic link between Britain and Nigeria.
1853	King William Dappa Pepple was exiled.
1860	The Ijaye War broke out between Ijaye and Ibadan.
1861	Lagos was ceded to the British Crown under King Dosumu and became a British Crown colony.
1865	The British established a consulate at Lokoja.
1869	Jaja left Bonny to found a new trading post at Opobo.
1879	George Taubman Goldie formed the United African Company.
1882	The United African Company changed its name to the National African Company.
1885	The Berlin Conference.
1886	British Government granted the National African Company, formerly known as the United African Company, a royal charter, giving the company political authority over the area under the company's influence. The Company became known as the Royal Niger Company.
1887	The British proclaimed the delta region of the Niger River and its surroundings The Oil Rivers Protectorate.
1890	The Anglo-French Agreement in which Britain was to claim the territories under the Royal Niger Company in the northern part of Nigeria.
1893	Oil Rivers Protectorate became Niger Coast Protectorate.
1895	The Akassa Massacre.
1897	Benin under Oba Ovonramwen was partially destroyed by the British.
1897	The name "Nigeria" appeared in the London *Times*.
1898	Railway construction began in Nigeria.
1899	The Anglo-French Convention.
1899	The name Nigeria received its first official recognition in London.
1900	The Royal Niger Company's charter was revoked and the Oil Rivers Protectorate together with the areas near it became the protectorate of Southern Nigeria. In the North, areas under the Royal Niger Company's

administration became the protectorate of Northern Nigeria.

1900 The Charter of the Royal Niger Company was revoked and Nigeria came under full British authority.

1901 The establishment of the West African Frontier Force.

1903 The Fulani Empire came under British rule.

1906 The Colony of Lagos was merged with the Protectorate of Southern Nigeria to become the Colony and Protectorate of Southern Nigeria.

1912 Lord Lugard, the High Commissioner of the Protectorate of Northern Nigeria, was appointed Governor of both the Northern and Southern Protectorates.

1914 The Colony and Protectorate of Southern Nigeria merged with the Protectorate of Northern Nigeria to become the Colony and Protectorate of Nigeria.

1917 Caseley Hayford founded the National Congress of British West Africa.

1922 The Clifford Constitution allowed four Africans to be elected to the Legislative Council in Lagos.

1925 The West African Students' Union was founded in London by Ladipo Solanke to provide a forum for West African students and promote African culture.

1926 The establishment of the Nigerian *Daily Times*.

1929 Aba women protested against the payment of tax. The riots led to many people dead and others injured.

1934 Yaba Higher College was established, followed by the formation of the Lagos Youth Movement.

1936 The emergence of the Nigerian Youth Movement.

1937 Shell Oil Company started oil exploration in Nigeria.

1939 Governor Bourdillon divided Southern Nigeria into the Eastern and Western provinces, each of which later became a region.

1942 The Nigerian Trades Union Congress was given official recognition by the colonial government.

1944 Ibo Federal Union was formed.

1944 The National Council of Nigeria and the Cameroons was formed.

1945 The General Strike took place.

1946 The Richards Constitution went into effect.

1947 The founding of the University College of Ibadan associated with the University of London.

1947	Northern representatives sat with the Southern representatives in the Legislative Council in Lagos for the first time.
1948	Egbe Omo Oduduwa was founded in Ile-Ife.
1948	Ibo Federal Union became Ibo State Union.
1949	The Northern Peoples Congress was formed.
1950	The formation of the Action Group Party.
1951	Macpherson Constitution went into effect.
Nov. 1951/ Jan. 1952	Nigeria's first general elections were held.
Jan. 1953	The majority in the House turned itself into an opposition to defeat all government bills, creating the Eastern Regional Government crisis.
April 1953	Chief Anthony Enahoro, an Action Group Party member, introduced a private member's bill demanding self-government by 1956. The motion was strongly opposed by the Northerners who asked for self-government to be introduced "as soon as practicable."
May 1953	Communal riots broke out in Kano against the southern minority in the Sabon-Gari area.
1953	The three major parties attended the London Constitutional Conference. It agreed on a federal constitution and the granting of self-government to any region that wished for it.
1954	The Lyttleton Constitution, which gave Nigeria a federal structure, came into force. The federation was made up of three regions.
1954	Lagos Constitutional Conference.
1954	COR State Movement was formed.
1955	Free Primary Education in Western Nigeria was launched.
1957	Second London Constitutional Conference. The British government set up the Minorities Commission known as the Willink Commission.
1957	Both the Eastern and the Western Regions became self-governing.
1958	Shell Oil Company started oil production in Nigeria.
1958	Third London Constitutional Conference.
1959	The Northern Region became self-governing.
Dec. 1959	Federal elections were held. No Party won an abso-

	lute majority, so the NPC and NCNC formed a coalition government.
1960	The fourth and the last London Constitutional Conference took place. University of Nigeria, Nsukka, was founded. Nigeria became independent on October 1.
1961	University of Ife was founded.
1962	University of Lagos and Ahmadu Bello University in Zaria were established.
1962	The Action group crisis in the Western Region and the declaration of a state of emergency in that region.
1962	Coker Commission of Inquiry was set up to look into the affairs of certain statutory corporations in the Western Region.
1962	Nigeria abrogated the Defense Pact with Britain.
1963	Mid-Western Region was created from the then-Western Region.
1963	A national census was taken, leading to the census crisis. This census remained (until 1992) the basis for national planning.
Jan. 1963	The state of emergency imposed on the Western Region was lifted.
Sept. 1963	Chief Obafemi Awolowo and some other Action Group Party leaders were jailed for treasonable felony.
Oct. 1, 1963	Nigeria became a republic.
Dec. 1964	Federal elections were held. The elections were widely boycotted in the East and West.
Oct. 1965	Elections were held in the Western Region. Amid widespread violence, Akintola and his party men were declared winners, and law and order broke down.
Jan. 15, 1966	The first military coup d'état by some army majors to overthrow Tafawa Balewa's government took place. Major General J.T.U. Aguiyi-Ironsi became the Head of State.
May 24, 1966	Major General Aguiyi-Ironsi abolished the regions by decree, thus introducing a unitary system of government in the country.
May 1966	Many northerners, believing the new system would bring the north under southern domination, rebelled against it and killed many southerners, mostly Igbo, who lived in the north.

July 29, 1966	The second military coup took place, staged by northern officers in the army. Aguiyi-Ironsi on a visit to Ibadan was killed together with his host, Colonel Adekunle Fajuyi, governor of the Western Region. Colonel Yakubu Gowon became the Head of State.
Aug. 1966	Lt. Colonel Odumegwu Ojukwu, Governor of the Eastern Region, refused to recognise Gowon's authority.
Jan. 1967	The Aburi Conference was held in Ghana and agreed to a loose confederation that would grant autonomy to the regions.
May 1967	General Y. Gowon issued a decree dividing Nigeria into twelve states—six in the North, two in the West, three in the East and the Mid-West Region.
1967	Col. Odumegwu Ojukwu, Governor of the Eastern Region, declared that region the sovereign Republic of Biafra.
July 1967	The Civil War began.
1967	Interim Administrative Council was established.
1968	Kampala Peace Talks and Addis Ababa Peace Talks.
1968	Interim Common Services Agency was established for the Northern Region.
1970	Colonel Odumegwu Ojukwu fled the country to Côte d'Ivoire. The end of the Civil War, Jan. 15, when Lt. Col. Phillip Effiong, Ojuku's deputy, surrendered to the Nigerian government.
1970	The Eastern State Interim Assets and Liabilities Agency Decree was promulgated.
1973	Nigeria changed from the pound sterling to the naira.
1973	Another population census was held.
1975	Economic Community of West African States came into being.
1975	Third military coup overthrew General Y. Gowon, and General Murtala Muhammed came to power.
1975	The Constitution Drafting Committee was set up.
1976	Nigeria became a federation of nineteen states.
1976	Federal Capital Territory was created in Abuja.
1976	Attempted coup, staged by Col. B.S. Dimka, February 13, in which General Murtala Muhammed was killed.
1976	Local government was recognized as the third tier of governmental activity in the nation.

1976	Universal Primary Education was launched.
1977	Local governments in the country elected 203 members to the Constituent Assembly, 30 other members were appointed by the Supreme Military Council.
1977	The Universal Primary Education was introduced.
Nov. 1977	FESTAC '77, The Festival of African Arts and Culture was held.
1977	Federal Electoral Commission was established.
1978	Land Use Decree was promulgated.
1979	The presidential constitution went into effect.
1980	Alhaji Shugaba Abdurrahman Darman, the majority leader of the Great Nigerian People's Party in the Borno State, was deported.
1981	Governor Abubakar Balarabe Musa of Kaduna State was impeached by the State House of Assembly.
Feb. 12, 1982	First-ever visit of the head of the Catholic Church, Pope John Paul II, to Nigeria.
April 15, 1982	Spiritual head of the Church of England, Archbishop Robert Runcie, visited Nigeria.
1983	The first and the last general elections were held under the Second Republican Constitution.
1983	The fourth military coup d'état on December 31st overthrew the Alhaji Shehu Shagari administration and brought General Muhammadu Buhari to power.
1984	Many political officeholders in the Second Republic were under probe, and many were sent to jail for corrupt practices.
Aug. 27, 1985	The fifth military coup d'état overthrew the administration of Major-General Muhammadu Buhari, bringing Major-General Ibrahim Babangida to power.
1986	Professor Wole Soyinka became the first Nigerian to win the Nobel Prize Award for Literature.
October 1986	Dele Giwa, editor-in-chief of the *Newswatch* magazine, was killed by a letter bomb.
1987	President Ibrahim Babangida began what later in 1993 became a futile transition program to civil rule.
1987	Two new states created, bringing total to 21.
Sept. 1987	A 46-member Constitution Review Committee was set up by the federal military government, headed by Justice Buba Ardo.

Oct. 1989	President I.B. Babangida announced the dissolution of 13 political associations that applied to the National Electoral Commission for recognition, and created two political parties—the Social Democratic Party and National Republican Convention.
April 22, 1990	Another attempted coup, staged by Major Gideon Orkar and his men was aborted. The coup leaders had announced a plan to excise the far north from the federation.
Aug. 27, 1991	President I.B. Babangida announced the creation of nine new states out of the existing 21 states, making the country a 30-state federation.
June 12, 1993	Presidential election to usher in the Third Republic took place.
June 23, 1993	The annulment of the presidential election that Chief M.K.O. Abiola appeared to have won.
Nov. 17, 1993	Sixth military coup overthrew the Interim National Government and brought into power Major-General Sani Abacha.
May 1994	The National Democratic Coalition (NADECO) was formed with the purpose of seeing democratic government return to Nigeria.
June 1994	National Constitutional Conference to draw up another constitution was inaugurated.
June 11, 1994	Chief M.K.O. Abiola, the undeclared winner of the June 12, 1993, presidential election, declared himself president and was later arrested and detained.
July 1994	The National Union of Petroleum and Gas Workers (NUNPENG) went on strike, asking, among other things, military handing over of government to the winner of the 1993 presidential election. The strike, which virtually paralysed the economy, lasted for two months.
Sept. 1994	Leading newspapers, *The Guardian,* the *Concord* and *The Punch,* were banned by the military government, and their publishing houses were closed down for six months.
March 1995	Government claimed it had foiled a coup plot to overthrow the Abacha regime. More than 40 people, military and civilian, including former head of state,

	General Olusegun Obasanjo and Major General Shehu Musa Yar'Adua, his second in command, were tried by a secret military tribunal and sentenced to varying terms of imprisonment.
July 1995	The Constitution Conference appointed in 1994 reported, recommending a rotational sharing of power.
Oct. 1, 1995	General Sani Abacha announced a three-year transition program to end on October 1, 1998.
October 1995	Abrogation of the Nigerian Enterprises Promotion Decree to encourage foreign investors to invest in Nigeria. Chief Alfred Rewane, one of Nigeria's nationalists of old and an opponent of the continuing military rule, was assassinated in his own house in Lagos.
November 1995	Nigeria's membership in the Commonwealth was suspended for the military government's civil rights abuses, and the hasty execution of Ken Saro-Wiwa, the Ogoni minority rights activist, together with eight of his colleagues.
March 1996	Local government nonparty elections took place as a prelude to the three-year transition programme to a democratic government.
April 1996	Alhaji Ibrahim Dasuki, the 18th Sultan of Sokoto, was removed from office by the Abacha government on April 20. Alhaji Muhammadu Maccido was installed as the 19th Sultan of Sokoto on April 21.
June 1996	The wife of the detained undeclared winner of the 1993 presidential election, Kudirat Abiola, was brutally murdered. The bans on political activities were lifted, paving the way for the formation of political parties.
October 1996	Military registered five political parties as part of its ongoing transition program.
March 1997	Local government elections were held.
May 1997	Nigeria initiated military actions against military government in Sierra Leone to restore democratically elected regime.
December 8, 1997	Politician and former Chief of Staff, Gen. (rtd.) Shehu Musa Yar'Adua died in detention.
May 1998	Group of 34, an association of powerful politicians, issued statement urging Sani Abacha to leave office.

June 8, 1998	General Sani Abacha died of an apparent heart attack, and was succeeded by General Abdulsalami Abubakar.
July 7, 1998	Moshood K.O. Abiola died in detention of an apparent heart attack.
July 20, 1998	General Abubakar announced a new democratic transition.
December 5, 1998	Local government elections were held.
January 9, 1999	Gubernatorial elections were held.
February 20, 1999	National Assembly elections were held.
February 27, 1999	Presidential elections were held, Gen. (rtd.) Olusegun Obasanjo of the PDP was the winner.
May 5, 1999	Constitution for the Fourth Republic was released to the public.
May 29, 1999	Olusegun Obasanjo was sworn in as the President of the Fourth Republic.

Introduction

Nigeria, with an area of 923,768 square kilometres (356,669 square miles), lies at the inner corner of the Gulf of Guinea in West Africa. The longest distance from the eastern to the western boundaries is 1,126 kilometres (700 miles), while the distance from the northern boundaries to the Atlantic sea is 1,046 kilometres (650 miles). It is bounded on the west by the Republic of Benin (formerly known as Dahomey), on the north by the Republic of Niger and the Chad Republic, on the east by the Republic of Cameroon, and on the south by the Atlantic Ocean.

The most southern part of the country in the Delta area is about 4° north of the equator and the northern boundary is about 14° north. The western and the eastern boundaries lie north and south between 3° and 15° east meridian. The official hour is one hour ahead of the Greenwich Mean Time (GMT).

The country can be said to have four main vegetational regions. The first is the coastline, which is intersected by a network of creeks and rivers, and the delta of the Niger River, which consists of a belt of mangrove swamp extending about 100 kilometres inland. After this comes the region of tropical forest in undulating land with scattered hills. The third region is the open woodland, the deciduous forest, stretching through an undulating plateau and hills of granite and sandstone at a general elevation of about 610 metres. The fourth region is the savannah grassland that spreads toward the Sahara Desert.

Nigeria takes its name from its most important feature: the Niger River. River Niger rises in the mountains northeast of Sierra Leone and flows through the republics of Guinea, Mali and Niger before it enters Nigeria from the west and then runs southeasterly to Lokoja, about 540 kilometres to the Atlantic Ocean, where it joins its main tributary, the Benue River. From Lokoja, the Niger flows southwards, to the delta where it splits into numerous channels before emptying itself into the ocean. The Benue, on the other hand, takes its source from the Cameroon Republic and flows southwesterly to its confluence with the Niger. The Niger is about 4,169 kilometres in length. Nigeria gets much of its electricity from the hydroelectric dam built on the Niger River at Kainji, about 112 kilometres north of Jebba.

In addition to the Niger and the Benue, the second major drainage system in Nigeria flows northeast from the central plateau into the Yobe River, which flows into Lake Chad through which the boundary between Nigeria and the Chadian Republic passes.

The climate of Nigeria varies from the south to the north. In the coastal areas of the south, the mean maximum temperature is about 30.55°C while it is 34.44°C in the north. Maximum temperatures are generally highest from February to April in the south, while they are highest in the north between March and June. In the whole country, the temperatures are lowest in July and August. The average minimum temperature in the south is about 22.2°C and in the north it is about 18.88°C. As such, the mean range of temperature is higher in the north where it averages about 7°C than in the south, where the average is about 4.77°C. The maximum relative humidity near the coast is between 95 percent to 100 percent through most of the year and usually decreases to between 70 percent and 80 percent in the afternoon. As one goes north, the humidity steadily decreases.

Nigeria can be said to have two main seasons, the rainy season and the dry season. This is due to the two principal wind systems in Nigeria: the southwesterly wind current and the northeasterly wind current. The southwesterly wind current is warm and very moist after its passage over the Atlantic Ocean. It therefore causes cloudy weather and frequently results in rain. Thus the rainfall is usually heavy in the south averaging about 177.8 centimetres a year in the western end of the coast and increasing to about 431.8 centimetres in the eastern section of the coast. The rainfall decreases sharply as one goes inland. It falls to about 127 centimetres in the central part of the country and to about 50.8 centimetres in the north. The rainy season generally begins in March and ends in October or November.

The northeasterly wind current is hot and dry after its passage over the Sahara Desert, and it is frequently laden with dust from the desert. The wind and the dust is generally referred to as the Harmattan. Under the influence of the wind current, the weather is dry and generally cloudless. Day temperatures are high in the afternoon, and low at night and in the early morning. The weather is often hazy, and visibility is reduced. The dry season is generally between November and April.

Nigeria has a wealth of mineral resources among which are petroleum, limestone, tin, columbite, gold, silver, coal, lead-zinc, marble, iron ore and uranium. The ownership and control of all minerals is vested in the federal government.

In spite of these mineral resources and the exploitation of the oil resources that has made Nigeria an important oil exporting country, Nigeria is basically an agricultural country. Farming is still the principal economic activity of most Nigerians. Before the Civil War in 1967, agricultural products used to be the principal export earner, but, since the war, petroleum oil has taken that pride of place. The growth in the foreign exchange earnings from oil financed a government-led effort to diversify the nation's economy. Building and construction, mining and quarrying, transportation, communication and industry have expanded considerably. For a long time, agriculture appeared to have been benignly neglected. However, because of Nigeria's growing dependence on food imports, the military government, before a civilian administration took over in 1979, began an agricultural recovery program known then as Operation Feed the Nation (OFN). OFN was designed to make the country self-sufficient in food and agricultural products for the growing local manufacturing industries. To make land readily available for large-scale commercial farming, the government in 1978 also issued the Land Use Decree, which vested all land in the state government. The commitment of the national government to self-sufficiency continued under the civilian administration of Alhaji Shehu Shagari, who renamed the OFN program the Green Revolution.

Nigeria is a nation of many nationalities or ethnic groups, each having its own culture and tradition and occupying a separate geographic area. These various groups speak languages that are mutually unintelligible to one another. The major ethnic groups are Hausa, Fulani, Igbo, Yoruba, Kanuri, Ibibio, Tiv, Itsekiri, Ijaw, Edo, Annang, Nupe, Urhobo, Igala, Idoma, Igbirra, Gwari, Efik, Birom and Yergam. The population of Nigeria, according to the 1991 census was 88.5 million, making it the most populous country in Africa.

The history of Nigeria started long before the time of Christ, but, because the people had not yet learned the art of writing, for many centuries oral history carried the story from one generation to the other. This accounts for the lack of accurate information about the origin of many of the peoples who inhabit Nigeria today. However, archaeological findings in various parts of Nigeria, like the Nok culture in the Jos Plateau of Northern Nigeria, Iwo Eleru in Western Nigeria, and Igbo Ukwu in Eastern Nigeria, have clearly shown that a high level of civilisation existed in various parts of Nigeria many centuries before Christ. For example, archaeological findings at the Jos Plateau show that the Nok people used iron tools in the eighth century B.C. Unfortunately, not much is known about these people and their civilisation other than what archaeological remains teach us. However, Islamic and Arabic scholars began to keep fairly accurate historical records with the advent of Islam, first to Bornu in the 11th century and later to Hausaland.

The modern history of Nigeria can, therefore, be said to begin when European explorers came to Nigeria and tried to open up trade with the people. Their control of the flow of trade eventually led to the colonisation of Nigeria and other parts of Africa. In the 15th century, the Portuguese first sailed along the Bight of Benin and the Bight of Biafra. The first Portuguese traders who sailed to the Bight of Benin in 1472 were reportedly Ruy Sequira and Fernando Gomez. They traded their goods for slaves. Sir John Hawkins was the captain of the first British ship to carry slaves from the West Coast of Africa. The ship left for Haiti in 1562.

Nigerians who lived in coastal areas became intermediaries in the slave trade. Kingdoms rose against kingdoms for the purpose of capturing their people for sale to the European slavers. From the 16th century to the 19th century, more than 20,000 able-bodied men and women were transported annually to the Americas. As a result, Benin, Lagos, Bonny and Calabar became thriving centers of the slave trade, a trade in which the Germans, Portuguese, French and British actively participated. The last Nigerian slaves were taken to the United States in 1862. During this 300-year period, more than six million Nigerian men and women were sold into slavery.

Towards the end of the 18th century, public opinion turned against this inhuman slave trade. British merchants began to look for markets in Africa for their industrial products and for new sources of raw materials for those industries. This led to the founding of the African Association in 1788, which later organised the exploration of the interior of Africa, most especially of the Niger River, and the pioneering work of such explorers as Mungo Park, Hugh Clapperton, the Lander Brothers, Heinrich Barth and William Baikie.

In 1807 Parliament in England abolished the slave trade and forbade its ships from trafficking in the trade. Britain soon set up a naval patrol to stop the continuation of the trade, but it was discovered that this alone was not enough to stop the Africans from offering their people for sale to the Europeans. The British needed a new type of legitimate trade to take slavery's place, and they wanted to Christianize the Africans.

In 1830 Richard Lander discovered the mouth of the Niger, thereby opening up legitimate trade in the hinterland. After pushing out other European commercial activities, the Royal Niger Company controlled this trade. In 1832 the first commercial British ship reached the confluence of the Niger and Benue rivers. British consular agents, first stationed at Calabar in 1849 and on the Island of Fernando Póo, took over the administration of the area from the Royal Niger Company. This was the beginning of British consular rule in Nigeria, during which the British with their gunboats on the sea forced local chiefs into many unequal treaties. Their effort in the Delta to expand their trading interest by opening up the interior of Nigeria to European free traders (instead of going through middlemen at the coast) created great conflicts between the British and such Nigerian traditional rulers as King William Dappa Pepple and Jaja of Opobo. The British began to interfere increasingly in the area's politics.

In 1851 the British turned west of the Niger to continue their gunboat diplomacy. When they reached Lagos, which the Portuguese had turned into a thriving center of slave trade, they began to interfere in local politics. The British consul for the Bight of Benin and Biafra, John Beecroft, supported the deposed Oba of Lagos, Akintoye, who wanted to regain his throne. Kosoko, who was well known for his slave-trading activities, had usurped Akintoye's power in 1845. Akintoye signed a treaty abolishing slavery in his domain, guaranteeing missionaries freedom to carry on their activities and giving the British special trading concessions. But the slave trade still continued. In 1853 the British government had two consuls in Nigeria, Beecroft for the Bight of Biafra and Benjamin Campbell for Lagos. In 1861 the son of Akintoye, Dosumu, who succeeded his father in 1853 and who the British consul supported as the most amenable to British interest among all the contestants for the throne, was made to cede Lagos to the British Crown, and so Lagos became a Crown colony. With Lagos and the delta area as their base, the British extended their influence further inland and began an active process of trade, missionary activity and interference in local politics. Until the 1870s, British merchants dominated trade in the delta area and in the interior of the country. However, the French soon began to offer them serious competition. At this critical time, Nigeria was saved for the British by the activities of George Dashwood Goldie Taubman who welded all the major companies in the area into the United African Company (UAC). By underselling the French companies, Taubman forced them out of the area. His series of treaties with the local chiefs promised British protection and free trade. In 1885 the Berlin Conference recognised the area controlled by the UAC as being under British influence. The British later proclaimed a protectorate over the Niger Districts—from the area around the confluence of the Niger and Benue rivers to the sea. In 1886 Britain granted the UAC, which had changed its name in 1882 to the National African Company, a royal charter, and it became the Royal Niger Company. Under the charter the company obtained political authority over the areas under its influence. In 1900 the company's charter was revoked, and Nigeria, made up of the colony of Lagos and the protectorates of Southern Nigeria and Northern Nigeria, came under direct British rule.

The British took little time to acquire and pacify Northern Nigeria, which came under its protection in 1900. The jihad, started by Usman dan Fodio in 1804, had already done much of the work for the British. Dan Fodio's men overthrew Hausa kings and put their states under Fulani rule. Dan Fodio divided his empire into emirates. After Fodio's death in 1817, his son, Muhammad Bello, became the Sultan of Sokoto, which became the religious and political center of the Fulani empire. The empire crumbled under British pressure, however, and by 1903 the British had installed a new sultan more amenable to their interest.

From this brief history of the British acquisition of Nigeria, it is clear that British imperial authorities created Nigeria. Furthermore, Nigeria's boundaries were determined not on the basis of any community of interest between its various peoples but rather upon European economic interests and power politics. In fact, the name "Nigeria," which first appeared in the London *Times* in 1897, received its first official recognition in 1899 during the debate in the House of Commons on the Royal Niger Company's charter revocation.

The central political problem that Nigeria has faced since its very creation is national unity, uniting the many groups within its borders under one administration while at the same time allowing each group a sufficient degree of autonomy to satisfy its cultural aspirations. In 1906 the British authorities made their first effort to unite the two southern administrations: the Colony of Lagos was merged with the Protectorate of Southern Nigeria to become the Colony and Protectorate of Southern Nigeria. In 1914 the second major effort was made when the Colony and Protectorate of Southern Nigeria was merged with the Protectorate of Northern Nigeria to form the Colony and Protectorate of Nigeria.

However, the amalgamation of 1914 was more on paper than in reality. The administrative system that emerged was more federal than unitary for it recognised the existence of two autonomous units called the Northern Provinces and the Southern Provinces, each being the same as the former northern and southern protectorates, respectively. Over each group of provinces was a lieutenant governor with responsibility for certain matters. Each had a separate secretariat and was required to submit a separate annual budget for incorporation into the national budget. What is most remarkable was that the north, except insofar as the national budget was concerned, was administered as a separate unit. The legislative council only legislated for the colony and the southern group of provinces while the governor continued to legislate for the north by proclamation. The only representatives of the north on the council were the lieutenant governor and some senior colonial officials. This isolation of the north from the south continued until 1947 when northern representatives sat side by side for the first time with southern representatives in the legislative council in Lagos.

The unity of the country has often been threatened: in 1953 over the self-government-in-1956 motion and over the Lagos issue after the 1953 constitutional conference in London; in 1964 over the federal election crisis; and in 1967 when the Eastern Region decided to secede, and declared itself the Republic of Biafra. It was won back after 30 months of civil war, and even today, many years after the Civil War, many Nigerians still worry about the precarious nature of their unity.

Nigeria has passed through a long period of constitution making. There was the Clifford Constitution of 1922, which introduced the elective principle into the constitutional development of the country and spurred on the emergence of political parties like the National Democratic Party of Herbert Macaulay, and the establishment of nationalist newspapers like the *Daily Times* in 1926. In 1936 a truly Nigerian nationalist organisation came into being when the Lagos Youth Movement, founded in 1934, became the Nigerian Youth Movement. But in 1941, a crisis within the movement ensued, which soon made the organisation moribund. In 1944 the National Council of Nigeria and the Cameroons (NCNC) was formed with Herbert Macaulay as its president and Dr. Nnamdi Azikiwe its general secretary. In 1946 the Richards Constitution came into being, and although it conceded majority membership of elected Nigerians on the legislative council, it fell far short of the nationalist expectations and was strongly criticized by the NCNC, which sent a delegation to the secretary of state for the colonies in London to protest the inadequacies of the constitution. Because of the failure of the constitution to meet the nationalist expectations, the Macpherson Constitution followed in 1951, but in spite of the care taken in its preparation, it was crisis-ridden, as illustrated by the Eastern Regional crisis of 1953 and the self-government-in-1956 motion crisis of the same year. What, however, was important during this period was the founding of the Action Group Party (AG), led by Chief Obafemi Awolowo and the Northern People's Congress (NPC) under the leadership of Sir Ahmadu Bello, the Sardauna of Sokoto. Furthermore, party government began to emerge.

As a result of the crises that took place in 1953, there was a constitutional conference in London that decided on setting up a federal system of government in 1954 made up of three regions: Northern, Eastern and Western. In 1957 both the Eastern and the Western Regions became self-governing, and the Northern Region joined suit in 1959. National independence finally came in 1960 with a parliamentary system of government at the federal and regional level. In 1963 Nigeria became a republic with a ceremonial head of state. It also became a federation of four regions after the Mid-Western Region was created from the Western Region.

After the euphoria of independence was over, the country went through nerve-racking crises, beginning with the Action Group crisis of 1962, the census crisis of 1963, the federal election crisis of 1964 and the Western Regional election crisis of 1965, which finally led to the military takeover of January 15, 1966.

The military government under the command of General Aguiyi-Ironsi, who became the Head of State, suspended certain parts of the constitution and asserted the supreme authority of federal military government decrees over any regional edict. In May 1966 the Ironsi government issued the Unification decree, which abolished the federal structure and set up a unitary system of government. Though done with good intentions, the act provoked protest and resentment, especially in the northern region, which saw it as a means for the south, especially the Igbo people, to dominate the country. In July 1966 another coup staged by northern elements took place in which General Aguiyi-Ironsi was killed and General Yakubu Gowon was brought to power.

Colonel Odumegwu Ojukwu, the head of the military government in Eastern Nigeria, refused to accept the authority of General Gowon because he was not the next in line to succeed Ironsi. In September of 1966, a wave of killing of people of Eastern Nigerian origin in the north swept through the area and Igbos who escaped the killing went back to the Eastern Region, their home of origin. This intensified the problem between the Federal Government in Lagos and the Eastern Nigeria Government in Enugu. When all efforts to resolve the various issues in dispute had ended in failure, the Eastern Region seceded from the Federation and a civil war broke out, which lasted until January 1970 when Colonel Ojukwu fled to Côte d'Ivoire, where he stayed in exile until 1982.

Before the Civil War began, the government of General Gowon made an important decision to divide the country into 12 states. The north was divided into six states, and the south was divided into six states. The big mistake then was to preserve the old line between north and south, which in essence has helped to sustain the old dichotomy between them. However, the creation of states helped, in no small way, to allay the fears of the minority ethnic groups who had struggled since the 1950s for their own separate states. It also freed the south of the fear of domination by the monolithic and impregnable north.

In 1975 General Gowon was overthrown, and was succeeded by General Murtala Muhammed who, within the short time of his administration, increased the number of states from 12 to 19, moved the federal capital to Abuja, purged the public services of old and incompetent officers, set up the Constitution Drafting Committee to return the nation to civilian rule and set in motion efforts to reform the local government system. Murtala Muhammed was killed in an abortive coup in February 1976, but his program to disengage the military from politics went on as planned under General Olusegun Obasanjo. A new constitution was drafted, debated by the Constituent Assembly, and was approved by the military government in September 1978 to take effect from October 1, 1979. With the approval of the constitution, the ban on political activities was lifted, and the contest for the 1979 elections began. Out of more than 50 political associations that sought recognition as political parties, only five of them—The National Party of Nigeria (NPN), Unity Party of Nigeria (UPN), Nigerian People's Party (NPP), Great Nigerian People's Party (GNPP) and the People's Redemption Party (PRP)—were recognised by the Federal Electoral Commission (FEDECO) as fulfilling the requirement of the electoral law.

Under the 1979 constitution, Nigeria changed from a parliamentary system of government to an executive presidential system, with a popularly elected president and a bicameral national legislature. Alhaji Shehu Shagari was elected president in the 1979 general elections, and was reelected in 1983 for his second and last term. He was sworn in on October 1, 1983, but, on December 31, 1983, a military coup d'état, the fourth successful one in the history of Nigeria, toppled his government and brought Major General Muhammadu Buhari to power. Eighteen months after this, General Buhari was overthrown by General Ibrahim Badamasi Babangida on August 27, 1985.

Babangida increased the number of the states in the Federation to 30 by just subdividing preexisting ones. It was during his tenure that Nigeria's economy virtually collapsed. In his effort to restructure the economy, he started the Structural Adjustment Programme (SAP), which, as a result of inefficient implementation and lack of accountability in government, was a complete failure. Worse still was his failure to complete his transition program to hand over power to an elected president. Rather than allowing the winner of the presidential election of June 12, 1993, to be officially declared, he stopped the National Electoral Commission (NEC) from declaring the results from all the states after publicly declaring those of 14 states and the Federal Capital Territory, Abuja. On June 23, 1993, he finally annulled the results of the election, which was widely believed to be the fairest and most peaceful in the nation's history. The annulment threw the nation into deep political crisis.

Before Babangida was forced to leave office on August 26, 1993, he had set up an interim national government, an appointed civilian government, to complete the transition programme, but the government had no popular support and a court in Lagos later declared it illegal. On November 17, 1993, General Sani Abacha overthrew the interim national government in a coup. Many people believed at the time that he was going to "right" the "wrong" done by the annulment of the presidential election of June 12, 1993, but upon assuming the leadership of the country he began to consolidate his power. Abacha liquidated all the democratic structures that his military boss and predecessor had painstakingly previously built. To gain support and legitimacy, he put together a cabinet with members of the major political groups in the country and declared support for a national constitutional conference. Many people believed Abacha supported the national sovereign conference, which many vocal people in the country had been asking for, that would reorder the nation's priorities and reorganise its political power structure.

In 1994 General Abacha set up the national constitutional conference to draw up a new constitution. The conference reported in 1995 and recommended a rotational power-sharing arrangement as a way to move Nigeria forward. The government accepted the recommendation and decreed that it would apply to all levels of government. The hope was that rotational power sharing would give every segment of the country a sense of belonging.

On June 11, 1994, Chief M.K.O. Abiola, the apparent but undeclared winner of the June 12, 1993, presidential election, declared himself president, and was soon arrested and charged with treason. In June 1996, two years after he was arrested, he still had not been tried in court. The court ordered that he be released on bail, but the government flouted the order. In June his eldest wife, Kudirat, who was struggling to focus government attention on her husband's plight, was mysteriously murdered, plunging the family into more anguish.

The uproar created by Chief Abiola's arrest and detention was followed by protests and strikes. The strike by the National Union of Petroleum and Gas Workers (NUPENG), which among other things demanded the handing over of government to the winner of the June 12, 1993, presidential election had the most far-reaching effect. The strike lasted for two months and virtually paralysed the nation's economy.

In March 1995, the Abacha government claimed that it had unearthed a plot to overthrow the government. The people it arrested included the former head of state, General Olusegun Obasanjo (1976–79) and his second in command, General Shehu Musa Yar'Adua, who was gearing up his political machine for the presidential campaign when the ban on political activities would be lifted. They and about 40 other people, military and civilian, were secretly tried by a military tribunal, found guilty, and sentenced to varying terms of imprisonment.

After almost two years of aimlessness and drift, the Abacha government finally responded to criticism on the thirty-fifth Independence Day anniversary, October 1, 1995, by announcing its transition programme to last for three years—October 1995 to October 1998. As part of the implementation programme, in March 1996, nonpartisan local government elections were held all across the nation. In June 1996, the bans on political activities were lifted. But the decision that dented the image of the government very seriously was the hasty execution of Ken Saro-Wiwa, a minority rights activist, and eight other Ogoni leaders who were charged for the murder of four other Ogoni leaders. They were tried secretly by a military tribunal, found guilty and sentenced to death by hanging. The government turned a deaf ear to all pleas for clemency and hanged them in November 1995, leading to an immediate suspension of Nigeria from the Commonwealth, and the imposition of sanctions on Nigeria by the United States, Britain, South Africa, and many other countries. Toward the end of June 1996, the Abacha government released seven of its many political detainees and promised early in July to release many more. However, nothing was said about the chief political detainee, Chief Moshood K.O. Abiola.

While some had hoped that Abacha's promised transition to democratic rule would signal a relaxation of his harsh authoritarianism it quickly became apparent that his style of governing would continue to be as dictatorial as ever. In the summer of 1996, a number of prominent politicians formed parties to contest in the upcoming elections. In September, however, all but five of the new political parties were dissolved. The five remaining parties were relatively weak, and had few significant political figures as members. The subservience of these officially approved parties to the military prompted the comment that they were "five fingers of the same leprous hand." Many saw this as an attempt by Abacha to prevent powerful politicians from challenging his bid to manipulate the transition to secure his own election as president.

In 1996, a series of bombings shook Nigeria. The specific motivations and culprits behind the bombings remained shrouded in mystery, but they contributed to an increasing climate of fear and insecurity within the country. In March 1997, the Abacha regime used the bombings as a pretext to indict a number of its political opponents, including exiles such as Wole Soyinka, Alani Akinrinnade and Anthony Enahoro, for treason. The military regime also increased its efforts to see Abacha elected as president. A number of government-funded groups emerged in 1997, lobbying for Sani Abacha to contest the presidency in 1998. One of the most prominent examples was Youths Earnestly Ask for Abacha (YEAA!) which staged a "two million man march" in support of the general in December 1997.

Internationally, Abacha's policies strained relations with a number of important allies, particular Britain, the United States and South Africa. Within West Africa, however, Abacha deployed Nigerian force in ways that underscored its role as a regional hegemon. In Liberia, Abacha continued to support the ECOMOG peacekeeping force with a large contingent of Nigerian troops (a mission that had been initiated under the Babangida regime), and thus contributed to the resolution of the civil war in that country in 1996. In Sierra Leone, the government responded to a May 1997 coup against a democratically elected government by initiating military actions against the coup leaders. Following some initial setbacks, the Nigerian forces returned the civilian regime to power in February 1998.

In December 1997, the government announced that it had uncovered a coup plot to unseat the government, led by Chief of Defence Staff, General Oladipo Diya. Diya was the second-highest ranking figure in the military government, and one of the few remaining Yoruba officers with any real clout. As with the regime's claims to have uncovered a coup plot in 1995, many were skeptical of the charges and suspected that Abacha was using them as a pretext to purge members of the junta who might be ambivalent about Abacha's plans to remain in power.

In early 1998, each of the official five parties announced that they had chosen Sani Abacha as their presidential candidate. This prompted a number of previously quiescent leaders and groups to come out publicly against the "self-succession" plan. In February, 18 of the most influential politicians in northern Nigeria formed the "Group of Eighteen" and released a statement urging Abacha to refrain from continuing in office past October 1998. In May, a coalition of 34 politicians under the leadership of former vice-president Alex Ekwueme (the "Group of 34") released their own statement criticising the Abacha self-succession plan. Similar anti-Abacha statements were voiced by former military heads of state Muhammadu Buhari and Ibrahim Babangida. But the most vigorous opposition to Abacha continued to originate from the southwest. In May, riots in Ibadan gave an indication of what could be in store if Abacha refused to yield power. Whether or not the growing opposition to Abacha by leaders within the society would have been enough to prevent his bid to rig his own election as president will never be known; on June 8, 1998, he died of a heart attack. Officially, the death was attributed to natural causes, although a number of unconfirmed reports implicated members of the military.

Following Abacha's death, Chief of Defence Staff General Abdulsalami Abubakar established himself as the new leader. In contrast to Abacha, Abubakar had a reputation for honesty and probity. He quickly undertook a number of actions that underscored the differences between his regime and that of his predecessor. Political detainees were gradually released, restrictions on the press were eased and the repression of basic human rights was curtailed. In terms of the military, most notable was the dismantling of the notorious Special Bodyguards, a security force of 2,000–3,000 men under the control of Major Hamza al-Mustapha that was used to terrorize the Abacha regime's opponents. Also notable were investigations into the rampant corruption of the Abacha years. Sums of hundreds of millions of dollars of stolen funds were seized from former members of the regime, including the family of the deceased dictator. The most notable political development was Abubakar's pledge to oversee the democratic election of a truly independent civilian regime.

Before details of Abubakar's transition plan could be released, however, tragedy struck. On July 7, 1998, M.K.O. Abiola died of a heart attack while meeting with a diplomatic delegation from the United States. He was still in detention at the time, but all indications are that he was to be released in a matter of days. Abiola's supporters immediately suspected foul play, and for the next several days riots rocked the southwest. While an autopsy conducted by international experts concluded that the death was due to natural causes, many continued to hold the military responsible due to the harsh conditions under which Abiola was imprisoned.

On July 20, Abubakar finally announced the details of his transition program. Having concluded that the Abacha transition was fatally flawed, and that the five political parties it had produced were likewise seriously compromised, a fresh programme was envisioned. New political parties would be created and a series of elections would be held, culminating in the transfer of power to a democratically elected civilian regime on May 29, 1999. When the new political parties were allowed to form, the regime adopted a hands-off attitude that contrasted sharply with the manipulation of parties during the Babangida and Abacha transitions. Eventually three parties emerged: the People's Democratic Party (PDP), formed out of the Group of 34, the Alliance for Democracy (AD) drawing heavily from the Yoruba cultural organisation Afenifere, and the All People's Party (APP), an eclectic mix of Abacha cronies and legitimate politicians. From the start, the PDP was the most powerful of the three, a situation that only became more pronounced after Olusegun Obasanjo emerged as their presidential candidate. Obasanjo, a former military head of state (1976–79), was one of the political prisoners released by Abubakar after assuming power. He had been in jail since 1995 on coup charges that many considered to have been fabricated. In order to combat the PDP juggernaut, the AD and the APP agreed to field a common candidate: Olu Falae, a former finance minister and pro-democracy activist. Nevertheless, in elections held on February 27, Obasanjo won decisively (just as the PDP had earlier emerged triumphant in elections for local government officials, governors and the National Assembly).

While the progress of the democratic transition held the promise of a bright future for Nigeria, it masked a number of more troubling developments. First the conduct of the 1999 presidential elections were marked by a number of irregularities. While most election observers reported that the ultimate outcome was not changed by the malpractices and fraud, the precedent was disturbing. The losing candidate, Olu Falae, never accepted the results, and mounted a challenge to them in courts, which he eventually lost. Second, ethnic conflict began to rise, most notably in the Niger Delta area. The Niger Delta is the site of most of the country's oil wealth. Groups indigenous to the area have been demanding a larger share of the oil revenues for some time. The most notable of these are the Ijaw, the country's fourth-largest ethnic group. In December 1998, the Ijaw Youth Council issued the Kaiama Declaration, which signaled an intensified struggle against the oil companies and the government. The Abubakar regime responded with a heightened military presence, resulting in a number of civilian deaths, and accusations of human rights abuses over the ensuing months. Third, the country's finances were in a parlous state, owing to a combination of low oil prices, high debt payments and years of kleptocratic misrule. The situation was made worse in the final months of the Abubakar regime, when the government's financial reserves were dramatically reduced. It was widely suspected that the money was being used to compensate departing military officers. A related controversy involved charges that a number of top military officers had been awarded lucrative oil blocks shortly before the departure of the regime.

But despite these enduring problems, the inauguration of the democratically elected Obasanjo regime on May 29, 1999, was a cause for celebration both in Nigeria and among its friends abroad. While the coming years could be expected to be very difficult, there was a sense that the country had been given one more chance to fulfill its tremendous potential. If the Fourth Republic fails, it is not clear how many more chances Nigeria will have. If it succeeds, however, Nigeria can expect to resume its role as the continental leader.

The Dictionary

-A-

ABACHA, GEN. SANI. Head of State and Commander in Chief of the Armed Forces. A Kanuri (q.v.), born on September 20, 1943, in Kano (q.v.), Kano State (q.v.), and educated at Government College in Kano (1957–62), Abacha started his military training in 1962 at the Nigerian Military Training College in Kaduna (q.v.). In 1963 he was sent to the Mons Defence Cadet College in the United Kingdom and in 1976 to the School of Infantry in Jaji, Nigeria. In 1981 Abacha attended the National Institute of Policy and Strategic Studies in Kuru, Nigeria, and the Senior International Defence Management Course in Monterey, California, USA, in 1982. Among the many important military posts General Abacha has held are battalion commander, brigade commander, and general staff officer of the Army School of Infantry. He was also director of army training and general commanding officer of the Second Mechanized Infantry Division. When he was still a brigadier, he announced the overthrow of the civilian administration of Alhaji Shehu Shagari (q.v.) on December 31, 1983. He also addressed the press in August 1985 after Brigadier Joshua N. Dogonyaro (q.v.) had previously announced the overthrow of Major General Muhammadu Buhari (q.v.). Under the General I. B. Babangida administration (q.v.) (1985–93), he was regarded as the de facto number two man in the administration, having served as chief of army staff, chief of defence staff and minister of defence at various times and a member of the highest decision-making body in the administration, the Armed Forces Ruling Council (q.v.). When General Babangida "stepped aside" after installing the Interim National Government (q.v.) headed by Chief Ernest A.O. Shonekan (q.v.), Abacha was the most senior military officer in that administration. On November 17, 1993 General Abacha became the Head of State and Commander-in-Chief of the Armed Forces (q.v.). Many people believed he would "right" the "wrong" done by General Babangida's annulment of the results of the presidential election of June 12, 1993, but upon assuming power, Abacha began to entrench himself in power, a move that would lead to political and economic crises.

The summer of 1994 marked an increase in the level of repression of the Abacha regime. On June 11, M.K.O. Abiola (q.v.) declared himself President, and was shortly thereafter arrested and charged with treason. There were protests against this arrest, the most notable of which was the strike of National Union of Petroleum and Natural Gas Workers (NUPENG) (q.v.), which demanded among other things handing over power to the winner of the June 12 election. The strike lasted for two months and virtually paralysed the economy of the nation before the military intervened forcefully to end it. A number of pro-democracy activists including Frank Kokori (q.v.), the general secretary of NUPENG, were arrested and put in detention. The government suspended the leaders of NUPENG and the Nigerian Labour Congress (NLC) (q.v.). Abiola would remain in prison until his death on July 7, 1998.

Over the ensuing years, Sani Abacha's government established itself as one of the most repressive in Africa. The regime began to rely increasingly on detention, torture and perhaps even assassination. Many of these abuses were carried out by the much feared Special Bodyguard, 2,000–3,000 troops trained in North Korea and directly answerable to Abacha. In March 1995, around 40 civilian and military critics of the regime were arrested on charges of planning a military coup (charges which continue to be disputed). These included former military head of state General Olusegun Obasanjo (q.v.), and his second in command, Major General Shehu Musa Yar'Adua (who died in prison under mysterious circumstances in December 1997) (q.v.). On November 10, 1995, the writer and minority rights activist Kenule B. Saro-Wiwa (q.v.) was executed together with eight other Ogoni (q.v.) leaders. They were accused of murdering four rival leaders, but they were prevented from presenting a reasonable defence at their military trial. Opposition leaders who were assassinated under mysterious circumstances include Kudirat Abiola (the wife of M.K.O. Abiola) and Alfred Rewane. Repression fell particularly hard on Abiola's supporters in the southwest, who were frequently imprisoned during this period, including Chief Ganiyu O. Fawehinmi (q.v.), Dr. Bekolari Ransome-Kuti (q.v.) and Olu Falae. Others, such as Wole Soyinka (q.v.), Anthony Enaharo (q.v.) and General Alani Akinrinnade (q.v.) were forced into exile. In December 1997, the government claimed to have uncovered another coup plot against it, and imprisoned a number of military officers, including General Oladipo Diya (q.v.), the second-highest-ranking member of the regime and the most prominent Yoruba military officer.

The human rights abuses of the Abacha regime brought increasing international condemnation. The 1995 assassination of Ken Saro-Wiwa led to Nigeria's suspension from the Commonwealth and the imposition of various sanctions by the United States, members of the European Union, South Africa, and other countries. Relations with the United States reached a nadir when Nigerian security forces forcibly dispersed a party for departing U.S. ambassador Walter Carrington in September 1997, a startling breach of diplomatic protocol. Within the West African region, however, Abacha retained a formidable power. Oil was provided to neighboring countries at concessional rates, and Nigerian troops were the backbone of the ECOMOG deployment in Liberia. In 1997, Nigeria initiated a military action to overturn a coup in Sierra Leone, and in 1998 the elected civilian government was briefly returned to power, before the country disintegrated into chaos.

Official statistics give the misleading impression that the economy performed respectably, but unimpressively, during the Abacha years. Inflation and the exchange rate were stabilized, and growth plodded along at the 2–3 percent range. In fact, however, Abacha's corruption and his apparent disregard for the welfare of the country had a terribly corrosive effect. During these years, the basic infrastructure of the country deteriorated at an alarming rate and the country's abysmal poverty levels continued to deepen. Billions of dollars were stolen by Abacha and his cronies (one prominent estimate puts Abacha's wealth at the time of his death at $6 billion). The apparent unwillingness/disinterest of Abacha in addressing the country's problems was indirectly acknowledged when he created the Petroleum Trust Fund (PTF) in 1996 under the leadership of former military head of state General Muhammadu Buhari. The PTF was independently funded and was responsible for addressing the country's declining infrastructure and growing poverty, problems that received no serious attention from the regime itself.

As with Ibrahim Babangida (1985–93), Sani Abacha sought to legitimate his regime by promising a transition to an elected civilian regime. The two transitions were remarkably similar: beginning with a National Constitutional Conference (1994–95), and progressing to the formation of political parties and series of staggered elections at the local, state and national government levels. From the start, many suspected that Abacha intended to manipulate the transition to have himself elected president, and perpetuate his tenure in office. These fears appeared to have been confirmed in early 1998, when all five of the official political parties endorsed Abacha as their presidential candidate. As widespread opposition to Abacha's candidacy mounted within the society and the elite, it appeared that Nigeria was headed for a potentially disastrous confrontation between the military and the civil society. On June 8, 1998, however, Abacha died from an apparent heart attack. While an autopsy was never performed, many observers both inside and outside Nigeria suspect that he was poisoned by his opponents in the military.

Abacha's regime was perhaps the most ruinous in the history of the country. One positive outcome of this period is that it appeared to have brought about recognition of the dangers that military rule posed for Nigeria in terms of corruption and human rights abuses. Abacha's successor, Gen. Abdulsalami Abubakar carried out a rapid transition to democratic rule that was completed on May 29, 1999.

ABA RIOT. The immediate cause of the riot was the belief, though mistaken, that the colonial government was ready to tax women. As far back as 1926, the government had decided that people in the Eastern Region (q.v.) and parts of the west who were not then paying tax should be made to pay in the form of a poll tax. This was to be levied on adult males only. But in 1929 a warrant chief by the name of Okugo of Oloko near Aba, while assessing the taxable wealth of the people of the area began to count women, children and their animals. Rumors spread that this was the beginning of the policy to tax all women. The women in Aba, a town about 65 kilometres northeast of Port Harcourt (q.v.), and Owerri, Aba's neighboring town to the north, rose up in arms against the administration. They attacked chiefs and Europeans and destroyed property and goods belonging mainly to expatriate trading firms. As the riot grew in intensity and expanse, the police were asked to open fire, leaving over 30 persons dead and many more wounded.

Two commissions of inquiry were set up to look into the causes of the riot. The first, an official one, tended to exonerate the officials involved. But the second one, which included two Nigerian barristers, was critical of the way the administration handled the uprising. It attributed the causes of the riot to: the low prices received by the people for their farm produce and the high prices they had to pay for imported ones; discontent arising from the taxation of men; and the persecution, corruption and extortion practised by native court members; and, finally, to the belief that the government was about to impose tax on women. The secretary of state for the colonies (q.v.) accepted the second report and blamed the riot on faulty intelligence. According to him, the government had insufficient knowledge of the indigenous institutions and the life of the people.

ABAYOMI, SIR KOFOWOROLA ADEKUNLE. An eye specialist and a politician. Born on July 10, 1896, in Lagos (q.v.), he attended the University of Edinburgh and the Moorfield Eye Hospital in London where he specialized in ophthalmology. He returned to Nigeria in 1930 and set up a private practice, which he combined with politics.

In 1933 he was a foundation member of the Lagos Youth Movement (q.v.), which later became the Nigerian Youth Movement (NYM) (q.v.)—the first truly nationalist organization. In 1938 he took over the presidency of NYM after the death of Dr. J.C. Vaughan. In the same year he was elected as a NYM member to the Legislative Council (q.v.) in Lagos. After serving for two years, he resigned and went to Britain for further studies.

He later served in many public positions, including on the Yaba Higher College Advisory Board and the Board of Medical Examiners. He was a member of the University College of Ibadan Council until 1961. He was the president of Nigeria's Society for the Blind in 1948. He was made the chairman of the University Teaching Hospital Board in 1951; and in 1964, he was the chairman of the Federal Electoral Commission (q.v.) but resigned a few months later. He died in January 1979.

ABAYOMI, LADY OYINKA MORENIKE. A teacher, social worker, administrator and politician, Lady Abayoni was born in 1897 and educated in the Church Missionary Society School (q.v.) in Lagos (q.v.), and Ryeford Hall College, Gloucester, England. She studied music in London, and, when she came back to Nigeria, she began to teach at the Anglican Girls School where she had received her primary education. She was the founder and president of the Girls Guide of Nigeria and was also national president and national consultant to the Young Women's Christian Association of Nigeria. As a young woman she devoted much of her time to social work. She later became a politician and was elected to public office. Lady Abayomi was nationally honored as Commander of the Order of the Federal Republic, and she is also a Member, Order of the British Empire.

ABDULLAHI BAYERO COLLEGE, KANO. Formerly known as Ahmadu Bello College, Kano, it was set up in 1960 by the Northern Regional Ministry of Education to prepare high school graduates for the advanced level of the General Certificate of Education (G.C.E. A Level) in Arabic, Islamic History, Hausa and English. In 1962 the Ahmadu Bello College became incorporated into the new University of Zaria, Ahmadu Bello University (ABU) (q.v.) and it changed its name to Abdullahi Bayero College, named after the former Emir of Kano, Abdullahi Bayero (q.v.). Thus, the post-secondary courses offered by the college became preliminary courses for entry into ABU. The college grew as a center for Arabic and Islamic studies, and in 1969 the center for Hausa studies was established in it. In 1975 it became a full-fledged university known as Bayero University, Kano, owned and financed by the Federal Government.

ABDULLAHI IBN MUHAMMAD. A scholar, poet, war leader and administrator, he was the younger brother of Usman Dan Fodio (q.v.) and one of the leaders of the Fulani (q.v.) Islamic revolution initiated by Dan Fodio. Abdullahi accompanied his brother on his missionary activities to many Hausa States (q.v.) like Gobir (q.v.) and Zamfara before the beginning of the jihad (q.v.) (holy war) in 1804. When the jihad began, he was one of his brother's military commanders and advisers because Dan Fodio was a scholar and had little understanding of military matters. In 1812, when most of the Fulani empire had been secured, Dan Fodio divided the empire between his son Muhammad Bello (q.v.) and Abdullahi. Abdullahi ruled his own part of the empire, including Nupe (q.v.) and Ilorin (q.v.), from Gwandu (q.v.). When his brother, Dan Fodio, died in 1817, Abdullahi was away from Sokoto (q.v.), but rushed back to contest for the leadership of the empire. But Muhammad Bello had already assumed leadership. The two men later reconciled. Abdullahi, some time after, retired to devote himself to study and writing, leaving the affairs of the caliphate to his son and nephew. He wrote many books, including a biography of Usman Dan Fodio. He died in 1829.

ABDUSALAMI. The first Fulani (q.v.) Emir (q.v.) of Ilorin (q.v.) from about 1824 to 1830. His father Alimi, a Fulani Muslim priest, had helped Afonja (q.v.), the Yoruba (q.v.) ruler of Ilorin to fight for Ilorin's independence from the Alaafin (q.v.) of Oyo. Later on, Afonja's troops, mostly Hausa (q.v.) and Fulani, revolted against him and Abdusalami seized power. He was recognized as an Emir by Muhammed Bello (q.v.), who was then at the head of the Fulani empire (q.v.) in Sokoto (q.v.). He died about 1830.

ABEOKUTA. The capital city of Ogun State (q.v.) since 1976, it is located about 106 kilometres north of Lagos (q.v.), the federal capital, and about 80 kilometres southwest of Ibadan (q.v.), capital of Oyo State. Abeokuta was said to have been founded in 1830 by one Sodeke who led a party of refugees fleeing from Ibadan during the Yoruba (q.v.) intertribal wars. Abeokuta, meaning in the Yoruba language "under the rock," derived its name from the cave dwellings of the Egba (q.v.) refugees under huge overhanging rocks. Later on, new groups of refugees from different parts of the Yoruba land followed them. At Abeokuta the refugees were kept together in separate communities and in different parts of the area. This explains why today there are many towns within the city of Abeokuta and why each has its own traditional ruler. The various towns in Abeokuta are Ibara, Ijaiye, Owu, Oke-Ona and Gbagura, while the traditional rulers are Alake of Abeokuta, the Oshile of Oke-Ona, Agura of Gbagura, Olowu of Owu and the Olubara of Ibara. However, because of the belief that the first Alake was the first settler in Abeokuta, the Alake has been given a central position among the Obas.

The people of Abeokuta have been prominent in the acquisition of Western-type education. They came in contact with white missionaries as early as 1842, who began the process of educating Nigerians. In 1846, the Rev. Henry and Mrs. Townsend (q.v.) and Rev. Samuel Ajayi Crowther (q.v.), a Nigerian clergyman went to the town and were given three acres of land at Ake for their first church. Abeokuta was the home of the first secondary grammar school in Western Nigeria, the Abeokuta Grammar School, which opened in 1908. However, in spite of this early acceptance of Western education, Abeokuta was for decades a depressed area. Things began to change rapidly when the city became the capital of the newly created Ogun State in 1976.

ABIA STATE. Created out of Imo State (q.v.) as one of the nine states created by the federal military government of General Ibrahim B. Babangida (q.v.) on August 27, 1991, Abia State is located in the southeastern region of Nigeria and lies within the latitudes 4° 40′ and 6° 14′N, and longitudes 7° 10′ and 8°E. It shares common borders with Imo State on the west, Anambra State (q.v.) on the northeast, Enugu State (q.v.) on the north, Cross River State (q.v.) and Akwa Ibom State (q.v.) on the east and southeast, and Rivers State (q.v.) on the south where the Imo River serves as a natural boundary.

With the capital in Umuahia, Abia State covers an area of 7,627 square kilometres, which is about 8.5 percent of the country's land area. The state is divided into 17 local government areas, and is topographically between 120 and 180 metres above sea level.

Abia State has two main seasons. The rainy season is from March to October, and the annual rainfall is between 1,900 and 2,200 millimetres. The dry season is between November and March, with January to March as the hottest months. The relative humidity is high throughout the year, reaching about 90 percent during the rainy season. The vegetation is part of the tropical rain forest dominant in the south of the country.

Abia State is rich in mineral resources including petroleum, natural gas, shale oil, coal, lead, copper, salt, limestone, kaolin, clays and phosphate.

The population of Abia State was 2,297,978 in 1991. The main population centres in the state are Umuahia, the state capital city, Aba, a large commercial center, Afikpo, Ohafia, and Arochukwu. The rest of the state is mainly village settlements, and the people are farmers and businessmen and women. The farmers, about 70 per cent of the population, plant food crops like yams (q.v.), cassava (q.v.), cocoyam, maize, rice, cowpeas, groundnuts (q.v.) and soybeans, and for cash crops they grow coconut, cashew, rubber (q.v.), raffia, oil palm (q.v.), cocoa (q.v.), kolanuts (q.v.), plantain, banana (q.v.) and mango. The Igbo (q.v.) are the ethnic majority, and Igbo is spoken throughout the state.

The musical instruments the people enjoy include the gong, leather drums, wooden drums, flutes and earthen pot drums. Some traditional dances are *Nkwa Umu Agbogbo,* known as maiden dance, Ekpe dance in Arochukwu and the waist dance of Isiala Ngwa. There are many traditional festivals, some before planting season and others at harvest. The New Yams festival thanks God for a good season. The people engage in different works of art like carved doors, stools, walking sticks, pottery and Akwete cloth of Ukwa East.

In 1992 Abia State had 855 primary schools and 178 secondary schools. It also has many colleges, technical and polytechnic schools and a state university at Uturu. Most of the people are Christians of different denominations, with some Muslims and people who practice traditional religions like the Oracle (q.v.) of Arochukwu.

On October 1, 1996, the Abacha regime combined part of Abia State with part of Enugu State to create the state of Eboniyi.

ABIODUN. Said to be the last great ruler of the Oyo empire (q.v.), he ruled 1770–89. Abiodun deposed Gaha, the Basorun (q.v.) (head of the Council of State known as Oyomesi) who himself had deposed other rulers of the Oyo Empire. During his reign there was peace, and trade flourished. But the army declined and was defeated in 1783 by the Borgu army. He died in 1789, and the Oyo Empire rapidly declined afterwards.

ABIOLA, CHIEF MOSHOOD KASHIMAWO OLAWALE. A chartered accountant, publisher, philanthropist, businessman, politician and president-elect during the 1993 general election. Born on August 24, 1937, in Abeokuta, Ogun State (q.v.), he was educated at Baptist Boys' High School, Abeokuta, and in 1961 proceeded to the University of Glasgow in Scotland to study accountancy. In 1965 he became deputy chief accountant of the University of Lagos Teaching Hospital, and in 1967 he became the controller of Pfizer Products Ltd. In 1969 he was the comptroller of the International Telephone and Telegraph Nigeria Limited (ITT). He was later appointed vice-president of the ITT for Africa and the Middle East and also chairman and chief executive of the ITT Nigeria Limited in 1971.

Chief Abiola became very wealthy and used his riches for such philanthropic purposes as donating and building public institutions, community development efforts and establishing educational institutions and generous individual charities.

When the ban on politics was lifted in 1978, Chief Abiola became a member of the National Party of Nigeria (NPN) (q.v.) and became a true believer of its objectives and methods of uniting the country, especially in giving every major or minor ethnic group a share in the national decision making through the system of zoning (q.v.). He set up the Concord Press of Nigeria Ltd., the publisher of the national and Sunday *Concord Newspapers* and *Isokan,* a Yoruba counterpart.

In July 1982, Chief Abiola became disillusioned when his aspiration to become the NPN presidential candidate for the 1983 elections was thwarted. He said he could no longer remain in the party where he could not contest as an equal. He resigned from the NPN and from all partisan politics. But he later changed his mind. On June 12, 1993, he contested the presidency of the Federal Republic of Nigeria. After declaring almost half of the results of the elections in the states (14 out of 30), the National Electoral Commission (q.v.) suddenly stopped the announcements, and on June 23, 1993, the military president, General Ibrahim Babangida (q.v.) annulled the election results. The annulment of the election, which was declared to be the fairest and most orderly Nigeria had ever had, and which ran across the traditional divide of ethnicity, religion and regionalism, plunged the country into very serious and debilitating political and economic crises. According to the results tabulated from the states, Chief Abiola was the clear winner. His victory showed that he was popular throughout the nation, in the north as well as in the south. The military claimed that they were the only force that could maintain national unity. On June 11, 1994, Chief Abiola announced himself the president and was later arrested, put in detention and charged with treason. As of June 1996, he had not been tried.

Chief Abiola's detention led to further political and economic crises. A wave of popular anger against the military rule swept across the country, and, as the political crisis escalated, many people expressed separatist tendencies. In July 1994, the National Union of Petroleum and Gas Workers (NUPENG) (q.v.) went on strike, demanding among other things that the military hand over power to the winner of the 1993 election. The strike lasted for about two months, virtually paralysing the economy.

Efforts were made many times to free Chief Abiola, but they all failed, including an order by the federal appeal court that he be released on bail. The successor to Gen. Babangida, Sani Abacha (q.v.) openly ignored the ruling. In February 1996, Abiola complained to some of his visitors that he had not been allowed to see his doctor since November 1995. He was reported to be held under cruel conditions: no books, no newspapers, no radio, no good medical care, and visitations were strictly limited. The Abacha government wanted him to renounce his 1993 mandate and guarantee that he would no longer engage in politics. Ironically, Abiola's wife, Kudirat Abiola, who was struggling to keep her husband's condition on the nation's agenda, was brutally murdered in June 1996.

After Sani Abacha's death on June 8, 1998, the government began to prepare for the release of Chief Abiola from prison. On July 7, 1998, however, while meeting with envoys from the United States, Chief Abiola suffered a heart attack that killed him later that day. In the days following the death, riots rocked the major cities of the southwest, including Lagos, Ibadan and Abeokuta. In order to address suspicions that the military may have had a hand in Abiola's death, an international team of doctors was asked to perform an autopsy on Abiola. They concluded that Abiola was likely to have died from natural causes, although the harsh conditions under which the military had imprisoned him undoubtedly contributed to his sudden death.

In death, Chief Abiola continued to serve as a powerful symbol representing the long struggle for democracy and the oft-frustrated political ambitions of the Yoruba.

Chief Abiola was the holder of many traditional titles in the western, eastern and northern parts of Nigeria. The titles by which he is most popularly known are Bashorun of Ibadanland and Aare-Ona-Kakanfo of Yorubaland. He has an Honorary Degree of Doctor of Laws from the University of Tuskegee in the United States.

ABOYADE TECHNICAL COMMITTEE ON REVENUE ALLOCATION. This group was set up in June 1977 to examine the then existing revenue allocation formula to determine its adequacy in light of the factors of population, equality of status among the states, derivation, geographical peculiarities, even development, national interest and any other factors bearing on the problem. The committee was to recommend new proposals for the allocation of revenue between the federal, state and local governments, and make recommendations on measures necessary for effective collection and distribution of the federal and state revenues.

The committee rejected the old principles of revenue allocation, which it found either as politically controversial or lacking in statistically concise definitions, and suggested new principles of allocating federally derived revenue. These were equality of access to development opportunities, national minimum standards for national integration, absorptive capacity, independent revenue and minimum tax effort, and fiscal efficiency. It also recommended that 30 percent of the federally derived revenue should be shared among the states and 10 percent be shared among the local governments.

The report was accepted by the federal military government but was rejected by the civilian government that succeeded it in 1979 on the basis that it was too technical and out of tune with the nation's political realities. When Alhaji Shehu Shagari (q.v.) became president in 1979, he set up another revenue allocation commission known as the Okigbo Commission (q.v.).

ABUBAKAR, GENERAL ABDULSALAMI ALHAJI. The military leader of Nigeria from June 8, 1998, to May 29, 1999. His regime was transitional, and will probably be best remembered for voluntarily relinquishing power to a democratically elected regime.

Abubakar was born on June 13, 1942, in Minna in Niger State. He joined the Nigerian Air Force in 1963 and was sent to Germany for a flight-training course from 1964–66. Upon his return to Nigeria, he was transferred to the Army and served in the infantry during the Civil War (q.v.). The ensuing decades saw Abubakar's military career steadily progress. From 1975–77 he attended officer-training courses in the United States and from 1978–79 he commanded the Nigerial Battalion of the UN Interim Force in Lebanon. On December 1, 1993, up until he became the Head of State, General Abubakar was the Chief of Defence Staff. During this time,

Abubakar established a reputation for military professionalism. He was a devout Muslim, did not appear to be especially corrupt and unlike many of his contemporaries, never held an overtly political position.

When the Provisional Ruling Council (q.v.) selected Abubakar to become the military head of state following the death of Sani Abacha on June 8, 1998, it marked a new direction for Nigeria. While Abacha had been known for his corruption, brutality and apparent amorality, Abubakar was considered to be honest and was respected for his integrity. Upon assuming power, General Abubakar began to undo some of the worst excesses of the Abacha regime. Prominent political prisoners were released. A number of corrupt officials were detained, and some were forced to repay money they had stolen from the government. The pro-Abacha political parties were dissolved.

Abubakar faced his first political crisis when M.K.O. Abiola (q.v.), the winner of the June 12, 1993, presidential elections, died in detention on July 7, 1998. Reports indicate that Abiola was days away from being released from prison. Riots engulfed the southwestern part of the country, and calm did not return until Abubakar announced his own timetable for a democratic transition on July 20. The timetable envisioned a staggered series of elections commencing on December 5, and culminating with presidential elections on February 27, 1999. The winner of those elections was former military head of state, General Olusegun Obasanjo (q.v.), who assumed power on May 29, 1999.

While Abubakar won praise within his country for his good faith in carrying out democratic elections, he faced more difficulty in his management of the economy, his efforts to maintain ethnic harmony and his handling of the military. During the Abubakar regime, the low price of oil left the government constantly short of cash. In October 1998, an increase was announced in the minimum wage, but the government was later forced to rescind the increase when it found itself unable to finance the higher wages for government workers. In December, the government appeared to sanction an increase in the prices of petrol, kerosene and diesel. It reduced the amount of the increase, however, when confronted with widespread protests. The regime invited another controversy with its excessive spending in the spring of 1999, which rapidly depleted the country's foreign reserves.

The Abubakar regime also struggled to deal with conflict in the Niger Delta (q.v.), the source of most of the country's oil. Minorities in the area had grown restive over the government's appropriation of their region's oil resources. While the Ogoni (q.v.) had been the most prominent minority protesting oil policies in the early 1990s, by 1998 the more numerous Ijaw (q.v.) had taken the initiative in challenging the government and the oil companies. Angry youths regularly disrupted oil production and violent clashes with security forces became a regular occurrence. In December 1998, the issuance of the Kaiama Declaration by the Ijaw Youth Council appeared to initiate a more militant chapter in the struggle. Over the ensuing months, troops were moved into the oil-producing areas to maintain government control, and there were regular allegations of human rights abuses, including beatings and the shooting of unarmed protesters. Despite these strong-arm tactics, the regions remained embroiled in turmoil.

But perhaps the biggest challenge that General Abubakar faced was controlling his own military. Many officers were openly ambitious and chafed at surrendering power to a civilian regime. An early controversy centered on whether regionally based armies should be allowed. While the idea was supported by a number of leaders in the southern part of the country, it enjoyed virtually no support within the military hierarchy, due to the fear that it would lead to the disintegration of the country. Other controversies dividing the PRC were the decision to release suspects in the alleged 1995 and 1997 coup attempts, whether service chiefs would retire with General Abubakar and accusations that lucrative oil exploration blocks had been awarded to powerful officers as a kind of "golden parachute."

To his credit, General Abubakar did not let his struggles with these problems delay his promised exit on May 29, 1999. Despite, or perhaps because of, his short tenure, Abdulsalami Abubakar is likely to be remembered as one of the country's more successful military leaders.

ABUBAKAR III, SULTAN SIDDIQ. The Sultan of Sokoto from 1938–88, the most powerful traditional ruler in northern Nigeria. He was born on March 15, 1903, in Dange. This was ironically the same day that the British captured Sokoto. In 1931, Abubakar was made the Sardauna, one of the most important positions in the hierarchy of the Sokoto Caliphate. In June 1938, he was selected to become the Sultan following the sudden death of Sultan Hassan. The other main contender for the position was Ahmadu Bello, who went on to become the most influential politician in the Northern Region.

Over the course of his reign, Sultan Abubakar III held power under the colonialists, two democratically elected civilian regimes and numerous military regimes. During this period, the powers of traditional rulers in Nigeria steadily decreased. Nevertheless, the Sultan continued to play an important role as a respected leader. In times of crisis (such as the 1966 coups and the Civil War) he would reassure the public and help to maintain public order. In religious matters he was often referred to as "sarkin musulmi" (or "leader of the [northern] Muslims"). In this role, he worked to resolve disagreements among the different Islamic factions of the north.

Sultan Siddiq Abubakar III died on November 1, 1988.

ABUJA. Nigeria's new Federal Capital Territory (FCT), Abuja lies east of Niger State (q.v.), south of Kaduna State (q.v.), west of Plateau State (q.v.) and north of Kogi State (q.v.). Lagos (q.v.), the former capital territory, wedged between the lagoon and the Atlantic Ocean on the one side and Ogun State (q.v.) on the other, had by 1975 become so congested that there was need for a new territory for the nation's capital. Upon coming into power in 1975, General Murtala R. Muhammed (q.v.) set up a panel, headed by Justice Timothy Akinola Aguda (q.v.), to look into the possibility of removing the capital territory from Lagos to some other place. The panel recommended that a new territory—centrally located with an area of about 8,000 square kilometres—should become the new federal territory.

The capital was planned to cover 250 square kilometres. The lowest elevation of 70 metres above sea level is found in the floodplain of River Guraja, while the highest is about 760 metres. The FCT records highest temperature of about 37°C during the dry season and the lowest of about 17°C. During the rainy season, March to October, it may fall to about 70°C. Its relative humidity during the dry season ranges from 20 to 30 per cent, while it may rise to 50 percent in the rainy season.

The population of the FCT in 1991 was 378,671 people. The area is divided into four local governments, each headed by a deputy mayor, while the administration of the whole territory is under a mayor.

The ethnic groups who live in the FCT are the Gwari (q.v.), Gwandara, Koro, Bassa, Ebira, Hausa (q.v.), Cade, Tiv (q.v.) and others, but the population is predominately Gwari. A substantial proportion of the people who live in the area are adherents of traditional religions, while the others are Muslims or Christians, but these two religions have not had much impact. Because the FCT is almost entirely rural, about 80 percent of the people are farmers. However, the federal capital city (FCC) is urban, occupied mainly by civil servants who moved there when the seat of the Federal Government changed in 1991. The FCC's surrounding areas are growing in population and changing to a more urban life-style.

ABURI MEETING. This meeting of the Supreme Military Council (q.v.) of Nigeria between January 4 and 5, 1967, at Aburi, Ghana (q.v.), was placed under the auspices of the Ghanaian head of state, General Ankran, when the conflict between the federal military government headed by General Yakubu Gowon (q.v.) and the former eastern regional government, headed by Lieutenant Colonel C. Odumegwu Ojukwu (q.v.) could not be amicably resolved.

At the meeting, the attendees agreed to renounce the use of force for settling conflicts between the two sides and to reorganize the armed forces. The army was to be governed by the Supreme Military Council, the chairman of which would be known as Commander-in-Chief and head of the federal military government. There would be a military headquarters with equal representation from each of the regions, and headed by a chief of staff. Each region was under an area commander. The personnel of the area command was to be drawn wholly from the people of the region and, so long as military rule lasted, military governors were to have control over internal security in their respective areas. Furthermore, all matters of policy, including appointments and promotions of persons in executive posts in the armed forces and police, were to be dealt with by the Supreme Military Council.

They also agreed that all decisions on matters affecting the whole country would be determined by the Supreme Military Council with the concurrence of every member of the council; for example, they agreed to set up a committee to look into the problem of rehabilitating displaced persons and recovering their property. Civil servants who had left their posts because of the disturbances would continue to receive their normal salary until the end of March 1967, provided they had not found alternative jobs.

Finally, all appointments to diplomatic and consular posts, and to senior posts in the armed forces and the police, together with those carrying superscale salaries in the federal civil service and federal corporations, required the approval of the Supreme Military Council.

These agreements were important for at least two reasons: the agreement that a region should constitute an area command under the control of the regional military governor in internal security gave the military governor of the Eastern Region control over the military unit in his area. Second, by introducing the principle of unanimity in decision making on matters that concerned the whole country, the military governors were each granted a veto power which was tantamount to a regional veto.

As was expected, interpretations of these provisions differed on both sides and there could be no agreement in carrying them out. The decree supposedly issued to implement the agreements was rejected by Colonel Ojukwu and, from then on, relations between the two sides worsened, leading progressively to civil war in 1967.

ACHEBE, PROF. CHINUA. A writer, born in November 1930 at Ogidi, near Onitsha (q.v.) in Anambra State (q.v.) where his father was teaching at a mission school, he received his secondary education in Umuahia in Imo State (q.v.) and later went to University College in Ibadan (q.v.). In 1954 he became a producer of the Nigerian Broadcasting Corporation (NBC) in Lagos (q.v.) and, in 1959, he was the regional controller of NBC's Enugu station. In 1961 he became the first Director of NBC's External Broadcasting Service, known then as the "Voice of Nigeria," in Lagos.

In 1967 Achebe became a Senior Research Fellow at the University of Nigeria, Nsukka (q.v.). During the Nigerian Civil War (q.v.), he supported the Biafran (q.v.) cause. In 1971 he became the director of African Studies at the University of Nigeria, Enugu Branch, as well as the editor of a literary journal, *Okike*.

In 1972 he was a visiting professor of English in the United States at the University of Massachusetts at Amherst, and in 1975 he was at the University of Connecticut at Storrs. Upon his return to Nigeria, he was appointed professor of english at the University of Nigeria, Nsukka, and became the director of Heinemann Educational Books Nigeria Limited.

Professor Achebe has written many books, among which are *Things Fall Apart* (1958), *No Longer at Ease* (1960), *Arrow of God* (1964), *A Man of the People* (1966), *Chike and the River* (1966), *How the Leopard Got His Claws* (1973), *Morning Yet on Creation Day* (1975), *Trouble with Nigeria* (1983), *Anthills of the Savannah* (1987), *Hopes and Impediments* (1987).

For his literary achievement, Achebe has received many national and international honours and awards, including the Nigerian National Trophy (1961), the "Jock" Campbell *New Statesman* Award (1965), the Commonwealth Poetry Prize (1972), the Honorary Fellowship of the Modern Language Association of America (1974), and honorary doctorate degrees from the University of Stirling in Scotland and the University of Southampton, England, in 1974. In 1975 he won the Lotus International Prize for Afro-Asian Writers and the Neill Gunn International Prize of the Scottish Arts Council in 1975. He was also an honorary fellow of the Ghana Association of Writers. Professor Achebe was a member of the People's Redemption Party (PRP) (q.v.) and the deputy national president of the party in 1983.

While visiting Nigeria in March 1990 Achebe was involved in a car crash, injuring his spine. As a result, he was confined to a wheelchair.

ACTION GROUP CRISIS OF 1962. A crisis developed after Chief Obafemi Awolowo (q.v.) surrendered the premiership of the Western Region (q.v.) to a deputy whom he did not like. He also failed, contrary to his expectations, to secure enough seats in the federal Parliament in 1959 to become the first prime minister of an independent Nigeria. This failure reduced him to continuing as the national president of the Action Group Party (q.v.) and leader of the opposition in the federal Parliament in Lagos (q.v.). As party leader, Chief Awolowo believed that he should exercise the power of supervision over all the activities of the Action Group, including those under the authority of the government of the Western Region. He asked that he should be duly consulted before major changes in policy and major appointments were made. Chief S.L. Akintola (q.v.), his deputy and premier of the Western Region, bitterly resented this.

Other areas of disagreement included the question of whether or not the Action Group should join in a national government which Prime Minister Alhaji A. Tafawa Balewa (q.v.) believed would strengthen national unity, but which would considerably limit the Action Group opposition to the National Council of Nigerian Citizens (NCNC) (q.v.) and the Northern People's

Congress (NPC) (q.v.) in their own regions. Even though Chief Akintola supported the idea, Chief Awolowo did not. He preferred the formation of a progressive alliance that would dislodge the NPC from its grip on the north. He, therefore, wanted a policy of collaborating with the NCNC with the hope that more states would be created in the north.

Ideologically, the two men were not in agreement. Chief Awolowo supported the ideology of democratic socialism, while he, as the Coker Commission of Inquiry (q.v.) showed, allowed party leaders close to him to amass wealth. Chief Akintola preferred to leave things as they were. Finally, there was the undying belief of Chief Awolowo that Chief Akintola wanted to supplant him as the party leader. This Chief Awolowo regarded as perfidy.

The crisis came to a head at the party congress in Jos (q.v.), Plateau State (q.v.) in February 1962. Because Sir Ahmadu Bello (q.v.), premier of the Northern Region, was then visiting Ibadan (q.v.), the capital of Western Nigeria, Chief Akintola and some of his close associates left the congress to give a courtesy reception to Bello. After Chief Akintola's departure, the congress decided to amend the party constitution to exclude regional ministers from membership in the Federal Executive Council (q.v.) of the party and to provide for the removal of any parliamentary leader by the body that put him in office. At the congress, Awolowo's supporters gained control of the party, and they began the move to oust Chief Akintola. In spite of several "peace" efforts to reconcile the two leaders and their factions, and in spite of the public apology of Chief Akintola to the party, Awolowo was determined to press the issue to a definite conclusion.

On May 19, 1962, at a joint meeting of the Western and Mid-Western Regional Executive Committee, Chief Akintola was asked, by a vote of 81 to 29, to tender his resignation as premier of the region and as deputy leader of the party. This decision was later confirmed by the Federal Executive Committee. Consequently, Chief Akintola was deposed as deputy party leader and, because he would not voluntarily resign from the post of premier, the governor of the region removed him after he received a no-confidence petition signed by 65 of 117 members of the House of Assembly (q.v.). Alhaji D.S. Adegbenro (q.v.) was then appointed as premier. But Chief Akintola argued that the only vote that could remove him from office was a majority vote in the Western Regional House of Assembly, and so he went to court.

On May 25 Adegbenro summoned a meeting of the House of Assembly and requested for a vote of confidence in his new government. But suddenly a member began to throw chairs, creating disorder in the House. Police dispersed the members with tear gas. Both sides had telephone conversations with the prime minister of the Federation (q.v.) in Lagos who acknowledged the right of the House to meet but refused to provide police protection within the chamber, and said that the Federal Government would not accept any decisions reached in the course of their deliberations if the police guarded them. Later, when fighting again broke out in the House, the "honorable" members were dispersed, and the House was locked up. On May 29 the Federal Parliament was summoned for its meeting, and a motion was carried that a state of public emergency existed in the region. Existing emergency regulations then came into operation, while others were passed. The federal government appointed Dr. M.A. Majekodunmi (q.v.), who at the time was a senator and the federal minister of health, to administer the affairs of the region for six months. Immediately after he assumed office, the governor, premier, ministers and other government officials were removed from office. Leaders of both factions were detained in various places, but Chief Akintola and his supporters were released in less than two months, giving rise to the accusation that the administrator and the federal government were not even-handed. As the emergency period passed, the Supreme Court (q.v.) in July ruled that the ex-governor of the Western Region had acted unconstitutionally when he removed Chief Akintola as premier without a vote of no confidence being passed on the floor of the House of Assembly. Furthermore, in December the Coker Commission of Inquiry, which was set up by the federal government during the period to look into the affairs of statutory corporations in the Western Region, reported incidence of malpractices and illegal syphoning of money to the Action Group Party. Even though the party president knew about the misconduct, it exonerated Chief Akintola from any blame.

Before this report was released, however, the police unearthed an alleged plot to overthrow the Federal Government. The plot involved some top members of the Action Group, some of whom had fled the country. Sam Ikoku (q.v.), the national secretary of the party went to Ghana (q.v.). Chief Anthony E. Enahoro (q.v.), the second vice president of the party and a member of the tactical committee, sought asylum in Britain but was later brought back into the country, tried and sentenced. Chief Awolowo and many of his followers were found guilty and sentenced to varying terms of imprisonment. Chief Awolowo was given 10 years. In December 1962, the prime minister, seeing that the Action Group party members in the House of Representatives had dwindled from 75 to 20, declared that he would no longer recognize Chief Awolowo as leader of the opposition.

When the emergency administration came to an end on January 1, 1963, Chief Akintola was reinstated as premier of the region, leading his own faction which had formed the United People's Party (q.v.). The party formed a coalition with the NCNC whose parliamentary leader was Chief R.A. Fani-Kayode (q.v.), popularly known as "Fani-Power," who became the deputy premier. At this juncture, only 38 of the 82 members of the party in the regional house remained loyal to the Action Group Party under the leadership of Alhaji Adegbenro, who then became the leader of the opposition. But, in May 1963, the Judicial Committee of the Privy Council (q.v.) in London, to which appeals from the Supreme Court in Nigeria lay, accepted the appeal of Adegbenro against Akintola and reversed the Supreme Court decision. The Western Regional House of Assembly then hurriedly amended the regional constitution retroactively—the premier could not be removed without a vote of no confidence in the House of Assembly. The federal Parliament endorsed this amendment and abolished all appeals from thenceforth to the Privy Council.

ACTION GROUP PARTY (AG). A political party formed in March 1950 by Chief Obafemi Awolowo (q.v.). At the first meeting eight members, including the founder, were present, and they decided to name it "Action Group" (a group that was disciplined and that meant action, not words). It operated in secret for a whole year, after which it was publicly launched on March 21, 1951. Its aims were:

1. To bring and organise within its fold all nationalists in the former Western Region (q.v.), i.e., the present Lagos, Ogun, Oyo, Osun, Ondo, Edo and Delta States so that they might work together as a united and disciplined group.
2. To prepare and present to the public, programmes for all government departments and to work hard to see them carried out.

Its undeclared aim was to capture political power in the Western Region under the electoral system of the 1951 constitution.

AG's slogan was "Freedom for All and Life More Abundant." According to AG followers, there was freedom for all when colonial rule was terminated; and there was life more abundant when there was education for all school-age children and general enlightenment of all illiterate adults. Furthermore, there was life more abundant when there was provision of health and general welfare for all, and total abolition of want in the society. Between 1951 and 1957, the party had become firmly established in the Western Region. The AG then turned its mind to winning the Federal Government election of 1959 but failed. Chief Awolowo became leader of the opposition in the federal parliament, while he reluctantly agreed that the deputy leader of the party, Chief S.L. Akintola (q.v.), should become the premier of the Western Region.

In 1962 a crisis ensued during which Chief Akintola was removed from the positions of premier and deputy leader of the party. After the state of emergency in the Western Region and Chief Akintola's United People's Party (q.v.) was installed in government, the AG became the opposition party under the leadership of Alhaji D.S. Adegbenro (q.v.). In 1964 the party formed an alliance with the National Council of Nigerian Citizens (NCNC) (q.v.)

and formed themselves into the United Progressive Grand Alliance (UPGA) (q.v.) to fight for the 1964 general elections. There were too many reports of election malpractices, but, in the end, the Nigerian National Alliance (NNA) (q.v.) made up of the Northern Peoples Congress (NPC) (q.v.) and Nigerian National Democratic Party (NNDP) was declared the winner. People, especially in the Western Region, the stronghold of the Action Group, hoped to deal a death blow to Akintola's NNDP party in the October regional election of 1965, but it was more brazenly rigged than any one before. The people then took the law into their hands, and there was a serious breakdown of law and order. On January 15, 1966, the army came into power, and through Public Order Decree Number 34 of 1966 (q.v.), the Action Group and all other political parties were banned. *See also* ACTION GROUP CRISIS OF 1962.

ADAMA, MODIBBO. *See* ADAMAWA STATE.

ADAMAWA STATE. Created as one of the nine states on August 27, 1991, by the administration of General Ibrahim B. Babangida (q.v.) from Gongola State (q.v.), Adamawa State has its capital in Yola (q.v.) and is divided into 15 local government areas. During the colonial administration, Adamawa State used to be Adamawa province with headquarters in Yola. Adamawa has a long history. It was founded by the followers and military commanders of Usman Dan Fodio (q.v.) in the early 19th century, Modibbo Adama and Lamido Kabi—both Fulani (q.v.) leaders who led the jihad (q.v.) (holy war) in the Upper Benue region of the country. Usman Dan Fodio (q.v.) recognized Adama as a learned Muslim who could lead the revolution there. Adama made many conquests to establish the Kingdom of Fombia, now known as Adamawa, with Yola as the ruling family's headquarters.

Adamawa is located at the northeastern part of Nigeria where the Benue River (q.v.) enters Nigeria from Cameroon (q.v.). It lies between longitudes 11° and 5.5°E, and latitudes 10° and 14.75°N. It is bounded by Taraba State (q.v.) in the south and west, Bauchi State (q.v.) in the northwest, Borno State (q.v.) in the north, and Cameroon in the east.

The land area is 39,742 square kilometres, and the climate is tropical, characterized by rainy and dry seasons. The rainy season is between March and November. The rainfall is between 759 millimetres in the north and 1,051 millimetres in the south. The relative humidity varies from 25 to 36 percent in the dry season—December to March—and from 82 to 92 percent between June and September, the peak of the rainy season. The temperature varies from 11°C to 33°C. The vegetation also varies from south to north. The south is a savannah forest, while the north has short grasses and trees.

The population of the state in 1991 was 2,124,049 people, made up of many ethnic groups—the Fulani (q.v.), Hausa (q.v.), Chamba, Higgi, Ewatiya, Lunguda Bachama, Mbula and Kilba. Each group has its own language, but Hausa (q.v.) and Fulani are widely spoken. Most people in Adamawa State are farmers who produce maize, rice, guinea corn, cowpeas and millet. Some people are nomads. The main population centers are Yola, the capital, Jimeta, Numan and Combi.

Adamawa State is not as educationally advanced as many other states in the Federation. In 1991 it had only about 57,000 students enrolled in secondary schools. It has some colleges of education, polytechnics and a federal university in Yola.

ADEBAYO, MAJ. GEN. ROBERT ADEYINKA. Adebayo was born in 1928 in Ile-Ife (q.v.), Oyo State (q.v.), but his hometown is Iyin-Ekiti, Ondo State (q.v.). He was educated at Christ's School, Ado-Ekiti and at Eko Boys High School, Lagos (q.v.).

He enlisted in the Nigerian Army (q.v.) in 1948. He attended various military courses both in Ghana (q.v.) and in Britain. He served in the Congo under the United Nations Peacekeeping Force between 1961 and 1963. Between 1964 and 1965, he was chief of staff of the Nigerian Army. In August 1966, he was appointed the military governor of Western Nigeria after the death of Adekunle Fajuyi (q.v.) in the July 1966 coup. After the Civil War, he was the chairman of the commission that was established to look into the conduct of all officers who fought on the Biafran (q.v.) side, with a view to readmitting into the Nigerian Army those who were not involved in the mutiny or convicted of any sadistic behavior. In 1971 he was posted to head the Defence Academy at Kaduna (q.v.) with promotion as major general. He was retired from the army in August 1975 by the late General Murtala R. Muhammed's (q.v.) regime.

After the ban on political activities was lifted in 1978, he joined the National Party of Nigeria (q.v.) and became the national vice chairman of the party.

ADEBO, SIMEON OLAOSEBIKAN C.M.G. A lawyer and a diplomat. Born on October 5, 1913, in Abeokuta (q.v.), capital of Ogun State (q.v.), he attended St. Peter's Day School in Abeokuta, and Abeokuta Grammar School, and finished his secondary education in King's College in Lagos (q.v.) in 1932. In 1933 he became a clerk at the Nigerian Railway Corporation (q.v.). He later in 1945 went to study law in London and was called to the bar at Gray's Inn in 1948. Upon his return to Nigeria, he became an administrative officer and rose to the position of permanent secretary in the Ministry of Finance, Western Region (q.v.) from 1957 to 1959 and in the Treasury from 1959 to 1960. He became head of the civil service and chief secretary to the government of Western Nigeria in 1961. In 1962 he was appointed permanent representative of Nigeria to the United Nations (UN) in New York, U.S.A. In 1968 he was made the UN Under-Secretary-General and executive director of the UN Institute for Training and Research. After the civil war in 1970, he was appointed chairman of the salary review commission known as the Adebo Salary Review Commission. The commission granted interim salary increases to the workers to offset the effect of postwar inflation. In 1973 he became chairman of the National Universities Commission (q.v.) but resigned in 1979 when he was appointed chairman of the National Institute of Policy and Strategic Studies of Nigeria. He died in October 1994.

ADEBOLA, ALHAJI HAROUN POPOOLA. A trade unionist, born on October 1, 1916, at Ijebu-Ode, Ogun State (q.v.). After his primary education, he went to Abeokuta Grammar School and Ijebu-Ode Grammar School. He joined the Nigerian Railway Corporation (q.v.) in 1941 and became an elected member of the Western House of Assembly between 1952 and 1954. In 1959 he was elected president of the Nigerian Union of Railway Staff and in 1960 president of the Trade Union Congress of Nigeria (q.v.). In 1962 he became the president of the United Labour Congress of Nigeria (q.v.), a position he occupied until 1969. He was a member of the Western House of Chiefs from 1963 to 1965 and was vice president of the International Confederation of Free Trade Unions (q.v.) from 1965 to 1970. In 1977 he was nominated to serve on the constitution drafting committee.

ADEDEJI, PROF. ADEBAYO. Adedeji was born on December 21, 1930, at Ijebu-Ode, Ogun State (q.v.). He attended Ijebu-Ode Grammar School and later the University College, Ibadan, from 1953 to 1954 and then went to Leicester University in Britain from 1955 to 1958 where he earned a B.Sc. in economics. He returned home and became an assistant secretary in the Ministry of Economic Planning in Western Nigeria from 1958 to 1960. He then went to Harvard University (1960–61) where he received a masters degree in public administration. He later returned to Nigeria as principal secretary (Revenue) at the Treasury Department of the Ministry of Finance in Western Nigeria. In 1963 he joined the University of Ife (q.v.) as deputy director, Institute of Administration, and in 1967 he became the Director of the Institute. In 1968 he was made professor of public administration, University of Ife. In 1971 he became the federal commissioner for Economic Development and Reconstruction. In June 1975 he left the service of the federal government to become the executive secretary for the United Nations Economic Commission for Africa (ECA).

Professor Adedeji is the author of many articles and books, which include *Nigerian Administration and Its Political Setting* (1969), *Problems and Techniques of Administrative Training in Africa* (1969), *Nigerian Federal Finance: Its Problems and Prospects* (1969), *The Tanzania Civil Service: A Decade after Independence* (1974), *Africa: The Crisis of Development and the Challenge of a New Economic Order* (1977) and *Towards the Dawn of the Third Millenium and the Beginning of the Twenty-First Century* (1986).

ADEDOYIN, PRINCE ADELEKE. A politician born on March 3, 1912, in Lagos (q.v.), he attended the Methodist Boys' High School in Lagos. He later studied law and was called to the bar at the Inner Temple in 1940. In 1942 he was appointed as magistrate, first in Lagos and later transferred to Ikot-Ekpene in Eastern Nigeria. He was also then appointed commissioner of the Supreme Court (q.v.) and was put in charge of many towns in the Eastern Region (q.v.). He resigned his appointment in 1944 to enter politics. In 1947 he became a member of the Lagos Town Council and in the same year was elected as member of the legislative council under the Richards Constitution (q.v.). In the same year he was the secretary of the National Council of Nigeria and Cameroon (NCNC) (q.v.) and was one of the party's pan-Nigerian delegation to London to protest against the Richards Constitution of 1946 and to demand self-government for the country. In 1951 he was elected to the Western House of Assembly on the platform of the NCNC, and in 1952 he was elected from the Western House of Assembly to the House of Representatives in Lagos. However, in 1956 he had changed his party allegiance and was elected to the Western House of Assembly as an Action Group Party (q.v.) member. In 1957 he became the Speaker in the Western House of Assembly. In the 1960 Western Regional election, he was also elected and kept his position as Speaker. He held this post during the Action Group crisis of 1962 (q.v.), but, during it, he joined the Akintola (q.v.) faction, which later formed itself into the Nigerian National Democratic Party (NNDP) (q.v.). In 1964 he was elected on this party platform to the Federal House of representatives. After the military came to power in 1966, little was heard of Prince Adedoyin until the ban on politics was lifted in 1978. He then became one of the foundation members of the National Party of Nigeria (q.v.). He contested the national chairmanship of the party but lost to Chief A.M.A. Akinloye (q.v.).

ADEGBENRO, ALHAJI DAUDA SOROYE. A politician, born at Ago-Owu, Abeokuta (q.v.), in 1909 in Ogun State (q.v.), he was educated at the Baptist Boys' High School, Abeokuta, and Abeokuta Grammar School. He worked for the Nigerian Railway from 1930 to 1937, United African Company (UAC) (q.v.) from 1937 to 1940, and rejoined the railway in 1943. He became a businessman in 1945 but in 1951 he was elected as an Action Group Party (q.v.) member to the Western House of Assembly. As a member of the House, he held many ministerial appointments, including minister of lands and housing and minister of local government. During the Action Group crisis of 1962 (q.v.), he was chosen to replace Chief S.L. Akintola (q.v.) as premier of Western Nigeria, but the declaration of a state of emergency in the region by the federal government and the appointment of an administrator prevented him from acting in that position. In 1963 when Chief Akintola was reinstated in power as premier of the region, Adegbenro became the leader of the opposition, a post he occupied until 1966. In 1967, when the military decided on inviting civilians into their administration, Adegbenro was appointed commissioner for the Ministry of Trade and Industry until 1971. Since then he remained a private citizen in Abeokuta, where he died in 1975.

ADEKUNLE, BRIG. BENJAMIN MAJA ADESANYA. A soldier born on June 26, 1937, he was educated at Dekina Primary School and Government College, Okene, from 1951 to 1957. He enlisted in the army and was sent to the Officer Cadet Training School at Teshie in Accra, Ghana (q.v.), in 1958. In 1959 he proceeded to the Officer Cadet Training School, Aldershot, England, and then to Sandhurst Military Academy in England from 1960 to 1961. He was aide-de-camp to the governor of Eastern Nigeria from 1962 to 1963. Between 1964 and 1965, he was at the Defence Services Staff College, Wellington, in India. He was promoted to adjutant-general of the Nigerian Army (q.v.) in 1966 and became a brigade commander in 1967. During the Civil War, he commanded the Third Marine Commando, which made seaborne assaults on Bonny (q.v.) and the Mid-West early in the war. Under him the Third Marine Commando had some spectacular successes by taking Calabar (q.v.), Port Harcourt (q.v.), Aba and Owerri.

Brigadier Adekunle was seen as a man with the great talent of getting things done. After the war, this talent was again put to use when he was appointed by the government to relieve the congestion at the Lagos (q.v.) ports, a task again accomplished with great success. Adekunle is said to have inspired great respect and fear in his men during the war. He was otherwise known as the "Black Scorpion," a name given to him as a result of his brilliant performance on the war front. He was retired from the Nigerian Army in 1975. When the ban on political activities was lifted in 1978, he identified himself with the Nigerian People's Party (q.v.). But he later left the party to join the National Party of Nigeria (q.v.).

ADELABU, ALHAJI ADEGOKE ODUOLA AKANDE. A politician, born in 1915 in Ibadan (q.v.), the capital of Oyo State (q.v.). He had his elementary education at the Mapo Central School, Ibadan, and later went to Ibadan Government College in 1931 on a government scholarship and graduated from there in 1935. He went from there to Yaba Higher College (q.v.) in Lagos (q.v.), which then was the highest educational institution in the whole country, under the United African Company (UAC) (q.v.) scholarship. He did not complete his studies there, for in June 1935 he returned to Ibadan and was appointed secretary to the UAC regional manager and became in

1936 an assistant produce manager. In 1939 he resigned his appointment and joined the Union of Cooperative Societies as produce inspector. He later came back in 1945 to the UAC where he was appointed as assistant production manager in Lagos. By this time he was becoming keenly interested in politics and he decided to leave the UAC for good in 1946. In 1951 he joined the National Council of Nigeria and the Cameroons (NCNC) (q.v.) under the leadership of Dr. Nnamdi Azikiwe (q.v.). He was then elected the party's assistant secretary for Western Nigeria from which he later rose to be the first national vice president and a member of the party's executive committee. In the 1951 elections to the regional House of Assembly (q.v.), the NCNC (q.v.) won the majority, but, owing to the practice of "carpet crossing" begun then by some members of his party, the Action Group Party (AG) became the majority party and the NCNC became the opposition party in the House. In 1954 he was elected to the federal House of Representatives (q.v.) in Lagos and was appointed minister of natural resources and social services in the national government under Sir Alhaji Abubakar Tafawa Balewa (q.v.). He was also elected to the Ibadan District Council where he became the chairman, thus holding two public posts. In 1956 he resigned from both posts following allegations of administrative irregularities in the Ibadan City Council, but he was reelected to the Western House of Assembly where he again became the leader of the opposition.

He was a good orator and a hard-working politician. He was very popular in Ibadan. He led the Western Nigeria NCNC to the constitutional conference in London in 1957, but on March 23, 1958, he died in a motor accident. Because of the circumstances surrounding his death, his supporters believed that his political enemies had a hand in his death, which led to the Adelabu Riot.

ADELE II, ADENIJI. Oba of Lagos. Born in 1893, Oba Adeniji Adele was the grandson of Adele I, who reigned as Oba (q.v.) of Lagos (q.v.) before Lagos was ceded to the British in 1861. He attended the Church Missionary Society (q.v.) Grammar School in Lagos and later worked as a surveyor for the colonial government. As a surveyor, he travelled to different parts of the country. During the First World War, he volunteered for service and was with the Royal Engineers in the Cameroons from 1914 to 1915. He later worked in the government service in various capacities. While he was working in Kano (q.v.) as provincial treasurer in 1949 he was nominated as Oba of Lagos, but he was not crowned until three years later as there were challenges to his nomination. In 1952 he became a member of the Western House of Chiefs (q.v.), for at that time until 1954 Lagos administratively was part of Western Nigeria. He was at the same time the president of the Lagos town council under the 1953 Local Government Law. He died in 1964 and was succeeded by Oba Oyekan.

ADEMOLA, SIR ADETOKUNBO ADEGBOYEGA. A Chief Justice of the Supreme Court of Nigeria, Sir Adetokunbo Ademola was born on September 1, 1906, at Abeokuta (q.v.), Ogun State (q.v.). The son of Oba Ademola II, he received his education at St. Gregory's Grammar School and King's College, all in Lagos (q.v.). He later proceeded to the University of Cambridge, England, to study law and was called to the bar at the Middle Temple in London in 1934. Between 1934 and 1935, he was a crown counsel, but later went into private legal practice. He was made a magistrate in 1939 and became a judge in 1949. In 1955 he was appointed Chief Justice of Western Nigeria and in 1958 he became Chief Justice of the Federal Republic of Nigeria (q.v.) from which position he retired due to health reasons in 1975.

Ademola played many important roles in the politics of Nigeria after independence and during the First Republic. In the Action Group crisis of 1962 (q.v.) during which Chief S.L. Akintola (q.v.) was removed as premier of Western Nigeria, he presided over the court cases that emanated from the crisis. He also featured prominently in the effort to bring together the two factions into which the Action Group (q.v.) had been divided by merging the two then existing Yoruba cultural groups—Egbe Omo Oduduwa (q.v.) and Egbe Omo Yoruba into Egbe Omo Olofin. Also in January 1965 during the election crisis, when the president refused to call on Sir Abubakar Tafawa Balewa (q.v.) to form a new government, Sir Adetokunbo Ademola was then quietly mediating between the president and the prime minister until the president finally decided to perform his constitutional duty. Again in May 1967, in an effort to avoid military confrontation between the federal government and the Eastern Region (q.v.), which was itching for a secession, Ademola was one of the people who convened the National Reconciliation Committee (q.v.), which sent a delegation to Lt. Col. Ojukwu (q.v.) in Enugu (q.v.) to attend the next committee meeting in order to discuss pressing problems and ensure that the country did not disintegrate.

In addition to these mediating roles, he was also called upon to serve the nation on many important occasions. He was chairman of the Federal Census Board from 1972, and it was under his chairmanship when the ill-fated 1973 census was conducted. It was later cancelled in 1975 by the regime of General Murtala R. Muhammed (q.v.) because it did not command general acceptance. In 1976 he was chancellor, University of Nigeria, Nsukka (q.v.). He won many foreign honours, including the Knight Commander of the Order of the British Empire in 1957, and in 1963 he was made the Queen's Privy Councillor. He died on January 29, 1993.

ADEMOLA II, OBA SIR LADIPO SAMUEL. The Alake of Abeokuta. Born to Oba Ademola I (q.v.) in the Ake palace in Abeokuta (q.v.) in September 1872, Oba Ademola II received his education at Igbore and Ikereku schools and later at St. Paul's School, Breadfruit Street in Lagos (q.v.). After being in business for some time, he became a printing apprentice to Richard Beale Olamilege Blaize (q.v.), before going back into business. In 1920, after the death of Oba Gbadebo, Prince Ademola was chosen as the Alake of Abeokuta, and crowned on September 27, 1920. It was during this time that Abeokuta celebrated the one hundredth anniversary of its founding in 1930. In 1937 he was created the Commander, Order of the British Empire, and in 1937 he attended the coronation of King George VI of England.

In 1948 there were riots by market women organised by Mrs. Funmilayo Ransome-Kuti (q.v.), wife of Reverend J. Ransome-Kuti (q.v.). As a result of this, the Alake was forced into exile for some years. Later, when peace had returned, he was allowed to come back into the city, and he ruled with greater support of his people. He died in 1962.

ADEREMI, OBA SIR ADESOJI TADENIAWO. A traditional ruler, born on November 15, 1889, in Ile-Ife (q.v.), Oyo State (q.v.), he belonged to the Oshinkola ruling house, one of the four ruling houses in Ile-Ife. Sir Adesoji Aderemi was one of the first pupils to enter the first school in Ile-Ife, St. Phillips, in 1901. Leaving the school in 1907, and being unable then to enter the secondary school of his choice, he began to attend evening schools in Lagos (q.v.), where he was working on the staff of the Nigeria Railways Corporation (q.v.), and he also took correspondence courses from overseas. By 1925 he had become a businessman. He was so successful that by 1927 he was being called "Obalola" or "king-to-be."

When the ruling Oba (q.v.) died on June 24, 1930, Aderemi vied for the throne and secured it. On August 23, 1930, the governor of Nigeria assented to the choice of the kingmakers and Aderemi became Ooni-Elect. On September 2, 1930, he was installed and crowned as the Ooni of Ife.

Aderemi was a moderniser. He modernised many of the traditional customs in Ile-Ife and saw to the economic and social development of the town. In 1932 he founded the Oduduwa College, the first secondary school in the whole Ife division. In 1934 he founded the Ife Central School and in 1938 the Origbo Central School, two primary schools meant to supply students to Oduduwa College. From then to his death on July 1, 1980, Ife Division abounded with numerous high schools and primary schools. The town is blessed with the prestigious University of Ife (now called Obafemi Awolowo University), which was opened in 1962.

Oba Aderemi played an important role in the politics of Nigeria. When the Richards Constitution (q.v.) came into existence in 1946, Oba Aderemi became a member of the Legislative Council (q.v.) in 1947. In 1948 he attended the African Conference in London, and, in the same year, he hosted the conference at which Egbe Omo Oduduwa (q.v.) was founded. (This Egbe later became the nucleus of the Action Group Party [q.v.]. Between 1951 and 1954, he was a member of the House of Representatives (q.v.) in Lagos where he was a minister without portfolio. In 1953 he led the Nigerian delegation to the coronation of Queen Elizabeth II, and, in the same year, he was a delegate to the Constitutional Conference (q.v.) in London, and all later ones in Nigeria, in 1954 and in London in 1957 and 1958. Between 1954 and 1960, he was president of the Western House of Chiefs (q.v.). In 1960 he became the first Nigerian governor of the Western Region (q.v.) of Nigeria but was suspended from office in 1962 when a state of emergency was declared in the region during the Action Group crisis (q.v.). From then to his death in July 1980, he became what he himself called "an elder statesman playing the role of adviser in many aspects of the nation's administration."

During his 50-year reign, Oba Aderemi was showered with many honours. In 1943 he was awarded the Companion of the Order of St. Michael and St. George (CMG) for his sound common sense, his statesmanlike ability and his invaluable advice to the British Chief Commissioner. In 1950 he was created Knight Commander, Order of the British Empire by King George VI, and in 1962 Queen Elizabeth II made him Knight Commander, Order of St. Michael and St. George.

ADETILOYE, RT. REV. JOSEPH ABIODUN. The Archbishop of the Church of Nigeria, Anglican Communion, born in 1929 at Odo-Owa in Ijero Ekiti area of Ondo State (q.v.), Adetiloye received his elementary education at St. Paul's School (Odo-Owa) and Christ School (Ijero Ekiti) and later attended Christ School Ado Ekiti for his secondary education before he answered the call to be a minister. He was trained for the ministry of the church at Melville Hall from 1954 to 1957 and then went to London, Wycliffe Hall, Oxford, and from there to King's College in London, 1957 to 1961 to complete advanced courses in theology. He was ordained a deacon in 1954 and an Anglican priest in December 1954. He was ordained Archbishop in 1988, to succeed the Most Reverend Timothy Omotayo Olufosoye (q.v.).

In the political crisis that ensued after the annulment of the June 12, 1993, presidential election, Reverend Adetiloye before 1996 had written four open letters to General Sani Abacha (q.v.), urging him to restore power to the people as the only way Nigeria could know peace.

AD HOC CONSTITUTIONAL CONFERENCE. After the second coup d'état of July 1966 which brought General Yakubu Gowon (q.v.) to power, the new Head of State announced to the nation that he would set in motion the process to review "our national standing" and return to civilian rule as soon as it could be arranged. His first step to bring this about was to set up a meeting of representatives of all the regions on August 9, 1966. The meeting, among other things, recommended the setting up of an ad hoc constitutional conference of delegates from all the regions to review the constitutional future of the Federation (q.v.).

The conference met from September 12 to 30, 1966. There were many proposals from each regional delegation. The conference reached agreement on a number of problems, but it could not complete its task because of the massacre of the Igbo (q.v.) people in the northern region which began on September 29, 1966. The conference later adjourned for three weeks, and when the conference resumed on October 24, the Eastern Region's (q.v.) government was not represented. All efforts aimed at persuading the east to resume participation failed.

ADUBI WAR. This was a revolt in 1918 by the people in Egbaland, in which a European and a traditional chief were killed. The revolt was a result of the loss of independence enjoyed under treaties with the British by the Egba (q.v.) and terminated by the administrative innovations of 1914 and the consequent introduction of indirect rule (q.v.). Other causes of the revolt were resentment of the imposition of direct taxation on the people in 1918 and the grievances felt by Egba abroad over the termination of their independence. It was quickly crushed. Investigations later showed that educated Egba residents in Lagos (q.v.) played a significant role in the revolt.

ADVISORY JUDICIAL COMMITTEE. Created under Decree Number 1 of 1966, it consisted of the chief justice of the Federation (q.v.) who was the chairman, the chief justices of the four existing regions and the chief justice of Lagos, the Grand Kadi (q.v.) of the Sharia (q.v.) court of appeal and the attorney general of the Federation with the solicitor general of the Federation acting as the secretary to the committee. The committee advised the military government on judicial matters.

AFENIFERE. The name of a cultural/political group representing Yoruba interests. In some ways it can be regarded as the successor to the Egbe Omo Oduduwa which Obafemi Awolowo created in 1945. Formed in February 1993, the Afenifere was very active in demanding the recognition of M.K.O. Abiola's June 12 election as president, and emerged as a prominent advocate for this position under the leadership of Michael Ajasin. Following Ajasin's death in 1997, leadership of the Afenifere was assumed by Abraham Adesanya. When the regime of Abdulsalami Abubakar initiated his own democratic transition (1998–99), the Afenifere became very influential within the Alliance for Democracy, which was one of the three main political parties.

AFONJA. The ruler of Ilorin (q.v.) province at the end of the eighteenth century was posted there by the Alaafin of Oyo (q.v.) to guard and defend the northern outpost of the Yoruba (q.v.) kingdom against the threatened invasion by the lieutenants of Usman Dan Fodio (q.v.) during the holy war (jihad) (q.v.) from Sokoto (q.v.). He, however, revolted against the Alaafin by proclaiming Ilorin independent of Oyo in 1817. To strengthen his position, he incorporated into his army some Hausa (q.v.) slaves and received assistance from Mallam Alimi (q.v.), a Fulani (q.v.) Muslim priest. As such, he was able to repel all attacks by the Oyo army. Later on, relations between him and his neighbors strained, and in his effort to seek reconciliation, he angered his Hausa troops who revolted and had him killed. The town thus fell to Abdulsalami (q.v.), one of the sons of Alimi. The Sultan (q.v.) of Sokoto (q.v.), Muhammad Bello (q.v.) recognized the new ruler and thus began Fulani rule in Ilorin, a Yoruba town, until this day.

AFRICAN ASSOCIATION. The African Association was formed in 1788 by British merchants who were desirous of exploring trade possibilities in the interior of Africa. The association was, therefore, prepared to finance the expedition of any person who would come forward for that purpose. One of the many volunteers was Mungo Park (q.v.), who in 1795 had his offer accepted and started on his first expedition to trace the course of the Niger River (q.v.). In this first expedition, he saw that the river flowed eastwards, but he later turned back and arrived in England in June 1797. He later on undertook a second journey during which he died at Bussa (q.v.) in Nigeria without accomplishing his mission.

Later on, other British expeditions followed the successes of Mungo Park. Among the explorers of Niger were Hugh Clapperton (q.v.), Richard Lander (q.v.), John Lander, William Baikie (q.v.) and MacGregor Laird (q.v.), who in 1832 accompanied a commercial expedition from the Niger Delta up the Niger River to Lokoja (q.v.) where it meets with its biggest tributary, the Benue River (q.v.). Soon after, the British government became interested in the exploration of Africa, but most of its efforts were frustrated owing to the attack of malaria fever (q.v.). It was not until quinine (q.v.) was discovered that loss of life was reduced to a minimum.

AFRICAN BANKING CORPORATION. The first commercial bank to be established in Nigeria, it became the sole distributor of British silver coins in Lagos (q.v.) and the sole repatriating agent in 1872. It started the banking business in Lagos in 1891. Being a pioneering private company in a country where money economy was yet to develop and receiving no government subsidy, the corporation had many problems. Sir Alfred Lewis Jones, a shipping magnate from Elder Dempster Company, came to its rescue by agreeing to take it over, hoping that, by extending credit facilities to small businesses, his own shipping business would continue to grow. Later, the British government asked that the company be made a joint-stock bank, and having reached an agreement, the company was registered in England as a limited liability company under the new name of the Bank of British West Africa (q.v.) in May 1894. Before this time, in 1892, the colonial administration in Nigeria had transferred its account in Lagos to the company's account. The bank is now known as the First Bank. It is today one of the leading commercial banks in the country, and, because of the Indigenization Decree (q.v.), Nigerians now hold a large equity share of the bank.

AFRICAN CHURCH. The African Church was founded in protest against the practice of color prejudice (racism) in the Anglican Church, the imposition of foreign culture and customary practices on the people, the effort to translate and enforce the principles of the Church of England on Africans and the colonial government's denial of self-government to the people. On October 13, 1901, about 800 worshippers of the Anglican Church, St. Paul's Breadfruit Church in Lagos (q.v.) broke away to form the African Church. From there the church spread to other parts of the country and outside it. The church was active in the educational and economic development of the nation. Its first school was built in 1902 and can boast of many primary and secondary schools together with teacher training colleges all over the nation. It was also through the activities of its evangelists like J.K. Coker that the cultivation of cocoa (q.v.) spread to places like Ondo (q.v.), Owo (q.v.) and Ekiti provinces. The African Church is remarkable for its protest against the imposition of foreign culture and rule. The founding of the church was no doubt the beginning of nationalist movements within the Christian Church in Nigeria.

AFRICAN CONTINENTAL BANK. Founded in 1948 by Dr. Nnamdi Azikiwe (q.v.), the then leader of the National Council of Nigeria and the Cameroons (NCNC) (q.v.), the bank started operating in September of the same year. As the Foster Sutton Commission of Inquiry (q.v.), set up to investigate the relationship existing between Dr. Azikiwe and the bank, found out in 1954, Dr. Azikiwe together with members of his family and the companies controlled by him were the principal shareholders of the bank. The commission therefore concluded that Dr. Azikiwe's conduct in connection with the affairs of the bank left much to be desired. Dr. Azikiwe later transferred all his rights and interests in the bank to the former Eastern Regional (q.v.) government. The bank presently has branches in many cities and towns all over the country.

AFRICAN EDUCATION CONFERENCE OF 1952. The conference met at King's College, Cambridge, in 1952 to study educational policy and practice in British tropical Africa. The conference considered five major themes: responsibility and control, the expansion of the educational system, the teaching profession, organisation and curriculum, and education and adult education. The recommendations of the conference were of great importance in setting up the aims of primary education in Western Nigeria (q.v.).

AFRICAN EDUCATION INCORPORATED. African Education Incorporated was an educational scheme launched by Dr. Nwafor Orizu in 1946, and designed to give scholarships to young Nigerians and to place them in American universities. Between 1947 and 1950, it was recorded that about 100 students had benefitted from the programme. But beginning in 1949, the scheme began to have serious financial and other difficulties due to poor management and inexperience. This brought great hardship to many of the students, and the Nigerian government, together with some American foundations, came to the rescue of the financially handicapped students by giving them loans, bursaries and other financial assistance.

AFRICAN FESTIVAL OF ARTS AND CULTURE (FESTAC-77). The First World Festival of Negro Arts and Culture was organized in Dakar, Senegal, in April 1966 and the Second World Black and African Festival of Arts and Culture, popularly known as FESTAC-77, was held in Nigeria from January 15 to February 12, 1977. The aims of FESTAC-77 were to ensure the revival, resurgence, propagation and promotion of black and African culture and black African cultural values and civilisation; to work toward better international and interracial understanding, encourage and facilitate periodic return of black artists outside Africa to the cultural sources, bring to the attention of the world the artistic and cultural achievements of the black man, and give black artists in Africa the opportunity of sharing their experiences and problems with other black artists operating outside of Africa.

AFRICANIZATION. This policy, before and after independence, placed Africans in positions formerly held by expatriates. Under colonial rule, non-Africans held many top positions in the civil service, trade and industry. After independence, Nigeria did not have sufficiently qualified persons to fill these posts and so foreigners were retained until qualified Nigerians could fill the positions. For a foreigner to work in Nigeria, he or she had to obtain a work permit, generally given for a specific period of time.

AFRICAN NATIONAL COUNCIL. *See* FOREIGN POLICY.

AFRICAN PETROLEUM COMPANY LTD. *See* NATIONALISATION OF BRITISH PETROLEUM COMPANY LTD.

AFRICAN STUDENTS' ASSOCIATION OF THE UNITED STATES AND CANADA. Organised in 1941, it had close association with the West African Students Union (q.v.) in London. Its aim was to fight for the independence of African countries. It asked the British government and its allies to grant internal self-government to the colonial peoples of Africa. It asked that the fundamental principles of democracy in the Atlantic Charter be applied to the African peoples immediately. Many members of the association, like the late Dr. Kwame Nkrumah (q.v.) of Ghana (q.v.), later became leaders in their countries. The association published a monthly paper called *The African Interpreter.*

AGBEBI, DR. MOJOLA. Mojola was formerly called David Brown Vincent, a name given to him by his Sierra-Leonean creole parents who had come back to Nigeria, their original home country. He was born at Ilesa in the present Osun State (q.v.) in April 1860. He went to Christian Missionary Society (CMS) (q.v.) Day School, Faji, Lagos (q.v.). In 1874 he entered a CMS Teacher Training School, and after three years, he was appointed as schoolmaster of Faji Day School. He worked not only for the CMS but also for other denominations like the Catholic, the Methodist and the American Baptist missions. He also worked with the first Independent Native Baptist Church of which he became a leader in 1888. In 1903, he left that church and founded his own Aroromi Church, but he later joined the American Baptist Church and remained there until his death in 1917.

He edited many papers during his lifetime. He worked with R.B. Blaize (q.v.) on the *Lagos Times,* and later he worked for the *Lagos Observer, Lagos Weekly Times* and the *Lagos Weekly Record.* He edited the *Iwe Irohin Eko.* Dr. Agbebi was also a close friend of Edward W. Blyden (q.v.) who invited him to spend some years in Liberia where he was awarded M.A. and Ph.D. honorary degrees for his literary ability. He also received a D.D. honorary degree from New York University in 1903.

Dr. Agbebi may be regarded as the forerunner of the later-year cultural nationalist, for he dropped his European names for Yoruba (q.v.) ones and was said to have abandoned European dress for Yoruba clothing.

AGE GROUPS. An age group is made up of children of about the same age. In some Yoruba towns (q.v.), men were divided into age groups, each age group being under the control of a slightly older person. Among the Igbo (q.v.), as each age group reached manhood, the members would select one of them as the group leader or head. Each age group performed important functions. They maintained discipline within the group and saw to it that each member obeyed the customary law of the community. The age groups were the only effective means of enforcing the law. The older age groups formed the governing age group, while the younger ones carried out the orders of the elders be it in judicial or other matters. The age group was also a means of organising the young people for war and for public work like cleaning footpaths. In short, the age-group system combined the function of defending the community, ensuring law and order and providing for public labour. They also were initiators of many useful community programs and projects.

Age grouping is also common among the Nupe (q.v.), Ibibio (q.v.), Beni, and Fulani (q.v.). Age is an important element in the life of many ethnic groups in Nigeria. For example, among the Yoruba (q.v.), reverence for those who are older is very important. In traditional Yoruba society, a younger man normally prostrates to an older person, woman or man, when greeting them, and a younger woman kneels or genuflects before an older person.

AGRICULTURAL CREDIT GUARANTEE SCHEME FUND. This fund was established in March 1977 to increase the volume of banks' lending to agriculture, and minimize the risks to which banks are exposed in lending for agricultural purposes. The scheme encourages banks to lend to all those who intend to or are engaged in the establishment or management of plantations for the production of crops like rubber (q.v.), oil palm (q.v.), cocoa (q.v.), coffee, tea and similar crops. It is also to be given to those who want to produce cereal crops, tubers, fruits of all kinds, cotton, beans, groundnuts (q.v.), benniseed, vegetables, bananas (q.v.), pineapples and plantain and for people who want to engage in animal husbandry like poultry, pig and cattle rearing, and fish farming. The extent of the liability of the fund in respect of guaranteed loans is 75 percent of any amount in default, subject, in case of a loan to an individual, to a maximum of N50,000 and in case of a loan to a cooperative society to a maximum of N1 million. Under the scheme, thousands of people benefitted.

AGRICULTURAL SECTOR EMPLOYMENT PROGRAM. *See* NATIONAL DIRECTORATE OF EMPLOYMENT.

AGRICULTURE. With about 70 per cent of its people in rural areas, Nigeria is still an agricultural society. Agriculture remains the source of livelihood for most Nigerians and, with the current downturn, in economic well-being, more and more people who can no longer make ends meet in the cities are going back to the land. During the colonial era, colonial policy favored the expansion of the agricultural sector so it could be a ready source of raw materials for industry at home. Nigeria became a dumping ground for Britain's manufactured goods. During this time, Nigeria was the largest producer of groundnuts (q.v.) (peanuts), second-largest producer of cocoa (q.v.) and supplier of about half the world's need for palm produce.

Agricultural production can be divided into food and cash crops. Food crops include rice, yams (q.v.), cassava (q.v.), maize, beans, plantains and all kinds of vegetables, while cash crops include cocoa, groundnut, oil palm (q.v.), palm kernel, beniseed, soybeans and citrus. Agricultural production also include animal husbandry and fishing.

However, with the discovery of petroleum oil and the consequent oil boom, the role of agriculture, which used to supply over 70 per cent of foreign earnings, has been supplanted by oil revenues, which has become the mainstay of Nigeria's economy since the 1970s. In 1996 oil receipts provided about 80 per cent of federal revenue. In 1976 the administration of General Olusegun Obasanjo (q.v.), seeing the rate at which rural young people were leaving for cities and the unwholesome amount of foreign exchange used to import food items that could be produced locally, launched the Operation Feed the Nation (OFN) (q.v.) program. OFN's aim was to make the country self-sufficient in its basic food needs. In the 1980s, the oil glut worsened the country's foreign exchange situation. To encourage local production the importation of many food items like rice, maize and wheat were banned, and the government set up many agricultural agencies and research institutions such as the Forestry Research in Ibadan (q.v.), Nigerian Institute for Trypanosomiasis in Kaduna (q.v.), National Veterinary Research in Vom and many others. In addition, the government in 1991 set up the National Agricultural Land Development Authority (NALDA) to execute a national agricultural land development program to moderate chronic problems of low utilisation of abundant farmland. The main target of the program was to develop about 30,000 hectares of land in each state during 1992 to 1994. NALDA was also to place over 7,500 farmers within the developed area. The states and local governments were to allocate suitable tracts of land to the authority for this purpose. In 1992 NALDA had been implemented in not less than 25 states, and by December 1994, it had expanded its programs to all 30 states of the Federation (q.v.). Added to this, among many others, is the Agricultural Development Project (ADP), a World Bank–assisted rural development project which has become a prominent organ for agricultural extension services and rural development. ADP provides infrastructure and distributes fertilizers and herbicides to farmers. In 1991, 1,014 kilometres of roads were constructed, over 3,000 boreholes were dug in the rural areas and 1.4 metric tonnes of fertilizers were distributed, while 153,800 litres of herbicide were sold to farmers. By January 1995, provision of roads in rural areas had risen to 1,786 kilometres while the provision of boreholes, wells and earth dams had increased to more than 4,000. In the same way, extension services greatly increased. As a result of all these efforts and favourable rainfall, agricultural production is noticeably on the rise.

AGUDA COMMITTEE. This group was set up in August 1975 to examine the dual role of Lagos (q.v.) City as a federal and state capital and advise on the desirability of Lagos continuing in that role. The committee recommended that Lagos should no longer maintain the dual role as the federal and state capital, and that the Federal Government should move its capital to an area of about 8,000 square kilometres in the central part of the country. The federal government later chose Abuja (q.v.) as the new capital. The head of the committee was Dr. Timothy Akinola Aguda.

AGUDA, DR. TIMOTHY AKINOLA. A highly respected jurist, born June 10, 1923 in Akure, Ondo State (q.v.), Aguda was educated at the Government College in Ibadan (q.v.) from 1939 to 1944, at Yaba Higher College (q.v.) in Lagos (q.v.) in 1946 and later went to the London School of Economics and Political Science at the University of London in England from 1949 to 1952. He was called to the bar in 1952 and became a private legal practitioner in Ibadan. He later joined the Ministry of Justice in 1955. In 1965 he was at the University of Ife (q.v.) in Ile-Ife (q.v.) as a teacher and in 1968 became a judge of the High Court in the Western State (q.v.). In 1972 he was chief justice of the Republic of Botswana and in 1975 chief justice of the Western State of Nigeria. In 1976 he became the first chief judge of Ondo State and in 1978 was appointed director-general of the Nigerian Institute of Advanced Legal Studies. From this time on, he has held many prominent public positions in and outside Nigeria. Justice Aguda is known for his forthrightness and courage. He has given many public lectures and written many articles and books, among which are *Principles of Criminal Liability in Nigerian Law* (1965), *Law of Evidence in Nigeria* (1966), *Practice and Procedure of the Supreme Court, Court of Appeal and the High Court of Nigeria* (1980), *Commercial, Business and Trade Laws of Nigeria* (1982), *The Challenge of the Nigerian Nation* (1985) and *The Crisis of Justice* (1986).

AGUIYI-IRONSI, MAJ. GEN. JOHNSON THOMAS UMUNANKWE. Former Head of State, born on March 3, 1924. After his elementary and secondary education, he enlisted in the Nigerian Regiment in 1942. He was promoted to captain in May 1953 and came into prominence. In 1956, when Queen Elizabeth II was visiting Nigeria, Aguiyi-Ironsi was chosen among others as equerry to the Queen. In 1958 he became a lieutenant colonel. In 1961 he served as military adviser to the Nigerian High Commission in London and was later promoted to the rank of brigadier. During the Congo crisis, he was the first African force commander of the United Nations peacekeeping operation. In February 1965, he became a major general and was appointed General Commanding Officer of the Nigerian Army. After the 1966 coup d'état (q.v.), General Ironsi became the head of the federal military government and supreme commander of the armed forces (q.v.). He held this position until he was kidnapped and killed on July 29, 1996, during the second military coup. It was his regime that issued the Unification Decree (q.v.) of May 1966, which abolished the federal structure and set up a unitary form of government for Nigeria.

AHIARA DECLARATION. On June 1, 1969, Lt. Col. C. Odumegwu Ojukwu (q.v.), as the commander-in-chief of the armed forces of the Republic of Biafra (q.v.) launched the Biafran Revolution in a village called Ahiara. The main principles of the revolution were that the people were supreme while the leaders were their servants. Biafrans from different parts of the country were to live together, work together, suffer together and pursue together a common cause of national survival. The revolution believed in the sanctity of human life and the dignity of the human person, and it placed a high premium on love, patriotism and devotion to the fatherland. One of the cornerstones of the revolution was social justice in Biafra: "all property belongs to the community." Whatever a person had, either in talent or material wealth, was held in trust for the community. This did not mean the abolition of personal property, but the state, acting on behalf of the community, could intervene in the disposition of property to the greater advantage of all. While the revolution would foster private economic enterprise and initiative, it was constantly alive to the dangers of accumulation of large private fortunes. Biafran revolution sought to create possibilities for citizens with talent in business, administration, management and technology, and it would create a society not torn asunder by class consciousness and class antagonisms. It was to be an egalitarian society.

AHMADIYYA. This religious movement within Islam (q.v.) was founded by Mirza Ghulam Ahmad Qadiani who said he was a Mahdi (q.v.) and the expected prophet that Scriptures had foretold. Ahmadiyya is similar to orthodox Islam with some differences in its interpretation of the Koran. The Ahamdiyya group, which formed in Lagos (q.v.) in 1916, has worked hard to make converts and has provided good services in education by establishing schools in many parts of the country. Some orthodox Muslims consider the group to be heretical because of its emphasis on the founder.

AHMADU BELLO UNIVERSITY, ZARIA. Established in October 1962 by the Northern Regional government, the university incorporated the Zaria (q.v.) branch of the Nigerian College of Arts, Science and Technology (q.v.), the Ahmadu Bello College, Kano (q.v.) (which later became Abdullahi Bayero College, Kano (q.v.)), the Institute of Administration in Zaria and the Institute of Agricultural Research at Samaru together with the Veterinary Research Institute at Vom. The federal military government took over the university in 1975.

AHMED BEN ALI. Ruler of Bornu (q.v.) from 1791 to 1808, he tried hard to defend the state against the agents of Usman Dan Fodio (q.v.) during the jihad (q.v.). In 1807 the Fulanis (q.v.) in Bornu province of Deya joined the holy war against the governor of the state. Ahmed decided to repel the attack of the Jihadists. He wrote Usman Dan Fodio and his son Muhammad Bello (q.v.), asking why they were waging war against Bornu, an Islamic state. In spite of this, the war continued, and the Fulani overran Bornu. Ahmed fled the city and abdicated in favor of his son Dunama (q.v.). His abdication created dissension in Bornu, which later opened the way for Muhammed Al-Kanemi (q.v.) to take power.

AIKHOMU, VICE ADMIRAL AUGUSTUS AKHABUE. A naval officer and vice president in the military administration of President Ibrahim B. Babangida (q.v.) from 1986 to 1993. He was born in Irrua-Ishan in Edo State (q.v.) on October 20, 1939, and received his education from various schools before joining the navy where he trained at home and abroad. He had held many appointments before he was retired from the navy to become vice president and a member of the Armed Forces Ruling Council (q.v.). He left office with Babangida in 1993.

AIR FORCE, NIGERIAN. *See* ARMED FORCES.

AIRSTRIP ANNABELLE. The Airstrip Annabelle was the Uli Airfield, a road sufficiently widened to be used as an airfield by the Biafrans during the Civil War (q.v.). The airstrip was where most relief planes landed. It was later captured by federal troops, and, for many years after, the remains of burnt airplanes bore evidence to the fact that it was one of the centers of activity during the war.

AJASA, SIR KITOYI. Ajasa was a lawyer and a journalist, born in 1866 and originally named Edmund Macaulay, the son of one Thomas Benjamin, a Sierra-Leonean slave who was freed from a slave ship. He received his education at Dulwich College in London and was called to the bar in 1893. Following the cultural nationalist practice of dropping foreign names for Yoruba (q.v.) ones—common then among many Lagos (q.v.) people who came from Sierra Leone to Nigeria—he too changed his name. In 1894 he was party to the launching of the *Lagos Standard,* but he soon fell out with the owner, George Alfred Williams because Williams was too critical of the British government. The British rewarded Ajasa for his loyalty—in 1902 he was appointed to the Board of Health. In 1906 he was appointed to the Legislative Council (q.v.) in Lagos (q.v.). He was a good friend of Lord Frederick Lugard (q.v.), and in 1914, when the ineffective Nigerian Council (q.v.) was created after the amalgamation (q.v.) of the Southern and Northern protectorates, he was appointed to that body. In the same year (1914), he established a new weekly newspaper, *Nigerian Pioneer (q.v.),* in partnership with some European businessmen. The paper, believing in moderate and loyal criticism of the colonial government, was disliked by other nationalists and their newspapers. In 1923 when the elective principle was conceded to Lagos and Calabar (q.v.) to send elected representatives to the Legislative Council (q.v.), Sir Kitoyi Ajasa was nominated by the governor to sit with the elected representatives. In the same year, 1923, he was created Officer, Order of the British Empire by the British government. In 1929 he was knighted. He died in August 1937.

AJASIN, CHIEF MICHAEL ADEKUNLE. An educationist and a politician, first governor of Ondo State (q.v.) in the Second Republic (q.v.). Born in Owo on November 28, 1908, he attended Saint Andrew's College in Oyo and later went to Fourah Bay College, Sierra Leone, and the University of Durham in Britain from 1943 to 1946, where he obtained a B.A. in english, history and economics. In 1947 he obtained a diploma in Education from the Institute of Education of the University of London. In the same year he became the first principal of Imade College in Owo, a post he occupied until December 1962. In January 1963, he became the founder, proprietor and first principal of Owo High School.

Chief Ajasin's interest in politics has an early history. He was the initiator and cofounder of the Nigerian Union of Students of Great Britain and Ireland in London in 1947. He was also the first vice president of the former Action Group Party (q.v.) when it was founded in 1951. He was the president of Egbe Omo Oduduwa (q.v.), an organisation named after the mythical ancestor of the Yorubas (q.v.), before it was banned by the military administration in 1966.

Chief Ajasin has also functioned in many public offices. He was chairman of Owo District Council (1954–59) and a member of the House of Representatives (q.v.) (1960–66). Following the reform of local government by the military administration in 1976, he was chairman of Owo local government in 1977, a post he held until 1978 when the ban on political activities was lifted. He became a member of the Unity Party of Nigeria (UPN) (q.v.) and was later elected Ondo State chairman of the party and a member of the party's National Executive Council (q.v.). In 1979 he was elected governor of Ondo State and was reelected in 1983 for a second term. After the military takeover of December 31, 1983, he was arrested and detained. He was tried with Governor V. Bisi Onabanjo (q.v.) of Ogun State (q.v.) and Governor Bola Ige (q.v.) of Oyo State (q.v.) by a military tribunal on charges of receiving a kickback of N2.8 million and passing it to the UPN, but he was acquitted. He was nonetheless still detained, awaiting further investigations on whether or not he had corruptly enriched himself while in office as governor. He was released in August 1985 by the Babangida (q.v.) administration. Old, but not tired, in 1994, Chief Ajasin became the leader of a new organisation, the National Democratic Coalition (NADECO) (q.v.) that fought for the restoration of democracy in Nigeria during the rudderless administration of General Sani Abacha (q.v.). He died on October 3, 1997.

AJAYI, PROF. JACOB FESTUS ADE. A historian, administrator and educationist, Ajayi was born in 1929 at Ikole-Ekiti, Ondo State (q.v.), and educated at St. Paul's School in Ikole-Ekiti, Christ's School in Ado-Ekiti, Igbobi College in Lagos (q.v.), Yaba Higher College (q.v.) in Lagos, and University College in Ibadan (q.v.) from 1948 to 1951. In 1952 he proceeded to University College in Leicester and in 1955 to King's College in London. In 1957 he was a Fellow at the Institute of Historical Research in London and came back to the University of Ibadan as a lecturer in 1958. He became a professor in 1963. He was vice-chancellor at the University of Lagos from 1972 to 1978 and a member of the Council of the United Nations University from 1974 to 1980. In 1985 he became pro-chancellor of Ondo State University in Ado-Ekiti. He has written many books, among which are *Milestones in Nigerian History* (1962), *Evolution of Political Culture in Nigeria* (1955), *Nineteenth Century Yoruba Warfare* (1964), *A Thousand Years of West African History* (1964), *Christian Missions in Nigeria, 1841–91: The Making of a New Elite* (1965) and *A Historical Atlas of Africa* (1985).

AJULUCHUKU, CHIEF MELIE CHEKELU KAFUNDU. A journalist, administrator and politician, Ajuluchuku was born February 10, 1924, in Nnewi, Anambra State (q.v.), and was educated at the Christian Missionary Society (q.v.) Central School in Nnewi, the Government College in Umuahia from 1938 to 1943, Higher College in Yaba from 1944 to 1946 and Bethune-Cookman College in Daytona Beach, Florida, in the U.S.A. in 1947. He then moved to Brooklyn College in New York from 1947 to 1949. He was the editor of *The African* in New York (1948–49), the *West African Pilot* in Lagos (1951–53) and *Nigerian Outlook* in Enugu (1954–60). He was the director of the federal government's Post Group of Newspapers, the Publishers of the morning and Sunday *Post* in Lagos from 1961 to 1964. In 1984 he became general manager of the Concord Press of Nigeria Limited.

As a politician, he was the founder and first secretary of the Zikist Movement (q.v.) and assistant national secretary of the National Council of Nigerian Citizens (q.v.) from 1947 to 1950. He was also a member of the executive committee of the United Progress Grand Alliance (q.v.) and director of research and publicity for the Unity Party of Nigeria (q.v.) in 1978. Among his publications are *Imoudu versus Governor* (1947) and *Ministers of Eastern Nigeria* (1960).

AKASSA MASSACRE. When the Royal Niger Company (q.v.) obtained its charter from the British government in 1886, the Brassmen, a subgroup of the Ijaw (q.v.), on the lower part of the Niger River (q.v.) who had from the very beginning resented the visits of European traders among them, saw that the customs regulations made and vigorously enforced by the company excluded them from their traditional markets. In 1889 they made a formal complaint to Mr. Macdonald, a British officer, who was then the special commissioner sent to investigate certain complaints against the company. However, nothing resulted from this, and the company continued to apply its regulations as strictly as possible. When the people saw that their complaint fell on deaf ears, they organized a force of about 1500 men who attacked and destroyed the company's property at Akassa. There followed a punitive expedition in which many people were killed. The Foreign Office then sent Sir John Kirk as a special commissioner to investigate the Akassa massacre. In its report the commission noted that the rules in force were practically prohibitory of native trade and the Brassmen were right in saying this was so.

AKENZUA II. Oba of Benin. Oba Akenzua II was born in Benin (q.v.) in 1899, the son of Oba Eweka II who ruled Benin between 1914 and 1933. As a young man, the Oba was educated at Benin Government School and at the King's College in Lagos (q.v.). He later became a transport clerk in the Benin Native Authority. In 1925 he worked under Oba Ademola II (q.v.), the Alake of Abeokuta, and was later appointed as head of the Ekiadolor District, a position he held when his father died. He became the reigning Oba in 1933. As Oba, he was appointed to many important public positions. He was a member of the Western House of Chiefs (q.v.), when that house was founded in 1946, and became a cabinet minister later. He was instrumental in carving out the Mid-Western Region (q.v.) from the old Western Region (q.v.) for the sponsoring organizations and parties that agitated for this. When the Mid-Western Region was created in 1963, he became the first president of the House of Chiefs in 1964.

As Oba of Benin, he was the custodian of the culture and tradition of the people of Benin. To promote this culture and tradition, he readily made available many ancient bronze and ivory carvings for the 1977 Second World Black and African Festival of Arts and Culture (FESTAC). For his many contributions to the political and the cultural development of his people, Akenzua was honored with the insignia of commander of the Republic of Nigeria (q.v.) and was also appointed chancellor of Ahmadu Bello University (q.v.) in Zatia. Oba Akenzua died in 1978 succeeded by Oba Erediauwa I (q.v.) of Benin in 1979.

AKHIGBE, ADMIRAL MIKE OKHAI. Born on September 29, 1946, in Fugar Etsako in the Western Region (q.v.) of Nigeria. He was appointed chief of general staff by Abdulsalami Abubakar in July 1998, a position that had remained vacant since the arrest of his predecessor, General Oladipo Diya (q.v.) in December 1997 on charges of planning a coup against the Abacha regime. Admiral Akhigbe retired, together with the other service chiefs, on May 29, 1999, when the military turned over power to an elected civilian regime.

AKIN-DEKO, GABRIEL. Born on October 30, 1913, he attended Yaba Higher College (q.v.) and the Brixton School of Building in England to qualify in building technology. He was a schoolteacher from 1937 to 1947. He then set up a private civil engineering firm in 1950. He was later elected as a member of the Western House of Assembly and was appointed minister of agriculture of the Western Region (q.v.) from 1952 to 1961. He later became chairman of the Western Nigeria Development Corporation. He was appointed the regional representative for Africa on the U.N. Food and Agricultural Organization in 1962. He was appointed the pro-chancellor of the University of Benin and the chairman of the National Sports Council of Nigeria (q.v.). He was later appointed as the pro-chancellor of the newly established Federal University of Technology, Abeokuta (q.v.) Ogun State (q.v.).

AKINFOSILE, OLUFEMI. A lawyer and a politician, born on March 5, 1926, at Igbolako Ikale in Ondo State (q.v.), he attended Baptist Academy in Lagos from 1934 to 1944, Birkbeck College, University of London in England from 1948 to 1952 and the Northwestern Polytechnic in London in 1953. He was called to the bar at Lincoln's Inn in London. He came back to Nigeria, and in 1959 contested the federal elections as a member of the National Council of Nigeria and the Cameroons (NCNC) (q.v.) and was later made the federal minister of communication. From 1962 to 1966, he was chairman of the NCNC's Western Working Committee. He was a member of the Ad Hoc Constitutional Conference (q.v.) called by General Yakubu Gowon (q.v.) from 1966 to 1967. He also was a member of the Constituent Assembly (q.v.) from 1977 to 1978. In 1978 he was appointed national chairman of the Nigerian People's Party (q.v.) and played a prominent role in the negotiation of the accord reached between his party and the presidential party, the National Party of Nigeria (NPN) (q.v.), in October 1979.

AKINJIDE, RICHARD OSUOLALE ABIMBOLA. A Senior Advocate of Nigeria (q.v.), born on November 4, 1931, in Ibadan (q.v.), Oyo State (q.v.), he was educated at St. Peter's School, Aremo, Ibadan, Oduduwa College in Ile-Ife (q.v.) and at the University of London in England from 1952 to 1956. He was called to the bar at the Inner Temple in London in 1956. Upon returning home he was elected member of Parliament in 1959 and became federal minister of education in 1965. He was president of the Nigerian Bar Association from 1970 to 1973 and a member of the governing council of the University of Ife (q.v.) from 1975 to 1976. He was appointed pro-chancellor and chairman of council at the University of Jos in 1976. In 1978 he became a member of the National Party of Nigeria (NPN) (q.v.) and its legal adviser. As legal adviser, he became famous for his interpretation of the constitutional requirement for a candidate for President where there were more than two candidates. To qualify, he must have the highest number of votes cast in the election and not less than one-quarter of the votes cast in each of at least two-thirds of all the states in the Federation (q.v.). As there were 19 states in 1979, he interpreted the two-thirds to mean 12 and two-thirds states and not 13 states as had previously been believed. His interpretation was upheld by the Federal Electoral Commission (FEDECO) (q.v.), the Election Tribunal and the Supreme Court (q.v.), and so Alhaji Shehu Shagari (q.v.), Akinjide's party's candidate, became the first executive president of Nigeria. Akinjide was later appointed minister of justice but was nicknamed Mr. Twelve Two-Thirds. He was not reappointed during Shagari's second term of office. After the December 1983 military takeover, he fled to Britain where he established a successful legal practice. He returned to Nigeria in 1993.

AKINRINADE, MAJ. GEN. IPOOLA ALANI. Born on October 3, 1939, at Yakoyo, Oyo State (q.v.), he attended the Offa Grammar School, the Royal Nigerian Military Forces Training College in Kaduna (q.v.) and from 1960 to 1962 the Royal Military Academy at Sandhurst in England. He later went to the U.S. Army Infantry School, Fort Benning, Georgia, from 1965 to 1966, and the Staff College in Camberley, England, in 1971. He served in many important positions in the Nigerian army, including rear commander and sector commander. In the February 1976 abortive coup staged by Lt. Colonel B.S. Dimka (q.v.), in which the Head of State, General Murtala R. Muhammed (q.v.) was killed, Akinrinade refused to allow his first army division in Kaduna to join, which caused the coup to fail. In 1979 he was appointed army chief of staff, a post from which he retired in 1981. He later became a BIG-TIME farmer, and in 1985 he was appointed minister of agriculture, water resources and rural development. In 1986 he became minister of industries and in 1989 minister of transport. After the crisis over the June 1993 presidential election and the taking over of power by General Sani Abacha (q.v.), General Akinrinade joined the demand for a democratically elected government. He later began to receive threats to his life, and fled Nigeria to become an exile in Europe. In May 1996, a terrorist squad of armed men with petrol bombs invaded his abandoned house in Ikeja, Lagos (q.v.), and burnt down the house. In March 1997 the government formally charged the exiled general with treason in connection with a series of bombings in the country.

AKINSANYA, OBA SAMUEL. Born August 1, 1898, he was educated at Ishara Anglican School. He worked as a shorthand typist from 1916 to 1931. He was the organizing secretary of the Nigerian Produce Traders and the president of the Nigerian Motor Transport Union from 1932 to 1940.

He was a foundation member of the Lagos Youth Movement (q.v.), which later became the Nigerian Youth Movement (NYM) (q.v.). He rose from general secretary of the organisation to being its vice president. He contested in 1941 with Ernest Ikoli (q.v.) the election within the movement to fill the vacancy in the Legislative Council (q.v.) created by the resignation of Sir K.A. Abayomi (q.v.) who was then the president of the NYM, but he lost to Ikoli. The same year he was appointed the Odemo of Ishara.

Oba Akinsanya was also a foundation member of the former Action Group (q.v.) and remained faithful to the party even during the party's crisis of 1962. In 1963 his salary as a traditional ruler was reduced to a penny (1p) by the government of the Western Region (q.v.) simply because he refused to join the government party.

In 1966 after the military takeover, the military government ordered that his salary should be paid in full, together with all the arrears since 1963. He died in January 1985.

AKINTOLA, CHIEF SAMUEL LADOKE. Born on July 6, 1910, at Ogbomosho in Western Nigeria, he received his primary and secondary education in his hometown, Ogbomosho. He became the editor of the *Nigerian Baptist,* published then by the Baptist mission in Lagos (q.v.). He worked as a clerk for the Nigerian Railway and later as editor of the *Daily Service,* which was at the time the organ of the Nigerian Youth Movement (NYM) (q.v.). He went to the United Kingdom to study public administration at Oxford in 1946 and later received a law degree. He came back to Nigeria in 1949. He served as the legal adviser to the Egbe Omo Oduduwa (q.v.), a Yoruba (q.v.) cultural society (society of the descendants of Oduduwa) and joined the Action Group (AG) (q.v.) early in its foundation.

Under the Macpherson Constitution (q.v.), Chief Akintola was a member of the Central Legislative Assembly (q.v.) and one of the four AG ministers that tendered their resignation after the "self-government in 1956" crisis in April 1953. In May 1953, he led the AG tour of the Northern Region (q.v.), which precipitated the Kano Riots of 1953 (q.v.).

In 1955 Chief Akintola became deputy leader of the party while Chief Obafemi Awolowo (q.v.) was leader. As deputy leader of the party, he served in many important positions. He was the leader of the AG parliamentary group in the federal House of Representatives (q.v.) in Lagos (q.v.) and served there as minister of communication and aviation in the national government formed by Alhaji A. Tafawa Balewa (q.v.) in 1957.

In preparation for the 1959 general elections (which were to lead the nation into independence in 1960), Chief Awolowo decided to vie for the topmost position in the country. He left the Western Regional (q.v.) government to go to the center. Chief Akintola then became premier of the region. The AG party did not win the majority of the seats to the national assembly and could not find a coalition partner. As such the party became the opposition party, while Chief Awolowo became the leader of the opposition. In 1962 a crisis erupted within the party as a result of a disagreement between him and the party leader, which led to fractionalization. On January 1, 1963, after the state of emergency in the Western Region had been lifted, Chief Akintola's newly formed party, United People's Party (UPP) (q.v.) formed a coalition government with the National Council of Nigerian Citizens (NCNC) (q.v.) in Western Nigeria.

By March 1964, Akintola was the leader of a new party, the Nigerian National Democratic Party (NNDP) (q.v.), which consisted of his UPP, some former members of the NCNC and the Southern People's Congress. The hand was the NNDP symbol. In the same year—and in preparation for the 1964 federal elections—the NNDP made an alliance with the Northern People's Congress (NPC) (q.v.), known as the Nigerian National Alliance (NNA) (q.v.), while the NCNC and remnants of the AG, together with other so-called progressive parties, formed an alliance called the United Progressive Grand Alliance (UPGA) (q.v.). The NNA won the election, which was marred by many allegations of election malpractices. In October 1965, many people believed the Western Regional elections would oust Chief Akintola from power. But the elections were so rigged that Akintola came back into power. There followed three months of bloody rioting in Western Nigeria, including arson and killing, until January 15, 1966, when the army staged a coup d'état, during which Chief Akintola was killed.

AKINTOYE. King of Lagos (q.v.) from 1841 to 1853, during whose reign the British consul began the practice of effectively interfering in local affairs. When Oba (king) Oluwole of Lagos died in 1841 without an heir, rival claims arose between Oluwole's cousin Kosoko (q.v.) and his uncle Akintoye, who with the assistance of the Oba of Benin was crowned as the Oba of Lagos in that year. Kosoko resented this and, in 1845, drove Akintoye from the throne. Akintoye went to Badagry, put pressure on the British to reinstate him with the promise that he would put an end to the slave trade still going on under Kosoko. When that was not successful, he made an alliance with Domingo José, a notorious Brazilian slave trader, to help him regain his throne, but that also failed. In 1849 John Beecroft (q.v.) was appointed consul to the Bights of Benin and Biafra and Akintoye came to an agreement with him that if he were restored to the throne of Lagos, he would put an end to the slave trade in Lagos. In 1851 Beecroft moved against Kosoko, expelled him from Lagos and reinstated Akintoye. Akintoye agreed to prohibit human sacrifice and stop the sale of slaves in his domain. Akintoye died in

1853, succeeded by his son, Dosunmu (q.v.), who among other contestants the newly appointed consul of Lagos, Benjamin Campbell, believed would be more amenable to the British interest. It was Dosunmu who ceded the city of Lagos to the British in 1861.

AKRAN, OBA C.D. A traditional ruler of Badagry, Lagos State (q.v.), and a member of the banned Action Group Party (AG) (q.v.) until that party's crisis in 1962. In 1963 he was instrumental in bringing about some kind of reconciliation between Chief S.L. Akintola (q.v.), leader of the United People's Party (UPP) (q.v.) and premier of Western Nigeria, and Alhaji D.S. Adegbenro (q.v.), AG parliamentary leader, together with their supporters. They issued a statement to the effect that they had resolved to collaborate in order to usher in an era of unity, peace, tranquillity, progress and the welfare of the people of Western Nigeria. They also resolved to evolve an all-embracing democratic organization to which all the people would belong. The agreement was criticized by opposition parties and so it was short-lived.

AKWA IBOM STATE. Created in 1987 by the administration of General Ibrahim Babangida (q.v.), the state, historically, has been in the forefront of the struggle for state creation (q.v.) in Nigeria. The oldest cultural organisation in Nigeria came from the state, the Ibibio State Union (q.v.), founded in 1928 but abolished in 1966 when the military came to power.

The state has a land area of 8,421 square kilometres and has between latitudes 4° 32′ and 5° 33′N, and longitudes 7° 25′ and 8° 25′E. It is bounded by Abia State (q.v.) to the north and northwest, Rivers State (q.v.) to the west, Cross River State (q.v.) to the east and the Atlantic Ocean to the south. There are two major seasons—the rainy season from March to October and the dry season from October to March. The annual rainfall varies from 2,340 millimetres to 3,170 millimetres. The temperature is fairly uniform all over the state, ranging from 7°C to 9°C in July when the rainy season is heaviest to 27°C during February and March towards the end of the dry season. As a result of the high temperature and plentiful rainfall, the interior vegetation is similar to a tropical rain forest, while mangrove forests abound along the coastal swamps.

The population of Akwa Ibom State was 2,359,736 in 1991 with a population density of 280 persons per square kilometre, which is much more than the national average of 95.8 persons. About 75 percent of the people live in rural areas, most of whom are farmers, creating a great demand for more agricultural land. The main economic crops are oil palm (q.v.), cassava (q.v.), yams (q.v.), cocoyam, maize and plantain. The people also have economic trees of the rain forest such as Iroko hardwood, Afara and many other fruit trees. The state has many mineral resources, including crude oil, condensate, natural gas, limestone, coal, silver, nitrate, glass sand, salt and clay. The State capital is Uyo. The most prominent urban centers are Abak, Ikot Ekpene, Eket, Uyo, Oron, Ikot Abasi and Itu. The state has 24 local government areas. It is composed mainly of the Ibibio (q.v.), but also the Oron, the Adon, Iheno, Anang, Eket and the Okobo people. Each group speaks its own language, but most understand Ibibio. Culturally, many people are Christian, comprising of Roman Catholics, Methodists, Presbyterians, Qua Iboe, Lutheran, the Brotherhood of the Cross and Star and many other denominations. Many also practise traditional religions, cults, secret societies and oracles, which, with Christianity, have created a hybrid of cultural values and artifacts. There are also masquerades like Ekpo, Ekong and Ibom, which generally appear at the time of the harvest. Missionaries were prominent in the educational development of the state. For decades they could boast of having some of the oldest schools in the whole country, such as the Presbyterian School at Ikot Offiong, founded in 1881, and the Methodist Secondary School at Oron, which was opened in 1905. In 1992 there were 1,055 primary schools and 253 secondary schools with 698,500 and 79,000 pupils, respectively.

ALAAFIN. The title of the ruler of the City of Oyo, the capital of the old Oyo empire (q.v.).

ALADURA CHURCHES. A number of indigenous Christian churches founded early in the 20th century. They are a combination of two cultural systems—European Christianity and various indigenous religious and cultural systems. Many of these churches originated from Yorubaland of Western Nigeria, hence, the Yoruba (q.v.) name *Aladura* churches, or Praying Churches. The founders of these churches wanted people to be free in expressing themselves culturally, expressing their fears and joys, rather than the restrictive nature of orthodox Christian churches. These churches include the Cherubim and Seraphim Churches, the Brotherhood of the Cross and Star and the Celestial Church of Christ. They have spread all over the nation.

ALAGOA, PROF. EBIEGBERI, J. A historian, born in 1933 at Okpoama, Brass, Rivers State (q.v.), Alagoa was educated at the Government College in Umuahia from 1948 to 1954 and the University College in Ibadan (q.v.) from 1954 to 1959. He later went to the United States to American University in Washington, D.C., in 1960 and then to the University of Wisconsin in Madison in 1962. In 1965 he was a lecturer in African history at the University of Lagos and moved to the University of Ibadan in 1966. He was appointed professor of history at the University of Lagos in 1972. In 1977 he became the dean of the school of humanities at the University of Port Harcourt and later held many important positions there. His publications include *The Small Brave City-State* (1964); *Jaja of Opobo: The Slave Who Became a King* (1970), *A History of the Niger Delta: A Historical Interpretation of Ijo Oral Traditions* (1972); and *A Chronicle of Grand Bonny* (1972).

ALAKIJA, SIR ADEYEMO. A lawyer and a founding member of the *Daily Times* of Nigeria, Sir Adeyemo Alakija was born on May 25, 1884, to a Brazilian family, which, remembering their ancestral origin to be Egbaland in Nigeria, had returned home. He was named Placido Adeyemo Assumpçao. He attended St. Gregory's Catholic School in Lagos (q.v.) and later went to the Church Missionary Society (q.v.) Grammar School for his secondary education. In 1900 he became a clerk in the government service and was for many years with the Post and Telegraph Department. He married in 1907, and in 1910 went to London to study law and was called to the bar in 1913. In that year he abandoned his Brazilian name and became Adeyemo Alakija. He was a successful lawyer, but soon became interested in politics. He was a good friend of Herbert Macaulay (q.v.), but the two men parted ways in the 1920s over the issue of British government treatment of the Oba of Lagos. In 1923 and 1926 he ran for one of the Lagos seats in the Legislative Council (q.v.), but he lost. In 1933, however, he was appointed member of the council representing Egba (q.v.).

Alakija's greatest contribution to the development of Nigeria was the part he played in the founding of the Nigerian *Daily Times* in 1926. He, together with Ernest Sesei Ikoli (q.v.) and Richard Barrow, who was an agent of Jurgen's Colonial Products Limited and the Chairman of the Lagos Chambers of Commerce, planned the paper. They then formed the Nigerian Printing and Publishing Company (NPPC) to start the publishing of the *Daily Times*. The new paper took over Ikoli's own paper, *African Messenger,* which Ikoli was editing. Ikoli became the first editor of the *Daily Times,* which started on June 1, 1926. Sir Alakija was the chairman of the board of NPPC. In 1936 the NPPC was merged with the West African Newspapers Limited of London, which used to publish the *West Africa* magazine and the *West African Review*. In 1948 the International Publishing Corporation of London took over the *Daily Times*.

Sir Alakija won traditional titles from Abeokuta (q.v.) and Ile-Ife (q.v.) and was many times honored by the British government. In 1945 he became a Knight of the Order British Empire. Though not very successful in politics, he contributed a great deal to the founding of Egbe Omo Oduduwa (q.v.), a Yoruba (q.v.) cultural organization. In 1948 when the Egbe was officially launched in Ile-Ife, Sir Alakija was made its first president and Chief Obafemi Awolowo (q.v.) its general secretary. This Egbe later became the nucleus of the Action Group Party (q.v.). Alakija died on May 10, 1952.

ALEXANDER, SIR DARNLEY ARTHUR RAYMOND, C.B.E., LLD. A former chief justice of Nigeria, Sir Alexander was born on January 28, 1920, at St. Lucia, West Indies. He was educated at St. Mary's College in St. Lucia and later at University College in London. In 1938 he was at the Middle Temple and was called to the bar in 1942. He practiced law in Jamaica between 1944 and 1957 and in Western Nigeria from 1957 to 1960. He was solicitor-general and permanent secretary in the Ministry of Justice in Western Nigeria from 1960 to 1963. In 1964 he became a judge of the High Court of Lagos (q.v.) the position he occupied until 1969. During this period he was appointed chairman of the Public Inquiries into the Owegbe Cult in the former Mid-Western Region (q.v.) (now Edo State) in 1965, and in 1968 he also was chairman of the Public Inquiries into Examination Leakages in Nigeria. In 1969 he became chief justice of the South Eastern State (later known as the Cross River State [q.v.]). He remained in this position until 1975 when he was appointed the chief justice of the Federal Republic of Nigeria and served in that position until 1979 when he retired. He is a member of many learned societies, among which are the Nigerian Society of International Law. He was a Commander, Order of the British Empire (CBE), in January 1963 and was also knighted.

ALHAJI, ALHAJI ABUBAKAR. Also known as "Triple A," Alhaji is the Sardauna of Sokoto (q.v.) and former minister of finance and economic development. Born on November 22, 1938, he was said to have learned the Koran by heart at an early age, even before he enrolled at the Sokoto Middle School. He attended Kano Junior Secondary School and later Katsina Government College. He went to the Bournemouth College of Commerce and Technology in Britain and the University of Reading, also in England, to study political economy.

He began his working career as a civil servant in the federal Ministry of Industries in 1964 and, six years later, he went to the Institute of Social Sciences at the Hague in Holland where he studied industrialisation. In 1971 he was posted to the federal Ministry of Finance, and, while there, he served as alternate executive director of the African Development Bank from 1972 to 1974. During that period he spent some time in the United States at the International Monetary Fund Institute (IMF) in Washington, D.C. He was later sent to the Ministry of Trade where he became deputy permanent secretary. In 1978 he was back at the Ministry of Finance, and in 1984 he became director-general in the Ministry of National Planning. In 1988 he was made minister of state for budget and planning and a special assistant to the president. In August 1990 he became the minister of finance and economic development. During these assignments, Alhaji served on various commissions, boards and agencies.

Alhaji Alhaji was very prominent in the international financial arena under the Babangida (q.v.) administration. He was always involved when Nigeria was looking for loans or rescheduling its debts with the Paris and London Clubs, the IMF and the World Bank.

In 1991 he became the Sardauna of Sokoto, a very prominent and powerful position in the Sokoto Caliphate (q.v.). In August 1992, he became Nigerian High Commissioner to Britain.

ALI EISAMI. A slave, freed by the British at Freetown (q.v.) in Sierra Leone (q.v.), he was the son of an Islamic teacher. Before his capture, he had received Arabic education. He was captured when the Fulani (q.v.) overran Bornu (q.v.), and was taken to Kano (q.v.), Katsina (q.v.) and later to Ilorin (q.v.). From Ilorin he was taken in 1818 to Porto-Novo (q.v.) where he was sold to European slavers. It was on his way to the Americas that the British antislavery squadron recaptured him and set him free in Freetown. There he took up a new name, William Harding. He later told his story of captivity and his life to S.W. Koelle, a German linguist working in Freetown. Koelle published Ali Eisami's story in *African Native Literature* (1854).

ALI GHAJI DUNAMANI. Ruler of the Kanuri (q.v.) people of Bornu (q.v.) from 1470 to 1503, his reign ended a period of internal wars. The Sefawa dynasty before his reign had split into two ruling houses. The system encouraged intrigues leading to warfare. When he became ruler, he was challenged by another candidate from the other ruling house. A war ensued in which he defeated and killed in battle the rival from the other ruling house. He then made sure that the powers of the other ruling house were drastically reduced so they could not challenge him again. Having accomplished this, he faced the Bulala (q.v.) nomads who posed great threat to his kingdom. The Bulala people had driven his people from Kanem to Bornu in the fourteenth century when Umar Ibn Idris (q.v.) reigned. Umar also defeated the Kanuri. Before his death in 1503, Ali Ghaji Dunamani founded Birni N'gazargamu, a capital city for his successors. The capital became a safe place for people to live and attracted many people and traders.

ALI GHAJI, MAI. Was the ruler of Bornu from 1465–97. Among his achievements was the siting of a new capital for the Sefuwa dynasty at Gazargamo, and a return to patrilineal succession.

ALIU BABBA. Ruler of the Sokoto (q.v.) Caliphate (q.v.) from 1842 to 1859, Aliu was the grandson of Usman dan Fodio (q.v.), the originator of the Fulani empire (q.v.) in northern Nigeria (q.v.). He was the son of Muhammad Bello (q.v.) who consolidated the empire and developed its administration. During Aliu's reign he fought hard to extend the empire and to quell revolts from places like Kebbi (q.v.) and Zamfara. His reign saw the Sokoto Caliphate firmly established in northern Nigeria. Before his death in 1859, he was said to have appointed no less than 16 emirs to various Hausa (q.v.) Emirates.

ALLIANCE FOR DEMOCRACY. One of the three political parties to emerge from Abdulsalami Abubakar's transition to democracy (1998–99). The Alliance for Democracy (AD) was created in September 1998, when a group of Yoruba politicians affiliated with the cultural organisation Afenifere opted not to ally themselves with either of the other two major parties, the All People's Party (APP) and the People's Democratic Party (PDP). While the AD quickly established itself as the dominant party in the southwest, it struggled to build a national base of support. This became clear in local government elections in December 1998 and governorship elections in January 1999. The AD swept the southwest, but won very little anywhere else. In order to bolster their chances for the presidential elections, in January 1999 the AD negotiated an agreement with the APP whereby the two parties would field a common presidential candidate. The working arrangement was made difficult by the presence within the APP of former supporters of the Abacha regime (1993–98), which had been particularly unpopular in the southwest. The two parties ultimately agreed to unite behind the AD's candidate, Olu Falae. Falae lost the February 27 election to Olusegun Obasanjo (q.v.). After the election, the AD was divided over whether to allow its members to participate in the newly elected Obasanjo government. Obasanjo's new cabinet included prominent AD members Bola Ige, and Mrs. Dupe Adelaja, daughter of Afenifere leader, Abraham Adesanya. While they were eventually allowed to join the cabinet (but not as representatives of the party) concerns remained that their affiliation with the regime might impair the AD's ability to function as a vigorous opposition.

ALL-NIGERIA TRADE UNION FEDERATION (ANTUF). Inaugurated 1953 in an effort to form a central labour organization after the disintegration of the Nigerian Labour Congress (NLC) (q.v.), its aims were to improve the position and the living conditions of the workers, organise and unite all the trade unions in the country, encourage the spirit of oneness and collective security among workers, fight for the social and economic security of workers and secure for workers improvement in wages and in their conditions of service. The leaders of the organisation were M.A.O. Imoudu (q.v.), who was president, and Gogo Chu Nzeribe, the general secretary.

The organisation did not last long for it disintegrated on the issue of its international affiliation. At the 1956 conference of the union, it was agreed that the union could affiliate with an international organisation. However, in the 1957 conference, some members wanted the federation to affiliate with the International Confederation of Free Trade Unions (ICFTU) (q.v.), while others wanted affiliation with the World Federation of Trade Unions (WFTU), which was communist-oriented. The motion for affiliation with ICFTU was made and defeated. But the general secretary of the ANTUF ruled that, since the conference voted against affiliation with ICFTU, it meant it approved affiliation with the WFTU. Many unions left in disgust and formed the National Council of Trade Unions of Nigeria (NCTUN) (q.v.). In 1959, through the effort of the government and some union leaders, the ANTUF and the NCTUN came together to form the Trade Union Congress of Nigeria (q.v.).

ALL PEOPLE'S PARTY. One of the three political parties to emerge from Abdulsalami Abubakar's transition to democracy (1998–99). It included many former supporters of the regime of General Sani Abacha (1993–98) (q.v.), earning it the derogatory title, "Abacha's People's Party." While there was some truth to the nickname, the party also boasted a number of powerful regional politicians such as Emmanuel Iwuanyanwu, Olusola Saraki, Umaru Shinkafi and Arthur Nzeribe. In January 1999, the APP reached an agreement with the Alliance for Democracy (AD) to field a common presidential candidate. When it became clear that the joint candidate would be Olu Falae of the AD, a number of prominent presidential aspirants from the APP (such as Saraki and Iwuanyanwu) deserted the party. Falae picked APP member Umaru Shinkafi to be his running mate, but lost the February 27, 1999, election to Olusegun Obasanjo (q.v.) of the People's Democratic Party (PDP). Following the election, the APP entered a long period of crisis as it splintered into factions. The most troublesome faction was that of Olusola Saraki, who was unhappy with the manner in which he had been denied the party's presidential nomination.

AMALGAMATION OF NIGERIA. The Amalgamation of Nigeria was the process of uniting the various parts of the country under one colonial administration.

Nigeria, before the amalgamation, was made up of many parts. There was the Crown colony (q.v.) of Lagos (q.v.), which was ceded to the British Crown in 1861. From Lagos the British authorities extended their jurisdiction to the hinterland as they developed their trading interest in the area. After the Berlin Conference (q.v.) of 1885, the zone of interest that British traders had established in the coastal areas became the Oil Rivers Protectorate (q.v.). In 1893 the protectorate was extended further to the interior and renamed the Niger Coast Protectorate (q.v.), and, when in 1900 the charter of the Royal Niger Company (q.v.) was revoked, it became the Protectorate (q.v.) of Southern Nigeria. In 1906 the Crown colony of Lagos was amalgamated with the Protectorate of Southern Nigeria and was then called

Colony and Protectorate of Southern Nigeria. This was really the first process in the unification of the various parts of Nigeria.

But while progress was going on in the south, Lord Frederick Lugard's (q.v.) administration was also busy consolidating its power in the north. On January 1, 1900, the Protectorate of Northern Nigeria replaced the administration of the Royal Niger Company. Between 1900 and 1914, with the use of the Royal West African Frontier Force, Lord Lugard was able to attack and defeat all centers of resistance to British rule and pacify the north. On January 1, 1914, the two administrations of the southern and northern protectorates were amalgamated and named the Colony and Protectorate of Nigeria with Lord Lugard as the governor-general, and two lieutenant governors were put in charge of the former areas of the former protectorates.

Certain factors were responsible for the amalgamation, such as that, before 1914, the Northern Protectorate was always in a deficit and was subsidized by annual grants from the imperial treasury and the southern administration, which had surpluses from the import duties on liquor and other goods. Thus, amalgamation was a means of relieving the imperial treasury of its burden.

The amalgamation did not mean complete unification of the former two administrations. Important departments like health, public works, forestry, education, agriculture, police and prison were still administered separately.

As a result of the amalgamation, the provincial system of government in the north was extended to the south. Each province was then headed by a resident. The government set up, in addition to the Executive Council (q.v.), a deliberative body known as the Nigerian Council (q.v.), composed of official and nonofficial members including traditional rulers from both the north and the south. The council was designed to give expression to African public opinion, but the chiefs who were in the majority of the nominated African members rarely attended its meetings. Lastly, after the amalgamation, the system of Indirect Rule (q.v.) was extended to the southern provinces. However, the Colony of Lagos was recognised as a separate unit from the southern provinces and placed under an administrator.

AMINA, QUEEN OF ZARIA. According to oral tradition, Amina was the queen of Zaria (q.v.) about 1588. She is believed to have fought many wars and expanded her jurisdiction as far as the Niger River (q.v.) in the south, and Kano (q.v.) and Katsina (q.v.) to the north. She is also remembered for the walled camps she established wherever she halted during her extensive campaign, as, for example, the wall around Katsina; and the famous Zaria wall is attributed to her reign. It is not certain whether or not she ever married, but tradition has it that she used to take new lovers wherever she stopped during her wars and had them disposed of when she left. During her reign

Zaria achieved considerable influence in Hausaland. She died in Attagara after 34 years of war and conquest.

ANAMBRA STATE. The present Anambra State was created during the administration of General Ibrahim Babangida (q.v.) on August 27, 1991, when Enugu State (q.v.) was carved out of the old Anambra State, which was created in 1976. The state derives its name from the Anambra River, one of the tributaries of the Niger River (q.v.). The state has a land area of 4,416 square kilometres and is bounded in the west by Niger River, in the north by Kogi State (q.v.), in the northeast by Enugu State, in the east by Abia State (q.v.) and in the south by Imo State (q.v.) and Rivers State (q.v.).

The population of the state in 1991 was 2,767,903, and the population density is 627 persons per square kilometres, making Anambra one of the most densely populated areas in Nigeria. The state is divided into 16 local government areas. Ethnically, the people are mainly Igbo (q.v.), but there are also the Mbembe, and migrants from various other states of the federation. The languages of communication are Igbo and English (q.v.). The people live in various rural communities. Towns are transformed villages that became urbanised during the colonial era. However, this does not mean that they never had big cities before the white man came. Archaeological findings have shown the existence of an ancient city known as Nri. Today Anambra State has many big cities such as Onitsha (q.v.), a commercial and industrial center east of the Niger River, Nnewi and Awka, the state capital and a commercial and industrial center.

The state is within the tropical rain forest zone. About 75 percent of the people are engaged in subsistence farming, raising crops of maize, rice, yams (q.v.) and cassava (q.v.). Large-scale farming, especially by corporate bodies is also developing. Anambra is rich in mineral resources like limestone, kaolin and pyrite.

Culturally, the state is a home of many cultural artifacts. Archaeological excavation at Igbo-Ukwu (q.v.) in Aguata—a local government area—uncovered great works of arts in bronze, dating back to the ninth century A.D. These artifacts are stored in several museums in Igbo-Ukwu, Nri and Nimo. The many traditional and religious festivals include the new yams festival (Iriji Ndigbo), the masquerade and the Ofala (a royal outing of traditional rulers) festivals. Christianity is widely accepted among the people.

Educationally, Anambra State is one of the most highly educated in the federation. In 1992 it had 874 primary schools with 385,216 pupils and 265 secondary schools with 124,546 students. There are many colleges of education, polytechnics, colleges of agriculture and Nnamdi Azikiwe University at Awka and the Madona University in Onitsha (q.v.). The Catholic Church also has a major seminary in Onitsha.

ANGLICAN CHURCH. *See* CHURCH MISSIONARY SOCIETY.

ANGLO-FRENCH AGREEMENT OF 1890. After the agreement at the Berlin Conference (q.v.) of 1885, recognising British claims to areas along the Niger River (q.v.), the French were still pushing hard in an effort to penetrate Nigeria to the west and south of the Niger. The two countries signed an agreement in 1890 that greatly strengthened the British position in northern Nigeria and effected a settlement of the northern boundaries. Under the agreement, Britain recognised French influence from its Mediterranean possessions south to a line drawn from Say on the Niger to Barrawa on Lake Chad (q.v.). Britain was to claim all the territories of the Royal Niger Company (q.v.) that fell within the Kingdom of Sokoto (q.v.), the exact units of which were to be determined by a joint commission. The French were not happy about this treaty because it strengthened the British claim to Borgu, which the French wanted very much.

ANGLO-FRENCH CONVENTION OF 1898. The struggle for territories in parts of West Africa continued to engender serious tension between the French and the British after the Anglo-French Agreement of 1890. The French still wanted to extend their power to Borgu, an area which included Bussa (q.v.), but the British, who had already signed a treaty with the ruler of Borgu, were determined to resist. To prevent the tension from leading to hostility between the two nations, the Anglo-French Convention of June 14, 1898, also known as the Borgu Convention, was drafted. Under the agreement reached, the French were granted the entrepôt on the Niger River (q.v.); the frontiers of Dahomey, now the Republic of Benin, were extended to the Niger north of Ilo; the Kingdom of Sokoto (q.v.) was awarded to Britain; the lease of ground south of Bussa was approved; and the British guaranteed equality of treatment on all matters dealing with navigation, commerce and tariffs. They further agreed that the delimitation of the West African territories should be entrusted to a joint commission. By this treaty, British claims to Nigeria became more secure.

ANGLO-NIGERIAN DEFENCE AGREEMENT. *See* DEFENCE PACT.

ANI, MICHAEL OKON NSA. Former chairman of the Federal Electoral Commission (FEC) (q.v.), which declared Alhaji Shehu Shagari (q.v.) as the nation's first executive president. Born on November 30, 1917, in Calabar (q.v.), Cross River State (q.v.), he was educated at the Sacred Heart School and at the Sacred Heart College, both in Calabar. He later went to the London School of Economics and Political Science in England. Upon his return to Nigeria, he joined the federal civil service and rose to the position of permanent secretary in 1960. In 1963 he was appointed United Nations expert on public administration for proposed federal civil service for Uganda, Kenya and Tanganyika. In 1967 Ani was appointed administrator of the liberated areas of Eastern Nigeria (q.v.) under federal command during the Civil War (q.v.) of 1967–70. He was director of the flour mills of Nigeria from 1973 to 1975 and member of the Federal Public Service Commission (q.v.) from 1975 to 1976. In 1977 he became chairman of the FEC, and it was his responsibility to conduct the first election that ushered in the Second Republic (q.v.) in 1979. He held this position until 1980 when the commission was dissolved. He died in 1985.

ANIKULAPO-KUTI, OLUFELA. A musician, composer, social critic and activist, popularly known as "Fela," Anikulapo-Kuti was born on October 15, 1938, in Abeokuta (q.v.), Ogun State (q.v.). He was educated at the Abeokuta Grammar School and the Trinity College of Music, in England, from 1959 to 1962. Upon arrival in Nigeria, he worked at the Nigerian Broadcasting Corporation (now Federal Radio Corporation of Nigeria [q.v.]) until 1967. He later founded his "Africa 70" group and became the creator of Afro-Beat music.

Fela's music is generally based on current themes, issues and events in his environment. Being a person born into local politics in Abeokuta where his mother, Olufunmilayo Ransome-Kuti (q.v.) was very active, he easily became interested in national and international affairs. In his "Jeun Koku" (chop and die), he asked the colonial masters to leave the Africans alone to manage their own affairs. He later began to preach pan-Africanism (q.v.) and from there turned his attention to the Nigerian government in his "Zombie," "Blackman-de-suffer" and "I.T.T." His house was attacked, and in 1977 his house known as "Kalakuta Republic" was burnt down. His mother later died of injuries received during an attack from government troops, where Fela was also beaten with many of his newly married "wives," who were dancers and singers.

In 1979 when the ban on politics was lifted, he formed his own party, Movement of the People, but it could not be registered as a political party. Fela has been a great campaigner against corruption, oppression and repression. In 1984 he was arrested and charged for violating currency regulations. Anikulapo-Kuti was sentenced to 10 years but served only 18 months, when he was released by the Babangida (q.v.) administration in 1986. Fela recorded over 40 albums, many of which consistently call attention to the evils in society. Fela died on August 2, 1997, as a result of complications from Acquired Immune Deficiency Syndrome (AIDS).

ANTI-SABOTAGE DECREE. *See* EXCHANGE CONTROL DECREE.

ANYAOKU, CHIEF ELEAZAR CHUKWUEMEKA. A diplomat, born in 1933 at Obosi Onitsha (q.v.), Anambra State (q.v.), he was educated at the

University of Ibadan in Nigeria, the Institute of Public Administration in London, and the Cavillam Institute in France. He joined the Nigerian Foreign Service in 1962 and became a member of the Nigerian Permanent Mission to the United Nations from 1963 to 1966. He was later seconded to the Commonwealth Secretariat as an assistant director in the International Affairs Division in London and in 1971 became the director of the Commonwealth Secretariat. He was elected deputy secretary-general (political) in 1978 and in 1989 was elevated to the post of secretary-general of the Commonwealth, following a secret ballot of the 49-member organisation in Kuala Lumpur, Malaysia. He has published many books, among which is *The Racial Factor in International Politics* (1977). He holds traditional titles and the national honor of the Commander of the Order of the Niger.

AOLE (AWOLE). Ruler of the Oyo empire (q.v.) during its decline (1789–1796). Before he became the Alaafin (king), the Oyo army under Abiodun (q.v.) had suffered a significant defeat by the Borgu forces. After Aole became Oba, the Nupe (q.v.) revolted against Oyo, and Aole's many unpopular decisions only made matters worse. One of his decisions was sending an expedition against Apomu in the Ife Kingdom, an act which was said to go against Yoruba (q.v.) tradition since the kingdom was regarded as the cradle of the Yoruba. His army later rebelled, and Aole was made to commit suicide after receiving an empty, covered calabash—an indication of his rejection. After his death, the empire declined further.

ARABIC LANGUAGE. The language originally spoken in Arabia and the language of the Koran. The spread of Islam (q.v.) and the movement of the Arabs to North Africa and Nigeria brought the language to Nigeria. It is written from right to left, and its characters are joined together. Because special prayers are said in Arabic, Muslim children in Nigeria go to Arabic schools to learn the language so they can pray and read the Koran.

ARABS. People of Arabia and their descendants. They first began their movement to North Africa in the 11th century and later moved south to the Sudan (q.v.) and northern part of Nigeria. As they came, they spread the Arabic language and the religion of Islam (q.v.) and mixed freely with the local population.

ARIKPO, DR. OKOI. A diplomat, born on September 20, 1916, he was educated at the Church of Scotland Mission, Ugefa. In 1923 he entered Hope Waddell Institute, Calabar, and in 1927 he went to the Government College, Umuahia. From 1934 to 1938, he was a student at the Yaba Higher College (q.v.), and he later left for Britain to study anthropology at London University. He was assistant lecturer in anthropology at the University College in London from 1949 to 1951. After his studies in London, he came back to

Nigeria, and in 1952 he was minister of lands, survey and local development, and in 1953 minister of mines and power. He later became commissioner for external affairs during the regime of General Yakubu Gowon (q.v.). As commissioner, he worked hard to restore better harmony with African and other countries after the Civil War (q.v.).

ARINZE, CARDINAL FRANCIS. A Catholic clergyman born in 1932 at Ezi Owelle Idemili, Anambra State (q.v.). He entered All Hallows Seminary, Onitsha (q.v.), in 1947, Bigard Memorial Seminary in Enugu (q.v.) and Urban University in Rome from 1957 to 1960. After his ordination, he taught for some years at the Bigard Memorial Seminary from 1960 to 1962 and became auxiliary bishop of Onitsha in 1965, Archbishop of Onitsha in 1967 and president of the Catholic Bishops' Conference of Nigeria in 1979. He was appointed cardinal by Pope John Paul II in 1985, becoming the second Nigerian Catholic cardinal. He is a member of the Sacred Congregation for the Evangelisation of Peoples. He has published many books, including *Sacrifice in Ibo Religion* (1971), *Answering God's Call* (1983), *Living Our Faith* (1983) and *Alone with God* (1987).

ARMED FORCES. When the Royal Niger Company (q.v.) received its charter to administer the northern part of the country, it organised the Royal Niger Constabulary (q.v.) with special emphasis on military activities. The constabulary consisted of five British and two African officers and about 400 men from Nigeria and the Gold Coast (now Ghana). Because of the French encroachment on the territory of the Royal Niger Company between 1894 and 1897, the British government decided to raise a local force to protect its area of influence. The government sent Colonel (later, Lord) Frederick Lugard (q.v.) to Nigeria, to raise and command the force. By the beginning of 1900 when all of Nigeria came under British authority, the force was well organised and well disciplined.

In 1901 all the colonial military forces in British West African colonies were constituted into the West African Frontier Force (q.v.). Each territory was, however, responsible for its force. The Nigerian force consisted of the Northern Nigeria Regiments, the Lagos Constabulary, which became the Lagos Battalion, and the Southern Nigerian Regiment. When in 1906 the Colony of Lagos was merged with the Protectorate of Southern Nigeria (q.v.), the Lagos Battalion became the Second Battalion of the Southern Regiment. However, on January 1, 1914, when the Northern and Southern Protectorates were merged, the two regiments were also merged and they both became the Nigerian Regiment. The Nigerian Regiment, as part of the West African Frontier Force, fought gallantly in the First and Second World Wars, and they won many Distinguished Conduct Medals, Military Medals, British Empire Medals and many Certificates of Good Service.

In 1955 the Nigerian Army was constituted into a separate command. In the same year, the Naval Defence Force, which was formed during the Second World War and made responsible for the security of Nigerian harbour entrances and the patrol of its coast, was formally established by parliament. On April 1, 1958, the control of the Nigerian military forces was surrendered by the British government to the Government of Nigeria, which still was under British rule, and the Naval Defence Force became the Royal Nigerian Navy. In 1963 when Nigeria became a republic, the Royal Nigerian Navy became the Nigerian Navy. In 1964 parliament established the Nigerian Air Force charged with the defence of Nigerian airspace.

Nigerian military personnel have served in various peacekeeping operations of the United Nations. In 1960 and 1963, they served in the Congo during the Congo crisis as members of the United Nations Peacekeeping Force. They also were sent to Tanganyika (now Tanzania) to help the government maintain law and order after the Tanzanian troops had mutinied. And during the Liberian civil war, Nigerian military personnel constituted a high proportion of the Economic Community of West African States Monitoring Group troops (ECOMOG).

During the Civil War, the Nigerian armed forces grew at a very rapid rate. Before the military took over the government in January 1966, the army consisted of about 10,500 men, but at the end of the war in January 1970, the army was composed of about 250,000 men. After the war, efforts were made to demobilise some of these soldiers, and by the time the military was handing power over to the civilian administration in 1979, more than 50,000 men had been demobilised while over 250 officers had retired. In 1980 the armed forces were estimated to be about 150,000 men and in 1984 about 100,000.

The role of the military in Nigerian politics has been mixed. It was only the military that could divide the four regions of the Federation in 1967 into 12 states, thus alleviating the fear of domination which many in the south had always felt. But lack of training and experience in the art of political bargaining, the art of give-and-take, compromise and toleration led to hasty decisions, always "with immediate effect," many of which have had disastrous effects on the Nigerian polity.

The military surrendered power to an elected government on October 1, 1979, after almost 14 years in power. However, on October 31, 1983, the army struck again, toppling the civilian administration of Alhaji Shehu Shagari (q.v.), which was accused of mismanagement of the economy, corruption and electoral malpractices. Thus from January 1966 to July 1996, a period of more than 30 years, the military has allowed civilian rule only for four years.

The prolonged rule of the military has changed its image as a corrective body, which comes in out of necessity to correct some mistakes and withdraws to something resembling an army of occupation. After the military tasted the forbidden fruit of political power, all the qualities of a good army have been badly devalued, and bastardized—qualities such as discipline, morale, esprit de corps, and loyalty to the nation have all suffered. The politics that goes on in the country has been really the politics within the military itself. There have been coups and countercoups, replacing one general with another, and leading to instability in political and economic decisions. For some undisclosed reasons peculiar to the ruling clique, the air force and the navy were neglected. Many planes were grounded, and ships became unseaworthy. Military men lobbied hard for political appointments, and many officers became corrupt. The effort of some military topnotchers to rebuild the armed forces professionally after General Ibrahim Babangida (q.v.) stepped down was soon after thwarted by the coming into power of General Sani Abacha (q.v.).

The continuous staying in power by the military has set back the country economically for many decades. The military, which based its legitimacy in 1966 and 1983 on a pledge to stamp out corruption, has developed a culture of corruption. Corruption has eaten deep into the fabric of the society, and it pervades every aspect of the nation's public life, including even the judicial system. From 1985, when General Ibrahim B. Babangida came to power, there has been a complete lack of financial accountability. Much of the revenue from oil has been diverted into private accounts in Europe, America and elsewhere. The standard of living has drastically fallen, while inflation continued to rise. Babangida, about a year before he was forced out of office, wondered how the economy was able to go on in spite of all the buffeting it had suffered under his administration.

The greatest disservice the military has done to Nigeria as an entity is the fractionalisation of the country, ethnically, politically and religiously. Nigeria was more divided in 1996 than ever before. This was a result of military leaders playing on ethnic and religious factors to stay in power. Still more, military rule has deprived the people of the opportunity to learn from mistakes, to bargain with one another and come to a compromise solution to problems, and it has deprived them of learning to tolerate each other and their opinions, and for the loser in the political contest to learn how to wait for his turn the next time around. Decision making has often been haphazard—without careful consideration of the pros and the cons—and the implication and implementation of the decisions made. *See also* ARMY, NIGERIAN.

ARMED FORCES CONSULTATIVE ASSEMBLY. Inaugurated in June 1989, the assembly was designed to provide interaction between the members of the armed forces, the police and the Armed Forces Ruling Council

(AFRC) (q.v.), the highest decision-making body under General I.B. Babangida's (q.v.) administration. The stated objectives for the AFCA were to serve as a channel of communication between the military government and military officers, promote through informal discussion *esprit de corps,* and find ways and means to ensure that during the transition to civil rule and after, the professional ethics of the military would be supportive of the democratic norms and values. The assembly was also to provide advice to the presidency and the AFRC on general policies, programs and decisions of government. The unstated objective, however, was for Babangida, the military president, to garner support for his administration even when he was planning not to quit power, which was contrary to what he always professed publicly. It is to the credit of the armed forces that they turned down his appeal in 1993 to continue in power.

ARMED FORCES RULING COUNCIL. *See* SUPREME MILITARY COUNCIL.

ARMED PLOT. On October 1, 1962, Prime Minister Alhaji Sir Abubakar Tafawa Balewa (q.v.) announced to the nation that the government had foiled an armed plot to forcibly overthrow the government by staging a coup détat. He announced that some persons who were principally implicated had absconded and were abroad. Many others had been arrested and were being detained under the emergency regulations powers of May 1962. On October 5, 1962, the police, after searching the homes of some Action Group Party (AG) (q.v.) members, discovered three stores of arms including submachine guns, tear gas, pistols, revolvers and other weapons. On November 2, 1962, Chief Obafemi Awolowo (q.v.) leader of the AG party and leader of the opposition in the federal House of Representatives (q.v.), was charged with 26 other persons with treasonable felony and conspiracy to overthrow the Federal Government by force. Some of the persons implicated and who were outside the country were Chief Anthony Enahoro, (q.v.) in London, Samuel Ikoku (q.v.) the federal secretary of the party in Ghana and Ayo Adebanjo.

ARO PEOPLE. The Aro people were an Igbo (q.v.) subgroup that had generally set themselves apart from other groups as a trading group. Before the British had extended their sway over the area, the Aro had traded in slaves and oil palm (q.v.). To perpetuate their monopoly in these trades, they developed a religion which claimed that God (Chukwu) had appointed them as his agents on earth, and had put them in charge of their famous Oracle (q.v.) in Aro, through which God revealed himself to men. This was not all; the Aro did not put all their confidence in the divine. They also entered into alliances with many other warlike clans within the Igbo and the Ibibio peoples. By these two means, they were able to control not only the slave trade but also the trade in palm oil. The Aro's dominant economic position was challenged when British officials began in the late 19th century to enter into treaties of friendship with various chiefs in the area and asserted their authority over the whole country.

ART. Art in Nigeria includes metal, wood, clay, stone, cloth, ivory and painting. Many works of art are produced for particular uses such as traditional or religious ceremonies and representation of rulers in particular societies or families. Much of Ife art (q.v.) and Benin art (q.v.) are of this kind. Among some people, artworks are buried with the dead. Nigerian art can also be seen in decorations of stools, walking sticks, clothes, doors and calabashes.

Different societies generally have distinct artworks. In the non-Muslim part of Nigeria, artworks include sculptures and painting of people and animals, but, in areas where Islam has been very strong, pictures that represent people or animals are not common. This is because Muslims are traditionally not allowed to make such figures or pictures. In such places artworks have consisted mainly in geometrical figures used to decorate calabashes, pots, leather saddles and bridles, clothes, necklaces, bracelets and beads.

ASHBY, LORD ERIC. An educationist, trained at the City of London School and the Imperial College of Science in London as a botanist, he was invited in 1959, on the eve of Nigeria's independence, to chair a commission that laid the groundwork for the country's postsecondary and higher education. The report of the commission titled "Investment in Education"—and known generally as the Ashby Report—painted a lucid demographical picture of the country's educational needs through the 1960s and the 1970s.

The recommendation of the commission led to the founding of the University of Lagos, Ahmadu-Bello University (q.v.) and University of Ife (q.v.) (now Obafemi Awolowo University) and the establishment of the National University Commission (NUC) (q.v.). The report drew attention to the important role of science and technology in the country's manpower development. The commission also insisted on the need to diversify the secondary school curriculum. *See also* ASHBY COMMISSION.

ASHBY COMMISSION. The official name of this commission is "The Commission on Post-School Certificate and Higher Education in Nigeria." There were nine members: three from the United States, three from Great Britain and three from Nigeria. The commission was set up in 1959 by the minister of education; its chair was Lord Eric Ashby (q.v.). It was the first commission on higher education (q.v.) to look into the higher education needs of Nigeria. Its mandate was to investigate the country's needs in the field of postschool certificate and higher education for the 20 years to 1980. The commission's report, based upon the objective of upgrading employed Nigerians who needed further training and of designing a system of postsecondary education that would meet the manpower needs of the country, drew much information from the Harbison Report (q.v.) on high-level manpower for Nigeria. The commission's recommendations were extensive, including primary and secondary education, teacher training, technical and commercial education, agriculture and veterinary education and university education. The government accepted the report in principle and declared that, with some amendments, the report would constitute the basis for the development of postschool certificate and higher education in Nigeria.

ASIKA, DR. ANTHONY UKPABI. A political scientist and an administrator, born in 1936 in Jos (q.v.), Plateau State (q.v.), Asika was educated at St. Patrick's College in Calabar and Edo College in Benin City (q.v.). Later, in 1956 he attended the University College, Ibadan, (now the University of Ibadan) and in 1961 went to the University of California, Los Angeles, in the United States. In 1965 he was a lecturer in political sociology at the University of Ibadan. In 1967 he was appointed administrator of the newly created East-Central State (q.v.) of Nigeria and served until 1975. He was at this post during the Nigerian Civil War (q.v.), which engulfed the East-Central State. He contributed greatly to the state's reconstruction and rehabilitation and to its people after the war.

ASIPA. Founder of the royal dynasty of Lagos (q.v.). From the middle of the sixteenth century to the middle of the eighteenth century, Lagos was under the rule of this Oba of Benin (q.v.). His origin is not clearly known. Benin tradition says Asipa was the grandson of an oba of Benin, while Lagos tradition says he was a Yoruba (q.v.) warrior who gained favor with the Oba of Benin by escorting home the body of an important Benin warrior. Asipa founded a new dynasty, which has continued to rule Lagos. Today the Oba of Lagos is a descendant of Asipa.

ASQUITH COMMISSION. The Commission on Higher Education in the colonies was set up in 1943 under the chairmanship of Hon. Mr. Justice Cyril Asquith. It was asked to consider the principles that should guide the promotion of higher education (q.v.), learning and research, and the development of universities in the colonies. It was also charged to explore ways by which universities in the United Kingdom could cooperate with the higher education institutions in the colonies. The colonial areas to be covered by the commission included Asia, Africa and West Indies. The most important recommendation for the universities that were later founded in the African colonies was that there should be an interuniversity council for higher education in the colonies, and that all colonial universities and university colleges should be under its jurisdiction. Members of such a council should be made up of representatives of all the universities in the United Kingdom and the council should keep in touch with the development of the new colonial institutions through regular visits of its members and should help in the recruitment of staff and in encouraging their staff members to take up appointment in the new institutions.

ASSOCIATION FOR BETTER NIGERIA. A political association founded in 1992 with the main objective of prolonging the stay of the military government in power under President Ibrahim B. Babangida (q.v.) or, if the military should quit politics, for Babangida to succeed himself as a civilian president. This association came at a time when most Nigerians wanted the military to go back to the barracks and after President Babangida had many times broken his promise to hand over power to a democratically elected government.

The ABN was under the leadership of Chief Francis Arthur Nzeribe (q.v.), a disqualified presidential candidate for the Social Democratic Party (SDP) (q.v.). The group launched a well-organised and well-funded campaign to show that Babangida was the only hope for solving the economic and political problems of the nation. While Babangida constantly told the nation that he was willing to quit, his administration was secretly funding ABN activities. This was revealed later by Chief Abimbola Davies, one of the top leaders of the ABN, who defected after the annulment of the June 12, 1993, presidential election (q.v.) results. When Babangida and the ABN could not stop preparations for the election, the ABN decided to go to court, asking for an injunction to stop the National Electoral Commission (NEC) (q.v.) from conducting the election as scheduled. Justice Bassey Ikpeme on the night of June 10, 1993, granted the injunction, but the NEC, relying upon the enabling Decree No. 13 of 1993, went ahead with the election. President Babangida and the ABN chiefs were not happy that Chief M.K.O. Abiola, the SDP presidential candidate, had a clear victory. Following the election, Davies, on behalf of the ABN, went to the court of the chief judge of Abuja (q.v.), Federal Capital Territory (q.v.), asking that the NEC be barred from publishing the election results from 14 states and Abuja. On June 23, the Babangida administration annulled the results of the election, plunging the nation into a serious political crisis.

ASSOCIATION OF EUROPEAN CIVIL SERVANTS IN NIGERIA. Formed in 1919 for the purpose of putting pressure on the colonial government to regrade the salaries of all European public servants in Nigeria, with the exception of the medical staff and the West African Frontier Force (q.v.). As a result of the activities of the association, the government not only regraded their salaries upward but granted them many concessions like travelling, transport and bush allowances, and travelling allowance on home leave. The government also agreed to pay a year's salary to the estate of a confirmed officer who died in the service.

ASSOCIATION OF NIGERIAN RAILWAY CIVIL SERVANTS. A splinter union from the Nigerian Civil Service Union, this association's objective was to take care of matters affecting railway office employees.

ASSOCIATION OF WEST AFRICAN MERCHANTS (AWAM). An association of European firms operating in the West African countries, formed during the Second World War to facilitate import agreements among the member companies and allocate export quotas to members. The member firms were the principal purchasers of export products at low fixed prices and principal importers of European goods at high and extortionist prices, leading to a lot of unrest in Ghana and Nigeria after the war. The government later withdrew support from the organisation, leading to its demise.

ATIBA. Ruler of the Oyo (q.v.) kingdom from 1836 to 1859, he was the son of Abiodun (q.v.), a former ruler of Oyo who was said to be the last great ruler of the empire. In 1858 Atiba abolished the traditional practice of the crown prince committing suicide at the death of his father, and, therefore, became one of the few obas in Yorubaland to modernise the traditional chieftaincy system. Upon his death in 1859, he was succeeded by his eldest son, Adelu. Because this was a breach of tradition, tension rose in Yorubaland; some important Yoruba towns (q.v.) like Ijaye refused to recognise him, but other towns like Ibadan did. This led to the outbreak of a civil war, which lasted for a long time. *See* IJAYE WAR.

ATIKU, ALHAJI ABUBAKAR. Born on November 25, 1946, in Jada, Northern Region (q.v.). In the late 1990s he emerged as the political heir to the northern politician Shehu Yar'Adua and in 1999 was elected to become vice president under President Olusegun Obasanjo (q.v.). Alhaji Atiku graduated from Ahmadu Bello University in 1969 with a law degree. For the next 20 years, he served in the civil service, retiring in 1989 as the deputy director of customs. In 1982, Atiku was bestowed with the traditional title, Turakin Adamawa.

Atiku first gained national attention in 1991 when he ran for the governorship of Adamawa State (q.v.). But the results of the gubernatorial primaries were overturned on charges of corruption in November 1991 and Atiku (along with his opponent, Bala Takaya) was temporarily banned from further participation in politics. In 1993, Atiku emerged as a candidate to be M.K.O. Abiola's running mate in the June 12, 1993, presidential election (q.v.). He enjoyed the strong support of Yar'Adua, the most powerful figure in the Social Democratic Party. Nevertheless, Abiola eventually picked Babagana Kingibe as his running mate, a decision that contributed to strained relations between Abiola and some leaders of the party. Alhaji Atiku remained active in politics under the Abacha regime, and was a leading gubernatorial candidate in Adamawa State at the time of Abacha's death.

Yar'Adua's death in prison in December 1997 allowed Atiku to assume control of the formidable political machine Yar'Adua had created. He established himself as powerbroker in the People's Democratic Party, which emerged as the dominant political party in Abdulsalami Abubakar's democratic transition. He was elected governor of Adamawa State on January 9, 1999, but later stepped down to serve as vice president under the newly elected presidency of Olusegun Obasanjo. There was a symmetry to Obasanjo's choice of Alhaji Atiku, for his political mentor, Yar'Adua had been second in command in Obasanjo's military regime (1976–79).

ATTAHIRU, AHMADU. Ruler of the Sokoto (q.v.) Caliphate (q.v.) at the time of the British conquest of the area. Attahiru had succeeded Abdurrahman, who died in 1902, shortly after Lord Frederick Lugard (q.v.) had begun the British conquest of Northern Nigeria (q.v.). Because of dissension in the Sokoto army, Attahiru's forces could not put up a strong defense against Lugard, and Attahiru was forced to flee to Burmi in 1903. Lugard entered the capital and persuaded the people to elect a new ruler, Muhamadu Attahiru II (q.v.), son of Aliu Babba, who then became a new sultan (q.v.) of Sokoto on March 21, 1903. In Burmi, Attahiru (who had been joined by some deposed chiefs, including the ex-Emir of Bida and the magaji of Keffi, under whom Captain Maloney, British resident in Keffi, died) was able to persuade many of his subjects to accompany him on a hijra, or a journey into political exile. British forces pursued him and, after Attahiru's men had put up a gallant show against British forces, his army was finally defeated, and Attahiru was killed in July 1903.

ATTAHIRU II, MUHAMMADU. The first Sultan of Sokoto (q.v.) to serve under the British system of indirect rule. His predecessor, Caliph Attahiru I refused to collaborate with the colonialists, and was killed by British forces in 1903 while embarking on a hijra, or journey into political exile. Muhammadu Attahiru II held office from 1903–15. Perhaps the most controversial aspect of his period in office was his role in the suppression of an anti-colonial revolt in the town of Satiru in 1906. The town was eventually razed, with a large number of deaths.

AVIATION. Nigeria's first experience with approaching airplanes was in 1925 when some British Royal Air Force pilots landed at the racecourse in Kano (q.v.). Before Nigeria Airways was incorporated in 1959, some foreign carriers operated together with the West African Airways Corporation (WAAC) (q.v.) as a regional carrier in the West African subregion. When Ghana became independent in 1957, it withdrew its membership from WAAC and established its own national carrier, Ghana Airways. Other shareholders, like Sierra Leone and the Gambia, also withdrew their membership and the assets of the defunct airline were shared among the shareholders. In 1958 the WAAC Nigeria Limited was incorporated, but, in May 1959, the name was changed to Nigeria Airways. At the time the airline was operating only a few lines, while it maintained a joint flight operation with the British Overseas Airways Corporation on its Lagos-to-London route.

As a result of the oil boom of the 1970s, Nigeria Airways enjoyed some relative expansion. The number of aircraft increased to about 27, but as a consequence of the economic downturn and mismanagement of the 1980s, the number of serviceable aircraft greatly decreased to only about seven planes in 1990. The Nigeria Airports Authority (NAA) (q.v.) was established in 1976 to take care of the increasing passenger traffic and to coordinate the activities and facilities of the then-existing 13 airports in the nation. The Murtala Muhammed International Airport was completed in 1979, and, between then and 1981, several other airports were built in many state capitals, more so for political reasons than economic. At present, from about 20 commercial airports in the country, only three are viable—Lagos, Kano and Port Harcourt—as national and international airports. The NAA is a partially commercialised government parastatal.

AWOKOYA, PROF. STEPHEN OLUWOLE. An educationist and a great supporter of adult education, born on July 9, 1913, in Awa, Ijebu-Ode in Ogun State (q.v.), he was educated at St. Andrew's College, Oyo, Yaba Higher College (q.v.) in Lagos (q.v.) and the University of London in England. He was former principal of Molusi College in Ijebu Igbo before getting into politics. Between 1952 and 1956, he was minister of education in Western Nigeria, and it was during his term of office that Western Nigeria launched its free primary education scheme, for all primary school children in the region. In 1958 he became the principal of the Federal Emergency Science School in Lagos, and in 1961 he was permanent secretary and chief federal adviser on education in Lagos. In 1967 he became director of the Department of Application of Science to Development of UNESCO, and in 1968 he was director of the Department of Scientific and Technological Research and Higher Education of UNESCO. In 1973 he was appointed a research professor of education at the University of Ife. He was a member of the Action Group (q.v.) from 1950 to 1956. He was honored with traditional and other titles: Aseto of Awa and Commander of the Order of the British Empire. In 1966 he published his book, *Science of Things Above Us*. He died in 1985.

AWOLOWO, CHIEF OBAFEMI. Born at Ikenne in Ijebu-Remo in Ogun State (q.v.) on March 6, 1909, he had his elementary education at Imo Western School, Abeokuta (q.v.), and also attended Wesley College, Ibadan. He began to work in various capacities from 1926 while taking correspondence courses in English, commercial knowledge, bookkeeping, business methods and shorthand. He wanted very much to be a journalist, a lawyer, a wealthy man and a politician. Accordingly, in 1934 he joined the staff of the *Daily Times* of Nigeria as a reporter-in-training. When he left the *Daily Times,* he became a freelance journalist while studying correspondence courses for a bachelor of commerce degree at the University of London, a degree which he successfully passed as an external student in 1944. The same year, he went to study law in London; he got his LL.B. degree in 1946 and was called to the bar at the Inner Temple in London on November 18, 1946.

During his short stay in London, he wrote *Path to Nigerian Freedom,* in which he said that every national group in Nigeria had an indigenous constitution that had been corrupted under colonial rule. He then advocated that the constitution of each cultural nationality should be its own domestic concern and every such nationality should be entitled and should be encouraged to develop its own political institutions within the framework of a Nigerian federation. He further maintained that it was the right of the educated minority of each cultural group to lead their fellow men into a higher political development. His belief then was that there should be political reforms at the local level, political unity at the cultural level and a federal constitution at the national level. This belief he restated in *The People's Republic* and *Thoughts on Nigerian Constitution.*

While in the United Kingdom, he founded the Egbe Omo Oduduwa (q.v.) (Society of the Descendants of Oduduwa), which had as its objective the unity and cultural development of the Yorubas (q.v.).

He returned to Nigeria in 1947 and became a practising lawyer and a politician. He was one of the leading nationalists and has had great impact on the constitutional development of Nigeria. In 1948, at a conference hosted by the then-Ooni of Ife, Sir Adesoji Aderemi (q.v.) in Ile-Ife (q.v.), the mythical cradle of the Yorubas, the Egbe Omo Oduduwa was inaugurated with Awolowo as its general secretary.

In 1949 he started the *Nigerian Tribune,* a daily newspaper, which later became the organ of his political party, the Action Group (q.v.), and the main organ of the Unity Party of Nigeria (q.v.). In March 1951, he publicly announced the forming of the Action Group (AG) Party, which had in reality been in secret existence for about a year. He was elected the party's president, the position which he held until 1966 when the military banned all political parties. In the same year Awolowo was elected into the then-Western

House of Assembly (q.v.). In 1952 he became leader of government business and minister of local government and finance. In 1954 he assumed office as the first premier of the Western Region (q.v.). In 1955 he introduced in the region free primary education (q.v.) for all school-age children. In 1959 he gave up his position as premier to run for the Federal Government election to the House of Representatives (q.v.) with the hope of becoming the first prime minister of independent Nigeria. He conducted a very well-organized and vigorous campaign but his party was unable to win a majority of the seats in parliament or to make other parties join in a coalition with him. He then became the leader of the opposition in the federal parliament. In 1962 a quarrel arose between him and his deputy leader Chief S.L. Akintola (q.v.) who became premier after Chief Awolowo had left for the capital. The quarrel grew into a serious crisis in the then-Western Region, which led to the declaration of an emergency in the region and his detention and that of many party members. He was later charged, along with about 26 other party members, with plotting to overthrow the Federal Government (q.v.). He was found guilty and sentenced to 10 years imprisonment. In August 1966 when Lt. Col. Yakubu Gowon (q.v.) became head of the federal military government, he was pardoned and set free from prison. In May 1967, he was appointed chancellor of the University of Ife (q.v.), and in the following month he was appointed federal commissioner for finance and the vice-chairman of the Federal Executive Council (q.v.). He held this post until the end of June 1971 when he resigned.

In September 1966, he led the Western Nigerian delegation to the Lagos Ad Hoc Constitutional Conference (q.v.) and served on the ad hoc committee charged with finding a workable constitution for Nigeria. Before this conference met, some Yoruba intelligentsia had chosen him as "Leader of the Yorubas." When the government of Eastern Nigeria, led by Lt. Colonel Odumegwu Ojukwu (q.v.), refused after the September 1966 massacre of the Igbo (q.v.) people in Northern Nigeria (q.v.) to continue participation in the conference and to attend regular meetings of the Supreme Military Council (q.v.). Chief Awolowo led a delegation of the National Reconciliation Committee (q.v.) to Enugu (q.v.) in May 1967 to persuade the government of Ojukwu to send representation to the National Reconciliation Committee.

After his resignation in 1971, he went into private practice. In 1975 General Murtala Muhammed (q.v.) appointed him one of the 50-member Constitution Drafting Committee (q.v.), but he declined to serve. When the ban on political activity was lifted in September 1978, he was the first to form his new political party, the Unity Party of Nigeria (UPN) (q.v.). As always, Chief Awolowo put up a hard but uncompromising campaign. His party captured the five states that made up the former Western Region, but he failed to win sufficient support in other states to make him the first civilian executive president of Nigeria. He also contested the 1983 presidential election, but he lost again.

Chief Awolowo was one of the few Nigerian politicians who were hard-working and intelligent. He was the most straightforward of all during his time. Even though much of his life's ambition had been realized (he was well educated, with professional standing as a lawyer and a politician, and very wealthy), one ambition he was not able to realize was that of leading Nigeria. He failed in 1959 to become the first prime minister of independent Nigeria, and, 20 years later, failed to become the first executive president of the Second Republic (q.v.). This is partly due to his straightforwardness, his uncompromising attitude in politics, and to a well-founded fear people had that he was vindictive and did not forgive, as shown in the Action Group crisis of 1962 (q.v.) and the many harsh references he made to the late Akintola, 15 to 17 years after the latter had been killed in the 1966 coup détat (q.v.).

In the pursuit of this last and overriding ambition of his, he was in the forefront of the Progressive Parties Alliance (q.v.), which hoped to wrench power from the National Party of Nigeria (q.v.) in 1983. The alliance, however, failed to get off the ground.

Chief Awolowo was showered with many traditional titles. He was Asiwaju of Ijebu-Remo, Losi of Ikenne, Apesin of Osogbo, Odole of Ife and Odofin of Owo. In 1982 he was awarded the highest national honour of Grand Commander of the Order of the Federal Republic of Nigeria. He had honorary degrees of LL.D. from the University of Nigeria, Nsukka (q.v.) and Ibadan, D. Litt. from the University of Lagos and D.Sc. from the University of Ife (q.v.). Among his many publications are: *Path to Nigerian Freedom* (1947), *Awo: An Autobiography* (1960), *Thoughts on Nigerian Constitution* (1968) and *The Strategy and Tactics of the People's Republic of Nigeria* (1970). He died in May 1987.

AZIKIWE, CHIEF (DR.) NNAMDI. First president of the Federal Republic of Nigeria (q.v.) and first indigenous governor-general of Nigeria. Born in Zungeru (q.v.) in Northern Nigeria (q.v.) on November 16, 1904, where his father was serving as a clerk in the Nigerian Regiment, he attended Mission Schools in Onitsha (q.v.), Lagos (q.v.) and Calabar (q.v.), and he later became a clerk in the treasury office in Lagos. He sailed for the United States in 1925, where he enrolled in Storer College, but he later transferred to Lincoln University and later still to Howard University in Washington, D.C. He lectured in political science at Lincoln University and later went to the University of Pennsylvania where he obtained a master of science degree. He returned to Nigeria in 1934 but he soon moved to Accra, Ghana (q.v.), where in 1935 he became the editor of the Accra *African Morning Post.* In 1938 he returned to Nigeria where he established the now defunct *West African Pilot,* a daily newspaper. He was a member of the Nigerian Youth Movement (NYM) (q.v.) but owing to the disagreement between him and other members of the movement as to who should fill the position left vacant in the Legislative Council (q.v.) by the resignation of Dr. K.A. Abayomi in 1941, he pulled out of the movement. In 1944 he, with Herbert Macaulay (q.v.), the leader of the Nigerian National Democratic Party (NNDP) (q.v.), founded the National Council of Nigeria and the Cameroons (NCNC) (q.v.), a party which came to be known for its nationalist agitations.

In June 1945, there was a general strike (q.v.) that many people believed was engineered by "Zik." On July 8, 1945, two of his daily papers—the *West African Pilot* and the *Daily Comet*—were banned by the government for allegedly misrepresenting facts that related to the strike. A few days later, Dr. Azikiwe wrote what he called his "last testament" and fled to Onitsha. In the testament he alleged that some unknown persons had planned to kill him. He then sent cablegrams to important personalities, news media and organisations in the United Kingdom, imploring them to prevail upon the government to give him police protection. The assassination plot increased his popularity among the rank and file, but he was criticized by the NYM members for propagating falsehood and inventing a story to make him a martyr and gain cheap popularity.

In 1947 Zik led his party's delegation of seven people, including Mrs. Funmilayo Ransome-Kuti (q.v.), to London to protest against the Richards Constitution (q.v.), but the Secretary of State for the colonies, Rt. Hon. Arthur Creech Jones (q.v.), told them to go back home and try to make the new constitution work. Dr. Azikiwe was also at the head of his party's delegation to all the constitutional conferences both in London in 1953, 1957, 1958 and in Nigeria in 1954.

Dr. Azikiwe was the premier of the Eastern Region (q.v.) from 1954 to 1959, but he resigned in December 1959 to take up the position of president of the Senate in January 1960. When Nigeria became independent in 1960, he became the first indigenous Nigerian governor-general of the Federation (q.v.), and in 1963, when the country became a republic, he was made the first president of the Federal Republic of Nigeria (q.v.), a position that was mainly ceremonial.

His term of office as president of the first republic was not without its crisis. After the 1964 election, which was riddled with irregularities in various parts of the country, President Azikiwe at first refused to appoint Sir Abubakar Tafawa Balewa (q.v.) as prime minister to form a new government. However, after a lot of discussions and compromise and the legal advice given to him that he had no constitutional power to order the army about, he performed his constitutional duty. On January 4, 1965, he stated that the constitution left him no alternative but to call on Alhaji Tafawa Balewa to form a new government.

In 1966 when the military seized power, Dr. Azikiwe was relieved of his post. Later, when the Civil War (q.v.) broke out, he supported the Biafran (q.v.) cause and used his great influence all over the world to seek diplomatic recognition and support for Biafra. However, when it became apparent that the federal side was winning the war, he began to look for a compromise solution with the Federal Government (q.v.) on ways to end the war. He later retired to his hometown, but when the ban on politics was lifted in 1978, he was persuaded to come back into politics by joining the Nigerian People's Party (NPP) (q.v.). He contested the position of the first executive president of the Federal Republic of Nigeria, but he lost to Alhaji Shehu Shagari (q.v.). As such, he remained the NPP leader. His party later on began to work together with three other parties, the Unity Party of Nigeria (UPN) (q.v.) led by Chief Obafemi Awolowo (q.v.) a faction of the People's Redemption Party (PRP) (q.v.) and a faction of the Great Nigerian People's Party (GNPP) (q.v.) in an effort to form the so-called Progressive Parties Alliance (PPA) (q.v.). But in the choice of who should be the PPA presidential candidate to beat the NPN in 1983, neither Azikiwe nor Awolowo could step aside for the other. The PPA, therefore, decided to field the two men as their presidential candidates, a fact which greatly weakened their support among the people, and led to the defeat of both candidates.

Dr. Azikiwe's contribution to Nigerian development is well recognised by the many honours bestowed on him. He is the Owelle of Onitsha, and was the Grand Commander of the Order of the Federal Republic of Nigeria in 1980. He has many honorary degrees of LL.D. and D. Litt. He also has written many books, including *Renascent Africa* (1939), *Political Blue Print of Nigeria* (1943), *Zik: A Selection of Speeches* (1961) and *My Odyssey* (1970).

Though a Nigerian nationalist, Azikiwe was always conscious of the fact that he was an Igbo. In 1948, in his address as the president of the Ibo State Union (q.v.), he said that it would appear that the God of Africa had created the Igbo nation to lead the children of Africa from the bondage of the ages and the Igbo nation could not shirk its responsibility from its manifest destiny. In 1978 he attributed his tax problem with the Federal Electoral Commission (q.v.) to the fact that he was an Igbo. He died in May 1996.

-B-

BABALOLA, APOSTLE JOSEPH AYO. Born in 1904 at Ilofa, Kwara State (q.v.), he, after his primary education, joined the public works department where he worked as a Caterpillar operator. He left there in 1930 to begin his missionary activities in Oke-Oye in Ilesha. He founded the Christ Apostolic Church (CAC) in 1930, but he later moved to Efon Alaye, which he made the base of his missionary activities. Believing him to be an instrument of healing the sick, people flocked to him for healing. He travelled all over Nigeria and to Ghana, preaching the word of God and healing the sick. In 1955 he founded the CAC Teacher Training College at Efon Alaye, the second-oldest teacher-training college in Ondo State (q.v.), to train teachers who would teach in his mission schools. He died in 1959 in Ede, Osun State (q.v.), but was buried in Efon Alaye according to his wishes. The CAC was one of the first indigenous churches in Nigeria and was a demonstration of revolt against Christian churches dominated by white value systems.

BABANGIDA, GENERAL IBRAHIM BADAMASI. First military president of Nigeria, Babangida was born on August 17, 1941, in Minna, the capital of Niger State (q.v.). He received his elementary education in Minna and proceeded to the Government College in Bida where he successfully obtained his high school diploma in 1962. In 1963 he enrolled in the Nigerian Military Training College, and, later in the same year, he was sent to the Indian Military Academy in India. Between 1966 and 1967 he was at the Royal Armoured Centre in the United Kingdom, and in 1972 he attended the Army Armored School in the United States. Between 1979 and 1980 he took courses in senior executive management at the National Institute of Policy and Strategic Studies in Kuru, Nigeria.

General Babangida has held many important military posts. He was troop commander of the Nigerian Army from 1964 to 1966, and, during the 1967–70 Nigerian Civil War (q.v.), he commanded the 44th Infantry Battalion called "The Rangers." Between 1970 and 1972, he was company commander and instructor at the Nigerian Defence Academy (q.v.). In 1973 he was regiment commander, and in 1975 he became commander of the Armoured Corps.

Babangida first came to public limelight when he was said to have singlehandedly disarmed the mutinous Lt. Col. B. Suka Dimka (q.v.), who had taken control of Radio Nigeria in the abortive coup that attempted to topple the government of the late General Murtala R. Muhammed (q.v.) on February 13, 1976.

In 1981 he was director of army staff duties and plans; in 1984 he became chief of the army staff, a position he held until August 27, 1985, when he became the president and Commander-in-chief of the armed forces (q.v.) after the coup he organized had successfully ousted Major General Muhammadu Buhari (q.v.) from office.

Due to his unpredictability during his presidency, Babangida was nicknamed Maradona after the Argentine soccer player, Diego Maradona. The nickname portrayed him as a person who was ready to use any means to achieve his objective. His administration affected the lives of every Nigerian as no previous administration had ever done. During his eight years in office, the economy virtually collapsed. The structural adjustment programme (SAP) (q.v.), which he initiated in 1986, was badly implemented and, rather than reviving the economy, worsened the lives of most people. The national currency, the naira, which was at par with the U.S. dollar, depreciated fast. In 1993 before he left office, it was worth about four cents. He brought the Central Bank of Nigeria (CBN) (q.v.) under the presidency, but his administration lacked financial accountability. For example, the $12.4 billion surplus earned during the Gulf War of 1990–91 could not be accounted for.

Socially, the Babangida administration divided the country more than any other before it. Nigerians became much more conscious of their ethnicity, and during the political crisis of 1993, many people, as a result of government propaganda, left their residences in fear of civil war.

Babangida's administration set Nigeria back politically many years. It had the notoriety of being the first in Nigeria to annul results of a presidential election that clearly showed that Nigerians wanted a change from military government to civilian government, from ethnic politics to pan-Nigerian politics, bridging the north-south divide and confounding the religious fanatics. National and international observers declared the presidential elections fair, free and the most peaceful in many years.

Babangida under pressure quit office on August 26, 1993, just a day short of his eighth anniversary in office. Among Babangida's published books are *Civil and Military Relationship: The Nigerian Experience* (1979) and *Defence Policy within the Framework of National Planning* (1985).

During the Abacha regime (1993–98) Babangida kept a very low profile. When General Abdulsalami Abubakar became the military leader of the country in 1998, however, Babangida became more politically active. Abubakar, like Babangida, is from the Gwari ethnic group and many suspected him of secretly advising the new president. Babangida was also suspected of using his connections and wealth to support a number of candidates in the 1998–99 elections, including the eventual winner of the presidential polls, General Olusegun Obasanjo (q.v.). But despite this growing influence, Babangida remained very unpopular with the public, and he was frequently referred to in the press as the "evil genius of Nigerian politics."

BABARI, SARKIN GOBIR. Ruler of Gobir (q.v.) from 1742 to 1770 when there was serious rivalry among the Hausa States (q.v.). When Babari ascended the throne, his first interest was to make his own state stable, and then later he began military campaigns against Katsina (q.v.), Kano (q.v.)

and Borgu. Being himself under pressure from the people along his northern borders, he began to look for expansion to the fertile lands of Zamfara on his southern borders. At first, his men began to move peacefully into Zamfara, and he himself gave his sister in marriage to the king of Zamfara. An agreement was reached that allowed his people to settle. However, in 1764, when they had sufficiently grown in number and strength, he led an army of Gobir citizens who lived in Zamfara against the state of Zamfara. He overran the capital of Zamfara, Birnin Zamfara, and later built a new capital, Alkalawa, within the territory.

BADAGRY. An ancient Yoruba (q.v.) town west of the city of Lagos (q.v.) and very close to the border between Nigeria and the Republic of Benin (q.v.), formerly Dahomey (q.v.). Badagry was a major slave-trading outpost in precolonial times and is famous today as the town in Nigeria where Christianity was first preached in 1842. On September 24, 1842, Rev. Thomas Birch Freeman (q.v.) arrived in Badagry as a representative of the Wesleyan Mission (q.v.), and by November a mission house and a bamboo chapel had been built.

BAFYAU, PASCHAL MYELERI. A trade unionist, born in 1947 at Larmude, Numan, in Adamawa State (q.v.), Bafyau was educated at St. Patrick's Primary School and Villanova Secondary School, both in Numan, and the School of Agriculture in Kabba in 1966. He began his career as a labor leader when he became a member of the Railway Permanent Way Training School in Zaria (q.v.) from 1967 to 1969. He then went to the International Center for Advance Technical and Vocational Training in Turin, Italy, and later to the National Institute for Policy and Strategic Studies in Kuru, near Jos (q.v.) in Nigeria. He rose up in the labor organisation at the Nigerian Railways, becoming national vice president of the Railway Permanent Way Workers Union in 1974 and general secretary of the Nigerian Union of Railwaymen in 1978. In 1988 he became vice president of the Nigerian Labour Congress (NLC) (q.v.) and in 1989 its president.

As NLC president, though a friend of many top men in government including President Ibrahim B. Babangida (q.v.), Bafyau preferred the middle road between labour and government. For this reason many people saw him as too close to the military government. What greatly impaired labour's credibility during his tenure was labour's apparent indecision during and after the June 12, 1993, presidential election (q.v.) crisis when Babangida annulled the results of the election. And even when General Sani Abacha (q.v.) in November took over power and raised the price of motor vehicle fuel from N0.70 to N7.50, labour's reaction was mild. When Chief M.K.O. Abiola (q.v.), the undeclared winner of the June 12, 1993, election declared himself president in June 1994 and was arrested, labour's attitude was lukewarm—so much so that affiliate industrial union members of NLC bypassed the NLC in their support of Abiola's actualising his mandate. While Bafyau was still negotiating with government for Abiola's release from detention, he lost his job after the government dissolved the NLC's executive committee.

BAGAUDA. Was the first recorded King of Kano. He was the son of Bawogari and the grandson of Bayajidda. He came to Kano (q.v.) in about 999 A.D. At the time the area that became the kingdom of Kano was under the control of a number of different chiefs. Bagauda forced these leaders to recognize his sovereignty, unifying political authority in the area. His descendants later reigned as the Kings (sarakuna) of Kano, and his grandson Gijimasu later established a settlement at the foot of Dala hill that helped establish the city of Kano.

BAIKIE, DR. WILLIAM BALFOUR. Born in Scotland, in 1825, he was a naval surgeon and naturalist who was asked in 1854 to command the *Pleiad,* a ship built by Macgregor Laird (q.v.) to go up the Niger River (q.v.), and open up trade with the people in the interior. The expedition was very successful, and no lives were lost. Baikie explored the Benue River (q.v.), almost getting up to Yola (q.v.), and opened up trade with people of the area. In 1857 he was also asked to command the *Dayspring,* a steamer which again sailed up the Niger River. Among the people on board was Samuel Ajayi Crowther (q.v.), who later became the bishop of the Niger. The *Dayspring* was wrecked near Jebba, but the crew members began to make contacts with the local people. Baikie installed himself at Lokoja (q.v.), which he hoped could become a permanent commercial site and a center of trade. Baikie travelled to many parts of Nigeria, including Bida, Zaria (q.v.) and Kano. He died in 1864.

BAKASSI. An oil-rich peninsula on the Nigerian border with the Republic of Cameroon (q.v.), claimed by Nigeria as part of its territory but also counterclaimed by Cameroon. The history of Bakassi goes back to the late nineteenth century when colonial agreements between Britain and Germany set the colonies' border at the Rio del Rey, which put Bakassi in British-administered Nigeria. But in 1913 another agreement shifted the maritime boundary with the Cameroon westward to Akpa Yafe River, a tributary of the Cross River in Nigeria, thus placing Bakassi in the Cameroon Republic. In December 1993, Cameroon, to press home its claim, invaded parts of Bakassi. As diplomatic efforts to resolve the crisis were conducted, France sent in troops, planes and helicopters to support Cameroon's claims. The dispute was later taken to the International Court of Justice. In 1995, the International Court of Justice ruled in favour of Nigeria.

BALEWA, SIR ALHAJI ABUBAKAR TAFAWA. The first prime minister of Nigeria, born in 1912 at Tafawa Balewa Town in Bauchi State (q.v.) in northeast Nigeria. He attended the Bauchi Provincial School for his elementary education and in 1928 went to the Katsina Higher College where he received a teacher's certificate in 1933. He then went to Bauchi Middle School to teach. In 1945 he was awarded a scholarship to study at the Institute of Education of London University in Britain. Upon his return, he was appointed an education officer in charge of Bauchi Province.

Soon after, he became involved in the politics of Northern Nigeria (q.v.). He was one of the foundation members of the Bauchi General Improvement Union (q.v.) in 1943. When the Richards Constitution (q.v.) came into effect in 1947, he became a member of the Northern House of Assembly (q.v.) from which he was elected to the Legislative Council (q.v.) in Lagos (q.v.). In 1949, following the pattern of cultural organisation going on in the south, he, along with Mallam Aminu Kano (q.v.) and some other leaders of the defunct Bauchi Improvement Union, joined together to form the Jami' yyar Mutanen Arewa (q.v.), a Northern People's Congress (q.v.). However, because of the conservative attitude of the organisation and its deference to the traditional political system, some members, led by Mallam Aminu Kano (q.v.) broke away to form the Northern Element Progressive Union (q.v.). In 1951 Alhaji Tafawa Balewa joined Alhaji Sir Ahmadu Bello (q.v.), the Sardauna of Sokoto (q.v.), in the reorganization of the Northern People's Congress (NPC) into a political party with Sir Ahmadu Bello as the leader and Amaji Tafawa Balewa as the deputy leader. After the implementation of the Macpherson Constitution (q.v.) of 1951, Alhaji Tafawa Balewa became minister of works in the central government. In 1954, when the country became a federation, he was appointed federal minister of transport. Following further constitutional developments, on September 2, 1957, being the parliamentary leader of the NPC, which had more representatives than any other party in the federal House of Representatives (q.v.), he was appointed the first prime minister of Nigeria. He went on to form a national government, consisting of all the major parties—six ministers from the National Council of Nigeria and the Cameroons (NCNC) (q.v.), four from the NPC, two from the Action Group (AG) (q.v.) and one from the Kamerun National Congress (q.v.). His belief was that all the major parties needed to cooperate on matters of planning and policy if Nigeria was to achieve independence at the appointed time. After the 1959 elections, the NPC still won a plurality of seats in the federal House of Representatives. Forming a coalition with the NCNC, Sir Tafawa Balewa was again appointed the prime minister, and on October 1, 1960, he became the first prime minister of independent Nigeria.

After independence, the Balewa administration was plagued by many crises. He worked as hard as he could for Nigerian unity, but that unity eluded him. In May 1962, there was the AG crisis (q.v.) in which the federal coalition government apparently took sides with Chief Samuel L. Akintola's faction in an effort to weaken the AG led by Chief Obafemi Awolowo (q.v.). There was also the census crisis of 1963, which made for the final disintegration of the coalition between the NPC and the NCNC at the center. Following this, in rapid succession was the election crisis of 1964, which led to open conflict between Balewa and the president, Dr. Nnamdi Azikiwe (q.v.), a former member of the NCNC.

The straw that broke the camel's back was the Western Region's (q.v.) election of October 1965, which was followed by a complete breakdown of law and order in the region. Many supporters of the jailed AG leader, Chief Awolowo, had thought that under the new leadership of Alhaji D.S. Adegbenro (q.v.), they would deal a deathblow to the Akintola government, but the elections were rigged more than ever before and Chief Akintola was back in power. Three months of rioting, arson and killing followed, until January 15 when the army decided to intervene. Some dissidents in the army, led by Chukwuma Nzeogwu (q.v.), staged a coup in which Sir Abubakar Tafawa Balewa was killed.

Balewa received many honours from the British government. He was made Officer of the Order of the British Empire in 1952, Commander of the Order of the British Empire in 1955, Knight Commander of the Order of the British Empire in 1960, and in 1961 he was appointed a Privy Councillor.

BALLOT, OPEN SECRET. The system of election used for the 1993 presidential election. Before this time, Nigeria had tried the secret ballot system and the open ballot system (q.v.). The secret ballot system was used during the first (1959–65) and the second republics (1979–83). The system was open to many corruptive practices. People could buy ballot papers from voters and, after collecting them, go to the booth to dump them in the box. Unauthorised ballot papers were secretly printed and used, and ballot boxes changed hands in transit, all leading to an inaccurate declaration.

Under President Ibrahim B. Babangida (q.v.), the country also tried the open ballot system (q.v.) and found the abuses that came with it worse than those that the country had witnessed using the secret ballot system. To avoid all this, people began to agitate for an open secret ballot, which was successfully in use by many associations and organisations in the country. Accordingly, the government introduced for the 1993 presidential primaries and elections the open secret ballot along with Option A4 (q.v.).

According to the open secret ballot system, a voter, after collecting his ballot, secretly marks the ballot for the candidate he wants to vote for and then drops his ballot in the ballot box, which is in an open place. After the voting hours, which last for a short time, end, counting is done in the open and necessary forms are completed and signed in the presence of all voters. Representatives of the candidates are each to keep a copy of the signed document, and the presiding officer takes the ballot—sealed in envelopes with the results declared and signed—to the local government collation center. From the federal centre each party relays its results to its state headquarters and then finally to its national headquarters. This was how Chief M.K.O. Abiola (q.v.), the undeclared winner of the presidential election of June 12, 1993 (q.v.), knew that he had a comfortable win in Abuja (q.v.) and 19 out of the 30 states and had more than one-third of the votes cast in nine out of the remaining 11 states.

BALLOT SYSTEM, OPEN. The open ballot system is the act of voting in the public, either by acclamation or by the voter filing past the presiding officers and stating their choice. All voters were expected to appear at a particular time. After accreditation, voters lined up behind the candidate's photograph and an electoral officer counted the voters for each candidate. In places where the elections were contested, voters could also show their preferences for particular candidates or issues by a show of hands.

Open ballot system was first used in the Western Region's (q.v.) election of 1951 when voting in the primaries was made open. The method was abandoned when it was seen to be undemocratic and giving room for wealthy members of the community to buy votes. Notwithstanding this lesson, the National Electoral Commission (NEC) (q.v.) in 1990 decided that open ballot system should be used for the local government election in December, and it continued to be used for all elections until 1993 when its evils could no longer be concealed by the government or the NEC.

In most places the counting was rigged, for one could hear "1, 2, 8, 12, 20, 30, 50," and so on. And worse still, the recording was also rigged, as long as the representative of the other party was sufficiently paid off, he signed anything put before him. During all the malpractice, the police officer in charge would conveniently turn a blind eye. Added to this were intimidation and harassment by landlords and powerful community leaders. The system was later changed into the open secret ballot (q.v.) for the 1993 presidential election.

BALOGUN, CHIEF (DR.) KOLAWOLE. A lawyer and politician, born on April 11, 1922, in Otan Aiyegbaju in Oyo State (q.v.), he attended Government College in Ibadan (q.v.) and the University of London from which he graduated with an LL.B. degree. He was called to the bar at Lincoln's Inn in London. While in London, he was the secretary of the London branch of the National Council of Nigeria and the Cameroons (NCNC) (q.v.) party. He became a chief in 1956, having been installed Ajaguna of Otan Aiyegbaju. He also has chieftaincy titles from Osogbo and Akure.

In 1953 he was a member of the Western House of Assembly (q.v.) as an NCNC member. Under the 1954 constitution, he was then sent to the federal House of Representatives (q.v.) in Lagos (q.v.) and became the federal minister of research and information from 1956 to 1958. In 1958 he and some others joined Dr. K.O. Mbadiwe in a petition to get Dr. Nnamdi Azikiwe (q.v.), the NCNC party leader, to resign, accusing him of splitting the party asunder and of losing interest in it. The national executive of the party expelled the leaders of the group, including Balogun. He and Dr. Mbadiwe later resigned from the Federal Government (q.v.).

In 1959 he was Nigerian high commissioner to Ghana (q.v.) and in 1962 he became the chairman of the Nigerian National Shipping Lines. In 1967 he was appointed commissioner for economic planning and social development and commissioner for education in 1968.

Chief Balogun was also a journalist and an author. He was assistant editor of the *West African Pilot* from 1946 to 1947, and editor of the *Spokesman* in Ibadan in 1948. He has authored numerous books including *My Country Nigeria* and *The Growing Elephant.* Balogun founded the magazine called the *Social Reformer* in 1966. In 1971 he became chairman, Sketch Group of Newspapers.

He was also a lecturer at the faculty of administration at the University of Ife (q.v.), and, when the ban on political activities was lifted in 1978, he left the institution to go back into politics. He was a foundation member of the Nigeria People's Party (NPP) (q.v.), and when the party broke into two factions, he left the NPP in the company of Alhaji Waziri Ibrahim (q.v.) to form the Great Nigeria People's Party (GNPP) (q.v.) where he was chosen as the national vice chairman. He was expelled from GNPP together with some few others on the grounds of antiparty activities. He later joined the National Party of Nigeria (NPN) (q.v.).

BANANAS. Bananas are one of the most important economic fruits in Nigeria. There are many varieties, each with its own color, shape and flavour. The bigger species is called plantain, which contains much starch when it is still green, and much sugar—almost as much as the smaller ones—when it is ripe.

Banana trees grow from about 3 metres to 9 metres high and are grown by planting their suckers which shoot up from below the soil as a replacement for the older ones. The fruits are carried in clusters called hands. They grow best where the temperature is between 23°C and 26°C and where the annual rainfall is about 1,800 millimetres. Although grown predominately in this weather, they are a staple food eaten raw and cooked throughout the country.

BANJO COMMISSION. Appointed in 1960 to review the educational system of Western Region (q.v.), with regard to the structure and working of the primary and secondary grammar schools, the adequacy or inadequacy of the teacher training programme and the interrelationship between primary and secondary education.

The commission gained the impression that the standard of education (q.v.) was falling in the region because of the rapid expansion of primary education without corresponding increase in facilities for teacher training. It recommended among other things more trained and better-qualified teachers, strengthening of the local education authorities to perform their duties more efficiently and enlarging the Inspectorate of Education to match the increased number of schools.

BANK-ANTHONY, SIR MOBOLAJI. An industrialist and philanthropist, born June 11, 1907, in Kinshasa, Congo, Bank-Anthony was educated in Lagos (q.v.) at St. Peters School, Methodist Boys' High School, Ijebu-Ode Grammar School and Baptist Academy. After his education he became a clerk at the Department of Post and Telegraph from 1924 to 1932. From this time on, his interest in trade grew, and he began to set up business organisations. By 1987, when he was celebrating his 80th anniversary, he had over 15 large companies. In addition to many philanthropic activities, Bank-Anthony donated a 180-bed accident ward to the Orthopaedic Hospital in Lagos. At the same time he was building a six-million naira, 130-bed obstetrics and gynaecology conveniences at the Ikeja General Hospital in memory of his late mother. Along with national and international honours, he was the recipient of many honorary degrees.

BANK OF BRITISH WEST AFRICA. Formerly known as the African Banking Corporation (q.v.), it was established in 1872 but reorganized as a limited liability company under the new name of Bank of British West Africa in May 1894. The bank was the first expatriate commercial banking institution in Nigeria. *See also* AFRICAN BANKING CORPORATION.

BANKING. In 1959 when the Central Bank of Nigeria (CBN) (q.v.) began operation, there were only 12 commercial banks operating through nearly 90 branches all over the country. At the time, there was only one merchant bank and few nonbank financial institutions. Between then and 1970, the number of commercial banks rose to 14 with over 273 branches and a total asset of N576 million. At the beginning of the 1990s, there were 47 commercial banks with an asset of about N65 billion, all having branches in over 1,800 places. There were also 34 merchant banks with a total asset of N22 billion operating with 56 branches. In addition, there were specialised banks such as the Nigerian Bank for Commerce and Industry (q.v.), the Federal Mortgage Bank, the Nigerian Industrial Development Bank and the Nigerian Agricultural and Development Bank (q.v.). In 1989 the government also set up the People's Bank of Nigeria (q.v.) to grant credit facilities without the usual collaterals to the underprivileged people in the society. The People's Bank was expected to be set up in every local government area of the country. Two years later, in 1991, the federal military government in an effort to further strengthen the People's Bank idea and to encourage small-scale businesses and artisans who would have difficulty in obtaining credit from conventional banks, established the Community Bank (q.v.), which was to be really owned and run by the people in their various communities. The idea quickly caught on, and, by the end of 1992, there were more than 400 such community banks spread across the country.

The rapid growth in the number of banks and the disproportionate growth in the quality of personnel to staff them led to mismanagement and inefficiency, leading to the collapse or near collapse of many banks. By 1995, 34 banks became distressed (insolvent or illiquid), leaving the number of operating banks to 116 licensed commercial and merchant banks. In addition to these, there were 279 mortgage banks, 183 bureaux de change, 970 community banks and 275 people's banks.

BAPTIST CHURCH. The American Baptist Church sent its first missionary to Nigeria, Reverend Thomas J. Bowen (q.v.), who arrived in Badagry in August 1850 with the objective of setting up missions in the interior of the country. The church established mission houses and schools in Ijaye, Ogbomoso, Oyo, Shaki, Igboho and in many other places. In the history of education (q.v.) in Nigeria, the Baptist church is one of the most prominent. The church also established hospitals to provide health care for people in many towns.

BAREWA COLLEGE. The school that has educated four Nigerian Heads of State (Alhaji Tafawa Balewa [q.v.], General Yakubu Gowon [q.v.], General Murtala Mohammed [q.v.] and Alhaji Shehu Shagari [q.v.]) was founded in 1922. It is the oldest secondary school in all of the northern part of Nigeria, and the school that many northern elites like Mallam Aminu Kano (q.v.), Sir Ahmadu Bello (q.v.), the Sardauna of Sokoto (q.v.), Alhaji Waziri Ibrahim (q.v.) and Alhaji Umaru Dikko (q.v.) have attended. Its motto was "Man jada-wa-jada," i.e., "He who tries, would succeed."

The school was originally founded in Katsina (q.v.) and called Katsina College. It later became Katsina Higher College, and Katsina Training

College. Before the Second World War, the school was moved to Kaduna (q.v.), the regional capital, and called Kaduna College. After the war, in 1949 it was moved to Zaria (q.v.) and became Zaria College, and later Zaria Secondary School. In 1970 it adopted its present name, Barewa College.

BARTH, HEINRICH. A German sent with two others to report on the general conditions of the countries in central Africa. Barth travelled hundreds of kilometres in the former northern part of Nigeria. In 1852 he reported that he had crossed the Benue River (q.v.) and speculated that it was the same river that flowed to the Niger River (q.v.) at Lokoja (q.v.). An expedition was financed by the British government to ascertain this fact. The expedition went as far as Yola with no loss of life, for the use of quinine (q.v.) against malaria fever (q.v.) had been found to be very effective.

BASORUN. The title of the leader of the traditional council of the Notables of Oyo Kingdom (q.v.), known as Oyomesi. The council was made up of seven prominent lineage chiefs of the capital city and had the power to act as a check upon the Alaafin's (king) (q.v.) power in several ways. The Basorun dominated the Oyomesi and ultimately kept the Alaafin in check. During certain periods of Oyo history, the Basorun became more powerful than the Alaafin. *See* HAHA.

BAUCHI GENERAL IMPROVEMENT UNION. Formed in 1943 by three young northerners then living in Bauchi: Mallam Saad Zungur (q.v.), the first northern Nigerian to attend Yaba Higher College (q.v.) where he came in contact with nationalist activities in the south; Mallam Aminu Kano (q.v.), a Fulani (q.v.) schoolteacher who later became the leader of the Northern Element Progressive Union (q.v.) and Alhaji Abubakar Tafawa Balewa (q.v.), also a teacher, who later became the first prime minister of Nigeria. The Emir (q.v.) of Bauchi, realising its political importance, became hostile to the union, and it soon became defunct. The union is important, however, for it started such pressure group activities in the north, which had long been protected by the British against nationalist activities in the south.

BAUCHI STATE. Created by the administration of General Murtala R. Muhammed (q.v.) in 1976 when the Northeastern State (q.v.) was split into three different states: Bauchi, Borno and Gongola. Bauchi State has remained intact since then. With an area of 64,605 square kilometres, it is located within latitudes 9° 30′ and 12° 25′ N, and longitudes 8° 45′ and 11° 50′ E. The state, about 600 metres above sea level, is surrounded by Borno State (q.v.) and Adamawa State (q.v.) to the east, Gongola State (q.v.) and Plateau State (q.v.) to the south, and Kaduna State (q.v.) and Kano State (q.v.) to the west and northwest. The major towns in Bauchi State are Bauchi, the state capital, with a population of 341,758 in 1991, Gombe, Talanga and some smaller towns, which are among the 23 local government headquarters—Azare, Misau, Jama'are, Tafawa Balewa, Toro and others.

There are two main seasons, the rainy season and the dry season. The rainy season is between May and September. The temperature ranges from 29.2°C in July and August to 37.6°C in March and April. Relative humidity ranges from 12 percent in February to 68 percent in August.

With a population of 4,294,413 in 1991, the state is made up of many ethnic groups. The major ones are the Gerawa, Ningawa, Hausa (q.v.), Fulani (q.v.) and Tangale, and about 60 smaller groups, including the Tula, Sawaya, Badawa, Barke, Bara and Bomboro. About 80 percent of the people are farmers who plant maize, rice, cassava (q.v.), groundnut (q.v.), and cotton in small peasant farms, even though large farms are springing up. In 1988–89, 28,000 metric tons of maize, 5,000 metric tons of rice and 5,000 metric tons of cassava were produced. Some people also engage in livestock farming of cattle, goat, sheep, donkey, pig and poultry. Bauchi is said to have more cattle than any other state in the Federation. The state is also blessed with clay, limestone, glass, sand, gems, tin (q.v.), columbite and galena.

Educationally, in 1986 there were about 1,800 primary schools and 58 secondary schools. It has many colleges of education and technical colleges, and has Abubakar Tafawa Balewa University in Bauchi, founded and named by the federal government (q.v.) in honor of Nigeria's first prime minister, Sir Abubakar Tafawa Balewa (q.v.) who was a native of the state. Culturally, as a result of the various peoples that make up the state, Bauchi has a variety of cultural values, practices and festivals—all nicely blended with the Muslim sallah festivals. There are also many places of interest for tourists like the famous Yankari National Park, about 207,000 hectares of open woodland where a large variety of wildlife reside. The Lame-Burra Reserve contains some types of animals not found in the Yankari National Park.

BAWO. *See* BAYAJIDDA and HAUSA STATES.

BAYAJIDDA. The legendary ancestor of the founders of the Hausa kingdoms (q.v.). According to legend, Prince Bayajidda came to town of Daura. Upon his arrival, he killed a snake that was preventing the people from drawing water from a well. Out of gratitude for this act, the Queen of Daura agreed to marry him. Their union produced a son, Bawogari (Bawo for short). Bawo, together with his six sons, founded the original seven Hausa states, or "Hausa bakwai." These are most commonly identified as Daura, Kano, Zaria, Gobir, Katsina (qq.v.), Biram and Rano. In addition, Bayajidda had a son by a concubine whose descendants became the founders of the "banza bakwai," or "seven bastards." These are usually identified as Kebbi, Zamfara, Gwari, Jukun, Yoruba, Nupe and Yawuri.

BAYELSA STATE. Was created out of Rivers State (q.v.) by the Abacha regime on October 1, 1996. Its capital is Yenegoa, and the primary ethnic group are the Ijaw (q.v.). It is the state of origin for much of the oil that is produced in Nigeria, and in recent years the indigenous communities of Bayelsa State have been embroiled in a bitter and violent conflict with the oil companies and the government over the distribution of oil revenues. This dispute forced the postponement of gubernatorial elections in January 1999.

BAYERO, ABDULLAHI. Born in 1881, the son of Emir Muhammadu Abbas who ruled in Kano (q.v.) between 1903 and 1919. Before he was appointed Emir of Kano in 1926, he was the district head of Bichi. As Emir (q.v.), he carried out some reforms of the government of the emirate (q.v.), and saw to the development of the Kano Native Authority (q.v.). By the time of his death on December 23, 1953, the authority was spending well over £1 million annually. He visited Britain in 1934 and was received by King George V. He went to Mecca in 1937 and again in 1951. The Bayero University in Kano was named after him. He was succeeded by his son Muhammad Sanusi.

BAYERO, ALHAJI ADO. Traditional ruler, born on June 15, 1930, in Kano (q.v.), Kano State (q.v.), he was educated at Arabic Schools in Kano, Kofar Kudu Elementary School in Kano, Kano Middle School and at the School for Arabic Studies. After his education, he joined the Bank of West Africa Limited, now the Standard Bank of Nigeria in Kano. He resigned in 1955 to become a clerk in the Native Authority (NA) (q.v.) in Kano. He went to the Clerical Training College in Zaria (q.v.) and was later promoted to the post of clerk to the Kano City Council. He was in 1955 elected into the Northern House of Assembly (q.v.), but he relinquished this post in 1957 when he was appointed chief of the NA Police Force. In 1962 he was appointed Nigerian ambassador to Senegal, but he returned to Nigeria when he was made Emir (q.v.) of Kano in 1963. He was chancellor of the University of Nigeria, Nsukka (q.v.) in 1966 and chancellor of the University of Ibadan in 1975.

BEECROFT, JOHN. Born in Yorkshire, in 1790, he was appointed the British consul for the Bights of Benin and Biafra (q.v.) by Lord Palmerston in 1849, thus opening up the first diplomatic link between the British government and Nigeria. It was Beecroft who established the pattern of British intervention in Nigerian affairs. Before his appointment, he was a British resident on the island of Fernando Póo (q.v.), which, with Spanish consent, had come under British rule in 1827. Fernando Póo was then used as a base for the suppression of the slave trade and the establishment of "legitimate" trade with the people of Benin (q.v.), Calabar (q.v.), Bonny (q.v.) and the Cameroons (q.v.).

In 1851 the deposed king Akintoye (q.v.) of Lagos (q.v.) petitioned Beecroft to restore him to the throne, promising to abolish the slave trade, which was still being carried on under Kosoko (q.v.) in Lagos, and to begin to carry on lawful trade especially with the British merchants. Beecroft accepted the petition, visited Lagos the same year with a naval force and deposed king Kosoko and restored Akintoye to the throne. In 1852 he had a treaty signed by Akintoye who undertook to abolish the slave trade in his territory and afford protection to missionaries. In 1853 he presided over the exile of William Dappa Pepple (q.v.), king of Bonny. He later died at Fernando Póo in 1854.

BELLO, SIR AHMADU. A politician, born on June 12, 1910, in Rabah near Sokoto (q.v.), he was the grandson of Usman Dan Fodio (q.v.), the leader of the Fulani Islamic revolution in northern Nigeria during the nineteenth century and the founder of the Fulani empire (q.v.). He graduated from Katsina Higher College in 1931 and became a teacher in Sokoto at the Sokoto Middle School. In 1938 when the then-reigning sultan (q.v.) of Sokoto died, he vied for the position, which was the most powerful in the Northern Region (q.v.) at the time. But he lost to Abubakar who later appointed him the Sardauna of Sokoto (leader of war).

In 1948 he secured a scholarship to study local government in England. In 1949 he was chosen by the Sultan of Sokoto to represent Sokoto in the Northern House of Assembly (q.v.), which was established under the Richards Constitution (q.v.). In 1951 Sir Ahmadu Bello was instrumental in forming the Northern People's Congress (NPC) (q.v.), which the north later used to dominate not only the region of origin but the politics of the country up until 1966.

In 1954, when the country became a federation composed of three regions, Sir Ahmadu Bello became the premier of the Northern Region. Because he preferred to remain in the north rather than go to the capital in Lagos (q.v.), the position of leader of the government fell to his able lieutenant, Sir Abubakar Tafawa Balewa (q.v.) who was then the NPC vice president. After the federal election of 1959, the NPC went into a coalition with the National Council of Nigeria and the Cameroons (NCNC) (q.v.) and Balewa became the first prime minister of independent Nigeria. Bello remained in the north, preferring to direct the affairs of the country through his lieutenants. During the first few years of independence, the belief was widespread that Sir Ahmadu Bello was the actual and effective ruler of the country because the federal prime minister had to constantly consult with him on major policy issues. In 1962 during the Action Group Crisis (q.v.), Sir Ahmadu and his party supported Chief S.L. Akintola's (q.v.) faction against Chief Obafemi Awolowo's (q.v.) faction and later formed an alliance with Akintola's faction to fight for the 1964 elections. In the dawn coup of January 15, 1966, Bello was assassinated together with prime minister Alhaji Tafawa Balewa, Chief S.L. Akintola and some others. Sir Ahmadu Bello was knighted in 1959. The first university in the north, Ahmadu Bello University, which was founded by his government, was named after him.

BELLO, MUHAMMAD. Son of Usman dan Fodio (q.v.) and one of the leaders of the Fulani (q.v.) Islamic Revolution in Hausaland and the man who built up the Sokoto (q.v.) Caliphate (q.v.). Born in 1781, he became commander of one of the revolutionary armies in 1804. After the revolution, which was successful in Hausaland and elsewhere, his father, Dan Fodio, divided in 1812 the conquered territories into two between his brother Abdullahi Ibn Muhammad (q.v.) and his son Muhammad Bello. He appointed Emirs to administer the conquered states while he himself retired from the day-to-day administration of the empire. Bello then began to build Sokoto as the capital of the caliphate. When Usman died in 1817, Bello succeeded him. He then took the title of Sultan (q.v.) of Sokoto (q.v.) and began in earnest to put down external threats to the empire and internal revolts. His greatest external threat was Bornu (q.v.), which had been saved from the Fulani conquest by Sheikh M.A. Al-Kanemi (q.v.), who began an offensive against the Fulani. In the long run, the Fulani settled for the control of the western part of Bornu. It was during his time that the British explorer Hugh Clapperton (q.v.) visited Sokoto in 1824 and 1827. Bello was reputedly a very capable administrator. He laid great emphasis on the education of his people and enjoined equal justice between the Hausa (q.v.) and their Fulani overlords. He died in 1837.

BENDEL STATE. This state was substantially the same as the former Mid-Western Region (q.v.). It was created in 1963 from the former Western Region (q.v.) and became the fourth region in the Federation of Nigeria (q.v.). In 1967 when the country was divided into 12 states, the region remained intact but its name was changed to Mid-Western State. However, in 1976, when some of the states were further subdivided, the Mid-Western State became the Bendel State, and it underwent some boundary adjustments in which some areas were merged with the Rivers State (q.v.) while some others were merged with Ondo State (q.v.).

The state shared common boundaries with Ondo, Anambra (q.v.), Kwara (q.v.) and Rivers states with the Niger River (q.v.) as the natural boundary between it and Anambra State. It had about 128 kilometres of coastline on the Atlantic Ocean in the south.

The state capital was the ancient city of Benin, known as Benin City (q.v.). The city was surrounded by a moat several metres deep, some of which is still extant today.

The population of the state was 2,535,839, according to the 1963 census. It had a density of 17 people to 2.6 square kilometres. The main ethnic communities who composed it were the Edo (q.v.), Urhobo (q.v.), Igbo (q.v.), Ijaw (q.v.) and the Itsekiri (q.v.).

The state was rich in petroleum (q.v.), rubber (q.v.), cocoa (q.v.) and oil palm (q.v.), and supplied about 60 percent of the nation's total timber. Other resources were natural gas, limestone and lignite. In 1991 the state was split into two: Edo State and Delta State (qq.v.).

BENIN ART. Benin art can be classified into early Benin art and the art that had great influence from the bronze art of Ife (q.v.). The early Benin arts and crafts were associated with the time of the Ogiso (king) of Benin during what may be regarded as the First Kingdom. The art of this period consisted of items basic for human survival and close to the social, political and religious life of the people. These included domestic implements like wooden kitchen utensils, iron tools, woven raffia clothes and ceremonial boxes. They also included brass jewellery, ceremonial swords and commemorative heads of ancestors made to honor the dead. There were also terra-cotta sculptures (q.v.) used on the royal ancestral altars.

Later on, the Ogiso dynasty was overthrown and the people asked the then-Ooni of Ife, Oduduwa (q.v.) to send them a wise and good prince to rule them. Oduduwa sent them Oranmiyan (q.v.) who began a new dynasty of the Second Kingdom, and whose son Eweka I (q.v.) became installed as Oba of Benin before Oranmiyan came back to Ile-Ife (q.v.). The establishment of this new dynasty brought Benin into contact with Ife bronze and brass art. Ife brass smiths were invited to the royal palace. The brass and the bronze sculptures of this period were ritual objects placed upon altars at the royal palace of the Oba of Benin. They consisted of heads of Benin kings and queens, and some were placed on palace pillars to commemorate important events. Some experts thought that Benin art was influenced by European brass and bronze technology of the time, but this cannot be correct. Before the Portuguese explorers reached Benin in the 15th century, Benin bronze and brass sculptures were already in existence at the king's palace. However, the British removed Benin's accumulated artwork of many centuries, including the royal palace's wood and ivory carvings after their 1897 punitive expedition. At present, Benin continues to be a centre of fine works of art.

BENIN CITY. An ancient city, which in the fifteenth century was said to be the greatest state and empire in the Gulf of Guinea. About 1300 A.D., Bini tradition says that, at the request of the people of Benin, Oduduwa (q.v.), the ancestor of the Yoruba (q.v.) Obas, sent his son, Oranmiyan (q.v.), to Benin where he became Oba (king). He later married the daughter of a Bini chief by whom he had a son called Eweka (q.v.). After some years in Benin, Oranmiyan, wanting to go back to Ile-Ife (q.v.), caused Eweka, his son, to be made king, and his descendants until now continue to rule Benin.

The Kingdom of Benin (q.v.) expanded into an empire under Oba Ewuare (q.v.) who conquered part of Yorubaland to the west and some part of Igboland to the east. He built roads and defensive walls around the capital, Benin, some of which are still extant and are tourist attractions today. Benin developed into a center for trade in ivory, pepper, cloth, metalworks, beads and later slaves. The first Portuguese explorer to visit Benin was João Alfonso D'Aveiro (q.v.) in 1485. Later on, Portuguese traders arrived, but they could not establish any control over the state. Benin empire further expanded under Oba Esigie (q.v.) in the 16th century and reached the city of Lagos (q.v.) from the Niger Delta. In the 18th century, Benin sold many slaves to European slave traders. Towards the end of the 19th century, the British authorities tried to reach some treaty agreements with Benin, and when that did not come easy, in 1897 they attacked the city and partially destroyed it. Its Oba, Ovonramwen (q.v.), was sent into exile. The British removed many of the Benin arts, and a few years later, Benin came under British colonial administration.

Today Benin is famous for its artworks in ivory, bronze and wood carvings. Benin artworks and carvings are some of the finest in the world, and some of the famous ones are kept in the national museum. The Benin people have great respect for the institution of the Oba, a fact that explains why many of their carvings relate to Obas and many ancient streets and institutions are named after past Obas.

Benin City became the capital of the Mid-Western Region (q.v.) in 1963, and today it is the capital of Edo State (q.v.). The population of the city, according to the 1991 census, was 780,976. The people of the city are mainly Edo-speaking. The city is one of the cleanest in Nigeria with wide streets and some very good roads. It is also a university city, being the home of the University of Benin, established in 1970.

BENIN DELTA PEOPLES PARTY. Formed in 1953 under the leadership of His Highness, Akenzua II (q.v.), the Oba of Benin, its aim was to seek a separate state for the Mid-Western Region (q.v.). In the 1954 federal elections, the BDPP, in alliance with the National Council of Nigeria and the Cameroons (NCNC) (q.v.), won most of the seats but was soon absorbed by the NCNC.

BENIN, KINGDOM OF. One of the most renowned kingdoms of precolonial Africa. It is remembered for its brass art, as well as its elaborate monarchical traditions. Located in the Mid-Western part of Nigeria, at the site of the current Edo State (q.v.), the first kingdom of Benin probably emerged sometime in the 10th century, under the ruling dynasty of the Ogiso. The Ogiso helped nurture a tradition of crafts, particularly woodcarving that would be influential in Benin's later tradition of brass work.

The second kingdom of Benin dates from around 1300, when oral tradition records that the people of Benin sent to Ife to request a new king. The man that was sent was the legendary Oranmiyan (q.v.), who established a new dynasty, eventually abdicating in favor of his son Eweka I (q.v.). From this point on, the influence and achievements of Benin began to flourish. The famous metal working industry prospered, and under the leadership of Oba Ewuare in the 15th century, strong and enduring government institutions were established. It was around this time that Benin began to conquer neighboring territories, forming the basis of an impressive empire.

By the 19th century, however, the leadership of Benin had become increasingly autocratic, initiating a period of decline. During this period, Benin also suffered from a disruption of trading patterns and some bitter succession struggles in the latter half of the century. These weakened the kingdom, leaving it vulnerable to conquest by the British in 1897.

BENIN, REPUBLIC OF. It has a land area of about 113,000 square kilometres. Its coastline is made up of lagoons, creeks and sandbars. It shares the same climatic condition with Nigeria, with high rainfall in the south, which declines as one moves north. The vegetation in the south is thick forest, while in the north it is savannah. *See also* DAHOMEY.

BENSON, CHIEF THEOPHILUS OWOLABI SOBOWALE. A lawyer and politician, popularly known as T.O.S. Benson, born on July 23, 1917, at Ikorodu, Lagos State (q.v.). He attended Christian Missionary Society (CMS) Grammar School in Lagos (q.v.), University College in London, Inns of Court School of Laws and was called to the bar at Lincoln's Inn, London, in January 1947. When he came back to Nigeria, he enrolled as a barrister and solicitor at the federal supreme court (q.v.). In 1951 he was elected to the Western House of Assembly (q.v.) as a member of the National Council of Nigeria and the Cameroons (q.v.). In 1953 he became the leader of opposition in the assembly. In 1954 he was elected to the federal House of Representatives (q.v.) and later became its chief whip from 1954 to 1959. In 1955 he was a member of the Lagos town council and in 1959, having won another election to the federal house, he was appointed the federal minister of information and broadcasting, a post he occupied until the military came to power in 1966 when he went into private practice.

Chief Benson has played a significant role in the development of Nigeria. He was a delegate to all the constitutional conferences from 1953 to 1962. He was a delegate to the Commonwealth prime ministers conferences and to the United Nations General Assembly from 1960 to 1965. He was a foundation member of the Organization of African Unity (q.v.) and at many times acted for the prime minister.

He was a staunch NCNC member who started as a legal adviser, then rose to be the chairman of the party's western working committee, the party's national secretary and the party's post of third national vice president. After the ban on politics was lifted in 1978, he became a member of the Nigerian People's Party (NPP) (q.v.). He supported the efforts of the minority parties—the NPP, the Unity Party of Nigeria (q.v.), the Great Nigerian People's Party (q.v.) and the People's Redemption Party (PRP)—to form the Progressive Parties Alliance (q.v.) to fight the National Party of Nigeria (q.v.) in the 1983 general elections.

BENUE PLATEAU STATE. One of the six states carved out of the former Northern Region in May 1967 when Nigeria became a federation of 12 states. In 1976 the state was further divided into two separate states, Plateau and Benue states. The capital of Benue Plateau State was Jos. *See also* BENUE STATE AND PLATEAU STATE.

BENUE RIVER. The chief tributary of the Niger River (q.v.), it rises in the Adamawa Mountains of the Cameroon (q.v.) and flows about 1,400 kilometres, first in a northerly direction and receives the Mayo-Kebbi River, which joins the Benue with the Logone during high waters. It later flows to Yola (q.v.), the capital of Adamawa State (q.v.) in Nigeria, where it becomes navigable by fairly large vessels for about 800 kilometres. From there it flows southwesterly, passing through Ibi and Markurdi to join the Niger at Lokoja (q.v.). Its major tributaries in Nigeria are Gongola, Taraba, and Dongo Rivers, all of which flood seasonally during the rainy season and dry up during the dry season. The German explorer Heinrich Barth (q.v.) discovered the Benue in 1851 and in 1852 reported that he had crossed the Benue and speculated that it was the same river that flowed to the Niger at Lokoja. Three years later, the river was further explored by William Balfour Baikie (q.v.) who proceeded from the Niger about 640 kilometres up the river in a small steamer called the *Pleiad* (q.v.). His exploration showed that a large and fertile region of Africa, previously unknown, was accessible by means of the Benue.

BENUE STATE. Created in 1976 by the administration of General Murtala R. Muhammed (q.v.) from the defunct Benue Plateau State, which had been created in 1967. The agitation for creation of new states in the Federation started from the 1950s when the minorities in each existing region after independence became fearful of their positions vis-à-vis the majorities. In the early 1960s, J.S. Tarka (q.v.) of the United Middle Belt Congress (q.v.) led the struggle in the Northern Region (q.v.). In 1967 the military administration under General Y. Gowon (q.v.) created 12 states out of the then-existing four regions and Benue Plateau was one of them. In 1976 Benue was separated from Plateau, but it contained the Igala (q.v.) and Bassa peoples who did not believe they should belong to Benue. In 1991 these two peoples' territories were carved out of Benue and became part of another new state, Kogi State (q.v.).

Benue State is situated between latitudes 6° 25′ and 8°8′N, and longitudes 7° 47′ and 10° 00′E. It is surrounded by five states—Plateau State to the north, Taraba State (q.v.) to the northeast, Cross River State (q.v.) and Enugu State to the south and Kogi State (q.v.) to the west. On the southeastern border, the state has a small boundary line with the Republic of Cameroon (q.v.).

The state gets its name from the Benue River (q.v.) that runs through it in the north. It is about 300 metres above sea level and has two main seasons, the rainy and the dry seasons. The rainy season is between April and October and the annual rainfall is between 1,200 and 2,000 metres. The temperature is between 21°C and 35°C and is fairly uniform all over the state. It is divided into 18 local government areas.

The population was 2,780,398 in 1991 with an average density of 89 persons per square kilometres. Among the many ethnic groups are Akweya, Yachi, Egede, Etolu, Hausa (q.v.), Idoma, Igbo (q.v.), Jukun (q.v.), Tiv (q.v.), Ufia and Utonkong, each of which speaks a native language. The culture of the people in the state, therefore, varies. There are Muslims, Christians and adherents of traditional religions. Among their traditional festivals are the Alekwu Ancestral festival of the Idoma people when the ancestors reestablish contact with the living in the form of masquerades. The Tiv also celebrate Tiv Day.

The state is not highly urbanized, even though it is well connected by land, air, rail and water. There are three major towns: Makurdi, the capital with a population of about 226,198 persons, Oboko and Oturkpo. Other small towns include Katsina Ala, Otukpa, Adikpo, Vandeikya, Naka, Adoka, Oju and Donga. About 70 percent of the people engage in small-scale farming over fertile land areas. Their cash crops include groundnut (q.v.), soybeans, and rice. Their food crops are yams (q.v.), cassava (q.v.), maize and sorghum.

They also keep goats, sheep, cattle, pigs and fish. The state has such mineral resources as coal, limestone, feldspar, bauxite, kaolin and mineral salt.

Benue State is one of the most educationally advantaged states in the north with high literacy levels and high enrollments in all three levels of education—primary, secondary and tertiary. The state has two universities—The Federal University of Agriculture and Benue State University.

BERLIN CONFERENCE. As a result of the European scramble for territories in Africa, much friction developed. Rather than allow the situation to become explosive, the Berlin Conference was called in 1884, finishing its work in 1885. The agreements at the conference greatly influenced British acquisition of Nigeria. At the conference, Britain made claim to all the territories under the Royal Niger Company (q.v.), and the conference recognized them as being under British influence. They also agreed that navigation on the Niger River (q.v.) must be free to all merchant ships of all nations, and they agreed on the important principle of effective occupation for delimiting the boundaries of their territory. The interpretation of this principle was not clear, but claims to sovereignty, maintained by sufficient military power to guarantee order, protection of foreigners and control over the indigenous population were considered. Treaties of protection made by the Europeans with the local chiefs were also considered as evidence of a valid title of sovereignty. After this conference, the British moved ahead rapidly to acquire the whole of Nigeria.

BIAFRA, BIGHT OF. The Bight of Biafra is the inlet of the Atlantic Ocean on the West African coast. It extends from the outlet of the Niger River (q.v.) in Nigeria to Cape Lopez in Gabon. The bight is bounded by southeastern Nigeria, Cameroon, Equatorial Guinea and south to the northwestern part of Gabon. Many rivers, including the Niger, Cross and Sanaga, discharge into the area. Within the bight are many islands and major ports like Malabo (Santa Isabel [q.v.]) in Equatorial Guinea, Port Harcourt (q.v.) and Calabar in Nigeria, and Libreville and Port Gentil in Gabon. Between the sixteenth and nineteenth centuries, the area was the scene of extensive slave-trading operations carried on mainly in Nigerian ports like Bonny (q.v.), Opobo (q.v.), Brass and Calabar. After the slave trade was abolished, the area became an important source of oil palm (q.v.), and today much of Nigeria's petroleum (q.v.) comes from the area.

Biafra was the name given to the former Eastern Region (q.v.) when Lt. Col. Odumegwu Ojukwu (q.v.) declared the secession of the region from the rest of the country on May 30, 1967, as the "Independent Republic of Biafra." As a result of this secession, a civil war ensued in 1967, which ended in January 1970, after the surrender of the Biafran army and the loss of thousands of lives. *See also* CIVIL WAR.

BIAFRA, REPUBLIC OF. The name given to the former Eastern Region (q.v.) when Lt. Col. Odumegwu Ojukwu (q.v.) declared the secession of the region from the rest of Nigeria on May 30, 1967, as the "Independent Republic of Biafra." As a result of this secession, a civil war ensued in 1967, which ended in January 1970 after the surrender of the Biafran soldiers. *See also* CIVIL WAR.

BIAFRAN ORGANIZATION OF FREEDOM FIGHTERS. In the last year of the Civil War, Lt. Col. Odumegwu Ojukwu (q.v.) launched a guerrilla operation composed of paramilitary young people under his own control. The group had some political education and ideological motivation. It was designed to move freely among civilians in the federally controlled areas north of Biafra, and along the west bank of the Niger River (q.v.) in the Mid-West. Though fairly successful, it was unable to help dislodge the federal troops from the occupied areas.

BIAFRAN OVERSEAS PRESS SERVICE. *See* MARKPRESS.

BINNS FISCAL REVIEW COMMISSION. Set up in June 1964 with K.J. Binns, an undersecretary and state commissioner of taxes in Tanzania as the sole commissioner. The commission was to review and make recommendations with respect to the provisions of Sections 140 and 141 of the constitution of the Federal Republic of Nigeria (q.v.) on mining royalties and rents, and on the distribution of funds in the distributative pool account. In doing its work, it was to take into account the experiences of the various governments of the Federation in the working of the revenue allocation that was then in force, the recent creation of the Mid-Western Region (q.v.) and the proportion of revenue allocated to it, the sources of revenue available to each of the governments and the legitimate requirements and responsibilities of each of the governments. It was also to consider the financial implications of the nonavailability of promised foreign aid for university education and other unfulfilled pledges for financial assistance to Nigeria and make recommendations on all the above matters. The commission recommended that:

1. The amount of 30 percent credited to the distributable pool account in accordance with the constitutional provision of Section 136(i) on import duties on certain commodities and Section 140(2) on mining royalties and rents should not be altered.
2. The portion of the distributable pool account payable to each region in accordance with Section 141 of the constitution should be altered as follows: the Northern Region (q.v.) and the Eastern Region (q.v.) were to continue to have a share of 40 percent and 31 percent, respectively, and the Western Region (q.v.) was to get 21 percent instead of the existing 18 percent and the Mid-Western Region (q.v.)

was to get 8 percent instead of the existing 6 percent. The Federal Government should introduce a bill to provide a payment of £3.75 million to the regions on an annual basis from 1965 to 1969. The Federal Government should discontinue, beginning with the 1965–66 financial year, the practice of paying to the regions a share of general excise revenue, but in doing so, the federal constitution should be amended to provide that when an excise duty was imposed on locally produced motor spirit and diesel oil, the Federation would pay to the regions the proceeds of that duty on consumption in the regions divided in proportion to regional consumption.

BLAIZE, RICHARD BEALF OLAMILEGE. Born in 1845 in Freetown, Sierra Leone, to Yoruba (q.v.) liberated-slave parents, he was raised as a Christian and was educated in mission schools. After schooling, he became a printer's apprentice. In 1862 he came to Lagos (q.v.) and started to work for Robert Campbell, as editor of the then *Anglo-African* newspaper. In 1863 he became head printer in the government printing office. In 1875 he left government service to start his own business as a merchant. Towards the end of the century, he was regarded as the wealthiest native businessman in Lagos. He was a member of the Lagos Chamber of Commerce and the owner of the *Lagos Weekly Record (q.v.),* which J.P. Jackson (q.v.), a Liberian-born journalist and a nationalist, edited. The *Lagos Weekly Record* was well known for its criticism of the British colonial authorities. Having become very successful as a merchant, Blaize was active in church and politics. He died in 1904.

BLYDEN, DR. EDWARD WILMONT. Born in Charlotte-Amalie, capital of St. Thomas in the Virgin Islands in the West Indies on August 3, 1832, Blyden wanted to join the ministry in 1849 and went to the United States to enter a theological training college but was rebuffed because he was black. He left the United States and migrated to Liberia in 1851. In Liberia he became the editor of the *Liberia Herald,* for which he had been a correspondent. In 1856 he wrote his famous pamphlet, "A Voice from Bleeding Africa on behalf of Her Exiled Children," which later had tremendous influence on black nationalists everywhere. In it he sought to restore pride and self-respect in the black race and disproved the myth of black man's inferiority to whites. He wanted to rediscover black history and correct many of the misrepresentations in books published by the white people. He also aimed at preserving African customs, culture and institutions and to develop what he called the "African personality." Dr. Blyden was not happy with colonial partitioning of Africa into ministates and advocated large groupings of people. Though himself a Christian, he was disenchanted with the racial discrimination practiced in the churches and so said that Christianity was unsuitable for Africans. In his book, *Christianity, Islam and the Negro Race* published in 1887, he criticized the established Christian churches for their attitude on African culture and their intolerance of certain African customs like polygamy. According to him, Christianity (q.v.) had retarded the emergence of African personality, while Islam had in fact worked in the opposite direction.

He visited Nigeria in 1876 and was one of the people who at the time agitated for the establishment of higher educational institutions in the country. In 1896 he was again in Nigeria. He recommended the establishment of a training college and an industrial institute in Nigeria to the governor of Lagos (q.v.). His writings together with his presence in Nigeria and his appeal to prominent African church leaders that they should establish a native church modelled on black churches in the United States, a church which would be composed of native Africans who would support it and govern it, helped a great deal to bring about the first religious protest movements against white-dominated Christian churches and the secession of the United Native African Church (q.v.) from the Anglican Church (q.v.). He died in 1912.

BONNY. A city-state in the Niger Delta, from which thousands of slaves were sold annually to Europeans in the late 18th and early 19th centuries. Long before the European slave traders (q.v.) came, Bonny had organized itself into trading houses, each representing a lineage with a head who was generally the most powerful and most prosperous person in the lineage. These houses were like trading companies that fiercely competed against one another. A successful house could absorb other weak and less prosperous ones. Each house had war canoes mounted with cannon to protect its commercial activities. By the close of the 18th century, Bonny was at the height of its power and could boast of many such war canoes.

In the early 19th century, there were two dominant trading houses in Bonny—Anna Pepple House and Manilla Pepple House. Under Opubu the Great, Anna Pepple House had been the more successful. When Opubu died, the headship of the house passed to Alali, who was very hardworking and energetic, though not of the royal family. When Alali also died, the house elected Jaja (q.v.), an ex-slave, to head the house. The rivalry between the two houses led to open conflict. In 1868 Manilla Pepple House attacked the Anna Pepple House with the support of the king, George Pepple (q.v.), who succeeded King William Dappa Pepple (q.v.) in 1866. Rather than Jaja fighting a civil war, he withdrew his house and reestablished it at Opobo, a site strategically chosen to cut Bonny off from the interior's palm oil trade. As a result, Bonny gradually declined.

BORGU CONVENTION. *See* ANGLO-FRENCH CONVENTION OF 1898.

BORNO STATE. Created in 1976 out of the Northwestern State (q.v.) previously created in 1967. In 1991 the administration of General Ibrahim Babangida (q.v.) carved out the western part of the state to form Yobe State. The State has an area of 69,435 square kilometres and is bounded in the east by the Republic of Cameroon (q.v.), in the northeast by Lake Chad (q.v.), in the north by Chad Republic, in the west by Yobe State and in the south by Bauchi State (q.v.) and Adamawa State (q.v.). It is about 300 metres above sea level.

There are two main seasons: the rainy and the dry seasons. The rainy season begins from about June to September, while the dry season begins in October and lasts until May. During the dry season, there is the cool dry harmattan wind down from the Sahara Desert between November and February. The temperature varies from 39°C to 40°C and is generally high year-round. The rainy season lasts for only about 80 days in the north and up to about 140 days in the south. Annual rainfall varies from 500 millimetres to 800 millimetres. The vegetation is savannah forest, short in the north but taller in the south. Its mineral resources include limestone, kaolin, iron ore, uranium, quartz, mica, and granite. The state is divided into 21 local government areas.

The population of Borno State was 2,596,589 in 1991, making the population density 37 persons per square kilometres. The major population centres are Maiduguri, the capital of the state, with about 629,486 people in 1991, Mukawa, Mongamu, Ngala, Damboa, Biu Gwoza and Bama. Many people who live in Borno State migrate to the Lake Chad shores and to the wetter local government areas in the south. Ethnically, the Kanuri (q.v.) are the dominant group and account for about three-quarters of the State's population. There are other ethnic groups, among which are Babur, Marghi, Shuwa, Fulani (q.v.), Hausa (q.v.) and Mandara. Each of these groups speaks a language native to its people. However, the people have been greatly influenced by Arabic culture and Islam (q.v.), which is the religion of most inhabitants. Most of the people are shepherds, fishers and farmers planting crops of sorghum, millet, maize, cotton, groundnut (q.v.), watermelon, tomatoes, wheat and rice. Animals generally reared are cattle, sheep and goats.

The state's educational system is making good progress, with 1,144 primary schools and 501,328 pupils, 30 secondary schools, many colleges of education and the Federal University at Maiduguri.

BORNU. Bornu was a kingdom located northwest of Lake Chad, the site of contemporary Borno State. Its origins date back to the eighth century. In the 13th century it was incorporated into the kingdom of Kanem to the north, which was ruled by the Sefuwa dynasty. When Kanem collapsed in the 14th century, the capital of the Sefuwa dynasty was relocated to Bornu. It was under the Sefuwa rulers (called Mai) that Kanuri (q.v.) people emerged as a nation to be reckoned with southwest of Lake Chad (q.v.). Bornu reached its apogee during the time of Mai Idris Aloma (q.v.). By the eighteenth century, all the various ethnic groups in today's Borno and Yobe states were under the Bornu empire. But the Fulani (q.v.) revolutionaries of Usman dan Fodio (q.v.) weakened the empire in the early 19th century. It was during this time that Al-Kanemi (q.v.), the founder of the Al-Kanemi dynasty and a great Islamic scholar, displaced the Sefuwa rulers and established his capital at Kukawa.

When the European colonizers came, the empire was dismembered and part of Bornu came under British rule. In 1902 the British reinstated Umar (q.v.), the son of Al-Kanemi, as the Shehu of Borno. But after the first World War and the defeat of Germany in 1918, the area of Bornu under the Germans came under British trusteeship and another Shehu was appointed for Dikwa. This explains the origin of two emirates and two Shehus in Bornu. This also, to some extent, explains Kanuri politics today.

The British rule brought about the relocation of the capital of Bornu to Yerwa, which the British renamed Maiduguri. Bornu was a province and part of the Northern Region (q.v.) until 1967 when six states were created from the region.

BORNU YOUTH MOVEMENT (BYM). Formed in 1954 by young Kanuri (q.v.) people who were dissatisfied with the system of Native Authority (q.v.) in the area, and the corruption they saw around them. Its major objective was the creation of a North-Eastern State (q.v.) which would consist of Bornu, Adamawa, Bauchi and Plateau provinces. The ruling Northern People's Congress (NPC) (q.v.) moved quickly to weaken the Bornu Youth Movement (BYM) by making efforts to eradicate corruption in the area, and, as a result, the party gradually declined enough so that the BYM did not make any representation to the Minorities Commission (q.v.) in 1958.

BOUNDARY ADJUSTMENT COMMISSION. Set up on February 12, 1976, to examine the boundary adjustment problems identified by the Irikefe Panel (q.v.), which looked into the creation of more states in addition to the 12 states created in 1967. The commission, headed by Justice Muhammadu Nasir, was also to specify areas to be merged, and to define interstate boundaries, especially where there were intergovernmental disputes. *See also* NASIR COMMISSION.

BOURDILLON, SIR BERNARD. Born in 1883, he served in India, Iraq, Ceylon and Uganda before coming to Nigeria as governor of Nigeria in 1935. He laid the foundation for the constitutional proposals which bear the name of his successor, Sir Arthur Richards (q.v.). During his term Bourdillon became convinced that the policy of isolating the north from the rest of the country had to change. He worked hard to convince the Northern Emirs about the advisability of coming to join the southerners in the Legislative Council (q.v.) of the country. But rather than recommend increasing the number of northern members on the Legislative Council, he, realizing the north's shortcoming in the use of English as a language of communication in the Legislative Council, proposed setting up regional councils with a central council in Lagos to which the deliberations of regional councils would be sent. This idea gave rise to the concept of regionalism which Arthur Richards embodied in the 1946 Constitution. In fact, it was Bourdillon, who in 1939 divided the south into eastern and western provinces. What he did later was to substitute region for province. He returned home in 1943 and died in 1948.

BOWEN, THOMAS J. An American Baptist missionary sent to Nigeria in 1850 with the objective of setting up missions in the interior of the country. He built his first station in Ijaye, and in 1854 he established another station in Ogbomoso. He wrote his *Yoruba Grammar and Dictionary,* which was published in 1858 by the Smithsonian Institution. *See also* BAPTIST CHURCH.

BRIDE PRICE. The bride price is the money paid by a bridegroom or his parents to the family of his would-be bride. This was part of traditional marriage custom. Part of the rationale for the parents paying it was to assert their authority over who the bride was going to be. The price varied from place to place. In Yorubaland, the amount was not that much, but among the Igbo (q.v.) of Eastern Nigeria, the price has always been high, so high sometimes that appeals are often made through the mass media for its reduction.

BRITISH COTTON GROWING ASSOCIATION. The British Cotton Growing Association (BCGA) was founded in 1902 with a capital of £50,000. It then began to conduct research into whether any British West African countries were suitable or adaptable to cotton growing. The objective was to supply British markets with cotton grown within the Commonwealth rather than from America. Experiments were then begun in both southern and northern Nigeria, and cotton ginneries were erected along the railroad at Abeokuta (q.v.), Ibadan (q.v.), Iwo and Osogbo in the south and Ilorin (q.v.), Kano (q.v.), Zaria (q.v.), Kaduna (q.v.), and Sokoto (q.v.) in the north. The Moore Plantations at Ibadan were said to have been founded by the BCGA as an experimental farm for cotton growing. The experiment in the south did not succeed as well because the interest in cocoa (q.v.) plantations occupied the minds of most farmers. However, the experiment was very successful in the north. The BCGA supplied cotton seeds to farmers free of charge in an effort to increase production. The association not only opened up profitable employments for people in the cotton-growing area, but offered the country another of its cash crops and so helped in the diversification of the Nigerian economy.

BRITISH PETROLEUM. *See* NATIONALISATION OF BRITISH PETROLEUM COMPANY LTD.

BROADCASTING CORPORATION OF BIAFRA. When Eastern Nigeria (q.v.) declared itself the Republic of Biafra (q.v.) in 1967, the Eastern Nigeria broadcasting service, "Radio Enugu," was renamed the Broadcasting Corporation of Biafra. The corporation played a very prominent role in secessionist propaganda.

BROWN, VINCENT DAVID. *See* AGBEBI, DR. MOJOLA.

BUBA, YERO. Buba was sent to Gombe as Emir (q.v.) to represent the Islamic leader, Usman Dan Fodio (q.v.), who initiated the Islamic revolution, jihad (q.v.) of 1804. After conquering Bauchi and Gombe, he became the Emir of Gombe.

BUHARI, MAJ. GEN. MUHAMMADU. Former Head of State, born on December 17, 1942, in Daura in Katsina Province (q.v.) of Kaduna State (q.v.) he attended the Katsina Middle School from 1953 to 1956 and later went to the Katsina Provincial Secondary School, now Government College, Katsina. He joined the army in 1962 and was trained at the Nigerian Military Training College in Kaduna, and at Mons Officer Cadet School, Aldershot, England. He was commissioned Second Lieutenant in January 1963. Before December 31, 1983, when he became the Head of State and Commander in Chief of the Armed Forces, General Buhari had served in many important positions. He served with the 2nd Battalion Nigerian Army in the Congo in the early 1960s. In April 1964 he was posted to the Corps of Supply and Transport where he served until August 1966. He later served in many staff and command positions in the army. In 1972 he attended the Defense Service Staff College in Wellington, New Zealand. He was Director of Supply and Transport of the Nigerian Army from September 1974 until July 30, 1975, when he was appointed military governor of the Northeastern State (q.v.). When the state was broken up into three different states in February 1976, he was named military governor of the new Borno State (q.v.). In March 1976, he was reassigned as federal commissioner for petroleum and energy. On December 31, 1983, after the administration of President Shehu Shagari (q.v.) had been overthrown by a military coup d'état (q.v.) he became the Head of State and Commander in Chief of the Armed Forces (q.v.). He was ousted from power on August 27, 1985, after 20 months in office, and retired in September 1985.

During his short period in office as Head of State, General Buhari, together with his second in command, Brigadier Tunde Idiagbon (q.v.), imposed very strict discipline on the populace, investigated the activities of various politicians while in office and tried and imprisoned those that were found guilty. His administration represented law and order. His asceticism, discipline and straightforwardness were not sufficiently appreciated until the later half of General I.B. Babangida's (q.v.) regime when indiscipline, corruption and lack of public accountability became the order of the day.

In 1995, Buhari was made the executive chairman of the Petroleum Trust Fund (PTF). The PTF was funded from an increase in the price of gasoline and was expected to help rebuild the country's declining infrastructure. It was hoped that Buhari's honesty would prevent the PTF from degenerating into the corruption characteristic of other branches of the government. Issues of accountability and charges of regional favoritism rendered the PTF controversial, however, and on May 27, 1999, Buhari resigned from his position as head of the organisation, and one month later the newly elected president dissolved the PTF.

BUKAR D' GIJIAMA. The Kanuri (q.v.) ruler of the State of Mandara, which was a province of Bornu (q.v.). For a long time Mandara had struggled to become independent of Bornu, and during the reign of Bukar (1773–1828), Mandara tried again and proclaimed itself independent. Bornu began a campaign to recapture it but failed. In 1807 the Fulani (q.v.) jihad (q.v.) overran Bornu, and in 1809 they turned their forces on Mandara. The attempt failed. The Fulanis later sent a delegation to Bukar to reach a settlement, but Bukar reportedly beheaded the emissaries. In the meantime, the Bornu people under Al-Kanemi (q.v.), in alliance with Bukar, had begun a successful campaign against the Fulani occupiers. Bukar died in 1828.

BULALA. The Bulala people were a nomadic tribe from around Lake Fittri. They were reputed to be strong, warlike and very independent. Towards the end of the 14th century, about 1389, they occupied Kanem and drove out the Kanem ruler to the west of Lake Chad (q.v.) where he founded the state of Bornu (q.v.), which has been the center of political power in the province ever since. The Bulala people continued to be a great national threat to the Kanuri (q.v.) people until the time of Mai Idris Katagarmabe, (q.v.) about 1507, when the Bulala were defeated and their capital city Njimi was reoccupied.

BUREAU FOR PUBLIC ENTERPRISES. *See* PRIVATISATION AND COMMERCIALISATION PROGRAMMES.

BUREAUX-DE-CHANGE. Licensed financial houses that specialize in foreign exchange dealings. In January 1989, the federal government (q.v.)

authorised the establishment of bureau-de-change by private entrepreneurs, to serve the needs of the people with small demand for and supply of foreign exchange. The establishment of the bureau-de-change was also intended to eliminate the parallel (black) market, or at least reduce the activities of the market. Furthermore, it was intended to protect Nigerians from buying fake foreign currencies from the parallel market. In 1992 there were 30 licensed bureaux-de-change in the country. By January 1995, there were 183.

BUSSA. The traditional city of the Bariba, situated in Niger State (q.v.), is famous in history as the place where Mungo Park (q.v.)—the leader of the first explorers of the Niger River (q.v.)—together with his men, died as they sailed down the Niger in 1805. In 1830 brothers Richard Lander (q.v.) and John Lander trekked overland from Badagry (q.v.) through Oyo to Bussa. They secured two canoes there and sailed down the Niger through its confluence with the Benue River (q.v.) until the Igbo (q.v.) took them captive at Asaba.

-C-

CALABAR. The capital of the Cross River State (q.v.), Calabar is a coastal town, which before the advent of the British colonial authorities was a trading and cultural center. In the 19th century, it was a seat of learning and culture and was one of the earliest British trading posts in the eastern part of the country. Like Lagos (q.v.), Calabar has always played an important role and enjoyed a special place in the political history of Nigeria. It was the headquarters of the Niger Coast Protectorate (q.v.) and the first capital of Southern Nigeria (q.v.) by the Orders-in-Council of 1899. The first British consul general, Major Claude MacDonald was appointed there in January 1891. The people traded palm oil with the Royal Niger Company (q.v.). After the Clifford Constitution of 1922 (q.v.) was in effect, Calabar enjoyed the status of a municipality with an elected representative in the Legislative Council (q.v.) of 1923. Calabar and Lagos were the first two cities where elections were held for members of the council.

Calabar has also been famous for being an early site of missionary activities. The first group of missionaries to land there were the Presbyterians, who came in 1846. From the time the people of Calabar embraced Christianity, the town became a center for the spread of Christianity (q.v.). Calabar is now a university city.

CALABAR-OGOJA-RIVERS STATE. Once the constitutional changes into a federal system were in effect, non-Igbo-speaking groups in the former provinces of Calabar, Ogoja and Rivers, who were minority ethnic groups in the Eastern Region (q.v.), began to agitate for a state separate from the region's numerically dominant Igbo areas. The demand for the Calabar-Ogoja-Rivers State (COR) was made first in 1953 at the area's conference of chiefs and representatives. In 1954 the COR Movement was formed and inaugurated at Uyo in Calabar (q.v.) province. The leader of the movement was Dr. Udo Udoma, a member of the House of Representatives (q.v.) for Opobo (q.v.), and a member of the United National Independence Party (q.v.) and the president of the Ibibio (q.v.) State Union.

The proposal for a separate state became an important issue in the eastern regional election of 1957. It was supported by the United Nigeria Independent Party, but was opposed by Dr. Nnamdi Azikiwe (q.v.) and his party on the ground that it would break up the Eastern Region (q.v.) and that the agitators for it were motivated by anti-Igbo sentiments and hate. However, in 1967, their demands became a reality when the 12-state structure took effect. Rather than a COR State, there were the Rivers State and the Southeastern State. The Southeastern State was later changed into the Cross River State in February 1976 when seven more states were created from the old 12 states.

CALIPHATE. The Caliphate was the administrative division of the Muslim areas in the Northern Region (q.v.). After the death of Usman Dan Fodio (q.v.), who initiated the holy war (jihad) (q.v.), the areas under his lieutenants were divided into two caliphates: Sokoto and Gwandu. Bello (q.v.), the son of Usman Dan Fodio, ruled in Sokoto, while his uncle, Dan Fodio's brother Abdullahi (q.v.), ruled in Gwandu.

CAMERON, SIR DONALD CHARLES, K.B.E., G.C.M.G. Born in 1875, he served in British Guiana, Newfoundland and Mauritius before he joined the colonial administration in Nigeria. He became interested in Lord Lugard's (q.v.) idea of indirect rule (q.v.). From Nigeria he lived in Tanganyika (now Tanzania) from 1925 to 1931, where he organised the country's civil service and introduced a legislative council and successfully opposed the effort to unite Tanganyika, Kenya and Uganda. He then returned to Nigeria where he served as governor from 1931 to 1935. His one great objective was reforming the administrative system, which he believed deviated from the original idea of the founder. He was concerned about the slow progress in the north where he felt the government had too long permitted a system of fiefdom. He abolished the system whereby British administrators sat as judges. He abolished the provincial courts (q.v.), where lawyers were not allowed to appear, and replaced them with the high courts and magistrate courts where lawyers could appear. He also set up a system for a Native Court (q.v.) of Appeal and subordinated all types of courts in the country to the authority of the Supreme Court (q.v.). Cameron did not believe in the policy set up by Lord Lugard of developing the north and the south on separate lines. He encouraged northern rulers and their staff to visit the south and the United Kingdom. His ideas were articulated in his "Principles of Native Administration and their Application" in 1934. He opened the Yaba Higher College (q.v.), which was the first postsecondary institution in Nigeria. He left Nigeria in 1935, and was succeeded by Sir Bernard Bourdillon (q.v.). He later served as a member of the Asquith Commission (q.v.) in 1943. He died in 1948.

CAMEROON. The Cameroon Republic is Nigeria's neighbor to the east from the Atlantic Ocean in the south to Lake Chad (q.v.) in the north. Before the advent of the Europeans, Cameroon had developed kingdoms and states. The earliest contact with the Europeans was in 1482 when the Portuguese established trading posts near Douala. Later on, Christian religious missions and slave traders followed. Many settlements near the coast participated in the slave (q.v.) and palm oil trade from the 16th century onwards. By 1869 the Germans competed with the British for trade, and in 1884 they hoisted their flag over the Cameroon and proclaimed a protectorate over the area, just a few days before the British arrived to declare it a British protectorate. The Germans ruled Cameroon until the end of the First World War when it came under a League of Nations mandate, which divided it in 1922 between the French (east) and British (west). The administration then brought British Cameroon under the administration of the government of Nigeria and administered it as part of Nigeria. In 1947 the League of Nations mandate was replaced with a trusteeship agreement between the United Nations and the governing powers.

However, as Nigeria moved toward independence, demands were made that British Cameroon should be granted autonomy from Nigeria. This demand became intensified in 1953 after the Eastern Regional Government Crisis (q.v.). Cameroon's representatives in the Eastern Region (q.v.) began to demand its autonomy from Eastern Nigeria. In 1953 they submitted a memorandum to the British secretary of state for the colonies asking for a regional legislature. At the Lagos Conference of 1954, the southern part of British Cameroon was granted an autonomous status and so ceased to be a part of the Eastern Region of Nigeria, but it remained as a quasi-federal territory of the Federation of Nigeria (q.v.). By this means, the federal legislature and the federal Executive Council (q.v.) would still have jurisdiction in the territory over matters in the federal and concurrent lists. The northern part of British Cameroon, on the other hand, did not opt to break away from the Northern Region (q.v.) and pull out of the federation. The view of the leadership was that they wished to remain part of the region.

According to the 1954 Constitution, the House of Assembly (q.v.) of Southern Cameroon consisted of the commissioner of the Cameroon, who was president of the house, three ex-officio members, 13 elected members, six members representing the Native Authorities (q.v.) of Southern Cameroon, and not more than two special members appointed by the governor-general to represent interests or communities not otherwise adequately represented. In 1957 Southern Cameroon was raised to region status within the federation and provisions were made for the position of premier as in other regions, but the ultimate responsibility for the territory still rested with the governor-general. In 1961, after Nigeria became independent, there was a referendum in both the northern and southern part of British Cameroon to determine whether either would stay in the Federation of Nigeria. Northern Cameroon preferred to stay in the federation, while Southern Cameroon joined the Republic of Cameroon which had previously been administered by the French. The two parts thus formed the Federal Republic of Cameroon.

In 1972 Cameroon became a unitary state with the capital at Yaounde. English is spoken in the West, while French is spoken in the East, thus making the country bilingual. Both languages are taught in all schools.

Nigeria's border with Cameroon in the south is still not settled. Both countries claim Bakassi (q.v.), an oil-rich peninsula. There have been many border clashes, resulting in many deaths and loss of personal property.

CAMEROONS PLEBISCITE. The former British Cameroons, made up of Northern Cameroon and Southern Cameroon, were United Nations (UN) trust territories, administered by Britain as an integral part of Nigeria. The Northern Cameroon then formed part of Northern Nigeria (q.v.), while the Southern Cameroon had its own separate administration within the Nigerian administrative system. As independence approached, there was a UN recommendation asking that both parts of the Cameroons should be constitutionally separated from Nigeria by October 1, 1960, when Nigeria would become independent, and that there should be separate plebiscites by March 1961 in each part of the territory to ascertain whether each wanted to achieve independence as part of Nigeria or as part of the Republic of Cameroon. As such, a plebiscite was held on February 11 and 12, 1961. The Northern Cameroon voted for unification with Nigeria and was formally incorporated into the federation (q.v.) in June 1961 and was later renamed Sardauna Province. The Southern Cameroon voted to be united with the Federal Republic of Cameroon and was incorporated into the Cameroon Republic on October 1, 1961, from which time it ceased to be administered as part of the Federation of Nigeria.

CAMPAIGN FOR DEMOCRACY. As President Ibrahim B. Babangida (q.v.) continued to break his promise to hand over power to an elected civilian administration, many people began to see that he would not give up power. They formed associations to put pressure on him to leave office. The Campaign for Democracy (CD) was one of the most well-known associations—

nationally and internationally. The association was founded in November 1991 and was made up of many other groups and associations like the Civil Liberty Organisation and Committee for Defence of Human Rights. CD's objectives include fostering and agitating for democratic governance and promoting fundamental human rights. The organisation has carried out practical programmes such as street protests, sit-down-at-home actions and symposia against dehumanising conditions of the people and putting pressure on the military government. CD has branches and affiliate bodies in Europe and America.

CARPET CROSSING. Carpet crossing denotes the movement of a parliamentarian from one party to the other. It might be from the opposition party to the government party or vice versa. The practice started in the Western Region (q.v.) after the 1951 regional election which the National Convention of Nigeria and Cameroons (NCNC) (q.v.) apparently won. But when the house met, some members of the NCNC crossed to the Action Group party (AG) (q.v.) giving the AG the majority it needed to form the region's government.

After independence and during the first republic (q.v.), carpet crossing was a common feature of Nigerian politics. The period witnessed a constant drift of opposition members in parliament or in the regional houses to the government side. As a result of this practice, the AGI which won 75 seats in the Federal House of Representatives (q.v.) in Lagos (q.v.) in 1959, was by 1963 (after the 1962 crisis) reduced to only 21 members.

To prevent this practice, which was open to great corruption, the 1979 Constitution, section 64(1a), provided that a member of any legislative house loses his seat when, "being a person whose election to the House was sponsored by a political party, he becomes a member of another political party before the expiration of the period for which that House was elected." The only exception to this was if a party breaks into two factions or two parties merge into one.

CARR, HENRY RAWLINSON. Born on August 15, 1863, in Lagos (q.v.), he was the son of an immigrant from Sierra Leone (q.v.) who originally was from England. He attended St. Paul's (Breadfruit) School and Olowogbowo Wesleyan Elementary School, all in Lagos, from 1869 to 1873. In 1874 he went to the Wesleyan Boys' High School in Freetown, Sierra Leone, and in 1877 he was admitted to Fourah Bay College (q.v.) where he obtained a bachelor of arts degree in 1882, being the first student of the institution to obtain an honors degree. He then went to Britain and enrolled at Lincoln's Inn, St. Mark's College in Chelsea and at the Royal College of Science in South Kensington in London. He returned to Nigeria in 1885 and joined the Church Missionary Society (q.v.) Grammar School in Lagos as a senior assistant master. In 1889 he joined the civil service as a chief clerk and became the first subinspector of schools in Lagos. In the following year he became an assistant secretary for native affairs. He was later transferred to the Department of Education as a provincial inspector and later as chief inspector of schools in the southern part of the country. Before he retired in 1924, he was the commissioner (q.v.) for the colony of Lagos.

Henry Carr believed that education (q.v.) was most necessary for the development of the individual, and therefore he devoted his life to the advancement of education in Nigeria. In 1928 he was appointed to the Legislative Council (q.v.) as an adviser on education until 1941. For his contribution to the development of education in the country, he was honoured with honorary degrees of master of science, and doctor of civil law and Commander, Order of the British Empire. He died on March 6, 1945.

CASLEY, HAYFORD. Founder of the National Congress of British West Africa (q.v.) in 1917, he was born in the Gold Coast (q.v.), now Ghana. During his tenure, the congress put pressure on the British colonial government for self-determination and political representation in the Legislative Councils (q.v.) in the various West African territories of the Gambia, Sierra Leone (q.v.), Gold Coast and Nigeria. The British governors in these countries derided the Congress's claims that it spoke for Africans. In 1922 the British government answered their demand by introducing the elective principle into the Nigerian Legislative Council in Lagos, and later on in all other territories. Casley died in 1930.

CASSAVA. Known also as tapioca, cassava is one of the most important root crops in Nigeria. It is a shrub and reaches a height of between two and three metres. There are two main types of cassava—sweet and bitter. The bitter one contains hydrocyanic acid and is usually treated before eating. The treatment depends on the kind of the final foodstuffs the cassava will make. Cassava and its derivatives contain very little protein. It is mainly starch and, therefore, requires the accompaniment of other protein-rich foodstuffs to make a balanced diet. In spite of this, it is widely eaten as fufu, lafun, garl and eba.

Cassava can grow in fairly poor soil and does not need much care before its shade begins to kill off some of the undershrubs. It is grown from stem cuttings planted at about one metre intervals on ridges or on flat ground. The crop is ready to harvest after about eight months, but a better result is obtained after a year and up to two years. Research at the International Institute of Tropical Agriculture (IITA) (q.v.) in Ibadan (q.v.), Oyo State (q.v.) is producing high-yielding and early maturing varieties to farmers. Depending on the soil and rain, the yield can be as high as 10 tons to 35 tons per hectare, and it is still rising.

CATHOLIC CHURCH. As early as 1472, Portuguese Catholic merchants visited Lagos (q.v.) and Benin (q.v.). By 1515 Catholic missionaries had established a school in the palace of the Oba of Benin for his sons and those of his chiefs, some of whom converted to Christianity (q.v.). As such, the Catholic missionaries were the first missionaries to enter Nigeria. However, their initial effort was almost completely destroyed by the slave trade (q.v.), and did not return for almost 300 years.

The second coming of the Catholic Church was in 1868. The church set up mission schools in Lagos, and from there it moved inland. A high percentage of Nigerian Catholics live in the eastern part of the country. Nine archbishops administer the nine ecclesiastical provinces into which Nigeria is divided. The church now has two cardinals, many bishops and both indigenous and expatriate priests and sisters. The Catholic Church is one of the major churches that have advanced the course of education (q.v.) in Nigeria.

CATTLE TAX. This is a tax known as "jangali" payable by cattle owners in the former Northern Nigeria (q.v.). This tax was imposed because the nomadic herdsmen normally did not pay the community tax (q.v.). Generally, the herds were counted from June of each year. The tax was collected from July to November unless extensions of periods were granted by the Ministry of Local Government.

CENSUS. There have been five censuses in Nigeria from 1952 to 1991, but only three of these have been accepted and used. The colonial authorities carried out the 1952 to 1953 census with the following results for the main divisions into which the nation had been divided: east—7,215,251, west—6,685,065, north—16,835,582, federal territory of Lagos—267,407. Total—30,403,305. Many people criticised this census because it was said to be inaccurate. Many people avoided being counted because they thought the purpose was to impose taxation on them. It was also criticised on the ground that the enumerators did not visit many villages. Nevertheless, the figures became the basis of the allocation of federal seats in the Legislature and Lagos (q.v.).

The 1962 census started on May 13, but, because of the apparent inflation of the figures in some of the regions, and the controversies arising from it, both the federal and the regional governments agreed in September 1963 to cancel it and authorise a new one. This census started on November 5 and ended on November 9, 1963. The operation was to be in the hands of regional officials, but each region was to send teams of inspectors to the other regions to observe the procedure and carry out checks. Demographic tests would also be applied to the figures when they arrived at the Lagos headquarters. The outcome of the census was announced on February 24, 1964, with the following figures: north—29,777,986, east—12,388,646, west (including the newly created Mid-Western Region—12,811,837 and Lagos—675,352. The total was 55,653,821. There was much uproar over these figures, for many people believed them to have been rigged and grossly inaccurate. When the Eastern Region (q.v.), which appeared most aggrieved, could not persuade the federal government and the other three regions to cancel it, it went to the Supreme Court (q.v.), asking that, because of the many irregularities in the process of the counting, the court should declare the exercise invalid. But the court refused to accept its plea and so dismissed the case. The figures were finally accepted, and they became the basis for the allocation of seats to the states in the federal legislative houses and the basis for national development planning.

In 1973 the military administration under General Yakubu Gowon (q.v.) carried out another census, but it was more widely rigged than ever before. As such, it generated much debate and hot blood. General Murtala R. Muhammed (q.v.), on his accession to lead the nation in July 1975, announced that it was clear that whatever results were made public for the 1973 population census, they would not command general acceptance throughout the country. The 1973 census was, therefore, cancelled, and the 1963 figures continued to be used for national planning. By 1990 speculations were rife that Nigeria's population was about 100 million people. However, the 1991 census, accepted by President Ibrahim B. Babangida (q.v.) put Nigeria's population at 88.5 million. The president, while accepting the figure, told the nation that it would not be used for political purposes. However, the National Electoral Commission (NEC) (q.v.) did use it in allocating registration cards to the states in 1992 on the basis that only about 45 percent of the population would be of voting age. In spite of the effort put into the census, there were complaints from almost all the states.

The major problem in taking a census in Nigeria is that it has become too politicised—the people have been made to believe that a census is used to allocate seats to their regions or states in the national assembly, and that it is the basis for sharing the national pie—whether at the national, state or local level.

CENTRE FOR THE PROPAGATION OF RELIGIOUS AND ETHNIC TOLERANCE (CENPETO). Set up in July 1991 by the Babangida (q.v.) administration, CENPETO has the task of propagating those values that would unite the people of Nigeria, sensitise the citizens to the positive values of ethnic and religious tolerance, facilitate the permeation of the spirit of oneness among the culturally diverse people of the country and contribute in the long run to the evolution of a new Nigeria rooted in ethnic harmony and religious tolerance. It is a center which the founders hoped would be one of "excellence to dissipate the spectre of fanaticism and bigotry, disseminate what unites them as a people and the positive common denominators, tenets and regulations for the compulsory study of religion and ethnic tolerance from Senior Secondary School (SSS) to the tertiary institutions."

CENTRAL BANK OF NIGERIA (CBN). Established in 1958 with the sole right to issue currency, CBN maintains the country's external reserves, controls commercial banks, safeguards the international value of the naira, promotes monetary stability, administers exchange control in Nigeria and serves as the financial adviser and banker to the Federal Government (q.v.). The bank already has branches in state headquarters like Ibadan (q.v.), Benin (q.v.), Enugu (q.v.), Jos (q.v.), Kaduna (q.v.), Kano (q.v.), Port Harcourt (q.v.), Abeokuta (q.v.), Maiduguri (q.v.), Sokoto (q.v.), and Calabar (q.v.). Under the military administration of President Ibrahim B. Babangida (q.v.) the bank was badly weakened after it was brought under the presidency in 1988, greatly impairing its autonomy. With the promulgation of the CBN Decree of 1991, the bank completely lost its independence. It became not only a unit in the office of the president but it became subject to the legally binding directives of the president. In practical terms, the president became the sole authority for deciding the nation's monetary and banking policy, and for issuing directives for its implementation.

CENTRAL-WEST STATE. The Central-West State was carved out of the former Northern Region (q.v.) in May 1967 and comprised of Kabba and Ilorin (q.v.) provinces. In March 1968, the name of the state was changed to Kwara State. *See also* KWARA STATE.

CHAD. *See* LAKE CHAD.

CHAHA, BENJAMIN AKARI. Speaker, House of Representatives (q.v.), October 1983 to December 1983 during the second term of the Second Republic (q.v.). Born in 1940 at Zaki Biam in Katsina Ala/Ukum, Benue State (q.v.), he was educated at Zaki Biam and later attended Teachers Training College at Mkar from 1952 to 1954 and Higher Teachers College at Gindiri from 1957 to 1958. He later served in many different positions including education officer, supervisor of education, and teacher. In 1978, when the ban on political activities was lifted, he joined the National Party of Nigeria (q.v.) and was elected to the national House of Assembly (q.v.). In 1983, after his reelection into the house, he became the speaker of the house, a post he occupied until December 31, 1983, when the military took over power.

CHERUBIM AND SERAPHIM CHURCH. The church was founded in 1925 by Moses Orimolade, a native of Ikare, Ondo State (q.v.), who was born in 1879.

Members of the church believe in the Holy Spirit and the use of oil and water for healing. They also believe in the significance of dreams and visions, which members consciously seek through prayers and fastings. Visions sanction their major doctrinal positions.

After three days of fasting and prayer for the purpose of choosing a name for the church, a woman claimed she saw the letters "SE," which were later interpreted to stand for Serafu. From then on, members of the church were called "Egbe Serafu," Seraphim Society. Later in the year, after a vision of Holy Michael Archangel was reported, church members added Kerubu (Cherubim) to the name to call it the Cherubim and Seraphim Church.

Though founded in Yorubaland, the church has spread to all parts of the country. Orimolade died in 1933.

CHICK COMMISSION. After the Constitutional Crisis of 1953, there was need for the review of the 1951 Constitution (q.v.). The regions wanted greater autonomy for themselves, and they also began to make demands for fiscal autonomy. Sir Louis Chick was, therefore, appointed as sole commissioner (q.v.) by the secretary of state for the colonies to review the financial effect of the proposed federal constitutional agreement. The commission was to draw up a revenue allocation scheme in which the principle of derivation would be followed to the fullest degree compatible with the needs of the central and regional governments.

The commission proposed that the system already in existence, under which revenue from the sale of tobacco and petrol were allocated to the regions, should be continued. Half of the excise duties on beer should also go to the regions in proportion to their consumption. Also half the net proceeds of export duties should go to the regions of origin of the products. Personal tax should go to the regions where the taxpayer resided. Mining royalties should go to the regions where the minerals were extracted. Regional High Court fees and fines together with fees for licenses on regional matters should go to the regions. Furthermore, one-half of the net proceeds on import duties, with the exclusion of tobacco and petrol, should be given to the regions. It should be divided as follows: 30 percent each to the Eastern (q.v.) and the Northern Regions (q.v.) while the Western Region (q.v.) would have the remaining 40 percent. The regions were to pay the federal government a proportion of the cost of collecting revenues that they shared and the Federal Government (q.v.) was given power to make grants to any regional government that might have financial difficulties arising from circumstances beyond its control.

The recommended principle of derivation was accepted. The west and the north did better under the principle than the east did. The east complained that the commission did not adequately take note of the needs of the centre and the needs of each of the regions.

CHIEF-AND-COUNCIL. Under the 1914 Native Authority (q.v.) Ordinance, which made provisions for the peculiarities of traditional administrative systems existing in the various provinces, the colonial authorities set up two types of native administration in the north: Chief-in-Council and Chief-and-Council. The paramount chief in both cases had to consult with his council on all matters except where the matter was not of much importance or was too urgent to allow for consultation of his council. In such cases he could consult with two members, act and later report to the council on what he had done. A difference arose in that under the Chief-in-Council system, the chief could disagree with the decision of his council and even act contrary to its decision if he believed this to be in the interest of his people. However, he had to make a report of his action to the regional government, which would then assess whether or not his action was justified. On the other hand, under the Chief-and-Council system, the chief could not act contrary to the decision of his council. This type of system was generally associated with areas where chiefs had been "artificially created," i.e., where tradition did not recognise such paramount chieftaincy. The Chief-in-Council system obtained generally where there was a system of traditional paramount chieftaincy like an Emir (q.v.) in his emirate. But where a chief abused his power by misgoverning his people, he could be reduced to a Chief-and-Council to curb such abuses in the future.

During the military regime, most native authorities in the north were reduced to Chief-and-Council system, but in 1976, the two systems were replaced with the local government system when the federal military government came up with its guidelines for the reform of local governments in the country.

CHIEF-IN-COUNCIL. *See* CHIEF-AND-COUNCIL.

CHIEFS. Before the advent of the British colonial authority, most of the peoples of Nigeria were ruled by a Chief, an Oba (king), an Emir (q.v.) or an Obi. The ruler may have military power and in some cases may also claim religious and spiritual power. The position of the chiefs in most societies is hereditary. In some it is limited to some ruling houses, clans, or lineages, and in others it may be by promotion. The system of chieftaincy and the power of chiefs vary from one ethnic group to the other.

Among the Yoruba (q.v.), for example, in every town, the administration is hierarchical from the Oba or Baale at the top to the lowest-ranking chiefs at the bottom. Each town has a number of chiefs who help the Oba in the town's daily administration. There are different kinds of chiefs in each town.

These range from quarter-heads to head messenger. For each quarter of the town, there is a chief who is responsible to the town council. There are war chiefs like the Balogun, ritual chiefs like the Arabs, and so on. The most senior chiefs are the king-makers. The chiefs confer with the Oba on many issues affecting the town. They are also members of the Oba's council, otherwise called town council. They enjoy a great deal of respect within the society.

The powers of the traditional ruler are not unlimited. In most societies, members of the traditional council may have hereditary powers so that the ruler must accommodate them. They may also have power to choose a new ruler or, in some cases, like Oyo in Yorubaland advise the ruler to commit suicide.

The chiefs perform such judicial functions as settling quarrels or disputes that emanate within their area of jurisdiction. However, difficult cases are referred to the paramount chief or the Oba for final arbitration and settlement. It should be noted that during colonial rule, the chiefs were involved in the administration of Nigeria through the indirect rule (q.v.) system. In the north, Emirs or chiefs of various grades functioned as the sole native authorities, and in the west, by 1939, five of the ruling chiefs or Obas had been appointed sole native authorities. In the east the situation was different. Because most people there did not have indigenous, centralized authority like the Hausa (q.v.) or the Yoruba (q.v.), the colonial authorities in pursuance of the system of indirect rule had to appoint what they called "Warrant Chiefs" (q.v.) and gave them great powers. This was resented, and it led to series of crises and riots, especially the Aba Riot (q.v.) in which many people were killed.

Today, in addition to the traditional titleholders described above, politicians, businessmen, professional people and even academicians actively seek to be honored with a chieftaincy title. This title of Honorary Chief is especially sought in the southern part of Nigeria.

CHRISTIAN ASSOCIATION OF NIGERIA (CAN). The most powerful organization representing Christian interest in Nigeria. Formed in 1976, CAN brought together three distinct groups: northern Christians (represented by the Northern Christian Association of Nigeria), southern Catholics (represented by the Catholic Secretariat of Nigeria) and Southern Christians of other denominations (represented by the Christian Council of Nigeria). CAN was created to unify the Christian community and defend its interests. In the late 1970s and 1980s, a number of issues contributed to growing activism on the part of CAN: perceived Muslim domination of the government, the debate over the inclusion of Shari'a law in the constitution, Nigerian membership in the Organization of Islamic Conference and increasingly violent clashes between Christians and Muslims in the northern part of the country.

CHRISTIANITY. The religion and way of life taught by Jesus Christ. Those who believe in Christianity are called Christians, and they belong to one of many denominations, beginning historically from the Catholic Church (q.v.), all the way to today's newest Christian movements.

Christianity had its root in Judaism; for like the Jews, Christians believe there is only one God who is the creator of heaven and earth. They both believe in the ten commandments God gave Moses. Unlike Judaism, however, the essence of Christian belief is in the Creed, which states there is only one God but three persons in one God: God the Father who created everything, God the Son who came down to earth and redeemed humankind from sin and God the Holy Spirit who sanctifies.

Christianity is not just a collection of beliefs and doctrines. The followers of Christ try to follow the examples of Jesus in loving fellow humans. Jesus told his disciples to love one another as he had loved them—not only their friends but even their enemies. Because of this, he taught that his followers should not retaliate. One of the marks by which Christians were known in the early days was how much they loved each other.

All that Christians believe and practise worldwide is carried on among Nigerian Christians. But in Nigeria, as elsewhere, Christianity has many different churches, and new churches are springing up almost every day. There are the orthodox churches like the Roman Catholic Church and the Anglican Church (q.v.), but there are offsprings of these and others, some in protest over European or expatriate cultural and power domination of the churches brought from abroad; and newer ones that claim a Christian "must be born again," a personal experience that happens on a particular day at a particular time. When you have been born again, you receive the gift of the Holy Spirit by speaking in tongues. There are others that are a blend of Christianity and traditional beliefs and religious practices like the Aladura Churches (q.v.), Cherubim and Seraphim Church (q.v.) and the Celestial Church of Christ.

Christianity is very strong in the eastern part of Nigeria and around the Niger Delta. In the western part, it coexists with Islam and traditional religions (q.v.) in a most amicable manner. In the north, where Islam is dominant, conflict between Christians and Muslims have become increasingly politicized and violent.

CHURCH MISSIONARY SOCIETY. The evangelisation of Nigeria by the Church Missionary Society (CMS) first originated in London and in Freetown, Sierra Leone (q.v.), where the church had been active among slaves who had been there since 1787. The church, known in England as the Anglican Church, sent its first missionaries to Nigeria in 1841—Rev. J.F. Schön and Samuel Ajayi Crowther (q.v.). In 1842 Henry Townsend (q.v.) and two freed Yoruba (q.v.) slaves, Andrew Wilhelm and John McCormack, arrived in Badagry (q.v.), Lagos State (q.v.) and moved on to Abeokuta (q.v.), Ogun State (q.v.) to explore the possibility of establishing a mission in the town to cater to the immigrant ex-slaves settling in the city. They arrived in the town in January 1843 and began to work in earnest, building churches, mission houses and schools and opening up the country to Christian missionaries. By 1858 Rev. Crowther had reached Onitsha (q.v.) on the Niger River in Anambra State (q.v.).

In the field of education (q.v.), the church was pioneer and leader. It established primary and secondary schools and teacher training colleges in many parts of the country. The first postsecondary institution, Fourah Bay College (q.v.) in Sierra Leone, which helped greatly in the education of Nigerians, was established by the church in 1827. The church is still growing strong. In 1979 the Anglican Church of Nigeria was carved out of the province of West Africa and became a full-fledged province of Nigeria with its own archbishop.

CIROMA, ALHAJI ADAMU. Born in 1934 in Potiskum in Yobe State (q.v.), Ciroma attended Barewa College (q.v.) from 1950 to 1955, the Nigerian College of Arts, Science and Technology in Zaria (q.v.) from 1957 to 1958 and the University of Ibadan where he graduated in history in 1961. In 1965 he was appointed editor of *New Nigeria* by the Federal Government (q.v.). Without any special training in banking or economics, he was later appointed a director of the Central Bank of Nigeria (q.v.) and subsequently became the governor of the bank in 1975.

During the Second Republic (q.v.), he went into politics, becoming a foundation member of the defunct National Party of Nigeria (q.v.) and the general secretary of the party. In 1978 he contested in the party primary for the party's presidential flag bearer but lost to Alhaji Shehu Shagari (q.v.). Under the Shagari administration, he served as minister in the ministries of industry, finance and agriculture. To usher in the Third Republic (q.v.), he ran as a member of the National Republican Convention (NRC) in the party primary as the party's presidential candidate in 1992, but the primaries were later cancelled by the military president. When General Sani Abacha (q.v.) took over power in 1993, Ciroma became minister of agriculture. Ciroma left this position in 1995.

In 1998, he was a member of both the Group of 18 and the Group of 34, coalitions of politicians opposed to plans by Abacha to remain in power. In

June 1999, Ciroma was selected to serve as minister of finance in the newly elected Obasanjo administration.

CITIZENSHIP. According to the 1979 Second Republican Constitution and the aborted 1989 Third Republican Constitution, the following are Nigerian citizens: Any person born in Nigeria before October 1, 1960, either of whose parents or any of whose grandparents belonged or belongs to a community indigenous to Nigeria; any person born in Nigeria after that date either of whose parents or any of whose grandparents is a citizen of Nigeria and any person born outside Nigeria either of whose parents is a Nigerian.

A woman married to a citizen of Nigeria or any person of full age and capacity born outside Nigeria, any of whose grandparents is a citizen of Nigeria may be registered as a citizen of Nigeria if the president is satisfied that she is a person of good character, with clear intention to be domiciled in Nigeria and takes the oath of allegiance. Furthermore, a person of full age and capacity, who satisfies the above conditions can be a citizen of Nigeria by naturalization if the governor of the state where he or she lives believes that such a person is acceptable to the local community, he or she has made or is capable of making useful contribution to the progress and well being of the country and has immediately preceeding the date of application either resided continuously in Nigeria for a period of 15 years or has resided in Nigeria continuously for a period of 12 months, and during the period of 20 years immediately preceeding that period of 12 months has resided in Nigeria for periods amounting in the aggregate to not less than 15 years. A person with dual citizenship, i.e., a citizen of Nigeria by birth who is also a citizen of another country, does not forfeit his Nigeria citizenship if when he attains the age of 21 years he renounces the citizenship or nationality of the other country.

In 1993 the government announced that Nigerians with dual nationalities did not have to renounce their foreign nationality. But no law was immediately made to back up the announcement.

CITIZENS' COMMITTEE FOR INDEPENDENCE. The Citizens' Committee for Independence was formed in Lagos (q.v.) in 1956. It was a small group of intellectuals and professionals like Chief R.O.A. Akinjide (q.v.), a lawyer, Eme O. Awa, a lecturer, D.A. Badejo, an engineer, H.A. Oluwasanmi (q.v.), a lecturer and A.B. Fafunwa, then a businessman. The committee published a pamphlet entitled "Forward to Freedom" in 1957 and distributed a free copy to the Nigerian delegates going to the 1957 Constitutional Conference (q.v.) in London. The group asked for the creation of more states in the country based on the old provinces so as to place the new Federation of Nigeria (q.v.) on a more harmonious basis to make for national unity. In the pamphlet, the committee also asked that the Federal Government (q.v.) have residual powers and that when allocating revenue, need should have greater weight than derivation. Furthermore, they asked that primary, secondary and technical education (q.v.) in the nation should be funded by the Federal Government.

CIVIL LIBERTIES ORGANISATION. The Civil Liberties Organisation (CLO), founded in October 1987 with headquarters in Lagos (q.v.), is a nongovernmental, nonpolitical human rights group. Its objectives are to promote the principles and practice of fundamental human rights (q.v.) in Nigeria, monitor conditions of human rights and civil liberties, issue reports on the state of these rights and liberties and provide legal aid when a breach of these rights occurs. The organisation has helped to raise public consciousness over the issue of human rights and has repeatedly drawn the government's attention to lapses in its human rights policy. It is particularly noteworthy that the CLO has championed the cause of many citizens who have been held in custody for many years without trial, securing freedom for some of them. The organisation has provided legal services to many poor persons who, ordinarily, would never have been able to pay their expenses in obtaining a fair trial. Besides other books, the organisation publishes the *Annual Report on Human Rights in Nigeria.*

CIVIL WAR. The Nigerian Civil War came about mainly as a result of ethnic suspicion and leadership tussle. In the first place, the Hausa (q.v.) and Fulani (q.v.) peoples saw the January 15, 1966, coup as a plot by the Igbo (q.v.) to dominate the country. The reactions of the northerners toward the January 15 coup led to a countercoup on July 29, 1966, which was led by the northern military officers. Many high-ranking Igbo officers were killed, including the supreme commander of the Armed Forces (q.v.) and head of the national military government, Major General J.T.U. Aguiyi-Itronsi (q.v.) who was an Igbo. Also, many civilians who were Igbo were murdered in Kano (q.v.) and Kaduna (q.v.). All this made the Igbo feel that they were victims of genocide. The Igbo then felt that they could no longer be secure within the Federation of Nigeria (q.v.). Also, General Y. Gowan (q.v.), who emerged as the nation's leader after the second coup of July 1966, was unacceptable to Lt. Col. Odumegu Ojukwu (q.v.) who was then the military governor of Eastern Nigeria (q.v.). According to him, there were officers superior to Gowon, and, as such, he would not agree to Gowon's leadership.

On January 4, 1967, Ghana's head of state, General Ankara, organised a reconciliation meeting between the Federal Government (q.v.) and the Eastern Region at Aburi, Ghana (q.v.). But the meeting failed to end the crisis because the resolutions reached at the meeting were interpreted differently by both parties.

On April 1, 1967, Ojukwu announced that all revenues due from any source whatsoever in Eastern Nigeria which were being collected for or on behalf of the Federal Government would be paid to the government of Eastern Nigeria. This edict also empowered the Eastern Regional government to take over all the Federal Government departments and statutory corporations situated in the region. The Federal Government reacted by suspending all flights between all parts of Nigeria and the Eastern Region and ordered the blockade of all the ports in the east. Furthermore, postal services to the east were grounded.

On May 27, 1967, General Yakubu Gowon declared a state of emergency throughout the federation and announced the division of Nigeria into 12 states. On May 30, 1967, Lt. Col. Ojukwu proclaimed the independent Republic of Biafra (q.v.) on the grounds that the people of Eastern Nigeria believed that they could no longer be protected in their lives and property by any government based outside Eastern Nigeria.

The Federal Government described the action of the Eastern Regional government as a rebellion and promised to crush it. On July 6, 1967, fighting broke out. The Federal Government described it as a "police action" against Ojukwu's act of rebellion. The end of the war, however, came on January 12, 1970, when Lt. Col. Effiong announced the surrender of Biafra, after Lt. Col. Ojukwu had fled the country. On the second day General Gowon accepted the surrender of the Biafran soldiers and promised amnesty for secessionist supporters.

During the war many efforts were made to reconcile the two sides. There was the Kampala Peace Talks (q.v.) of May 23 to 31, 1968, the Niamey meeting between July 16th and 26th of 1968, and the Addis Ababa talk of August 5th to 13th, 1968. All these meetings did not yield any appreciable success. Biafra put up a strong propaganda effort to achieve international recognition, but only five countries—Tanzania, Gabon, Ivory Coast and Zambia in Africa and the Republic of Haiti—recognized her.

CLAPPERTON, HUGH. Born in Scotland, in 1788, he was one of the leading pioneering explorers of the interior of Africa for the purpose of opening up trade with the people of the area. He together with Major Dixon Denham and Dr. Oudney left for Nigeria from Tripoli across the Sahara in 1821. They arrived at Lake Chad (q.v.) in 1823, and from there they went to Bornu (q.v.) where they were received by Al-Kanemi (q.v.). From there they went to Kano (q.v.), and later to Sokoto (q.v.) where Sultan Muhammah Bello (q.v.) received them well and expressed desire to establish a commercial relationship with Britain. Clapperton then returned to England. The report made the government equip another expedition led by Clapperton with the object of reaching the interior from the sea through the Niger River (q.v.).

When he got to the coast, he did not discover the port which the Sultan Bello had told him would lead him up the Niger River, and so he decided to go by foot from Badagry (q.v.) to Sokoto. Upon arrival in Sokoto, he saw that the attitude of the Sultan to him had changed. He soon fell ill and died in 1827.

CLARK, PROF. JOB PEPPER. A dramatist, poet, and literary critic, Clark was born April 6, 1935, in Kiagbodo, western Ijaw (q.v.) Delta State (q.v.). He was educated at Government College in Ughelli from 1948 to 1954, University College, Ibadan (now University of Ibadan [q.v.]) from 1956 to 1960 and Princeton University in the United States from 1962 to 1963. On arrival in Nigeria, he was appointed information officer for the Federal Ministry of Information in Lagos (q.v.), and later taught in the University of Ibadan and University of Lagos, where he became a professor in 1972.

He has written many plays and poems, including *Poems* (1962), *America, Their America* (1964), *Three Plays: Song of a Goat, The Raft, Masquerade* (1966), *A Reed in the Tide* (1965), *Ozidi* (1966), *Casualties* (1970), *The Examples of Shakespeare* (1970), *The Ozidi Saga* (1976) and *The State of the Union: Return to Dear Native Land* (1988).

CLIFFORD CONSTITUTION. Sir Hugh Charles Clifford (1886–1941) was Governor of Nigeria from 1913 to 1925. The Clifford Constitution came in 1922 as a result of strong pressure from organisations like the National Congress of British West Africa (q.v.) for greater representation in the Legislative Council (q.v.). Under the constitution there was a Legislative Council for the Colony of Lagos (q.v.) and the Protectorate of Nigeria made up of 46 members, 27 of whom were officials and 19 unofficials. Out of the 19 unofficial members, 15 were nominated by the governor while four were elected on the basis of three members to represent Lagos, the capital, and one to represent Calabar (q.v.). The Legislative Council legislated for the colony and the southern provinces while the governor extended parts of the legislation that were relevant to the northern provinces by proclamations. What the country generally had in common was the whole country's annual budget. In addition to the Legislative Council, there was an Executive Council (q.v.), which was an advisory body to the governor. The Executive Council was composed of officials who were all expatriates since there were no African principal officials or heads of departments at the time. The constitution was remarkable for one thing: its introduction of the elective principle into the composition of the Legislative Council. However, the exclusion of the northern provinces from its overall authority helped to exacerbate the north-south dichotomy.

CLIMATE. *See* GEOGRAPHY AND CLIMATE.

COAT OF ARMS. The coat of arms has an eagle mounted on a shield bisected by two wavy silver bands. Two white chargers support the shield. The base of the shield is a wreath of flowers. The black shield represents Nigeria's fertile soil, and the wavy silver bands are the rivers Niger and Benue. The eagle stands for the country's strength, while the chargers are Nigeria's symbol of dignity. The wreath depicts the national colors of green and white. The motto beneath all is "Unity and Faith."

COCOA. Cocoa was introduced into Nigeria in the 19th century, and for many years Nigeria was second only to Ghana (q.v.) as a cocoa-producing and exporting country. Today Nigeria is the third-largest producer of cocoa in the world with Côte d'Ivoire and Ghana being first and second, respectively.

The cocoa tree is a tropical plant that grows best south or north of the equator where the temperature is about 27°C. It requires a moderate rainfall of between 1,140 to 1,500 millimetres and grows best on soils with a high clay content. In 1965 Nigeria produced almost one-quarter of all the world's total, but this production level rapidly fell, partly due to the aging of the trees and failure to replace them with new ones. Cultivated varieties must be replaced after about 30 years. Production slumps were also partly due to the oil boom in the 1970s, which drove farmers away from their farms to the cities where they could earn high wages in construction and other jobs.

In the second half of the 1980s, the administration of General Ibrahim B. Babangida (q.v.) dismantled the Commodity Boards (q.v.) as part of its International Monetary Fund–inspired deregulation and structural adjustment programme (SAP) (q.v.). Its effect on the national currency, the naira, quickly raised the price of cocoa beans locally, and production began to move up. But, in the 1990s, as a result of ecological problems and increased cost of production, production has begun to fall. In the late 1980s, production rose to 256,000 tons, but it fell to 221,000 tons in 1990 and to 180,000 in 1991. In spite of this, however, cocoa still remains the country's largest nonoil foreign exchange earner. Cocoa is grown mostly in the states of Ondo (q.v.), Oyo (q.v.), Ogun (q.v.) and Osun (q.v.).

COCOA MARKETING BOARD. The board was established in 1947 for the purpose of controlling all exports of cocoa. The establishment of the board removed the purchase of cocoa from the West African Produce Control Board. The board was to recommend the fixed price of cocoa to the government. The board was dissolved in 1954 when the Western Nigeria Marketing Board (q.v.) was established to take charge of the purchase of cocoa and other agricultural produce in the region.

CODE OF CONDUCT BUREAU. Established under the Second Republic's (q.v.) constitution, this bureau received declarations by public officers within three months of their taking office, at the end of every four years in office, and at the end of the term of office. The officers' conduct concerned all properties, assets and liabilities, and those of a spouse or unmarried child under the age of 21 years.

The bureau retains custody of such declarations and makes them available for inspection by any Nigerian citizen on such terms as the National Assembly might prescribe. It also receives complaints about noncompliance with or breach of the code. The bureau is comprised of a chairman and nine members, appointed by the President but subject to the approval of the Senate.

The Code of Conduct Bureau was unable to prevent rampant corruption during the Second Republic (q.v.).

COKER COMMISSION OF INQUIRY. Set up by the Federal Government in June 1962 after a state of emergency had been declared in the Western Region (q.v.), its purpose was to look into the affairs of certain statutory corporations in Western Nigeria. The chairman of the commission was Justice G.B.A. Coker.

The report of the commission was a serious indictment of the Action Group Party (AG) (q.v.) administration of the region. The commission found that the National Bank (q.v.) owned by the government of the region made unsecured loans to the AG through the medium of fictitious accounts, and that on one occasion it concealed the actual indebtedness of the party to the bank from federal government examiners. Further still, it found that the National Investment and Properties Company Limited (NIPC)—created in 1958 apparently to develop properties owned by the National Bank—was, in fact, owned by four leading members of the AG, who also happened to be its directors. However, the chief purpose the company served was to subscribe or guarantee money for charitable political causes. The commission found that the shares held by the four directors were purchased with funds diverted from the company itself.

The company borrowed freely from the Western Nigeria Marketing Board (q.v.) which had the responsibility of purchasing export crops from farmers at stabilised prices for sale abroad and was empowered to supply capital to statutory corporations in an effort to further the economic development of the region. The company received from the board over £2 million allocated to the Western Development Corporation by the board had also been diverted to the NIPC and that the NIPC was making great profit over the sale of property to the Western Regional government at inflated prices.

On March 17, 1963, the Western Nigerian government announced that it would acquire for public purposes all property owned by the NIPC in the region, in accordance with the recommendation of the commission.

COLONIAL DEVELOPMENT CORPORATION. The corporation was created by the United Kingdom's Overseas Resources Development Act of 1948. Its purpose was to formulate and carry out projects for the development of the colonial resources. The corporation played a significant role in the development of Nigeria: it invested in engineering, industry, housing development and sawmills. It permitted and encouraged participation by commercial firms and by the government and its agencies so that these could eventually assume full responsibility for them.

COLONIZATION. With the abolition of the slave trade (q.v.), the intensification in the search for legitimate trade, and the increased growth of the palm oil trade, the British government in 1849 appointed John Beecroft (q.v.) as the consul for the Bight of Benin (q.v.) and Bonny (q.v.), with the task of regulating commercial relations with the coastal people. However, Beecroft was not satisfied with such a modest assignment; he began to interfere in the internal affairs of the coastal states and, backed by British gunboats, he began the process that finally led to the imposition of British colonial rule on the whole of the country. In 1861, as a result of the internal conflicts in Lagos (q.v.) and the pressure brought to bear on the British authorities by commercial and missionary interests, the British acquired Lagos Island by cession and proclaimed it a Crown colony (q.v.). From there the British moved to the hinterland.

Because of the pressure of competition brought to bear on the British by the French and the Germans in the area, the British government abandoned its earlier policy not to expand its colonial possessions in the area. Thus, through the initiative of the United African Company (UAC) (q.v.), formed by George T. Goldie (q.v.) by the amalgamation of a number of British firms in 1879, to secure trading rights in parts of the country that subsequently became Northern Nigeria (q.v.), Nigeria was recognized as within the British sphere of influence during the Berlin Conference (q.v.) of 1885. In 1886 the UAC received a royal charter to administer the territory, but, in 1899, the charter was revoked and the British government began to directly administer it under the name "Protectorate of Northern Nigeria (q.v.)."

Similarly, in 1885, the delta area of the country was proclaimed the Oil Rivers Protectorate (q.v.) after local rulers and the British consular officials signed many treaties. In 1893 the protectorate had been extended inland and was then known as the Niger Coast Protectorate (q.v.). In 1906 Lagos Colony was merged with this protectorate and became known as the Colony and Protectorate of Southern Nigeria. In 1914 the two British administrations, the Protectorate of Northern Nigeria and the Colony and Protectorate of Southern Nigeria, were merged to form a single entity known as Nigeria under British rule. British rule ended on October 1, 1960.

COLONY AND PROTECTORATE OF SOUTHERN NIGERIA. *See* PROTECTORATE.

***COMET*, THE.** On July 14, 1933, Duse Mohammed Ali, an Egyptian internationalist, launched his weekly *Comet,* which Nnamdi Azikiwe (q.v.) acquired in 1945 and turned into a daily newspaper. The paper, which was then published in Lagos (q.v.), was transferred to Kano (q.v.), making it the first daily newspaper in Northern Nigeria (q.v.).

COMMANDER OF THE FAITHFUL. *See* EMIRATE SYSTEM.

COMMISSIONER. The term *commissioner* has been used to refer to the occupier of different offices in the history of Nigeria. It referred to the administrative head of each of the Northern and Southern protectorates (q.v.) (1900–09), and under Sir Donald Cameron (q.v.) (1931–35). In this sense it is equivalent to a lieutenant governor (q.v.), which the head of each unit was called from 1909 to 1931. It has also referred to political appointees like commissioners of native courts and provincial commissioners. Under the military administration, a civil commissioner was a civilian member of the military cabinet known then as the Executive Council (q.v.). Under the 1979 Constitution (q.v.), a commissioner was a political appointee of the state governor and a member of the governor's cabinet. The term can also refer to a member of a federal or state commission, be it an ad hoc commission, as a commission of inquiry, or a full-time commission, as the Public Service Commission. *See also* COMMISSIONER, CIVIL.

COMMISSIONER, CIVIL. After one-and-a-half years of military rule, the Supreme Military Council (q.v.) decided in July 1967 to invite civilians as full members of the federal and state Executive Councils (q.v.) (cabinet). These civilians were called civil commissioners to distinguish them from military men who were also members of the executive councils.

Even though they were supposed to be in charge of the ministries just as ministers used to be under the First Republic (q.v.), their effectiveness was very limited. Many of them suffered from what may be called a crisis of identity: they were neither military men who naturally belonged in a military administration nor civil servants without whom the military could not function. Their position depended on the fiat of the governor or the Head of State. Because they could not effectively supervise the activities of the civil servants, their effectiveness gradually waned.

COMMISSIONERS, DISTRICT. Colonial administrative officers appointed to be president of native councils and performing many other administrative duties. For many years before the amalgamation of Nigeria in 1914 (q.v.) the former Eastern Nigeria (q.v.) and Mid-Western Nigeria (q.v.) were subject to direct administration by the so-called native councils, which were native courts (q.v.) with legislative, executive and judicial powers. The council was generally made up of influential members selected from the various communities in each area. The British then appointed a district commissioner to each of the native councils as president and chairman. However, when Lord Lugard (q.v.) introduced the indirect rule (q.v.) system to the area, believing that native courts should really be native, he removed the district commissioners from the chairmanship of the native councils and appointed warrant chiefs (q.v.), hand-picked from the community without caring about their acceptability to the people, as chairmen of the councils. The councils were then under the supervision of the district officers (q.v.) who replaced the district commissioners.

COMMODITY BOARDS. Following state creation (q.v.) in Nigeria, the reorganisation of the various states' marketing boards became a pressing problem, more so since the increasing expenses and administrative overheads of each board eroded the income of the farmers. Many feared the erosion would be worse if each state had its own marketing board. The military government, therefore, in 1976 set up a committee to study the operation of the state marketing boards system and the Nigerian Produce Marketing Company. Following the report of the committee, the government began a thorough reorganisation of the system on a nationwide basis. The government set up a new commodity marketing system made up of a price-fixing authority and seven commodity boards, each responsible for different commodities—cocoa (q.v.), groundnut (q.v.), cotton, palm produce, rubber (q.v.), grains and root crops. The objective of the new boards was not only to market raw materials for the world market as previously done but, more important, to encourage the production of the commodities and organize the marketing of such commodities for local consumption and local processing, with maximum benefit to the farmers. As a result of this reorganisation, the Nigerian Produce Marketing Company and the then-existing state marketing boards were phased out in 1977. The commodity boards were dissolved in 1986 as part of the government's deregulation of the economy.

COMMON SERVICES. When Nigeria was divided into 12 states in 1967, there came the problem of sharing the assets and liabilities of the former Eastern (q.v.) and Northern Regions (q.v.) by the new states. To solve the problem, the federal military government promulgated two decrees establishing agencies that could take care of these assets and liabilities.

The first decree was the Decree Number 12 of 1968, which established for the Northern Region the Interim Common Services Agency to take care of the assets and liabilities of the former Northern Region, which was then divided into six states. According to the decree, the agency consisted of one person from each of the six states of the former region appointed by the head of the federal military government. The chairman was to be appointed by the members from amongst their members. The agency was charged with the control, operation and general management of the services, statutory bodies and institution, jointly owned by the states which were inherited from the former Northern Region. It was empowered to dispose of property that it no longer required on such terms as it thought fit; to erect, provide, equip and maintain and keep in repair buildings necessary for carrying out its duties and invest its funds in government securities in Nigeria or in any other manner approved by the agency.

Among the services, institutions and statutory bodies that were vested in the agency were Ahmadu Bello University and its affiliated schools and services, Advanced Teachers Colleges in Kano (q.v.) and Zaria (q.v.), Government Press in Kaduna (q.v.), Sharia (q.v.) Court of Appeal, Kaduna Polytechnic, Livestock and Meat Authority, Northern Nigeria Housing Corporation, Northern Nigeria Marketing Board (q.v.) and the Northern Nigeria Radio Corporation. The agency was dissolved in 1976 with the promulgation of Decree Number 19 of 1975. The decree ended the term of the Agency on March 31, 1976.

The second decree on the Common Services was promulgated in 1970 and titled "Eastern States Interim Assets and Liabilities Agency Decree 1970." It was Decree Number 39 of 1970. According to the decree, the agency consisted of the military governors of South-Eastern State (q.v.) and Rivers State (q.v.) together with the administrator of East-Central State (q.v.). The office of chairman of the agency was to be held by each member in rotation for such periods as members might agree among themselves. All the assets and liabilities of the former Eastern Region, which were vested in the agency in trust for the Eastern states, included statutory corporations established by law for the former region of Eastern Nigeria, the University of Nigeria, Nsukka (q.v.), former government-controlled limited liability companies and those jointly owned by the former government and any person—corporate or incorporate.

COMMONWEALTH. An association of countries, including the United Kingdom, which were once ruled by Great Britain before they each became independent. About one-quarter of the world's population live in the countries of the Commonwealth. The Commonwealth countries' historical background has left them with many similar political and social organisations and, in most cases, trade links. It is their interest to preserve these advantages and their common interest in peace, economic development and political cooperation.

The prime ministers of the Commonwealth countries discuss such matters of interest to the organisation as trade, scientific cooperation and defence at conferences. Each member is sovereign, and, as such, no member or group of members can force other members to follow certain policies or rules. The members have no definite duties to one other, and they have no central government or military force. A secretariat and a secretary general work to increase understanding and cooperation between members, especially in politics, economics and technical development. Some developing member countries received economic and other kinds of aid from the developed members. There is also cooperation in technical development, agriculture, medicine, and education.

When Nigeria became independent in 1960, it became a member of the Commonwealth. Nigerian membership in the Commonwealth was suspended in November 1995 as a result of human rights abuses, particularly the execution of the writer and Ogoni Rights activist Ken Saro-Wiwa (q.v.). Lobbying by representatives of the Nigerian government narrowly thwarted the imposition of sanctions by the Commonwealth in June 1996. Following the assumption of power by the democratically elected regime of Olusegun Obasanjo (q.v.) in May 1999, the suspension was lifted.

COMMUNITY BANKS. Established in 1991 by the federal military government of President Ibrahim B. Babangida (q.v.) to cater to the needs of the informal sector and the rural population. It was to further strengthen the People's Bank of Nigeria (q.v.) and encourage small-scale businesses and artisans who would have difficulties in obtaining credit from conventional banks. The banks are community owned because the majority of the shares are owned by the people within the community. By the end of 1992, 401 such banks were operating in various communities all over the nation. Their loans and advances have reflected their initial orientation toward rural activities and small enterprises. Agriculture and petty trading in 1992 received a large sum of their loan facilities, followed by small restaurant businesses and cottage industries. Some amount was also lent to small-scale manufacturing enterprises and transportation. By early 1995, the number of the banks had risen to 970.

COMMUNITY TAX. Receipts from the community tax, formerly called Haraji in the north where it was in practice, paid persons who were not salary earners, including those whose income did not exceed N800 per year. In some places, the tax was a flat rate for all, but in others, a fixed amount was levied on a community or village, and the community or village head would decide how much each taxpayer would pay. Under the British, the Native Authority (q.v.) kept seven-eighths of the tax collected, and the British government received the rest.

CONSENSUS GOVERNMENT. *See* NATIONAL GOVERNMENT.

CONSOLIDATED REVENUE FUND. The Consolidated Revenue Fund consists of all revenues or monies that have not been otherwise provided for by the constitution (q.v.) but which are raised, collected or paid into the coffers of the Federal Government (q.v.). The fund represents the largest bulk of all the monies available to the Federal Government and, as such, almost all government expenditures are drawn from it. However, it is a special fund since no money can be drawn from it except to meet expenditures charged upon it by the constitution. Some public officers whose salaries are charged to it include the president and the vice president, justices of the Supreme Court (q.v.), Court of Appeal and the Federal High Court, along with all expenditures of the federation's judicial officers and chairmen and members of certain federal commissions such as the Civil Service Commission, the National Electoral Commission (q.v.), the Police Service Commission (q.v.) and the National Population Commission. All other government expenditures must be authorized by the Appropriation Act of the National Assembly. Each state of the Federation (q.v.) also has a consolidated revenue fund, and it is operated just like the Federation's.

CONSTITUENCY DELIMITATION COMMISSION. At the 1957 constitutional conference (q.v.), agreement was reached that the country should be divided into 320 single-member constituencies for the purpose of federal elections, based on about one member to 100,000 people. As such, a Delimitation Commission headed by Lord Merthyr, a deputy speaker of the House of Lords, was appointed. The commission recommended 174 seats to the Northern Region (q.v.), 73 seats to the Eastern Region (q.v.), 62 seats to the Western Region (q.v.), 8 seats to the Cameroons (q.v.) and 3 seats to Lagos (q.v.).

CONSTITUENT ASSEMBLY. On September 14, 1976, the Constitution Drafting Committee (CDC) (q.v.) submitted its report and on October 7, 1976, the Constituent Assembly was set up to receive and collate comments from the public on the draft constitution and, in the light of these, revise the draft. The assembly was made up of 203 elected members. Each state had five members on the basis of equality, while the remaining seats were computed on the basis of population. Members of the assembly were elected by the various local government councils, which constituted themselves into electoral colleges. In addition to the elected members, 20 other members were appointed to the assembly to represent interests that were inadequately represented through the election process. These included women, labor, commerce, press, education, students, public servants and traditional rulers. Justice Udo Udoma, a judge of the Supreme Court (q.v.) of Nigeria was appointed chairman of the assembly by the Supreme Military Council (q.v.) on September 11, 1977. When the assembly met on October 6, 1977, it totalled 230 elected and nominated members. On August 29, 1978, after 11 months of open debate, it submitted its report and was then formally dissolved. In 1987, during the transition to civilian rule, there was another constituent assembly that put finishing touches to the draft of the Third Republic's (q.v.) Constitution. The constitution was never adopted, however.

CONSTITUTIONS. Nigeria has gone through a long and tedious route in constitution making. There was the Clifford Constitution (q.v.) of 1922, the Richards Constitution (q.v.) of 1946, the Macpherson Constitution (q.v.) of 1951, the Lyttelton Constitution (q.v.) of 1954—each progressively made certain concessions to nationalist demands—and finally before independence, the Independence (q.v.) Constitution, which conceded full sovereignty to Nigeria.

The Independence Constitution followed very closely the British constitution in that it was parliamentary, but unlike the British, the Nigerian constitution was written. At the time of independence in 1960, Nigeria was a federation of three regions. The Head of State was the governor-general (q.v.) who was ceremonial head and represented the Queen of the United Kingdom. There was the prime minister, the leader of the majority party or coalition in Parliament, who was responsible for the national government and who appointed members of his cabinet, which was collectively responsible to the Parliament. Parliament, which was under a firm control of the majority party or coalition, was said to be supreme. In 1963 the country became a republic. The only major change to the Independence Constitution was that the Head of State was no longer the governor-general but the president, who still was a ceremonial head as before.

In 1966, following the military takeover, much of the Republican Constitution was suspended, but in 1979 a new constitution, the Second Republican Constitution, was adopted. This constitution set up an executive presidential form of government. The president was popularly elected for a term of four years and could serve for only a second term. The president appointed his cabinet members with the approval of the Senate (q.v.). Members of the cabinet were not members of the legislative assembly, which was made up of the Senate and a House of Representatives (q.v.). The constitution guaranteed individual freedom of thought, conscience, association, movement, and expression. After the 1983 military coup d'état (q.v.), parts of the constitution were suspended and other parts could be amended by decrees. The Third Republican Constitution, which should have been in effect in 1989, never was adopted because the June 12, 1993, presidential election (which would have ushered in the constitution) was annulled by General Ibrahim

B. Babangida (q.v.). In 1994 the military government of General Sani Abacha (q.v.) set up a new constitutional conference (q.v.), again to fashion a new constitution. The conference reported in 1995 and recommended a rotational power sharing as a way to reduce tension and the southern fear of northern domination of the political life of the country. The military government accepted the recommendation and decreed that it would apply to all levels of government, with the hope that all segments of society would feel a sense of belonging. The government also endorsed a modified presidential system in which six key executive and legislative offices would be zoned and rotated between six identifiable geographical groupings. The country would be grouped into northeast, northwest, middle-belt, southwest, southeast and southern minority. The offices that would be rotated were those of president, vice president, prime minister, deputy prime minister, Senate president and speaker of the House of Representatives.

By the time of Sani Abacha's death in 1998, the 1995 draft constitution had still not been released to the public and had become somewhat controversial due to the belief that it had been altered to serve the late leader's personal ambitions. In order to address these concerns, the regime of Abdulsalami Abubakar inaugurated the Constitutional Debate Coordinating Committee (CDCC) under the leadership of Justice Niki Tobi on November 11, 1998. The CDCC submitted its report to the military government on December 30, 1998. These recommendations were debated by the military Provisional Ruling Council (PRC), and the constitution that would serve as the basis of the Fourth Republic was belatedly released on May 5, 1999. The new document closely resembled the 1979 constitution in that it retained a presidential system of government, with a separate bicameral legislature and a federal devolution of power to the states. As in the Second Republic, Shari'a law was not imposed throughout the country, but was left as an option for any state that chose to administer it. The recommendation of the 1995 constitution for the zoning and rotation of offices was rejected. In addition, a new principle of derivation was adopted that would allow the oil producing areas to keep 13 percent of the oil revenues generated from their states. This was enacted to address the ongoing unrest in the Niger Delta region of the country. Because of the heavy role the military played in drafting this constitution, it lacked the legitimacy of the constitutions of earlier republics.

CONSTITUTIONAL CONFERENCES. The calling of constitutional conferences was the British government's method of soliciting public opinion from their overseas territories about the kind of government they would like. In the constitutional history of Nigeria, there were many such conferences.

The first took place in Ibadan (q.v.), capital of the Western Region (q.v.), to review the Richards Constitution (q.v.) which was strongly criticized for lack of consultation with the people before it was drawn up. Sir John Macpherson (q.v.) decided that full consultation should be made in its review. The procedure for its review involved village meetings, provincial conferences, regional conferences and, finally, the general conference which was composed of all unofficial members of the Legislative Council (q.v.) together with additional representatives of the regional conferences and the Colony and Lagos conference. The general conference agreed on a number of issues that were incorporated into the Macpherson Constitution (q.v.) of 1951.

The Macpherson Constitution, however, was not destined to last, for in its operation, many unforeseen problems, like the Eastern Regional Government Crisis (q.v.) of 1953, cropped up. As such, there was need for another review of the constitution. The secretary of state for the colonies announced the Macpherson Constitution would be redrawn to provide for greater regional autonomy and for the removal of powers of intervention by the center. He, therefore, invited Nigerians to come to London for a constitutional conference. The conference met in London from July 30 to August 22, 1953, under the chairmanship of the secretary of state for the colonies, Lord Chandos, to consider the defects of the Macpherson Constitution, changes that would be required to remedy the defects, steps that would be taken to put the changes into effect and the question of self-government in 1956. Before the conference adjourned, it agreed to reconvene in Lagos (q.v.) in January 1954 to consider the advice of fiscal commissioner Sir Louis Chick, appointed by the colonial secretary with regard to the allocation of financial resources to the regions and the central government. The 1953 conference agreed on a federal system of government with residual powers in the hands of the regions. It agreed that the regions should be more independent of the centre. It drew up a list of specific functions to be allocated to the centre and a concurrent list. It also agreed on neutralizing Lagos, the capital city, instead of merging it with the west. On the question of self-government, the British government agreed to grant any region self-government on regional matters in 1956.

On January 19, 1954, there was the Lagos Conference, which could be regarded as a continuation of the 1953 London Conference. The conference reached decisions on fiscal agreement under the new constitution, regionalisation of the public services and the judiciary and on granting a quasi-federal status to Southern Cameroon.

In 1957 there was another constitutional conference in London. It took place from May 23 to June 26. It was attended by all political parties and chaired by the secretary of state for the colonies, Mr. Lennox-Boyd. This conference agreed on a Senate (q.v.) for the federal Parliament and the enlargement of the House of Representatives (q.v.) to 320 members. The position of the chief secretary was to be abolished. There was to be a House of Chiefs (q.v.) for the Eastern Region (q.v.) and the Southern Cameroon, and an all-African Executive Council (q.v.) for both the Eastern and the Western Regions. It agreed on setting up an independent civil service commission, the retention of the police as a federal subject and on setting up commissions of inquiry to look into the fears of minorities, and on revenue allocation. It agreed on the Western and Eastern Regions becoming self-governing that year, provided they would do nothing to prejudice the functions of the Federal Government (q.v.). The governor was to appoint as premier the person who appeared to him to command a majority in the House of Assembly (q.v.) and the Queen's power to disallow regional legislation was to remain. Southern Cameroon (q.v.) was to be raised to the status of a region. The Northern Region (q.v.) was to be self-governing in 1959, and election to the federal legislature was to be by universal adult suffrage in the Eastern and Western regions, and the Southern Cameroon, while it was to be by adult male suffrage in the Northern Region. There was also agreement that the office of the prime minister for the Federation of Nigeria (q.v.) should be created and the governor-general (q.v.) was to appoint as prime minister any member who appeared to him to command a majority in the House of Representatives. Before the conference closed, the secretary of state said that if a new Nigerian parliament to be elected in 1959 would pass a resolution asking for independence on a date in 1960, the British government would do its best to implement it.

In 1958 another constitutional conference was held in London from September 29 until October 27 to consider the reports of the Fiscal (q.v.) and Minorities Commissions (q.v.) appointed in 1957 and other outstanding matters from the previous constitutional conferences. It was also to discuss the request for independence which Nigerian delegates were making to the British government at the 1957 conference.

The conference made decisions on matters like the inclusion of fundamental human rights (q.v.) in the constitution, the police, self-government for Northern Nigeria, the position of Lagos, the position of Southern Cameroon, electoral arrangements, fiscal arrangements, the minorities problems (q.v.), Nigerian independence and other pertinent matters. There was to be a single police force under an inspector-general of police responsible to the Federal Government, but each regional contingent was to be under the control of a commissioner who, though under the general supervision of the inspector-general of police, would be responsible for the recruitment of the force under his charge within the region. The conference accepted the main recommendations of the fiscal commission chaired by Sir Jeremy Raisman. It also agreed on a uniform set of electoral qualifications for all future elections to the regional houses of assembly and the federal House of Representatives.

On state creation (q.v.), the conference, rather than throw away the opportunity to become independent in 1960 agreed to accept the Minorities Commission's report that there was no need to create new states. With this accepted, the colonial secretary announced the willingness of Her Majesty's government to grant full independence to Nigeria on October 1, 1960.

The final Nigerian constitutional conference under the colonial administration opened in London from May 10 to May 19, 1960. The conference authorized a committee of legal draughtsmen to submit a draft of the Independence Constitution to the conference for approval. There was agreement on military cooperation between Britain and Nigeria, which would be of mutual advantage to both countries, and it was agreed that, if Northern Cameroon joined Nigeria, it would form part of the Northern Region, but if Southern Cameroon joined, it would have the status of a fully self-governing region like other regions in the federation.

In 1993, after the annulment of the results of June 12, 1993, presidential election (q.v.), and the court declaration in November that the Interim National Government (q.v.) under Chief Ernest A.O. Shonekan (q.v.) was illegal, General Sani Abacha (q.v.) overthrew the Shonekan administration and installed himself as Head of State. In his effort to garner support for his tottering administration, he moved quickly to give apparent support for a national sovereign conference which many vocal people had been asking for to reorder the nation's priorities and reorganise its power structure. Many people interpreted the national constitutional conference as a national sovereign conference. The conference began in 1994 and lasted until 1995. Its purpose was to write a new constitution for Nigeria. In its report the conference recommended the principle of rotation of important government positions as a way of alleviating the fear of northern domination of the public life of the country strongly held by the people in the south. The government accepted the recommendation.

CONSTITUTIONAL REVIEW STUDY GROUP. This group was set up in March 1966 by General Aguiyi-Ironsi (q.v.), the first military Head of State. It had a membership of 10 under Chief F.R.A. Williams (q.v.), a distinguished constitutional lawyer. The group was to identify those problems which militated against the unity of the country and which might make for the emergence of a strong central government. In addition, it was to look into the extent to which territorial division of the country into constituent parts of the federation and the division of powers between the centre and the regions fostered regionalism and contributed to the weakness of the centre. Furthermore, it was to look into the merit of a unitary versus a federal system of government and a one-party system versus a multiparty system. The group met in June when specific assignments were given to individual members to study and report on. Before members had enough time to do the work assigned to them, there was the July coup in which the general and others were killed.

CONSTITUTION DRAFTING COMMITTEE. The Constitution Drafting Committee was set up in September 1975 under the distinguished chairmanship of Chief F. Rotimi A. Williams (q.v.), a prominent constitutional lawyer. The committee was initially composed of 50 members, but it was later reduced to 49 members when Chief Obafemi Awolowo (q.v.) declined to serve. The committee was chosen on the basis of at least two members from each of the then-existing 12 states. Beyond this state and geographical representation, there were no other criteria for the selection of members except to ensure that major professional and other groups were represented. Thus, there were lawyers, businessmen, professional men, administrators, university lecturers and so on. The committee was assigned the job of drafting a constitution that would be federal and democratic, in which basic human rights would be guaranteed and which would make for political stability and the development of the principle of constitutionalism. The committee was not unanimous in its recommendations. Dr. Segun Osoba and Mr. Yesufu Usman submitted a minority report, which was not contained in the official report of the committee. In spite of this, the report generated much debate all over the nation.

CONSTITUTION (SUSPENSION AND MODIFICATION) DECREE NO. 1 OF 1966. After the military came to power in 1966, the first decree issued suspended certain provisions of the Republican Constitution, especially those dealing with the legislative and executive branches of the regional and national governments. Other provisions not suspended were to continue to have effect. Section six of the decree stated that the validity of a decree made by the federal military government or an edict made by the regional governors could not be questioned by any court of law in the country.

CONTRACT SYSTEM. This is the system that allows the employer, be it public or private, to hire a person on a contract which could be periodically renewed for as long as the employee's services are needed, that is, as long as no "indigenous" replacement could be found for him. This means a person on this kind of contract cannot expect to be confirmed or allowed to have tenure. Effective use of this system by many state governments has greatly limited the geographical mobility of labour in the country and deprived various agencies of the expertise readily available in the country. In fact, many states have preferred to hire expatriate Indian and Pakistani nationals instead of Nigerians who may wish to settle where they work.

COOPERATIVE MOVEMENT. With the growth of the cocoa (q.v.) crop in Nigeria in the early part of this century, farmers in Western Nigeria (q.v.) began in the early 1920s to organize collective sale of their cocoa under the supervision of the Department of Agriculture. In the early 1930s the organisation had become fairly well established in many places, so the government had to appoint an administrative officer as registrar of cooperative societies. Later, a Cooperative Department was created and made responsible for the affairs of cooperative societies. The new department saw to the training of Nigerian officials to teach the various associations how they could apply the basic principles of cooperation to solving practical problems and teach them a sound and simple system of accounting. Farmers who desired to form cooperative societies were also encouraged.

The cooperative society was based on the principle that the share capital of the society was provided by its members, the principle of one man, one vote, regardless of capital holding, and the society did not make profit. Surpluses were allocated at the end of the financial year to members in accordance to the proportion of their sales or their purchases.

Other cooperative associations were formed. The Association of Nigerian Cooperative Exporters became a licensed buying agent for the Western Nigeria Marketing Board (q.v.) and was responsible for selling the products supplied by the Produce Marketing Societies. The Cooperative Thrift and Loan Societies catered primarily to salary earners. Members of the Thrift and Loan Societies were encouraged to save part of their salary and borrow from the society. Other cooperative associations also grew up like the Cooperative Thrift and Credit Societies for nonsalary earners and the Cooperative Consumer Societies. The movement even went into banking, with the establishment of the First Cooperative Bank in Western Nigeria in 1953. To improve efficiency of the various societies, the government in 1953 opened a Cooperative Training School in Ibadan (q.v.), the capital of Western Nigeria, to train cooperative inspectors, auditors and other staff.

COST OF LIVING ALLOWANCE. A sum of money the colonial government granted in 1941 to civil servants, employees of native authorities and teachers due to the rising cost of living caused by the Second World War.

COUNCIL OF CHIEFS. Under the Richards Constitution (q.v.) of 1946, there were Houses of Chiefs (q.v.) in the Northern (q.v.) and in the Western Regions (q.v.). The Constitutional Conference (q.v.) of 1958 also granted one to the Eastern Region (q.v.). These houses constituted second legislative chambers in the regions. When the military took over power in 1966, and the legislative houses were dissolved, the chiefs in each region (and later each state) formed themselves into a council known as the Council of Chiefs, with different names in each region like the Council of Obas in the west and Emirs Council in the north.

Under the 1979 Constitution, the council is made up of a chairman and such number of persons as may be prescribed by the state's House of Assembly law. The main function of the council is to advise the governor on any matter relating to customary law, cultural affairs, intercommunal relations and chieftaincy matters. The council could also advise the governor upon request on matters relating to the state's public order on any other matter the governor may direct.

COUNCIL OF MINISTERS. The Council of Ministers was the principal instrument of public policy. It was established under the Macpherson Constitution (q.v.) of 1951. The council consisted of the governor, six official members and 12 ministers appointed by the governor. Of these ministers, four were appointed from each of the regions from the members of the House of Representatives (q.v.) chosen by the regional legislatures to represent them.

The ministers were not responsible for any ministries. Their responsibility was limited to dealing in the legislature with matters concerning their "subject" or "subjects" or introducing in the Council of Ministers matters concerning their subject or subjects. Furthermore, when a decision concerning their subject had been taken in the Council of Ministers, they were to ensure, in association with the appropriate officials, that effect was given to such a decision.

Under the 1954 Federal Constitution, the Council of Ministers consisted of the governor-general (q.v.), three official members and three ministers from each region and one from the Cameroon (q.v.). They were appointed by the governor-general on the advice of the regional executive. The Council of Ministers during this period served as a kind of second chamber, while, at the same time, it was the only policy-making body for the whole country. One of the weaknesses of this arrangement was that the Council of Ministers had regional basis, and members were beholden to the regional executives by whose grace they were appointed. This necessarily facilitated the drift to the regionalism that later became characteristic of later politics.

COUNCIL OF OBAS. *See* COUNCIL OF CHIEFS.

COUNCIL OF STATE. The Council of State was originally created in 1975 by the military regime of General Murtala R. Muhammed (q.v.). Before that time, military governors used to be members of the Supreme Military Council (q.v.), which was the highest policy-making body. In 1975 the Supreme Military Council no longer included the military governors. It was, therefore, thought necessary to set up an advisory body in the Council of State where each state would have input into decisions of major political importance.

Under the 1979 Constitution, the Council of State is a federal agency, composed of the president who is also the chairman, the vice president, all former presidents and heads of the government of the Federation, the chief justice of Nigeria, president of the Senate, speaker of the House of Representatives, all state governors, the attorney general of the Federation (q.v.) and one person from each state appointed by the Council of Chiefs of each state. Its function is to advise the president on the national population census, the grant of prerogative of mercy, award of national honours, appointment to the Federal Electoral Commission (q.v.), the Federal Judicial Service Commission (q.v.) and National Population Commission. It also can advise the president when requested on the maintenance of public order and any other matters that are put before it.

COUP D'ÉTAT. Nigeria has witnessed six successful coups d'état and as many as five attempted ones. The first coup occurred on January 15, 1966, when a section of the Nigerian Army (q.v.) revolted in Lagos (q.v.), Enugu (q.v.), Ibadan (q.v.) and Kaduna (q.v.) and killed many army officers and many leading politicians including the prime minister, Sir Abubakar Tafawa Balewa (q.v.), the premier of Northern Nigeria (q.v.), Alhaji Sir Ahmadu Bello (q.v.), the premier of Western Nigeria (q.v.), Chief S.L. Akintola (q.v.), and the federal minister for finance, Chief Festus S. Okotie-Eboh (q.v.). The leader of the coup, Major P.C.K. Nzeogwu (q.v.), said that they seized power to stamp out tribalism, nepotism and regionalism. However, rather than Nzeogwu becoming the head of government, it was the general commanding officer of the Nigerian Army, Major General Johnson Thomas Umunankwe Aguiyi-Ironsi (q.v.) who became the head of the federal military government and supreme commander of the Nigerian armed forces (q.v.).

He immediately announced decrees for the suspension of the offices of the president, prime minister and members of Parliament. He decreed that there should be military governors to head the governments of all the regions and that regional military government would be responsible to the federal military government.

The first coup was seen by some people as having been staged for the single purpose of bringing about Igbo domination. This impression was sadly reinforced by certain appointments and actions of the Ironsi regime. A good example of such actions was the Unification Decree (q.v.) of May 24, 1966, which abolished the federal structure of the country and set up a unitary form of government in its place. People from the Northern Region (q.v.) saw this as concrete evidence of the Igbo (q.v.) people's attempt to dominate the rest of the country, and there were demands for secession to avoid such domination.

After the promulgation of the Unification Decree, violent protest demonstrations began in the Northern Region. Many Igbos were killed, and their properties destroyed. This hostility toward the Igbos continued until July 29, 1966, when the Ironsi regime was overthrown by northern elements in the army. Their intention was to lead the north out of Nigeria through secession. Their keyword was "araba," the Hausa (q.v.) word for secession. This second coup claimed the lives of Major General Ironsi, Lt. Col. Adekunle Fajuyi (q.v.) and many other military men. After much negotiation, Lt. Col. Yakubu Gowon (q.v.) became the new Head of State. Gowon repealed the Unification Decree and brought back the federal structure.

The third coup, a bloodless one, took place on Tuesday July 29, 1975. It toppled the government of General Gowon, and General Murtala R. Muhammed (q.v.) emerged as the new Head of State. Many reasons were advanced for this coup:

1. In 1974, General Gowon in his National Day address to the nation dismissed as "unrealistic" the 1976 deadline previously made to return the government to civilian rule.
2. As the coup makers put it, the nation had been groping in the dark, and the situation inevitably would result in chaos and bloodshed unless it was arrested. The administration had been characterised by indecision, indiscipline, lack of consultation and neglect. The Head of State had become inaccessible even to his official advisers and, when advice was given, it was often ignored.

The coup brought Muhammed and Brigadier Olusegun Obasanjo (q.v.) to power.

On February 13, 1976, there was an attempted coup, organised by Lt. Col. B.S. Dimka (q.v.) and others. In it, General Murtala R. Muhammed was killed, but it failed to gain support. All the organisers still in the country were apprehended and tried. Those found guilty were publicly executed.

The next successful coup occurred on December 31, 1983, after Nigeria had experimented with the presidential system of government for four years and three months. It was a bloodless coup, which brought Major General Muhammadu Buhari (q.v.) into the leadership of the country. The coup was a sequel to the farcical electoral processes the nation went through in the second half of 1983—mismanagement of the economy which turned an oil-rich country into a beggar nation filled with corruption and indiscipline.

One major contribution of this coup to the political development of Nigeria was the insistence that past and present leaders must be made accountable for their stewardship. As soon as the coup became successful, past political leaders, beginning from the former executive president of Nigeria, Alhaji Shehu Shagari (q.v.) the vice president of Nigeria, Dr. Alex Ekwueme (q.v.), state governors, ministers and commissioners who were in Nigeria, were arrested and detained. Their accounts were all frozen, and investigations were initiated to find out whether or not they had corruptly enriched themselves while in office. Many of these were found guilty and sentenced to varying terms of imprisonment.

On August 27, 1985, Maj. General Ibrahim B. Babangida (q.v.) successfully carried out a palace coup against the Buhari regime. Among the reasons given for the coup was Buhari's growing authoritarianism. Babangida was the first military leader to take the title of president, and he changed the name of the Supreme Military Council to the Armed Forces Ruling Council. Two major unsuccessful coups were attempted during his time in office. In December 1985, Babangida announced that he had uncovered a coup plot against the regime led by Christian officers from the Middle Belt region of the country (particularly Benue State). The coup appeared to have been motivated by personal ambitions, and it resulted in the execution of 10 officers in 1986. On April 22, 1990 a more serious coup was attempted by officers led by Major Gideon Orka. The motivations were openly ethnic: the plotters were primarily southern minorities opposed to domination by the Hausa/Fulani. Among the more novel goals of this coup was the expulsion of five northern states (Bauchi, Borno, Kano, Katsina and Sokoto) from the country. Sixty-seven officers were eventually executed for their role in the plot.

General Babangida promised that his would be the last military government, and to this end he put in place an elaborate transition to civilian rule program. When he refused to surrender power to the winner of presidential elections on June 12, 1993, however, he was forced to transfer power to an Interim National Government (ING) on August 26, 1993. The ING was very unpopular and was eventually declared illegal by the courts following a case brought against it by the undeclared winner of the June 12 election, M.K.O. Abiola (q.v.). A few days after this decision, on November 17, 1993, a palace coup was carried out by General Sani Abacha (q.v.). Abacha had been the defense minister and the highest ranking military officer in the administration. Many believed that the coup was intended to recognise Abiola's election as president, but this was not to be. Over the coming months General Abacha moved to entrench himself in power, eventually imprisoning Abiola and putting in place the most repressive regime in Nigeria's history.

During the course of his regime, Abacha claimed to have uncovered two coup attempts. The first in March 1995, involved civilians, active military officers and retired military officers including former head of state Olusegun Obasanjo. Forty-four people were tried for the coup, but as a result of international pressure, none were executed. The second in December 1997 was alleged to have involved senior officers including General Oladipo Diya (q.v.), Abacha's second in command. Both the 1995 and 1997 coup allegations were regarded with widespread skepticism and many consider them to have been concocted to afford Abacha the opportunity to settle scores with his political opponents. Eventually the coup plotters were released by the Abubakar regime (1998–99).

Following Sani Abacha's death on June 8, 1998, General Abdulsalami Abubakar assumed power. Abubakar moved quickly to organise elections and hand over power to the democratic regime of Olusegun Obasanjo on May 29, 1999. In response to the growing consensus that military coups had become one of the greatest threats to the country's stability and prospects for development, one of Obasanjo's first acts as president was to purge the military of all officers who had ever held political office under previous military regimes. It was hoped that this would discourage future coups from occurring.

COURTS, CUSTOMARY. Before the advent of colonial authorities in Nigeria, cases of disputes over land and family matters were heard in the courts of the paramount Chiefs (q.v.), Obas, Obis and the Emirs. When the British came, rather than destroy the system which they saw had existed since time immemorial and which worked fairly efficiently, they decided only to reform it and allow it to exist side by side with the British types of courts, magistrate and high courts. These indigenous courts were first called native courts but later came to be known as customary courts. These courts still exist to administer customary laws dealing with such matters as divorce contracted in the traditional manner. In the Muslim areas of the north, Muslim law is administered as customary law. The Shari'a (q.v.) Courts in the Muslim areas of the north are the courts to which appeals come from the Alkali or Muslim courts. *See also* COURTS, NATIVE.

COURTS, NATIVE. In the early years of colonial administration in Nigeria, two systems of judicial administration existed side by side. There was the British system of judicial administration beginning from the magistrate courts to the Supreme Court (q.v.). These courts had jurisdiction over natives and nonnatives and applied the statutory laws and the common law of England. The second court system consisted of the native or customary courts which administered the native law and custom prevailing in their area of jurisdiction. They were organised into grades A, B, C or D, and they had power to impose fines and punishments with the exception of mutilation, torture or any other punishment repugnant to natural justice and humanity. Appointments to these courts were made by the Head Chief or the Emir (q.v.), but with the approval of the colonial officers in charge of the area. In the north the Muslim courts fell into this category, but the colonial official was vested with the power of appointing members to the court. Native courts had no jurisdiction over nonnatives, and they were under the supervision of British officials. Later on, in 1933, a hierarchy of appeals was set up, beginning from native courts to native courts of appeal and, if necessary, to British-type courts. However, appeals from Muslim courts on matters governed by Muslim law are sent to the Muslim Court of Appeal, which was later replaced in 1958 by the Shari'a Court of Appeal. In the early 1950s, the term *customary* replaced the word *native* in native courts and native law in both the Eastern (q.v.) and the Western Regions (q.v.).

Native courts were of great importance in the colonial administration of the local people for maintaining law and order and in settling local disputes, which the British types of courts were not equipped to handle. Today, the courts still handle a high proportion of the work of the judicial system.

COURTS OF EQUITY. The Court of Equity was first set up at Bonny (q.v.). It was a commercial association organised by merchants in the Oil Rivers Protectorate (q.v.). It was composed of both white and black traders, but the whites occupied the chair in monthly rotation. All trade disputes came before the court, and, with the consent of the traditional rulers, fines were levied on defaulters and collected. Similar courts composed of agents of various firms were set up in other areas like Calabar (q.v.), Brass (q.v.), Akassa and Opobo (q.v.). Initially, the courts possessed no legal status, but its rules were submitted to the British government for approval or disapproval. In 1872 the courts were legalized by an Order in Council, which helped to strengthen the administrative and judicial powers of the consul by giving him power to levy fines of a limited amount and to imprison for 21 days or even banish an individual for one whole year from an area for a breach of the regulations set up between the British and the people.

COWAN INQUIRY. Set up in 1948 to investigate and report on the methods of negotiation between government and its employees on questions affecting conditions of service in government industrial establishments. In his report Mr. T.M. Cowan of the United Kingdom Ministry of Labour and National Service stressed the need for improving industrial relations by improving the organisation of trade unions, continuity of leadership, and the need for discipline and education of the workers on the principles of trade unionism. The report also laid down the duties of government with regard to labour relations as being those of making laws that give room for union development, improving its own side of labour-management relations by employing the right kind of personnel officers in some of the principal industrial developments, provision of independent assistance to the growing trade union movement (q.v.) and the need to have adequate consultation and negotiation between government, its departmental representatives and the unions.

COWRY SHELLS. Cowry shells were used before the advent of the Europeans as a medium of exchange among the Yoruba (q.v.), Igbo (q.v.) and Benin (q.v.) peoples of Southern Nigeria. Even after the British came, cowry shells were still being converted or being equated with British coins. Among the Yoruba, six pence used to be equated with 2,000 cowries (Egbaa) and one shilling was 4,000 cowries (Egbaaji, Egbaa meji), three pence was 1,000 cowries (Egberun). Cowry shells were generally used for small exchanges locally, while costly beads were used on distant journeys for trade. The shells used to be collected from the coast and especially along the Indian Ocean. Cowries gradually faded out as commerce grew more complex with modern technicalities and expanded scope. Today, the shells can be found as ornamentations in palaces, shrines, museums, and they are even used for decorative purposes in various houses, both public and private. They are also used as part of Yoruba musical instruments called sekere and dundun.

CROSS RIVER STATE. Cross River State was a part of the Eastern Region (q.v.) until 1967 when a 12-state federal structure replaced the previously existing four regions. In 1976, when the 12 states became 19, Cross River State was formed, embracing the present-day Cross River and Akwa-Ibom States (q.v.). In 1987, when Nigeria became a federation of 21 states, Akwa-Ibom was carved out of the Cross River State.

Located on the southeastern frontier with the Republic of Cameroon (q.v.), Cross River State is bounded in the north by Benue State (q.v.), in the west by Enugu (q.v.) and Abia States (q.v.) and in the south and southwest by the Atlantic Ocean and Akwa-Ibom State. The state has an area of 21,481 square kilometers and lies within the tropical rain forest zone with plenty of wildlife, coastal mangrove forests, and upland of tall trees and forests. The state derives its name from the Cross River, which comes down from the Cameroon mountains and forms a delta with the Niger River (q.v.). The state's mineral resources are tin, gold, columbite, tantalite, kaolin, graphite, manganese, marble, limestone, salts, lead, uranium and petroleum (q.v.). It is divided into 14 local government areas.

The population of the state in 1991 was 1,865,604, and its density was 65 persons per sq. km. The major population centers are Calabar (q.v.), the capital with 320,862 persons, Ogoja, Ikom, Obudu, Ugep, Obubra, Akampa and Odukpani.

CROWN, THE. The Crown in Nigeria under colonial rule legally meant the Nigerian government, which was subject to policy direction and the power of disallowance exercisable by His/Her Majesty's Government in London. However, because that government was alien, the Crown came to mean, for many people, British imperialism.

CROWN COLONY. This is a colony under the power and authority of a king or queen. Its main characteristics are that the legislature of the colony is subordinate to its executive council and the colonial government is subordinate to the imperial government. Lagos (q.v.) became a Crown colony when it was ceded to the British Crown in 1861. The British then extended their jurisdiction into the interior from Lagos.

CROWTHER, BISHOP SAMUEL AJAYI. The first African bishop of the Anglican Church (q.v.) in Nigeria, he was an explorer and a missionary. He was born in Yorubaland about 1809 but was captured in 1821 during the civil war that devastated the area in the early 19th century and was sold into slavery to the Portuguese slave traders. But the ship transporting him to America was seized by a British antislavery patrol ship and was released in Freetown (q.v.), the capital of Sierra Leone (q.v.). Crowther was educated there by the Church Missionary Society (CMS) and was baptized in 1825. He later went to Fourah Bay Institute, and, after graduating, he became a schoolteacher. Due to how devoted, hardworking and intelligent he was, he was invited to join the British Niger expedition in 1841. He later went to England where he was ordained in 1844. He was then sent back to the west coast as a missionary. His first post was Badagry (q.v.) in Nigeria before being sent to Abeokuta (q.v.) in 1846. In 1854 and later 1857 he joined the W.B. Baikie (q.v.) expedition up the Niger River (q.v.). The CMS later decided to create a West African diocese with indigenous African pastorate and selected Crowther to be the first indigenous bishop in 1861. He was very successful in promoting Christianity (q.v.) and missionary education along the Niger River. Owing to his hard work and enthusiasm, he attracted many people to the church and the clergy. But not being able to supervise all the men and women working under him, discipline waned. He was criticised by white missionaries who opposed the setting up of an indigenous African pastorate and people like Sir George Goldie (q.v.) who believed that missionaries in Nigeria should help to extend British political influence, but he did not heed these criticisms very much. He resigned in 1890 and died the following year.

Bishop Ajayi Crowther was known not only for his religious activities but also for his intellectual and scholarly achievements. His work included the translation of the New Testament into Yoruba. Crowther was also an African nationalist. He had the strong belief during his missionary days that Africa must be saved by Africans. He was given an honorary degree of doctor of divinity by Oxford University.

CRUDE OIL SALES COMMISSION OF INQUIRY. The commission, headed by Mr. Justice Ayo Irikefe, a judge of the Supreme Court (q.v.), was appointed by the Federal Government (q.v.) on April 16, 1980, to probe the alleged loss of N2.8 billion by the Nigerian National Petroleum Corporation (NNPC) (q.v.). The commission found that all crude oil sold by NNPC and payments therefrom were in all respects made in accordance with the terms of their contract, that no proceeds of any sales were missing or improperly accounted for, that no person had been found guilty of fraud or wrongdoing with regard to the auditing or accounting for the sales of crude oil, that no proceeds of sales of crude oil were ever paid into the NNPC account with the Midland Bank, International Division in London and that the corporation as set up was extensive and far beyond normal span of management control. The government accepted the report and stated that no N2.8 billion was ever missing from the account of the company. Following this the government began to study necessary changes in the organisation of the company.

CURRENCY. From January 1, 1973, Nigeria changed from the pound sterling to the decimal currency known as the naira, which is subdivided into 100 kobo. The word *naira*, written with the symbol N, was adapted from Nigeria, and Kobo has always been a popular name for a penny in the old currency. Both terms are the same in singular and plural forms. The naira is presently issued in the N50, N20, N10, N5 denominations of notes, while the coins presently in use are in the N1.00, 50 kobo, 25 kobo and 10 kobo denominations. When the new currency was issued, the naira was to be equivalent to 10 shillings (£0.5) in the old currency and to be worth about 1.5 American dollars. Between 1973 and 1985, the Nigerian government still exchanged the naira for the British pound or the American dollar at a rate not too far below this exchange rate, even though the price of the naira had considerably fallen in the black market. Beginning with the Babangida (q.v.) administration's Structural Adjustment Programme (q.v.) and the deregulation of the naira in 1986, the price of the naira steadily declined. In the second half of 1994, the official exchange rate stood at $1.00 to N22.00, while in the black market it fluctuated from about $1.00 to $80.00 and N100.00. In November 1994 it was $1.00 to N110.00. In 1995 to 1996 the rate stabilised at about $1.00 to N80.00.

CURRICULUM CONFERENCE OF 1969. The report of this conference marked the beginning of the nation's action in the history of educational research. The report reviewed the objectives and purposes of primary and secondary education (q.v.) teacher training and higher education (q.v.) and made recommendations on each sector. It also examined the role of science and technology in national development, and also the role of women in education. As a result of the report, in 1972 the Nigerian Educational Research Council (q.v.) was formed, charged with the duty of encouraging, promoting and coordinating educational research programs carried out in Nigeria.

CUSTOMARY LAW. The customary law in Nigeria is the set of rules by which all people in a particular community must live by. A community's way of life is preserved by the observance of these laws. In Nigeria, customary law varies from place to place. In communities where there are chiefs, the paramount chief and his council are the custodians of the rules. Where there are no chiefs, the elders are the guardians of the law. And in communities where Islam is dominant, Islamic personal law becomes the customary law of the people.

CUSTOMARY RIGHT OF OCCUPANCY. Under the Land Tenure Law (q.v.) of 1962 in Northern Nigeria (q.v.), one of the ways an individual or a community could hold land was by the Customary Right of Occupancy, which means the right of a member of an indigenous community or a community to use or occupy a piece of land in accordance with customary law prevailing in the community. This right, however, could be revoked by the minister if the land was needed for public use, but, in such cases, compensations must be paid—not for the land itself but for the improvements and crops on it. In 1978, under the Land Use Decree (q.v.), all the land in a state was then vested in the governor as a trust for the people, but any right of occupancy already acquired, either under customary law or under statute law especially in the south where land was allowed to be purchased in "fee simple," was recognised.

-D-

DAHOMEY. Dahomey, now the Republic of Benin, is Nigeria's neighbour to the west. Dahomey's history before colonial rule was closely related to that of Western Nigeria. Dahomey's leading ethnic group, the Yoruba (q.v.), were divided when the colonial powers in Berlin, Germany, partitioned the region in 1885. The Yoruba who lived in the area west of the Nigerian-Dahomey border fell under French rule in Dahomey, while those in the area east of the border fell under British rule in Nigeria. Centuries before, this area was the site of many wars and raids for slaves between neighbouring kingdoms. The Oyo empire (q.v.) encompassed much of Dahomey's territory. Dahomey became independent of the Oyo empire in 1818. *See also* BENIN, REPUBLIC OF.

DAILY EXPRESS. Formerly known as the *Daily Service,* this daily newspaper was the official organ of the Nigerian Youth Movement (NYM) (q.v.). Its first editor was Ernest S. Ikoli (q.v.). With the dissolution of the NYM, the *Daily Service* then became the official organ of the Action Group Party

(AG) (q.v.). The *Daily Express* was used throughout the First Republic (q.v.) as the official AG organ.

DAILY TIMES. One of the leading national newspapers, it was established in 1926 by Richard Barrow, Sir Adeyemo Alakija (q.v.), a Nigerian barrister and some European businessmen. The first publication of the paper came out on June 1, 1926. Originally, it was an independent newspaper, but in 1977, the Federal Government (q.v.) bought the largest share in the company, thus bringing the paper under its control. Though still a national daily, it has come to be regarded as a government paper.

DANJUMA, LT. GEN. (RTD.) THEOPHILUS YAKUBU. The chief of army staff and the third most powerful figure in the Obasanjo regime (1976–79) behind Head of State Gen. Olusegun Obasanjo (q.v.) and chief of staff Gen. Shehu Yar'Adua. Born on December 9, 1937 in Takum, Taraba State, Danjuma was, like many military officers, a member of a northern minority group (the Chamba). Danjuma entered the military in 1960. He received military training in Nigeria, the United Kingdom and the United States at various points during the 1960s, and also commanded Nigerian peacekeeping forces sent to the Congo (1961–62) and Tanzania (1964).

Danjuma played an important role in the July 1966 countercoup against the Ironsi regime that brought Yakubu Gowon (q.v.) to power. During the Civil War (q.v.) he served with distinction, and in fact led the successful assault on Enugu (q.v.), the capital of the secessionist state of Biafra. Following the July 1975 coup that brought General Murtala Mohammed (q.v.) to power, Danjuma was made chief of army staff. He continued to hold this position in the Obasanjo regime (1976–79). In this role, Danjuma had the difficult responsibility of maintaining the support of the armed forces, and his influence in the military led him to be both respected and feared. When the Obasanjo regime ceded power to a democratically elected civilian government, Danjuma, together with the other service chiefs, retired in 1979.

Following his retirement, Danjuma was active in business and is reported to have served on the board of directors of some 20 companies. He remained outspoken about developments in the country, voicing prominent criticisms of the Shagari, Buhari and Babangida regimes. During the aborted Babangida democratic transition (1986–93) Danjuma was one of the kingpins of the Middle Belt Forum, an association that worked to organise Northern minorities politically. In the late 1990s, he chaired a subgroup of the Abacha regime's Vision 2010 panel. In 1997, he was again the subject of controversy when he was accused of supporting members of his own ethnic group, the Chamba, in a violent dispute with the Kuteb in Taraba State.

When former Head of State Olusegun Obasanjo launched his own bid to be elected president of the country in 1998–99, Danjuma was one of his most prominent supporters. At one point he famously declared that if Obasanjo did not win, he would go into self-imposed exile. When Obasanjo succeeded in becoming elected president in 1999, Danjuma emerged as one of the most powerful figures in the new regime. He played an important role in the selection of the new cabinet, and was himself selected to serve as minister of defence.

DANTATA, ALHAJI ALHASSAN. Said to be the wealthiest Nigerian from the north in his time, Dantata's exact date of birth is not known, but it is said to be about 1880. As early as 1912, he had developed a business in kola nuts (q.v.), trading in Kumasi, Ghana (q.v.), and shipping kola nuts to Nigeria by sea. He returned to Nigeria in 1912 and turned his attention also to groundnut (q.v.) purchasing and became the main supplier of groundnuts to the Royal Niger Company (q.v.). He went to Mecca after the First World War, via London, where he was presented to King George V. His businesses in kola nuts and groundnuts continued to grow. He even became one of the two major agents buying groundnuts for the marketing board. He founded with other merchants the Kano Citizens' Trading Company for industrial enterprises and the Kano Textile Mill in 1950. Before he died, he was appointed to some important positions, including director of the Nigerian Railway Corporation (q.v.), and a council member of the Emir (q.v.) of Kano. He died in October 1955.

DASUKI, SULTAN IBRAHIM. The 18th Sultan (q.v.) of Sokoto (q.v.) and a direct descendant of Usman Dan Fodio (q.v.), the founder of the caliphate, Dasuki was born on December 31, 1923, at Dogan Daji in Sokoto State (q.v.). Early in his childhood, he was enrolled at a Koranic School in "Dogon Daji" before he started his primary education. He later gained admission to the Kaduna College (now Barewa College [q.v.]) and graduated in 1945. He later went to London for higher education.

Dasuki has served in many important public positions. He was appointed personal secretary of Sir Ahmadu Bello (q.v.), the Sardauna of Sokoto and Premier of Northern Nigeria (q.v.) from 1953 to 1955. He was deputy secretary of the Northern Executive Council (q.v.) in 1957, and in 1958 he was seconded to the diplomatic service and posted to Saudi Arabia as the pilgrims' officer at Jeddah. He also served in Khartoum, Sudan, before he was posted back home. In 1970 he was made the chairman of the local government reform committee in the former North-Western State (q.v.). He was a member of the 1977 constituent assembly (q.v.) that approved a presidential system of government for Nigeria. He was also a member of the Constitution Drafting Committee (q.v.) in 1987 and a member of the constituent assembly for the Third Republican Constitution.

Dasuki was a prominent leader in Muslim affairs and was appointed secretary general of the Jama'atu Nasril Islam in 1971 and the Nigerian Supreme

Council of Islamic Affairs in 1973. At the height of the controversy created as a result of the surreptitious entry of Nigeria into the Organization of the Islamic Conference (OIC) (q.v.), Alhaji Dasuki was appointed by the federal military government as co-chairman of the advisory committee on religious affairs in Abuja (q.v.). Understanding fully well that Nigeria is a multireligious country, Alhaji Dasuki has always preached religious tolerance.

After the death of the former Sultan of Sokoto, Alhaji Siddiq Abubakar III, Dasuki vied for the post of sultan with Alhaji Shehu Malami and Alhaji Muhammadu Maccido (q.v.), the son of the late Sultan, and won. His victory led to more than three days of rioting in Sokoto with many lives and much property lost. As Sultan of Sokoto, he became the focal point of the Islamic population, most especially in the northern part of the country. His views carried much weight with the government of the day.

Relations between Alhaji Dasuki and General Sani Abacha (q.v.), the new Head of State after General I.B. Babangida (q.v.), became strained. In April 1996, Dasuki was dethroned, having been accused of conduct unbecoming his position, poor leadership, unauthorised journeys, misuse of funds, causing disaffection among Muslims, demeaning the exalted throne through failed bank's trials, decline of Islamic religion under him and inviting foreign diplomats without government knowledge. Unmentioned in these allegations was that Dasuki's son, Sambo, who retired from the military in 1993 was implicated in the February 1995 coup plot, and was sought by police. Dasuki was quizzed about the coup plot and the whereabouts of his son. Dasuki was sent into exile from Sokoto to Wukari and his more popular rival, Alhaji Muhammadu Maccido, succeeded him. Shortly after being deposed, Dasuki was imprisoned in Taraba State on charges of financial mismanagement. He was not released until June 1998, following the death of Sani Abacha.

DAURA. Said to be the oldest of the Hausa (q.v.) states. In addition, it was the offspring of the Queen of Daura and Prince Bayajidda in around the 10th century who are reputed to have founded the other Hausa states. The kingdom of Daura fell to the Fulani (q.v.) jihadists in 1809, who divided it into three parts, the Daura Fulani, Daura Baure and Daura Zango. The British conquered Daura in 1903.

D'AVEIRO, JOÃO ALFONSO. A Portuguese explorer, he was recorded to be the first Portuguese explorer to visit Benin City (q.v.) in 1485. Upon his return to Portugal, he reported to the king of the great possibilities for opening up trade in ivory and pepper with the people of the area and of evangelizing them. He returned to Benin—to establish a trading post—where he later died.

DAVID-WEST, PROF. TAMUNOEMI SOKARI. An educationist and newspaper columnist, born on August 26, 1936, at Buguma, Kalabari, in the Rivers State (q.v.), he was educated at Kalabari National College in Buguma, University College of Ibadan (q.v.), Michigan State University and Yale University in the United States and McGill University in Canada. Upon returning to Nigeria, he joined the staff of the University of Ibadan and rose to the position of professor of virology. He served as commissioner (q.v.) for education and was later a member of the Constitution Drafting Committee (q.v.). He has received many academic awards, including a World Health Organisation fellowship and a Commonwealth medical research fellowship, and he is a member of many national and international organisations. In January 1984, after the military had overthrown the government of President Alhaji Shehu Shagari (q.v.), he was appointed by the new Head of State as minister for petroleum and energy.

David-West competed for the presidential nomination of the People's Democratic Party in 1998–99, but was soundly defeated at the party's February 1999 convention in Jos (q.v.).

DAVIES, CHIEF HEZEKIAH OLADIPO. A lawyer and businessman, born on April 5, 1905, he was educated at the Methodist Boys' High School, Lagos (q.v.), King's College, Lagos (q.v.) and at the London School of Economics and Political Science in England. He was called to the bar at the Middle Temple in London in 1946.

Chief Davies started as a teacher at the King's College in Lagos from 1925 to 1926. In 1934 he cofounded the Nigerian Youth Movement (NYM) (q.v.), the first nationalist organisation in the country. And, while in London, he was president of the West African Student Union (q.v.) from 1944 to 1945, and in 1946, its secretary general. Upon his return to Nigeria, he was made NYM chairman from 1946 to 1948. Also, when the Egbe Omo Oduduwa (q.v.), which gave birth to the Action Group Party (q.v.), was founded in 1948, he was its legal adviser. He was also legal adviser to the Lagos and Colony State Movement from 1953 to 1956. He became a Queen's counsel in 1958 and fellow of the Institute of International Affairs of Harvard University. He later joined the Nigerian National Democratic Party (q.v.), led by Chief S.L. Akintola (q.v.), and was elected a member of the Ekiti West constituency into the federal House of Representatives (q.v.); he was later appointed minister of state in the federal Ministry of Industries from 1964 to 1966. He was at the head of many business companies: chairman of the board of directors, Arbico Limited, director of the Total Oil Products (Nigeria) Limited, chairman of Safrap (Nig.) Ltd. and chairman of the Hassan Transport Limited. He died in 1988.

DECOLONIZATION. The city of Lagos (q.v.) was ceded to the British in 1861, and from there they extended their influence and jurisdiction to the hinterland. This process of extension of jurisdiction met with much resistance from the traditional chiefs, Obas and Emirs all over the country, but because the British had the Maxim guns, they overcame the resistance, though at great cost. Thus, by 1903 they had asserted their power over Sokoto (q.v.), the capital of the Fulani empire (q.v.).

Even though the country was subjugated, resistance to British rule continued. However, it took a new turn. Various nationalist organizations, newspapers and political parties took up the struggle. The first of these was the National Congress of British West Africa (q.v.), founded in the Gold Coast (Ghana) (q.v.) in 1917 by Caseley Hayford, a lawyer, with a branch in Lagos. The aims of the congress included putting pressure on the British government to grant the right of self-determination to its four West African colonies—Nigeria, Gold Coast, Sierra Leone (q.v.) and the Gambia. Its branch in Nigeria was critical of the composition and the role of the Nigerian Council (q.v.) set up by Lord Lugard (q.v.) after the 1914 Amalgamation of Nigeria (q.v.).

In 1921 the first militantly nationalist newspaper, the *Lagos Weekly Record* (q.v.) of John Payne Jackson (q.v.) was established, followed by Herbert Macaulay's (q.v.) *Lagos Daily News*. The same Macaulay founded a political party, the Nigerian National Democratic Party (NNDP) (q.v.) in 1923, which, though concentrating its activities on parochial Lagos affairs, nonetheless put pressure on the colonial authorities at the seat of government. In 1926 the *Daily Times* was also founded, which together with the *West African Pilot,* became the forum for nationalist expression of discontent and agitation. The West African Student Union (q.v.), formed in 1925 by Oladipo Solanke (q.v.), acted as a pressure group from London.

In 1934 the Lagos Youth Movement (LYM) (q.v.) was formed in opposition to the colonial government educational policy with regard to the alleged deficiencies of the Yaba Higher College (q.v.). The LYM in 1936 changed its name to Nigerian Youth Movement (NYM) (q.v.), and was therefore the first really nationalist organisation in Nigeria. It quickly superseded the NNDP but was short-lived.

Between 1944 and 1951, the development of political parties was rapid. Beginning with the formation of the National Council of Nigeria and Cameroons (NCNC) (q.v.) in 1944, the Action Group (q.v.) in 1951 and the Northern Peoples Congress (q.v.) in 1951—all of which fought relentlessly to gain independence for Nigeria—Western (q.v.) and Eastern Nigeria (q.v.) became internally self-governing in 1957, and Northern Nigeria (q.v.) in 1959. National independence finally came on October 1, 1960.

DEEPER LIFE CHURCH. A religious movement founded in 1973 by W.F. Kumuyi (q.v.), then a lecturer at the University of Lagos, Lagos State (q.v.). The Deeper Life, like evangelical and pentecostal movements that have very much influenced the founder, bases its doctrine on three main pillars: conversion, sanctification and baptism. Conversion means to be "born again," a definite experience that happens on a particular day of the believer's life. For Kumuyi, it was April 5, 1964. When a person is born again, he places himself unreservedly under the demands of the Gospel. This is sanctification, which is the time a person consciously avoids sin as he grows in grace. Baptism in the Holy Spirit is evidenced by speaking in tongues. The Deeper Life Church is different from other pentecostal churches in that its believers keep away from unchristian practices like mixing traditional religious practices with Christian practices. The church has spread not only to all the states of the Federation (q.v.) but to many countries of Africa and Europe.

DEFENCE ACADEMY. The Nigerian Defence Academy was established in Kaduna (q.v.) in January 1964 to cater for the joint training of potential officers belonging to the three services—army, navy and air force. The academy runs regular commission courses. In the regular army courses, cadets pursue two and a half years of training at the end of which successful candidates are commissioned as second lieutenants. The naval and air force cadets do only a one-and-a-half-year joint training program at the end of which successful candidates leave for further specialisation training in their respective services. The academy also runs short-service commission courses of six months duration for men who rise from the ranks. At the end of the training, the cadets are commissioned as second lieutenants.

DEFENCE PACT. As far back as 1958, Nigerian political leaders had initialled an agreement for mutual defence arrangements between Britain and Nigeria. This agreement became a matter of great debate, and, in the 1960 Constitutional Conference (q.v.) in London, the colonial secretary had to assure Nigerians that the granting of independence was without any strings attached. At the conference, agreement was reached that each country would give the other assistance in mutual defence—Britain to give help in training, equipment and supplies, while the two countries would give each other staging facilities for aircraft in their respective areas. The agreement was to be sent before the federal Parliament after independence.

Immediately after independence, the defence agreement was put before the federal House of Representatives (q.v.). It was to afford each country such assistance as may be necessary for mutual defense and to consult together on the measures to be taken jointly or separately to ensure the fullest co-operation between the two countries. Britain was to help in training the

Nigerian Army while Nigeria was to provide overflying rights and facilities for the Royal Air Force. The pact generated much heat in the House where the opposition party strongly attacked it as an attempt to swindle Nigeria out of its sovereignty. Both the press and university students were critical of the agreement, and as a result of adverse opinion against it, the agreement was abrogated in 1962.

DE GRAFT, WILLIAM. A Methodist missionary who accompanied Reverend Thomas Birch Freeman (q.v.) to Badagry (q.v.), Lagos State (q.v.) in September 1842. When Rev. Freeman returned to the Gold Coast (q.v.) in 1843, de Graft and his wife built the first western-type school in Badagry named "Nursery of the Infant Church."

DELEGATION TO LONDON. The Richards Constitution (q.v.) of 1946 was bitterly criticised by Nigerians, especially by the National Council of Nigeria and the Cameroons (NCNC) (q.v.), on the grounds that by formalising the regional concept into the Nigerian constitutional development, it might lead to the disintegration of the country. Further, they criticised it as being the work of only one man without seeking the consent of the people who were to live under it. The NCNC also said that the constitution should not only secure greater participation by Africans in the discussion of their own affairs, but, more important, it should secure for them greater participation in the management of their own affairs. Finally, the party objected to the continuation of nominated members in the Legislative Council (q.v.). They asked that nominated members should be replaced with popularly elected members.

Because the colonial government would not yield on these matters, the NCNC began a tour of the country to secure a mandate to go to London and present the people's grievances against the constitution. The delegation to London was received by the secretary of state, Rt. Hon. Arthur Creech Jones (q.v.), who advised them to go back home and cooperate on making the constitution work.

DELTA STATE. Delta State used to be part of the old Western Region (q.v.). In 1963 the Mid-Western Region was created out of the Western Region, and it embraced the present Edo (q.v.) and Delta States. In 1967, when the administration of General Yakubu Gowon (q.v.) created the 12-state structure, the Mid-Western Region became Mid-Western State, and in 1976 it became Bendel State (q.v.). In 1991 Bendel State was split into two, Edo State and Delta State. Delta State is divided into 19 local government areas.

The state has a land area of 16,842 square kilometres and is located between latitudes 5° and 6° 30′N, and 5° and 6° 45′E. It is bounded in the north by Edo State, in the east by the Niger River (q.v.), in the south by the Rivers

State (q.v.), and in the southwest by Ondo State (q.v.) and the Atlantic Ocean. Its Atlantic coastline comprises about 160 kilometres of the Bight of Benin (q.v.).

Portuguese explorers visited the area in the 15th century, and it was the center of many battles between the indigenous population and British colonial authorities in their effort to stop the slave trade (q.v.) in the area and gain control of the trade within the hinterland.

The state's vegetation varies from mangrove swamps at the coast to evergreen forests in the center and savannah forest in the northeast. The riverine area is about 35 percent of the state; it is rich in crude oil. Part of the state's natural gas is exported, part is used for domestic consumption and the rest is still to be flared.

The population of the state was 2,570,181 in 1991, and its density is 152 persons per square kilometre. The people are multiethnic, made up of the Urhobo (q.v.), Igbo (q.v.), Isoko, Itsekiri (q.v.), Ogoni (q.v.) and Izon, each of which has its own native language. Christianity (q.v.) has the largest following, but there are many who still practise traditional religions (q.v.). Because of the wide cultural background of the people, they have many festivals which they celebrate like the Okere-Juju among the Itsekiri, the Ikenga and Ukunta in Aboh, Iwuyi in Agbor and Soghein in Izon, as well as many Christian festivals. The area abounds in art works—carvings, handwoven cloths, table mats, ashtrays and flower pots. Most people in the state are fishers, traders and farmers, growing rubber (q.v.), oil palm (q.v.), cassava (q.v.), maize, rice, yams (q.v.) and bananas (q.v.).

Major towns are Asaba, the state capital, Warri, Sapele, Ughelli, Abraka, Kwale and Orerokpe. Education is of primary importance to the people. Because Delta State was formerly a part of the old Western Region, which was under the Action Group (q.v.) government and later under the government of the Unity Party of Nigeria (q.v.), both of which continued free education from the colonial days, the state now has about 870 primary schools and 290 secondary schools.

DEMOCRATIC PARTY OF NIGERIA AND THE CAMEROONS. Formed out of a split in the National Council of Nigeria and the Cameroons (NCNC) (q.v.) in 1958 by Dr. K.O. Mbadiwe (q.v.), federal minister of commerce and industry, Chief Kolawole Balogun (q.v.), federal minister of information, Mr. U.O. Ndem, parliamentary secretary to Dr. Mbadiwe and Mr. O. Bademosi, parliamentary secretary to Chief Balogun.

On June 14, 1958, 31 NCNC members petitioned Dr. Nnamdi Azikiwe (q.v.), the national president and Eastern Regional (q.v.) premier, to resign from the government and the party because, as they alleged, he was splitting the party asunder and was losing interest in the party. They referred to the findings of the Foster-Sutton Commission of Inquiry (q.v.) against him, and they also blamed him for the failure of the universal free primary education scheme. The national executive committee of the party expelled the four members from the party, and they then formed a new organisation called the NCNC Reform Committee. In July 1958 Dr. Mbadiwe, Chief Balogun, and their parliamentary secretaries resigned from the Federal Government (q.v.), and on August 4, 1958, the Reform Committee turned itself into a new political party known as the Democratic Party of Nigeria and the Cameroons under the leadership of Dr. Mbadiwe. It advocated a federal form of government based on socialist ideology.

The new party found little support. It could not secure a footing in the Western Region (q.v.) and so found itself limited to the Eastern Region (q.v.) where Dr. Mbadiwe could not adequately compete with Dr. Azikiwe. The new party met with complete failure in the federal elections (q.v.) of December 1959, and in 1960, Dr. Mbadiwe became reconciled with Dr. Azikiwe and the DPNC was dissolved.

DEMOCRATIC SOCIALISM. Democratic socialism was adopted as a political ideology by the Action Group Party (q.v.) at the Jos Conference in 1962. The ideology envisaged the construction of a mixed socialist economy that would combine elements of both public and private enterprise within the framework of a comprehensive national plan. The adoption of the ideology split the party into two: those who supported the ideology were led by the party leader and the national president Chief Obafemi Awolowo (q.v.), while those who did not support it were led by the Western Regional premier and deputy leader of the party, Chief S.L. Akintola (q.v.). *See also* ACTION GROUP CRISIS OF 1962.

DEVELOPMENT PLANS. Since independence in 1960, Nigeria has had four Five-Year Development Plans—1962–68, 1970–74, 1975–80 and 1981–85. The first National Development Plan (1962–68) aimed at a growth rate of at least 4 percent per annum as against the 3.9 percent per annum achieved in the preceding 10 years. To achieve this objective, the plan aimed to invest 15 percent of the country's gross domestic product and raise per capita consumption by 1 percent per year.

The Second National Development Plan (1970–74) was drawn up by the military administration of General Y. Gowon (q.v.). It aimed at the transformation of the whole society. The planners recognised the possibility of using planning as a weapon of social change and as a means for correcting existing defects in production, distribution and exchange. To this end it sought to make Nigeria a united, strong and self-reliant nation; a great and dynamic society; a just and egalitarian society; a land bright and full of opportunities for all its citizens and a free and democratic society. The Third Plan retained the objectives of the second plan but broadened its scope. It aimed to invest N30 billion, which was 10 times the level of investment of the second plan. The plan included every aspect of government endeavour. For example, N7 billion was allocated to transport; education, N2.5 billion, agriculture, N2.2 billion, urban development, N1.8 billion and health, N700 million. The private sector's participation stood at N10 billion of the total planned expenditure.

The Fourth Plan (1981–85) envisaged the expenditure of about N82 billion—N70.5 billion would be accounted for by the various governments of the Federation, while N11.5 billion would be added from the private sector. This plan came at a time when the revenue from oil on which the plan heavily depended was rapidly declining as a result of the world oil glut. It was, therefore, impossible to achieve many of the objectives of the plan.

DIKE, PROF. KENNETH O. Born on December 17, 1917, he received his education at the Dennis Memorial Grammar School in Onitsha (q.v.), Achimota College in Ghana (q.v.) and Fourah Bay College (q.v.) in Sierra Leone (q.v.). He went for further studies at the Universities of Durham, Aberdeen and London where he obtained his M.A., Ph.D. and LL.D. degrees. He returned to Nigeria and became a lecturer at University of Ibadan from 1950 to 1952 and senior research fellow at the West African Institute of Social and Economic Research (q.v.) from 1952 to 1954. He was made chairman of the Nigeria Antiquities Commission in 1954, in 1955 the president of the Historical Society of Nigeria and a professor of history in 1956.

In 1960 Dike was chosen as the vice chancellor at the University of Ibadan, a post he occupied until 1966. He was also the director of the Institute of African Studies at the University of Ibadan from 1962 to 1967. Professor Dike published many articles and books, including *Trade and Politics in the Niger Delta from 1830 to 1895, A Hundred Years of British Rule in Nigeria* (1956) and the *Origin of the Niger Mission* (1957).

DIKKO, ALHAJI UMARU. Born on December 31, 1936, in Kaduna State (q.v.), he attended the Barewa College (q.v.) in Zaria (q.v.) from 1949 to 1954, the Nigerian College of Arts, Science and Technology (q.v.) in Zaria from 1954 to 1958 and the University of London, where he obtained a degree in 1965. In 1967 he was appointed commissioner (q.v.) for finance in the North-Central State and served until 1972 when he became commissioner for information until 1975. In 1979 he was appointed by president Shehu Shagari (q.v.) as minister of transport. He later became the chairman of the presidential task force for the importation of essential commodities such as rice. Suddenly, he became a very wealthy person.

After the military takeover on December 31, 1983, he went underground and later surfaced in London where he preferred to stay. From London he reportedly threatened the overthrow of the government of General Muhammadu Buhari (q.v.). In Nigeria he was accused of large-scale corruption, hoarding of essential commodities and illegally enriching himself. He became the most wanted man among the many wealthy Nigerian fugitives in Europe and America. In July 1984, there was an attempted abduction of Dr. Dikko but the attempt failed. He had been drugged and loaded in a crate on a cargo plane that would have flown him from London to Nigeria. While in exile in Britain, he studied law and in 1991 was called to the bar at the Middle Temple. He came back to Nigeria in 1994 as a government-nominated member to the constitutional conference (q.v.) that took place in Abuja (q.v.).

DIKKO, DR. RUSSELL ALIYU BARAU. A Fulani (q.v.), converted to Christianity (q.v.), the first university-educated person and the first medical doctor from Northern Nigeria (q.v.), Dr. Dikko was born on June 15, 1912, in Zaria (q.v.). He was educated at the Church Missionary Society (CMS) School at Wusasa outside Zaria from 1922 to 1929. He then went to King's College in Lagos (q.v.) from 1929 to 1931 and then to the University of Birmingham, England.

Upon his return to Nigeria, he joined the government medical service in 1940. Because of his educational attainment in the Northern Region (q.v.), Dr. Dikko could not but take part in the political activities going on in the north and in the country as a whole at the time. In 1949 he, together with people like Mallam (Alhaji Muhammed) Aminu Kano (q.v.), Tafawa Balewa (q.v.) and Yahaya Gusau created a pan-Northern Nigeria cultural organisation known as Jam'iyyar Mutanem Arewa (q.v.), which later became the Northern People's Congress (NPC) (q.v.). Dr. Dikko headed the organisation for two years until 1951 when the NPC became a political party, and he, being a civil servant, resigned.

In 1960 Dr. Dikko was posted to the curative service division in the Northern Region, and in 1962 he became a permanent secretary in the ministry of health. In June 1967 during military rule, he became the federal commissioner (q.v.) for mines and power, and in 1971 he became commissioner for transport. He retired from the Federal Government (q.v.) in January 1975 and died in 1977.

DIMKA, LT. COLONEL B.S. An officer of the physical education corps of the Nigerian Army, he with others made an attempt to overthrow the government of General Murtala Muhammed (q.v.) on February 13, 1976. The attempted coup (q.v.) led to Muhammed's death. Immediately the coup was aborted; Dimka went into hiding but was later arrested on March 5, 1976, at a checkpoint at Abakaliki in Anambra State (q.v.). He was tried by a military tribunal, which found him guilty and sentenced him to death by firing squad. He was executed along with six others on March 15, 1976.

DINA COMMITTEE. Set up in 1968 under the leadership of Chief Isaac Dina, during the Civil War (q.v.) and after the country had been divided into 12 states, to look into and suggest changes in the then-existing system of revenue allocation (q.v.) in the country. It was also to suggest new revenue resources for both the federal and state governments. In its effort to foster national unity through fiscal allocations, the committee recommended, among other things, a uniform income tax legislation for the whole country and federal government assumption of full responsibility for the financing of higher education (q.v.). Mining rents were to be distributed on the basis of 15 percent to the Federal Government (q.v.), 10 percent to the states of derivation and 70 percent to the distributable pool account (q.v.). Offshore rents and royalties were to be distributed on the basis of 60 percent to the federal government, 30 percent to the distributable pool and 10 percent to a special account. It also suggested that the pricing and financial policies of marketing boards (q.v.) should be harmonised, and recommended the setting up of a permanent national planning commission for the whole country. The report was, after thorough examination, rejected because it was said to have exceeded its powers and in some cases ignored its terms of reference.

DIPCHARIMA, ZANNA BUKAR SULOMA. Born in 1917 in Dipcharima Village in the Bornu Province of Northern Nigeria (Borno State) (q.v.), he was educated at the Maiduguri Middle School and later trained as a teacher at the Katsina Teacher Training College. He taught from 1938 to 1946 when the Richards Constitution (q.v.) came into being and when he decided to go into politics. He first joined the only party existing then, the National Council of Nigeria and the Cameroons (NCNC) (q.v.), under the leadership of Dr. Nnamdi Azikiwe (q.v.). He was a member of the NCNC delegation to London in 1947. In the same year he left the party and joined the John Holt Company. In 1954 he came back to party politics by joining the dominant party in the north, the Northern People's Congress (NPC) (q.v.), and was elected on its platform to the Native Authority (q.v.) in Bornu and won a seat to the federal House of Representatives (q.v.) in Lagos (q.v.) in the same year that he was made a parliamentary secretary in the Ministry of Transport. His popularity made him rise very fast. He became president of the NPC branch in the Bornu Province and was appointed the head of the Yerwa District with the title of Zana in 1956. In 1957 he was made minister of state without portfolio and later minister of commerce and industry. In 1964 he accepted the portfolio of the Ministry of Transport. When the military took over power in January 1966, he was still in this position, and, in the absence of the prime minister, Alhaji Tafawa Balewa (q.v.), who had then been abducted, it was Dipcharima's fate to preside over the cabinet meeting that handed over power to the armed forces (q.v.). He died in 1969 in an air accident.

DIRECTORATE OF FOOD, ROADS AND RURAL INFRASTRUCTURE. President Ibrahim B. Babangida (q.v.) established and launched the National Directorate of Food, Roads and Rural Infrastructure (DFRRI) in February 1986. Its activities covered all 30 states of the Federation (q.v.) and the nation's 589 local government areas.

The need for setting up such an organisation as DFRRI arose after the mass migrations of people from rural areas—which had little or no infrastructure—to cities like Lagos (q.v.), Ibadan (q.v.), Jos (q.v.), Kano (q.v.), Enugu (q.v.), Kaduna (q.v.), and Port Harcourt (q.v.) where services are better. The belief was that if conditions in the rural areas were improved, people would stay there and produce to boost the nation's economy. DFRRI was, therefore, charged with providing rural communities with the necessary infrastructural facilities. It embarked upon such projects as rural electrification, rural water supply and sanitation, construction of feeder roads, rural housing, food, agriculture and industrialisation. In 1990 DFRRI built a total of 30,728.34 kilometres of feeder roads, 55,576.24 kilometres in 1991 and 85,592.82 kilometres in 1992. In 1992 18,680 communities benefitted from rural water and sanitation programmes and 506 rural communities had electricity.

After the change of leadership from Babangida to General Sani Abacha in 1993, there was a lack of continuity in policy. The Central Bank showed that by 1995, rural development activities had slowed down drastically following the lull in 1994 in the operations of the directorate and the Better Life Program, which was transformed under Mrs. Abacha into the Family Support Program.

DIRECTORATE OF SOCIAL MOBILISATION (MAMSER). Established by Decree no. 31 of 1987, to help create a new cultural and productive environment which would promote pride in productive work, self-reliance and self-discipline; awaken in the citizens their rights and obligations to the nation; encourage people to take active part in the discussions and decisions affecting their welfare and promote new sets of values, attitude and culture for the attainment of the goals and objectives of the nation. The directorate had a governing board made up of representatives of many ministries and a chairman appointed by the president. In spite of the huge sums of money invested in the organisation during the presidency of General Ibrahim B. Babangida (q.v.), the founder, there is not much to be said for it. It was dissolved in 1993.

DISTRIBUTABLE POOL ACCOUNT. This was the account to which all revenues shared by the states were paid. Some percentage of federally generated revenue—import duties on certain commodities and mining royalties, for example—were paid into this account, while some percentage was paid to the federal government and some to the state of origin. The proportion of money distributed to the regions or states varied from time to time. For instance, in 1958 it was shared in the ratio of 40 to the north, 24 to the west and 31 to the east. Under the 1963 Constitution, the north received 40, the east 31, the west 18 and the mid-west (which was in 1958 part of the west) 6, with five percent always left in the account. But under the 1979 Constitution, the Distributable Pool Account was called the "Federation Account" (q.v.), into which all revenues collected by the Federal Government (q.v.), with some few exceptions, were paid. The amount in this account was distributed among the federal, state and the local government councils in accordance with the prescription of the National Assembly (q.v.). In 1982 the National Assembly agreed on a ratio of 55 percent to the federal government, 35 percent to the state governments and 10 percent to local governments.

DISTRICT HEADS. In the Northern Region (q.v.), these were senior native authority (q.v.) officials who were responsible for collecting taxes and other forms of revenue, with the exception of court fines, and for maintaining law and order in their districts.

DISTRICT OFFICERS. Under the system of Native Administration (q.v.), the resident (q.v.) was the political officer in charge of a province, while the district officer was in charge of one of the divisions or districts within the province. The district officer generally had a university education and was given special training in administration. He was required to perform all the functions of all the departments. These included judicial, postal, customs, police and engineering. He saw to the enforcement of ordinances, kept records and issued licences. He was the medium of communication between the military or departmental officers and the native chiefs on a number of matters. He rendered assistance to missionaries, miners and traders in his area. He also undertook regular tours to administer justice, settle disputes and correct any injustices that came to his notice.

DIVINATION. Divination is a way of getting guidance and advice from the gods. In traditional Nigerian societies, divination is used in many different situations. Parents may want to know what kind of life their newborn baby will live. If they have twins, the parents may want to know certain additional do's and don'ts. A man or woman may need advice and guidance in starting a business or a journey, or choosing a mate. People may want to know the cause of an illness or details about some other misfortunes. Each Nigerian society has different gods with whom they consult. In Yoruba (q.v.) society, for example, many people go to an Ifa priest known as Babalawo. The Babalawo may throw some kola nuts (or some other special objects) a number of times. The way in which the nuts fall will indicate traditional *Odu Ifa* verses to recite, which serves as advice for the person from the god, Ifa. The Babalawo will then prescribe what to do, gifts to give, or sacrifices to offer. Some diviners are also experts in traditional medicine, and they are able to treat many kinds of illnesses. Such men and women command great respect among the people, and are often sought after.

DIYA, MAJ. GEN. DONALDSON OLADIPO. A soldier and second in command in the administration of General Sani Abacha (q.v.), Diya was born in 1944 and educated at Yaba Methodist Primary School, Lagos (q.v.), Odogbolu Grammar School and the Nigerian Defence Academy (q.v.), Kaduna (q.v.), 1964–67. He was later sent to the United States Army School of Infantry, Fort Benning, Georgia, from 1971 to 1972. He then moved steadily up the promotion ladder until 1988 when he was promoted to major general. He was governor of Ogun State (q.v.) between 1984 and 1985 and became a member of the Armed Forces Ruling Council (q.v.) between 1985 and 1987. In 1993 when General Abacha took over power from the Interim National Government (q.v.) of Ernest Shonekan (q.v.), Diya became the chief of general staff, the number-two position in the administration.

Despite his prominent position, Diya never gained the complete trust of Abacha. In December 1997 he was arrested on charges of plotting a coup. Many, however, suspected that the charges were fabricated. On March 4, 1999, he was released from prison by the regime of General Abdulsalami Abubakar (q.v.).

DOGONYARO, MAJOR GENERAL JOSHUA NIMYEL. A soldier, born on September 6, 1942, at Dakan-Kuka in Plateau State (q.v.), he attended Boys Secondary School, Gindiri, after which he entered the Nigerian Army in 1964 and moved up the ranks as he gained new experience and qualifications. He had served in many command positions before the August 1985 coup d'état (q.v.) that ushered in the administration of General Ibrahim B. Babangida (q.v.). Until the coup, he was relatively unknown, but he came into the limelight when he announced to the nation on August 27, 1985, the overthrow of General Muhammadu Buhari (q.v.). He then became a member of the Armed Forces Ruling Council (q.v.). He served in Liberia in 1990 with the Economic Community of West African States Monitoring Group forces. He was retired from the military by the General Sani Abacha (q.v.) administration, which came to power in November 1993.

DOSUNMU. The ruler of Lagos (q.v.) (1853–85) under whom Lagos was ceded to the British Crown in 1861. When his father Akinoye (q.v.) died in 1853, he ascended to the throne of Lagos with the help of the British consul of Lagos, who believed him among other rivals to be more tractable to the British interest. Like his father, he was a weak ruler who heavily depended on the British, thereby allowing them to interfere more and more in local affairs. Thus, in 1861, with their warship steaming at the Lagos harbor, the British demanded that Dosunmu sign the treaty ceding Lagos to them. When he refused, he was threatened with force, and three days later, August 6, 1861, he yielded. In return the British gave him a pension. He was allowed to continue to use his title as king of Lagos and to continue to decide disputes between the inhabitants of Lagos with their consent, but subject to appeal to British law. He died in 1885, succeeded by his son, Oyekan.

DRUG CONTROL. In 1966 the military government promulgated the Indian Hemp Decree No. 19 (The Dangerous Drugs Act. Cap. 48), which stipulated imprisonment of not less than 10 years with hard labour for possession and use of Indian hemp. In 1975 the Indian Hemp Amendment Act, No. 34 of 1975 reduced the jail sentence to not less than six months or with an option of fine. With the promulgation of the Special Tribunal (Miscellaneous Offence) Decree No. 20 of 1984, the penalty for the illegal possession, use and trafficking in narcotics was changed to death.

Decree No. 20 also established the Miscellaneous Offences Tribunal for the trial of offenders. According to the decree, any person who without lawful authority, deals in, buys, sells, exposes or offers for sale or induces any other person to buy, sell, smoke or inhale the drug popularly known as cocaine (or other similar drugs) commits an offence and is liable upon conviction to suffer death by firing squad.

Although the decree was promulgated in July 1984, it was made retroactive from Dec. 31, 1983. On April 10, 1985, Bartholomew Owo, Bernard Ogedengbe and Akanni Ojuolape were publicly executed notwithstanding the public condemnation of the sentence passed on them by the special military tribunal. As a result of the pressure brought to bear on the government locally and internationally, the Babangida administration issued Decree No. 22 of 1986, under which hard drug offences no longer attracted death sentences, but punishments ranging from a few years to life imprisonment. Apart from these and other laws, the government has made serious efforts to patrol its airports and its borders. At the border there is the customs National Drug Unit (Narcotics Section) under the Directorate of Enforcement and Drugs of the customs department set up in 1988. The section has the responsibility of investigating, arresting and prosecuting drug offenders.

Furthermore, the government in 1989 signed the Mutual Legal Assistance Treaty in Washington, D.C., between Nigeria and the United States, while a similar treaty was also signed with the United Kingdom. The treaty provided for joint efforts of both governments in investigating, confiscating, arresting and prosecuting drug offenders with a view to stemming the illicit drug trade between the two countries.

More important was the creation of the Directorate of Enforcement Agency and the enactment of Decree No. 48 of 1989, which aimed at controlling drug trafficking and abuse in the country and stipulating life imprisonment for drug traffickers and their barons, and offenders' forfeiture of property to the state. Hard drug users face between 15 and 25 years of imprisonment. People or organisations who helped to conceal or disguise proceeds or illicit drug trafficking face the prospect of up to 25 years of imprisonment. The decree also established the National Drug Law Enforcement Agency.

The agency started well, but it was later found to be riddled with corrupt officials. It was a common occurrence for drugs seized from traffickers to disappear from custody. The latest of such was the celebrated case of 246 kilograms of heroine seized in 1993. Twelve raps of the drug—worth about N700 million—disappeared, leading to the establishment of a commission of inquiry in early 1994 to probe the agency's activities.

DUAL MANDATE, THE. According to Lord Lugard (q.v.) in his book, *The Dual Mandate,* the British had a dual purpose in Africa: to promote the interests of the British industrial class and those of the native races in their progress toward self-government.

DUDLEY, BILLY J. Professor of political science, Dudley was one of those pioneers in the study of Nigerian politics, and a national figure who was often called to serve in important positions in the affairs of the country. In 1966 he was adviser to the Mid-Western Region's (q.v.) delegation to the Ad Hoc Constitutional Conference (q.v.). While other regions were thinking of a breakup of the country or a confederal arrangement, his delegation was the only one that stood firmly by the idea that the country should remain a federation. He was also in 1975 appointed to the Constitution Drafting Committee (q.v.) and was a member of the subcommittee on citizenship, citizenship rights, political parties and the electoral system. In 1977 he became the director of the Nigerian University Commission in London where he later died at the age of 49 in December 1980. Among his books are *Politics and Parties in Northern Nigeria, Politics and Crisis in Nigeria* and *An Introduction to Nigerian Government and Politics.*

DUNAMA BEN AHMED. Ruler of the Kanuri (q.v.) people of Bornu between 1808 and 1809, and between 1813 and 1820. It was during his reign that state power moved to Muhammad Al-Kanemi (q.v.), an Islamic scholar and warrior, thereby putting an end to the thousand years of the Sefawa dynasty. In 1808 Dunama's blind old father Ahmed Ben Ali (q.v.), seeing that he could not keep away the Fulani (q.v.) Jihadists from his domain, abdicated in favour of Dunama. The abdication was not popular, and Dunama, anxious for victory against the Fulani to shore up his waning prestige, invited the help of Al-Kanemi. Their combined effort freed Bornu from the Fulani, but the Fulani later attacked. Dunama called on Al-Kanemi again to come to his aid. After their victory, he gave some land to Al-Kanemi in appreciation for his help. In 1809, because of Dunama's dependence on Al-Kanemi and their unhappiness about his accession to the throne, his people deposed him and put his uncle Muhammad Ngileruma in power. But the new ruler did not get on well with Al-Kanemi who joined forces with the supporters of Dunama to reinstate him in 1813.

Because the Fulani were still a threat, Dunama continued to rely on Al-Kanemi, but he saw that Al-Kanemi was also a threat to his dynasty and so planned to get rid of him. The plan leaked to Al-Kanemi, and, in the fight that ensued, Dunama was killed in 1820. His younger brother, Ibrahim Ben Ahmed, succeeded him, but Al-Kanemi and his forces were effectively in power.

DUNAMA DIBALEMI. The ruler of the Kanuri (q.v.) of the Kanem-Bornu empire (q.v.) between 1221 and 1259. During his reign he worked hard to extend the boundaries of the empire that he inherited from his father, Ahmad Alimi (q.v.). The empire was very large, extending to Tragham, about 1,300 kilometres away from the capital city. He appointed military commanders to administer conquered territories. Many of these commanders broke away and established their own states.

Dunama also had serious problems with the Bulala (q.v.) people, a nomadic group within his empire. Tradition says he violated a religious taboo by opening a talisman, considered a sacred symbol of the power of their religion. A conflict ensued, and he died later in 1259.

-E-

EAST-CENTRAL STATE. Created out of the former Eastern Region (q.v.) of Nigeria on May 27, 1967, it covered an area of about 28,459 square kilometres with a 1963 population of about 7.5 million. In October 1967, when the Civil War (q.v.) was ending after the fall of Enugu (q.v.), Anthony Ukpabi Asika (q.v.), a lecturer in political science at the University of Ibadan, was appointed the administrator of the state, a position he occupied until the fall of General Yakubu Gowon (q.v.) in 1975.

The state, for all practical purposes could be said to have existed for only six years because the Civil War raged between 1967 and 1970 and the administrator could not take up effective administration of the state. He frequently stayed in Lagos (q.v.), until the war ended in January 1970.

The state is rich in agricultural resources like oil palm (q.v.), yams (q.v.), cassava (q.v.), plantain, maize, citrus and cocoa (q.v.). Among its many industries are coal, cement, asbestos, pottery and oil processing.

The state capital was Enugu, best known as the administrative center of the former Eastern Region (q.v.) and of the present-day Enugu State (q.v.). Its commercial centers were Aba and Onitsha (q.v.) with its famous market. Other major towns included Aba, Owerri and Abakaliki. On February 3, 1976, the state was divided into two—Anambra State (q.v.) and Imo State (q.v.).

EASTERN HOUSE OF ASSEMBLY. The Eastern House of Assembly was created under the Richards Constitution (q.v.) of 1946, which divided the country for administrative purposes into three regions—Eastern (q.v.), Western (q.v.) and Northern (q.v.). The Eastern House of Assembly was composed of the chief commissioner (q.v.) as president, 13 official members and 15 to 18 unofficial members, 10 to 13 of which were selected from the native authorities (q.v.) and five of whom were to be nominated by the governor to represent interests and communities that were inadequately represented. The house was intended to be a link between the native authorities and the Legislative Council (q.v.) in Lagos (q.v.), and it was to advise the governor on any matter referred to it or introduced by a member in accordance with the constitution.

In 1951 the house became a truly legislative body. It was, however, dissolved in 1966 when the military took over power.

EASTERN HOUSE OF CHIEFS. Eastern Nigeria (q.v.) did not have a House of Chiefs under the 1946, 1951 and 1954 constitutions (q.v.) as the Western (q.v.) and Northern Regions (q.v.) had. However, realizing that this kind of institution could be helpful in controlling voters, politicians decided to consider another House of Chiefs.

At the 1957 Constitutional Conference (q.v.) in London, it was agreed that the Eastern Region should also have a House of Chiefs. The house met in January 1960, but in 1966 it was dissolved by the military administration just as all other legislative bodies were dissolved.

EASTERN NIGERIA. *See* EASTERN REGION.

EASTERN REGION. The Eastern Region extended from the east of the Niger River to the boundary with the Cameroons (q.v.), and from some miles south of the Benue River (q.v.) to the Atlantic Ocean in the south. The region was about 29,484 square miles in area with about 12,388,000 inhabitants, according to the 1963 census. The pressure of population on the land was very great, which partly accounted for the fact that many people in the region readily left the area to look for employment in other parts of the country. The dominant ethnic group in the region was the Igbo (q.v.), but there were other important groups like the Ibibio (q.v.), Efik (q.v.) and the Ijaw (q.v.), who were generally looked at as the minority groups in the area. The people of the region, as with all the other regions, were mostly farmers, with palm oil the chief agricultural export product. The region was also blessed with coal and petroleum (q.v.), which has today become Nigeria's most important foreign exchange earner.

The first premier of the region was Dr. Nnamdi Azikiwe (q.v.), who served from 1954 to 1959, and the dominant party in the region (up to the military takeover in 1966) was the National Council of Nigerian Citizens (NCNC) (q.v.), founded and led by Dr. Azikiwe until he became the governor-general (q.v.) of Nigeria in 1960. Dr. Michael Okpara (q.v.) led the NCNC after Azikiwe.

Some of the main towns of the region were Enugu (q.v.), the regional headquarters, Calabar (q.v.), which according to the 1922 Constitution (q.v.), was allowed to elect and send a representative to the Legislative Council in Lagos (q.v.), Port Harcourt (q.v.) with its harbor, Onitsha (q.v.), famous for its markets, Owerri (q.v.), Aba, Abakaliki and Nsukka, which became a university town, the seat of the University of Nigeria, Nsukka (q.v.) in 1960.

Even though the region had always fought for a united Nigeria, which was propitious for citizens in other parts of the country, in 1964, following the outcome of the 1963–64 census, which the region described as unacceptable, and the emergence of petroleum as the most important foreign exchange earner, the Eastern Region threatened to secede from the rest of the country. In 1967, following the vendetta against the Igbo in the north in 1966 and the failure of the Federal Government (q.v.) and the Eastern Regional government to peacefully resolve the differences between them, the region under Lt. Colonel Odumegwu Ojukwu (q.v.) declared itself independent as the Republic of Biafra (q.v.) on May 30, 1967. This was a few days after the Federal Government had divided the region into three separate states, creating 12 states out of the four previously existing regions. The "rebellion" was, however, crushed in January 1970 after a 30-month war.

EASTERN REGIONAL GOVERNMENT CRISIS. On January 28, 1953, the National Council of Nigeria and the Cameroons (NCNC) (q.v.) Parliamentary Committee requested resignation from all nine regional ministers so that the regional Executive Council (q.v.) could be reshuffled as part of an effort by Nnamdi Azikiwe to establish his authority over the party. After all the ministers resigned, information leaked that six would not be included in the new council. These six sent letters to the lieutenant governor (q.v.) withdrawing their resignations. As it happened, the letters of withdrawal reached the governor's office before the letters of resignation. On February 4, 1953, the regional assembly, controlled by the NCNC, passed a vote of no confidence in the six ministers, but the ministers insisted that the vote of no confidence should be by secret ballot (q.v.) instead of by show of hands. The party refused to go by the secret ballot method, and it later turned itself into the opposition party, opposing and defeating every bill that was presented to the house, including the appropriation bill. The lieutenant governor was forced to use his reserve powers to decree appropriation for the running of the government. In May 1953 the house was dissolved, and, after the election that followed, the NCNC was overwhelmingly returned to power, headed by the party leader, Dr. Nnamdi Azikiwe (q.v.).

EASTERN STATES INTERIM ASSETS AND LIABILITIES AGENCY. When Nigeria was divided into twelve states in 1967, the Civil War (q.v.) did not allow the federal military government to concentrate its effort on how best to solve the problem of sharing the assets of the former Eastern Region (q.v.), which had been divided into three different states. After the end of the war in 1970, the federal government issued Decree No. 39 of 1970, which set up the Eastern States Interim Assets and Liabilities Agency. This agency vested all the assets and liabilities of the former Eastern Region—all statutory corporations, the University of Nigeria, Nsukka (q.v.) and government-controlled companies. The agency ceased to exist in 1976 by the promulgation of Decree No. 19 of 1975. *See also* INTERIM ADMINISTRATIVE COUNCIL.

EBONIYI STATE. Was created out of Abia and Enugu States by the Abacha regime on October 1, 1996. Its capital is Abakaliki.

ECOBANK NIGERIA LIMITED. In October 1989, ECOBANK Nigeria Limited, the Nigerian associate of ECOBANK Transnational Incorporated, Lomé, Togo, was formally opened. The bank is 60 percent owned by Nigerian citizens and 40 percent owned by the parent organisation in Lomé. The establishment of ECOBANK Nigeria Limited was aimed at enhancing the payment system within the Economic Community of West African States (ECOWAS) subregion, and facilitating the emergence of ECOWAS as a single economic and trade bloc.

ECONOMIC BLOCKADE. One of the weapons used by the Nigerian government against secessionist Biafra (q.v.) during the Civil War (q.v.) was to impose economic sanctions. After Colonel Odumegwu Ojukwu (q.v.) had declared the secession of the former Eastern Nigeria (q.v.) as the "Republic of Biafra," the Nigerian government ordered the closure of all the ports in the region. Communication links to the region from outside Nigeria and from other parts of the country were cut off. Later during the war, the Federal Government (q.v.) imposed restrictions on transportation or the sending of food to the region, and it instructed the oil companies not to pay any royalties due to the secessionist region. All these measures helped in no small way to bring an end to the war.

ECONOMIC COMMUNITY OF WEST AFRICAN STATES. A 16-nation association of West African states, ECOWAS came into being in 1975 following the signing of the ECOWAS Treaty by 15 of the members, including Nigeria, Niger, Benin (q.v.), Togo, Ghana (q.v.), Ivory Coast, Liberia, Sierra Leone (q.v.), Guinea Bissau, Upper Volta and Cape Verde Island. The ECOWAS Treaty was the result of the initiative of both Nigeria and Togo. Its aim was to unite the countries in West Africa into one large economic community, patterned after the European Economic Community. As such, ECOWAS is a common market of West Africa and a customs union. It is to promote the free flow of persons, property and capital within the community. This implies an integration of the economic policies and programmes of member states and an indigenisation of the ownership and control of capital in the area. The two main organs of ECOWAS are the Summit of the Heads of State which is the highest body, and the Council of Ministers. Like the Organization of African Unity's Council of Ministers, ECOWAS Council of Ministers makes recommendations to the Summit and gives direction to subordinate institutions of the organisation. The Summit meets at least once a year while the Council of Ministers meets about twice a year. The headquarters of the organisation is in Abuja (q.v.), Nigeria.

Many ECOWAS citizens who took advantage of the free flow of persons came to Nigeria and decided to stay and work beyond the time permitted so as to take advantage of the apparent oil boom in the country. In February 1983, these illegal aliens were asked to go back while those who were still legally in the country were allowed to stay. Nigeria has special immigration arrangements for all ECOWAS citizens.

In May 1990, ECOWAS dispatched a major peacekeeping force to help resolve the Liberian civil war. The force, known as the ECOWAS Monitoring Group (ECOMOG), was primarily composed of Nigerian troops and supported with Nigerian funds. ECOMOG was controversial in both Liberia, where it was sometimes seen as corrupt, and in Nigeria where it was derided for its expense. Nevertheless, by 1996 elections had been held and peace restored to Liberia—an outcome the ECOMOG forces helped to achieve.

ECONOMY. Many of the peoples of the coastal areas of Nigeria have traditionally depended on fishing. But as one moves inland, more work in agriculture (q.v.), where the main food crops in the nation's southern half are corn, yams (q.v.), vegetables, beans, millet, rice, and many others. Traditionally, under a system of shifting cultivation, farmers clear a few acres of bush and grow crops there for a few years before moving to another patch of land that has been lying fallow. The main cash and export crops are cocoa (q.v.), palm oil, palm kernel, rubber (q.v.), timber and citrus fruits.

In the north the main food crops are millet, maize, guinea corn and beans. Groundnut (q.v.) was traditionally produced for export, but most of what is produced today is consumed locally. Other export crops are cotton and tobacco. The north also raises cows, sheep and goats, and it supplies most of Nigeria's needs.

Nigeria is also rich in natural and mineral resources, such as tin ore, cassiterite, columbite, limestone, iron ore, marble, petroleum (q.v.), gold, uranium and coal. Oil refineries convert crude oil to all grades of oil; there are also petrochemical industries in the nation.

Nigeria began rapid industrialisation in the 1970s after the Civil War (q.v.) and, with the then oil boom, many manufacturing industries began to spring up and the economy was buoyant. But due to gross mismanagement of the resources, especially revenue from crude oil, the economy became depressed and on the verge of collapse. The naira, which used to exchange for $1.50 in the early 1980s, was by 1993 not worth much more than $0.01. Many industries began to produce much below their installed capacity—between 30 and 50 percent—and because many could not get raw material, they closed down. The situation worsened as a result of the political crisis arising from the annulment of the presidential election of 1993, which in turn led to the economic crises of 1994. Many industries and manufacturing concerns reported a slowdown of activities in 1994 and 1995. The nationwide survey conducted by the Central Bank of Nigeria (q.v.) in 1995 showed that the average rate of capacity utilisation in the manufacturing establishments had fallen from 37.2 percent in 1993 to 30.4 percent in 1994. Most industries operated less than 30 percent of their installed capacity. According to the 1996 budget, the performance of the real sector continued "to be sluggish as industrial output fell by 2.6 percent," while inflation rose from 57 percent in 1994 to 74.3 percent in 1995. It described the economy as "too weak."

ECOWAS MONITORING GROUP (ECOMOG). The name of the peacekeeping force sent by ECOWAS to help resolve the Liberian civil war. It is the most ambitious indigenous peacekeeping operation ever undertaken in the West African region. ECOMOG was dispatched in May 1990, and was primarily composed of Nigerian troops and supported with Nigerian funds. The early years of ECOMOG produced few positive results. Within Liberia the troops were seen as ineffective, and were accused of being corrupt and involved in drug smuggling. Within Nigeria, the costs of the operation made it very controversial. By 1996, it is estimated that ECOMOG had cost Nigeria $3 billion and claimed the lives of 1,000 Nigerian soldiers. In 1996, however, elections were successfully held in Liberia, bringing the bloody civil war to an end. While a number of factors contributed to this outcome, ECOMOG deserves a share of the credit.

EDET, INSP. GEN. LOUIS OROLA. Born on August 29, 1913, at Duke Town, Calaban (q.v.), Cross River State (q.v.), he obtained his elementary education at the Sacred Heart School in Calabar and his secondary education at the Bonny (q.v.) Government Grammar School. He joined the Nigerian Police Force in 1931 as a clerk, and later proceeded to the Police College in Hampshire in England. He became a subinspector in 1945 and an assistant superintendent of police in 1949. He again attended a senior training course at the Ryton-on-Dunsmore in Britain between 1953 and 1957 and later in 1960. In 1957 he was promoted to senior superintendent of police. In 1960 he led and commanded the first contingent of the Nigerian Police Force to the Congo under the United Nations auspices. Edet returned to Nigeria in 1961 and became a police commissioner in Lagos (q.v.). In 1962 he was promoted to deputy inspector general of police and became inspector general of police in 1964, being the first Nigerian to hold such a high post.

When the military took over power in 1966, he was a member of the Federal Executive Council (q.v.). After the second military coup (q.v.) in July 1966, General Yakubu Gowon (q.v.), on taking over power, accepted Edet's retirement. After his retirement he was appointed as recruitment attaché in the Nigerian High Commission in London. In 1968 he was appointed commissioner (q.v.) for home affairs and information in the South-Eastern State (q.v.), one of the 12 states newly created in 1967.

Edet was a highly honoured person. He was awarded the Order of the Federal Republic of Nigeria, the Queen's Police Medal, Commander of the Order of the British Empire and was also awarded a medal by Pope Paul VI. He died on January 17, 1979.

EDO. The Edo people constitute one of the major communities in present-day Edo State (q.v.) and Delta State (q.v.). These people are centered in the old kingdom of Benin. Edo is also the name given to the language spoken by the people of Benin (q.v.), Ishan (q.v.), Etsako, Akoko-Edo, Owan, the Urhobo (q.v.) and the Itsekiri (q.v.) of the Niger Delta. The first dynasty of the kingdom of Benin (q.v.) came to an end when the people decided to banish Owodo, the last Ogiso (king), for maladministration. After his banishment, the people sent emissaries to the then-Ooni of Ife, Oduduwa (q.v.), pleading that he should send a wise prince to them to be their ruler. Oduduwa sent Oranmiyan (q.v.) to them, who became the founder of the Second Benin Kingdom. This lends credence to the Yoruba (q.v.) tradition that describes the Edo-speaking peoples as an off-shoot of the Yoruba people. Further still, there are certain Edo institutions and works of art that are markedly similar to those of the Yoruba. Today, however, the Edo and Yoruba languages are mutually unintelligible.

EDO STATE. Edo State was one of the two states created out of the old Bendel State (q.v.) in 1991; the other was Delta State (q.v.). Bendel State was the same as the old Mid-Western Region (q.v.), carved out of the Western Region (q.v.) in 1963. The state is located within longitudes 6° 04′ and 6° 43′E, and latitudes 5° 44′ and 7° 34′N. It is bounded by Delta State in the south and east, Ondo State (q.v.) in the west, and Kogi State (q.v.) in the north and northeast. Its vegetation is tropical rain forest in the Benin lowlands and savannah forest in the Akoko-Edo uplands. It is rich in many cash-crop trees like rubber, oil palm (q.v.) and mango. The state is divided into 14 local governments.

The population of the state was 2,159,848 in 1991 with a density of 109 persons per square kilometre. The inhabitants of the state are made up of many ethnic groups such as Bini/Edo, Ishan (q.v.), Etsako, Etuno, Igbo (q.v.) and Okpamheri, but many of these groups trace their origin to the ancient kingdom of Benin, and, therefore, have linguistic and cultural affinity toward one another. The main language of the state is Edo with local variations in many places. Other languages spoken are Igbirra (q.v.), Okpamheri, Uneme, Ososo and Yoruba (q.v.). Three religious groups coexist in the state. Some people still cling to the traditional religious worship (q.v.) of their fathers. Christianity (q.v.) reached Benin City (q.v.) as early as the 15th century through Portuguese explorers and missionaries. Islam (q.v.) came to the state through the Nupe (q.v.) warriors in the 19th century.

Edo State is rich in traditional festivals like Igue among the Bini, Ukpe among the Ishan and Okpameri, and Uda in Ekpoma. It is also very rich in arts and crafts. Benin is famous for its wood carvings and brass and bronze castings. These works of art are said to date back to the 10th century. The art of brass casting was traced to the coming of the Ife smiths to Benin City (q.v.) in the late 13th century. Other local crafts are cloth weaving in Igarra and Auchi, pottery in Ojah Udo and Uhonmora, mat and basket making, smithry and jewelry-making. Major urban centers include Benin City, the state capital, Auchi, Uromi, Ekpoma Ibillo, Ososo, Jattu, Igara and Okpella.

Edo State is the home of Okada Village, referred to as Okada Wonderland. Many modern facilities are provided by Chief Gabriel O. Igbinedion (q.v.), the Esama of Benin.

Because Edo State was a part of the old Western Region, it has enjoyed free primary education since 1956 and, therefore, enjoys a high level of literacy. There are presently two universities in the state—the University of Benin and Bendel State University at Ekpoma.

EDUCATION. Education is the process that provides the young with the knowledge, skills and values that a society believes are necessary. In Nigeria there are various forms of education. Traditional education is usually informal. The child learns from his parents and elders the importance of tradition, religion and respect for elders and other people. As the child grows up, he or she learns about the customs and ways of life of his or her people.

Formal education takes place in schools, colleges and universities. Here the child is taught such knowledge and skills that will help him or her secure a job and live in other societies and environments. Nigeria's present economic, social and political development has depended very much on the quality of these schools, colleges, and universities.

The foundation of education in Nigeria was laid by the European missionaries who came to Nigeria in the 19th century. Even though the aim of the missionaries was to save souls by making converts, they saw that they had to teach the people how to read and write, thus opening up opportunities for young men and women to enter schools. Prominent among the missionary groups that led in this field were Wesleyan Methodist missionaries who visited Badagry (q.v.) and Abeokuta (q.v.) in 1841, the Church Missionary Society (CMS) (q.v.) who landed at Badagry in 1842, the Presbyterians who began work in Calabar (q.v.), Eastern Nigeria (q.v.), in 1846, the Baptist and Catholic (q.v.) missionaries. Even when the need of expatriate commercial firms and the government for literate people to staff their agencies, departments and companies became felt, government still considered it cheaper to subsidise mission schools rather than set up its own schools. Thus, until 1898, all education in Nigeria was under the direct control of missionaries, and, as late as 1942, missionaries controlled more than 90 percent of the schools.

But while the south readily accepted the education that missionaries brought, the Muslim north appeared to identify that education with the Christian religion and so were reluctant to accept it. In 1903 Lord Lugard (q.v.), realizing how sensitive the issue was, promised the Emir (q.v.) of Sokoto (q.v.) that government would not interfere with the Muslim religion and the colonial government kept out missionaries from most of the Muslim north. This explains why the north, even today, lags behind the south in westernized education. Many of the states in the north are still officially regarded as educationally backward states.

While missionaries led in the field of primary and secondary education, the government has had a virtual monopoly in postsecondary education. Beginning in 1934 with the establishment of the Yaba Higher College (q.v.), government went on in 1947 to set up the University College of Ibadan (q.v.) in association with London University, with Yaba Higher College becoming a nucleus of the new University College. Later on, regional governments stepped into founding universities. In the east was the University of Nigeria, Nsukka (q.v.), founded in 1960, in the west was the University of Ife (q.v.), founded in 1961 and in the north was Ahmadu Bello University (q.v.), founded in 1962. The Federal Government (q.v.) in 1962 set up another university, the University of Lagos while making the University College, Ibadan an autonomous university. Today there are 32 universities in the country—most federally owned and financed with many technical colleges and teacher-training colleges.

Education today has a high priority in the country's development plan. There has been free primary education in the Western Region (q.v.) since 1955. The Federal Government launched its Universal Primary Education (UPE) Program in 1976. This effort was unsuccessful because many young children, who for one reason or another, did not attend school, and Nigeria soon became one of the few countries in the world where illiteracy is high.

In recent years, the Nigerian educational system has suffered a serious setback because of the political instability and economic downturn that have afflicted the country. Schools, colleges and universities have deteriorated physically and educationally. Buildings are rundown and equipment has broken down without any hope of replacement. Since 1992, elementary and secondary schools have suffered from constant strikes because the government has failed to pay the teachers or for some other reasons. Universities are closed down for weeks and months as a result of strikes by the academic, administrative or technical staff. Pay was very low; for example, between 1993 and 1996, a full professor earned the equivalent of $100 a month. The "brain drain" began first among medical doctors and other personnel and has engulfed all academic disciplines. Highly skilled Nigerians are scattered all over Europe, the United States, Canada, the Middle East and Asia, leaving the educational system in Nigeria in a very perilous state.

EDUCATION, HIGHER. Higher education in Nigeria has gone through a very rapid expansion in the past three decades. Before 1960, there was only the University of Ibadan (q.v.), but in the early 1960s, there were universities in Nsukka, Ile-Ife (q.v.), Zaria (q.v.), Lagos (q.v.), Benin (q.v.) and Kano (q.v.). In the 1970s, the federal military government established new universities in Jos (q.v.), Calabar (q.v.), Maiduguri, Sokoto (q.v.), Port Harcourt (q.v.) and Ilorin (q.v.). During the Second Republic (q.v.), the Federal Government of Alhaji Shehu Shagari (q.v.) pledged to establish a university in any state that did not already have one. Furthermore, some state governments began to set up new state universities. In addition to rapid expansion in university facilities, both the federal and state governments set up polytechnical and technical schools to train people to operate the growing technical industries.

As a result of this expansion, enrollment rose sharply from about ten thousand in 1970 to over sixty thousand in 1980. Admission to these universities is done through a central admission board known as the Joint Admissions and Matriculation Board (JAMB) (q.v.). The board would avoid duplicate offers, helping to "nationalize" the admission system by taking account of the "federal character" of Nigeria. At present, admission through JAMB is based on the criteria of merit, catchment areas, and educationally backward areas. Every university is, therefore, expected to admit some candidates on the basis of merit, no matter what states they come from. Other candidates are admitted from the areas or states close to the university and from some educationally backward states.

Since university education is tuition-free, and almost all universities, colleges of education, polytechnics and technical schools are owned and financed by the government—national and state—financing so many universities and colleges has posed a great problem, especially when the country's economy has fallen into a recession. This has been the case since the second coming of military rule in Nigeria. Facilities have broken down and cannot be replaced. As a result of sky-rocketing inflation, faculty and staff are frustrated because their pay can no longer feed them, much less help them maintain a minimum standard of living. This has led to a massive brain drain to other countries in Africa, Europe, the Middle East, Asia and North America. In 1996 every department in the university has suffered serious attrition in personnel, leaving higher education in a deplorable situation. In the past, degrees awarded by Nigerian universities were highly regarded all over the world, but beginning in 1994, serious doubts were raised abroad about the standard of Nigerian higher education. *See also* ELLIOT COMMISSION.

EDUCATION, NATIONAL POLICY ON. Published in 1977 as a result of the Nigerian Educational Research Council (q.v.), the policy had as its major objective the improvement of the productive capacity of the nation through improved education so as to consolidate the nation's independence while reducing its dependence on outside sources for most of its needs.

The proposals for executing it were made in 1979 in the Blueprint of the Implementation Committee. According to the blueprint, secondary school education would be reorganised into junior and senior secondary schools, each providing a three-year course, beginning in 1982, when the graduates of Universal Primary Education (q.v.) would be ready to enter high school. It was estimated that about 40 percent of the children would enter junior secondary schools, while about 40 percent of these would go on to senior secondary schools.

EFIK. The Efik people of the Cross River State (q.v.) are closely related to the Ibibio (q.v.) in their language and much of their culture. The Efik have a centralized authority system, and the traditional ruler of Calabar is the Obong. From the 17th to the 19th century, many Efik villages became important centers of trade with Europeans who sought slaves and palm oil. Trade then was organised into trading houses by people of the same lineage. These houses competed among themselves for trade with the Europeans. The main trade center of the Efik then was Calabar (q.v.), which was an amalgamation of many towns like Duke Town, Greek Town and Big Qua Town.

It was the custom among the Efik that when a king or a prominent person died, the deceased's trading house demonstrated its wealth by the number of slaves it sacrificed to accompany the deceased to the afterlife and render him services thereafter. The competition between the various houses to sacrifice more and more slaves came to a head in the early 1850s when runaway slaves organised against the practice, thus ending the custom within a few years. Another Efik tradition was the fattening house to which prospective brides were sent for fattening and receiving necessary instructions before they got married.

EFIK LANGUAGE. Efik is used widely along the Cross River of eastern Nigeria. It was popularized through schools run by the Presbyterian Mission in Calabar (q.v.) in 1846.

EGBA. The Egba are a subgroup of the Yoruba (q.v.) people. During the Yoruba civil war in the early 19th century, the Egba left Ibadan (q.v.) in 1830 with their leader, Sodeke, a hunter, and moved to a place now known as Abeokuta (q.v.), meaning "under the rock." It has become the chief town of the Egba. The rock is the Olumo Rock, which is on the outskirts of Abeokuta, and served as a protective device for the Egba during any war or invasion. The Egba provided places for refugees from other parts of Yorubaland during the Yoruba civil war. For instance, refugees from Ijaye and Owu were given settlement by the Egba.

The Egba were the first Yoruba people to have contacts with the European Christian missionaries. Western civilization spread from Abeokuta to other parts of Yorubaland, and because of their early contact with the West, the Egba were able to preserve the autonomy of the Egba kingdom until 1914 when their independence was taken away by the British who took full control of the country after the Amalgamation (q.v.) of the Northern and Southern protectorates (q.v.). In 1918 there was a revolt in Egbaland called the Adubi War (q.v.), which was caused partly because of resentment over the termination of Egba independence and partly over the system of indirect rule (q.v.), newly introduced to the area.

Each section of the Egba has their own traditional ruler but the supreme head of all the Egba is the Alake of Egbaland. The Egba are mostly farmers and because of their proximity to Lagos (q.v.), many of them have become successful in business. The Egba's traditional rulers (Alake, Osile, Gbagura, Olubara and Olowu) now live in Abeokuta in peace with each other.

EGBA UPRISING. *See* ADUBI WAR.

EGBE OMO ODUDUWA. Egbe Omo Oduduwa (which means the Descendants of Oduduwa, the ancestor of the Yoruba [q.v.]) was a Pan-Yoruba cultural society founded in 1945 by Chief Obafemi Awolowo (q.v.) when he was in the United Kingdom. Its main objectives, according to its constitution, were to promote the unity and the social progress of the Yoruba people, and to cooperate with other regions in the country so that the aims set out for Yorubaland would be applied to the whole country. It also aimed at fostering the study of the Yoruba language, culture and history and to accelerate the emergence of a virile, modernised, and an efficient Yoruba State with its own individuality within the federal state of Nigeria.

In June 1948, the society was inaugurated at a conference held in Ile-Ife (q.v.), Osun State, under the auspices of the late Ooni of Ife, Sir Adesoji Aderemi (q.v.). Sir Adeyemo Alakija (q.v.) was made president of the organisation, while Chief Awolowo was chosen as the general secretary. The society had among its members many important people including Obas, chiefs, businessmen and politicians. The society had branches in many Yoruba Towns (q.v.). It promoted the study of the Yoruba language, culture and history and awarded scholarships to deserving students in secondary schools and universities.

Although the Egbe society was said to be nonpolitical, the National Council of Nigeria and the Cameroons (q.v.) saw it as a threat and, therefore, launched a vigorous campaign against it through the *West African Pilot* (q.v.). The Egbe later became the nucleus of the Action Group Party (q.v.) formed in 1951.

EGBE OMO OLOFIN. *See* ADEMOLA, SIR ADETOKUNBO ADEGBOYEGA.

EGBE OMO YORUBA. *See* ADEMOLA, SIR ADETOKUNBO ADEGBOYEGA.

EGHAREVBA. Tradition says he was the third ruler of Benin who, in the thirteenth century, initiated Benin sculptures and brass castings as historical records of events.

EIGHT-POINT PROGRAMME. Consequent on the Constitutional Crisis of 1953 at which Chief Anthony E. Enahoro (q.v.) moved in the National House of Assembly (q.v.) a proposal for self-government in 1956 and the northern representatives moved an amendment "as soon as practicable," the Action Group (q.v.) and the National Council of Nigeria and the Cameroons (q.v.) members walked out of the house in protest. The colonial secretary in London called Nigerian leaders for a constitutional conference (q.v.) in London. While preparations for the conference were being made, the Northern People's Congress (q.v.) put forward its Eight-Point Programme, which they believed would remedy the defects in the constitution. The programme proposed that each region should have complete legislative and executive autonomy in all matters except defense, external affairs, customs and some research institutions. They asked that there should be no central legislative and executive or policy-making body for the country. A nonpolitical body that would have no legislative or executive power operating in a neutral territory should constitute a central agency for the country and should be responsible for matters not allocated to the regions. Matters like railways, air services, ports, electricity, posts and telegraphs and coal mining should be organized on an interregional basis and all revenues except customs duties should be collected by the regions. Finally, each region should have its own separate public service. This programme, if accepted, would have created three independent states rather than a federal state. In the 1953 Constitutional Conference in London, the north abandoned the Eight-Point Programme.

EJOOR, MAJ. GEN. DAVID AKPODE. Born on January 10, 1934, at Ovu in Bendel State (q.v.), he was educated at the Government College, Ughelli, and joined the Nigerian Army in 1953. He did his officer's training in Accra, Ghana, before going to Sandhurst in England. He returned to Nigeria and was commissioned in 1956. He was company commander in the Cameroons (q.v.) in 1960 and was with the Nigerian Peacekeeping Mission to the Congo under the United Nations Peacekeeping Force from 1960 to 1961. He was the military governor of the Mid-Western Region (q.v.) from 1966 to 1967.

When the Civil War (q.v.) broke out, he was firmly on the side of the Federal Government (q.v.) but some of the men he trusted double-crossed him by allowing the Biafrans (q.v.) to invade the Mid-West (q.v.). He escaped to Lagos (q.v.). In 1969 he became commandant of the Nigerian Defence Academy (q.v.) and chief of staff of the Nigerian Army in 1972. He retired in 1975.

EKANDEM, HIS EMINENCE DOMINIC. The first West African Catholic (q.v.) bishop and first Nigerian cardinal, Ekandem was born in 1917, at Obio Ibiono, Itu, in Cross River State (q.v.). He was educated at the Christ the King College in Onitsha (q.v.), Senior Seminary Okpala Ngor in Owerri (q.v.) and the Bigard Memorial Seminary in Enugu (q.v.). He was ordained a priest December 1947 and served at St. Andrew's Parish. He was later appointed Rector of the Queen of Apostles Seminary, Afaha Obong. He was consecrated Auxiliary Bishop of Calabar (q.v.) by Pope Pius XII in February 1954 and was consecrated Bishop of Ikot Ekpene in 1963. He was made a cardinal by Pope Paul VI in April 1977. He is the president of the National Episcopal Conference. He is a member of the Sacred College of the Cardinals and member of the Sacred Congregation for the Evangelization of the People. He is honoured with the Commander, Order of the Niger, and he is a Member of the Order of the British Empire.

EKITI STATE. Was created out of Ondo State by the Abacha regime on October 1, 1996. Its capital is Ado-Ekiti, and the majority of the population are Yoruba (q.v.).

EKWENSI, CYPRIAN ODIATU DUAKA. A pharmacist, public relations consultant and most popularly known as a novelist, Ekwensi was born on September 26, 1921, at Minna, Niger State (q.v.). He was educated at the Government School in Jos (q.v.), the Government College in Ibadan, Yaba Higher College (q.v.) in Lagos (q.v.), the School of Forestry in Ibadan (q.v.), Achimota College in the Gold Coast (q.v.) and Chelsea School of Pharmacy at the University of London in England.

After graduation he worked in many places, including as head of features at the Nigerian Broadcasting Corporation (now Federal Radio Corporation of Nigeria [q.v.]). During the Civil War (q.v.) from 1967 to 1970, he was the director general of the Broadcasting Corporation of Biafra. He was appointed commissioner (q.v.) for information in Anambra State (q.v.) in 1983. He has written many books, including *The Drummer Boy* (1960), *Yaba Roundabout Murder* (1962), *Trouble in Form Six* (1962), *Jagua Nana* (1961), *Survive the Peace* (1975), *Motherless Baby* (1980), *Divided We Stand* (1980) and *Jagua Nana's Daughter* (1985). He is the winner of the Dag Hammarskjold International Award for Literary Merit.

EKWUEME, DR. ALEX IFEANYICHUKWU. First vice president of Nigeria, born on October 21, 1932, in Oko, Anambra State (q.v.), he attended Anglican School, Oko, Anglican Central School, Ekwulobia, King's College, Lagos (q.v.), and later studied sociology, architecture and urban planning at the University of Washington in the United States. He earned a Ph.D. from the University of Strathclyde in Glasgow, Scotland. When the ban on political activities was lifted in 1978, he joined the National Party of Nigeria (NPN) (q.v.) and was elected vice president of Nigeria with Alhaji Shehu Shagari (q.v.), who was president. After the December 1983 military takeover, Dr. Ekwueme was arrested and detained, and investigations went on to determine whether he had corruptly enriched himself while in office. In 1994 he was a member of the Constitutional Conference (q.v.) set up by the Abacha (q.v.) regime to fashion a new constitution for the country.

In December 1995, Ekwueme chaired the prestigious All Nigeria Politicians Summit, which was ultimately unsuccessful in uniting the political class against military rule. Ekwueme was more successful in his leadership of the Group of 34, a collection of very prominent Nigerian politicians who publicly opposed Sani Abacha's plan to manipulate his transition program to have himself elected president. In May 1998, the newly-formed Group of 34 released a lengthy memorandum detailing why Sani Abacha should not continue in power. The act clearly unnerved the military regime.

Following Sani Abacha's death in June 1998, the Group of 34 emerged as one of the most powerful political forces in the country. They formed the nucleus of the People's Democratic Party (PDP), which became the dominant political party under General Abdulsalami Abubakar's (q.v.) transition to democratic rule (1998–99). Enjoying the backing of much of eastern Nigeria and prominent northern politicians, Ekwueme was an early favorite to win the presidential elections. This changed in October 1998, when former military head of state Olusegun Obasanjo (q.v.) announced his candidacy. Eventually Obasanjo won the presidential nomination of the PDP at a tumultuous party convention in Jos (q.v.) in February, 1999. Ekwueme's hard fought campaign, however, had confirmed his position as the most powerful Igbo (q.v.) politician since the death of Nnamdi Azikiwe in 1996.

ELECTORAL MALPRACTICES. Electoral malpractices are devices by which elections are made unfair and most often farcical. In Nigeria the popular expression is "rigging," and this includes falsification of election results, double voting, voting by the underaged, or unregistered persons. For example, in the federal elections of 1964 and the Western Regional (q.v.) election of 1965, there were allegations of electoral malpractices by politicians; it was alleged that government parties in many constituencies prevented other party candidates from filing their nomination papers or that, when such candidates presented the papers in the office of the electoral officer, the officer would not be available. The result was that, in many constituencies, government candidates were declared unopposed. Furthermore, there were charges of falsification of election results in many constituencies and that ballot boxes were stuffed with "fake ballot papers." At the 1979 general elections to usher in the presidential system of government, all the parties complained of electoral malpractices in the states where their parties failed to win. Worse still was the allegation that the gubernatorial primary elections of the Unity Party of Nigeria (q.v.) in 1982 were rigged in four out of five states, a situation that rocked the solidarity of that party. The losers—Chief S.M. Afolabi and Chief Busari Adelakun in Oyo State (q.v.) and Chief Akin Omoboriowo in Ondo State (q.v.)—opted out of the party. In the 1983 national and state elections, allegations of electoral malpractices were common, which led to many court cases in which the petitioners asked the court to nullify the results.

In the 1992 presidential primary elections, the National Electoral Commission (q.v.) identified many electoral malpractices, such as the use of money by wealthy aspirants to buy votes, threats and intimidations, favoritism on the part of parties' executive committees, use of state government machinery by some state governors in favour of some aspirants, falsification of figures and allocation of votes where elections did not take place, arbitrary cancellation of results, and mutilation of election results. The NEC was created in 1987 to monitor Bubangide's transition program. FEDECO monitored the transition program in the Second Republic (1977–83) (q.v.).

ELECTRICITY. Production and transmission of electricity was formerly in the hands of the Electricity Corporation of Nigeria, but, in 1972, the company was merged with the Niger Dams Authority, which was then producing hydroelectric power from the Niger Dam at Kainji. The new company was called the National Electric Power Authority (q.v.).

In 1970 the original capacity of the four generating units at Kainji—647 megawatts—was sufficient to double the then-installed capacity in the country, but because of the rapid economic development due to the oil boom, the demands soon outstripped the supply. To remedy the production side of this problem, new hydroelectric projects have been set up in some places and gas-fired stations were built in Ughelli, Afam and Sapele. In 1988 thermal and hydroelectric energy generated was 11,237.9 million kilowatt hours, while 85.2 million kilowatt hours were purchased. In 1991, 13,672.2 million kilowatt hours were generated and 260.7 million kilowatt hours were still purchased. However, owing to gross inefficiency, shortage of technically qualified staff, and the need to import all parts, many areas in cities remain without electricity for days and sometimes weeks.

ELECTRICITY CORPORATION OF NIGERIA. *See* NATIONAL ELECTRIC POWER AUTHORITY.

ELIAS, DR. TASLIM OLAWALE. A scholar and a jurist, former chief justice of the Federation (q.v.), he was born on November 11, 1914, in Lagos (q.v.) and was educated at the Christian Missionary Society Grammar School (q.v.) in Lagos, Igbobi College, Yaba, Lagos, and at the University College, London. He was called to the bar at the Inner Temple in London in 1947. After receiving his Ph.D. in Law at London University, the first Nigerian to have done so, he taught law at Manchester University from 1951 to 1953 and was the recipient of many research fellowships, among which were the Oppenheim Research Fellow, Institute of Commonwealth Studies, Queen Elizabeth House and Nuffield College. He was in 1956 a visiting professor to the University of Delhi where he helped to establish a department of African studies. Returning to London, he served as governor of the School of Oriental and African Studies from 1957 to 1960.

Back in Nigeria he became attorney general and minister of justice from 1960 to January 1966 when the military took over. In the same year he became professor and dean of the faculty of law at the University of Lagos, but in October 1966, he was reappointed attorney general and later commissioner of justice from 1967 to 1972. In 1972 he became the chief justice of the federal republic. In 1975 he was appointed a judge of the International Court of Justice (ICJ) at the Hague, and in 1979, he was elected vice president of the ICJ, and in 1982 became the president of the Court.

Professor Elias has held many important national and international posts, including membership of the governing council of the University of Nigeria, Nsukka (q.v.), from 1959 to 1966, and the chairman of the Committee of the United Nations (UN) Conference on Law of Treaties from 1968 to 1969. He was also chairman of the UN committee of constitutional experts that drafted the Congo Constitution from 1961 to 1962 and a member of the expert committee that drafted the charter of the Organization of African Unity (q.v.).

Elias also found time to write many books, including *Nigerian Land Law and Custom* (1951), *Nigerian Legal System* (1954), *Makers of Nigerian Law* (1956) and *The Impact of English Law upon Nigerian Customary Law* (1960). He died August 14, 1991.

ELLIOT COMMISSION. Set up in 1943 to look into higher education (q.v.) in West Africa, the commission, headed by Sir Walter Elliot, with three African educationists and British members of the Conservative, Labour, and Liberal parties, made a fairly comprehensive survey of higher education in West Africa and reported in 1945. The commission agreed on the urgent need for the extension of higher education and university development in West Africa. The majority agreed that there should be a university college established in Nigeria and in Ghana (q.v.), respectively, and that higher educational development should also be carried through in Sierra Leone (q.v.) in connection with the Fourah Bay College (q.v.). The commission suggested the faculties that should be set up in each institution. They also recommended how the colleges were to be administered and financed. This report was finally accepted, leading to the establishment of the University College in Ibadan (q.v.) in 1947, which opened in January 1948.

EMERGENCY ADMINISTRATION IN WESTERN NIGERIA. The disorder in the Western House of Assembly (q.v.) in May 1962 arising from the Action Group (AG) Crisis of 1962 (q.v.) made the Federal Government (q.v.) invoke sections 64 and 65 of the 1960 Constitution by declaring that a state of emergency existed in the region. The regional government was suspended, and an administrator, Dr. M.A. Majekodunmi (q.v.), was appointed to look after the affairs of the region. The administrator restricted most of the leading politicians to places outside Ibadan (q.v.), the regional capital, but by the end of two months, virtually all the members of the Akintola (q.v.) factions and those of the National Council of Nigerian Citizens (q.v.) were released while AG members remained restricted. The period of the emergency witnessed two important events: the setting up of the Coker Commission of Inquiry (q.v.) to look into the affairs of certain statutory corporations in Western Nigeria (q.v.), and the Treason Trial (q.v.) of Chief Awolowo (q.v.) and many other AG leaders charged with the plan to overthrow the government of Nigeria. At the end of the emergency, a new government headed by Chief S.L. Akintola was installed in office.

EMIR. The title that the Fulani (q.v.) rulers of Northern Nigeria (q.v.) took, after they had conquered the Hausa (q.v.) city-states and other states during the jihad (q.v.) (holy war), which was initiated by Usman Dan Fodio (q.v.) in 1804. In Arabic language, Emir means the governor or military commander of a territory.

EMIRS COUNCIL. *See* COUNCIL OF CHIEFS.

EMIRATE SYSTEM. The system of administration used in Northern Nigeria (q.v.) before the British took over the administration of the country. During the jihad (q.v.), or holy war, of Usman Dan Fodio (q.v.), which overran most of the region, Dan Fodio's lieutenants in each Hausa state (q.v.) and other places were appointed as Emirs. Before his death in 1817, he divided the emirates into two—those to the west of Gwandu (q.v.) paid tribute to Abdullahi (q.v.), Dan Fodio's brother, while those to the east paid tribute to his son Muhammad Bello (q.v.), who resided in Sokoto (q.v.). But Sokoto was supreme as the seat of Dan Fodio, the Commander of the Faithful. Each emirate had a high level of independence, but they were tied together under the caliphate (q.v.) by a common religious allegiance to the Commander of the Faithful.

After the conquest of Northern Nigeria by the British at the beginning of the 20th century, much of the emirate system was retained. Under Lord Lugard's program of indirect rule, traditional structures were preserved, and incorporated into the colonial bureaucracy. While this ensured the survival of the emirate system, it also undermined its legitimacy for many Northern Nigerians.

ENAHORO, CHIEF ANTHONY ERONSELE. Journalist and politician, born on July 22, 1923, at Uromi in Bendel State (q.v.), he was educated at the King's College, Lagos (q.v.). In 1942 he took up journalism, and became editor of the *Southern Nigerian Defender* in 1944. In 1945 he joined the *Daily Comet* (q.v.) in Kano (q.v.) and became associate editor of the *West African Pilot* (q.v.) in 1949. In 1951 he was appointed editor-in-chief of the *Nigerian Star.*

Chief Enahoro was a foundation member of the Action Group (AG) (q.v.) Party in 1951. He was elected under the AG ticket to the Western Regional House of Assembly (q.v.) in 1951 and from there was later sent to the House of Representatives (q.v.) in Lagos. As a member of the central legislature, he moved the "self-government-in-1956" motion (q.v.), asking that the British give self-government to Nigeria. While this motion eventually led to self-government for the regions and the country, it immediately created a crisis leading to the resignation of the four AG ministers from the government and a temporary alliance between the AG and the National Council of Nigeria and the Cameroons (NCNC) (q.v.) and the northern loss of confidence in the legislative assembly. It also speeded up the demise of the Macpherson Constitution (q.v.).

Back in Western Nigeria (q.v.), Chief Enahoro was made minister of home affairs in 1954, and in 1957 he added the portfolio of Mid-Western Affairs. After the 1959 federal elections in which his party became the opposition party, Chief Enahoro was the opposition spokesman on foreign affairs from 1959 to 1963. He attended all constitutional conferences (q.v.) beginning in 1953 to independence.

During the AG crisis of 1962 (q.v.) in the Western Region (q.v.), and the declaration of emergency following it, Chief Enahoro was arrested and detained along with Chief O. Awolowo (q.v.) and was to be tried with others for treasonable felony, but he escaped, first to Ghana (q.v.) and finally sought asylum in Britain. He was arrested in Britain and detained during extradition proceedings. After a lot of row in the press and in the British Parliament over the decision to extradite him, and after many court cases to keep him in Britain, he was extradited to Nigeria on May 16, 1963. He was then tried for treasonable felony, found guilty and sentenced to seven years' imprisonment. However he did not stay that long in jail for on August 2, 1966, two days after General Yakubu Gowon (q.v.) became head of state, he released both Chief Enahoro and Chief Awolowo.

Chief Enahoro led the Mid-Western Delegation to the Ad Hoc Constitutional Conference (q.v.) of September 1966 and served on the committee that was charged with finding a workable constitution for the country. In 1967 he was appointed federal commissioner for information, labour, and cultural affairs. As such, he worked hard to keep Nigeria united. He ensured that Nigeria got its arms supply from Britain and from Russia and presented the federal case at the Kampala Peace Talks (q.v.) in May 1968 when the Biafrans (q.v.) were asked to give up secession and accept the new order in the Federation. He also later led a delegation to Addis Ababa, Ethiopia, to present similar proposals. In 1975 he was made federal commissioner for special duties, to prepare for the African Festival of Arts and Culture (FESTAC) (q.v.). The July 1975 coup relieved him of his duties, and he went into private business. When the ban on politics was lifted in 1978, Chief Enahoro became a member of the National Party of Nigeria (q.v.) and was made chairman of the party's branch in the then-Bendel State (q.v.). In 1994 Chief Enahoro was arrested and detained by the Abacha (q.v.) regime for joining in the campaign for the military to quit politics and restore the country to civilian government. In May 1996, when Chief Enahoro became convinced that his life was in danger, he fled the country into exile to join many of his National Democratic Coalition (q.v.) colleagues. Chief Enahoro received an honorary degree of doctor of science from the University of Benin in 1972. He also wrote the *Fugitive Offender* (1965).

Chief Enahoro declined to participate in the Abubakar regime's 1998–99 democratic transition based on his belief that it would not "provide the framework for the kind of Nigeria for which our people yearn."

ENDELEY, DR. EMMANUEL MBELA LILAFFE. A Cameroonian physician and politician, born on April 10, 1916, at Buea in the Cameroons (q.v.), he was educated at the Bonjongo Government College, Umuahia, from 1931 to 1934. In 1935 he entered the Yaba Higher College (q.v.) to study medicine. After his training he served in many places as a medical officer. He later founded the Cameroons National Federation, which later became the Kamerun National Congress (KNC) (q.v.) and was its president. He was leader of the South Cameroon Delegation to the 1957 Constitutional Conference (q.v.) in London and became the first Premier of the Southern Cameroons in 1958. He successfully fought for the separation of his country, Southern Cameroon, from Nigeria.

ENGLISH LANGUAGE. Nigeria is made up of many nationalities or ethnic groups whose languages are mutually unintelligible. And even though Hausa (q.v.) is the lingua franca of most of the former Northern Nigeria (q.v.), the only common language between the peoples of the south and north and the language of communication between one group and another is the English language, inherited from the British colonial authorities. For most Nigerians, English is a second language that is learnt in schools beginning from the primary school. A "credit" pass in English language at the secondary school level is required for admission into Nigerian universities. Today a growing portion of the population speaks English.

ENUGU. Enugu is one of the new towns east of the Niger River (q.v.), which was established in 1912. It is presently the capital of Enugu State (q.v.). The city owes its origin to the discovery of coal east of the Nguro village in 1909. In 1917 Enugu attained the status of a township, and in 1929 it was made the administrative headquarters of the southern provinces (q.v.). In 1939 it became the headquarters of the eastern provinces. In 1951 it became the capital of the Eastern Region (q.v.) and in 1967 the capital of the East-Central State. In 1976 it became the capital of Anambra State (q.v.) and in 1991 the capital of Enugu State. At one time or another, Enugu has served as capital for all seven states east of the Niger.

With a population of about 465,000 people, according to the 1991 census, Enugu is well served by trunk roads which run west to Onisha and east to Abakaliki. It is linked to the north through Opi Junction, near Nsukka. There is a modern airport linking Enugu with other parts of the country, and a railroad runs down from Jos (q.v.) in the north to Port Harcourt (q.v.) in the south. Enugu is a thriving city. It has many institutions of higher learning, and besides the coal-mining industry, there is a steel-rolling mill and many other industries.

ENUGU STATE. Created in 1991 by the administration of General Ibrahim B. Babangida (q.v.), Enugu State is bounded in the north by Kogi (q.v.) and Benue States (q.v.), in the east by Cross River State (q.v.), in the south by Abia State (q.v.), and in the southwest by Anambra State (q.v.). It lies within the tropical and semitropical rain forest. In the south the vegetation is characterised by evergreen forests, but in the north—the Nsukka region—the vegetation is grassy. The temperature during the hottest period is about 33°C while the annual rainfall is between 1,520 millimetres and 2,030 millimetres. The rainy season begins around March to April and ends in October. The state's mineral resources include coal, salt, lead, zinc, limestone, but heavy rainfall, bush burning, and agricultural activities cause soil erosion. The state is divided into 10 local government areas.

The population of the state was 3,161,295 in 1991 in an area of 12,791 square kilometres. Thus, the population density was 214 per square kilometre. The state has four main city centers, Enugu (q.v.) the state capital,

Abakaliki, Nsukka, a university city and Udi. Enugu, traditionally a coal-mining center, had a population of 500,000 people in 1991. Enugu is also a commercial, financial and industrial center. The people of the state are mainly Igbo (q.v.), and they speak both Igbo and English (q.v.). In spite of the fact that they are basically ethnically homogeneous, they are culturally dynamic. They have many festivals: the masquerade (q.v.) and yam (q.v.) festivals that mark the end of the farming season. Traditional industry includes wood carving, blacksmithing, pottery, cloth dyeing, and basket and mat making. Christianity (q.v.) has deep roots in the state.

The state is fairly well developed educationally, with about 40 secondary schools, 46 commercial schools and two universities—Enugu State University of Technology and University of Nigeria, Nsukka (q.v.), including many colleges of education. The state is well connected to other states by road, rail and air.

On October 1, 1996, the Abacha regime combined part of Enugu State with part of Abia State to create the new state of Eboniyi.

ENWONWU, PROF. BENEDICT CHUKA. A sculptor and painter, born on July 14, 1921, in Onitsha (q.v.), Anambra State (q.v.), he was educated at St. Mary's Primary School in Port Harcourt from 1929 to 1930, Holy Trinity Primary School in Onitsha from 1930 to 1931 and later went to Government College in Umuahia from 1934 to 1939. He also attended Ruskin College, University of Oxford in England and Slade College of Art at the University of London. In 1959 he was the art supervisor for the Federal Government (q.v.) of Nigeria and in 1968 became its cultural adviser. He was appointed professor of fine art at the University of Ife (q.v.) (now Obafemi Awolowo University) from 1971 to 1975. He was a visiting professor of African studies in the United States at Howard University in Washington, D.C., in 1971. He has exhibited his artistic works in London, Glasgow, Paris, New York, Boston and many other places. He has received many national and international honours and awards and is a member of many cultural organisations.

EREDIAUWA I, OBA SOLOMON IGBINOGHODUA AISIOKUOBA AKENZUA. The Oba (king) of Benin, formerly an administrator and a lawyer, born in Benin (q.v.) in 1923 and educated in Benin, the Government College in Ibadan from 1942 to 1945, Yaba Higher College (q.v.) in Lagos (q.v.) and University of Cambridge, England from 1948 to 1951. He came home to become an administrative officer in the Nigerian Public Service Commission (q.v.). In 1965 he was deputy permanent secretary in various ministries until 1968 when he became permanent secretary of the Federal Ministry of Mines and Power. He was crowned Oba of Benin in 1979. His traditional title is Omo N'Oba N'Edo Uku Akpolokpolo Erediauwa.

ESIGIE. He ascended the throne as Oba of Benin (q.v.) about 1504. During his reign, trade in ivory, Benin cloths and beads flourished between his people and the Portuguese, who came to his kingdom as traders and missionaries.

Esigie was the first Oba in West Africa to establish diplomatic relations with a European country. His son was the first accredited black envoy to Portugal.

It is believed that Onitsha (q.v.) was founded by his people who immigrated there from Benin, and this may explain the fact that, like Benir with an Oba, Onitsha has an Obi. His mother, Idia, was a warrior queen who became immortalized in the ivory carving of her face, adopted as the African Festival of Arts and Culture (q.v.) symbol.

Oba Esigie contributed much to the arts and culture of Benin, and he encouraged the brass work that his predecessors had introduced into the kingdom, all of which continue to make Benin such a popular tourist attraction.

ETHNIC GROUP. Generally, a group of people who have a common language and common cultural values. In Nigeria there are 250 to 350 ethnic groups; some are regarded as ethnic majority groups and others as ethnic minority groups. In the old regional arrangement, the ethnic majority groups were those that constituted a majority in each region, such as the Hausa (q.v.)-Fulani (q.v.) in the north, the Yoruba (q.v.) in the west and the Igbo (q.v.) in the east. Ethnic minority groups are the less populated ethnic groups in each region. Because each ethnic majority group controlled the political parties that controlled the regional government, ethnic minority groups feared domination by the ethnic majority groups as independence drew nearer. The minorities then agitated for their own separate states to be carved out of each region. But with state creation (q.v.), some minority ethnic groups have become majority ethnic groups in their respective states, encouraging further struggle for the creation of more states.

EWEKA I. The first indigenous ruler of the second kingdom of Benin. According to oral tradition, around 1300 the Ife king Oranmiyan established a new dynasty in Benin. This was Benin's second kingdom, which would last until 1897. After ruling for a number of years, Oranmiyan turned over power to Eweka I, his son by a local woman.

EWUARE. The ruler of the kingdom of Benin (q.v.) about the middle of the 15th century. Tradition remembers him as one of the greatest rulers of Benin because he expanded the kingdom. He conquered parts of Yorubaland to the west and parts of Igboland to the east, thereby extending his territory much beyond that of the Edo-speaking people of Benin. Furthermore, he built roads and defensive walls around his capital, Benin, some of which are still extant.

EXECUTIVE COUNCIL. The Executive Council, now known as the Cabinet in both the state and the federal governments, has its origin in colonial administration. Under the British colonial system, when a colony was set up, there was a Legislative Council (q.v.) and an Executive Council. The Legislative Council legislated for the colony while the executive council formulated government policy and carried out the law. The relationship between the Legislative and Executive councils was based on clearly defined principles, e.g., the Legislative Council was subordinate to the Executive Council, and the colonial government itself was subordinate to the British government in London.

When Lagos (q.v.) became a Crown colony (q.v.), it had a Legislative Council and a small Executive Council. The Executive Council was an advisory body to the governor, and it consisted of the governor and some departmental heads of the government. After the 1914 Amalgamation (q.v.), the lieutenant governors (q.v.) of the Northern and Southern provinces (q.v.) and the administrator of Lagos were also included. The first African to be a member of the Executive Council was appointed in 1943. Under the 1951 Macpherson Constitution (q.v.), the Executive Council became the Council of Ministers (q.v.) and the policy-making body for the government. In the First Republic (q.v.), the Executive Council, known as the Cabinet, was collectively responsible to Parliament for its actions. This lasted until January 1966 when the military took over power. During the military regime, the Executive Council for the Federal Government (q.v.) was known as the Federal Executive Council, while in the states, it was called Executive Council. Under the Second Republic's (q.v.) Constitution, the Executive Council was called the Cabinet, made up of the president of Nigeria (q.v.) and his ministers. The ministers were responsible only to the president who appointed them and not to the legislative assembly.

EXERCISE HARMONY. During the tense period before the December 30, 1964, federal elections, Sir Abubakar Tafawa Balewa (q.v.) on December 28 announced that the troops would make a countrywide tour to give the Nigerian people an opportunity to see their army, and show the people that the army was at the ready in case there was any trouble anywhere. This show of force and military readiness for troublemakers was termed "Exercise Harmony." The exercise did show that things were not well in the country, that politicians could not conduct their business by negotiation and compromise, and it put ideas in the minds of young army officers who were politically minded to plan a coup (q.v.), which finally came in January 1966.

EX-OFFICIO MEMBERS. During the colonial administration, membership in the Legislative (q.v.) and Executive councils (q.v.) were made up mostly of officials and some few nonofficials. The official members of these councils were known as ex-officio members, that is, they were there because of the posts or offices they held. For example, the Executive Council of Nigeria before the Second World War consisted of entirely official members like the chief secretary, lieutenant governors (q.v.) of the Northern and Southern provinces (q.v.) of the protectorate (q.v.), the administrator of the colony, the attorney general, and the commandant of the Nigeria regiment. The Legislative Council consisted of officials (ex-officio members) as majority, and nominated nonofficials together with four elected members. However, as Nigeria advanced toward independence, the number of the ex-officio members of the legislative houses and Executive Councils gradually dwindled and they were almost completely eliminated at independence.

EXPORT REGISTRATION. A prospective exporter must be duly registered. Application for registration is available at the Nigerian Export Promotion Council, and applicants must meet the following requirements: evidence of incorporation of the company certificate; memorandum and articles of association; current tax clearance certificate; evidence of business contact with a potential buyer and a signed agreement with the producer. Exporters who are unable to provide evidence of business contact with a potential buyer and a signed agreement with the producer will still be registered as would-be exporters whose only activities in export business are their intention to export after identifying exportable products. Registration is for two years, after which it is renewed with evidence of performance and a current tax clearance certificate.

EXPORT TRADE. Nigeria's export trade dates back to some five centuries ago when the old northern empires, particularly the old Bornu empire, traded with the North African merchants through the Trans-Saharan trade routes. Later, the southern forest kingdoms also began to exchange goods with European merchants. These included pepper, palm oil, palm kernel and many more, which were exchanged for European exotic products. The slave trade (q.v.) took over thereafter and formed the bulk of the exports until the end of the 19th century.

With colonial rule from 1900 to 1960, the emphasis of the Nigerian economy shifted to the export of major cash crops such as palm kernel, palm oil, cocoa (q.v.), groundnuts (q.v.), groundnut oil, raw cotton, rubber (q.v.), kola nuts, beniseed, soya bean and fresh bananas (q.v.). There were also exports of timber in various forms, namely, sawn timber, logs, plywood, and veneer. Hides and skins were quite prominent on the schedule of exports, while tin ore and coal formed the major minerals that were exported.

From 1900 to 1965, non-oil exports accounted for more than 90 percent of the country's foreign exchange earnings. Nigeria was once the largest producer of groundnuts (averaging 712,600 metric tonnes per year), the second largest producer of cocoa (203,600 metric tonnes) after Ghana (q.v.), and the largest producer of columbite. Her oil palm (q.v.) supplied half the world's export of palm oil (152,700 metric tonnes).

However, with the discovery of crude oil in the late fifties and its subsequent exportation, the trend changed dramatically. It not only reduced the relative importance of agricultural produce but also led to a considerable neglect of agriculture. For example, in 1960, non-oil exports contributed about 93 percent to the country's foreign exchange earnings, while minerals accounted for the balance. But in 1969, minerals contributed about 41 percent of the total export earnings, which rose in subsequent years to over 90 percent between 1974 and 1985. The non-oil exports consequently became practically neglected due to the prominence which the oil sector secured. This trend was further exacerbated by mass exodus of rural labour to the urban centres, precipitating a vicious cycle for the agricultural sector. Between 1970 and 1979, while the 'Petro-naira' kept on increasing, the naira from non-oil exports went the opposite way to the extent that Nigeria started to import groundnut oil, palm oil, sawn timber, etc. Also, within this period, the export of manufactured goods was insignificant. In fact, importation of finished products was more lucrative. Trade with the West African subregion was rather minimal. In the period from 1980 to 1983 only two percent of Nigeria's exports went to ECOWAS.

The oil glut reared its ugly head in 1983 because projected revenue from oil was not realised. And, since oil was the mainstay of the economy, reduced earnings resulted in a deficit balance of payments. Inexorably, a convoluted inflationary spiral precipitated an economic crisis. Nigerians began to seek other ways of attracting foreign exchange so as to reverse the deficit and revamp the economy. In 1984 the government started to initiate programmes to launch Nigeria's non-oil exports into the world market. However, the boldest attempt came in 1986 with the federal budget and subsequent decrees that rolled out a package of incentives for interested Nigerian exporters.

EXTERNAL DEBT. The problem of external debt started in the early 1970s but has worsened by the depreciating value of the nation's exports while the value of imports continue to rise.

Nigeria resorted to external borrowing early in its history to speed up the pace of its economic development. The debt before the oil boom of the early 1970s was easily serviced during the boom, but in 1978 the oil boom collapsed, putting serious pressure on government finances. This led to more borrowing from the international capital market to support the country's balance of payments. Thus, in 1974, the debt stood at only $1.6 billion, but by 1979 it had jumped up by over 325 per cent to $6.8 billion. During the Shagari (q.v.) administration (October 1979 to December 1983), the debt rose astronomically to $18.5 billion, and, according to the 1996 budget, Nigeria's total external debt stock as of December 31, 1995, stood at $32,585 billion, despite the fact that the government has been servicing its external debt for the past five years with $2 billion every year.

The causes of the rapid rate of growth of the nation's external debt can be attributed not so much to new loans but rather to poor debt servicing management, accumulated payment arrears, penalties of payment due but not made, unrealistic exchange rate of the naira, decline in foreign exchange earnings and corruption in diverting loans from solving the problems for which they were taken to other uses and personal foreign bank accounts. Debt servicing and loan repayment constitute a huge problem for Nigeria and have created a serious economic crisis for the country.

-F-

FADAHUNSI, SIR ODELEYE. A former governor of Western Nigeria (q.v.), Fadahunsi was born in 1901 at Ilesha, Osun State (q.v.). He was educated at Osu Methodist School and Wesley Teacher Training College, Ibadan (q.v.). He was a teacher at Methodist schools at Ikorodu and Lagos (q.v.) between 1925 and 1926; he also worked as a produce buyer, a storekeeper and a salesman in the GBO, United African Company and UTC companies from 1927 to 1948. He formed and was the managing director of the Ijesha United Trading and Transport Company Ltd. in 1948. He was also a member of the Nigerian Cocoa Marketing Board from 1948 to 1953 and the director of the Nigeria Produce Marketing Company from 1952 to 1953; chairman of Ijesha Divisional Council from 1955 to 1960; and chairman of the Nigeria Airways Corporation in 1961.

Sir Odeleye Fadahunsi was a member of the Western House of Assembly (q.v.) and deputy leader of the National Council of Nigeria and the Cameroons (q.v.), the opposition party in the house from 1951 to 1961.

After the state of emergency was lifted in January 1963 and Chief S.L. Akintola (q.v.) was reinstated, Sir Odeleye was appointed governor of Western Nigeria, a position he held until the military took over power in January 1966.

Sir Odeleye was knighted by Queen Elizabeth II in 1963 and was earlier awarded the Queen's Coronation Medal in 1953. He also is a traditional

Chief and has been the recipient of a national honor, the Grand Commander of the Niger.

FAGUNWA, DANIEL O. A Yoruba (q.v.) novelist, born about 1910, Fagunwa became a teacher and later worked for the Ministry of Education in Ibadan (q.v.) in the then-Western Region (q.v.) of Nigeria. He wrote *Ogboju Ode Ninu Igbo Irunmole* (1939), and *Igbo Olodumare,* which were both based upon Yoruba tradition, fables and folktales.

FAJEMIROKUN, CHIEF HENRY OLOYEDE. A businessman, born in Ile-Oluji in Ondo State (q.v.), on July 14, 1926, he attended the Christian Missionary Society Grammar School (q.v.) in Lagos (q.v.) and Ondo Boys' High School in Ondo. In 1944 he joined the Royal West African Frontier Force and in 1945 served during the war in India. From 1946 to 1956, he served in many positions as a civil servant. In 1956 he left government service to start his own business. He was a successful businessman, and, by his death in 1978, his business, known as Henry Stephens and Sons, included insurance, engineering and shipping firms. In 1970 he became president of the Lagos Chamber of Commerce and Industry. In 1972 he was president of the Nigerian Association of Chambers of Commerce, Industry and Mines and was also elected the president of the Federation of West African Chambers of Commerce. In 1974 he was elected vice president of the Federation of Commonwealth Chambers of Commerce. He was also a copresident of the Nigerian British Chamber of Commerce and a member of the board of governors of the Nigerian American Chamber of Commerce. In recognition of his contribution to his home areas, he was honored with chieftaincy titles: Yegbato of Ile Oluji and the Asiwaju of Okeigbo. The University of Ife (q.v.) granted him the honorary degree of doctor of science.

FAJUYI, LT. COL. ADEKUNLE. Born in Ado Ekiti, Ondo State (q.v.) on June 26, 1926, he was educated at St. George's Catholic School, Ado Ekiti. He later enlisted in the Nigerian Army, received military training at the Command Training School at Teshie, Ghana (q.v.), and went for a course at the Officer Cadet School at Chester in England. He was commissioned in 1954. He later returned to Nigeria and joined the Third Battalion of the Queen's Own Nigeria Regiment. He was appointed to a number of posts between 1955 and 1960, and also went back to Britain for further training. He served in the United Nations (UN) Peacekeeping Force in the Congo where he won a military cross for his performance as head of his company in North Katanga (q.v.). He even became military assistant to the supreme commander of the UN forces in the Congo. Back in Nigeria in 1964, he was made commander of the First Battalion of the Second Brigade of the Nigerian Army in Enugu (q.v.). He was later sent on a senior military tactical course in Pakistan. Before the January 1966 coup (q.v.), he was at Abeokuta (q.v.) to command the Abeokuta Garrison. After General Aguiyi-Ironsi (q.v.) took over the government in 1966, Lt. Col. Fajuyi was appointed military governor of the Western Region (q.v.). On July 29, 1966, while the supreme commander and Head of State, General Ironsi was his guest at the government house in Ibadan (q.v.), a second coup was staged. Both Lt. Col. Fajuyi and General Ironsi were arrested and killed. The coup makers would have spared his life, but he told them if they took General Ironsi, they should take him too, and so they did.

FAKEYE, LAMIDI. An artist who specialises in wood sculpture (q.v.) depicting Yoruba (q.v.) lifestyle and myths, Fakeye was born in Ila in 1925 in Osun State (q.v.). He was an apprentice sculptor to his father. As a wood carver, he had his first exhibition in 1960, the year of Nigeria's independence. Two years later, he won a scholarship to study stone carving technique in Paris, France, and from there he moved to London in 1963 where he held an exhibition at the Commonwealth Institute. He later went to Western Michigan University in the United States. In 1978 he became a fellow at the Department of Fine Arts at the University of Ife (q.v.) (now Obafemi Awolowo University), where he teaches wood carving and other courses. Lamidi has carved doors for many public places in Nigeria, and his work is famous in Europe and America. Perhaps the most imposing and the most acclaimed of his works was the 13-foot high statue of Oduduwa (q.v.), the traditional ancestor of the Yoruba Obas, unveiled in 1987; it now sits in Oduduwa Hall, Obafemi Awolowo University, Ile-Ife (q.v.), Osun State. Lamidi, even though a Muslim, still draws from Yoruba tradition, symbols and myths in his artistic expression.

FALAE, CHIEF SAMUEL OLUYEMISI. A prominent civil servant and presidential contender. Olu Falae was born September 21, 1938, in Ilua-Aabo, Western Region (q.v.). He earned his bachelor's degree in economics from the University of Ibadan in 1963, and obtained a master's degree from Yale University from 1971–72. Falae was in the civil service from 1963–81, leaving from 1981–86 to serve as the chief executive of Nigerian Merchant Bank. In 1986, Ibrahim Babangida (q.v.) appointed him secretary to the Federal Military Government, and later he was made Minister of Finance, resigning in 1989 to participate in the Babangida transition program. During his tenure serving the Babangida administration, Falae is best remembered for his role in the design and implementation of the controversial Structural Adjustment Programme (SAP). SAP was the most aggressive effort yet undertaken to liberalise the Nigerian economy, and it remained the object of much controversy for years after it had been discontinued.

In 1992, Falae was a leading candidate for the presidential nomination of the Social Democratic Party (SDP), but appears to have lost out to Shehu Yar 'Adua (q.v.) when the military annulled the primaries and banned all the candidates in the fall of 1992. Falae was active in the campaign to force the government to recognize the election of M.K.O. Abiola (q.v.), which resulted in his imprisonment in January 1997. He was not released until after Abacha's death in June 1998. Under the Abubakar democratic transition (1998–99) Falae was a leading figure within the Alliance for Democracy (AD), one of the three officially recognised parties. In January 1999, he was selected as the presidential candidate of the AD, beating out Bola Ige (q.v.). While Bola Ige was considered to have stronger support within the southwest, which was the base of the AD, Falae was seen as having more national appeal. When the AD and the APP agreed to field a common presidential candidate, Olu Falae was selected to represent the alliance. He picked Umaru Shinkafi as his running mate, but lost to the candidate of the People's Democratic Party, Olusegun Obasanjo (q.v.) on February 27, 1999. Falae felt that the elections were fraudulent and initiated a court case to challenge the results but in April 1999, the charges were dismissed.

FANI-KAYODE, CHIEF REMI ADE. A legal practitioner and politician, born on December 22, 1921, in London, England. He was educated at the Christian Missionary Society Grammar School (q.v.) and King's College in Lagos (q.v.), and later proceeded to Cambridge University where he obtained M.A. and LL.B degrees. He was called to the bar at the Inner Temple in 1945. He later went into politics, becoming a member of the federal House of Representatives (q.v.) in 1954 and a member of the Western Regional House of Assembly (q.v.) in 1960, and the National Convention of Nigerian Citizens (q.v.) opposition party leader. After the state of emergency in the Western Region (q.v.) was lifted in January 1963, he came to the height of his power as the deputy premier of the region during the coalition government of his party with the United Peoples' Party (q.v.), and played an important role in the postemergency politics. He was popularly known then and after as "Fani-Power." In 1966 after the military took over power, he went into private legal practice and business. In 1978 when the ban on politics was lifted, he became a member of the National Party of Nigeria. He was later chosen as one of the party's national vice presidents. He died in October 1995.

FATAYI-WILLIAMS, JUSTICE ATANDA. A jurist, born on October 22, 1918 in Lagos (q.v.), educated at Methodist Boy's High School in Lagos (q.v.) from 1929 to 1938, Trinity Hall, University of Cambridge in England from 1943 to 1947 and Middle Temple in London, England, in 1948. He was appointed Crown Counsel in Lagos in 1950. He was an adviser to the Western Region (q.v.) at the London Constitutional Conference (q.v.) of 1957.

In 1958 he became chief registrar of the High Court of Western Nigeria, and judge of the High Court in 1960. In 1967 he was a justice of appeal at the Western State Court of Appeal, and a justice of the Supreme Court (q.v.) in 1969. In 1979 he was appointed chief justice of Nigeria. It was under his leadership that the Supreme Court heard Chief Obafemi Awolowo's (q.v.) appeal in 1979 of the interpretation of the constitutional provision by the Federal Electoral Commission (q.v.) that two-thirds of 19 states meant 12 and two-thirds. The court affirmed the interpretation, leading to a constitutional amendment of the provision by the military government, and greatly influencing the course of events during the Second Republic (q.v.) and after. He retired as chief justice in 1983.

FAWEHINMI, CHIEF GANIYU OYESOLA. A lawyer, author, publisher, philanthropist and human rights activist, Fawehinmi was born in 1938 at Ondo in Ondo State (q.v.) and educated at the Ansar-Ud-Deen School from 1946 to 1953, Victory College in Ikare, University of London as an external student and Nigerian Law School in Lagos (q.v.) in 1964. He was called to the bar in 1965.

Gani Fawehinmi hates government oppression, repression and misrule. He eschews corruption in government and likes to take up cases against the government that the victim may be financially unable to take up in court. He very often single-handedly will sue government for what he believes is against the law or against the constitution, very often to call public attention to the action of government. Because of his fight against human rights abuses, he is frequently arrested and detained in prison for weeks and months. His latest ordeal started on January 30, 1996, when he was arrested the day he was to address a mass rally at the University of Lagos as part of his campaign for a mass boycott of the local government elections scheduled for February. In March the government flouted the court order that he be produced in court, and so he continued to languish in detention.

Gani Fawehinmi has published and edited many books, including the *Digest of the Supreme Court Cases, 1956–84*, Vols. 1–10 (1983); *Supreme Court of Nigeria Law Reports* (1983) and *The Nigerian Constitutional Law Reports*, Vols. 1–6 (1985).

FEDERAL CAPITAL TERRITORY. *See* ABUJA.

FEDERAL CHARACTER. In an effort to promote national unity, the 1979 constitution (q.v.) provided that appointments to positions in the Federal Government (q.v.) and federal agencies must reflect the federal character of the country. This meant that there should be no predominance of persons from a few states or from a few ethnic or sectional groups in the government or its agencies. The same requirement applied to the executive organs of political parties. This provision made sure that no major ethnic group or no state was left out in decision making at various levels of government.

FEDERAL CIVIL SERVICE COMMISSION. *See* FEDERAL PUBLIC SERVICE COMMISSION.

FEDERAL COUNCIL OF MINISTERS. Under the 1951 constitution (q.v.), a Council of Ministers was the principal instrument of policy for the central government. Under the 1954 federal constitution, the Council of Ministers became the federal Council of Ministers and was made up of the governor-general of Nigeria (q.v.), three ex-officio members (q.v.) and ten ministers, three from each of the three regions and one from the Southern Cameroon (q.v.). During the First Republic (q.v.), 1960–1966, the Federal Council of Ministers consisted of the prime minister (q.v.) and the cabinet ministers, which, following the British system, were collectively responsible for government policy.

FEDERAL COURT OF APPEAL. Established in 1976 by the military administration, it is an intermediate appellate court. Under the 1979 constitution (q.v.), appeals come from the Federal Court of Appeal to the Supreme Court while appeals come to it from the State High Courts, Shari'a Court of Appeal, Customary Court (q.v.) of Appeal, Code of Conduct Tribunal (q.v.) and other tribunals. The court has jurisdiction all over the nation and is composed of not less than 15 members, of which not fewer than three members must be learned in Islamic (q.v.) personal law and not fewer than three must be learned in customary law (q.v.).

FEDERAL DEPARTMENT OF ANTIQUITIES. The Nigerian Antiquities Services was set up in 1945 under K.C. Murray who was then the surveyor of antiquities. In 1953 the Federal Department of Antiquities was established by an ordinance, and following this law, a 17-member antiquities commission was set up with powers to control archaeological excavations and export of antiquities. The Department of Antiquities acts as the executive arm of the commission in its effort to prevent illegal export of valuable works of art from the country. In addition, the department is responsible for discovering and preserving traditional cultural materials all over the country. It has responsibility for studying these and publishing the results of its work. Museums have been built in many parts of the country: Owo and Esie in 1945, Jos (q.v.) in 1952, Ile-Ife (q.v.) in 1954, Lagos (q.v.) in 1957, Oron in 1958, Kano (q.v.) in 1960, Kaduna (q.v.) in 1972 and Benin City (q.v.) in 1973. The National Museum in Lagos houses most of the collections of the department. It holds over half a million such collections, but only a few of them are on display to the public.

FEDERAL ELECTIONS. Federal elections refer to elections to the federal Houses of Representatives (q.v.) before and during the First Republic (q.v.). The results of these elections determined which party leader could be called upon as prime minister to form the government. The first truly federal election took place in December 1959 with the following results: Northern Peoples Congress (NPC) (q.v.)—142 seats, National Council of Nigerian Citizens (NCNC) (q.v.)—89, Action Group Party (AG) and allies—72 and Independents—9, totalling 312 seats. As such, a coalition government was formed by the NPC and the NCNC with the NPC presenting the prime minister. Another federal election took place in 1964, which was reportedly riddled with abuses, and which the United Progressive Grand Alliance (UPGA) (q.v.) boycotted in many places. In 1965 a federal election was conducted in places that boycotted in 1964.

In the 1979 elections, the distinction between the federal and state elections was not that pronounced partly because the Federal Electoral Commission (FEDECO) handled both and they both took place within the same four-week period. FEDECO supervised three separate "federal" elections to the Senate (q.v.), House of Representatives (q.v.) and the presidency, and two separate "state" elections to the Houses of Assembly (q.v.) and the governor's offices.

FEDERAL ELECTORAL COMMISSION. Established in 1977, it consisted of 24 members with Chief Michael Ani, a retired civil servant as its chairman. The commission was to register political parties and conduct elections into the state and federal Legislative Houses in an effort to return the country to civilian rule in 1979.

The Federal Electoral Commission (FEDECO) was one of the federal commissions established under the 1979 Second Republican Constitution (q.v.). It was empowered to organise, undertake and supervise all elections to the offices of the president and vice president, governors and members of the federal and state Legislative Houses. It had power to arrange for the annual examination and auditing of the accounts of political parties and to publish a report for public information. FEDECO was responsible for the registration of voters and for making the list ready and available for all elections even to local government (q.v.) councils.

FEDERAL EXECUTIVE COUNCIL. Established under Decree No. 1 of 1966 as the executive organ of the federal military government, it consisted of the head of the federal military government who was the president of the FEC, the heads of the Nigerian Army, Navy and the Air Force, chief of staff of the Armed Forces (q.v.), the chief of staff of the Nigerian Army, the attorney general of the federation and the inspector general and the deputy inspector general of the police. In 1967 the secretary to the federal military government and other appropriate officials of the federal and regional governments could attend the meetings of the FEC in an advisory capacity. Later, civilian and military commissioners (q.v.) (ministers) were added to the council.

FEDERAL GOVERNMENT. Under the 1954 constitution (q.v.), Nigeria, which had been run as a unitary government since 1914, became a federation (q.v.) made up of three regions, the Eastern (q.v.), the Western (q.v.) and the Northern (q.v.). Since then, with only a brief period from May 1966 when the Unification Decree (q.v.) was issued in July 1966 when the second coup (q.v.) took place, Nigeria has remained a federal state. Accordingly, the powers of government are shared between the central government (centre) and the regions/states. The exclusive legislative list spells out federal government powers, the concurrent legislative list relates to areas where the centre and the constituent parts can exercise powers but, in case of conflict, federal laws prevail. Residual powers are left for the states to exercise. The government at the centre is the federal government. The chief executive during the First Republic (q.v.) was the prime minister, but during the Second Republic (q.v.), he was called the president, who was popularly and nationally elected. He freely chose his cabinet provided that all the states of the federation were represented in it. His term of office was four years and he could be reelected into office for a second term only. Under the military administration, the federal government effectively dominated the states.

FEDERAL HIGH COURT. *See* FEDERAL REVENUE COURT.

FEDERAL HOUSE OF REPRESENTATIVES. The federal House of Representatives was one of the legislative chambers for the Federal Government (q.v.). During the First Republic (q.v.), the house was made up of 312 members, but during the Second Republic (q.v.), it was made up of 450 members, with the speaker as its leader. The only difference between the House during the First and Second Republics was that they were working under different political systems. The First Republic operated under the Westminster-type of parliamentary democracy, while the Second operated under the executive presidential system.

FEDERAL INSTITUTE OF INDUSTRIAL RESEARCH. Established in 1956, it was given the function of furthering the government policy of diversifying the nation's economy by encouraging businessmen to set up industries that especially relate to the processing of Nigerian raw materials. The FIIR offers technical advice to existing industries by providing laboratory facilities for analysing samples of products and seeking solutions to basic technical problems. The major criteria used for the choice of its research projects are import substitutability, primary processing of raw materials for local industries and the development of native technology. Contract research is, however, acceptable at any time.

FEDERAL JUDICIAL SERVICE COMMISSION. Under the 1960 constitution (q.v.), the appointment of judges of the superior courts was the responsibility of a body known as the Judicial Service Commission. Before a judge could be removed from office, his case was examined by a tribunal whose membership was restricted to judges and ex-judges. However, in 1963, the Judicial Service Commission was abolished when Nigeria became a Republic (q.v.); it was then the prime minister who advised the president on the appointment of federal judges, and the question of whether or not any of them should be removed from office was left to a two-thirds majority vote on the floor of the two Houses of Parliament (q.v.). This was a retrogressive step, which affected the independence of the judiciary.

When the military took over in 1966, they established the Federal Judicial Service Commission, charged with the responsibility of appointment and disciplining judges of the nation's superior courts. But it was the responsibility of the Head of State to appoint the chairman of the commission.

Under the 1979 constitution, the Judicial Service Commission became entrenched. It was and is responsible for advising the president on nominations for appointment of justices to the Supreme Court (q.v.), including the president of the Federal Court of Appeal (q.v.), judges of the Federal High Courts (q.v.) and members of the Code of Conduct Bureau (q.v.). However, such nominations require the approval of the Senate (q.v.). It can also recommend their removal for inability to discharge their duties, misconduct or contravention of the code of conduct.

FEDERAL PARLIAMENT. The national legislature during the First Republic (1960–66). It was composed of two houses: a 312 member House of Representatives which was elected from single member districts, and a federal Senate comprised of 12 senators from each region plus eight additional senators (four from the capital territory, and four appointed by the president).

FEDERAL PUBLIC SERVICE COMMISSION. The 1954 constitution (q.v.) provided for the establishment of the Public Service Commission of the Federation, with the power to appoint, promote and discipline public servants in the federal public service. Under the 1979 constitution, the scope of the commission was limited to the civil service. It was then called the Federal Civil Service Commission, composed of a chairman and not more than nine members. Its responsibilities were to appoint persons to offices in the federal civil service and to exercise disciplinary control over them.

FEDERAL RADIO CORPORATION OF NIGERIA. The name Federal Radio Corporation (FRCN) came to be used in 1978 for the Nigerian Broadcasting Corporation (NBC) after the latter was reorganised. The NBC was established by an act of Parliament in April 1957. It was owned and financed by the Federal Government (q.v.). Before the corporation came into being in 1957, its functions used to be carried out by the Federal Broadcasting Service (FBS), which was a government department.

Among the major functions of the FRCN are to provide broadcasting services by radio for reception in Nigeria, based on the national objectives and aspirations, and to areas outside the country in accordance with Nigeria's foreign policy. Its broadcasting is to contribute to the development of Nigerian society and to promote national unity by ensuring balanced presentation of views from all parts of the country. It is also to provide commercial and educational broadcasting services.

The corporation has a policy-making body, known as the board of governors, made up of nine members. Its headquarters is in Ikoyi Lagos, but its zonal broadcasting houses are in the former regional capitals of Ibadan (q.v.), Enugu (q.v.) and Kaduna (q.v.).

FEDERAL REPUBLIC OF NIGERIA. The full official name for Nigeria following October 1, 1963, when it became a republic. Prior to that time it was known as the "Federation of Nigeria."

FEDERAL REVENUE COURT. The Federal Revenue Court was set up in 1973 with jurisdiction over all revenue matters. It handles both civil and criminal matters relating to company taxes, banking, copyright, merchandise marks, trademarks and cases of admiralty, relating to ships within the country's waters. The Federal Revenue Court became known as the Federal High Court under the 1979 constitution (q.v.), and it is given power to hear all cases pertaining to the revenue of the government of the Federation and any other matter which the National Assembly (q.v.) may by law prescribe.

FEDERATION ACCOUNT. The Federation Account consists of all revenues collected by the government of the Federation (q.v.), except the proceeds of the personal income tax from the residents of the Federal Capital Territory (q.v.), Abuja (q.v.). Any amount standing to the credit of the Federation Account will be distributed among the federal, state and local governments on such terms and in such manner as may be prescribed by the National Assembly (q.v.). The National Assembly also has power to prescribe how the state and the local governments (q.v.) would share their allocation. In 1983, under the administration of Alhaji Shehu Shagari (q.v.), the states altogether received 35 percent, while local governments received ten percent.

In 1992, during the Babangida (q.v.) administration states received 24 percent, while the share of local government rose to 20 percent.

On October 1, 1995, during the 35th independence anniversary broadcast, General Sani Abacha (q.v.), the military Head of State, announced that his government had decided to set aside a fixed sum of 13 percent of all revenue accruing to the Federation Account directly from natural resources to compensate communities that suffer severe ecological degradation as a result of exploitation in their areas. This was an indirect response to the demand of the Ogoni (q.v.) people for compensation for the destruction of their environment, an issue that led to the execution of Ken Saro-Wiwa (q.v.). The plan was never implemented by the Abacha regime. Eventually, however, it was incorporated into the 1999 constitution of the Fourth Republic.

FEDERATION OF NIGERIA. The official name for Nigeria from October 1, 1960, until October 1, 1963. At that time it became a republic, and its name was changed to "Federal Republic of Nigeria." By convention, however, the term "First Republic" is often used to refer to the entire period of civilian rule from 1960–66.

FERNANDO PÓO. Is an island in the Bight of Bonny that played a prominent role in the history of contacts between Europeans and Africans. The Portuguese first laid claims to the island in 1471. The island was later the site of sugar plantations making use of slave labor from the coast. In 1778, Spain was granted control of the island in a treaty with Portugal. From 1827–43, Spain allowed Britain to maintain a base on the island that was used as part of the British campaign to suppress the slave trade. In 1968, the island was granted independence as Equatorial Guinea.

FIRST BANK. *See* AFRICAN BANKING CORPORATION.

FIRST REPUBLIC. Generally refers to the period between independence on October 1, 1960, and the military takeover on January 15, 1966, but the First Republic formally began on October 1, 1963. By becoming a republic, Nigeria broke the few remaining legal ties to Great Britain. Instead of the governor-general (q.v.), who legally represented the Queen, the country had a president who was more or less a figurehead. Second, appeals sent to the Privy Council in London were abolished. The Federal Supreme Court (q.v.) became the final Court of Appeal for Nigeria. The short period of the republic was filled with crisis—it was born in crisis, for events of military takeover of 1966 were the culmination of the events that started with the Action Group crisis of 1962 (q.v.). These crises were: the 1962–63 census controversy leading to alienation between the federal coalition of Northern People's Congress (NPC) (q.v.) (representing the north) and the National Convention of Nigerian Citizens (NCNC) (q.v.) (representing the east); the election conflict of 1964 among the various parties, again which led to two broad political alliances: the Nigerian National Alliance (q.v.) composed of the NPC and the Nigerian National Democratic Party (q.v.) formed during the Action Group (AG) (q.v.) crisis of 1962 (q.v.) by the Akintola (q.v.) faction and the United Progressive Grand Alliance (q.v.), composed of the NCNC, the AG and the United Middle Belt Congress (q.v.) and the Northern Element Progressive Union (q.v.). The president was convinced that the 1964 federal elections were grossly rigged in many places and boycotted in parts of the country. He refused at first to call the leader of the majority party after the election to form a new government. The differences were mediated, and business returned to "normal." But the Western Regional (q.v.) election campaign and the rigging of the election in 1965 led to a breakdown of law and order in the west. The government appeared unable to put an end to the thuggery, killing and arson that followed, and so the military on January 15, 1966, put an end to the life of the First Republic.

FISCAL COMMISSION. *See* RAISMAN COMMISSION.

FOMBIA. *See* ADAMAWA STATE.

FOOT, SIR HUGH M. Born in 1907, he was educated at St. John's College, Cambridge. He served as an administrative officer in Palestine from 1938 to 1939, an assistant British Resident in Trans-Jordan from 1939 to 1942 and in Cyrenaica in 1943, colonial secretary in Cyprus from 1943 to 1945, as acting governor of Cyprus in 1944, colonial secretary in Jamaica from 1945 to 1947 and chief secretary of Nigeria from 1947 to 1951. He later went back to Jamaica. As chief secretary, one of his first assignments was to head a commission on Nigerianisation (q.v.) of the higher civil service with the recommendation that only where no suitable and qualified Nigerian was available should non-Nigerians be considered for any government post. Furthermore, in the process of reviewing the Richards Constitution of 1946 (q.v.), Sir Hugh Foot moved a resolution in the Legislative Council (q.v.), that a Select Committee of the Legislative Council should study the methods of reviewing the constitution (q.v.). He proposed various ways to consult public opinion, through village meetings, divisional meetings, provincial meetings and other organisations. He contributed in no small way to the making of the Macpherson Constitution of 1951 (q.v.). While still in Nigeria, on February 18, 1950, a member of the Zikist Movement (q.v.) made an unsuccessful attempt on his life, an incident that confirmed the colonial authorities' suspicion of the organisation as dangerous to the good government of the country and led to the banning of the movement in April 1950.

FOOT COMMISSION. After the Second World War, the government finally yielded to the demand of the Nigerians for the Nigerianisation (q.v.) of the higher civil service. As such, in June 1948, Sir John Macpherson (q.v.), soon after his coming to Nigeria, set up the Foot Commission of Inquiry, headed by the chief secretary to the government, Sir Hugh M. Foot (q.v.). The commission was to look into the problem of recruiting Nigerians into the higher levels of the civil service, and make recommendations with regard to the steps that had to be taken to implement the government policy to appoint Nigerians to posts in the government senior service as fast as suitable candidates were available. The commission recommended among other things that no non-Nigerian should be recruited for any government post except where no suitable and qualified Nigerian was available. The government accepted the recommendation and the process of Nigerianisation was speeded up. *See also* NIGERIANISATION.

FORD FOUNDATION. Among the donors of aid to educational institutions in Nigeria, the Ford Foundation has played very significant roles. Between 1948 and 1964, it gave millions of naira as research grants to the University of Ibadan (q.v.). And when regional universities at Ife (q.v.), Ahmadu Bello (q.v.) and Nsukka (q.v.) were established in the early 1960s, the foundation was quick to come to their aid. It helped to develop the faculty of education in the University of Nigeria, Nsukka, and in the building of the former Institute (now Faculty) of Administration and the Institute of African Studies in the University of Ife (now Obafemi Awolowo University).

FOREIGN POLICY. Nigeria's foreign policy is based upon what it regards as its national interest, which is generally agreed to include defence of the country's sovereignty, independence, territorial integrity and the restoration of human dignity to black men and women all over the world, particularly (until 1994) the eradication of colonialism and white minority rule in southern Africa.

From the time of independence—October 1960 to the present—Nigerian foreign policy has been based on certain well-established principles: Africa as the centerpiece of Nigeria's foreign policy, nonalignment, legal and sovereign equality of states, noninterference in the domestic affairs of other states and the principle of multilateralism. From the first post-independence government of Sir Abubakar Tafawa Balewa (q.v.), Africa has occupied a place of pride in Nigeria's foreign policy. With the highest concentration of black people anywhere in the world, Nigeria has regarded it as its duty to lead and champion African interests in international organisations. To achieve this objective, Nigeria played a prominent role in the formation of the Organization of African Unity (OAU) (q.v.) in 1963, which was then seen as machinery to advance the interest of the continent. Nigeria has made political, economic and diplomatic contributions to the OAU.

In the struggle to liberate all of Africa from white minority rule, Nigeria has played a prominent part. It contributed financially to the funding of liberation organisations in southern Africa, such as South-West African Peoples Organisation (SWAPO) of Namibia and the South African Revolutionary Youth Organisation of South Africa. In addition, it permitted the SWAPO and African National Congress (ANC) to open offices in Lagos (q.v.), the former capital of the country. What is more, as a result of her involvement in the liberation struggle in southern Africa, Nigeria became a member of the frontline states and its ambassador at the United Nations (UN) became the chairman of its Committee against Apartheid.

Nigeria is also a strong member of the UN. It subscribes to the UN principle of peaceful resolution of disputes. As such, it has been closely associated with mediating in African disputes since the 1960s. It mediated the Algerian-Morocco border conflict in 1963, the Chadian crisis in 1979, and has participated in almost all UN peacekeeping efforts all over the world, including the Congo in 1963 and Yugoslavia and Somalia in 1993. Nigeria has even struggled for a permanent seat on the UN Security Council.

On the economic front, Nigeria also has taken the lead in promoting African economic cooperation through bilateral and multilateral economic arrangements. In 1975 Nigeria promoted the formation of the Economic Community of West African States (q.v.). In 1980 it organised the first economic summit of the OAU in Lagos.

With regard to nonalignment, Nigeria's attitude has been inconsistent. The first post-independence government of Balewa (q.v.) was more pro-West in its foreign policy as shown in its relations with the United States, Canada, Britain, France and Germany. Nigeria moved East during the Civil War (1967–70) (q.v.) when France supported Biafra (q.v.) and the United States and Britain refused Nigeria's request to buy arms and ammunition.

With the end of the Cold War and the disintegration of the centralized economies of the Soviet Union and Eastern Europe, Nigeria has been one of the major countries to call for an understanding of the world's poor countries by its developed countries, most especially at the Non-Aligned Movement Conference held in Accra, Ghana (q.v.), in 1991. Unfortunately, the economic downturn and gross mismanagement during the Babangida (q.v.) administration and the annulment of the June 12, 1993, election (q.v.) cannot but affect Nigerian foreign policy and capabilities in the future.

FOSTER-SUTTON COMMISSION OF INQUIRY. The Foster-Sutton Commission of Inquiry, chaired by Sir Stafford Foster-Sutton, chief justice of the Federation of Nigeria (q.v.) was set up in 1956 to inquire into the relationship between Dr. Nnamdi Azikiwe (q.v.), the then-premier of Eastern Nigeria (q.v.), the government of Eastern Nigeria (q.v.) and the African Continental Bank (ACB) (q.v.). The commission was to look into the allegations of improper conduct on the part of Azikiwe in connection with ACB affairs and examine the circumstances in which securities belonging to the Eastern Region's marketing board (q.v.) were transferred to the Eastern Region Finance Corporation and the circumstances in which such proceeds were invested in or deposited with the ACB by the Eastern Region Finance Corporation. It was also to look into the relationship between Azikiwe and ACB, its directors, shareholders or officers and the relationship between the Eastern Region Finance Corporation and the ACB. In addition, it also looked into the relationship between any person or organisation, corporate or not in which Azikiwe had some interest at any material time whether direct or indirect and the ACB, and the use made of the resources of the ACB whether before or after the investments and deposits referred to were made insofar as such use appeared to the tribunal to be material for the foregoing purposes. Finally, the commission was to determine whether in respect of any persons holding ministerial or other public offices had infringed the standards of the conduct demanded of the holder of such offices and, if so, in what respect.

On January 16, 1957, the report of the commission was published. After noting that Dr. Azikiwe's motives for founding the bank were to make available an indigenous bank with the purpose of liberalising credit for the people of the country, it still went on to conclude that his conduct in connection with the affairs of the bank fell short of the expectations of honest, reasonable people. As a means of contesting the findings of the commission and to test the support of the people for Dr. Azikiwe, the Eastern House of Assembly (q.v.) was dissolved and fresh elections were called. The people voted him and his party back into power with a fairly large majority. Furthermore, the Executive Council (q.v.) advised Dr. Azikiwe to transfer all his rights and interests in the ACB to the Eastern Region's government, which Dr. Azikiwe readily accepted.

FOURAH BAY COLLEGE. The Fourah Bay College was established in 1827 in Sierra Leone (q.v.) by the Church Missionary Society. Its original aim was to train teachers, priests and layworkers for the church. However, in 1876, the status of the college was raised by affiliating it to Durham University in England. As such, it prepared students to take the external examinations for the B.A. degrees awarded by Durham University. Furthermore, the college offered diploma courses in theology and education.

Fourah Bay College has played a very significant role in the history of higher education (q.v.) in Nigeria. As it was the first higher institution in all British West Africa—Nigeria, Ghana (q.v.), Sierra Leone and the Gambia—the students came from the four territories, but, for quite over a century, Nigerian students constituted about 50 percent of all student population. In fact, the first graduate of the college was Bishop Ajayi Crowther (q.v.), a Nigerian, in 1828.

Fourah Bay College has also grown not only in enrollment and staff, but in status, for in 1960 it was granted University College status even though it was still affiliated with Durham University, and in 1966 it severed this legal bond by becoming a constituent college of the University of Sierra Leone, which was granted autonomous status that same year.

FOUR-ONE-NINE (419). The newspapers regularly report the activities of people whose business is to defraud expatriates abroad and Nigerians at home. Their crime is termed Advance Fee Fraud, popularly known as Four-One-Nine (419) from Section 419 of the Criminal Code of Nigeria, which makes it an offence for any person to obtain money or other things under false pretences.

The perpetrators of the crime have offices with letterheaded papers, and pose as honest businessmen. They carefully collect information about what their intended victim would be interested in and they make him an offer, claiming that they have special relationships with government officials or officials of the Central Bank of Nigeria to facilitate the processing of their papers and their businesses. But to get the processing done, some money must be paid by their intended victim. In some other cases, they may send fake letters from relations of the victim who are abroad, asking him to expect some shipment of some goods, but, before receiving the goods, the victim must pay money to an agent in an appointed place. Because of the bad publicity the crime has given Nigeria at home and abroad, the government has issued a decree intended to combat it.

FOURTH REPUBLIC. The democratic regime that came into existence with the inauguration of President Olusegun Obasanjo (q.v.) on May 29, 1999.

FREEDOM MOVEMENT. When the colonial government in April 1950 declared the Zikist Movement (q.v.) unlawful because its purposes and methods were dangerous to the good government of the country, the group met in Port Harcourt (q.v.) the following month and reorganised itself into the Freedom Movement with the aim to destroy all forms of imperialism and to establish a free socialist Republic of Nigeria (q.v.), which would fight in and out of Parliament, employing nonviolent revolutionary tactics. Memberships were the same in both. Branches were set up mainly in the Eastern Region (q.v.), even though there were some in the west. The movement was short-lived, owing to waning enthusiasm among its members and the factional feuds between the leaders in Lagos (q.v.) and those in Port Harcourt. Its death was, however, hastened by the reorganisation of the National Council of Nigeria and the Cameroons on the basis of individual membership rather than organisational membership in 1951.

FREEMAN, REV. THOMAS BIRCH. A Methodist missionary of mixed race. Accompanied by William de Graft (q.v.), a Ghanaian, he was the first missionary to arrive in Badagry (q.v.) in September 1842. He built a mission house and started a small prayer service. In December of that year he visited Abeokuta (q.v.) and was well received by the Oba Sodeke and his people. In 1843 Freeman returned to the Gold Coast (Ghana) (q.v.) and left William de Graft behind.

FREETOWN. The capital of Sierra Leone (q.v.), founded by the British abolitionists as a place of refuge for slaves who had been set free in England. In 1787 an expedition of 400 freed slaves disembarked on a piece of land purchased from a local chief. In spite of the hostility from the Africans, sicknesses and other adversities in 1792, over 1,000 people were sent there to join the initial settlers. In 1808 the British assumed responsibility for the colony, which became the naval base for antislavery patrols. By 1850 more than 70,000 freed slaves had settled there. Among the ex-slaves were many Nigerians, including Bishop Ajayi Crowther (q.v.), who later came back to Nigeria either as missionaries or traders, and, therefore, were of great assistance in the educational development of the Yoruba (q.v.) of Western Nigeria (q.v.) and many other parts of Nigeria. From 1866 till 1888, all British territories in West Africa, including Nigeria, were administered from Freetown. Furthermore, Freetown was the seat of Fourah Bay College (q.v.) founded in 1827, which contributed a great deal to the training of many first-generation university graduates in Nigeria.

FULANI. The Fulani live in many parts of West Africa from Senegal to the Lake Chad (q.v.) area. The original home of the Fulani is not well known, but it is generally assumed to have been in the Senegal River valley and the Highland in Guinea known as Futajalon Highland of West Africa. From this area they moved eastwards about the 12 century A.D. until they reached Northern Nigeria (q.v.) and the Lake Chad area. Many Fulani became Muslim, and they have played important roles in the spread of Islam (q.v.) both by teaching as Islamic teachers and priests, and by war.

The Fulani are one of the major ethnic groups in Nigeria, and they were one of the first to accept the Islamic religion, which they did much to spread in many parts of the country. They can be found mostly in the northern part of the country, which includes the following states: Sokoto (q.v.), Kebbi (q.v.), Katsina (q.v.), Kano (q.v.), Jigawa (q.v.), Bauchi (q.v.), Gongola (q.v.), Borno (q.v.), Yobe (q.v.), Niger (q.v.) and Plateau Zamfara, Gombe (q.v.).

The Fulani are generally divided into two categories: the nomadic or pastoral Fulani and the town Fulani. The pastoral Fulani are found in the savannah area of the country where the population density is fairly low; they derive their livelihood from their cattle, sheep and goats. The town Fulani are sedentary. They engage in farming and trade. Some Fulani are classified as semisedentary because they do farming as well as keep animals.

The physical appearance of the Fulani is much different from all their other neighbors. They are light in complexion with straight hair, narrow noses and thin lips. In spite of this, their language, Fuldulde, is classified with the West Atlantic group of the Sudanic languages, which are included in the Niger-Congo family. The language is said to have six main dialects: Central Nigeria, Adamawa, Niger-Sokoto, Mali, Guinea and Senegal.

The Fulani came to religious and political prominence in the early part of the 19th century through the jihad (holy war) (q.v.) of Usman Dan Fodio (q.v.). As a result of the war, the Fulani were installed as Emirs (q.v.) in almost all the Hausa (q.v.) city-states and in many other places of Northern Nigeria (q.v.) in place of the former traditional rulers. The Fulani empire (q.v.) became weak toward the end of the 19th century and was conquered by the British in 1903. In spite of this, the Fulani's role in the politics of Nigeria today is still preponderant. The Fulani and the Hausa have acculturated each other's values, and it is now very difficult to distinguish an Hausa town from a Fulani town. This is partly because the Hausa live in the same environment as the Fulani with Emirs.

FUNDAMENTAL HUMAN RIGHTS. When Nigeria became a federation in 1954, the minorities in each region became restive: there were demands to create new regions in the three existing regions. The demand became so loud that the British government set up the Minorities Commission (q.v.) in 1957 to look into the fears expressed. The commission, as was expected, did not recommend the creation of new regions, but it recommended some palliatives, one of which was that fundamental rights of the citizens everywhere in the country should be protected by the constitution (q.v.). Accordingly, in the 1958 Constitutional Conference (q.v.), a proposal to include a list of Fundamental Rights in the Constitution was adopted. Chapter IV of the 1979 constitution dealt with these fundamental rights, among which are right to life, personal liberty, a fair hearing, and freedom of thought, conscience and religion, expression and the press.

-G-

GAHA. Head of the Council of State (q.v.) in the Oyo empire (q.v.), he became Basorun (q.v.) in 1754 and used the position to dominate the affairs of the empire for about 20 years. During that time, he was said to have deposed four Alaafins (kings) and became so powerful that people accorded him the honor due to the Alaafin. The conflict between him and the kings arose over whether the Oyo Empire should continue to expand or should begin to consolidate so as to take advantage of the profitable slave trade (q.v.) taking place in Badagry (q.v.) and Porto-Novo (q.v.). Gaha favored expansion, while the kings favoured consolidation.

During the time he was head of the council, the Oyo empire maintained its power. Gaha fought wars successfully as far away as Togo. However, he was later challenged by Alaafin Majeogbe. Gaha became disabled physically. When Abiodun (q.v.) ascended the throne, Gaha was effectively defeated in a brief civil war.

GANA, PROFESSOR JERRY. Emerged as one of Nigeria's most durable politicians since the late 1980s. He was born on November 30, 1945, in Busu, Niger State (q.v.). He attended Ahmadu Bello University, Zaria (1968–70) and later the University of Aberdeen, Scotland, where he received his Ph.D. in geography in 1974. From that time until 1987 he taught at ABU Zaria.

Professor Gana first gained national prominence as the Chairman of the Directorate for Social Mobilisation (DSM, also known as MAMSER), an organization created by the Babangida regime to inculcate democratic values in the population. He resigned from this position in 1992 to compete for the Social Democratic Party's (q.v.) presidential nomination, but was unsuccessful. Gana was a vocal defender of M.K.O. Abiola (q.v.) in the June 12 imbroglio (1993) but apparently reversed himself when he later agreed to serve in the first Abacha (q.v.) cabinet as Minister of Information (1993–95). This role required him to defend the regime's much maligned "War against Indiscipline" (WAI) program. Gana redeemed his democratic credentials somewhat in 1998, when he emerged as a member of both the Group of 18 and the Group of 34, coalitions of politicians opposed to the continuation of the Abacha regime.

In 1999, Gana was appointed to serve as minister of Cooperatives and Integrated Rural Development in the Obasanjo (q.v.) administration.

GARBA, MAJ. GEN. JOSEPH NAUVEN. Born on July 17, 1943, at Langtan near Shendam in Plateau State (q.v.). He was educated at the Sacred Heart School, Shendam, and later at the Nigerian Military School in Zaria (q.v.) from 1957 to 1961. In 1962 he was sent to the Mons Officer Cadet School, Aldershot, in England after which he became a commissioned officer. In 1963 he attended Staff College at Camberley, England. From 1963 to 1968, he moved up very rapidly and served in many capacities and places including Kashmir in India under the United Nations Observer Forces. From 1968 to 1975 when General Yakubu Gowon (q.v.) was toppled from power, he was the commanding officer of the brigade of guards at the Dodan Barracks in Lagos (q.v.). He participated actively in the 1975 coup (q.v.) and was the one who announced the ouster of General Gowon from power in a bloodless coup on July 29, 1975. He later became commissioner (q.v.) for external affairs. In 1978 he was commandant, Nigerian Defence Academy (q.v.) in Kaduna (q.v.) and was promoted to major general in 1979. He retired from the Nigerian Army in 1980, but after the December 1983 coup, he was appointed Nigerian ambassador to the United Nations.

GENERAL STRIKE. During the Second World War, and as a result of the austerity measures adopted by the colonial government, the condition of life for Nigerian workers increasingly deteriorated. In 1942 the government approved a cost-of-living allowance (COLA) (q.v.) to workers, but this did not improve the quality of life much. Because government price control efforts were also ineffective, workers asked for a 50 percent increase in the cost of living allowance and a minimum daily wage of 2/6d for a labourer. When the demands were not met, union leaders called for a strike by the railway workers, postal and telegraph workers, and technical workers in government departments. The strike, lasting 37 days, virtually paralysed the economy (q.v.). The government later set up the Davies Commission of Enquiry to examine the workers' grievances. As a result of its submission, workers' salaries were regraded upward and the cost-of-living allowances were also increased. Nationalists like Dr. Nnamdi Azikiwe (q.v.) and his newspapers gave strong support to the workers. And so, even though the colonial government helped the development of labour organisations in Nigeria, labour unions became one of the pressure groups fighting not only for economic betterment but also for social and political reforms.

GENOCIDE ALLEGATION. During the 1967–70 Civil War (q.v.), the former Eastern Nigeria (q.v.), known as Biafra (q.v.), mounted a series of propaganda claims to arouse the sympathy of people all over the world to its cause. One such propaganda issue was the allegation that they were seceding from Nigeria because of Nigeria's determination to wipe out the Igbo (q.v.) people. They alleged that their security could no longer be guaranteed by a government outside their regional boundaries, and they considered the war being waged against them by the Federal Government (q.v.) as a war of genocide. To disprove this allegation, the federal military government allowed visits by international observers to the so-called liberated areas.

GEOGRAPHY AND CLIMATE. The Federal Republic of Nigeria (q.v.) has an area of 924,000 kilometres, with a population of 88.5 million people, according to the 1991 census.

At the Gulf of Guinea are the Bight of Benin (q.v.) and the Bight of Biafra (q.v.). Along the gulf is a sandy coastline, and behind it are swamps and creeks covered with mangrove forests. In the southeast, swamps cover a great deal of the Niger Delta. In Nigeria's southwest and southeast, the land rises gradually up to about 300 metres above sea level. Along the Niger River (q.v.) and the Benue River (q.v.) are lowlands. In the west the land rises to a plateau of about 300 metres above sea level. In the north the Jos Plateau rises from about 300 metres to about 1,500 metres.

The climate in the south is hot and humid year round, while the average temperature is between 30°C in the south to 34°C in the north. Average annual rainfall is higher in the Niger Delta and reaches about 2,000 millimetres, while in Lagos it is about 1,800 millimetres. The heaviest rainfall is between May and July, even though the rainy season begins in March and ends in October. The driest period is between November and February, at which time comes the harmattan (q.v.), a wind that comes with dust from the Sahara Desert and moves toward the Atlantic Ocean. In the north the climate is much hotter and less humid. Rain falls for a lesser period as one moves from the south to the north. In the far north the average rainfall is about 900 millimetres per year, while the average monthly temperature is about 21 to 24°C for the coolest months and 29 to 32°C for the hottest months.

Nigeria's natural vegetation can be divided into two zones. In the south are rain forests, but farther north is savannah forest. Farming, road building and urban development in the south has greatly altered this natural vegetation.

GHANA. *See* GOLD COAST.

GOBIR. One of the seven original Hausa States (q.v.), and the center and starting point of the Fulani (q.v.) uprising initiated by Usman Dan Fodio (q.v.). The people of Gobir were said to be strong and warlike, and their state served as a buffer for the remaining Hausa states to the south and against other tribes to the north. However, in the 18th century under pressure from the northern tribes, Gobir looked down toward the fertile south to Zamfara. By the middle of the century, Zamfara had transferred its capital to Birnin Zamfara. At this time Barbari (q.v.) the Sarkin Gobir, in his effort to take over Zamfara, gave his sister in marriage to the king of Zamfara, Mairoki, and received permission for himself and his people to settle in Zamfara. As the number of the Gobir people increased, they began to gain confidence in their ability to take over Zamfara. In 1764 they attacked and captured the capital under their king and leader Barbari. At the time of Usman Dan Fodio's revolution in Gobir, much of the northern part of Zamfara was occupied by Gobir.

Toward the end of the 18th century, Usman Dan Fodio had become a teacher and preacher of great distinction, and the king of Gobir had entrusted the education of his son Yunfa to him. When the king died, Yunfa became king, and, in an effort to prevent the Muslims in the state from developing into a separate group, he made an attempt on Dan Fodio's life. This led to an open rupture and the beginning of the jihad (q.v.) in 1804. In 1808 the Fulani overtook Gobir after killing Sarkin Gobir Yunfa and his chiefs.

GOLD COAST. Gold Coast is the colonial name of the modern Ghana. The name was changed to Ghana in 1957 when the country became independent. In 1874 Lagos (q.v.), Nigeria, was brought under the administration of the governor of the Gold Coast, but in January 1886, Lagos was detached from the Gold Coast and became self-administering. In 1894 the Nana of Itsekiri (q.v.) was deported to the Gold Coast because of his resistance to the British. He stayed in the Gold Coast until 1906 when he was allowed to come back home.

Both Nigeria and the Gold Coast share a common colonial experience under the British colonial administration. During the nationalist struggle, the Gold Coast gave Nigeria the lead. One of the most popular nationalists in Nigeria, Dr. Nnamdi Azikiwe (q.v.), first worked in the Gold Coast as a nationalist before coming back to Nigeria. In 1957 the Gold Coast became the first of the British West African countries to become independent and changed its name to Ghana. Ghana was an inspiration to Nigeria in its struggle for national independence. In 1959 Ghana hosted the Pan-African Conference (q.v.) at which nearly all the nationalist leaders in Africa were present.

In addition to the above common experiences, Ghana and Nigeria also share common experiences in agriculture for both are major cocoa-producing countries for the world market. However, the two countries almost unconsciously see each other as rivals. This rivalry is best seen in their sporting activities, which have for a long time been organised between the two countries. In fact, one may say that it was this Nigeria-Ghana sports rivalry that gave birth to the All-West African Sports Competition.

Again during Nigeria's agonising years in which great efforts were made to bring about a reconciliation between the Federal Government (q.v.) headed by General Yakubu Gowon (q.v.) and the Eastern Regional government headed by Lt. Col. Odumegwu Ojukwu (q.v.), it was Ghana among all African countries that first organised a peace talk at Aburi (q.v.) to settle the dispute. However, relations strained later when in 1970 Ghana ordered thousands of Nigerians who had for decades lived and worked in Ghana to pack and go back to Nigeria. Nigeria then showed a sign of maturity by not reacting under such provocation. But with the coming into operation of the Economic Community of West African Countries (q.v.), many Ghanaians flooded to Nigeria to avoid the political instability and the economic hardship going on in the country, most of them staying in the country illegally.

In February 1983, the government of Nigeria, itself suffering from economic recession due to the world oil glut, ordered illegal aliens to leave the country. This was a big blow to Ghana, which was forced to make room for about two million citizens who had to go back home. The government of Lt. Jerry Rawlings calmly accepted the challenge and began the process of absorbing them.

GOLDIE, GEORGE TAUBMAN. Goldie was born in 1846 on the Isle of Man. As a youth in the early 1860s, he trained for two years at the Royal Military Academy, Woolwich, as an engineer. Two years later, a relation of his died, leaving him a fortune, and Goldie went straight to Egypt where he learned from Hausa (q.v.) pilgrims and scholars on their way to Mecca that the Egyptian Sudan was just the fringe of the vast Sudanic belt extending from the Niger River (q.v.) to the Nile. After three years he left Egypt and returned to England. In 1871 he married. In 1875 the opportunity he had been looking for came through his family connection. His eldest brother, the then-head of the family, had married Min Amelia Grove-Ross, whose father, Captain Joseph Grove-Ross, was the secretary of a small firm, Holland Jacques and Company, which had been trading on the Niger since 1869. By 1875 the company was in financial difficulty and Joseph Grove-Ross appealed to his son-in-law for help. The Taubman family then decided to take over the company and Goldie decided to go back to Africa, specifically to the Niger and if possible cross over through the Sudan to the Nile. Within two years of his stay in Nigeria, he had created what may be called a trading empire on the river. He saw to the amalgamation of four competing companies—Miller Brothers of Glasgow, James Pinnock, Holland Jacques Central African Trading Company and his own West and Central African Company—into a United African Company (UAC) (q.v.). But the UAC was later found to be incapable of coping with the situation, and so in 1881 a new company, the National African Company (NAC) (q.v.) was formed. It took over UAC's business in Central Africa and the Niger. The success of his company attracted foreign competition by the French and the Germans who were pursuing a vigorous colonial policy in Africa. By underselling the French companies, he was able to make them agree to merge with the NAC in 1884 or leave the scene. He concluded treaties with many Chiefs along the Niger, all which later became the basis for the British claim at the 1884–1885 Berlin Conference (q.v.) at which Goldie represented the British. In 1886 the British government granted a charter to his company which became the Royal Niger Company (q.v.). The charter empowered the company to govern, keep order and protect the territories under it and to acquire new ones subject to the sanction of the secretary of state. In 1900 the company's charter was revoked. The British government took over the administration of the country, while the company concentrated on business. By this time Goldie had become fairly wealthy. He died in August 1925.

GOMBE STATE. Created out of Benue State (q.v.) by the Abacha (q.v.) regime on October 1, 1996. Its capital is Gombe.

GOMWALK, JOSEPH DESHI. Born on April 13, 1935, at Amper Pankshin Division in Plateau State (q.v.), he was educated at the Sudan United Mission (SUM) School in Amper and in Gindiri where he finished his secondary education in 1955. He then went to the Nigerian College of Arts, Science and Technology (q.v.) in Zaria (q.v.) in 1956 and University College, Ibadan (q.v.) in 1958 where in 1961 he obtained a bachelor's degree in zoology, specialising in parasitology. He later worked as a research officer at the Kaduna Veterinary School. After some time he was transferred to the Northern Nigerian administrative service from 1961 to 1965. In February 1966, he joined the Nigeria Police Force and quickly rose to the rank of chief superintendent. When states were created in 1967, he was appointed governor of Benue-Plateau State (q.v.). Together with other governors, he was compulsorily retired in 1975 when General Yakubu Gowon's (q.v.) regime was overthrown. After the abortive coup (q.v.) of February 13, 1976, led by Lt. Col. B.S. Dimka (q.v.) in which General Murtala R. Muhammed (q.v.) was killed, Gomwalk was said to be connected with the plot. He was arrested, secretly tried and found guilty. He was shot by firing squad on May 14, 1976.

GONGOLA STATE. Gongola State was created on February 3, 1976, out of the former North-Eastern State (q.v.). The state was the second largest in the Federation (q.v.) with an estimated area of 91,390 square kilometres. It had a population of about three million people. The state had a large variety of ethnic groups who lived in segmented communities—large and small—speaking different languages. Most of the groups fell into two linguistic groups—the Afro-Asian group and the Niger-Congo family. Among the first group were people like the Higgi, Margi, Gude, Kilba and Bata/Bachama. Within the other group were the Chamba, Bura and Vere. There were others such as the Fulani (q.v.), Jukun and the Mambilla.

The main towns in Gongola State were Yola, Mubi, Numan, Ganye, Jalingo, Gembu and Wukari. Gongola State had many secondary and postsecondary schools, such as the Advanced Teachers' College, Federal College of Arts and Science and the Advanced College of Preliminary Studies, which prepared students for entrance into universities and other institutions. Being an agricultural land area, the state had farm training centres and many farms, which produced food crops and livestock. The state was also rich in mineral resources like iron, lead, zinc, limestone and others.

The state capital was Yola. In 1991 the administration of General Ibrahim Babangida (q.v.) split Gongola State into two states: Adamawa State (q.v.) and Taraba (q.v.) State.

GORSUCH COMMISSION. In 1954 agreements at the Constitutional Conference (q.v.) had been reached that Nigeria should become a federation (q.v.) of three regions, and that the civil service and the judiciary should be regionalised. Furthermore, the existing division of the civil service into senior and junior staff, where the senior staff were mainly expatriates and the junior staff were Nigerians, was most criticised and it called for a change, especially since independence was just a few years away. As such the government decided in 1954 to set up the Gorsuch Commission under the chairmanship of L.H. Gorsuch to inquire into the structure and remuneration of the public services with special reference to the problems arising from the constitutional changes proposed at the 1954 Conference on the Nigerian constitution (q.v.). It was also to examine the problems from the individual aspects of the future federal and regional governments, while taking into consideration factors of similarity and divergence that were involved, and make recommendations in a form that would be suitable for submission to the future federal and regional governments.

The commission did not like the structure of the civil service—broad at the top and at the bottom but little or nothing at the middle level. In its place the commission recommended a hierarchical structure similar to the one in the United Kingdom. The old classification was replaced by a new classification into generalist and specialist branches. The generalist branch in descending order was made up of the superscale, the administrative, the executive, the clerical and the subclerical. The specialist branch was made up of the superscale, the professional, higher technical, technical and minor technical. The commission recommended advancement through training from one level to another.

These recommendations were accepted both by the federal and regional governments, and they became the basis of the civil service structure until the Udoji Commission (q.v.) recommended the abolition of the many classes and substituted a single grading system for both generalist and specialist branches. The commission was important for many reasons. It enabled the new regions to mold their services on a similar pattern, based on the system in the United Kingdom. By broadening the middle level, it freed the administrators and their professional counterparts from routine duties which people at the executive level could do.

GOVERNMENT. The frequent constitutional changes that Nigeria has experienced since her independence in 1960 have led to experiments with different types of government. At independence, Nigeria inherited the parliamentary system of government. The Queen, represented by the governor-general (q.v.), was the constitutional Head of State, while the prime minister was the head of government collectively responsible to Parliament. In 1963 Nigeria became a republic. The Queen was no longer the Head of State. The Head of State became the president, elected by a secret ballot at a joint meeting of both houses of parliament (q.v.). The president appointed the prime minister, a member of the House of Representatives (q.v.) who appeared to him likely to command the support of the majority of the members of the house, and other ministers on the advice of the prime minister. The prime minister and the other ministers formed the Council of Ministers (q.v.), which was collectively responsible to Parliament for any advice given to the president.

The First Republic (q.v.) was riddled with many crises, and it finally broke down in January 1966 when the military came to power. The federal military government suspended certain provisions of the 1963 constitution, especially those dealing with the executive and legislative institutions of government. In their place was the Head of State who was the head of the federal military government and the Commander-in-Chief of the armed forces (q.v.). Under him was the chief of staff supreme headquarters, who served in a position analogous to that of a prime minister.

The highest policy-making body for the country was the Supreme Military Council (q.v.), made up of the Head of State, top military officers, the attorney general of the Federation and the inspector general of police. The executive authority of the government was exercised by the Federal Executive Council (q.v.), members of which were appointed by the Head of State. The Head of State also appointed military governors to the constituent units of the Federation (four regions in 1966, 12 states in 1967, 19 states in 1976, 21 states in 1987 and 30 states in 1991, and thus enabling the military to maintain its command structure. In 1979 the military voluntarily gave up power after having successfully drawn up a new constitution (q.v.) and supervised elections that ushered in the constitution.

Under the 1979 constitution, Nigeria had an executive presidential system of government, very much like the system in the United States. The Federal Republic of Nigeria (q.v.) was headed by an executive president who was Head of State, the chief executive of the Federation and the Commander-in-Chief of the armed forces. He was elected for a term of four years and could be re-elected for a second term. He was assisted by ministers who were the heads of various federal ministeries. The president, in choosing his ministers, was required to choose at least one member from each of the states that made up the federation and submit his nominations for approval to the Senate (q.v.).

The legislative assembly was made up of two houses: the Senate and the House of Representatives (q.v.). Members of the legislative assembly could not at the same time be members of the executive authority.

In the states, there were governors who were each the chief executives of their respective states. The governor's term of office was four years and could be re-elected for a second term only. He was assisted by a cabinet of commissioners (q.v.), the appointment of whom had to be approved by the state House of Assembly (q.v.), which was unicameral. Each state was divided into all-purpose local government (q.v.) authorities. Under the constitution, local governments were given special functions and were required to share in the national revenue collected by the Federal Government.

This new type of government was not understood by the operators. The legislative assembly did not appreciate its role as a check on the executive authority and its independence of it. Right from the beginning, the Senate yielded to executive pressure by approving some of the presidential nominations for ministerial posts, which it had previously rejected. The executive authority saw this weakness, and exploited it. By the end of the first four years, the executive branch, by all kinds of tactics including corruptive ones, was in virtual control of the houses. The system broke down after the 1983 elections, which were perhaps the most rigged elections in the history of the country. On December 31, the soldiers again came into power.

The new military government was based on the same model as the one the country had during the first period of military rule. There was the Head of State and Commander-in-Chief of the armed forces. He was also the chairman of the Supreme Military Council, the highest policy-making body, the chairman of the Federal Executive Council, and the national council of state, a consultative body that included state military governors.

The new administration started with great popular support and enthusiasm. It decided that every person who had held elective or appointive public offices from October 1979 to 1983 should account for his or her stewardship. Thus, it asked all former governors and their deputies, political appointees at the federal and state levels and members of federal and state houses of assembly, together with party officials to report to security officers. Those who were suspected of having illegally enriched themselves while in office were detained. Most of these were later set free, while some were tried by military tribunals and if found guilty were sentenced to varying terms of imprisonment.

The government would also be remembered for launching the campaign of war against indiscipline (WAI) (q.v.), the currency exchange regulations and its austerity measures. In March 1984, the WAI was launched to inculcate discipline and instill in all Nigerians orderly and respectable conduct in every sphere of life. The currency exchange decree of April 1984 was to stop currency trafficking and reduce the excess money in circulation by changing the colours of the various denominations of the naira and thus making worthless about half the N6 billion in circulation at the expiry of the change. Finally, the government austerity measures forced Nigerians to begin to look for ways to provide locally for their needs rather than depend on imports.

However, the administration soon began to show signs of stress. It lost steam and began to drift. The Supreme Military Council was deeply divided on policy issues, and the economy showed no sign of improvement. On August 27, 1985, the fifth military coup (q.v.) in Nigeria took place, ousting from power the regime of Major General Mohammadu Buhari (q.v.) and his second in command, Major General Tunde Idiagbon, bringing into power General Ibrahim B. Babangida (q.v.). The new Head of State became president and Commander-in-Chief of the armed forces. The second most important position—the chief of staff supreme headquarters—was abolished, and a new one, Chief of General Staff (CGS), was created. The CGS was responsible only for the general administration of the country, but not for the armed forces (q.v.) as was previously the case. The highest policy-making body was no longer called the Supreme Military Council, but the Armed Forces Ruling Council (q.v.). The Federal Executive Council became the National Council of Ministers, while the National Council of State retained its name and its role.

After a costly and elaborate preparation to hand over power to a civilian government, President Babangida annulled the results of the June 12, 1993, presidential election (q.v.) and set up an Interim National Government (ING) (q.v.) as he gave up power.

The ING lacked both legitimacy and strong leadership. In early November, a high court declared it unconstitutional and several days later on November 17, 1993, it was overthrown by General Sani Abacha (q.v.), who was the minister of defense and the highest ranking military officer in the administration. While many initially believed he intended to hand over power to M.K.O. Abiola (q.v.), the winner of the June 12 election, instead he moved to consolidate his own grip on power, using tactics that were often brutal. The top military ruling body was the Provisional Ruling Council (PRC) rather than Babangida's AFRC, and it was initially notable for including civilian members. Abacha eschewed the title of "president," preferring "head of state." Abacha's initial cabinet included some of the country's most prominent civilian politicians, but by early 1995 the majority of these had either resigned or been forced from office. In 1996, Abacha increased the number of states to 36, and the number of Local Government Areas to 774.

Following Abacha's death on June 8, 1998, the regime of General Abdulsalami Abubakar carried out a rapid transition to a democratically elected government, which assumed power on May 29, 1999. The Fourth Republic has a constitution modeled on that of the Second Republic (q.v.). Like its predecessor, it is a presidential system in which the executive is directly elected to a four-year term. The National Assembly consists of a Senate of 109 members and a House of Representatives with 360 members. Following years of de facto unitary rule under the military, the new constitution sought to reestablish a genuine federal system, reserving certain powers for the states.

GOVERNMENT, LOCAL. Up until 1976, local government in Nigeria was within the complete authority of the state government, and as such, local governments had suffered the continuous whittling down of their powers. They lacked adequate funds and appropriate institutions to carry out their functions efficiently and effectively, and excessive politicking characterised the life of local governments during the First Republic (q.v.). Furthermore, each state decided on the type of local government it wanted, and exercised the power of life and death over it.

In 1976 the federal military government decided to rescue local government from some of the problems that plagued it, by recognising it as the third tier of governmental activity in the nation. The government then issued its *Guidelines for Local Government Reform,* which laid down a uniform type of local government for the nation. Each local government was to have a clearly defined area of authority, and each was given specific functions to be administered by a popularly elected council. Under the 1979 constitution (q.v.), the system of local government by a democratically elected Local Government Council was guaranteed. The constitution went further to assign them specific functions and to guarantee them a share in the public revenue collected by the Federal Government (q.v.), which in 1992 stood at 20 percent. However, state governments still have the power to create local governments and to supervise their activities. In May 1999, there were 774 local government areas.

GOVERNMENT, NATIONAL. On September 2, 1957, Alhaji Abubakar Tafawa Balewa (q.v.), deputy leader of the Northern People's Congress (NPC) (q.v.) and federal minister of transport, was appointed Nigeria's first prime minister by the governor-general (q.v.), Sir James Robertson (q.v.). He immediately formed a national government, consisting of six ministers from the National Council of Nigeria and the Cameroons (NCNC) (q.v.)—four from the NPC, two from the Action Group Party (q.v.) and one from the Kamerun National Congress. Explaining why he formed a national government, the prime minister stated that he regarded the period before independence as a time of national emergency when Nigerians must show the world that they were united and could work together for their common good. He argued that if Nigeria was to achieve independence in 1960, it was most essential that the three major political parties in the country should work together in close cooperation on all matters of policy and planning.

After the 1959 federal elections, efforts were made to form a national government, but they failed. What resulted was a coalition government made up of the NPC and the NCNC. In 1979 Alhaji Shehu Shagari (q.v.) was declared the winner of the presidential election. Serious controversy called into question the legitimacy of the government he was to form, so he tried to form a national government to comprise all the five recognised parties, but again his effort failed. What emerged was an accord between his party, the National Party of Nigeria (q.v.), and the Nigerian People's Party (q.v.), led by Dr. Nnamdi Azikiwe (q.v.). Again, as the country moved slowly through a long transition from military rule to the Third Republic (q.v.), people began to clamour for a national government, which some people referred to as a consensus government.

When General Ibrahim Badamasi Babangida (q.v.) hurriedly relinquished power in August 1993, he handed over to an Interim National Government (q.v.) the political impasse created as a result of the annulment of the June 12, 1993, presidential election (q.v.) results. More voices were added to the call for a national government to be formed when the winner of the election would be finally announced. The result was not announced. Instead, the military came back to power in November 1993 and formed a broad-based government.

GOVERNMENT OF NATIONAL CONSENSUS. *See* NATIONAL GOVERNMENT.

GOVERNOR-GENERAL OF NIGERIA. Consequent upon the Amalgamation (q.v.) of the Protectorate of Northern Nigeria with the Colony and Protectorate of Southern Nigeria on January 1, 1914, the post of governor-general of Nigeria was created, with Sir Frederick Lugard (q.v.) as its first incumbent. However, all his successors, beginning with Sir Hugh Clifford to Sir Arthur Richards were all referred to as governors of Nigeria. But when the 1954 federal constitution (q.v.) was adopted, Sir John Macpherson (q.v.), who since 1948 had been governor of Nigeria, became the governor-general. The governor-general or the governor of Nigeria was the Queen's representative and all his powers derived from Her Majesty's Government. Before 1957, the governor-general combined the functions of Head of State and the chief executive. In 1957 the position of prime minister was created and the governor-general became the Head of State and a ceremonial head of government, for he had to be advised by his responsible ministers.

After Nigeria became independent on October 1, 1960, Sir James Robertson (q.v.), the then-governor-general, stayed on until November 15, 1960, when he retired. As such, Dr. Nnamdi Azikiwe (q.v.) became the first indigenous governor-general of Nigeria.

In 1963 when Nigeria became a republic, the position of governor-general was abolished and the position of the president of the republic was created. Dr. Azikiwe again stepped into this new position. However, he remained Head of State and a ceremonial chief executive only, but he did not owe his authority to the British monarch.

GOWON, GENERAL YAKUBU. Head of the federal military government and supreme commander of the Nigerian Army from August 1966 to July 1975. Born on October 19, 1934, in the Lur Pankshim division of Plateau State (q.v.), he was educated at St. Bartholomew's School, Wusasa, and at the Government College in Zaria (q.v.). He enlisted in the army in 1954 and was sent to take many officers' courses in Ghana (q.v.) and England. He served twice with the Nigerian contingent serving on the United Nations Peacekeeping Force in the Congo, first from 1960 to 1961, and second in 1963. He was promoted to major in 1962 and lieutenant colonel in 1963.

Gowon was out of the country in January 1966 during the first coup (q.v.), and since he was not involved in it, the new leader, General Aguiyi-Ironsi (q.v.) appointed him chief of staff of the Nigerian Army and a member of the military government.

In the second coup of July 29, General Ironsi was killed and the coup makers, most of them from the north, decided he was the only leader acceptable to them even though Brigadier Babafemi Ogundipe (q.v.), a Yoruba (q.v.) man and his senior in rank, was available. As Head of State, his first priority was to restore discipline in the army and allay the fear of the civilian population. On August 2, 1966, a day after he came to power, he released from jail Chief Obafemi Awolowo (q.v.), leader of the banned Action Group Party, convicted of treasonable felony of planning to overthrow the Federal Government (q.v.) of Nigeria in 1962. He also released many other political prisoners.

The discipline he tried to restore in the army eluded him. Lt. Colonel Odumegwu Ojukwu (q.v.), the Eastern Region (q.v.) military governor, believing that Brigadier Ogundipe should have assumed command, refused to accept Gowon's leadership. In October 1966, a violent massacre of the Igbo (q.v.) people erupted in the north, causing them to flee home. It prepared the way for the movement toward the secession of Eastern Nigeria (q.v.), later called Biafra (q.v.). Efforts were made to reconcile the wishes of the two men, including the meeting at Aburi (q.v.) Ghana, but all failed. On May 27, 1967, Ojukwu was mandated by the meeting of the Consultative Assembly held at the instance of the governor in Enugu (q.v.) to declare at an early practical date Eastern Nigeria as a free sovereign and independent state by the name of the Republic of Biafra. In the evening of the same day, General Gowon announced a state of emergency throughout the nation and a decree dividing the country into twelve states, thus removing the old fear of northern domination and assuring Gowon the support of the minority areas, two of which were in the Eastern Region, that had long agitated for their own states. Two days later, Ojukwu proclaimed the Republic of Biafra.

Hostilities started in July, and General Gowon took what he called "a police action" to end the Biafran secession. But the war continued for two and a half years, after which Lt. Colonel Ojukwu fled the country to the Ivory Coast and the Federal Government accepted the surrender of Biafra.

During the Civil War (q.v.), to allay the fears of the Igbo who were being told that the federal government was waging a war of genocide against them, and to assure the world that there was no intention to commit such atrocities, General Gowon issued a "Code of Conduct" to his troops, insisting that Biafran soldiers were not to be treated as external enemies but former comrades and the civilians were to be treated as Nigerians and cared for. He also allowed international observer teams to come to the war zone and observe his troops' conduct of the war. His only objective was to keep Nigeria united by bringing back Biafra. Once the war was over, he began the process of rehabilitation and reconstruction of the war-torn areas.

On October 1, 1970, General Gowon announced the program that would lead to civilian rule in 1976. These included a new constitution, a new census and elections. But on October 1, 1974, he told the nation that 1976 was no longer a realistic date to hand over government to civilian rule. This announcement was a great disappointment to many people.

On July 27, 1975, General Gowon left Lagos for Kampala in Uganda to attend the 12th summit meeting of the Organization of African Unity. Two days later on July 29, Colonel Joseph Nanven Garba (q.v.), head of the Brigade of Guards announced at six a.m. in a radio broadcast that General Gowon had been ousted from power in a bloodless operation. Brigadier Murtala Muhammed (q.v.) succeeded him as Head of State and Commander-in-Chief of the armed forces (q.v.). General Gowon in Kampala pledged support and loyalty to the officers who ousted him and the new Head of State said that General Gowon would be retired in his rank with pension and he would be free to return home as soon as conditions permitted.

Leaving Kampala, he went into exile in Britain and enrolled as a student of political science at the University of Warwick, Coventry, in October 1975. In the abortive coup of February 13, 1976, staged by Lt. Col. B.S. Dimka (q.v.) in which General Murtala Muhammed was killed, it was alleged that one of the purposes of the coup was to restore General Gowon back to power, but General Gowon denied any knowledge of the coup. However, Dimka, after his arrest, confirmed that he had visited General Gowon in London and discussed plans with him. On May 15, 1976, the Head of State announced the dismissal of General Gowon from the army, and he was declared a wanted person. However, President A. Shehu Shagari (q.v.), the first civilian Head of State of the Second Republic (q.v.), pardoned him in 1981 and declared that he was free to come home from exile. He came back home in 1983, but soon went back to England to finish his Ph.D. thesis. He received his Ph.D. degree in political science at the University of Warwick in England in July 1984. In November 1987, he had his military honour and ranks reinstated by President Ibrahim B. Babangida (q.v.). While in office, he received many honorary degrees from Nigeria, the United States and Britain. Gowon was a prominent supporter of Olusegun Obasanjo's (q.v.) campaign for the presidency in 1998–99.

GRAHAM-DOUGLAS, NABO BEKINBO. Born on July 15, 1926, at Abonnema in the Rivers State (q.v.), he was educated at Nyemoni School, Abonnema, and at Kalabari National College, Bugama. He later went to the University College, Exeter, England, and to King's College, University of London. He then went to the Institute of Advanced Legal Studies in London. He was called to the bar at the Inner Temple in London.

Upon his return to Nigeria, he took up a successful law practice in Port Harcourt (q.v.), the capital of the Rivers State. In 1966, after the first coup d'état (q.v.) and Colonel Odumegwu Ojukwu (q.v.) became the military governor of the Eastern Region (q.v.), he was appointed attorney general for the Eastern Region. He became unpopular in the Ojukwu administration by advising against secession after the massacre of the Igbo (q.v.) in the north, and he resigned in September 1966. When Ojukwu finally declared secession in 1967, Graham-Douglas was arrested and detained. His law library in Port Harcourt was burned by Biafran troops. In 1968 he was liberated from detention and became federal government envoy touring Europe and America to explain the federal government's side in the war. In 1972 when Taslim O. Elias (q.v.) succeeded the retired chief justice of the Federation, Sir Adetokunbo Ademola (q.v.), Graham-Douglas was appointed attorney general of the Federation, a position he occupied until 1975. Graham-Douglas wrote *Triumph or Turpitude*, an account of his personal involvement in the Civil War (q.v.) and also *Forensic Aspects of Nigerian Land Law* (1972).

GRAND KHADI. The Grand Khadi is the judge who presides over the Shari'a (q.v.) Court of Appeal which hears cases concerning Muslim private law. He has vast powers under Islamic laws.

GREAT NIGERIA PEOPLE'S PARTY. A political party, one of the many parties formed when the ban on politics was lifted in 1978, and one of the five political parties recognised in the 1979 elections. The GNPP was formed by the faction that broke away from the Nigerian People's Party (q.v.) on the issue of whether or not the same person should combine in himself the position of presidential candidate and party leader. Alhaji Waziri Ibrahim (q.v.), the party leader, believed that the two posts should be combined and held by himself, while the other faction disagreed.

After the senatorial election on July 7, 1979, and the House of Representatives (q.v.) election on July 14, it became clear that the only party that all the other parties had to beat was the National Party of Nigeria (NPN) (q.v.). Alhaji Waziri Ibrahim on July 17, 1979, announced that the other four parties, the GNPP, the Nigerian People's Party, the Unity Party of Nigeria (UPN) (q.v.) and the People's Redemption Party (q.v.) were making moves to work together to prevent the NPN from coming to power. In spite of the move, not only did he lose the presidency, but the NPN was declared the winner of the presidential office. The GNPP won two gubernatorial elections in Borno (q.v.) and Gongola (q.v.) states and won eight out of 95 senatorial seats and 44 seats out of 449 in the House of Representatives. It also won many seats in state legislatures. Although the party slogan during the campaign was "Politics without Bitterness," the party leader was very bitter about the alleged rigging of the election, especially in Sokoto State (q.v.) where the party believed it was most favored to win. The postelection politicking led the party and the UPN to enter into an accord of some sort. In the 1983 elections, the party fared very poorly, for it could not win any state gubernatorial election, not to talk of the presidency. The party was banned after the coup d'état (q.v.) of December 31, 1983.

GREEN REVOLUTION. In December 1979, President Shehu Shagari (q.v.) announced plans for a programme to increase food production in an effort to provide food for every Nigerian. The government would speed up shipments of new materials and animal feeds and help each state to expand its productive areas. An additional 4,000 hectares of land would be tilled at the beginning of the programme. The government, he said, was determined to establish a self-reliant economy. This programme is popularly known as the Green Revolution.

Thus, on January 31, 1980, the Operation Feed the Nation (q.v.), launched in May 1976 by the military regime of General O. Obasanjo (q.v.) was abolished and replaced by the National Council on Green Revolution. The National Council would consist of the federal minister for agriculture and state commissioners for agriculture and would be headed by the president himself. The government would harness the services of the Ministry of Science and Technology to provide necessary equipment for farmers with the services of the Ministry of Water Resources to provide water for farming and animal husbandry.

GROUNDNUTS. Groundnuts (peanuts) used to be one of the most important foreign exchange earners in Nigeria. They were grown mostly in the northern part of the country, and, when packed into sacks ready for transportation to the coast, they were stacked up into beautiful pyramidal forms in many places in northern Nigeria. However, as a result of the 1972–74 drought, which badly affected the crop, farmers were discouraged from continuing to grow them. Today Nigeria does not grow much groundnut for export, for most of what is produced is locally processed and consumed. To encourage greater production, the government's River Basin Projects were designed to ensure the supply of water to farmers year round, and the government has also provided fertilizer and other agricultural assistance at subsidized rate. From 1986 when the marketing boards (q.v.) were dissolved as a result of government deregulation policy, groundnut production has steadily increased from about 696 tonnes to 1,016 tonnes in 1988 and 1,309 tonnes in 1991.

GROUP OF 18. A collection of northern politicians who came out in open opposition to General Sani Abacha's (q.v.) apparent plan to remain in office. The Group of 18 sent a letter to Abacha in February 1998 outlining their opposition to a continuation of Abacha's rule past October 1998. The Abacha regime was considered by some to favour the northern region of Nigeria, so it was unexpected when a collection of the north's most respected politicians openly challenged the regime. Later, members of the Group of 18 joined with southern opponents of Abacha to form the Group of 34. Among the most prominent members of the Group of 18 were Solomon Lar, Adamu Ciroma, Lawal Kaita, Abubakar Rimi, Iyorchia Ayu, Sule Lamido and Abubakar Umar.

GROUP OF 34. A collection of politicians who came out in open opposition to General Sani Abacha's (q.v.) apparent plan to remain in office past October 1998. While officially named the Institute for Civil Society, they were more commonly known as the Group of 34 (or G-34). Sani Abacha had promised to surrender power to a democratically elected regime in October 1998, but by early 1998 it had become clear that he planned to manipulate the transition to secure his own election as a civilian president. This prompted a group of 18 prominent northern politicians to draft a letter to Abacha in February 1998 urging him not to remain in office. These northern politicians later joined with a group of southern politicians opposed to Abacha's plans to perpetuate his hold on power. This coalition became the Group of 34 and in May 1998 they drafted their own letter to Abacha opposing his presidential bid. The Group of 34 was an impressive collection of politicians, former military officers and political activists from every region of the country. As a result, their actions had an electrifying effect on the country.

After the death of Sani Abacha on June 8, 1998, the Group of 34 emerged as one of the most powerful political forces in the country. The membership of the Group of 34 eventually served as the core for the People's Democratic Party (PDP), the dominant political association of the Abubakar transition program (1998–99). The Group of 34 was led by former Vice President Alex Ekwueme. Other well-known members included Solomon Lar, Adamu Ciroma, Lawal Kaita, Bola Ige, Iyorchia Ayu, Jerry Gana, Abubakar Umar, Ango Abdullahi, Balarabe Musa, C.P. Ezeife and Basil N. Ukegbu.

GUINEA WORM INFECTION. A disease that is spread to human beings through untreated water. When a person swallows guinea worm larvae, the larvae develop in the intestine. They then bore through the walls of the intestine to body tissue. They finally settle as parasites mostly in the legs around the ankle. The worm becomes adult about a year later, each about 70 centimetres long. When the worm begins to discharge its larvae into the leg tissue, the patient develops blisters and later on the blisters develop into wounds. The worm will then begin to come out of the wound very slowly. The patient is not expected to remove it by himself for it may break and cause more problems and complications. The wound generally heals within a few weeks or months. In Nigeria today guinea worm is generally not present in places where there is tap water, but it is still found in many rural areas that depend on untreated water. In such places it is advisable to boil all drinking water. The World Health Organization is helping Nigeria to eradicate the disease.

GUMI, SHEIKH ABUBAKAR MAHMOUD. An erudite Islamic scholar, born on November 5, 1922, in Gumi, Zamfara, about one hundred kilometres south of Sokoto (q.v.) town, he started his primary school education in 1931. Before then, he had read through the Koran in Arabic from cover to cover and reportedly could recite any verse by heart. In 1939 he entered the central Middle School in Jatau, and, in 1942, he became a student of Arabic and Islamic studies at the Kano School for Arabic Studies. In 1943 he started his Islamic law course at the Shari'a Law School in Kano (q.v.) from where he graduated in 1947 as an Islamic lawyer. He later went back to Sokoto to teach Islamic law before he went back for a postgraduate course in 1949. In 1951, after his graduation, he taught for two years before embarking upon another course in Islamic law and Arabic Studies in the Sudan. In 1955 he went to Saudi Arabia on the sponsorship of the Sudanese Institute where he studied. While there, he met Sir Ahmadu Bello (q.v.), the Sardauna of Sokoto and premier of Northern Nigeria (q.v.) who, with some others, was a member of the Nigerian delegation to the 1957 Constitutional Conference (q.v.) in London, and who was visiting Saudi Arabia after the conference. Upon his return to Nigeria, Gumi joined the School for Arabic Studies in Kano, and, while there, he was appointed the first West African pilgrims officer by the colonial administration. In 1960, when the Shari'a (q.v.) Court of Appeal was set up in the north, he was appointed the deputy Grand Khadi (q.v.) (deputy chief judge) of the court. In 1963 he became the Grand Khadi and a close adviser to Sir Ahmadu Bello who was still the premier. In 1976, when Nigeria became a federation of 19 states with 10 of them in the old Northern Region, he stepped down as the overall Grand Khadi.

During this long service period, he was a member of the judicial advisory council of the Supreme Military Council (1966–75) and chairman of the Nigerian Pilgrims Board in 1975. He has honorary doctor of laws (LL.D) degrees from the University of Ibadan (q.v.) and Ahmadu Bello University (q.v.) in Zaria. He was honored nationally as Commander of the Federal Republic, and, before his death, he won the prestigious King Faisal International Memorial Award for distinguished service to Islam (q.v.). Towards the end of his life, he became controversial when he stated in an interview that Muslims, especially in the North, would not vote for non-Muslim presidential candidates, and that the place of women was not to assume leadership roles.

Gumi was committed to the modernisation of Islam in northern Nigeria, and he consequently played a role that was alternately conciliatory and divisive. In 1962, he was appointed to be the first leader of the Jama'atu Nasril Islam (JNI), an organisation that worked to unify the various Islamic factions of northern Nigeria. By the 1970s, however, Gumi had taken to vocally criticising the Islamic brotherhoods of the North for "heterodox" practices. His attacks were seen as a challenge to the religious establishment and eventually led to the establishment of the radical Izala movement in 1978. By the end of his life Sheikh Gumi appears to have moved toward a reconciliation of sorts with the establishment, and the Izalas were seen as a less radical movement.

Sheikh Gumi translated the Koran into Hausa (q.v.) and has written many other publications. He died in September 1992.

GWANDU. Before his death, Usman Dan Fodio (q.v.) had in 1812 divided the administration of the empire which he created into two caliphates (q.v.), one under his brother Muhammad Abdullahi (q.v.) and the other under his son, Muhammad Bello (q.v.). Abdullahi was placed in charge of the western caliphate including Nupe (q.v.) and Ilorin (q.v.) with its capital in Gwandu, while Bello was in charge of the emirates to the east, which included

Zamfara, Katsina (q.v.), Kano (q.v.), Daura (q.v.), Bauchi Katagum and Adamawa (q.v.) with their capital in Sokoto (q.v.). The two caliphates lasted until the British occupation. However, Bello, the Sarkin (q.v.) Musulmi in Sokoto, and his successors were always accepted as supreme.

GWARI. An ethnic minority group, it is located in the present Niger State (q.v.). The people were said to have come from Bornu (q.v.) and to be indigenous to Nigeria. They were never conquered by the Fulani (q.v.) during the jihad (q.v.).

-H-

HABE KINGDOMS. Refers to the Hausa kingdoms before their conquest by the Fulani-led jihad (q.v.) of Usman Dan Fodio (q.v.) in the early 19th century. By contrast, Hausa kingdoms is used to refer to these kingdoms both before and after the jihad.

HARBISON REPORT. This report on high-level manpower study for Nigeria was submitted by Frederick Harbison of Princeton University in the United States to the Federal Government (q.v.). Professor Harbison was required to estimate the country's manpower needs between 1960 and 1970. He divided what he regarded as high-level manpower into two categories—senior and intermediate. He estimated that Nigeria would need 31,200 personnel in the senior category by 1970 and 54,000 persons in the intermediate category as opposed to the 30,000 personnel in both categories in 1960. He estimated that Nigerian universities would have to turn out at the rate of 2,000 graduates a year to meet these demands and other postsecondary institutions an estimate of about 5,400 graduates a year in the intermediate category. He, therefore, recommended upgrading the employed manpower through in-service training, and the establishment of a Manpower Development Board to coordinate other interregional machinery for manpower development. The government accepted Harbison's analysis of the country's manpower position but could not accept his estimates of future needs of the country. The government felt that the target set was too low.

HARDING, WILLIAM. *See* ALI EISAMI.

HARMATTAN. Harmattan is the name given to the wind that blows across the Sahara Desert toward the Atlantic coast. The weather is characterised by very strong, cold and dust-laden winds that blow in a northeasterly direction. The atmospheric moisture is low with a high range of temperature, which is cold at night and hot and dry during the day. In the northern part of the country, it may start as early as October or November and last until February or March. In the south it is generally between November and February. The harmattan period is the driest part of the year when many trees shed their leaves and grasses dry up. It is a period when there are many bush fires, sometimes caused by accident, but very often by farmers who use the opportunity to clear their farmlands by fire. The dry air also dries and cracks people's skin and lips. Because of the dust that hangs in the air like a fog, visibility is very low, making it difficult sometimes for aircraft to land, especially at the Kano International Airport. The harmattan generally lasts each time for only a few days, interspersed with warm and less dry weather.

HARRAGIN COMMISSION. Set up in November 1945 to review and make recommendations on the structure and remunerations of the civil services of the four British West African colonies. It was to look specifically at the standards of remuneration and superannuation payments, the relationship between the salaries and conditions of service of locally recruited and externally recruited officers, machinery for adjusting remuneration to variations in the cost of living, provision of suitable arrangements between governments and staff organisations, and provision by means of the Public Service Commission (q.v.) for regulating, selecting and promoting candidates for posts in the service.

Sir Walter Harragin, who was then the chief justice of the Gold Coast (q.v.), (Ghana) was the sole commissioner. His report was published in 1947. It recommended substantial wage increases for government employees and a higher entry point of salary for African technical staff in an effort to encourage them to stay with the government for its many development programmes. It recommended the introduction of expatriation pay for expatriates who were recruited outside Nigeria. It also recommended the setting up of an advisory council modelled on the British Whitley Councils in each territory to advise government on all matters like salaries and conditions of employment of civil servants.

The government accepted most of its recommendations but the Nigerian Civil Service Union and some others were strongly opposed to higher entry points for African technical officers.

HAUSA. The Hausa are the most numerous people in Northern Nigeria (q.v.). They are found mostly in Sokoto (q.v.), Kebbi (q.v.), Kano (q.v.), Jigawa (q.v.), Katsina (q.v.), Bauchi (q.v.) and Kaduna (q.v.) States. They are also found in sizeable numbers in all areas of the northern part of the country and some other important towns and cities of the federation. Outside Nigeria, they are in Ghana (q.v.), Benin (q.v.), Niger Republic and many parts of West Africa. Historians are not too sure of their exact origin. Some say they came from Libya or Mecca; others say the Hausa migrated from the

Chad Basin and settled among the local population, while others say that the Hausa trace their origin through Bayajidda (q.v.), son of Abdullahi, king of Baghdad, who had journeyed about the 13th century, first to Bornu (q.v.), then to Daura (q.v.) where he married the Queen of Daura, by whom he had a son Bawo. Bawo later had six sons who, together with him, founded the seven Hausa City-States (q.v.), or Hausa Bakwai. These seven states are Katsina, Daura, Gobir, Kano (qq.v.), Zamfara, Zaria (q.v.) and Rano.

The Hausa have a common language, which is classified as belonging to the Chad subfamily of Afro-Asiatic languages. At present, the Hausa language is widely spoken, not only in Northern Nigeria where it has become a lingua franca, for the most part, but also in many parts of West Africa.

Taking advantage of the savannah that they occupy, the Hausa are mostly farmers, planting crops like rice, cowpeas, millet and guinea corn. A good proportion of them engage in trading, and some are artisans. As artisans, they excel in the making and dyeing of cotton textiles, which in the precolonial days found a ready market across the Sudan belt to North Africa. Leather goods are also another Hausa specialty. They are great blacksmiths, silversmiths, iron smelters and mat and basket makers. Being highly skilled traders, they have settled in almost all urban centres throughout West and Central Africa.

Traditionally, political authority among the Hausa belonged to local chiefs who supported larger state organisations like Kano or Katsina. Such large states maintained their administration through collection of taxes by officials in the various regions or districts. The settlement pattern among the Hausa varied. In some places there were villages of round huts. There were also big cities like Kano that surrounded themselves with high city walls.

Islam (q.v.) came to the Hausaland about the 13th century, but traditional religious (q.v.) beliefs and practices were still prevalent until the Fulani (q.v.) jihad (q.v.) of the early 19th century (q.v.) which aimed at establishing Islam more firmly in the Hausa States by imposing Fulani rulers, called Emirs (q.v.), on them. Today the Hausa are mainly Muslim.

Like many other ethnic groups in Nigeria, the Hausa trace their descent patrilineally and their marriages are patrilocal, while inheritance is mainly by male heirs. Thus, hereditary title passed from father to son, which, to a great extent, explains why today they still allow the sons of the Fulani Emirs to succeed their fathers.

When Hausa people travel to other places they like to stay together in what is called Sabon-Gari (q.v.) in the big cities. In the northern part, sabongaris are created for southerners who migrate and work there.

The Hausa possess an intense cultural consciousness and pride in themselves. Consequently, the impact of Christianity (q.v.) upon them has been small.

HAUSA BAKWAI. Hausa Bakwai refers to the seven original Hausa States (q.v.): Kano, Rano, Zaria, Daura, Gobir, Katsina and Zamfara, but owing to the destruction of records of Hausa history by the Fulani (q.v.) who conquered them, authorities are not agreed on Zamfara as one of the seven original states. Some will substitute Biram or Yareem for Zamfara and include Zamfara as one of the Hausa Banza or Banza Bakwai, which were the seven states which had great Hausa influence but were not the seven original states. These seven states are listed as Zamfara, Kebbi, Nupe, Gwari, Yauri, Yoruba and Kororofa by some authors, while others say they are Zamfara, Kebbi, Nupe, Yauri, Yoruba, Borgu and Ghoorma.

HAUSA CITY-STATES. The Hausa city-states emerged as powerful entities between 1200 and 1600. According to tradition, they were established by the son and grandsons of Bayajidda (q.v.) who, reputedly, came from the east and journeyed first to Bornu (q.v.), and later to Daura (q.v.) where he married the Queen of Daura. Their son Bawo and his sons founded the seven Hausa states of Daura, Kano, Rano, Gobir, Zamfara, Zaria and Katsina. States like Kano (q.v.) and Zaria (q.v.) became rich and powerful and took part in the trans-Sahara Desert trade. By the 17th century, they had trade links with other states like Oyo (q.v.), Dahomey (q.v.) and Ghana (q.v.). Trade routes also extended from Kano to the east to the Nile Valley.

Hausa city-states also became centers of craft and industry (q.v.), like leatherwork, metalwork and weaving. The cities were surrounded by high walls which enclosed not only the people but also plenty of farmlands in case the city was under a siege so that it could survive for an indefinite period of time without the people having to go out. The gates were strongly built and fortified against possible enemies. However, in the early 19th century, most of these states were overcome during the jihad (q.v.), initiated by Usman Dan Fodio (q.v.) who made Sokoto (q.v.) the center of the Fulani (q.v.) empire. Sokoto in 1903 was itself captured by Lord F. Lugard (q.v.) and became part of the British protectorate (q.v.) of Northern Nigeria (q.v.).

HAUSA CONSTABULARY. The Nigerian Police, founded in Lagos (q.v.) in February 1861 as a consular guard of 30 men, was to maintain public peace in Lagos which had just become the Crown colony (q.v.). Two years later the police force became known as Hausa Police. In 1879 the colonial authority set up the Hausa Constabulary for the colony of Lagos, consisting of 1,200 officers and men under the command of an inspector general. The constabulary was mainly military in character, but it performed some civil police duties also. In 1896 the Lagos Police Force was created under the command of a commissioner who also was responsible for the prisons and for the fire brigade. The Lagos Police Force was also equipped like the Hausa Constabulary.

HAUSA KINGDOMS. *See* HAUSA CITY-STATES.

HAUSA LANGUAGE. The Hausa language is the most widely spoken in Northern Nigeria (q.v.). In fact, it has become the lingua franca in most parts of the area. Hausa is also spoken in Niger Republic and in many parts of West Africa. Hausa belongs to the Chadic subfamily of the Afro-Asiatic languages. It is rich in both oral and written literature and degrees are offered in it. Many Arabic words have been incorporated into it because most Hausa people are Muslim.

HEAD OF SERVICE. The head of service is the head of all the civil servants of the state or Federal Government (q.v.). During the colonial days, the head of service was known as the chief secretary, but during the First Republic (q.v.) and the military regime, the posts of head of service and secretary to the government were concentrated in one person. However, under the 1979 constitution (q.v.), the two posts were separated. The constitution made the head of service a civil service appointment, while the post of secretary to the government was termed "political." The appointment of a head of service was made by the governor in case of the state government and by the president in case of the Federal Government. The head of service, directly responsible to the governor or the president, as the case may be, coordinated the activities of the permanent secretaries in the various ministries.

HEALTH CARE. Health care delivery has grown a great deal since Nigeria became independent, thanks to the oil boom. When Nigeria became independent in 1960, life expectancy was about 35 to 40 years, but this rose to about 57 in the early 1990s. This was a result of general improvement in personal and environmental health care services all over the nation. Smallpox that used to be dreaded has been eradicated and the World Health Organization was able in 1976 to certify that Nigeria was a smallpox-free country.

Much of Nigeria's emphasis in health care delivery has been on the preventive rather than on the curative. The government has invested much in medical research in various institutions, coordinated by the Nigerian Medical Research Council, set up in 1972. Many training facilities have also been provided. There are at present 15 university teaching hospitals, all produce about 11,500 medical doctors and other medical personnel such as nurses, pharmacists, dentists and radiologists every year. Today Nigeria has about 800 general hospitals, over 3,000 maternity centers and many specialist hospitals.

At present, the main focus of Nigeria's health care services is the Primary Health Care System, which was launched in 1987, with the objective of taking health care services to the rural areas at affordable prices. It is a grassroots-oriented scheme, and it includes health education, family planning, immunisation, nutrition education, prevention of diseases, provision of potable water, basic training in sanitation and the provision of essential drugs. Most of the country's local government areas have set up such schemes in rural areas and most of the target population for immunisation has been reached and immunised against different kinds of diseases.

HICKS-PHILLIPSON COMMISSION. During the period between 1948 and 1951, after the recommendation of the Phillipson Commission (q.v.) to allocate revenue to the regions based on derivation (and even progress) was adopted, the north felt that it was receiving less than its just share of the central revenue. Thus, at the Ibadan Conference of 1950, a review was recommended. The government thus set up the Hicks-Phillipson Commission, charged with responsibility to inquire into and submit proposals on how government revenue was to be divided over a period of five years. The commission could not say whether or not the north had been unfairly treated. To cater to the principle of national unity and national well-being in which the well being of one part depended on the other, the commission suggested that allocation should be based on the principle of independent revenue, needs, national interest and special federal grants. Thus, it recommended that all revenue already regional should continue to be regional together with taxes on petroleum (q.v.); half of the proceeds from duties on manufactured and nonmanufactured tobacco should be assigned to the regions in proportion to their rate of consumption. Furthermore, to cater to national interest, the Federal Government (q.v.) should make annual grants to the regions on population basis and refund part regional expenditure on the Nigerian Police Force and half of the expenses on the Native Administration Police Force. It also recommended special grants of £2 million to the Northern Region (q.v.). The government accepted these recommendations with some modifications. The report was short-lived because the government set up another revenue allocation commission in 1953 known as the Chick Report (q.v.).

HORTON, JAMES AFRICANUS BEALE. A West African nationalist, born in Sierra Leone (q.v.) by an Igbo (q.v.) ex-slave father who was rescued at sea by the British anti-slavery patrol and set free in Sierra Leone. He was educated in mission schools and later went to study Christian ministry at Fourah Bay College (q.v.) in Freetown (q.v.). In 1853 he was one of three African students who went to study medicine in Britain. He received his degree in medicine at the University of Edinburgh in 1859 and returned to West Africa as an army medical doctor. He worked in many army locations along the coast for 20 years and retired as a lieutenant general. After his retirement, he went into private business. Among his books is *West African Countries and Peoples* (1868). He died in 1882.

HOUPHOUET-BOIGNY, FELIX. Former president of the Ivory Coast (q.v.). During the Nigerian Civil War (q.v.), he accorded diplomatic recognition to the "Republic of Biafra" (q.v.) after President Nyerere of Tanzania and President Albert Bongo of Gabon had done so. He also gave asylum to Lt. Col. Odumegwu Ojukwu (q.v.) after he fled from Biafra before its surrender to the Federal Government (q.v.).

HOUSE OF ASSEMBLY. A legislative House of Assembly was created for each of the three regions under the Richards Constitution (q.v.) of 1946. Each of the regional houses had both official and unofficial members, but, for the first time in the history of the country, unofficial members outnumbered official members, and the number of official members gradually dwindled until they practically disappeared at independence. Every one of the 36 states in the Federation (q.v.) has a house of assembly today.

HOUSE OF CHIEFS. The House of Chiefs was the second legislative chamber in each of the three regions constituting the Nigerian Federation (q.v.). Its history began in 1947 when the Richards Constitution (q.v.) created a Council of Chiefs (q.v.) for the Northern Region (q.v.). In 1951 under the Macpherson Constitution (q.v.), the west got its own House of Chiefs. In the Constitutional Conference (q.v.) of 1958, a recommendation for an upper chamber was made for the Eastern Region (q.v.), and in 1960, a second upper house was created for that region. Under the 1979 constitution, there were no Houses of Chiefs. Each state legislative house was unicameral.

HOUSE OF REPRESENTATIVES. The House of Representatives was originally created under the Macpherson Constitution (q.v.) of 1951. It then consisted of a president, six ex-officio members (q.v.), 136 representatives elected from the regional houses and six special members appointed by the governor to represent interests and communities that were inadequately represented. Under the Independence Constitution of 1960 and the Republican Constitution of 1963, the House of Representatives consisted of 312 members, from whom the governor was to choose a member who appeared to him to command the support of the majority of the members as prime minister, who together with his cabinet was responsible to the House. However, under the executive presidential system of the Second Republican Constitution, the House of Representatives was independent of the executive branch, for the president and his cabinet were not members of the House of Representatives.

HOUSE SYSTEM. The house system operated in the city-states in the Niger Delta and all the way to Calabar (q.v.). Traditionally, the people in these areas had a segmentary system of authority based on lineages. The lineages, in their effort to organise trade for export, developed into houses. Each house had a chosen head who had much power over members, and was the custodian of their property and finances. These houses, in effect, were like trading firms or corporations and engaged in very fierce competition with one another. Those that could not compete successfully were swallowed up by the more successful ones.

The power and prestige of a house was judged by the number of men and war canoes mounted with cannon at its disposal and the number of soldiers ready to protect its trading interest in time of war. It has been said that in the 18th century when competition for slaves and palm oil was very keen, a house in Bonny (q.v.) could have as many as 10 war canoes, if not more. Before this time, only people of royal blood were chosen as head of the family, but, as time went on, people of servile origin, such as Oko Jumbo (q.v.) and Jaja of Opobo (q.v.) who showed exceptional abilities, were chosen as heads.

HOWELLS, BISHOP ADOLPHUS WILLIAMSON. Born in Abeokuta (q.v.) on August 9, 1866, he attended the Ake School there before he went to the Christian Missionary Society (CMS) Training Institute in Lagos (q.v.) in 1882. He later became a teacher at a mission school in Badagry (q.v.). In 1887 he was transferred to St. Paul's School on Breadfruit Street in Lagos. In 1891 he went to study at Fourah Bay College (q.v.), Freetown (q.v.) in Sierra Leone (q.v.) and later to Durham University in England. He returned to Lagos in 1894 and was appointed a tutor at the CMS Grammar School (q.v.), while he supervised the CMS mission's training institutions in Lagos. In 1897 he became a deacon of the church and was ordained priest in 1899. He became curate of the Christ Church Pro-Cathedral in Lagos in 1900 and later was appointed pastor of St. John's Parish, Aroloya. In 1919 he was appointed the first African vicar of the Pro-Cathedral Church of Christ. His superiors did not fail to recognise his work and his worth to the church, and in 1920 he was consecrated bishop by the Archbishop of Canterbury at St. Paul's Cathedral in London. He was then posted to the Niger Diocese where he served until 1933. He returned to Lagos as assistant to Bishop Melville Jones who was then the Bishop of Lagos. He had under him the churches in Abeokuta, Ibadan (q.v.) and Ijebu (q.v.). In the same year, 1933, he became a resident bishop of Abeokuta, his hometown. He served there until he retired. He lived long enough to ordain his own son, Rev. A.W. Howells, a priest at Onitsha (q.v.) in 1931. He died on December 3, 1938.

-I-

IBADAN. Capital city and administrative headquarters of Oyo State (q.v.), Ibadan, according to the 1963 population census, was the largest city in the whole of West Africa and the most populous in Africa south of the Sahara. Its population then stood at 1.3 million people.

There are many stories about the founding of Ibadan, but what is certain is that Ibadan was originally an Egba (q.v.) village with a market in the centre. This village was destroyed during the intertribal wars that destroyed Owu and other places, and after the Egba withdrew to Abeokuta (q.v.) and settled there the conquering army occupied the village. The leader of the army that settled in Ibadan was Lagelu, an Ife warrior and a farmer, said to have been the founder of the town. The place where he first pitched his camp was known as "Eba-Odan," meaning "by the field" (in between the forest and the savannah). From this came the Ibadan known today. Some sources went further to say that this settlement was later destroyed by the Olowu, and Lagelu had to move to Eleyele Hill, where the Egba suffered much hardship, and had to feed on snails and a wild apple called "oro." Hence, one hears about the Ibadan: "Omo a joro sun, omo a je'gbin yo, omo a fikarahun fori mu,"—Ibadans eat oro for supper, feed on snails and use the snail shells as bowls for eating corn porridge.

Because of the military foundation of Ibadan, the traditional titles and order of precedence in the town are mostly military. The traditional ruler of the town is called the Olubadan, whose selection is through promotion from among a long line of hierarchy of Chiefs divided into two lines, one military and the other civil, instead of the usual succession of the Yoruba (q.v.) Obas. Not one family in which the previous title of Baale, now Oba, is hereditary, and until recently there was no official residence of the Oba. Thus succession to the throne in Ibadan is devoid of the acrimony seen in other towns where there are hereditary lines. In Ibadan the Balogun always succeeds the Oba.

Ibadan is a commercial and an administrative town, but a good percentage of its inhabitants are farmers. The most important traditional festivals in the town are Oke'badan and the Egungun (masquerade). The town is blessed with many educational institutions. It has three teacher-training colleges, scores of secondary schools, hundreds of primary schools, a polytechnic and a university. Places of interest in the city are: University of Ibadan (q.v.), which was founded in 1948; University Teaching Hospital, Nigerian Television (formerly WNTV first in Africa); Liberty Stadium, which was opened on September 30, 1960; Cocoa House, a 27-story skyscraper reputed, when built, to be West Africa's tallest skyscraper, the Premier Hotel, the Government Secretariat and a host of other places.

IBADAN PROGRESSIVE UNION—WOMEN'S SECTION. *See* NATIONAL COUNCIL OF WOMEN'S SOCIETIES.

IBEKWE, DAN ONUORA. Born in Onitsha (q.v.), Anambra State (q.v.) he had his primary education at St. Mary's School, Onitsha, and his secondary education at Christ the King College, Onitsha. He later went to the Council of Legal Education Law School in London and was called to the bar in 1951. Upon his arrival in Nigeria, he and J.I.C. Taylor became partners in a private legal practice in Lagos (q.v.). In 1954 Ibekwe moved to Aba where he set up his legal practice. In 1956 he was legal adviser to the premier of Eastern Nigeria (q.v.), Dr. Nnamdi Azikiwe (q.v.). In 1958 he was made solicitor-general of Eastern Nigeria. During the constitutional crisis over the federal elections of 1964, he advised the president that he had no constitutional powers to form an interim government nor to assume power himself. He was strongly criticised for this advice, and he resigned. He later became a senator in the federal Senate (q.v.) and was appointed minister of Commonwealth relations. He was in this post when the coup (q.v.) came in January 1966 after which he became solicitor to the firm of Irving and Bonner. In 1966 he was arrested by the government of Eastern Nigeria and was detained until after the Civil War (q.v.) in 1970 when he was released. He was later appointed commissioner for works, housing and transport in the East-Central State (q.v.). In 1972 he was made a justice of the Supreme Court (q.v.) of Nigeria. In 1975 he became federal attorney general and commissioner for justice. In 1976 he became president of the Federal Court of Appeal (q.v.) and also the chairman of the Nigerian Institute of International Affairs (q.v.) in Lagos. He died on March 23, 1978.

IBIAM, DR. AKANU. Physician and statesman, Sir Francis Ibiam was born on November 29, 1906, at Unwana, a town in Afikpo division of Anambra State (q.v.). He was educated at Hope Waddell Training Institute, Calabar (q.v.), King's College, Lagos (q.v.), University of St. Andrews, Scotland, and the London School of Tropical Medicine and Hygiene, England. He returned to Nigeria to become the medical missionary to the Church of Scotland Mission (CSM), Calabar, from 1936 to 1966. He founded the Abiriba Hospital in 1936. He later became medical superintendent at the CSM Hospital at Itu from 1945 to 1948. In 1947 he became a member of the Legislative Council (q.v.) of Nigeria and a member of the Executive Council (q.v.) of Nigeria between 1949 and 1952. Between 1952 and 1957, he was the medical superintendent at the CSM Hospital at Uburu. In 1957 he became the principal of the Hope Waddel Training Institute, Calabar, and was also president of the Christian Council of Nigeria from 1955 to 1958 and chairman of the provisional committee of the All-Africa Church Council from 1958 to 1962. Between 1958 and 1961, he was the chairman of the Council of University College, Ibadan (q.v.) and was appointed one of the six presidents of the World Council of Churches in 1961.

He became the governor of Eastern Nigeria (q.v.) in 1960, the post he held until 1966 when the military took over, and was appointed adviser to the military governor of the Eastern Province (q.v.) in 1966. He was the special adviser to the Biafran Head of State, Colonel Odumegwu Ojukwu (q.v.) from 1967 to 1970.

Sir Francis Ibiam was nationally honored as the Grand Commander of the Order of Niger. Foreign honors include Knight Commander of the Order of the British Empire and Knight Commander of St. Michael and St. George. He was awarded an honorary LL.B. degree by the University of St. Andrews, Scotland, D.Litt. by the University of Ibadan and an LL.D. by the University of Ife (q.v.). He died in July 1995.

IBIBIO. The Ibibio live in the Cross River State (q.v.). They are closely related in their culture and language to the Efik (q.v.). However, unlike the Efik, they were not united under one traditional authority. Their traditional organisation was based on family groups and villages with elders who have the authority to discuss important political problems and make decisions. Traditionally, every village had a member of the traditional secret society known as Ekpo, which assumed responsibility for protecting the community against disaster by performing certain rituals at special occasions such as planting time and harvest. Today the Ibibio are all over Nigeria, but their main centers of population are Uyo, Ikot Ekpene and Itu. Occupationally they are mainly farmers and traders. Among their food crops are yams (q.v.), cassava (q.v.) and palm oil, and some engage in pottery, wood carving and cloth weaving.

IBO FEDERAL UNION. The Ibo Federal Union was founded in 1944 as a cultural organisation. It aimed mainly to promote solidarity among the Igbo (q.v.) and their educational development. When the National Council of Nigeria and the Cameroons (NCNC) (q.v.) was founded later that year by Dr. Nnamdi Azikiwe (q.v.), who was an Igbo, the Ibo Federal Union was one of its member organisations. In 1948 the union changed its name to Ibo State Union and redefined its purpose to include organising Igbo linguistic groups into a political unit in accordance with the NCNC Freedom Charter. The union gave its unflinching support to the NCNC and elected the party leader, Dr. Azikiwe, its national president. The organisation worked relentlessly to promote Igbo solidarity especially outside the Igbo land and to provide for the educational advancement of the Igbo people through scholarship at home and abroad. The union was banned in 1966 after the military seized power.

IBO STATE UNION. In 1948 the Ibo Federal Union became the Ibo State Union. It consisted of representatives from all local unions. Many leading members of the National Council of Nigeria and the Cameroons (NCNC) (q.v.) were members of the union. In fact, Dr. Nnamdi Azikiwe (q.v.), the NCNC president, was also president of the union from 1948 to 1952.

IBRAHIM, ALHAJI WAZIRI. Businessman and politician, born at Yerwa, Borno State (q.v.), on February 26, 1926, he attended Maiduguri Middle School and Kaduna College in Kaduna (q.v.). He worked as a labour staff manager at the United African Company (UAC) (q.v.) in Benue Area between 1953 and 1954, and served in many capacities under the UAC establishment. In 1959 he was elected into the federal House of Representatives (q.v.) where he was appointed federal minister of health, and later minister of economic development between 1962 and 1966. He went into business after the military came to power in 1966. When the ban on political activities was lifted in 1978, he fulfilled one of his life ambitions by forming a political party, the Nigerian People's Party (NPP) (q.v.). But owing to dissension on whether or not the same person should be chairman of the party and the presidential candidate, Ibrahim, believing that he should be both chairman and presidential candidate, left to form a new party, the Great Nigerian People's Party (GNPP) (q.v.). He contested the presidential election in 1979 under the banner of his new party. He lost the election, but his party won the gubernatorial elections in Borno State (q.v.) and Gongola State (q.v.).

After the presidential defeat of 1979, the GNPP became a close ally of the Unity Party of Nigeria (UPN) (q.v.), and both became the nucleus of the four-party alliance forged in 1982. But Ibrahim later in 1982 became disillusioned and withdrew from the alliance effort. However, a faction of his party, led by the two governors of Borno and Gongola, continued to cooperate with the other parties to work out a basis for the alliance known as the Progressive Parties Alliance (PPA) (q.v.). Ibrahim was also a candidate for the presidency in 1983, but he again lost to Alhaji Shehu Shagari (q.v.) who was reelected for a second term. Alhaji Ibrahim was famous for his slogan: "politics without bitterness." He died July 9, 1992.

IBRAHIM BEN AHMED. Ruler of Bornu from 1820 to 1846. Before him, his older brother Dunama Ben Ahmed (q.v.) had allied with Al-Kanemi (q.v.) to ward off the incessant attack of the Fulani (q.v.) who had carried to Bornu the jihad (q.v.), initiated by Usman Dan Fodio (q.v.). Al-Kanemi, however, gradually gained in power, and Dunama, in an effort to kill Al-Kanemi, was himself killed in battle, leading to the accession of Ibrahim in 1820. Ibrahim was only a figurehead. When Al-Kanemi died in 1837, his son Umar (q.v.) succeeded him, and Ibrahim seized the opportunity to reassert the Sefawa dynasty's (q.v.) authority over Bornu, but he failed. Ibrahim then plotted with the Sultan of Wadai, Muhammad Sheriff, to invade Bornu in order to remove Umar. Umar knew about the plot and had Ibrahim killed in 1846. From then on, Umar became the effective ruler of Bornu, thereby firmly establishing the Al-Kanemi dynasty in power.

IBRAHIM, SIR KASHIM. An educationist, politician and the first indigenous governor of Northern Nigeria (q.v.), Sir Kashim Ibrahim was born in 1910 at Maiduguri, Borno State (q.v.). He was educated at Borno Provincial School and at the Katsina Training College. He became a teacher in 1929, and in 1933 he became the senior provincial visiting teacher and education officer from 1949 to 1952. He was a founding member of the Northern People's Congress (NPC) (q.v.) and became the central minister of social services in Lagos (q.v.) from 1952 to 1955 and northern regional minister of social development from 1955 to 1956. He was the Waziri of the Borno Native Administration (q.v.) between 1956 and 1962, chairman of the Nigerian College of Arts and Science between 1958 and 1952 and chairman of the provisional council of Ahmadu Bello University, Zaria (q.v.), from 1960 to 1962. He was appointed governor of Northern Nigeria (q.v.) from 1962 to 1966, and when the military took over power, he was appointed adviser to the military governor of Northern Nigeria from 1966 to 1967. Additionally, he was chancellor of the University of Ibadan in 1966 and in 1977 he became the chancellor of the University of Lagos. He was awarded several honors, among them: Grand Commander of the Order of the Niger, Knight Commander of the Order of St. Michael and St. George, Member of the Order of the British Empire and Commander of the Order of British Empire. He was awarded honorary LL.D. degrees by the University of Nigeria, Nsukka (q.v.), University of Ibadan and Ahmadu Bello University, and a D.Litt. by the University of Lagos. He died in July 1990.

IDAH, A. A sculptor born in 1908 who, from age seven, lived and worked in the palace of the Oba of Benin, Oba Eweka II (q.v.). He began to learn carving by practising with calabashes and other materials. In 1923 he went to Lagos and carved with ebony. He was perhaps the first to carve ebony in Nigeria and to use cement for sculpture.

IDIA. Idia was the Queen Mother of Oba Esigie of Benin (q.v.) who ruled at the beginning of the 16th century. Idia was said to be a great warrior, immortalized by an ivory carving of her face, which was adopted in 1977 as the African Festival of Arts and Culture (q.v.) symbol.

IDIAGBON, MAJ. GEN. TUNDE. Born September 14, 1943, chief of staff, supreme headquarters, and the number-two man in the military administration that replaced the Shagari (q.v.) administration. He was born in Kwara State (q.v.) and had served in many important positions prior to the December 1983 coup (q.v.). He was, for example, the military administrator for Borno State (q.v.) in 1978 in a preparatory effort to hand over power of the military to civilians in 1979. In January 1984, Idiagbon became the chief of staff, Supreme Headquarters, in the Buhari (q.v.) administration, a position in which he was responsible for both the general administration of government and the administrative functions of the armed forces (q.v.). He lost this position as a result of the palace coup that replaced Major General Muhammadu Buhari, the Head of State, when Idiagbon was on a pilgrimage to Mecca. While in power, Idiagbon was seen as a very disciplined, nonsmiling and no-nonsense officer. He launched the War against Indiscipline (WAI) (q.v.) campaign to instill discipline in Nigerians and promote unity and patriotism. He also insisted on the accountability of public officers of all ranks. He, however, was accused of stubbornness and a refusal to listen to advice. His greatest undoing was the wide power he gave to the security officers, the NSO, to arrest and detain, a power that was grossly abused. He retired in September 1985, after he had come back from his pilgrimage, and was in political detention for 40 months before he was released in December 1988. He died on March 24, 1999.

IDRIS BEN ALI ALOMA. Ruler of the Bornu (q.v.) empire from 1570 to 1603. Before this time, the empire was in great decline. Idris ascended the throne at a time when Bornu was under all kinds of threat from the Bulala (q.v.) people—who had driven the Kanuri people out of Kanem—from the Hausa States (q.v.) that regularly raided Bornu, and from the Tega nomads who were harassing the empire at its northern boundaries.

When Idris went on a pilgrimage to Mecca, he was exposed to firearms. He decided to build a very strong army, and invited Turkish musketeers to come and train his army. He personally led many campaigns, but the most important for him was the victory against the Bulala of Kanem, which then came under the authority of Bornu. He also introduced administrative reforms to make a revolt less likely. The territories outside his immediate control were placed under trusted people rather than his relations who could one day revolt against him. His expenses were financed through taxes, tributes and income from the slave trade (q.v.). A good Muslim, he instituted the Islamic judicial system and built mosques together with a hostel in Mecca. He was a famous ruler who had diplomatic contact with places like Turkey and Morocco. He died about 1603.

IDRIS KATAGARMABE. A great warrior and son of Mai Ali Ghaji Dunamami (q.v.), Idris succeeded his father in Bornu (q.v.) in 1504. About 1507 he thoroughly defeated the Bulala people (q.v.) who, about a hundred years before, had driven out the Kanuri (q.v.) people of Kanem into Bornu. His victorious army reoccupied Njimi, the old capital of Kanem, and brought Kanem back as a province (q.v.) of the Bornu empire instead of Bornu a province of the Kanem empire. The capital of Bornu remained Birni, Ngazargamu, founded by Ali Ghaji Dunamami. Idris died in 1526.

IFE ART. The history of the development of Ife art is not very clear. It predates the bronze and brass sculptures found in the Benin (q.v.) royal palace by many centuries. Ife brass and bronze smiths greatly influenced the development of Benin bronze and brass sculptures. Ife traditional art consists of terra-cotta (q.v.), bronze and brass heads of kings of Ile-Ife (q.v.). They are described as the most naturalistic and refined of African sculptures. There are also masks for Egungun rituals (Masquerade). Still very important are the Ibeji figures, which are wooden representatives of dead twins, cared for as if they were live babies.

Ife has lost much of its brass and bronze technology, but people still specialise in beautiful beadworks, making beaded crowns, pectoral badges and ornamental materials.

IGALA. Igala people live mainly in Kogi State (q.v.). Their traditional kingdom was at Idah and was a powerful state as far back as the 15th century. The traditional ruler is called Ata. Igala society is divided into clans or groups of people who are descended from the same ancestor. Each clan holds traditional authority, thereby making sure that power is shared among the various groups and clans. Most Igala people are farmers who grow such crops as yams (q.v.), cassava (q.v.), maize and millet.

IGBINEDION, CHIEF GABRIEL OSAWARU. A businessman and philanthropist, born September 11, 1934, at Okada in Edo State (q.v.), Igbinedion was educated in Eko Boys High School from 1952 to 1954 and joined the Nigerian police force in 1958. In 1964 he was a sales representative and later a sales manager at the Leventis Group of Companies. He later founded the Okada Group of Companies, which is involved in soft drink bottling, farms, airlines, bread making, motor sales, shipping, education and so on. He was honoured with a merit award of outstanding achievement in air transportation by the Benin Chambers of Commerce, Industry Mines and Agriculture. He has a traditional title of Esama of Benin.

Igbinedion was a powerful political broker in Edo state under the Babangida (q.v.) administration, where he worked to support a number of National Republican Convention candidates (including his son Lucky, who narrowly lost the gubernatorial election). Igbinedion remained active in politics and was a prominent supporter of the People's Democratic Party during the transition program of Abdulsalami Abubakar (1998–99). His clout was finally successful in securing the election of his son Lucky as the governor of Edo State in January 1999, and contributed to Olusegun Obasanjo's (q.v.) victory in the presidential elections of February 1999.

IGBIRRA. One of the minority ethnic groups that inhabit the areas north and east of the Niger-Benue confluence in the old Northern Nigeria (q.v.). The Igbirra are now part of the Kogi State (q.v.). Even though most of the north was subjugated by the Fulani (q.v.) in the early 19th century, the Igbirra were never so subjugated. They are made up of the following subgroups: Egu, Okene and Panda.

IGBO. One of the three main population groups in Nigeria, the Igbo occupy the present Abia (q.v.), Anambra (q.v.), Enugu (q.v.) and Imo (q.v.) States, with a combined population of about 11 million people, according to the 1991 census. Because they live in an area of about 3,000 square kilometres, this area is the most densely populated in Nigeria. Igbo people, perhaps as a result of the population density in the area, have readily migrated to other parts of the Federation (q.v.) in great numbers, especially trade businessmen and women, teachers and technicians.

The origin of the Igbo is not precisely known, but it is commonly believed that they migrated from the north around the confluence of the Niger (q.v.) and Benue Rivers (q.v.). Early Igbo people appeared to have first occupied the Awka-Orlu plateau area many centuries ago, which is often referred to as the Igbo heartland. Archaeological remains found in Igbo Ukwu (q.v.) show that a high level of civilisation existed in the area more than one thousand years ago. Linguistically, the Igbo language belongs to the Kwa subfamily of the Niger-Congo family. However, numerous dialects are spoken, reflecting the small-scale nature of their organisation.

The Igbo people are mostly farmers who plant yams (q.v.), cocoyams, maize, cassava (q.v.) and oil palm (q.v.). They are also skilled traders, and are making great strides in technological development. Furthermore, they are skilled in wood carving and pottery. Igbo dancing groups are well known all over the nation for their music and dancing.

Politically, the Igbo people have been slow in developing a highly centralised political organisation like the Yoruba (q.v.) of Western Nigeria (q.v.) with the institution of an Oba (king) or the Hausa (q.v.) or Fulani (q.v.) peoples of Northern Nigeria (q.v.), with their Emirs. The basic unit of authority among the Igbo was the family, while the largest was the village group, a collection of villages that was their highest form of political organisation. All the family heads or elders sat together to carry out each village's government business. Usually the most senior of the elders would preside at meetings. Though the oldest among the elders, he was not a chief because he did not rule, and had not much authority outside his extended family. At the village meetings, everybody was free to speak and men were respected for their talents, ability, wealth or wisdom.

The Igbo people can be divided into many groups. There are those west of the Niger River with a tradition of kingship as in Agbor, which is likely due to the influence of nearby Benin (q.v.). There are the people to the east called the Aro Igbo who participated greatly in the Atlantic slave trade with the Europeans in the 18th century, assisted by their oracle (q.v.) at Aro Chukwu, which they used to promote the trade until it was abolished in the early 19th century when palm oil began to replace it. The people around Nnewi and Nsukka area have distinctive titles, which may have been influenced by the rulers of Nri, whose political and ritual authority was at its highest about the 13th century. The Igbo people of Owerri (q.v.) also have a system of traditional titles in their communities.

The social unit among the Igbo is the extended family, and their system of descent is patrilineal. The family traditionally tends to be polygamous and residence is patrilocal. For a marriage to become legal, the future husband must pay a bride price (q.v.) to the bride's father.

The Igbo traditionally believe in God, but they still pay respect to ancestors and have beliefs in spiritual and supernatural powers. Some of their rituals are connected with yam production, for example, before planting and harvesting.

The Igbo have played important roles in the history of Nigeria. They continued to resist British rule, which culminated in the Aba Riot (q.v.) of 1929. And even though many groups in Nigeria had threatened secession by pulling out of the Federation, the Igbo were the only people who declared secession as a result of the coup and countercoup in 1966 and the massacre of many Igbo in Northern Nigeria, all leading to the fratricidal Civil War (q.v.) from 1967 to January 1970. *See* CIVIL WAR.

IGBO-UKWU. At Igbo-Ukwu in Anambra State (q.v.), archaeologists have found remains of a culture that was highly civilised and over one thousand years old. Some of the findings are metalworks, decorated bronze pots and copper works. Remains of a man buried with many precious objects point to a well-organised society with certain religious beliefs and a ruler who might have wielded some political power.

IGE, CHIEF BOLA. Lawyer, politician and the first governor of Oyo State (q.v.) in the Second Republic (q.v.), Chief Ige was born on September 13, 1930, at Esa Oke in Obokun Local Government Area, Ilesha Division of

Osun State and received his primary education at St. Joseph's Catholic School in Kaduna (q.v.) and his secondary education at the Ibadan (q.v.) Grammar School from 1943 to 1948. From 1949 to 1955 he attended University College, Ibadan (q.v.) where he graduated with a B.A. in classics. He taught in Ibadan Grammar School from 1955 to 1956 then went to the United Kingdom where he graduated in law from University College, London, and was called to the bar at the Inner Temple in 1961. He returned to Nigeria and set up a private legal practice.

His political activities started at the University of Ibadan where he took active part in student union politics and also served as the publicity secretary and general secretary of the Action Group (AG) (q.v.) youth club at the university. In 1962 he was elected federal publicity secretary of the AG at the Jos Conference, a post he held until January 1966 when the military took over the government. During the 1962 emergency period in Western Nigeria (q.v.), Chief Ige was one of those restricted. After his release, he was a delegate to the Nigerian Constitutional Conference (q.v.) held in Lagos (q.v.) in 1963. Under the military administration, Chief Ige was appointed commissioner (q.v.) for agriculture and natural resources for the Western State (q.v.) from July 1967 to January 1970 when he became commissioner for lands and housing until May 1970. He was a member of the Constitution Drafting Committee (q.v.) appointed to draft a new constitution for the country in 1975.

When the ban on politics was lifted in 1978, Chief Ige became a member of the Unity Party of Nigeria (UPN) (q.v.) in Oyo State. He ran for the governorship of the state under his party's platform and won. He was also state chairman of his party. In the 1983 gubernatorial elections, he lost to Dr. V. Omololu S. Olunloyo (q.v.) the candidate of the National Party of Nigeria (q.v.).

After the December 1983 coup d'état (q.v.), he was arrested and detained. He was tried with Governor V. Bisi Onabanjo (q.v.) of Ogun State (q.v.) and Governor Michael Ajasin (q.v.) of Ondo State (q.v.) for receiving a kickback of N2.8 million from a contract. He was acquitted, but he was later convicted on a two-count charge of conspiracy and corruptly enriching the proscribed UPN. He was sentenced to 21 years imprisonment, but was later released. After Alhaji Shehu Shagari (q.v.) was removed from office in 1983, Chief Bola Ige refused to serve under any military administration, and he was at the forefront of those who, after the annulment of the results of the June 12, 1993, presidential election (q.v.) in which Chief Moshood Abiola (q.v.) was the apparent winner, began to work toward the actualisation of Chief Abiola's mandate.

Out of principled opposition to the military Chief Ige refused to participate in either the Babangida or the Abacha democratic transitions, a stance that is informally known as "siddon look" ("Sit and watch"). Bola Ige was one of the Group of 34 (q.v.) politicians who came out publicly against the Abacha regime in May 1998. He was imprisoned shortly thereafter in connection with anti-government riots in Ibadan. Chief Ige was released from prison after the death of Sani Abacha (q.v.). He joined the Alliance for Democracy and emerged as a top presidential candidate, but lost the party's nomination to Chief Olu Falae, who was judged to have greater national appeal. After Obasanjo assumed office, Chief Ige was offered, and accepted, a position in the cabinet as federal minister of power and steel. The decision was very controversial within the AD. The leaders of the AD were apparently afraid that Ige's participation in the cabinet would hamper their ability to play a vigorous opposition role.

IJAW. The Ijaw people make up a large part of the present Rivers State (q.v.). Some of them are also found in the Delta State (q.v.). They live in Bonny (q.v.), Brass (q.v.), Okrika, Kalabari and Akassa. Tradition says they came from the east and the north about the fifteenth century, but their language, compared to other Nigerian languages, does not give credence to this. The Ijaw language belongs to the Kwa branch of the Niger-Congo family.

Most of Ijaw land is in the Niger Delta, which consists largely of mangrove swamps and farmlands, divided by creeks and rivers. The Ijaw traditionally depended on fishing. They built small villages, with their houses built on stilts above the swamps. Because of their geographical location, many villages joined in the slave trade (q.v.) with the Europeans in the 18th century, and they became intermediaries between the seaside Europeans and the hinterland.

Today the development of the petroleum (q.v.) industry in the area has created many changes in the life of the people. Oil and water pollution destroys the fish, making life much harder for the fishers. Land and atmospheric pollution is due to oil prospecting and the flaring of natural gas, all of which has raised anger and much unhappiness with the area.

IJAYE WAR. The war in 1859 between Ibadan (q.v.) and Ijaye over the successor to Atiba (q.v.), the Alaafin (q.v.) of Oyo. When the Oyo empire (q.v.) dissolved in the first half of the 19th century, the Ibadan and Ijaye kingdoms helped resettle the former location of the Oyo empire. In 1836 Kurunmi, the ruler of Ijaye, helped to place Atiba on the throne of Oyo, and Atiba rewarded him with a chieftaincy title of Are-Ona-Kakanfo (generalissimo of the army). When Atiba died, contrary to the tradition of Oyo that the first son of the dead Alaafin should follow his father to the grave, Ibadan rulers pleaded that the first son of the dead Alaafin should be allowed to succeed his father. Adelu, Atiba's first son, was thus installed Alaafin of Oyo. This action enraged Kurunmi who refused to recognise the new king. Ibadan sent emissaries to Ijaye, asking that Kurunmi accept the new ruler. Rather than recognise him, he vowed to wage war against Adelu all his life. War, therefore, broke out, and Ibadan and its allies lay siege to Ijaye. The Egba (q.v.) came to support Ijaye, but they could not raze the siege. Thousands of the Ijaye people died of starvation. In 1861 Kurunmi died. Ijaye fell in March 1862, and the town was deserted. Most of the refugees fled to Abeokuta (q.v.).

IJEBU. A subgroup of the Yoruba (q.v.) ethnic group, the Ijebu, together with the Egba (q.v.) make up most of the people of Ogun State (q.v.). Because of their proximity to Lagos (q.v.) and the sea, the Ijebu, like the Egba, played the role of middlemen between the white traders and the people in the interior, a position which they jealously protected. Thus, during the Yoruba civil wars of the 19th century, they occupied a better position than other Yoruba states in getting modern weapons from the coast. In 1891 the British finally secured a treaty abolishing human sacrifice, opening up the road to the sea from the hinterland and allowing trade to go through their territory. But in 1892, the Ijebu reneged, and a war between them and the British ensued in which the Ijebu were defeated, marking a significant event in the British occupation of the Yorubaland.

During the colonial era, the whole of the Ijebu area was constituted into a province (q.v.) with a resident (q.v.). Important traditional rulers in Ijebu are the Awujale of Ijebu-Ode, Akarigbo of Ijebu-Remo, Odemo of Ishara and Orimolusi of Ijebu-Igbo.

IJEMO MASSACRE. Under the treaty of 1893 between the Egba (q.v.) Chiefs and the governor of Lagos (q.v.), Egbaland was a semi-independent state. It therefore set up the Egba united government. In 1914 Mr. Ponlade, one of the opponents of the secretary to the united government, Mr. Edun, was arrested and later died in prison. People began to demonstrate against the death, and because the Egba united government could not contain the demonstration, additional troops were requested from Lagos. The troops fired on the people, killing many demonstrators. This was the Ijemo Massacre, and it led to the abrogation of the independence of Egbaland and the British assertion of authority over the land.

IKEJA. Though historically distinct, Ikeja has become part of metropolitan Lagos (q.v.). It used to be provincial headquarters in the former Western Region (q.v.) of Nigeria and the industrial center of the region. But by the creation of the Lagos State (q.v.) in 1976, Ikeja became the administrative capital of the new state and still so remains. Ikeja is also the location of the Lagos International Airport, also called the Murtala Muhammed Airport, so named after the late Head of State, General Murtala R. Muhammed (q.v.), who was killed in the 1976 abortive coup (q.v.)

IKOKU, ALVAN AZIMWA. An educationist, born in Amanagwu in Arochukwu on August 1, 1900. He was educated at Government School, Calabar (q.v.), Cross River State (q.v.), and later went to Hope Waddell College to train as a teacher. In 1920 he joined the Presbyterian Church of Scotland in Itigidi and became a staff member of St. Paul's Teacher Training College in Awka in 1924. While at the college, he took correspondence courses with the Wolsey Hall in London and earned the University of London degree in philosophy in 1928 with honours. Believing that education was essential to the development of the country, in 1931 he resigned from his work with the mission to establish his own college in Arochukwu, the Aggrey Memorial College, named after Dr. Aggrey, the Ghanaian educationist. When a branch of the Nigerian Union of Teachers (NUT) (q.v.) was opened in Calabar, Ikoku joined it, and in November 1940, he was elected the national second vice president of the organization. In 1944 he became one of the three men appointed to serve on the board of education for the Southern Provinces. In 1946, following the Richards Constitution (q.v.), Ikoku was nominated to the Eastern House of Assembly (q.v.) and was appointed to the Ministry of Education. In 1947 he became a member of the Legislative Council (q.v.) in Lagos (q.v.), being one of the three people who were representing the Eastern Region (q.v.) in the council. As a member of the council, he used his position to advance the interest of NUT and education in the country.

Ikoku later became interested in politics, becoming the leader of the United National Party, which won some seats in the former Eastern House of Assembly, but the party did not live long, owing to the Eastern Regional Government Crisis of 1953 (q.v.). In 1955 he became president of NUT, and during his tenure the organisation made recommendations to the government to set up a uniform educational system for the country. The recommendations were rejected, but when the military took over power in 1966, Ikoku was a member of the Study Group, set up to look into the feasibility of setting up a unified educational policy for the country. Unfortunately, the Civil War (1967–70) (q.v.) interrupted their work. Ikoku died on November 18, 1971.

Ikoku was a dedicated educationist. Besides founding the Aggrey Memorial College, he established other schools and initiated private scholarship schemes for needy students. In 1965 the University of Ibadan (q.v.) awarded him an honorary degree of doctor of laws, and for his lasting contribution to the development of education in Nigeria, the federal military government declared him a national hero and his picture is engraved on the Nigerian 10 naira note.

IKOKU, SAMUEL GOMSU. An educationist and a politician, born on July 24, 1924, he was educated at Aggrey Memorial College, Arochukwu, Achimota College, Accra, Ghana (q.v.), and at London University where he received an M.S. degree in economics. He later on in Nigeria joined the Action Group (q.v.) Party and in 1962 during that party's crisis, he was the secretary general of the party as well as the leader of the party in the Eastern Region (q.v.). He was one of those charged with Chief Obafemi Awolowo (q.v.) in 1962 as conspiring to overthrow the Federal Government (q.v.) by force. He fled the country to Ghana and became a wanted man. He was repatriated in March 1966 and detained, but was later released by the military administration that later came to power. He was appointed East-Central State (q.v.) commissioner for economic development and construction in 1970. When the ban on political activity was lifted in 1978, he became a member of the People's Redemption Party (q.v.) and was later elected the national secretary of the party.

When the party was banned in January 1984 by the military administration of Major General M. Buhari (q.v.), Ikoku went back into private business. In 1994 he was a member of the Constitutional Conference (q.v.) set up by General Sani Abacha (q.v.) to review the Nigerian constitution (q.v.).

IKOLI, ERNEST SESEI. A journalist, born on March 25, 1893, at Brass (q.v.) in Rivers State (q.v.). He was a son of a successful businessman and a European-educated mother. He attended the Bonny Primary School and was later a foundation student of the King's College (q.v.) in Lagos (q.v.) in 1909. After his secondary education, he was appointed a teacher at the school but resigned in 1919 to become an editorial assistant in the *Lagos Weekly Record* (q.v.), which was at the time edited by Thomas Horatio Jackson, the son of the paper's founder, John Payne Jackson (q.v.). In 1921 he left to found his own newspaper, the *African Messenger,* which he edited until 1926 when he became editor of the newly founded *Daily Times* (q.v.) of Nigeria. He wrote the first editorial of the paper on June 1, 1926. His own paper, the *African Messenger,* by this time had been taken over by the *Daily Times.* In 1928 he left the *Daily Times* to found the Nigerian *Daily Mail* and edited the *Daily Telegraph* for J.A. Doherty, the owner. In 1931 the *Daily Telegraph* became defunct.

Ikoli also played a prominent role in Nigerian political awakening. He was secretary of the Lagos branch of the Universal Negro Improvement Association set up by Marcus Ikoli Garvey. In 1934 Dr. J.C. Vaughan (q.v.), Chief H.O. Davies (q.v.) and Oba Samuel Akinsanya (q.v.) formed the Lagos Youth Movement (LYM) (q.v.), which was opposed to the colonial government education policy with regard to some alleged deficiencies of the Yaba Higher College (q.v.). The LYM in 1936—in an effort to convert itself to a nationalist organisation—changed its name to Nigerian Youth Movement (NYM) (q.v.) under the leadership of Vaughan. Ikoli in 1941 vied with Akinsanya for the vacancy on the Legislative Council (q.v.), created by the resignation of Dr. K. Abayomi (q.v.), and won. In 1943 he became the president of the NYM, which could not fully recover from the schism created by the 1941 contest. For six years (1938–44), he edited the NYM organ, the *Daily Service* with Chief S.L. Akintola (q.v.). He was also reelected into the Legislative Council in 1946. He was later appointed chairman of the rediffusion Service, and became public relations adviser to the Nigerian Railway Corporation (q.v.). He was a Member of the Order of the British Empire. He died on October 21, 1960, just a few weeks after Nigeria became independent.

ILE-IFE. Known as the Cradle of the Yoruba, Ile-Ife is believed to be the final home of Oduduwa (q.v.), the ancestor of the Yoruba Obas (kings). All Yoruba (q.v.) people regard Ile-Ife as their original home from where they all dispersed to various settlements. Ile-Ife was probably occupied as far back as the sixth century, and, by the 11th century, it had become a centre of fine terra-cotta sculptures (q.v.) and copper and bronze heads, especially of the ruler, the Ooni of Ife. Today this art is famous all over the world.

According to history, the traditional ruler, the Ooni of Ife, is the spiritual leader of the Yoruba, a fact evidenced by the ancient city's many shrines. By the 16th century Ile-Ife began to lose political power to the Oyo empire (q.v.). In spite of this, the Ooni continued to have great religious authority.

Ile-Ife is located at longitude 4.6°E and latitude 7.5°N, and is situated on an elevation of about 275 metres above sea level. It has a tropical temperature and is within the tropical rain forest zone. The population of the city, according to the 1991 census, was about 250,000 people.

The Ifes are the indigenous people of Ile-Ife and its districts. The Ifes are a subgroup of the Yoruba ethnic group. They are predominantly farmers who live mostly in the villages; traders, craftsman, businessmen and such other people live in the township. Although the Ife place much importance on traditional religious (q.v.) practices, they also embrace the two nonindigenous religions in Nigeria—Islam (q.v.) and Christianity (q.v.).

Ile-Ife is the home of the Obafemi Awolowo University (formally called the University of Ife [q.v.]). Among the places of interest in the town are: Opa Oranmiyan, Ife Museum of Antiqinties, the Aafin of the Ooni of Ife and the Natural History Museum at the Obafemi Awolowo University.

ILORIN. A Yoruba (q.v.) town in the old Northern Region (q.v.), and now the capital of the Kwara State (q.v.). Originally, Ilorin was one of the military outposts of the Old Oyo empire (q.v.) under the Alaafin (q.v.), but it came under Fulani (q.v.) rule after the defeat of Afonja (q.v.), who was posted there to guard and defend the northern outpost against the threatened invasion by the lieutenants of Usman Dan Fodio (q.v.) during the holy war (jihad [q.v.]). Afonja himself, with the assistance of Alimi (q.v.), a Fulani herdsman, had revolted against the Alaafin of Oyo and proclaimed the independence of the town. However, soon after, Alimi attacked Afonja and won, and so the town came under the rule of the Fulani with the title of Emir (q.v.) of Ilorin, even to this day.

During the colonial era, Ilorin was part of the Northern Protectorate (q.v.), which in 1946 came to be regarded as a region. In 1967, when the then-existing four regions were divided into 12 states, Ilorin became the capital of the Kwara State. It is also a university town. The Ilorin people are famous for their pottery industry.

ILORIN TALAKA PARAPO. One of the small parties that combined to form opposition in the Northern House of Assembly (q.v.) during the First Republic (q.v.). In the 1956 Northern Region (q.v.) election, ITP, backed by the Action Group (q.v.), gained 2.6 percent of the seats in the Northern House. In the 1957 elections the ITP captured the Ilorin District Council, but the Council was suspended after many clashes between it and the Emir (q.v.), who was aided by Northern People's Congress politicians. The leaders of the ITP were Chief J.S. Olawoyin and Alhaji Sule Maito.

IMAM. A term in Nigeria which refers to the Muslim prayer leader. A Muslim with necessary theological education and sufficiently versed in the technique of the Sal'at can be an Imam.

IMAM, ALHAJI ABUBAKAR. Born in 1911 in Kagara in the Northern Region of Nigeria. He is best remembered for his contributions to Hausa literature, particularly the three-volume collection of stories *Magana Jari Ce* which is probably the best loved work written in the Hausa language.

Alhaji Imam was among the first northern Nigerians to receive a European education, attending the famous Katsina Training College. He first came to prominence by winning an award from the colonial government in 1934 for his short comic novel, *Ruwan Bagaja* (The water of cure) which is still widely read. In 1937–38, his three volume collection of stories *Magana Jari Ce* (The ability to speak is money). In addition to authoring these classics of Nigerian literature, Alhaji Imam also served as the first Hausa language editor of the newspaper *Gaskiya Ta Fi Kwabo* (The truth is better than a penny) from 1939–54.

Abubakar Imam was also active in the north's first political associations. In 1948, he was one of a handful of northerners who helped found the Jam'iyyar Mutanen Arewa, a cultural organization that eventually evolved into the Northern People's Congress (NPC) in 1949. Imam was the first treasurer of the NPC and served as an elected representative to the Northern House of Assembly and the Nigerian House of Representatives in the early 1950s. From the mid-1950s until the late 1970s, Alhaji Imam held a number of different positions in the civil service, helping to shape the first generation of civil servants from northern Nigeria. He died on June 19, 1981.

IMO STATE. One of the seven states created in 1976 by the administration of General Murtala R. Muhammed (q.v.), Imo State was once a part of the East-Central State (q.v.), a part of the Eastern Region (q.v.), one of the four regions in the Federation (q.v.). In 1991 Abia State (q.v.) was carved out of Imo State. The state is located between latitudes 4° 45′ and 7° 15′N and longitudes 6° 50′ and 7°25′E. It is 5,100 square kilometres, and is bounded in the southwest by Rivers State (q.v.), in the east by Abia State and in the north by Anambra State (q.v.). The rainfall is between March and October with its peak between July and September. Violent storms generally herald the coming of the rainy season. The annual rainfall is between 1,990 millimetres and 2,200 millimetres. The temperature is about 27°C and the relative humidity is about 75 percent, rising to about 90 percent in the rainy season. The people grow maize, rice, legumes, cassava (q.v.), yams (q.v.), plantain and groundnuts (q.v.). They also have oil palms (q.v.), oranges, rubber (q.v.), and raise sheep, goats, and poultry. The state's mineral resources include coal, lignite, kaoline, gravel, marble, petroleum (q.v.) and gypsum. The state is divided into 21 local government (q.v.) areas.

The population of the state was 2,485,499 in 1991 and its density is 230 persons per square kilometres, thus making the state one of the most densely populated in the country. Ethnically, Imo State is predominantly Igbo (q.v.), and even though the state is mainly Christian (q.v.), there are Muslims (q.v.) and people who still cling to traditional religions (q.v.). One of their most popular festivals is Ahiajoku. The traditional dress of the Igbo men is an overall jumper or long sleeve shirt over a wrapper, tied round the waist and reaching down to the ankles. This is complemented with a hat and a walking stick. For the women it is a blouse over a wrapper tied round the waist, with a head tie and earrings to match. The main population centers are Owerri (q.v.), the capital, Okigwe and Oguta.

Educationally, the state is one of the most well endowed in the country. In 1992 it had 1,205 primary schools with 570,345 pupils and 287 secondary schools with about 154,375 students. There are two universities in the state and many technical colleges and colleges of education.

IMOUDU, CHIEF MICHAEL OMINUS. A trade unionist and a politician, born on November 20, 1902, at Ora in Bendel State (q.v.). He was educated at the Government School, Ora, Catholic (q.v.) School in Onitsha (q.v.), and the Agbor Government School. In 1928 he joined the Nigerian Railway as a labourer and later became an apprentice turner. Chief Michael Imoudu played a prominent role in the establishment of the Railway Workers' Union (q.v.) in 1932.

In 1941 Imoudu was elected the vice president of the African Civil Servants Technical Workers' Union (ACSTWU) comprised of the Railway Workers' Union, P. & T. Workers' Union, the Nigerian Marine African Workers' Union and the Public Works Department Workers' Union. In January 1943, he was summarily dismissed for alleged misconduct and insubordination and was served with a detention order under the Nigeria General Defence regulations. He was accused of action prejudicial to public safety or defence and was immediately taken to Benin province. In March 1943, the detention order was replaced by a restriction order, and he was required to report twice a week to the police in Auchi. The ACSTWU and the Railway Workers' Union began a vigorous campaign for his release. Their efforts later bore fruit. He was released from restriction and returned to Lagos (q.v.) on June 2, 1945, amid the cheers of his supporters.

In the nationalist struggle after the Second World War, Chief Imoudu played a very important role. He led the nationwide strike of 1945 and was among the National Council of Nigeria and the Cameroons (NCNC) delegates who toured Nigeria between April and December to educate the people on the Richards Constitution (q.v.) of 1946 and the so-called "obnoxious bills." In 1949 Imoudu was elected the president of the Nigerian National Federation of Labour (q.v.) and at the inauguration of the Nigerian Labour Congress (q.v.) on May 26, 1950, he became its president. In 1953 he was made the president of the All-Nigerian Trade Union Federation (ANTUF) (q.v.). When the ANTUF and the National Council of Trade Unions of Nigeria (q.v.) merged together in January 1959, to form the Trade Union Congress of Nigeria (q.v.), Chief Michael Imoudu was also elected its president. In May 1962, he formed the Independent United Labour Congress (q.v.) and became its president. In 1976, in an effort by the military administration to reorganise the Nigerian trade unions, he and other labour leaders were retired.

In 1978 the University of Ife (q.v.) conferred on him an honorary degree of doctor of law. In the same year when the ban on politics was lifted, Dr. Imoudu became one of the leaders of the People's Redemption Party (PRP) (q.v.) led by Mallam Aminu Kano (q.v.). In 1980 when the party broke into two factions, over whether the party should accede to the National Party of Nigeria's (q.v.) invitation to take part in a national government, Dr. Imoudu, believing that the two parties were not ideologically compatible, led the breakaway faction and remained its leader. In the four-party alliance worked out in 1982, the Imoudu faction of the PRP was one of the parties. However, in the preparation for the 1983 elections, efforts were made to reunite the factions to improve the party's electoral chances in the states and in the nation as a whole. On May 18, 1983, just about a month after the death of Aminu Kano (q.v.), the two factions were reunited and Chief Imoudu became a national vice president of the party.

INDEPENDENCE. In 1958 the British government agreed that if a resolution asking for independence was passed by the new federal Parliament that was to come into being early in 1960, Her Majesty's government would agree to such a resolution. Accordingly, at the first meeting of the federal legislature in January 1960, both Houses of Parliament (q.v.) unanimously passed a resolution calling for independence. Her Majesty's government later introduced a bill known as the Nigerian (Constitution) Order in Council, 1960, in Parliament and it was passed on September 12, 1960. The order came into effect on October 1, 1960, and Nigeria became an independent and sovereign nation.

INDEPENDENT NATIONAL ELECTORAL COMMISSION (INEC). The body created by the Abubakar administration in 1998 to supervise transitional elections. It replaced the thoroughly discredited National Electoral Commission of Nigeria (NECON), which was used by the Abacha regime to manipulate election results. INEC was under the leadership of Ephraim Akpata, a former Supreme Court Justice. While most observers affirmed the impartiality and integrity of INEC, the series of elections held in 1998–99 suffered from logistical problems, difficulties in registering voters and accusations of fraud. Nevertheless, the results were creditable enough to allow the transition to be complete on schedule.

INDEPENDENT UNITED LABOUR CONGRESS. Formed on May 4, 1962, as a protest movement against the decision of the United Labour Congress (q.v.) to affiliate with the International Confederation of Free Trade Unions (q.v.). The principal officers of the new group were M.A.O. Imoudu (q.v.) as president and Amaefule Ikoro as secretary. The IULC preferred to affiliate only with the All-African Trade Union Federation (q.v.).

INDIANS. Indians from South Asia came into the country as early as 1911, but, beginning from the 1920s, they began to arrive in increasing numbers. The influx was not arrested until the immigration restrictions of 1947. Originally, they were retail traders, but today few Indians are found in commercial activities in Nigeria. Nigeria is presently experiencing a new influx of Indians who are teachers in many schools, doctors in hospitals and engineers or architects all over the nation.

INDIGENISATION DECREE. *See* NIGERIAN ENTERPRISES PROMOTION DECREES, 1972 AND 1977.

INDIRECT RULE. The system of ruling the indigenous population through the already existing traditional local structures, Chiefs, Obas, Emirs and native courts, adopted in all British West African territories by the colonial authorities. When Britain took over the administration of Nigeria from the Royal Niger Company (q.v.), in 1900 Lord Lugard (q.v.) became the High Commissioner of the then-Northern Protectorate (q.v.). As commissioner (q.v.), he was faced with two major problems: he lacked sufficient knowledge of the local population to be able to rule them effectively and efficiently and he had very limited financial and human resources to directly rule what he called a "vast" country. He, therefore, decided to rule through the northern Emirs (q.v.) and the existing Muslim courts so that his need for European officers would be limited to a supervisory role. The system was based on the belief that Chiefs and Emirs were the rulers of their people, and, if the colonial authorities would officially recognise them as having authority to make laws, enforce them, punish offenders, collect local revenues and provide certain services, they would be a great asset to the colonial authorities who only had to control the Chiefs and Emirs to control the people.

After the Amalgamation (q.v.) of the Northern and Southern protectorates, the system was nationalized by extending it to the south, and the fallacy of the British assumption became clear. In Western Nigeria (q.v.), Chiefs (Obas) did not have absolute authority and therefore could not always make the people do what they did not want to do. In Eastern Nigeria (q.v.), there were no such Chiefs in many towns and villages as there were in the north and in the west. Thus, colonial authorities embarked on a policy of creating chiefs by issuing them warrants—called the Warrant Chiefs (q.v.)—who were very much resented by the people, a situation that partly accounted for the Aba Riots (q.v.) of 1929.

While the system, for a long time, protected the traditional political and legal system from too much interference from the outside, it nonetheless worked against the principles that the British believed in. It limited the participation of educated elements in the government in their locality, made for fragmentation of the country into discrete cultural groups, thereby, making the problem of national integration a more serious one, and, while it strengthened traditional authorities vis-à-vis their people, these traditional rulers became mere puppets in the hands of colonial authorities. Finally, the system preserved the indigenous system of land ownership and so encouraged a peasant and subsistence production system rather than freeing land for large commercial agricultural undertakings.

INDUSTRIAL RESEARCH COUNCIL OF NIGERIA. Established in 1971, it is a federal government statutory body affiliated to the federal Ministry of Industries. Its principal functions are to promote and coordinate all industrial research activities in Nigeria, and develop and apply such industrial research results. The 12 members of the council come from faculties of science and engineering of Nigerian universities, the public and the private sectors of the economy, with four ex-officio members (q.v.) made up of permanent secretaries from the federal Ministries of Trade, Communications, Works and Housing, and Mines and Powers.

INDUSTRY. The authorities during the colonial period had greater interest in developing Nigeria as a raw materials source for their industrial concerns at home, while Nigeria was kept open for British manufactured goods rather than seeing the country turn the raw materials to finished goods. Even cocoa (q.v.), which Nigeria produced in abundance, was sent to Britain to be processed into Ovaltine, chocolates and cookies, and then sent back to Nigeria. The nationalists of the 1950s were determined to reverse this practice. In the first national development plan (q.v.) after independence (1962–68), the government was determined to create and stimulate an industrial climate that would enable Nigerians to participate to an ever-increasing extent in the ownership, direction and management of Nigerian industry and trade. The government did not give a legal backing to this until 1972, issuing the Nigerian Enterprises Promotion Decree (q.v.), which classified enterprises into those which could be wholly owned by Nigerians and those they could own jointly with expatriates. As a result of this encouragement and the oil boom of the early 1970s, many industrial concerns sprang up and government began to get involved in many capital-intensive industries like oil refineries and petrochemical plants, fertilizer and steel plants, and paper mills and machine tools. Nigeria also began to try its hands in vehicle assembly plants.

In addition to many of these efforts, the government set up and funded many industrial and technical research institutes to provide technological support for industrial activities, especially to manufacturing establishments. Their main services include promotion and transfer of technology, use and adaptation of local raw materials and technologies in manufacturing processes, and the introduction of innovative cost-saving devices in industries. Some of these Institutes are the National Office for Technology Acquisition and Promotion (q.v.), which, established in 1979, facilitates the acquisition of foreign technology in order to promote rapid industrialisation and economic development, and Project Development Institute (PRODA), which, established in 1971, carries out industrial research and development into power equipment and machines. In the pursuit of its objective, PRODA has fabricated many machines, including commercial *gari* plant, palm oil mills, maize milling plants, four-wheel drive vehicle series, computer softwares and many others.

In spite of all these efforts, there is noticeable deceleration in the rate of growth in recent years. This is due, in part, to the high cost of foreign exchange for procuring basic raw materials and spare parts for machinery for maintenance and replacement. The situation is also made worse by massive importation and smuggling of a wide variety of products into the country through its porous borders. As a result overall manufacturing capacity utilisation of most firms ranged from 38 per cent to 50 per cent in 1991 and 1992. Only a few industries exceeded 50 per cent capacity utilisation rate.

The slowdown in the tempo of activities in the industrial sector continued until 1995. The CBN survey of the manufacturing subsector in 1994 showed that the average capacity utilisation in the manufacturing establishments had fallen from 37.2 per cent in 1993 to 30.4 per cent in 1994. Many industries produced much below this, including auto vehicle assembly plants, producing at about 15 per cent, while glass and glass products produced at 8 per cent. Still worse, the 1996 budget stated that the performance of the real sector continued in 1995 to be sluggish, as industrial output fell by 2.6 per cent.

INTERIM ADMINISTRATIVE COUNCIL. Established in May 1967 concerning the territories formerly known as Northern and Eastern Nigeria (q.v.), which were divided into new states.

The council, composed of the permanent secretaries of the territory or the newly created states, was charged with responsibility to arrange the share to which each state was entitled in the assets of the former region out of which the new states were created. It was responsible for establishing new departments of government or other government institutions necessary in the new states. It was also to allocate members of the public service in the former regions to the new states, and to consider from time to time problems of general administration in all or any of the states. By further amendments, the council had vested in it all immovable public property held in trust by the governors of the former Northern and Eastern regions. While the council was able to function in the north, the Civil War (q.v.) that broke out immediately after the states were created did not permit the decree to take effect in the Eastern Region (q.v.). In 1968 the council was succeeded by the Interim Common Services Agency (q.v.). In the Eastern Region, after the Civil War ended in 1970, Decree No. 39 of 1970, which set up the Eastern State, Interim Assets and Liabilities Agency (q.v.), was promulgated.

INTERIM COMMON SERVICES AGENCY. When Nigeria was divided into 12 states in 1967, there arose the problem of how best to share the assets and liabilities of the former Northern and Eastern regions (q.v.) where the new states were created. To solve the problem in the north, the federal military government issued Decree No. 12 of 1968, creating the Interim Common Services Agency to take care of the assets and liabilities of the former Northern Region, which had then been divided into six states. The agency was charged with the control, operation and general management of the services, statutory bodies and institutions that were owned by the states which formerly formed the Northern Region. It had power to dispose of any property that was no longer required by it, invest its funds in government securities and maintain its various properties. Included under the authority of the Agency were Ahmadu Bello University (q.v.) in Zaria (q.v.), the Government Press in Kaduna (q.v.), Shari'a (q.v.) Court of Appeal, Kaduna Polytechnic (q.v.), Northern Nigeria Housing Corporation, Livestock and Meat Authority, Northern Nigeria Marketing Board (q.v.) and Northern Nigeria Radio Corporation. The agency was dissolved in 1976 with the promulgation of Decree No. 19 of 1975, which caused the term of the agency to expire on March 31, 1976.

INTERIM NATIONAL GOVERNMENT. After the annulment of the June 12, 1993, presidential election (q.v.), pressure was brought to bear on the military president, General Ibrahim B. Babangida (q.v.) to quit office. This he did on August 26, 1993, when he transformed the Transitional Council (q.v.), headed by Chief Ernest Shonekan (q.v.), into the Interim National Government (ING), which again was headed by Ernest Shonekan. The ING was to resolve the political crisis created by the annulment, but support for the ING was thin. Before it had time to settle down, a court in Lagos (q.v.) ruled, in a case instituted by Chief Moshood K.O. Abiola (q.v.), the undeclared winner of the presidential election, that the ING was illegal. A few days after, November 17, 1993, General Sani Abacha (q.v.) pushed the ING aside and became the Head of State and Commander-in-Chief of the armed forces (q.v.).

INTERNATIONAL COMMITTEE OF THE RED CROSS. During the Nigerian Civil War (q.v.), the Red Cross was one of the relief agencies that supplied relief materials to the war-affected areas of the country. The Committee made use of Fernando Póo, a Spanish island near Nigeria, as their storing depot where the relief materials were stored before onward transmission to the war areas.

The ICRC, having received approval from the two sides in the war, received donations from organisations and individuals throughout the world to carry out its humanitarian assignment.

However, the involvement of Carl Gustaf Von Rosen (q.v.) in the relief effort, who in May 1969 led an air raid on Port Harcourt (q.v.), created problems for the organisation. The federal government troops shot down a Swedish Red Cross aircraft in June 1969, after the aircraft, heading for Uli airport had refused to land at the Port Harcourt airport. The government later formally banned all unauthorised night flights through its air space and ended the ICRC's mandate to coordinate the relief operations in the country. The government then handed over the ICRC's coordination effort to the Nigerian Red Cross, and expelled the ICRC's representative to Nigeria, August Lindt.

INTERNATIONAL CONFEDERATION OF FREE TRADE UNIONS. The International Confederation of Free Trade Unions sent a delegation to Nigeria in 1951 to recommend a base in West Africa where the organisation could begin its operations. The Nigerian Labour Congress (q.v.) was opposed to this, and there were demonstrations against the visit at the airport in Lagos (q.v.). As a result of this opposition, the ICFTU left for Accra, Ghana (q.v.), where they were well received. The Gold Coast Trade Union Congress decided to affiliate with it, and it recommended Accra to be the base of their operations in West Africa.

INTERNATIONAL INSTITUTE OF TROPICAL AGRICULTURE. Before the military came into power in 1966, the Federal Government (q.v.) had begun negotiations with the Ford Foundation (q.v.) and the Rockefeller Foundation to establish and maintain in Nigeria an international institute of tropical agriculture. A proposal to this effect had been submitted as far back as March 1965. The federal military government, seeing the need for the establishment of the institute in Nigeria, issued Decree No. 32 of 1967 to set it up. Its functions were to undertake studies of and research into tropical agriculture and to provide information to authorised representatives of governments, or groups or bodies of persons, interested in tropical agriculture. It was to look for ways and means to increase the output and improve the quality of tropical food crops, to provide, in cooperation with universities and other educational institutions, high-level professional training to persons who were expected to become staff members of the institutions and organisations concerned with increasing food production and distribution in the tropics. The institute was to publish its research findings and distribute improved plant materials to other research centres.

ITTA was governed by a board of trustees composed of the permanent secretary of the Ministry of Agriculture and Natural Resources, two members appointed by the Federal Government, two members, one each from Rockefeller Foundation and Ford Foundation, both serving as ex-officio members (q.v.), the director of the institute and another person chosen outside Nigeria but from a tropical area of the world. Its headquarters or principal office is in Ibadan (q.v.), Oyo State (q.v.).

INTERNATIONAL OBSERVER TEAM IN NIGERIA. During the Civil War (q.v.), the Federal Government (q.v.), in order to counteract the effective propaganda of Biafra (q.v.) against the alleged federal government atrocities, resorted to allowing various groups of foreign observers to come and see for themselves and report on their experience in the warzone. These were groups of military observers drawn from Britain, Canada and Poland to inspect the behaviour of federal troops at the fronts and investigate Biafran charges of genocide.

The idea of an observer team was first suggested by the British government and accepted by General Yakubu Gowon (q.v.). It was opposed by some who saw the presence of such observers as an infringement on Nigeria's sovereignty and independence.

The team spent 16 months working at the fronts and producing objective reports on the conduct of federal soldiers' treatment of Biafran civilians, prisoners of war and the relief situation, and investigation of charges of brutality. The team was only on the federal side and did not go to the Biafran side because the Federal Government was opposed. The team exercised a moderating and cautionary influence on the federal troops and undermined Biafran claims of genocide.

INTER-UNIVERSITY COUNCIL FOR HIGHER EDUCATION IN THE COLONIES. The Inter-University Council for Higher Education in the Colonies was set up in 1946 as a follow-up to the recommendation of the Asquith Commission (q.v.). Members included representatives of all the universities in the United Kingdom. It was charged with the duties of keeping in touch with the development of new colonial institutions of higher learning through regular visits by its members. The council was to help in the recruitment of staff and encourage members of the home universities to take up appointment in the colonial universities. The council was also to strengthen cooperation between universities in the United Kingdom and those in the colonies and to foster the development of higher colleges in the colonies to advance to university status. Members of the council visited West Africa in 1946. Their purpose was to make recommendations to the secretary of state for the colonies on the issue of university colleges for West Africa. As a result of their recommendation, two university colleges were established, one in the Gold Coast (q.v.) (Ghana) and the other in Ibadan (q.v.), Nigeria, in 1948.

INVESTMENT COMPANY OF NIGERIA LIMITED. The Investment Company of Nigeria Limited, organised by the Commonwealth Development Finance Company Limited in consultation with British and Nigerian business interests, was incorporated in 1959. Its objectives were to encourage and, if necessary, to sponsor the development of local industrial commercial and agricultural enterprises. It was to provide financial assistance to exploit the country's natural resources and attract expatriate investment capital to private enterprises. Furthermore, it sought technical and managerial expertise and encouraged the development of stocks and shares market.

IRIKEFE PANEL. Set up by the federal military government in August 1975 to examine the burning issue of state creation (q.v.) in the Federation (q.v.). The panel, headed by Supreme Court (q.v.) judge, Ayo Irikefe, was, if it found a need for more states, to advise the government on the delimitation of such states, on the location of their administrative capitals, on their economic viability and on all other matters that might appear to the panel to be relevant. The panel submitted its report on December 23, 1975. On February 3, 1976, following some of the recommendations, seven new states were created from the existing 12 states.

ISHAN. The Ishan people constitute an ethnic group in Edo State (q.v.). They form part of the Edo-speaking people of the state. *See also* EDO.

ISLAM. An Arabic word meaning submission, and the name of the religion preached by the Prophet Muhammed in the seventh century. A follower of Islam is called a Muslim (Moslem). To a Muslim, Allah (God) is the most high, the creator and ruler of everything. Muslims also believe in angels, the holy Koran and prophets of Allah, including Abraham and Jesus. The five duties of a Muslim are regarded as the pillars of Islam. One must (1) believe there is no god except Allah, and Muhammed is the Prophet of Allah; (2) say one's prayers regularly five times a day; (3) fast during the month of Ramadan; (4) give alms to certain people especially the poor and (5) make a pilgrimage to Mecca if and when one can afford it.

The two main sources of Islamic law (q.v.) that govern all Muslim life are the Koran and the Sunna. The Sunna is the way in which Prophet Muhammed translated the teaching of the Koran into practical use. This will be found in the sayings and actions of Prophet Muhammed, as recorded in the Hadith (tradition).

One of the duties of a Muslim is to spread the religion to non-Muslims and convert them, if possible. But Islam does not ask its followers to spread the religion by force, even though Muslims can fight holy wars (jihad [q.v.]) to get rid of aggression, transgression of the Koran or hostility to believers. Places that are opposed to Islam are called places of war. Christians and Jews in an Islamic state are to be permitted to practise their religion, but they must respect the Muslim authority.

Islam was the earliest external influence to reach Nigeria; it followed the caravan trade routes that came from North Africa across the Sahara Desert into Western and Central Sudan (q.v.). Islamic faith and ideas began to come into the Kanem-Bornu empire (q.v.) of the Central Sudan around the 11th century, and from there it spread to the Hausa States (q.v.). It introduced a new way of life and brought with it literacy in the Arabic language. As such, the first written sources of historical study of the area were by Arabic scholars. For many centuries in Northern Nigeria (q.v.), Islam remained a religion of a small elite found around the courts of the Hausa (q.v.) rulers. However, toward the end of the 18th century, things began to change as Islamic access to Nigeria through the Senegal Basin continued to spread. By the beginning of the 19th century, the knowledge of Islam in the area was widespread enough to accept the reforms introduced by Usman Dan Fodio (q.v.). Dan Fodio launched an Islamic jihad (q.v.) in the Hausa States through his Fulani co-religionists living in the area. After taking over the states, the jihad moved westward to the Borgu Kingdom and eastward to Bornu (q.v.) where their initial successes were later reversed by the forces of Al-Kanemi (q.v.). To the south it reached Ilorin (q.v.), a Yoruba (q.v.) town. The Yoruba successfully fought against the jihad, but they could not stop the spread of Islam in Yorubaland. Thus, today Islam is not only widely accepted and practised in Northern Nigeria, but it peacefully coexists with Christianity (q.v.) and traditional religion (q.v.) in western Nigeria. The only place where it does not have many adherents is in eastern Nigeria where Christianity is predominant.

ISLAMIC LAW. Prior to the establishment of colonial rule, there was already in existence in the northern parts of Nigeria a well-developed system of judicial administration. Under the caliphate (q.v.) system, Islamic courts, manned by scholars known as alkalis, administered Islamic law, the Shari'a. The Shari'a is codified law that covers ways and modes of worship, standards of morals and life and laws that govern general human conduct. Its main sources are the Koran and the Hadith.

This code of Islamic law survives into the modern age. In most of Northern Nigeria, native courts administer Islamic law. Provisions are also made in the constitution (q.v.) for the establishment of Shari'a Courts of Appeal in any state of the Federation that desires it, and for the composition of the Court of Appeal and the Supreme Court (q.v.) in such a way as to make the application of Islamic law possible when necessary.

ITA, PROF. EYO. Born in Calabar (q.v.), Cross River State (q.v.), he was educated first at Duke Town School and then at the Hope Waddell Training Institute to become a teacher. He taught at the Baptist Academy in Lagos before proceeding to the United States for studies. Upon his return in 1933, he founded the Nigeria Youth League Movement. He taught for some time in Ogbomosho, but in 1938 he went back to Calabar where he became the head of a national institute. He later started his educational institution known as the West African People's Institute. He set up a press which, among other things, published his many works.

Professor Eyo Ita was a member of the National Council of Nigeria and the Cameroons (NCNC) (q.v.) and became in 1948 the first national vice president of the party. In 1951 he was elected to the Eastern House of Assembly (q.v.) and became minister for natural resources and leader of government business for the region. During the Eastern Regional Crisis of 1953 (q.v.), he, together with some regional ministers and expelled NCNC central ministers and their supporters, formed a new party known as the National Independence Party (q.v.). Professor Eyo Ita became the president of the new party. In conjunction with the United National Party of Alvan Ikoku, they were able to maintain themselves as opposition parties in the region. The two parties later joined together to form the United National Independence Party (q.v.). When later in the year the Calabar-Ogoja-Rivers (q.v.) Movement was launched, comprised of the non-Igbo-speaking minorities of the region, and asking for a separate state of their own, Professor Ita was a leading figure of this movement. In 1959 he went back to the NCNC and, after independence in 1960, he concentrated his effort on the development of his school. During the Civil War (q.v.), he supported the cause of Biafra (q.v.). He died in 1972.

ITSEKIRI. The Itsekiri people live on the western side of the Niger Delta (q.v.) in the Delta State (q.v.). Traditionally, they were fishers and traders. During the period of the slave trade (q.v.), the Itsekiri kingdom of Warri (q.v.) was one of the major sources for slaves, as the people acted as middlemen between the Europeans and the peoples in the hinterland. The kingdom was said to have been founded in the 15th century by a Benin prince, who, with his followers, migrated to Warri, and married into a branch of the Yoruba (q.v.) people. They later grew up to become a new group, speaking a Yoruba dialect modified by Benin influence, known as Itsekiri. Today the area has become an important centre of the nation's petroleum (q.v.) industry.

IVORY SCULPTURE. Ivory, the dentine material that composes the tusks of elephants, has been used in Nigeria for centuries for sculpture. It lasts longer than wood and can be easily carved with a sharp knife. Beautiful ivory sculptures, made in Benin and many parts of Nigeria, include horns for playing music, decorative adornments, or sculptures for display in places of worship.

IWO ELERU. Iwo Eleru was a rock shelter about 24 kilometres from Akure, capital of Ondo State (q.v.). Excavations have shown that it was inhabited at recurring intervals thousands of years before Christ. What the place, however, is most famous for are the remains of the Late Stone Age covering a period of about 10,000 years. It is said that the oldest Nigerian skeleton yet discovered, and perhaps the oldest skeleton showing negroid characteristics so far discovered in Africa, was found there. It was dated at about 9,000 B.C.

IWUANYANWU, CHIEF EMMANUEL CHUKWUEMEKA. Born on September 4, 1942, in Imo State. He is an engineer and wealthy industrialist. Among his enterprises have been ABC Merchant Bank Limited, Hardic and Enic Construction Company and Oriental Airlines. He is the publisher of the *Champion* and *National Post* newspapers. Chief Iwuanyanwu has been active in politics and has established himself as one of the top powerbrokers among the Igbo. He competed unsuccessfully for the presidential nomination of the National Republican Convention as part of the Babangida democratic transition program, and also vied for the presidential nomination of the United National Congress Party during the Abacha regime. During the transition programme of the Abubakar regime (1998–99) Iwuanyanwu pursued the presidential nomination of the All People's Party. He was angered by his failure to win the party's nomination, however, and shortly before the February 1999 presidential election he switched his support to the rival People's Democratic Party.

IZALA. The popular name for the Islamic association, Jama'at Izalatil Bid'a wa Iqatamus Sunnah, or "Movement Against Negative Innovations," which was formed in 1978. The inspiration for the organisation was the ideas of the Grand Khadi of Northern Nigeria, Sheikh Abubakar Gumi (q.v.). Throughout the 1970s, Gumi had carried out a number of polemical attacks on the main Islamic brotherhoods (Qadiriyya and Tijaniyya) for their "heterodox" practices. Although Sheikh Gumi did not formally participate, the formation of the Izalas was seen as a direct challenge to the brotherhoods. Because the brotherhoods were closely connected to the political and religious hierarchy of northern Nigeria, some saw the Izala movement as a challenge to the status quo. While the Izalas were associated with a number of violent clashes with followers of the brotherhoods in the 1980s, by the 1990s it had become a respectable advocate for the reform of Islamic practices in the north.

-J-

JACKSON, JOHN PAYNE. Born in 1848 in Liberia (q.v.), and after his formal education, he went into business, travelling to Ghana (q.v.) and Nigeria, but he finally settled in Nigeria. After serving under J.S. Leigh, a businessman, he set up his own business and became a palm produce trader. He was later forced out of competition. He went to Lagos (q.v.) in 1882 and took up a job with the *Lagos Times* which was then owned by Mr. R.B. Blaize (q.v.). In 1891 he founded his own weekly newspaper, the *Lagos Weekly Record* (q.v.), which became an important force in the nationalist struggle. In the early 1900s, he was critical of British administration and was very much involved in petitions and protest activities against the government in Lagos. He died in 1915.

JAJA. Ruler of the Niger Delta state of Opobo (q.v.) from 1869 to 1887, Jaja was born in 1821 in Amaigbo village group in the former Eastern Nigeria (q.v.). At 12 years of age, he was sold as a slave to a chief in the trading state of Bonny (q.v.). He later transferred to the Anna Pepple trading house in Bonny. In 1861, after the head of the Anna Pepple house died, he became a Chief of Bonny. Two years later he became the head of the Anna Pepple trading house. He expanded his trading business by absorbing other trading houses. By his successes, he became the envy of the Manilla Pepple trading house, headed then by Oko Jumbo (q.v.). In the competition between the two houses, there was need for a neutral person to intervene, but King George Pepple (q.v.), who succeeded King William Dappa Pepple (q.v.) in 1866, could not intervene because he was known to listen more to the head of the Manilla Pepple house. The king requested that the British consul, Charles Livingstone, intervene, but he refused. War broke out in 1869, and Jaja left Bonny to establish a new trading state at Opobo, where he could take over the palm oil trade coming from the interior into Bonny. He, therefore, became ruler of Opobo even though he had no royal blood in him.

By cutting off palm oil from reaching Bonny, many European companies became bankrupt. When British trades boycotted Opobo, Jaja broke the boycott by getting a trader who would continue to buy from him. In 1870 he officially proclaimed the Kingdom of Opobo, a name which still linked him to Bonny because Opobo was the name of one of Bonny's famous kings. In 1873 he agreed to settle with Bonny, but the settlement enhanced Opobo.

As ruler of Opobo, he established plantations, built ports and trading settlements. Jaja had good relations with the British once he was recognised as the king of Opobo. But his control over the oil trade created serious problems for him. In 1884 he signed a treaty putting his kingdom under British protection. The following year Britain declared a protectorate (q.v.) of the Oil Rivers, which included Jaja's kingdom.

Jaja did not like the idea of the free trade that the British were peddling and the British decided to get him out of their way as middleman so as to have direct access to the market instead of through him. By trickery, the British acting vice consul, Harry Johnston, invited him on board the gunboat H.M.S. *Goshawk* with assurances that he would have safe conduct and no evil would happen to him. He was arrested, taken to Accra, in the Gold

Coast (q.v.), now Ghana, tried and was banished in 1887 to the West Indies. The British, after petitions, finally agreed that he could return home. He died on his way back on July 7, 1891. His body was taken home and buried in Opobo.

JAKANDE, ALHAJI LATEEF KAYODE. A journalist and a politician born on July 23, 1929, in Lagos (q.v.). He was educated at Banham Memorial Methodist School, Port Harcourt (q.v.), Ilesha Grammar School and King's College (q.v.) in Lagos. He served as a reporter for the *Daily Service,* (1949–50), subeditor, (1950–51) and acting editor, (1951–52). He joined the *Nigerian Tribune* as editor in 1953 and became managing editor in 1954. In 1956 he became the editor in chief of the Amalgamated Press of Nigeria and managing director of the Allied Newspapers of Nigeria in 1960. He became the managing director and editor in chief of the African Newspapers of Nigeria, chairman of the Lagoon Book and Stationery Company Ltd. and chairman of the John West Publications Ltd. He was the former chairman of the Nigerian Institute of Journalism, former president of the International Press Institute, patron of the Nigerian Union of Journalists in Lagos State (q.v.) and the Nigerian Guild of Editors. He is a member of the International Association for Mass Communications Research.

Alhaji Jakande was a prominent member of the defunct Action Group Party (q.v.). He was also one of those tried and jailed with Chief Obafemi Awolowo (q.v.) for treasonable felony in 1963. He was also released and fully pardoned along with Chief Awolowo in August 1966. With the coming of the Second Republic (q.v.), he became a prominent member of Unity Party of Nigeria (q.v.), under whose ticket he won the governorship election of Lagos State in 1979. As governor, Alhaji L.K. Jakande talked little but worked hard. This peculiarity earned him nationwide acclaim as the "action man" of Lagos State.

After the December 1983 military takeover, he was arrested and detained while investigation continued about his management of the financial resources of Lagos State when he was governor. The Babangida administration released him in August 1985, and he went back into private business.

When the ban on politics was lifted in 1989 and two parties were launched by the military government, Jakande joined the Social Democratic Party (q.v.). In 1992 he ran in the presidential primaries, but the military government cancelled them for many irregularities. In 1993 when Chief M.K.O. Abiola (q.v.) became the presidential candidate of his party, Jakande became his staunch supporter, even after the military had annulled the results of the election that Chief Abiola had won. But when General Sani Abacha (q.v.) became Head of State and appointed him minister of housing and transportation, his support for Abiola perceptibly waned.

Alhaji Lateef K. Jakande wrote many books, including *The Role of the Mass Media in a Developing Country* and *The Trial of Obafemi Awolowo.* Jakande emerged as a prominent member of the All People's Party in 1998, but his association with the Abacha regime had seriously undermined his standing with his supporters in the southwest.

JAMA'ATU NASRIL ISLAM (JNI). An organization created by Islamic leaders affiliated with Ahmadu Bello in 1962 (formally launched in 1964). Among its goals are the propagation of Islam in Nigeria and the promotion of unity among the various Islamic factions of the country. It enjoyed its period of greatest influence up until 1966. Following the death of Ahmadu Bello, however, the JNI was divided by the ongoing dispute between its chairman, Abubakar Gumi, and the leaders of the Islamic brotherhoods. While this division kept the JNI from regaining its former influence, it has remained a prominent representative of Islamic interests. Its current activities including promoting Islamic education, humanitarian activities and the publication of the weekly newspaper, *Haske.*

JAM'IYYAR MUTANEN AREWA. The Jam'iyyar Mutanen Arewa originally was a cultural organisation meant to embrace all of the Northern Region (q.v.). Its name means northern people's congress, and it was formed in 1948 as a way to provide for the cultural and educational development of the region just like the Igbo (q.v.) people had done in 1944 by forming the Ibo Federal Union (q.v.) and the Yoruba (q.v.) in the west in 1948 by forming Egbe Omo Oduduwa (q.v.). Its leaders included Mallam Aminu Kano (q.v.), as well as Alhaji Sir Abubakar Tafawa Balewa (q.v.) and some others. Its aim was not to usurp the authority of the traditional rulers, the Emirs (q.v.), but rather to enhance their authority, whenever possible. Members would also help the traditional rulers in the discharge of their duties and the enlightenment of the masses of the people.

As election under the 1951 constitution (q.v.) was approaching, the Jam'iyyar reorganised itself into a political party, the Northern People's Congress (q.v.), which, from then until 1966 when the military banned all political parties and cultural associations, controlled the pace of political development in the Northern Region.

JANGALI. *See* CATTLE TAX.

JEHOVAH'S WITNESSES. A religious organisation founded in the United States by C.T. Russell. They believe that, according to the Bible, Jesus Christ will rule God's kingdom on earth. Only those who work hard, are dedicated and baptised will live happily in that kingdom. Because they see themselves as citizens of Jehovah's kingdom, they obey only laws that do not conflict with their faith. The organisation came to Nigeria in 1928 and has spread to many parts of the country. Witnesses to Jehovah's teachings are often seen in pairs, making house-to-house visits.

JEMIBEWON, MAJ. GEN. DAVID MEDAIYESE. A soldier, born on July 20, 1940, at Iyah-Gbedde in Kaba division of Kogi State (q.v.). After his elementary education, he attended Offa Grammar School in Kwara State (q.v.) from 1955 to 1959. He later enlisted in the Nigerian Army and received military training in Nigeria, Britain and the United States.

During the Civil War (q.v.), he was the assistant adjutant and quartermaster-general of the First Division based at Makurdi. He later commanded the 27th Infantry Battalion under the Second Section, which liberated Abakaliki in March 1968. He fought in many other places during the war. After the war, he served in a number of capacities, most prominently as military governor of Western State from 1971–72, and of Oyo State from 1976–78. In 1978, he returned to regular military service and was appointed Commander, Army School of Infantry in Jaji. He retired from the army in September 1983, and from 1983–87 he attended the University of Lagos to earn his law degree. When General (rtd.) Olusegun Obasanjo (q.v.) announced his candidacy for the presidency in 1998, Jemibewon emerged as one of a number of retired military officers who actively campaigned on his behalf. Jemibewon played an instrumental role in securing Obasanjo's victory in Kogi State in the February 1999 elections. In June 1999, Jemibewon was appointed minister of police affairs by the newly elected Obasanjo regime.

General Jemibewon was the recipient of many honours, including the Defense Service Medal, the National Service Medal and the United Nations Congo Medal. He wrote *A Combatant in Government.*

JIGAWA STATE. One of the nine states created in August 1991, Jigawa had been part of Kano State (q.v.). It is located between latitudes 11° and 13°N, and longitudes 8° and 10°35′E. With an area of 22,410 square kilometres, it is bounded in the west by Kano and Katsina States (qq.v.), in the north by the Republic of Niger, in the east by Bauchi (q.v.) and Yobe States (qq.v.) and in the south by Bauchi State (q.v.). There are two main seasons—rainy and dry. The rainy season begins in May and lasts until October. Annual rainfall varies from 635 millimetres to 890 millimetres. The temperature also varies from 31.5°C to 33°C, but it can drop as low as 10°C during the harmattan period, especially in December and January. The vegetation falls within the savannah forest zone with extensive open grassland and scattered stunter trees. During the dry season many bushes burn and so only resistant trees survive the yearly destruction. Soil erosion is a big problem for the state. Jigawa has many mineral resources: kaolin, potash, silica, iron ore, copper, white quartz and clay. There are 21 local government (q.v.) areas.

Jigawa has a population of 2,829,929 with 80 percent in the rural areas. The people are mostly Hausa (q.v.), Fulani (q.v.) and Kanuri (q.v.), but Hausa is widely spoken. Recently, education has been given a high priority with 1,453 primary schools and over 359,000 pupils in 1992, 77 postprimary institutions, many colleges of education, and Islamic and legal studies programmes. The state is predominately Muslim (q.v.), but Christianity (q.v.) is also taking root. The main population centers are Dutsi, the capital, Birni-Kudu, Hadejia, Malladuri and Gumer.

JIHAD. The jihad was the Muslim holy war initiated in 1804 by Usman Dan Fodio (q.v.), a Fulani (q.v.) Muslim priest and reformer. Its aim was religious purification and social justice, together with a desire to see improvement in the economy, which was adversely affected by the wars among the various Hausa (q.v.) city-states. To this end the Shehu selected 14 trusted lieutenants to carry the flag to the 14 Hausa States (q.v.). After they conquered the area, they would be installed as Emirs (q.v.) there. The war was waged in the name of Allah and his prophet and was directed not only against the pagans (unbelievers) but also against lukewarm followers of the prophet Mohammed. During the war, Bornu (q.v.), which was then a Muslim country, was attacked and conquered but later regained its independence under Al-Kanemi (q.v.), a fact which has always coloured the relationship between the Hausa-Fulani and the Kanuri (q.v.) peoples. Usman Dan Fodio died in 1817, leaving the care of the state to his brother Abdullahi (q.v.) and his son Bello (q.v.), the grandfather of the late Sir Ahmadu Bello (q.v.), the Sardauna of Sokoto. The Fulani empire, created by the jihad included Katsina (q.v.), Kano (q.v.), Zaria (q.v.), Hadeija, Adamawa (q.v.), Gombe, Katagum (q.v.), Nupe (q.v.), Ilorin (q.v.), Daura (q.v.) and Bauchi (q.v.).

The war helped to spread Islam (q.v.), and in giving Northern Nigeria (q.v.) a unity that it never had before. Sokoto (q.v.), the city founded by Usman Dan Fodio, became the focal point of Islam in Nigeria.

JOHNSON, JAMES. Born in 1836 in Sierra Leone (q.v.) to Yoruba (q.v.) parents who were former slaves but released by the British antislavery patrol, he was converted to Christianity (q.v.) and was educated in Church Missionary Society (q.v.) schools. He went to Fourah Bay College (q.v.) in 1858, and, after graduation, became a schoolteacher, but in 1863 he became a catechist. He was later ordained as a pastor and sent to join the mission in the Yorubaland of Nigeria. He worked in Lagos (q.v.) and Abeokuta (q.v.), but in 1880, he was posted back to Lagos to look after the Breadfruit Church. In 1890 he became assistant bishop in charge of the Niger Delta and Benin territories. Johnson was one of the earliest Africans who began to ask the colonial authorities to establish universities in their territories and to begin the process of industrialisation.

JOHNSON, SAMUEL. Born in 1846 in Hastings, Sierra Leone (q.v.), Samuel Johnson came to Lagos (q.v.), Nigeria, with his parents in 1857 and later from there to Ibadan (q.v.) now the capital of Oyo State (q.v.). He was there during the Ijaye war (q.v.) until 1862 when he was sent to the Church Missionary Society (CMS) (q.v.) Training Institute in Abeokuta (q.v.) where he studied for three years. In 1866 he was appointed schoolmaster in Ibadan, a position from which he rose to be the superintendent of schools at Kudeti and Aremo. He was made a catechist in 1875 and mediated on behalf of the colonial government in the war between Ibadan, Ijesha and the Ekitis in 1885. In 1886 he became a deacon and was ordained in 1888. He was later sent to Oyo where he remained until his death. He was a great historian and wrote *The History of the Yorubas,* a book which today remains the truest eyewitness account of the intertribal wars among the Yorubas in the second part of the 19th century. The book was completed in 1897 and sent in 1899 to the CMS in London for publication but the manuscript got lost. Johnson died in 1901. It was his brother Obadiah Johnson who compiled the present book from his notes.

JOHNSTON, HENRY HAMILTON. An explorer, author and colonial administrator. Between 1885 and 1902, he was vice consul over the Niger Delta (q.v.) and the Cameroons (q.v.). It was during this time that the Europeans in the Delta were having problems with King Jaja of Opobo (q.v.). In his effort to remove obstacles to free trade on the Niger River (q.v.), he invited Jaja for a meeting, and promised he would not be detained by him. When Jaja came on board the British gunboat, Johnston arrested him and sent him to Accra for trial. Johnston later served in Mozambique, Malawi, Tunis and Uganda. He was the author of *Comparative Study of the Bantus and Semi-Bantu Languages*. He died in 1927.

JOINT ACTION COMMITTEE. Formed in September 1963 at a meeting of the United Labour Congress (q.v.) for the purpose of prosecuting wage demands for Nigerian workers. The pressure mounted by the JAC for a review of wages prompted the government to set up the Morgan Commission of Inquiry (q.v.) to look into the existing wage structure, remuneration and conditions of service in wage-earning employments. The commission submitted its report in April 1964, and when the government failed to publish the report in time, the labour unions, on June 1, 1964, began a general strike, which prompted the government to release the report two days later. In 1965 the committee was disbanded.

JOINT ADMISSIONS AND MATRICULATION BOARD (JAMB). Established by a decree in 1977, JAMB is responsible for the general control of the conduct of matriculation examinations for admissions of undergraduate students into all universities in Nigeria. It can appoint examiners, moderators and invigilators, and it can set up panels and committees with respect to matriculation examinations and other matters incidental to it. It is also responsible for the placement of successful candidates in the universities and collection and dissemination of information on matters relating to admissions into the universities. The board, however, is not responsible for examinations or any other selective processes leading to postgraduate or professional courses.

Members of the board, appointed by the minister of education, consist of a chairman who is a vice chancellor of a Nigerian university, the vice chancellor of each university in Nigeria, or his representative, two representatives each of intermediate postsecondary institutions, teachers' colleges and the Nigerian Conference of Principals of Secondary Schools, the permanent secretary in the Ministry of Education or his representative, the registrar of the West African Examination Council (q.v.), which conducts high school diploma examinations, the executive secretary of the National Universities Commission (q.v.) or his representative, the registrar of the board and three other persons, representing interests not otherwise represented in the above list.

In practical terms, the board sets examinations and sees to their marking, sends computer printouts of the results to each university in accordance with the choice of candidates. Each university through its various faculties selects candidates on approved criteria, and presents its list of candidates to JAMB panels or committees for approval. Candidates so approved are duly notified by JAMB.

This system of recruitment of candidates to the universities was set up to make for national character in the admission of students to the various universities and prevent a student from being offered admission to two or more universities at the same time. In this way a university is sure that most of the candidates offered admission will take advantage of the offer there.

JOINT CHURCH AID. The Joint Church Aid was one of the humanitarian organisations that supplied relief materials to Biafra (q.v.) during the Nigerian Civil War (q.v.).

JONES, RT. HON. ARTHUR CREECH. Creech Jones was the secretary of state for the colonies in 1947 when the National Council of Nigeria and the Cameroons (q.v.) sent a delegation to London (q.v.) to protest certain provisions of the Richards Constitution (q.v.). He advised the delegation to go back to Nigeria and cooperate with the government to make the constitution work.

JOS. The capital of Plateau State (q.v.) with a population of about 622,000 people, according to the 1991 census. Jos is a relatively young city, officially founded as a township in 1915. It is situated on the northern edge of the Jos Plateau. It is about 4,000 feet above sea level, and is famous for its fairly temperate climate. The yearly temperature ranges between 50° to 95°, while the annual rainfall ranges between 40 and 70 inches. Jos is blessed with large deposits of tin ore on the Jos Plateau, which has encouraged tin mining (q.v.) and has attracted the Makeri Tin Smelting Company into the area. In 1972 a branch campus of the University of Ibadan was established there; it has become a full-fledged university known as the University of Jos.

JOSE, ALHAJI ISMAIL BABATUNDE. A distinguished journalist, born on December 13, 1925, he was educated in a Yaba Methodist school and the Saviours' Boys High School in Lagos (q.v.). In 1941 he began to train as a printer with the *Daily Times* (q.v.). Between 1948 and 1952, he was the political correspondent for the same paper, and was in 1957 promoted to the position of editor of the paper. In 1962 he became the managing director of the company, but retired in 1975 when the federal military government acquired 60 percent of the company's shares. He was honoured with a doctorate degree in 1980 by the University of Benin.

JUDICIAL COMMITTEE OF THE PRIVY COUNCIL. The Judicial Committee of the Privy Council is the final court of appeal for all British dependencies and independent members of the Commonwealth (q.v.) that choose to retain the appeal. Before October 1, 1963, when Nigeria became a republic (q.v.), the highest court of appeal for Nigeria was Her Majesty's Judicial Committee of the Privy Council in London, to which appeals come from the Supreme Court (q.v.) in Nigeria. The Privy Council was famous for its impartiality and forthrightness, and was the defender of the legal rights of the citizens against the colonial administration. The court, no doubt, contributed immensely to the constitutional development of the country, especially in making sure that the Nigerian government (q.v.) kept its own laws.

JUDICIARY. The Nigerian judicial system is organised as follows: at the federal level, there are the Federal High Courts (q.v.), Federal Court of Appeal (q.v.) and the Supreme Court (q.v.). Appeals lie from the Federal High Courts to the Federal Court of Appeal and from there to the Supreme Court. On the state level there are three types of courts: at the bottom level are Magistrate Courts, Customary Courts (q.v.) and Shari'a Courts (q.v.). At the top are State High Courts, State Customary Courts of Appeal and State Shari'a Courts of Appeal. Appeals move from the Magistrate Court to the State High Court, from the Customary Court to the State Customary Court of Appeal and from the Shari'a Court to the State Shari'a Court of Appeal. However, there is a link between the federal and the state judicial organisations: appeals move from the State High Court, State Customary Court of Appeal and State

Shari'a Court of Appeal to the Federal Court of Appeal and from there to the Supreme Court.

JUKUN. The Jukun are one of the minority ethnic groups in the northeastern part of Nigeria along the Benue River (q.v.) valley. According to their tradition, they came from Yemil, east of Mecca, and, with their leader, Agudu, passed through the Sudan and Bornu (q.v.). But Hausa (q.v.) myth says that Kororofa, the ancestor of the Jukun, was one of the seven illegitimate children of Biram. Therefore, another name for the Jukun is Kororofa—the name also given to the Jukun Kingdom capital city. The Jukun were first mentioned in history in the latter half of the 14th century when Yaji Sarkin Kano raided their capital.

The Jukun were warlike. They subjugated many ethnic groups and towns, including the Angaras and Miriam, and the towns of Zaria (q.v.) and Kano (q.v.). The kingdom once extended to the south of the Cross River and the borders of Bornu. However, the city of Kororofa was destroyed during the Fulani (q.v.) jihad (q.v.) (holy war) of the early 19th century.

JUNE 12, 1993, PRESIDENTIAL ELECTION. June 12, 1993, was the day of the presidential election that should have ushered in the Third Republic (q.v.). Soon after General Ibrahim B. Babangida (q.v.) took over power in 1985, he came up with a long and tortuous quarter-by-quarter transitional program to hand over power to a civilian administration in 1989. For this reason, the Third Republic's constitution was dated 1989. The constitution stipulated that only two parties would be allowed to operate. In 1989 none of the 13 political associations that applied to the National Electoral Commission (q.v.) was found recognisable by the government. The Babangida government then founded two parties, the Social Democratic Party (SDP) (q.v.) and the National Republican Convention (NRC) (q.v.), funded them and gave them constitutions and manifestoes. Elections were held on different days and months by local government (q.v.) councils, state assemblies, the governorship positions in the states and to the national houses of assembly (q.v.). The presidential election slated for June 12, 1993, was between Chief M.K.O. Abiola (q.v.), a southern Yoruba (q.v.) Muslim (q.v.) of the SDP and Alhaji Bashir Tofa (q.v.) a northern Hausa (q.v.) Muslim from Kano (q.v.).

Long before the election, it had become clear that President Babangida did not want to quit power. An organisation emerged, known as the Association for Better Nigeria (ABN) (q.v.), secretly funded by the Babangida administration. It campaigned for a continuation of the Babangida administration arguing that he was the only saviour who could protect the country from economic and social collapse. ABN, seeing that preparations for the June election were going on well, decided to foil all efforts. It went to court to stop the elections, and, when that failed, and after results showed clearly that Abiola had son, Babangida and the ABN began new tactics. ABN went to court again to stop further announcement of the results after almost half of the state results had been announced. On June 23, 1993, President Babangida annulled the results of the June 12 elections, plunging the country into serious political, social and economic crises.

For many Nigerians, June 12 represented a vote for change in the political leadership of the country, and a shift in the regional base of power from the north to the south. The writer Wole Soyinka, for instance, enthused that it was a "national triumph." For these reasons, the date remained a potent political symbol for years after the annulment.

-K-

KABI, LAMIDO. *See* ADAMAWA STATE.

KADUNA. The capital of the old Northern Region (q.v.) and now of Kaduna State (q.v.), it is one of the most important towns in Nigeria as the centre of the northern intelligentsia. It is also the town in which the Defence Academy (q.v.), a modern military training institution and the Nigerian Air Force Tactical and Training Wing are located. Furthermore, Kaduna has become a booming industrial center in the north, having many modern factories such as the Peugeot Assembly Plant.

In 1900 Kaduna was selected as the headquarters of the Northern Protectorate (q.v.) and when the old Northern Protectorate became the Northern Region (q.v.), it remained as the regional headquarters. In the First Republic (q.v.), Kaduna was at the center of power as the home of the Northern Regional government and of the Northern People's Congress (q.v.), which was the major coalition partner at the centre. Even the prime minister of the Federation consulted constantly with the party leader in Kaduna, Sir Ahmadu Bello (q.v.), the Sardauna of Sokoto and the premier of Northern Nigeria. But after 16 states were created from the old Northern Region, Kaduna's power has considerably dwindled.

KADUNA MAFIA. A term referring to a segment of the northern elite that emerged in the 1970s. As opposed to the older elite that emerged under the leadership of Ahmadu Bello (q.v.) in the 1950s and 1960s, the Kaduna mafia were younger, western educated and owed their influence to positions in the civil service and government created agencies. They are associated with Kaduna (q.v.) because of that city's role as the administrative headquarters of the Northern Regional government. Despite the conspiratorial connotations of the term "mafia," the members of the group do not have a recognised leader and do not regularly meet. Among the more prominent figures said to be members of the Kaduna mafia are Shehu Yar'Adua, Adamu Ciroma and Bamanga Tukur.

KADUNA POLYTECHNIC. Established by the federal military government in 1968, it consisted of the College of Science and Technology made up of the Polytechnic of Kaduna and the Irrigation School at Sokoto (q.v.), and the Staff Development Centre, made up of the Staff Development Centre in Kaduna (q.v.), the Local Government Training Centre in Zaria (q.v.), the Cooperative Training Centre in Zaria, the Social Welfare Training Center in Zaria and the Community Development Institute. The Polytechnic provides diverse instructions, training and research in technology, the sciences, commerce and the humanities. It also provides in-service training for members of the public services in Nigeria. The institution is run by a board of governors composed of members from all the northern states appointed by the governor of each state and other members from some industries and the Ahmadu Bello University (q.v.).

KADUNA STATE. In 1976, when the administration of General Murtala R. Muhammed (q.v.) created seven new states, the North-Western State (q.v.) with its capital at Kaduna (q.v.) was renamed Kaduna State, made up of the two colonial provinces (q.v.) of Zaria (q.v.) and Katsina (q.v.). But, in 1987 Katsina province became Katsina State (q.v.), while the old Zaria province became Kaduna State. It is located within longitudes 6°05′ and 8°48′E and latitudes 9°03′ and 11°32′N. It is bounded in the north by Katsina and Kano States (q.v.), in the east by Bauchi State (q.v.), in the south and southeast by Plateau State (q.v.) and the Federal Capital Territory (q.v.) and in the west and northwest by Niger State (q.v.) and Sokoto State (q.v.). The annual rainfall varies from 1,530 millimetres in the Kafanchan area to 1,015 millimetres in the Ikara-Makarfi district. The vegetation is savannah grassland with scattered trees and shrubs. The state is divided into 18 local government (q.v.) areas.

The population was 3,969,252 in 1991 and is made up of many ethnic groups. The major ethnic groups are Kamuku, Gwari (q.v.), Kadara, Hausa (q.v.) and Kurama, while others are Jaba, Kaje, Koro, Kamanton, Kataf (q.v.), Morua and Chawai. The people are Muslims (q.v.), Christians (q.v.) and adherents of traditional religious (q.v.) beliefs. They have many traditional festivals (q.v.) like Tuk-Ham, and their artworks consist of leatherworks, pottery and indigo pit dyeing. Most of the people of the state live in the rural areas planting such crops as yams (q.v.), cassava (q.v.) and cotton. They also raise animals such as cattle, goats, sheep, rams and pigs. The main urban centers are Kaduna, the state capital, Zaria, Kafanchan and Sabon-Birni-Gwari.

Educationally, Kaduna State had a headstart over many other states in the then-Northern Region (q.v.) because of the activities of mission voluntary agencies that founded many primary and secondary schools in places like Kwoi, Zonkwa, Kagoro, Kaduna, Makera, Tudun Wada, Sabon-Gari (q.v.) and Kafanchan. It is estimated that about 70 percent of the children of school age are receiving formal education in the state. The state has Ahmadu Bello University (q.v.) in Zaria, the Army Staff College at Jaji and many other colleges, polytechnic and technical schools. Kaduna State is a major cultural center where the Nok (q.v.) terra-cotta are found in the State's southern region.

Kaduna State inherited all the infrastructure the colonial and postcolonial authorities in Northern Nigeria built. As such, it has become one of the most industrial and commercial centers in Northern Nigeria. It is the home of Peugeot Automobile Assembly Plant and the center for petroleum (q.v.) refinery, and textile mills. More important, it is a political power center—not only in the north but the nation.

KAFANCHAN RIOTS. A series of clashes in March 1987 between Christians and Muslims in the town of Kafanchan in Kaduna State (q.v.). While tensions between the two religions had been building for some time, the ferocity of the Kafanchan riots marked the start of a period of more intense and violent inter-religious conflict in Nigeria. They also presaged other violent clashes between Christians (q.v.) and Muslims (q.v.) in the cities of Kano, Bauchi, Katsina, Zaria, and the town of Zangon-Kataf.

The immediate catalyst for the riots were a week of pro-Christian celebrations at the campus of the College of Education, Kafanchan, organised by the Federation of Christian Students. Muslims found aspects of the celebrations, such as a banner declaring the College "Jesus Campus" to be provocative, and a series of dispute quickly escalated to violence and ultimately engulfed the town of Kafanchan. By the time order had been restored, at least twelve people were dead and a number of churches and mosques had been destroyed. Although the riots were local, they accelerated the growing polarization between Muslims and Christians throughout the country. They were also a contributing factor in the politicisation of the Christian Association of Nigeria (CAN) and the formation of the Northern Elders' Committee, a coalition of northern elites committed to preserving their region's political unity.

KAINJI RIVER DAM. The Niger River (q.v.) was dammed at Kainji about 112 kilometres north of Jebba for the purpose of generating hydroelectric power, which is distributed to different parts of the country. The generating capacity of the dam at its inception in 1969 was 647 megawatts, which doubled the installed capacity in the country. Nigeria was, therefore, able to supply electricity to the Niger Republic. In 1976 two more turbines were installed, making the total six, thereby, considerably raising the generating capacity of the dam. In spite of this, demand continues to outstrip supply.

KAMERUN NATIONAL CONGRESS. A political party formed in the early 1950s under the leadership of Dr. E.M.L. Endeley (q.v.), it began agitation for the separation from Nigeria of the Cameroons (q.v.), a British trust territory, administered as part of Nigeria. During the 1954 federal elections, the party won all six seats allocated to the Southern Cameroon, and when the Southern Cameroon was given regional autonomy, the party was the governing party. In 1961 its objective was realised: Southern Cameroon became separated from Nigeria and joined the Republic of Cameroon while the Northern Cameroon preferred to remain as an integral part of Nigeria.

KAMPALA PEACE TALKS. The Kampala Peace Talks were held between May 23 and 31, 1968. The meeting was convened by the president of Uganda, Dr. Milton Obote, in an effort to find a political solution to the Civil War (q.v.), then tearing the country into pieces. The two sides to the war—the Federal Government (q.v.) and Biafra (q.v.)—sent delegates to the talks. Dr. Obote, in declaring the meeting open, appealed for an agreement on cessation of hostilities and a cease-fire as a basic preliminary stage for a broad understanding on the nature of a government the principals would set up later. His appeals fell on deaf ears. Neither side was prepared to yield on their major demands. During the talks a member of the Federal Government delegation, Mr. Johnson Banjo, was reportedly abducted and later reported killed. When the talks resumed after this incident, Chief Anthony Enahoro (q.v.), the leader of the federal delegation, put forward his proposals for a cease-fire and Sir Louis Mbanefo (q.v.), a justice of the High Court who led the Biafran side, told him that Biafra had not come to Kampala to surrender to Nigeria. The meeting then broke up on May 31, 1968, without reaching any important agreement.

KANEM-BORNU EMPIRE. Established as a state to the northeast of Lake Chad (q.v.) about A.D. 800 by the Kanembu-speaking people under their leader, Saef Ben Dhu Yasan, who founded the Sefawa dynasty (q.v.) in Njimi, the capital of his kingdom. Islam (q.v.) came to the kingdom in the 11th century at a time when the Sefawa dynasty was beginning to grow in power. The power of Kanem-Bornu was based on its fast and very efficient army of horsemen. By the 12th century, it controlled most of the areas around Lake Chad, and it grew rich with the trans-Saharan trade, through which slaves were sent north while cloth, horses and metal goods moved south to Kanem.

Kanem was most powerful in the 13th century under Dunama Dibalemi (q.v.), but, after his death, the empire began to decline. In the 14th century a new capital was built in Bornu, west of Lake Chad at Birnin. About this time Kanuri (q.v.) influence was growing, and the rulers began to speak the Kanuri language. In the 16th century, Bornu expanded under Idris Ben Ali Alooma (q.v.), whose army reportedly was the first to use guns in this part of Africa. Bornu developed as a very powerful state and a center of Islamic teaching and culture. But the successors to Alooma were not strong enough, and the empire began to decline. It did not regain much of its power until the time of Al-Kanemi (q.v.) in the early part of the 19th century when Mai Dunama Ben Ahmed (q.v.) in 1808 called on Muhammad Al-Amin Al-Kanemi to come to his aid and rescue the kingdom from the Fulani (q.v.) Jihadists of Usman Dan Fodio (q.v.). In 1810, when the Fulani began a new attack on the kingdom, Dunama called for Al-Kanemi's help to drive them back. Though the most powerful person in Bornu, Al-Kanemi preferred to remain a Sheikh. It was not until Sheikh Umar Ben Al-Kanemi, Al-Kanemi's son, succeeded his father as leader of the Bornu troops that the Sefawa dynasty of 1,000 years was replaced by the Al-Kanemi dynasty after the death of Mai Ali in 1846. *See also* BORNU.

AL-KANEMI, SHEIKH MUHAMMED AL-AMIN. Al-Kanemi was a scholar and a religious and political leader who helped contain the Fulani empire (q.v.) from engulfing Bornu (q.v.). He was the son of Sheikh Ninga. He became a Muslim scholar, went to Mecca, and, upon his return, saw that the jihad (q.v.) of Usman Dan Fodio (q.v.) had spread to the capital of Bornu, Birni Ngazargamu. The ruler of Bornu, (Mai) Ahmed Ben Ali (q.v.), was becoming old, and, after trying in vain to persuade Usman and his son Muhammad Bello (q.v.) that they should not attack an Islamic state, he abdicated the throne for his son Dunama Ben Ahmed (q.v.) in 1808. Dunama formed an alliance with Al-Kanemi against the Fulani. In 1809 Birni Ngazargamu was recaptured, and Al-Kanemi became a most important personality in Bornu. In 1811 the capital was again occupied but Al-Kanemi's forces, together with those of Mai Dunama, drove the Fulani warrior, Ibrahim Zaki, back to Katagum (q.v.), thus preventing the Fulani empire from spreading to Bornu.

Many people in Bornu did not like the growing influence and power of Al-Kanemi and the fact that their Mai (king) needed Al-Kanemi to repel the attack of the Fulani and so decided to depose Dunama in 1809 and replace him with his uncle, Muhammad Ngileruma. Al-Kanemi never got along well with the new ruler and, therefore, joined forces with Dunama's supporters to depose the new ruler and reinstate Dunama, making Al-Kanemi the most powerful man in the state.

Seeing the growing power of Al-Kanemi, Dunama was persuaded by his followers to look for a way to get rid of his friend. He planned with Burgomanda, the neighbouring ruler of Baghirmi, to attack Bornu and in the process surround Al-Kanemi's forces and get rid of him. The plan, however, leaked. Dunama was killed in battle in 1820, and Al-Kanemi installed Dunama's younger brother, Ibrahim, as a figurehead ruler. When D. Denham and Hugh Clapperton (q.v.) visited Bornu in the early 1820s, they saw Al-Kanemi as an effective ruler who was feared, though loved and respected, and who substituted laws of reason for practices of barbarity.

This was not the end of his problems. The Fulani continued to attack Bornu. Believing that Muslims should not be fighting Muslims, Al-Kanemi tried to come to terms with the Fulani, but, when his effort was spurned, he took up arms against them and successfully penetrated into the Hausaland, almost reaching Kano (q.v.). The Fulani were allowed to remain in the western part of Bornu. Al-Kanemi died in 1837, succeeded by his son Sheikh Umar Ibn Muhammad Al-Amin Al-Kanemi (q.v.) who ruled through Mai Ibrahim. In 1846 Mai Ibrahim, wanting to take advantage of the revolt of the state of Zinder, tried to regain control from Sheikh Umar. Mai Ibrahim was killed in the attempt, just like his sons. After his death, Sheikh Umar established the Al-Kanemi dynasty of Shehus of Bornu.

KANO. The capital of Kano State, and one of the most ancient and famous of Nigerian cities. The first recorded king of Kano was said to be Bagauda, son of Bawo and grandson of Bayajidda (q.v.). Bagauda's reign started about A.D. 999. Islam (q.v.) came to Kano about the 13th century. In the 15th century, Kano emerged as a prosperous and influential power. There were many mosques built, and Islamic scholars and influential people came to Kano. For many centuries, Kano was the commercial center of the Western Sudan and an important stop along the West African caravan route. It was also one of the southern terminals of the trans-Saharan trade and was second only to Timbuktu in all of West Africa. In the 16th and the first half of the 17th century, Kano fought many wars with Katsina (q.v.), which greatly weakened it and opened it up for attacks from many other states like Kebbi (q.v.) and Kwararafa. In 1734 Kano was under the Sultan of Bornu (q.v.), receiving its tribute until the early 19th century when the jihad (q.v.) began.

By the time of the jihad, there were many Fulani (q.v.) clans in Kano territory, and in 1807 Dan Zabuwa of the Daneji clan was sent to Shehu Usman Dan Fodio (q.v.) to receive a flag for the conquest of Kano. Kano fell, and the city came under the rule of the Fulani. In 1903 the British expedition to take Kano was underway. The Emir (q.v.) fled the city, and Muhammadu Abbas submitted to Lord Frederick Lugard (q.v.), who installed him as Emir of Kano.

With the coming of the British, Kano still maintained its traditional trading role and is now the commercial centre of the whole of Northern Nigeria (q.v.). Kano is made up of the old walled city with its 16 gates. The walls were built for the purpose of protection against any aggression. This area is about 21 square kilometres and contains the traditional markets that offer all kinds of goods, including locally made goods and foreign goods. The other part is the modern industrial and commercial centre known as Sabon-Gari (strangers' quarters) where mostly people of southern origin live. To the north of the old city and on the edge of the Sabon-Gari is the Mallam Aminu Kano (q.v.) International Airport, the second international airport in the nation.

Being one of the seven historical Hausa States (q.v.), Kano is predominantly Hausa-speaking, and, even though there are Fulani and Kanuri (q.v.) in the city, Hausa culture and tradition are dominant and the Hausa language is the lingua franca, even for most of the north. The traditional industries of weaving, cloth embroidery, tanning of animal skins and the production of ornamental leatherwork—all of which made Kano famous in the past—are still carried on today in the city. Kano City was famous for its pyramids made of groundnut bags, ready for export to the world market.

KANO, MALLAM MUHAMMED AMINU. Popularly known as Mallam Aminu Kano, he was a teacher and a politician, the founder of the Northern Element Progressive Union (NEPU) (q.v.), and the former leader of the People's Redemption Party (q.v.). A Fulani (q.v.), born on August 9, 1920, he was educated at Shahuchi Primary School, Kano Middle School and at Kaduna College from 1937 to 1942. He later received a teacher's certificate from the Institute of Education at London University in England and taught at Bauchi Middle School from 1942 to 1946. While at the school, he, together with Mallam Sa'ad Zungur (q.v.) and Mallam Abubakar Tafawa Balewa (q.v.), founded the Bauchi Improvement Union (q.v.) in 1943. He was also the founder of the Northern Teachers' Association (q.v.) and he was its first secretary-general from 1948 to 1953.

Following the pattern of group associations formed in the south, Mallam Aminu Kano, together with Alhaji Abubakar Tafawa Balewa, Dr. Russell A.B. Dikko (q.v.) and Yahaya Gusau founded the Jam'iyyar Mutanen Arewa (q.v.), meaning Northern People's Congress (NPC) (q.v.) in 1948. Because this organisation was too conservative for Mallam Aminu Kano, he, together with people who felt like him, broke away from the organisation and founded the NEPU in 1950. He remained the leader of the party until 1966 when the military dissolved all political parties. As such, he led his party's delegation to all the constitutional conferences (q.v.), both in London and in Nigeria.

Mallam Aminu Kano had many years of service to the nation. In 1959 he was elected to the federal House of Representatives (q.v.), and his party, in alliance with the National Council of Nigeria and the Cameroons (NCNC) (q.v.), which was the junior partner in the coalition government that emerged after the election, he became deputy government chief whip, from 1959 to 1964, while his party in the Northern House of Assembly (q.v.) continued to maintain the radical proletarian image of the party in that house. In 1963, with the coalition between NPC and NCNC disintegrating, NEPU's alliance with the NCNC became stronger, and Mallam Aminu became first vice president of the NCNC. In 1964, the coalition completely broke down, and, in the realignment efforts made before the 1964 federal elections, NEPU and some other progressive parties in the north and south, including United Middle Belt Congress (q.v.), NCNC and the Action Group (q.v.), formed the United Progressive Grand Alliance (UPGA) (q.v.). UPGA lost, and Mallam Aminu Kano also lost his seat in Kano (q.v.).

During the military rule, Mallam Aminu Kano was appointed federal commissioner for communications, (1967–71) and federal commissioner for health, (1971–74). He was a member of the Constituent Assembly (q.v.), (1977–78), and when the ban on political activities was lifted in September 1978, Mallam Aminu Kano formed the People's Redemption Party (PRP) (q.v.), under which he was nominated as candidate for the presidential election in 1979. He lost the election to Alhaji Shehu Shagari (q.v.). In the effort to realign the parties that lost the presidential election against the presidential party—National Party of Nigeria (NPN) (q.v.)—Mallam Aminu Kano refused to support an alliance against the NPN. In the process his party, the PRP, broke into two factions, one led by him and the other led by Chief Michael Imoudu (q.v.), the old trade unionist. Just as Mallam Aminu Kano refused to gang up in 1979, in the same way he refused in 1982 to join the so-called Progressive Parties Alliance (q.v.), whose main objective was nothing other than to wrest power from the NPN. Aminu later worked hard to reunite the factions in his party and prepare it for the 1983 election. He was on the verge of doing so when he died on April 17, 1983. The factions became reunited on May 18, 1983.

Mallam Aminu Kano was a great nationalist and a defender of the poor and downtrodden. The international airport in Kano, Mallam Aminu Kano Airport, was named after him.

KANO PEOPLE'S PARTY. A splinter party from the Northern People's Congress (q.v.), formed in opposition to the NPC deposition of Alhaji Sir Muhammadu Sanusi, the Emir of Kano, in 1963. The party contested the 1964 elections and won seven seats in the Kano province of Northern Nigeria (q.v.). The party was banned along with other political parties when the military came to power in 1966.

KANO RIOTS OF 1953. In 1953 Chief Anthony Enahoro (q.v.) tabled a motion in the federal House of Representatives (q.v.) in Lagos (q.v.) for "Self-government-for-Nigeria-in-1956" (q.v.). The northern representatives wanted self-government "as soon as practicable." The motion generated a lot of heat, and after it had been amended to read "as soon as practicable," Action Group Party (AG) (q.v.) members and some National Council of Nigeria and the Cameroons (NCNC) members walked out of the house. The two parties later decided to form an alliance to bring about self-government in 1956. To this end, they undertook to send delegations to tour the northern cities to campaign for self-government in 1956. One such delegation led by the late Chief S. L. Akintola (q.v.), a member, went to an AG/Kano (q.v.). The mission of these southern politicians was resented by northerners, and the tense atmosphere that it generated resulted in a four-day riot at Sabon-Gari Kano during which 36 persons died and over 200 were injured. At the Constitutional Conference (q.v.) in London in July 1953, Britain agreed to give self-government to any region wishing to have it.

KANO STATE. Created in 1967 when the Federation (q.v.), made up of four regions, was divided into 12 states. The state survived further subdivisions of the country in 1976 and 1987. But in August 1991, Jigawa State (q.v.), made up of the emirates of Hadejia, Gumel and Kazaure, was carved out of Kano State, leaving the Kano Emirate conterminous with Kano State. It is bounded in the north and northeast by Jigawa State, in the southeast by Bauchi State (q.v.), in the south by Kaduna State (q.v.) and in the west by Katsina State (q.v.). The vegetation of the state is savannah, but this has been much replaced by peasant farms. The annual rainfall is between 800 millimetres in the north and 1,000 millimetres in the south, and the temperature varies from 26°C to 33°C. The state is divided into 35 local government (q.v.) areas.

The population in 1991 was 5,632,040 with a density of 270 persons per square kilometre. Ethnically, the state is predominantly Hausa (q.v.)-Fulani (q.v.) even though other groups like the Nupe (q.v.) and Kanuri (q.v.) occupy some portions of the state. Many Yoruba (q.v.) and Igbo (q.v.) people are also in the state along with such expatriates as the Lebanese and Arabs (q.v.). Hausa is widely spoken, and Hausa and English (q.v.) are the official languages. Kano State is predominately Muslim, but Christianity (q.v.) also has many adherents. A high percentage of the people engage in agriculture, planting crops of guinea corn, groundnuts (q.v.), cow-pea, millet and cotton. Kano State used to be the home of the famous groundnut pyramids. The state also has much livestock, such as cattle, goats and sheep. Parts of the state are well connected by roads, since 1906, rail in 1911 and by air since 1949, and it has one of the country's international airports, Mallam Aminu Kano (q.v.) International Airport. The major population centres are Kano (q.v.), the capital—and for many centuries the greatest commercial center of the old Western Sudan (q.v.)—Dawakin Tofa, Rano, Wudil, Bichi and Dambatta.

For centuries the education of the people was based on Koranic studies; a large proportion of the people are literate in Arabic. The State has two universities, about five polytechnic and four technical colleges and other colleges. In 1993 there were 185 secondary schools, and about 2,090 primary schools. Craftsmen engage in beautiful leatherworks, metalwork, colourful and decorated garments and wood and bone carving.

KANTA. Said to be the founder and the first ruler of the Hausa (q.v.) state of Kebbi (q.v.). During his reign, he built up a great army with which he subjugated many Hausa States (q.v.) during the first half of the 16th century. In 1514 he joined hands with Askia Muhammad, who was ruler of Songhai, to conquer the Tuareg in the north. But the two soon parted ways. Kanta repulsed Muhammad's efforts to control Hausaland. He established his capital at Surame and surrounded it with seven encircling walls built at various times during his reign. When he heard that Daura (q.v.) had risen up against him, he set out on an expedition but died of an arrow wound during the encounter.

KANURI. Kanuri people live mainly in the region of Lake Chad (q.v.), and they are the main ethnic group in present-day Borno State (q.v.) and the eastern part of Niger Republic. They are scattered in great numbers in many States in the north and in some parts of the south. The Kanuri live in small agricultural villages. The Kanuri people are mostly farmers, growing crops of guinea corn, millet, groundnuts (q.v.) and cotton. They also tend cattle, sheep and goats. In their long tradition of centralised political authority within kingdoms and empires, the traditional political authority in the village was the chief assisted by a council of elders. The Kanuri, however, have also had large towns that were centers of commerce and trade.

The Kanuri trace their origin to Yemen where Saef Ben Dhu Yasan, a Yemenite noble, came to found the Sefawa dynasty (q.v.) in the ninth century. The dynasty became the ruling line in Kanem-Bornu for over a thousand years until the 19th century when the Muhammad Al-Kanemi (q.v.) line eventually overthrew by the Sefawa dynasty. The Kanuri have had many great rulers and empire builders such as Dunama Dibalemi (q.v.), Ali Ghaji Dunamami (q.v.) and Idris Ben Ali Aloma (q.v.) under whose reigns the Bornu empire grew east and west, even to Kano.

Islam (q.v.) came to the Kanem-Bornu empire (q.v.) as early as the 11th century, and, by the time of the jihad (q.v.) initiated by Usman Dan Fodio (q.v.), most of the people and their rulers were Muslim. This was why Ahmed Ben Ali (q.v.), the ruler of Bornu in 1807, wrote to Usman Dan Fodio and his son, Muhammad Bello (q.v.), asking why they were waging a war against an Islamic state. When the Fulani did not relent, his successor and son, Dunama Ben Ahmed (q.v.), sought the assistance of Muhammad Al-Kanemi to repel the Jihadists and protect the state from falling under Fulani rule and domination.

KATAF. *See* ZANGO-KATAF.

KATAGUM. A town in Bauchi State (q.v.), established in 1803 by Malam Zaki who, after the death of his father, went to Shehu Usman Dan Fodio (q.v.) in Sokoto (q.v.), the originator of the jihad (q.v.) of the early 19th century, received a flag from him and became the Emir (q.v.) of the town. This was an important victory for the Fulani-led jihad in that it extended the area under their control into the western frontier of the kingdom of Borno. The headquarters of the Katagum was removed to Azare in 1910 for administrative convenience.

KATSINA. Katsina, capital of Katsina State (q.v.), was reportedly founded by Kumayo, one of the grandsons of Bayajidda (q.v.), whose dynasty lasted until about the middle of the 15th century, when Sanau, the last ruler was killed. Korau from Yandoto killed Sanau, thus establishing another dynasty. For about 80 years—1570 to 1650—Katsina and Kano (q.v.) engaged in one conflict or another, but this ended when they faced a common threat from Kwararafa. With the fall of the Songhai empire at the end of the 16th century, many scholars moved to Katsina, creating a center of learning and civilization. Before the Fulani (q.v.) jihad (q.v.), it was a large commercial centre.

When the Fulani living in Katsina and surrounding areas heard about Usman Dan Fodio's (q.v.) revolution, they went to Dan Fodio for a flag to take over Katsina. Umaru Dallaji became the first Emir of Katsina. When the British came to take over the city, Abubakar was the Emir (q.v.) and was confirmed Emir by Lord Frederick Lugard (q.v.). Katsina, now the capital of Katsina State, is growing in commerce, industry and education.

KATSINA, MAJ. GEN. HASSAN USMAN. A soldier, born on March 31, 1933, in Katsina, Katsina State, he was educated at Kankiya Elementary School, Katsina Middle School, Kaduna College, the Institute of Administration in Zaria (q.v.) and at the Nigerian College of Arts, Science and Technology (q.v.) in Zaria (q.v.).

He joined the Nigerian Army in 1956 and trained as an officer in Ghana and in England. He later returned to Nigeria, and in 1961 was sent to the Congo as a member of the United Nations Peacekeeping Force. In 1962 he was sent for further training on infantry maneuvers in the United States at Fort Benning, Georgia. He returned later and was appointed company commander of the Fifth Battalion. In 1964 he was at the Staff College in Camberley, England. In 1965 he became a squadron leader and later in the year a regimental commander.

General Katsina did not participate in the January 15, 1966, coup (q.v.) and was later appointed governor of the Northern Region (q.v.) by General Aguiyi-Ironsi (q.v.) the Head of State. After the death of Aguiyi-Ironsi in July 1966, General Yakubu Gowon (q.v.) kept him in his place as governor, and Katsina helped to keep the north behind Gowon and the Federal Government (q.v.). When the north was divided into six states in 1967, he was the chairman of the Interim Common Services Agency (q.v.) until 1968 when he became army chief of staff and helped in the prosecution of the Civil War (q.v.). In 1971 he was appointed a major general, and in 1973 he became a federal commissioner (q.v.) for establishment. He retired later from the army and became a businessman. He died in July 1995.

KATSINA STATE. Formerly a part of the old Kaduna State (q.v.), Katsina State was created in 1987 and covers Katsina and Daura (q.v.) provinces (q.v.) of the colonial administration. It covers an area of 23,938 square kilometres, and it is located between latitudes 11°08′ and 13°22′N, and longitudes 6°52′ and 9°20′E. It is bounded by the Niger Republic in the north, Jigawa (q.v.) and Kano States (q.v.) in the east, Kaduna State in the south and Sokoto State (q.v.) in the west. The elevation varies from 360 metres to 600 metres above sea level. It has many rivers—the Koza, Sabke, Tagwai and Gragara—but they are all seasonal. The rivers dry up during the dry season. Climatically, it is within the semiarid zone with rainfall ranging from 800 millimetres to 1,000 millimetres in the south and 600 millimetres to 700 millimetres in the north. Vegetation is savannah forest, which has been altered due to human interference and degradation through fuel wood, grazing and cultivation. Mineral resources include kaolin, asbestos, manganese, gold, uranium, nickel, cromite, silica sand and latrite clay. The state has ecological problems of drought and desertification. It is divided into 26 local government (q.v.) areas.

The population in 1991 was 3,878,344 with a density of 162 persons per square kilometre. The state is inhabited predominantly by the Hausa (q.v.) and Fulani (q.v.) and most speak the Hausa language (q.v.). There are migrants from other states, especially the Yoruba (q.v.) and the Igbo (q.v.) from the south.

Most of the people in the state are Muslim, even though a good proportion of the population are adherents of other religions. A good number of the people are traders, while about 75 percent of the people are farmers, cultivating such crops as guinea corn, millet, maize, cowpea, cotton and groundnuts (q.v.). They also rear animals for food and cash. The state's population centers include Katsina (q.v.), the capital, Daura, and Funtua.

A substantial proportion of the people are literate in the Arabic language, and the state is rapidly developing its educational system. It now has about 100,000 pupils in primary schools and over 50,000 in secondary schools. It also has teacher training colleges and technical colleges.

KEBBI. An ancient kingdom said to be founded by Kanta (q.v.). Kebbi used to be under the Songhai empire, but its governor, Kanta, revolted and set up Kebbi as an independent state. Under Kanta, Kebbi grew into a large kingdom, requiring a great number of men to police the area. After Kanta's death, Kebbi continued to stand up against Songhai when it tried to control Kebbi. In 1805 Sarkin Kebbi Muhammad Fodi Dan Salema was driven out of Birnin Kebbi by Abdullahi Dan Fodio (q.v.) during the Fulani (q.v.) revolution of the early 19th century. But Muhammad Fodi continued to fight until he died in 1826. His people never completely succumbed to the rule of the Fulani after Fodio's death and, when the British came in 1900, the Kebbi people readily welcomed them.

KEBBI STATE. One of the nine states created in 1991 by the administration of General Ibrahim B. Babangida (q.v.), Kebbi State was formerly a part of the Sokoto State. It is located between latitudes 10° and 13°15′N, and longitudes 3°30′ and 6°E. It is bounded in the north and east by Sokoto State (q.v.), in the south by Niger State (q.v.) and in the west by the Republic of Benin (q.v.). It has a land area of 44,145 square kilometres and its vegetation is within the savannah zone, characterised by medium-sized trees to open woodland with scattered trees like acacia, borassus and other plants. The original vegetation has, however, been greatly altered by cultivation and farmlands, pastoral system and annual bush fires. The state has two main seasons—rainy and dry. The rainy season is from April to October in the south, and May to September in the north. The annual rainfall is about 800 millimetres in the north to 1,000 millimetres in the south. The temperature is about 26°C in the state, but, during the harmattan (q.v.), it may fall as low as 21°C. The state, like some others in the northern part of the country, suffers from desertification and wind erosion. Kebbi State is divided into 16 local government (q.v.) areas.

The population of the state was 2,062,266 in 1991 and has a density of 50 persons per square kilometre. It is, therefore, fairly sparsely populated.

Ethnically, the state is composed of the Hausa (q.v.), Fulani (q.v.), Kambari, Dandawa Zarmawa, Dukawa, and many others. These various peoples have languages native to them but the Hausa language (q.v.) is widely spoken all over the state. It is rich in culture and in such works of art as goldsmithing, weaving, carving, sculpturing and knitting. About eighty percent of the people live on subsistence farming, cultivating sorghum, millet, maize, rice, wheat, beans, cassava (q.v.), onion, cotton, tobacco, and some people rear animals while others engage in fishing. Some people migrate seasonally to large cities in other states to look for work, and some farm labourers move to less humid areas. The major towns are Birni-Kebbi, the capital, Argungu, Yauri, Zuru, Jega and Kamba.

For centuries, education in the state had been based on Koranic studies, and a high proportion of the people are literate in the Arabic language. At present, there are many Islamic schools. The state is also rapidly developing in western-based education with 803 primary schools, 59 postprimary schools and many tertiary institutions.

KINGIBE, BABAGANA. A diplomat and an administrator, born June 25, 1945, at Maduguri, Borno State (q.v.), he was educated at the University of Sussex in England and trained at the British Broadcasting Corporation Television Training School in London. In 1969 he was a lecturer at the Ahmadu Bello University (q.v.) in Zaria (q.v.) before he joined in 1970 the Northern Nigeria Broadcasting Corporation of Nigeria. In 1972 he was at the Ministry of External Affairs and in 1975 was sent to London as senior counsellor, Nigerian High Commission. In 1976 he was the principal political secretary at the Supreme Military Headquarters in Lagos (q.v.) and later was appointed principal political secretary, Executive Office of the President. In 1981 he was the ambassador to Greece with concurrent accreditation to Cyprus. In 1984 he was ambassador to Pakistan but in 1988 was appointed secretary to the Constituent Assembly (q.v.) to review the 1989 draft constitution (q.v.).

In 1989 when President Ibrahim B. Babangida's regime dictated a two party-system for Nigeria and founded the Social Democratic Party (SDP) (q.v.) and the National Republican Convention (q.v.), Kingibe joined the SDP, and became its chairman. However, when the presidential primaries of 1992 were cancelled, he entered the presidential race as a candidate. He lost the primary election to Chief Moshood Abiola (q.v.) who later made him his running mate in the June 12, 1993, presidential election (q.v.). They won, but the election was annulled before all the results were declared. In November 1993 when General Sani Abacha (q.v.) seized power from the Interim National Government (ING) (q.v.), Kingibe was offered the post of minister of external affairs, which to the surprise and disappointment of many people, he gladly accepted.

In response to his critics, Kingibe claimed to have had Abiola's blessing in accepting the position. Kingibe was one of the few civilian politicians to serve throughout the entire Abacha regime. He held a number of different posts, including Minister of External Affairs, Minister of Internal Affairs and Minister of Power and Steel. His long association with the unpopular Abacha regime did substantial damage to his public image and he did not participate in the 1998–99 democratic transition under Abdulsalami Abubakar.

KING'S COLLEGE, LAGOS. Established in Lagos (q.v.) by the colonial government in 1909. It was the first government-owned secondary school in the country. The college admits students from all over the nation. When the Yaba Higher College (q.v.) was established, parts of King's College served as temporary buildings for it. Today the college runs secondary school certificate courses as well as other courses for those who would like to seek admission to one of the nation's universities.

KINGSLEY, MARY H. An explorer and writer (a niece of author Charles Kingsley) who worked to change the racist attitude of British colonial officers. Born in 1862, she began her trips to Africa in 1893 and visited various trading posts on the coast of Africa, including Nigeria. From these she developed an interest to travel up the Niger River (q.v.). During her second visit to Africa, beginning in 1894, she arrived in Calabar (q.v.) in January 1895 and, after spending about five months there, she changed her mind on the Niger plan and went to Gabon and other places. Her decision to discontinue with her tour up the Niger River reportedly had to do with her personal sympathy toward the Brass people of the Niger Delta (q.v.) who rioted and attacked the trading post of the Royal Niger Company (RNC) (q.v.) at Akassa (q.v.) in protest against their exclusion from the palm oil trade which the British had given exclusively to the RNC.

Mary Kingsley worked hard to correct the view propagated by missionaries and British officials that Africans were culturally and racially inferior to Europeans. She gave lectures and wrote books to propagate her ideas, including *Travels in West Africa* (1897) and *West African Studies* (1899). Her third trip was to South Africa as a nurse, where she died in 1900.

KOGI STATE. Created in August 1991, the state covers the area of the former Kabba province (q.v.) in the British colonial administration. In 1976 the people of the province were split between Kwara State (q.v.) and Benue State (q.v.). The split put a temporary break between the people of the province who for over 70 years had lived peacefully together. Thus, the creation of the state was a restoration of old ties. The state is bounded in the north by

Niger State (q.v.), Plateau State (q.v.) and the Federal Capital Territory (q.v.), in the east by Benue and Enugu States (qq.v.), in the south by Anambra, Delta and Edo States (qq.v.), and in the west by Ondo and Kwara States (qq.v.). Kogi State is where the two major Nigerian rivers—the Benue (q.v.) and the Niger (q.v.)—meet at Lokoja (q.v.), the capital, which as far back as 1917 was declared a second-class township. The rainfall in the state is between 1,100 millimetres and 1,300 millimetres and the rainy season is from April to October, while the dry season is from November to March. The vegetation of the state varies from rain forest in some parts with deciduous forests, having many economic trees like oil palm (q.v.), Iroko and mahogany; on the other hand, there are areas of savannah forest with tall grasses and some trees, where the land becomes dry during the dry season. The state's mineral resources include coal, limestone, marble, kaolin, iron ore, feldspar, clay, gold and columbite. The state is divided into 16 local government (q.v.) areas.

The population was 2,099,046 in 1991, and it is over 80 percent rural. Ethnically, the state is predominately Igala, Kwa and Igbirra, but there are other groups, each speaking languages native to them. The population centers are relatively small, the biggest among them are Lokoja, the capital, Kabba, Okere, Egbe, and Ayamgba. Islam (q.v.) has a firm foundation, but Christianity (q.v.) is also taking a firm root.

Educationally, Kogi State has been in the forefront of educational development in northern Nigeria. The first primary school in northern Nigeria was built at Lokoja during the 1860s. There are also colleges of education and polytechnics.

KOKO, FREDRICK WILLIAM. Ruler of the Niger Delta (q.v.) trading post of Nembe from 1888 to 1898, he was born in 1853 and became ruler of Nembe in 1888 where George T. Goldie's (q.v.) Royal Niger Company (RNC) (q.v.) was virtually forcing the Nembe traders out of their traditional palm oil market by monopolising the market. In preparation for an attack against the RNC in 1894, he unsuccessfully tried to form alliances with the neighbouring states of Bonny (q.v.) and Kalabari. When these states refused to go along with Koko, he joined forces with the neighbouring state of Okpoma and attacked the company's trading post at Akassa (q.v.). The RNC—with the support of the British-supported Niger Coast Protectorate (q.v.), which was in control of Nembe—counterattacked and destroyed Nembe while Koko fled to the village of Etiema. He died in 1898.

KOKORI, FRANK. A trade unionist, born December 7, 1944, at Warri (q.v.), Delta State (q.v.), was educated at Urhobo College, Warri, from 1959 to 1962, Eko Boys High School, Lagos (q.v.), from 1963 to 1964, the University of Ibadan in 1974 and the Institute of Social Studies at the Hague, the

Netherlands, in 1984. He became the national secretary of the National Union of Petroleum and Natural Gas Workers (NUPENG) (q.v.) in 1978. He led his union in a national strike that virtually paralysed the nation's economy in 1994 over the detention of Chief M.K.O. Abiola (q.v.), the undeclared winner of the June 12, 1993, presidential election (q.v.). His union executive was disbanded, and he himself was arrested and detained. Before this time he had served in many important national and international positions such as a member of the Constitution Review Committee in 1977, member of the national executive council of the Nigerian Labour Congress (q.v.), a member of the petroleum committee of the International Labour Organisation and a member of the Constituent Assembly (q.v.) from 1988 to 1989.

KOLANUTS. In Nigeria there are many species of kola trees, which produce kolanuts. The tree grows to about 15 metres in height, while its branches and leaves almost reach down to the ground. It grows well in deep, well-drained soils with a rich humus. It needs an annual rainfall of about 1,200 to 1,500 millimetres and a temperature of about 24°C. Kola tree is usually grown from its fruits and about seven to 10 metres apart.

Kolanuts are produced in clusters, each pod containing up to 10 or more nuts, which may be pink, yellowish, red or white. The nuts contain caffeine and theobromine, and, when chewed and eaten, they help keep a person awake and alert. The nuts are used in the manufacture of beverages and for medicinal purposes. Traditionally, kolanuts are offered to visitors to show that they are welcome. They are also used for marriage ceremonies, naming ceremonies, traditional festivals (q.v.) and for certain sacrifices to some gods.

KOSOKO. The son of King Idowu Ojulari, who was born in Lagos (q.v.) and ruled over Lagos between 1819 and 1832, during the time the British were trying to put an end to slave trade (q.v.) and have legitimate trade substituted in its place. After his father's death in 1832, Kosoko did not support King Oluwole, who succeeded his father. He and others conspired to overthrow him but failed. He was deported from Lagos to Porto Novo (q.v.) where he came in contact with Portuguese slave traders. Oluwole died and Akintoye (q.v.) succeeded him in 1841. The new king allowed his nephew Kosoko to come back to Lagos in 1845. He led a rebellion against his uncle Akintoye and, being victorious, he deported Akintoye to Abeokuta (q.v.). Slave trading continued to flourish during his reign. In 1851 the British consul in the Bight of Benin (q.v.), John Beecroft (q.v.), wanted to bring back Akintoye after the latter had sent a petition to the consul to restore him to the throne in return for which he would put an end to the slave trade. With a naval force of about 400 men, the consul stormed the city, drove Kosoko out from Lagos and restored Akintoye to the throne. Kosoko was exiled to Epe where he continued his campaign against the British. Akintoye died in 1853 and was succeeded by his son Dosunmu (q.v.). In 1862 Kosoko returned to Lagos but did not reclaim the throne.

KUFORIJI-OLUBI, CHIEF DORCAS BOLAJOKO AYODELE MAJIYAGBE. A chartered accountant and economist, born in Lagos (q.v.) in 1936, she was educated at Our Lady's High School, Kaduna (q.v.), St. Theresa's Catholic High School, Jos (q.v.), and St. Agnes Teachers Training College, Maryland, Ikeja (q.v.), Lagos. She attended the University of London, England, from 1960 to 1963. She has served professionally in many and varied capacities in both private and public agencies as an accountant. She chaired the Ogun-Oshun River Basin Development Authority from 1976 to 1980, a member of the governing council of the Nigerian Institute of Social and Economic Research (q.v.) from 1980 to 1983, economic adviser to the Federal Government (q.v.) and chairman of the United Bank for Africa Ltd. In 1993 she was appointed to the cabinet of the Interim National Government headed by Chief Ernest Shonekan (q.v.). She was awarded the national honour of Member of the Order of the Niger.

KUMUYI, W.F. Founder and leader of the Deeper Life Church (q.v.) movement, born in 1941 into an Anglican family, he earned his first degree in mathematics at the University of Ibadan, Oyo State (q.v.), and a M.S.Ed. at the University of Lagos, Lagos State (q.v.), where he later became a lecturer in 1973. As a teacher at the university, many people began to come to him for advice and counselling on religious matters. Because of the pressure on his time, he decided that people should come to his flat once a week for Bible study, thus beginning a Bible study group known later as the Deeper Christian Life Ministry and the Deeper Life Bible Church, which is generally referred to simply as Deeper Life. From Lagos the Deeper Life movement spread to other parts of Nigeria and Africa and to parts of Europe.

KURUNMI. Ruler of the Yoruba (q.v.) kingdom of Ijaye, who precipitated the first of the Yoruba civil wars. After the Yoruba Kingdom of Oyo (q.v.) fell and dispersed in the early 1800s the kingdoms of Ijaye and Ibadan helped to reconstitute it. These two kingdoms were, in the heydays of the Oyo empire, subordinate to Oyo. In 1836 Kurunmi helped to place Atiba (q.v.) on the throne of Oyo, and Atiba rewarded him with a high office of Are-Ona-Kakanfo (generalissimo of the army).

When Atiba died in 1859, Kurunmi protested against Adelu, his first son, taking the throne. By tradition, Adelu would have been killed to follow his father to the grave. Ibadan supported Adelu as ruler and installed him, but Kurunmi refused to recognise him. In 1860 war broke out between Ibadan (q.v.) and Ijaye. Kurunmi received help from the Egba (q.v.), while Ibadan troops laid siege to Ijaye. In 1861 Kurunmi died, and the following year Egba and Ijaye abandoned the city for Abeokuta (q.v.), thus leaving it for the Ibadan forces to destroy.

KWARA STATE. One of the 12 states created in 1967 out of the then-four existing regions, Kwara State (q.v.) then comprised the old Ilorin (q.v.) and Kabba provinces. In 1976 Kwara lost the state's Igala-speaking people to the former Benue State (q.v.). In August 1991, Kwara still suffered further dismemberment by losing Borgu and Agwara local government areas to Niger State (q.v.) and the remaining part of Kabba province to the new Kogi State (q.v.), which substantially comprised old Kabba province during the colonial era. The state is situated between latitudes 11°7′ and 11°45′N and longitudes 2°45′ and 6°40′E. It has the Niger River (q.v.) as its natural boundary in the northeast, Kogi State and Niger States in the east, Ondo (q.v.), Osun (q.v.) and Oyo (q.v.) States in the south and an international boundary with the Republic of Benin (q.v.) in the west. Its land area is 31,600 square kilometres with a population density of 48 persons per square kilometre. Its annual rainfall varies between 800 millimetres and 1,200 millimetres in the northern part and 1,000 millimetres to 1,500 millimetres in the southeastern part. The temperature ranges from 30°C to 35°C. The vegetation is savannah forest, and its mineral resources include kaolin, feldspar, quartz, granite and clay. The state is divided into 12 local government (q.v.) areas.

The population is 1.57 million people, according to the 1991 census, with about 70 percent in the rural areas, producing crops of cotton, coffee, cocoa (q.v.), kolanuts, tobacco, beniseed, maize, rice and millet. There are three major ethnic groups in the state. The Yoruba (q.v.), Nupe (q.v.) and the Baruba, and all these have cultural festivals peculiar to them. They include the Pategi regatta, Egungun (masquerade [q.v.]) and the Leyewu, Ogun and Shango festivals. The Muslims and Christians in the state also have their own festivals. The population centers are Ilorin (q.v.), the capital, Jebba, Omuaran, Ajase-Ipo, Offa, Pategi and Yashikera.

Educationally, it was one of the most widely educated states in the old Northern Region (q.v.), and it continues to develop its educational system. At present, it has over 250,000 pupils in primary schools and about 90,000 in the secondary schools, while about 15,000 are in polytechnics and colleges of education. The University of Ilorin has presently enrolled about 10,000 students.

-L-

LADIPO, DURO. A composer and writer of musical plays. His most famous play is *Oba Koso,* based on the Yoruba (q.v.) legend of Shango who was one of the early rulers of Oyo (Alaafin of Oyo). Other plays are *Oba Moro* and *Oba Waja,* all of which have been translated into English. Duro Ladipo has performed in Europe and America.

LAGOS. A Yoruba (q.v.) town and the capital of Nigeria from 1914 to 1976. An ancient city originally inhabited partly by the Awori people and partly by the Ijebu (q.v.), Lagos in the 16th century was a part of the Kingdom of Benin (q.v.). Benin tradition says that about A.D.1550 the Oba of Benin Awhrogba (Oshogba) stayed in Lagos after his return from a visit to Portugal. The Oba appointed one of his sons, Asipa (q.v.), to be in charge of Lagos as the Eleko of Lagos. Yoruba tradition, however, says Asipa was a Yoruba warrior who gained favor with the Oba of Benin by escorting home the body of an important Benin warrior. Asipa founded a new dynasty in Lagos, which has continued to rule.

From 1820 Lagos was an important slave port on the West African coast. The British effort to put an end to the slave trade (q.v.) and make the people turn their attention to legitimate trade brought about patterns of British intervention in the politics of Lagos and has greatly shaped the history and development of Lagos. In 1845 Kosoko (q.v.) who favoured the slave trade took up arms against his uncle Akintoye (q.v.) and ousted him from the throne. In his effort to regain the throne, Akintoye in 1851 agreed with the British to put Lagos under their protection. If he was restored to the throne, he would abolish the slave trade. The British helped to drive Kosoko out of Lagos while Akintoye was restored to the throne.

In 1853 Akintoye died and was succeeded by his son, Dosunmu (q.v.), during whose reign Lagos was ceded to the British Crown in 1861. Lagos then became a Crown colony (q.v.). In 1866 the colony was placed under the British administration in Sierra Leone (q.v.), but it retained a separate Legislative Council (q.v.) and an administrator was responsible for its affairs. In 1874 Lagos came under the governor of the Gold Coast (q.v.). In 1886 it was finally set up as a separate colony under its own governor.

In 1914 Lagos became the capital of Nigeria. In 1919 it became a first-class township with a representative town council. Under the Macpherson Constitution (q.v.) of 1951, Lagos formed part of the Western Region (q.v.), but in 1954, it was constituted a neutral federal territory. In 1967 Lagos served in the dual role as capital for the Federation (q.v.) and for Lagos State (q.v.). In 1976 it was constituted a "special area" along with Kaduna (q.v.) and Port Harcourt (q.v.).

Lagos is a large commercial and industrial centre and has the largest and main seaport. Though now a cosmopolitan city, the tradition of the Yoruba, the original settlers, have been preserved through the institution of Obaship.

LAGOS ISSUE. The Lagos Issue was the controversy concerning the position of Lagos, the capital of Nigeria in the 1954 federation. Under the Macpherson Constitution (q.v.) of 1951, Lagos was part of the Western Region (q.v.), but owing to the Constitutional Crisis of 1953 over the question of securing self-government in 1956, the northern people (who did not want to oppose the position of Lagos) began to ask that the capital be neutralized so that in the event of the west seceding, they would still be able to get their exports to Lagos, the most important Nigerian seaport. The National Council of Nigeria and the Cameroons (NCNC) (q.v.), which had never been in favor of Lagos merging with the west, supported the neutralisation of Lagos, but the Action Group (q.v.), which controlled the west, argued for the merging of Lagos with the west as it had been since 1951. When the delegation to the London Conference could not agree on the issue, they appealed to the colonial secretary to arbitrate. The secretary supported the idea of a neutral Lagos, that is, the federal capital separating from the Western Region.

LAGOS STATE. One of the states created in 1967 when Nigeria became a federation (q.v.) of 12 states, it embraces areas that have been significant in the history of Nigeria, beginning with Lagos (q.v.), ceded to the British Crown (q.v.) in 1861, and Badagry (q.v.), being an important slave-trading post. The state is made up of the old Federal Territory of Lagos, which is today the financial and commercial hub of the country, together with the old colony province (q.v.) of the old Western Region (q.v.). Since its creation, its land area has not been affected by subsequent state creation (q.v.) exercises, which have now made Nigeria a 30-state federation.

Situated in the southwestern part of the country, the state is bounded in the east by the Republic of Benin (q.v.), in the south by about 180 kilometres of Atlantic coastline and in the east and north by Ogun State (q.v.). The state is within latitudes 6°20′ and 6°40′N, and longitudes 2°45′ and 4°20′E. The area of the state is 3,577 square kilometres, the smallest in Nigeria and has water covering about 22 percent of the land area. The coastal plain is covered by sand banks, lagoons and creeks, and most areas of the state are below 320 millimetres above the sea level. It enjoys a tropical climate, characterised by year-round rainfall and high relative humidity and temperature. Annual rainfall ranges from 1,524 millimetres to 2,031 millimetres in the western part to 2,032 millimetres to 2,540 millimetres in the east. The temperature is between 23.8°C and 30°C, and the relative humidity is about 88 percent. There are swamp mangrove forests in the coastal belt and rain forest in the dry lowland. Only about 30 percent of the state is used for agriculture; such crops as maize, cassava (q.v.), rice, vegetables, cowpeas, soybeans, kolanuts, oil palm (q.v.) and cocoa (q.v.) are grown. A good number of the population engage in fishing. The state is divided into 15 local government (q.v.) areas.

The population was 5,685,781, in 1991, making it the most densely populated area of the country with 1,590 persons per square kilometre. In built-up areas, it can be as high as 20,000 person per square kilometre. The indigenous population of the state is Yoruba (q.v.), but because Lagos City (q.v.) had been the capital of Nigeria from 1914 until 1991, it has been a place that has attracted and still attracts all sections of Nigerian population, as well as non-Nigerians from Africa and the rest of the world. These people are mainly wage and salary earners in the public and private sectors, businessmen and industrialists. In fact, the state is today the commercial, financial and industrial nerve centre of the country. It has the nation's chief port, which handles most of the country's export and import businesses. Lagos State is also the home of the Murtala Muhammed International Airport at Ikeja (q.v.). The state's population centers are Lagos, Ikeja (the capital), Badagry, Ikorodu and Epe. Because the state is a melting pot of all the peoples of Nigeria, it has adherents of all religious beliefs. The people's artistic works are found in their pottery, sculpture, mat and basket-weaving, and raffia work. Their major traditional festivals are Adamu Orisa (Eyo masquerades [q.v.] and the Eluku and Okoso festivals. Educationally, Lagos State has one federal university, the University of Lagos, and Lagos State University, with over a million pupils in both primary and secondary schools.

LAGOS TOWN COUNCIL. Established by ordinance in 1917, it had power to have among its members elected councillors to represent the various wards into which the town was divided. The election to the council was dominated from 1922 by Herbert Macaulay's (q.v.) Nigerian National Democratic Party (NNDP) (q.v.) until 1938 when the Nigerian Youth Movement (q.v.) successfully challenged the party's monopoly. Because the Macpherson Constitution (q.v.) of 1951 placed the city of Lagos (q.v.) in the Western Region (q.v.), the Western Regional Local Government Law of 1953 brought the Lagos Town Council under the control of the region, abolished the office of the mayor and in its place put the Oba of Lagos as the president of the council. Later the Town Council was known as the Lagos City Council. With the 1976 local government (q.v.) reforms, the Lagos City Council was dissolved, and new local governments were established.

LAGOS WEEKLY RECORD. Established in Lagos in 1891 by John Payne Jackson (q.v.) who was its first editor, the paper was most popular among the Nigerian nationalists for its campaign in defence of West Africans against alien white rule. In 1915 when John Payne Jackson died, his son Thomas Horatio Jackson took over the editorship and the ownership of the paper. The paper stopped publishing in 1930.

LAGOS YOUTH MOVEMENT. Lagos Youth Movement was formed by four eminent Nigerian nationalists—Ernest S. Ikoli (q.v.), Dr. J.C. Vaughan (q.v.), Oba Samuel Akinsanya (q.v.) and H.O. Davies (q.v.)—to oppose the government education policy with regard to the deficiencies evident in the setting up of the Yaba Higher College (q.v.) in 1934. The institution was to award its own Nigerian diplomas in medicine, arts, economics, agriculture and engineering without it being affiliated at least initially with any British university. This arrangement was attacked because it was believed that the institution would be inferior in status to British universities and its diplomas would be inferior even though the time taken to acquire the diplomas was longer than the time required for a university degree in the same subject. In 1936 the Lagos Youth Movement changed its name to the Nigerian Youth Movement (q.v.).

LAIRD, MACGREGOR. After the Lander (q.v.) brothers returned to England with the news that the riddle of the Niger River (q.v.) had been solved, Macgregor Laird, a Liverpool businessman, financed an expedition from the coast to the interior of Nigeria in 1832. Many of the members of the expedition died of malaria (q.v.). Out of the 48 Europeans who set sail, only nine survived. The failure of the expedition slowed down the efforts to open up the interior of the country to trade. In 1854 Laird built the *Pleiad* (q.v.) and sent out an expedition to the Niger under the command of Dr. William Balfour Baikie (q.v.). The expedition was a great success; trading posts were established in many places, including Lokoja (q.v.) at the confluence of the Niger and Benue Rivers (qq.v.). In 1857 Laird was given a contract by the British government to maintain a steamer on the Niger for five years, and again he placed Dr. Baikie in command. The first steamer was the *Dayspring,* and the expedition included Samuel Ajayi Crowther (q.v.) who later became the first bishop of the Niger. Laird met with much opposition from the people of the area, who served as middlemen between the interior and the white men on the coast, and the Liverpool supercargoes who resented his efforts. In 1860 he was able to convince the British government to provide him with a naval escort, but the local commander never provided any because he felt it was too risky at the time. As a result, his expedition involved him in heavy losses of capital. However, Dr. Baikie, who had been wrecked in the *Dayspring,* established himself in Lokoja and appeared to be doing well. Born in Scotland in 1808, Laird died in 1861.

LAKE CHAD. Lying across the central Sudan (q.v.), the Lake Chad region has for centuries been a crossroads of trade in Africa. The lake is on the northeastern border of Nigeria and lies partly within Nigeria's boundaries and that of the Chad Republic. The lake receives its main supply of fresh water from the Logone River and the Chari River, both of which meet in

N'Djamena and run along the border with Cameroon into the southern part of the lake. There is also some supply from the Kamadougou Yobe, which marks the boundary between Nigeria and Niger and supplies the northern part of the lake.

Climatic changes have greatly altered the reality of the lake. The lake is in danger of drying up. The size has, in the recent past, fluctuated from about 25,000 to 15,000 square kilometres and continues to grow smaller as a result of droughts. In 1964, when the lake was overflowing with water, Lake Chad Basin Commission was set up to coordinate the exploitation of the lake's resources. But now as the lake recedes, the lake communities—fishers, farmers and herders—move closer around the decreasing shorelines. This means smaller catches for the fishers, but more fertile land for the farmers and herders. The objective now is to maintain the small-scale development projects and continue to sustain the life of the lake community.

LAMBO, PROF. THOMAS ADEOYE. A neuropsychiatrist and an educationist, he was born on March 29, 1929, at Abeokuta (q.v.), Ogun State (q.v.) and educated at the Baptist Boys' High School, Abeokuta. He later went to the University of Birmingham in England and then to the Institute of Psychiatry, University of London.

Back in Nigeria in 1950 he became a medical officer for the Nigerian Medical Services, specialist-in-charge at Aro Hospital for Nervous Diseases and a consultant physician to the University College, Ibadan, from 1956 to 1963. In 1963 he became professor and head of the department of psychiatry and neurology at the University of Ibadan and dean of the medical faculty in 1966. In 1968 he was appointed the vice chancellor of the University of Ibadan and was also the chairman of the West African Examinations Council (q.v.).

Professor Lambo has held important positions in many international organisations and has been the recipient of many honors. In 1961 he convened the first Pan-African Conference of Psychiatrists and was founder of the Association of Psychiatrists in Africa in 1961. He was chairman, Scientific Council for Africa from 1965 to 1970 and was a member of the executive committee, Council for International Organization for Medical Science (UNESCO) from 1965 to 1968. He was also chairman, United Nations Advisory Committee for the Prevention of Crime and Treatment of Offenders from 1968 to 1971. In 1971 he was appointed assistant director-general of the World Health Organization (WHO) and in 1973 became deputy director of the organisation. He was also a member of the Royal Medico-Psychological Association of Great Britain and a Fellow of the Royal College of Physicians. Among the honors Lambo received were Officer, Order of the British Empire and honorary degrees of D.Sc. and LL.D. from various universities. He also received the Haile Selassie African Research Award in 1970. He coauthored *Psychiatric Disorder among the Yorubas* (1963).

LANDER, RICHARD. The servant of Hugh Clapperton (q.v.), one of the leading explorers of the interior of West Africa, he was with Clapperton in the latter's journey from Badagry (q.v.) to Sokoto (q.v.) in 1825. When Clapperton died in 1827, Lander tried to reach the coast by going down through the Niger River (q.v.). He was captured by the local inhabitants at the confluence of the Niger and Benue Rivers (qq.v.), and was made to go down the coast by land. He went back to England and persuaded the British government to support his journey to Nigeria. In 1830 he and his brother John travelled by land from Badagry to Bussa (q.v.) where Mungo Park (q.v.) died. They got two boats there and sailed down the Niger until they reached Asaba where they were captured by the local inhabitants, who agreed to hand them over to the master of the English ship at Brass (q.v.) at the mouth of the Niger. Lander died in 1834.

LAND TENURE SYSTEM. Traditional basis of land tenure was common ownership whether by the community as a whole or by families, and the allocation of land was controlled by traditional authorities who acted as trustees for the community. All the members of the community or family had a right to the land, and once an individual was given a piece of land, he could use it as he saw fit but he could not sell it or alienate it in any way from the family or the community. The right an individual had over the land in his possession was usufructuary.

When the colonial authorities came, they decided to preserve as much as possible the traditional land ownership system. In the Southern Protectorate (q.v.), an alien, that is, an expatriate, was prohibited from acquiring an interest in land from a native or from a fellow alien except under an instrument previously approved by the governor. This meant that some families, who wished to, could collectively alienate their land to Nigerians. As such, some community lands were divided up among families, and some of these began to offer them for sale to other Nigerians in "fee simple" (absolutely). In the Northern Protectorate the government was empowered to hold all the land in trust for the natives and no title to the use and occupation of land was valid without the consent of the government.

The policy of preventing aliens from purchasing land in fee simple had two major effects. It prevented the growth of a white settler community in Nigeria and so deterred the investment of private European capital in the development of the economy. Second, by defining an alien as a person whose father belonged to a tribe not indigenous to Northern Nigeria, the law in the north inhibited freedom of migration and residence of Nigerians in their own country and therefore made the problem of national integration all the more difficult. *See also* LAND USE DECREE.

LAND USE DECREE/ACT. As a result of the recommendation of the Rent Control Panel (q.v.), the federal military government set up the Land Use Panel headed by Justice Chike Idigbe. The outcome of the panel's recommendations was the promulgation of the Land Use Decree (now Act) in March 1978.

As a result of the traditional Land Tenure System (q.v.), as amended by different statutory laws in the Southern and Northern protectorates (q.v.), certain problems that urgently needed solution arose. In the urban areas, there was too much speculation in land, and this made for the rise in land value all over the nation. Second, the governments of the federation were experiencing difficulty in acquiring land for public use, especially in the south where there was no coordinated tenurial system of land, which consequently led to endless land litigations. Finally, the land tenure system as it operated in the country imposed great impediments on agricultural modernisation and the effort of the nation to be self-sufficient in food. It was these impediments and other problems that the Land Use Decree was designed to remove and solve.

According to the decree, ownership of all land in each state of the Federation (q.v.) is vested in the government of the state which holds it in trust for the people and administers it for the use and common benefit of all the people. By this decree a uniform system of land ownership for the whole country was established and an individual could no longer legally sell land in fee simple. All urban areas were further placed under the control and management of the governor of the state, while rural lands were placed under the control and management of the local government that had jurisdiction in the area where the land is situated. As far as rural land areas were concerned, the decree did not disturb the right of users of land traditionally occupied or developed, but it transferred the right of allocating unoccupied land from traditional authorities like Chiefs (q.v.) and heads of families to local governments, which are empowered to grant customary right of occupancy to persons or organisations of not more than 500 hectares for agricultural purposes or 5,000 hectares for grazing purposes. By this decree, traditional authorities are deprived of the right to their undeveloped land and such land is opened to anyone who needed it for development, including strangers.

There is great resistance to this decree by traditional landowners, lawyers who lost income through the new system and some others. There are efforts to amend the decree, but an amendment is made difficult since it is protected by the constitution (q.v.).

The implementation of the decree has been woefully poor. Part of the problem is that the government of each state has no survey map of unoccupied lands before or even after the decree went into effect. As such, land continued to be sold by traditional landowners and the receipts were backdated to a time before 1978.

LANGUAGES, NIGERIAN. There are probably more than 350 languages that are spoken by as many, if not more, ethnic groups in Nigeria. If we add the various dialects of each language, the number goes into many hundreds, if not thousands. Some languages like Hausa (q.v.), Yoruba (q.v.), Igbo (q.v.), Edo (q.v.), Fulani (q.v.) and Kanuri (q.v.) are spoken by millions of people, while there are others spoken by only a few thousand.

Nigerian languages fall into many language groups. Hausa, Fulani and Kanuri fall into the West Chadic group spoken west, south and east of Lake Chad. The Bantu-speaking people occupy the southeastern area of Nigeria. These are Effik-Ibibio and Tiv (q.v.). Yoruba, Ijaw (q.v.), Itsekiri (q.v.), Edo and Igbo belong to the Kwa branch of the Niger-Congo family.

Because Nigeria is a multiethnic society, many people are multilingual—able to speak languages other than their own native tongue. Hausa in Northern Nigeria is one of such languages. Hausa is the lingua franca in most parts of the north. Where there is no such common language between various language groups like Hausa, Edo, Yoruba and Igbo, English or its variant becomes the only medium of communication.

LAR, CHIEF SOLOMON DAUSHEP. Born April 1933 in Pangna, Plateau State (q.v.). Chief Lar is one of the top politicians of the country, and is particularly influential in the middle belt. Even as a young man, Lar was active in the politics of the First Republic. He was elected to the Federal House of Representatives from 1959–64 as a member of the United Middle Belt Congress. He earned a law degree in 1971 and returned to politics under the Second Republic (1979–83) as a member of the Nigerian People's Party (q.v.). From 1979 to 1983, he served elected civilian governor of Plateau State.

Lar was one of the politicians who were initially banned from participating in the transition program of Ibrahim Babangida (q.v.). Nevertheless, he was active in politics behind the scenes, which led to his being briefly detained in December 1991. In 1993, he was appointed Minister of Police Affairs in the first Abacha cabinet, serving until 1995. Chief Lar later became alarmed by Abacha's excesses and in 1998 he was one of the driving forces behind the formation of the Group of 18 (and later the Group of 34) (q.v.), an association of prominent politicians opposed to the Abacha Regime. When the Group of 34 metamorphosed into the People's Democratic Party in September 1998, Lar was chosen as the national chairman. In this role, he helped secure the election of Olusegun Obasanjo (q.v.) as president in February 1999.

LEGAL SYSTEM. One main feature of the Nigerian legal system is its dualism, i.e., a combination of indigenous and British laws in the administration of justice. Before the advent of the British colonial authorities, each community had its own legal system through which disputes were settled. In the southern part of the country, these are called customary laws, administered through the indigenous court system presided over by traditional rulers, Chiefs (q.v.) and/or community leaders. In the north, a well-developed legal system is based on the Islamic system of judicial administration. Under the Emirate system (q.v.), the Islamic laws (q.v.) (Shari'a) were administered by learned jurists called *alkali*. This advanced system of judicial administration was not destroyed by the British authorities. Nonetheless, the colonial administration superimposed the British legal system by creating a series of British-type courts, and integrated them with the customary/native courts (q.v.) through a system of appeal that terminated at the Judicial Committee of the Privy Council (q.v.) in London.

At present the customary courts lie at the bottom of the hierarchy of courts in Nigeria. In the north, appeals move from the Shari'a courts to the Shari'a Courts of Appeal of each state. The same applies in the south where appeals from customary courts move to the Customary Court of Appeal of each state. Ordinarily, appeals are sent from these indigenous courts of appeal to the Federal Court of Appeal (q.v.), and from there to the Supreme Court (q.v.).

The head of the judicial system is the chief justice who is appointed by the president with the assent of the Senate (q.v.). A judge may retire at 60, but he must retire at 65. Any judge who retires at 65 is entitled to pension for life at the rate equivalent to his last annual salary in addition to any other retirement benefits to which he may be entitled. *See also* JUDICIARY.

LEGISLATIVE COUNCIL. After the annexation of Lagos (q.v.) in 1861 whereby Lagos became a Crown colony (q.v.), the colonial authorities in accordance with the British policy in Crown colonies set up a small body known as the Legislative Council. Its purpose was to advise the governor in framing legislation for the colony, but the governor did not need to accept its advice. It was not a representative body. It was composed of the governor, government officials and unofficial nominated members.

In 1923 the council was reorganised to provide for four elected African members, three from Lagos (q.v.) and one from Calabar (q.v.). Its advisory role was to cover the whole of the Southern provinces (q.v.). This arrangement lasted until 1947 when the Richards Constitution (q.v.) came into force. The council was replaced by a more representative All-Nigerian Council in which both the Northern and the Southern representatives sat to discuss Nigerian affairs.

LIEUTENANT GOVERNOR. After the Amalgamation (q.v.) of the Southern and the Northern protectorates (q.v.), one lieutenant governor for each of the former protectorates was appointed to be responsible to the governor-general (q.v.) in Lagos (q.v.). Each lieutenant governor was charged with the administration of the former protectorate to which he was appointed. When Sir Donald Cameron (q.v.) became governor of Nigeria in 1931, he abolished the offices of lieutenant governors and renamed them chief commissioners (q.v.). Under the Macpherson Constitution (q.v.) of 1951, the office of lieutenant governor was reinstated and each lieutenant governor was in charge of each of the three regions in which Nigeria was divided. Under the 1954 federal constitution (q.v.), the lieutenant governors became governors over their regions while the governor at the centre became the governor-general.

LINGUISTIC GROUPS. In Nigeria there are many linguistic groups commonly referred to as ethnic groups or tribes. These groups range in size from a few thousand people to many millions. The three major groups are the Hausa (q.v.)-Fulani (q.v.) group predominately inhabiting the northern part of the country, the Yoruba (q.v.) inhabiting the southwest, and the Igbo (q.v.) living in the southeast. Several other linguistic groups are the Edo (q.v.), Efik (q.v.), Gwari (q.v.), Ibibio (q.v.), Itsekiri (q.v.), Kanuri (q.v.), Tiv (q.v.), Urhobo (q.v.), Nupe (q.v.) and others. There are about 350 groups, each speaking an indigenous language. These languages have been variously classified: Hausa, Fulani and Kanuri fall into the West Chadic group spoken west, south and east of Lake Chad. Efik, Ibibio and Tiv in the southeastern part of Nigeria fall into the Bantu-speaking group, while Ijaw, Itsekiri, Edo, Igbo and Yoruba belong to the Kwa branch of the Niger-Congo family.

LIPEDE, OBA MICHAEL MOFOLORUNSO OYEBADE. Born in 1915 in Abeokuta (q.v.), Ogun State (q.v.), Oba Oyebade Lipede, the only surviving son of his parents, attended St. Peter's School, Ake, Abeokuta and later went to Abeokuta Grammar School and the Christian Missionary Society Grammar School in Lagos (q.v.). In 1937 after his secondary school education, he joined the Department of Customs and Excise. He later worked in many parts of Nigeria, especially in Warri (q.v.), Sapele, Port Harcourt (q.v.) and Calabar (q.v.), as a staff member of the Nigerian Produce Marketing Company Limited. While still under this company, he served also in England, Belgium, and Hamburg in Germany. In 1956 Oba Lipede was one of the first two Nigerians promoted as Shipping Officers, and after 34 years in government service, Oba Lipede retired in 1971. He became an Oba, the Alake of Egbaland in 1972.

LISHABI. Liberator of the Egba (q.v.) from the Oyo empire (q.v.). Before his revolt, Egba people in their various villages and towns were under the Oyo empire. The revolt took place about the time of Abiodun (q.v.), the Alaafin (q.v.) of Oyo, between 1775 and 1780. Lishabi organised the farmers into the Egbe Aro Society, which was apparently a farmers' cooperative society, but in reality an underground army. Later each town turned its Egbe Aro into the military society, Egbe Olorogun, and met every 17th day. They were secretly armed, and, when the time was propitious, they attacked, killing over 600 representatives of the Alaafin in the various towns and villages. Abiodun later tried to reconquer Egbaland but failed.

Lishabi later became ruler of the Egba people and during his time, he gave laws to the people, taught them how to defend their freedom by arms and built fortifications so that they could repel attacks not only from Oyo but also from Dahomey (q.v.), which constantly raided the area. During his time, trade flourished, and his own people regarded him as father and liberator of their nation. The manner of his death is not known.

LITTLE ELECTION. The Little Election was held in March 1965 as a result of the federal elections (q.v.) boycott in the Eastern Region (q.v.) in December 1964 by the United Progressive Grand Alliance (q.v.). The boycott was occasioned by the then-unprobed allegation of election malpractices in many parts of the Federation (q.v.), especially in the north and in the west and the government's refusal to postpone the elections.

LOKOJA. Capital of Kogi State (q.v.), situated at the confluence of the Niger and Benue Rivers (qq.v.). The members of an 1841 expedition (which included Samuel Ajayi Crowther [q.v.] who, 23 years later became bishop of the Niger territories), sent by the British government, bought a piece of land from the local chiefs in Lokoja and later set up what they called a model farm. Lokoja became the headquarters of British trade and influence, and from there they established routes into the Hausa States (q.v.) of the north and to Lagos (q.v.). In 1865 the British established a consulate at Lokoja, but, because of the hostilities of Africans toward white settlers, it was closed in 1869. Lokoja was originally made the capital of the Northern Protectorate (q.v.), before the capital was moved to Zungeru (q.v.). The first primary school in the then-Northern Nigeria (q.v.) was built in Lokoja. It was no wonder then that Lokoja, in spite of its being a small town, was chosen as the capital of the newly created Kogi State in 1991.

LUGARD, LORD FREDERICK. A British colonial administrator, born in India in 1858, he began a career in the army after his education. He served in Nyasaland (Malawi) in 1888, in Kenya in 1889 and in Uganda in 1890. He entered the service of the Royal Niger Company (q.v.) in 1894 and negotiated a number of treaties of protection with local rulers and succeeded in bringing Borgu under the Royal Niger Company. He later left Nigeria to lead an expedition to extend the pacification and trading role of the South African Company upon Bechuanaland (Botswana). In 1897 he was called upon by the British government to organise and command the West African Frontier Force (q.v.) with which to defend British interest and possession against the French and the German claims to territories in Northern Nigeria (q.v.). In 1900 when the British government revoked the charter of the company, he was appointed the first High Commissioner of the northern territories. Between 1901 and 1903 he was engaged in the pacification and conquest of the Sokoto (q.v.) Caliphate (q.v.), which was created by Usman Dan Fodio (q.v.). In 1903 he told the newly appointed Sultan (q.v.) of Sokoto that Fulani (q.v.) rule established in the territories during the jihad (q.v.) had come under the British. He also annexed territories outside Sokoto.

In 1907 Lord Lugard left Nigeria to be governor of Hong Kong, but in 1912 he was brought back to Nigeria with the task of unifying the north with the south. After the Amalgamation (q.v.) of the two territories in 1914, he became the governor general of the Colony and Protectorate of Southern Nigeria (q.v.). In addition to the Legislative Council (q.v.) which then existed, he set up the Nigerian Council, which was a larger body with the hope that the newly united country should have a larger advisory body that would be fairly representative of the Chiefs (q.v.) and other people, but with an official majority.

Lord Lugard played a very prominent role in the making of modern Nigeria. He is generally associated with the system of Indirect Rule (q.v.), which was later accepted by the British as the best method of administering African countries. He resorted to this method out of necessity: he did not know enough of the culture of the people and he did not have sufficient British officials to administer directly such a vast territory. According to the system, British officials ruled the people indirectly, through the Chiefs. The British government assumed power to appoint Emirs (q.v.) and Chiefs who ruled over their people—provided their rule was not repugnant to British moral standards. The Chiefs were to collect taxes as appointed by the High Commissioner and they were to be advised by the British officials known as residents. The system succeeded fairly well, but met with opposition when extended to the south, especially in Eastern Nigeria (q.v.) where the people had not developed such centralised administration as existed under the Emirs or the Obas in Western Nigeria (q.v.).

In 1919 Lord Lugard retired from public service, and three years later he published his famous book *The Dual Mandate in British Tropical Africa*. The thesis of the book was that Europe was in Africa for the mutual benefit of her own industrial classes and of the native races in their progress to a higher plane. He argued that the benefit could be made reciprocal and that it was the aim of civilised administration to fulfill this dual mandate. He died in 1945.

LUKMAN, ALHAJI RILWANU. An engineer, economist, administrator and former minister of mines, power and steel, he was born in Zaria (q.v.), Kaduna State (q.v.) in 1938 and received his primary education at Tudun Wada Elementary School in Zaria from 1944 to 1948 and later went to Narewa College in Zaria where he received his secondary school education. He attended the Nigerian College of Arts, Science and Technology (q.v.), now Ahmadu Bello University (q.v.). He studied at the Imperial College of Science and Technology, University of London from 1959 to 1962 where he received a B.Sc. degree in engineering. He also did a postgraduate course in mining and mineral exploitation at the Institute of Prospecting and Mineral Deposits, University of Mining and Metallurgy, Leober, in Austria from 1967 to 1968. He also studied mineral economics at McGill University, Montreal, Canada.

His work experience started with the A.B. Statagruvor, Hoaksberg, in Sweden (1962–64), and he joined the Federal Ministry of Mines and Power in Jos (q.v.) in 1964. In 1974 he became general manager and chief executive of the Nigerian Mining Corporation. During the Buhari (q.v.) regime, he was minister of mines, power and steel, and when the Babangida (q.v.) regime began in 1985, he kept his post. In 1986 he was deployed to the Ministry of Petroleum Resources, and later became the chairman, board of directors of the Nigerian National Petroleum Corporation (q.v.). In the same year he was elected president of the Organization of Petroleum Exporting Countries (q.v.). He was awarded the Knight Commander, Order of the British Empire in the United Kingdom in 1989 and has many honorary doctorate degrees.

In 1999, he was appointed presidential advisor on petroleum and energy by the Obasanjo (q.v.) administration.

LYTTELTON CONSTITUTION. The Lyttelton Constitution, named for Lord Oliver Lyttelton, a British Statesman, came in 1954 as a result of the two constitutional conferences (q.v.) held in London between July and August 1953 and in Lagos between January and February 1954. At the conferences, the defects of the Macpherson Constitution (q.v.) were highlighted and agreements were reached on major changes that were necessary to remedy those defects.

Under the constitution, Nigeria became a federation (q.v.) of three regions: Northern (q.v.), Eastern (q.v.) and Western (q.v.). Lagos (q.v.), which was formerly part of the Western Region, became a federal territory, while Southern Cameroon (q.v.) which was previously administered as part of the Eastern region, ceased to be part of that region; it, however, remained part of the Federation of Nigeria as a quasi-federal territory.

The federal legislature was unicameral and consisted of a speaker, three ex-officio members (q.v.) and 184 representative members elected independently of the regional legislatures on the basis of single-member districts. The north had 92 representatives while the west and the east had 42 representatives, respectively; Southern Cameroon sent six members while Lagos sent two. The House could legislate on the exclusive and the concurrent legislative lists, while the regional houses could legislate on areas not in the exclusive legislative list and also on the concurrent list. However, federal laws would prevail over regional laws.

The Council of Ministers (q.v.) consisted of the Governor-General (q.v.) who presided, three official members, three members from each region and one member representing Cameroon (q.v.). These ministers were appointed by the governor from members directly elected to the house, on the advice of the regional executive.

While the constitution did not provide for the post of a prime minister for the Federation, it however established the position of a premier for each of the regions. The regional governor was given the power to appoint the leader of the party that commanded the regional house as premier.

By this constitution, the public service in Nigeria and the judiciary (q.v.) were also regionalised.

-M-

MABOGUNJE, PROFESSOR AKINLAWON LADIPUPO. A world-renowned geographer, author and teacher, Professor Mabogunje was born October 18, 1931, in Kano (q.v.), Kano State (q.v.). He started his education there at the United Native African Church School (q.v.) from 1936 to 1941 and moved south to Mapo Central School in Ibadan (q.v.) in 1942, Ibadan Grammar School from 1943 to 1948 and University College Ibadan (now University of Ibadan) from 1949 to 1953. He later joined the university and became a professor of geography in 1965, dean of the faculty of social sciences from 1968 to 1970. Since then, he has headed various organisations, both nationally and internationally. These include the international Geographic Union, Nigeria Geographical Association, the National Council for Population Activities and the National Council for Management Development. He was also chairman of the International Committee for Overcoming Hunger. He has served as consultant to the United Nations, UNESCO, and the World Bank. He is a National Merit Award Winner of the most prestigious French Geographical Society Award, La Grande Médaille, in January 1993. Professor Mabogunje has also been the recipient of many other awards and honours in Europe, America and Africa.

MABOLAJE GRAND ALLIANCE. Organised in 1953 in Ibadan (q.v.), the then-capital of Western Nigeria (q.v.), by Alhaji Adegoke O.A. Adelabu (q.v.), Mabolaje Grand Alliance was a political party with its base in Ibadan. It was in alliance with the National Council of Nigerian Citizens (NCNC) (q.v.), which at that time was the party in opposition to the Action Group (AG) (q.v.), and it was gradually increasing its hold on the region. The alliance was very popular as can be seen from the sweeping victory in the Ibadan District Council elections of 1954 and 1958 where it won 35 and 28 seats, respectively, out of 43 seats, in spite of the efforts of the AG to win substantial support in the capital. Adelabu, however, died in a motor accident in 1958, and the alliance broke into two factions, one led by Adeoye Adisa who succeeded to the Adelabu's seat in the regional house of assembly (q.v.) and the other by Mojeed Agbaje, chairman of the Ibadan District Council, who was elected in 1958. This spelled the end of the alliance for, with Adelabu out of the way, the AG increased its support and the NCNC began to assert more and more freedom and independence.

MACAULAY, HERBERT. Born on November 14, 1884, he lost his father at the age of 13 and graduated from Lagos Grammar School at 14. He worked as a clerk with the public works department in Lagos (q.v.). He was later granted a scholarship by the governor of the colony of Lagos, Sir Alfred Moloney, to train in England as a land surveyor and a civil engineer. Upon returning from England, he took appointment with the colonial government as a surveyor in Lagos. He resigned his appointment in 1898 after working for the government for five years and set up his own private practice as a licensed surveyor and civil engineer in Lagos.

Macaulay became interested in politics and successfully opposed a number of unpopular measures proposed by the colonial government in Lagos. The one that made him most popular was the Apapa Land Case of 1920, in which a chief in Lagos, Chief Amadu Oluwa, demanded compensation for land compulsorily acquired by the government. Macaulay and the Chief successfully fought the government in court up to the Privy Council in London and he returned home a hero.

Herbert Macaulay was first in many ways. He was the grandson of Bishop Ajayi Crowther (q.v.), who was the first African bishop in West Africa, the son of the first principal of the first Grammar School in Nigeria, King's College (q.v.) and the first Nigerian to be given a scholarship to receive professional training in England. He founded the first political party in Nigeria, the Nigerian National Democratic Party (NNDP) (q.v.), which had as its goals local self-government, expanded educational and commercial opportunities for the people and Africanisation of the civil service. Strictly speaking, however, it was a Lagos organisation for it concentrated much of its efforts on Lagos affairs and received much of its support from the traditional leaders. Macaulay also was the founder of the first daily newspaper in Nigeria, the *Lagos Daily News* (q.v.), which he used effectively to arouse nationalist sentiments in the country and which today remains a reference journal for the pioneering phase of the country's nationalist movement.

Macaulay was the chairman of the meeting held at the Glover Memorial Hall in 1944, called at the instance of the National Union of Nigerian Students (q.v.) in connection with the King's College boys' strike. This meeting gave birth to a new political party, the National Council of Nigeria and the Cameroons (NCNC) (q.v.). Macaulay was elected the president of the party while Dr. Nnamdi Azikiwe (q.v.) was general secretary.

In 1945 when the Richards Constitution (q.v.)—which fell short of nationalist expectations—was being proposed for Nigeria, the NCNC led a campaign against it. In 1946 Macaulay and other NCNC leaders began a campaign tour of the country against the constitution, sought support of the people for the position of the party and raised funds for representation to London. Macaulay fell sick in Kano (q.v.) and was rushed back to Lagos. He died on May 7, 1946. Before the military relinquished power in 1979, Herbert Macaulay had been declared a national hero by the federal military government. His portrait is on every Nigerian naira.

MACCIDO, ALHAJI MUHAMMADU. The 19th sultan (q.v.) of Sokoto (q.v.) and son of the late sultan, Abubakar Sidiq III, the predecessor of Alhaji Ibrahim Dasuki (q.v.). When his father died in 1988, he, with Shehu Malami from Mohammed Bello's (q.v.) lineage, challenged the right of Dasuki to the throne because the line of Dasuki through Muhammadu Buhari, one of the sons of Usman Dan Fodio (q.v.) who was the founder of the Sokoto Caliphate in 1804, had never occupied the throne.

Born in 1926 in Dange, Maccido acquired his elementary education in the town of his birth, and his secondary education at Katsina Teachers' College, and later at Sokoto Middle School. In 1947 he was at a clerical training college in Zaria (q.v.) where he studied office administration, and in 1948 he was in his father's office as a clerical assistant. In 1952 he was sent to England to study public administration, and upon his return, he was made district head of Talata Mafara where his father was district head before becoming the sultan.

Maccido rose quickly, becoming a councillor for works in the Sokoto Native Authority (q.v.) in 1956 and later councillor for rural development before he was put in charge of agriculture in 1960. He later studied agriculture in the United States and Europe. He served as commissioner of agriculture and later of health under General Yakubu Gowon (q.v.) until Gowon was overthrown in 1975. In 1976 he was the chairman of the Local Government Service Commission until 1979 when he entered politics as a member of the disbanded National Party of Nigeria (NPN) (q.v.) and became the Sokoto State (q.v.) party chairman and the presidential liaison officer for Sokoto State until 1983. He was back in the local government (q.v.) system in 1985 and was in 1988 appointed into the Sokoto inner emirate council. He had much experience in his father's palace before his father died.

Upon his father's death on November 1, 1988, the struggle for the throne began. The Sokoto Council of King Makers, made up of nine members and headed by the Waziri, was to deliberate on the successor and forward three names to the state government, which was to pick one of them as the next sultan. It was the general belief that Maccido's name topped the list, followed by Shehu Malami and the last, Ibrahim Dasuki. But Dasuki, the No. 3 candidate, with the greatest clout—the support of the military Head of State, General Ibrahim Babangida (q.v.), and that of the state governor—was finally chosen as sultan. The choice was unpopular and was followed by several days of rioting in which many lives and property worth millions were lost. In the long run, peace was restored. In August 1993, the administration of President Babangida who installed Dasuki in power changed, and in November, General Sani Abacha (q.v.) became Head of State. The relationship between the two leaders was tense, and on April 20, 1996, Dasuki was dethroned, paving the way for Maccido's enthronement on April 21, 1996. There was jubilation in many parts of Sokoto city, especially among the many that Dasuki had alienated.

MACPHERSON CONSTITUTION. Sir John Macpherson became governor of Nigeria in 1948 and announced that, rather than wait for nine years after the Richards Constitution (q.v.) of 1946 before making any changes, as was formerly proposed, he was prepared during the second three-year period to agree to constitutional changes if it was the wish of the country. Accordingly, before the constitution was adopted, there were a series of conferences both at the provincial and regional levels and at the All-Nigerian Constitutional Conference at Ibadan in 1950. The constitution that ensued was thus named after Sir John Macpherson.

The constitution promulgated in 1951 provided for a Council of Ministers (q.v.) made up of six ex-officio members (q.v.) and 12 Nigerian ministers, four from each regional House of Assembly (q.v.). The responsibility of each minister was limited to dealing in the legislative assembly with matters concerning his ministry and introducing in the Council of Ministers matters concerning his ministry and to see that the decisions taken by the Council of Ministers were carried out by appropriate officials. The constitution did not make the minister responsible for the framing of the policy of his ministry.

The constitution provided for a House of Representative (q.v.) consisting of 142 members of which 136 were Nigerians. In both the north and the west, the constitution also provided for a bicameral legislature, the House of Assembly (q.v.) and the House of Chiefs (q.v.), while in the east, there was only one legislative house, the House of Assembly (q.v.). The constitution also provided for the Public Service Commission (q.v.) to advise the governor on matters affecting the public service.

In spite of the consultations that went into its making, the constitution later proved unworkable and had to be replaced in 1954.

MACPHERSON, SIR JOHN. Born in 1898, Sir John Macpherson became the governor of the Colony and Protectorate of Southern Nigeria (q.v.) in 1948. His first major concern was the reform of the local government (q.v.) system. His government initiated first in the Eastern region the transformation of the native authority (q.v.) system to the local government council system, which was modelled on the British system. He then proposed that beginning in 1950 there would be a review of the 1946 constitution (q.v.) if the people so wished. This review led to the 1951 constitution, christened the Macpherson Constitution. Owing to the Constitutional Crisis of 1953, new efforts were initiated in 1953 to review the constitution in London and in 1954 in Lagos. This gave rise to the Federal Constitution of 1954, at which time Sir John Macpherson became the governor-general (q.v.) of the Federation (q.v.). He officially opened the Ibadan branch of the Nigerian College of Arts, Science and Technology (q.v.) in 1954. He left Nigeria in 1955 and was succeeded by Sir J.W. Robertson (q.v.).

MAHDI. Islamic title used for the messiah spoken about in the Bible. Even though the Koran does not speak of a Mahdi, and it is not in any orthodox tradition, the belief in a coming redeemer is strong among some Muslims. The founder of the Ahmadiyya (q.v.) group is said to be a Mahdi.

"MAITATSINE." *See* MARWA, MUHAMMADU.

MAJA, DR. AKINOLA. A medical practitioner, a politician and one of the early Nigerian intellectuals. He was a foundation member of the Nigerian Youth Movement (q.v.) and its president from 1944 to 1951. In 1949 after the shooting incident in Enugu (q.v.) during which many miners were killed, many leading Nigerians formed the National Emergency Committee (q.v.) to investigate, report and see that justice was done. Dr. Maja was elected the committee's chairman. He was also a foundation member of the Egbe Omo Oduduwa (q.v.) and later became its president. He used to be referred to as

"Father" of the Action Group (AG) Party (q.v.), and when the AG crisis was brewing in 1962, he was called upon to intervene. He was also one of the founders of the National Bank of Nigeria (q.v.) in 1933, and later became the chairman of the board of directors of the bank.

MAJEKODUNMI, CHIEF MOSES ADEKOYEJO. Physician and politician, born August 17, 1916, at Abeokuta (q.v.), Ogun State (q.v.), he was educated at Abeokuta Grammar School, St. Gregory's College, Lagos (q.v.), Trinity College, Dublin, where he received a diploma in child health and master of obstetric art. He then became a house physician at the National Children's Hospital in Dublin from 1941 to 1943. Upon his return to Nigeria, he was appointed federal medical officer from 1943 to 1949 and then a consulting obstetrician at the Massey Street Maternity Hospital in Lagos, General Hospital in Lagos and Greek Hospital in Lagos from 1949 to 1960. He was also appointed a senior specialist obstetrician of the Nigerian Federal Government Medical Services.

In 1960 Dr. Majekodunmi became a senator and leader of the Senate (q.v.) in the First Republic (q.v.) and was appointed federal minister of state for the army, and in 1961 he was federal minister of health. During the Action Group crisis of 1962 (q.v.) in Western Nigeria, when a state of emergency was declared for the Western Region (q.v.), Dr. Majekodunmi was appointed administrator for Western Nigeria. In 1965 he was made the federal minister of health and information.

Dr. Majekodunmi was the former director of Barclays Bank of Nigeria, former director of the Westminster Dredging Company Limited and was appointed a member of the board of governors of St. Gregory's College in Lagos. He was a fellow of the Royal College of Obstetricians and Gynecologists and a fellow of the Royal College of Physicians. He was awarded many honorary degrees including LL.D. from the University of Dublin and D.Sc. from the University of Lagos. His foreign honours include Companion Order of St. Michael and St. George. He published many books, including *Premature Infants: Management and Prognosis.*

MALARIA FEVER. A disease caused by the bite of the Anopheles mosquito. The disease starts with a chill in which the patient's temperature may rise to about 40°C. The chill may be accompanied by a headache. After some hours, the patient will start to sweat profusely. The headache may then disappear, and the temperature may return to normal. But this does not mean it is over unless it is properly treated. The treatment is aimed at destroying the parasites in the blood of the patient by the use of drugs like Chloroquine, Quinine and such other drugs.

The lifecycle of the parasite begins when the mosquito bites an infested person. Malaria parasites enter the stomach of the mosquito as the blood from the bite does. If it bites a second person within seven to 14 days, some of the malaria parasites will enter the second person's blood stream. They make their way to the person's liver where they develop for about a week before returning to the bloodstream. The parasite grows in the red blood cells and multiplies. The fever begins about 14 days after the bite. The fever lasts for between 48 to 72 hours interval.

Before the discovery of quinine in 1854 and its variants, many people died of the disease in Nigeria and West Africa. It was one of the most dreaded diseases by white Europeans in West Africa. Because of the number of Europeans who died of the disease while exploring West Africa, Nigeria and other West African countries were called the "Whiteman's grave." Today the incidence of this disease has been greatly reduced. Drugs destroy the parasites in the blood or serve as prophylactics against the disease, even when bitten. Campaigns on environmental hygiene have also reduced the incidence of stagnant water where mosquitoes breed. Yet, the dread of the disease helped in no small way to discourage permanent white European settlement in Nigeria in contrast to many other places.

MALIKI, ALHAJI ABDUL. Born in 1914, he was the son of the Atta of Igvirra, a traditional ruler in the Kwara State (q.v.). He received his education at Katsina Training College and taught for some years at Okene Middle School, (1934–1935). In 1936 he was appointed supervisor of Native Authority Works. In 1939 he was provincial clerk in Katsina. In 1940 he became the chief officer of Igbirra Native Authority (q.v.) and also chairman of Okene Town Council. In 1950 he took a local government (q.v.) training course in Britain. On his arrival, he joined the Northern People's Congress (NPC) (q.v.) and became a member of the Northern Regional House of Assembly (q.v.), and in 1952 a member of the federal House of Representatives (q.v.). In 1955 he was appointed commissioner (q.v.) to the United Kingdom for Northern Nigeria (q.v.). In 1958 he joined the federal diplomatic service and, after independence, he became the first High Commissioner to the United Kingdom. In 1966 he was transferred to France as ambassador. He died in 1969 while on leave at home.

MANUWA, SIR SAMUEL LAYINKA AYODEJI. Born on March 4, 1903, in Ijebu-Ode, Ogun State (q.v.), he received his education at many schools including the Christian Missionary Society Grammar School and Kings College (q.v.), all in Lagos. After his secondary education in 1921, he went on to the University of Edinburgh to study medicine. In 1926 he went to the University of Liverpool, England, where he received a diploma in tropical medicine and hygiene. Upon arrival in Nigeria in 1927, he was appointed a medical officer and a senior surgical specialist. He served in many capacities and was a member of many scholarly associations. He served on the

Federal Public Service Commission (q.v.) and was pro-chancellor and chairman of the University Council of the University of Ibadan (q.v.), 1961 to 1975. He published many books including *Hernia in the West African Negro* (1929), *Mental Health in Commonwealth* (1967), and *Mass Campaign as an Instrument of Endemic Disease Control in Developing Countries*. He died in 1975.

MARIERE, CHIEF SAMUEL JERETON. The first governor of the Mid-Western Region (q.v.), Chief Samuel Jereton Mariere was born in 1907 at Evwreni, Urhobo Division of the Delta State (q.v.). He was educated at St. Andrew's School, Warri (q.v.). He then taught at the African School at Okpari, (1927–28). In 1929 he began to work for Mukoro Mowoe & Co., founded by Chief Mukoro Mowoe, a relation of his, where he stayed until 1938. He later joined the John Holt Company and stayed there until his retirement in 1961.

Chief Mariere was active in political activities as far back as the 1930s. He was a member of the Urhobo Progressive Union and became its secretary-general in 1935. He later joined the National Council of Nigeria and the Cameroons (NCNC) (q.v.). He was elected an NCNC member of the House of Representatives (q.v.) for Urhobo (q.v.) East in 1954 and later in 1959 for Urhobo Central. When the Mid-Western Region was created in 1963, he became its first governor. When the military seized power in 1966, he, like other governors, lost his job, but was later appointed adviser to the military governor. In 1968 he became the chancellor of the University of Lagos and also chairman, state school board, Mid-Western State (q.v.). He was honored with many traditional titles and was awarded an honorary LL.D. degree of the University of Nigeria, Nsukka (q.v.), and of the University of Ibadan, both in 1964. He died in 1971.

MARKETING BOARDS. Before the 1954 Federal Constitution (q.v.), marketing boards were organised on a nationwide basis. The Nigerian Cocoa Marketing Board was established by law in 1947, the Nigerian Groundnut (peanut) Marketing Board in 1949, the Nigerian Oil Palm Produce Marketing Board in 1949, and the Nigerian Cotton Marketing Board in 1954. These boards were set up to secure the most favourable arrangements for the purchase and exportation of agricultural produce. As such, they were placed in a monopolistic position since they had complete control of purchases of such agricultural export products. The Board fixed the buying prices at the beginning of each season. In the second place, they generally adopted different grades for the same products and paid different prices for each grade in order to improve the quality of the products. This system was much criticised because, while it stabilised prices of agricultural produce and so lessened the impact of price fluctuation on farmers, it nonetheless set and maintained producer prices throughout each season at a rate much below the world market prices and thus accumulated a lot of surpluses, which should have gone to the farmers but which never did. Under the 1954 Federal Constitution, agriculture became a regional matter and the purchase of agricultural produce was reorganised on a regional basis, leading to establishment of regional marketing boards and the division of the assets of the former boards among the regional boards. However, the export of crops was a federal matter and, therefore, there was then a Central Produce Marketing Board to export the crops purchased by the regional marketing boards.

In 1977 the military administration, in a reform effort, reverted to what had existed before the 1954 constitution. Seven new commodity marketing boards, each operating on a nationwide basis, were set up.

It should be noted that the surpluses generated by the purchase and exports of the produce were used by regional governments to finance regional development corporations to further agricultural and industrial development, and, as the Coker Commission of Inquiry (q.v.) showed, some of the surpluses indirectly found their way to party accounts. The marketing board system was abolished under the administration of General Ibrahim Babangida (q.v.).

MARKETS. In Nigeria a market is a place where sellers and buyers go to sell or buy. They both bargain over prices in an effort to maximise their gains and satisfaction. Nearly all Nigerian towns have their own marketplaces. The markets are generally of two types: the daily markets and the periodic markets. The daily markets are common in all parts of Nigeria, while the periodic markets are more common in Southern Nigeria. The periodic markets are either open every four, five or nine days, weekly or fortnightly. The commodities common in Nigerian marketplaces are assorted types of foodstuffs, meat, vegetables, clothes and various other goods ranging from provisions to cosmetics. The various crafts people use the market day to display or carry on their trade such as blacksmiths, bicycle repairers, tailors, sewing mistresses and tinkers. The essential difference between the market in a Southern town and in a Northern town is that both men and women are sellers of commodities in the south but in the north, men predominate. This may be explained by the fact that in the north, Muslim women are expected to stay in their *purdah*.There are other social activities that do take place in the Nigerian traditional markets, especially the periodic markets. They serve as centers of communication and information networks. Markets do provide opportunities for religious and ritual performances by people meeting on particular days and for political or other announcements by rulers and leaders. They also provide an opportunity for the exchange of views between friends and kinsmen from neighbouring villages and towns. Also, both males and females utilise the market day and marketplace as an opportunity for recruiting sexual partners.

MARKPRESS. Markpress, an abbreviation for Market Press, was the Biafran Overseas Press Service. It was Biafra's public relations firm based in Geneva to propagate the Biafran cause. The owner and director of Markpress was William Bernhardt, an American public relations expert. Though the first press release was made in February 1968, the effort was not successful until April, when the first organised group correspondents' reports about starvation in Biafra (q.v.) became a good propaganda issue.

The agency was linked by telex to Biafra via Lisbon, which was the main Biafran base and communications center. Markpress's success in selling Biafra to the world was due in part to the hard work and dedication of Bernhardt, who also served as a kind of roving ambassador for Biafra, attending the peace conferences and meeting important personalities.

MARWA, MUHAMMADU. A religious fanatic whose followers incited a number of violent disturbances in Northern Nigeria between 1980–85. Marwa, who was more popularly known by the alias "Maitatsine" (or "the one who scorns"), claimed to be the right and true prophet of Allah, a claim that orthodox Muslims considered to be heretical.

Marwa was a Cameroonian citizen who illegally immigrated to Kano (q.v.). In 1962, the Emir of Kano ordered him arrested and deported on the charge of disturbing the peace. By the 1970s, however, Marwa had returned to Kano and his unorthodox views began to attract a larger following. In December 1980, Maitatsine's followers (estimated to number 3,000) embarked on a series of vicious attacks on the citizens of Kano. Battles raged from December 18–29, paralysing the city. By the time the police had restored order, 4,000 people had been killed, including Muhammadu Marwa. Despite a presidential decree outlawing the movement in 1982, violent clashes involving the followers of Maitatsine continued up until 1985, most prominently in Kaduna (q.v.), Maiduguri and Yola (q.v.).

MASQUERADE. In many parts of Nigeria, masquerades are an important part of certain festivals. Masquerades supposedly call upon dead ancestors to periodically visit the living—who wear masks—to bless them. Hosting these returning ancestors is often a very colourful affair. Before the festival, the oracle (q.v.) must have been consulted to know the proper date to commence.

The identity of the person who wears the mask is a secret to women and young children because they have been taught to believe that all masquerades are ancestors who come up from the ground in communion with the living and go back into the ground at the end of the ceremonies held in their honour. As such, men are the most visible at the ceremonies except a few women believed to have soared so high in spirituality that the rituals and the person behind the mask are no longer secrets.

Among the Yoruba (q.v.), the period of the festival is usually seven days of traditional music, songs, incantations, dancing, eating and drinking.

Even though the festival is a yearly affair, certain masquerades may be consulted on special occasions, in times of emergency, or plague and may come out to perform necessary rituals to ward off the evil.

Many other ethnic groups in Nigeria also have masquerade festivals. For example, among the Ebirra people of Kogi State (q.v.), the Ekuechi festival is an important, popularly celebrated masquerade festival in the year.

MASS PURGE. The massive retirement of public officeholders during the second half of 1975 is known as the Mass Purge. The decision to purge the public services in the Federation (q.v.) of all undesirable elements was taken by the new military regime of Murtala R. Muhammed (q.v.) and Olusegun Obasanjo (q.v.) which overthrew the General Yakubu Gowon (q.v.) regime on July 29, 1975. The second day, new Head of State Brigadier Muhammed announced the compulsory retirement of all officers of the rank of general and the equivalent in other services, the military governors, the inspector general and the deputy inspector general of police. He also announced the dismissal of all federal and state civil commissioners (q.v.). The purge of other officers started on August 5, 1975, and it cut across various ranks, ranging from other senior army officers, senior public servants, including the chief justice of the Federation who was retired for health reasons, to junior staff all over the nation. Various criteria were used to decide the fate of those retired. These included divided interest (that is, public servants who still had their private businesses) old age, poor health, inefficiency, corruption, incompetence and confidential reports based on the public servants' records. Unfortunately, many people in power turned the whole exercise into a kind of witch-hunt and personal vendetta, and when the government saw that the purposes of the purge were being abused, it was called to a halt, but not until about 10,000 public officers had been retired or dismissed.

While the purge had its salutary effects, it nonetheless undermined the sense of security which had hitherto characterised seeking a career in the public services and it disposed any public servant to begin to look out for a greater sense of security for himself and his family. Some left the services, some of those who remained saw the period of service as a period to make as much money as possible and get out to start their own businesses, while some others continued their private businesses pari passu with their public services at the expense of the latter. Thus, rather than reduce indiscipline and corruption in the public services, it appears to have increased them.

This corruption and indiscipline had a field day during the civilian administration that succeeded the military in October 1979. And when the military intervened again in December 1983, there were calls that many public officials should be investigated and retired, especially for the role many of them played in the general elections of 1983. The new military administration began a slow and quiet retrenchment of public officers, including teachers.

MBADIWE, DR. KINGSLEY OZUMBA. A politician, administrator and businessman, born March 15, 1917, at Orlu, Imo State (q.v.), he attended St. Mary's Catholic School in Aba, Hope Waddel Training Institute in Calabar (q.v.), Aggrey Memorial College in Arochukwu and Igbobi College in Lagos (q.v.). He later went to Lincoln University in the United States of America in 1939 and later to the Business College at Columbia University and New York University. In 1936 he founded the *Daily Telegraph* newspaper in Lagos, and in 1937 he was a representative of Dr. Nnamdi Azikiwe's (q.v.) *West African Pilot* for Port Harcourt (q.v.), Aba, and Onitsha (q.v.). He was also the founder of Greater Tomorrow Transport Company. He lead the "Operation Fantastic" Atilogwu Dancers to the World Fair in New York City in 1964. He was also founder of the African Academy of Arts and Research.

Dr. Mbadiwe's political career started in 1941 when he was a founding member of the African Students' Association of the United States and Canada (q.v.) and in 1945 became the first president of the African Students Union in the United States. In 1958 he founded the unregistered Democratic Party of Nigeria and Cameroons (DPNC) (q.v.). He was a great nationalist, and it was he who stated that Nigeria's twin goal was self-government and independence, and a united Nigeria. He was one of the members of the 1950 and 1957 constitutional conferences (q.v.), a member of the 1978 Constitution Drafting Committee (q.v.) and later of the Constituent Assembly (q.v.). In 1951 he represented Orlu in the then-Eastern House of Assembly (q.v.) and became a member of the federal Parliament and minister of land and industries in 1952. In 1963 he became adviser on African affairs to prime minister Alhaji Tafawa Balewa (q.v.). In 1979 he joined the National Party of Nigeria (NPN) (q.v.) and in 1983 was President Shagari's ambassador extraordinary. He died in 1990.

MBAKWE, SAMUEL ONUNAKA. Born in 1926 at Avuta, Etiti, in Imo State (q.v.), he attended Fourah Bay College (q.v.) in Sierra Leone (q.v.) from 1952 to 1953, Manchester University from 1953 to 1956 and Hull University from 1956 to 1959. He obtained his B.A. in 1956 and LL.B. (London) in 1959 and became a legal practitioner.

In 1977 he represented Etiti Local Government (q.v.) area at the Constituent Assembly (q.v.), and in 1979 he became the first executive governor of

Imo State under the platform of the Nigerian Peoples Party (q.v.). When the army came back to power in 1983, he was sentenced to 10 years imprisonment by the Exchange Control (Anti-Sabotage) Tribunal (q.v.). In July 1986, he was released from jail. When the government of President Ibrahim B. Babangida (q.v.) imposed two parties on Nigeria, the Social Democratic Party (SDP) (q.v.) and the National Republican Convention (q.v.), Mbakwe joined the SDP and worked hard for his party's presidential flag bearer, Chief M.K.O. Abiola (q.v.). In 1994 he became a member of the National Constitutional Conference (q.v.) set up by General Sani Abacha (q.v.).

MBANEFO, SIR LOUIS NWACHUKWU. A jurist born in 1911, he went to St. Mary's School in Onitsha (q.v.), the Methodist Grammar School and later to King's College (q.v.), both in Lagos (q.v.). In 1935 he obtained a bachelor of law degree from the University of London and was called to the bar at the Middle Temple. He then went to King's College, Cambridge where he got a B.A. in history, followed by an M.A. in 1937.

Upon return to Nigeria, he set up his law practice in Onitsha. In 1939 he became a member of the Onitsha Town Council (q.v.). In 1950 he was a member of the Eastern House of Assembly (q.v.) and represented the Eastern Region (q.v.) at the Legislative Council (q.v.) in Lagos in 1950 and 1951. In 1952 he was appointed judge of the Supreme Court (q.v.), and in 1956, following the regionalisation of the judiciary (q.v.) consequent on the adoption of a federal constitution (q.v.) in 1954, he became a judge of the federal High Court (q.v.) of Eastern Nigeria. In 1958 he was transferred to Lagos as a judge of the federal Supreme Court of Appeal (q.v.), but he went back to the East in 1959 as the chief justice of the region. In 1961 he was appointed an ad hoc judge of the International Court of Justice.

In addition to his services on the bench, he was appointed to many important positions. In 1946 his hard work and devotion to the Anglican Church (q.v.) earned him recognition, and he was made the chancellor of the Anglican Diocese of the Niger. He was pro-chancellor of the University of Ibadan (q.v.), 1965–67, chairman of the board of governors of Iyi Enu Hospital in Ogidi, Anambra State (q.v.), and, during the Biafran Civil War (q.v.), he represented Biafra on several trips abroad, including the meeting in Kampala (q.v.), Uganda, in 1968. In 1970 he took part in the formal surrender of Biafran soldiers to the federal government in Lagos. He was knighted in 1961 by Queen Elizabeth II, and in 1963 he received an honorary degree of doctor of laws from the University of Nigeria, Nsukka (q.v.). In 1972 he was made a fellow of the University of London. He died in 1977.

MBU, MATTHEW TAIWO. A lawyer, politician and diplomat born November 20, 1929, at Okundi Village in Ogoja Division of Cross River State (q.v.), he attended the Catholic School at Okundi and received postal tuition from

Wolsey Hall, Oxford University and Middle Temple Inns Court, London, and was called to the bar in 1960. He was a member of the Eastern Regional House of Assembly (q.v.) in 1952 as a member of the National Council of Nigeria and the Cameroons (NCNC) (q.v.). From 1953 to 1954, he was one of the people who represented the Eastern Region (q.v.) in the House of Representatives (q.v.) in Lagos (q.v.), where he became minister of labour, and in 1959 after the pre-independence election, minister for the navy. In 1955 he became the first Nigerian High Commissioner to the United Kingdom and in 1959 the first Nigerian chief representative to Washington, D.C. In addition, he has represented Nigeria in many international bodies and conferences. Returning home after service abroad, he was chairman of the Eastern Nigeria Public Service Commission (q.v.) from 1966 to 1967, member of the Constituent Assembly (q.v.) from 1977 to 1978 and pro-chancellor and chairman of Council at the University of Ife (q.v.) (now Obafemi Awolowo University) from 1980 to 1984. He has been chairman and director of many private companies. He received an honorary doctor of laws degree from the University of Ibadan (q.v.) and has many traditional chieftaincy titles.

MEDICAL RESEARCH COUNCIL OF NIGERIA. Established by the federal military government under Decree No. 1 of 1972 as a statutory body to take over the functions hitherto performed by the West African Council for Medical Research in Nigeria, it was inaugurated on January 26, 1973. The council has the duty of advising on, promoting, supervising and coordinating research in the medical sciences, and it is under the general surveillance of the Nigerian Council for Science and Technology (q.v.). The objectives of the council include: the promotion of research programmes, which are designed to solve important health problems confronting the people of Nigeria; the promotion of simple clinical research in hospitals, health centres and dispensaries and of special research projects in well-equipped laboratories.

MEDICINE, TRADITIONAL. In many parts of Nigeria, as it is in many parts of Africa, people have believed and still believe that diseases, injuries, misfortunes, failures in one's enterprise have not only physical and natural causes but also are a result of some spiritual forces. These spiritual forces may have come as a kind of punishment from God or from the spirit of an ancestor or even sent by some other person(s) to harm them. Accidents, the inability to have children or some other misfortunes may be seen as the work of the enemy through witchcraft. Even in some Christian churches, protection from "the enemy" or "powers and principalities" is taken seriously.

To free oneself from such forces, a patient goes to a healer, who often may be a traditional priest who will not only understand the physical causes of the illness or problem, but who also can explain why God or some other spirit is sent to molest the patient. The healer/priest will then tell the patient how to get rid of the misfortune by taking some medicines or another concoction and/or offering sacrifices of chickens, goats or food.

When a person believes that an illness is caused by witchcraft, the healer must find out the sources of the witchcraft and appease the source. The healer must have all relevant information about possible enemies or people who may have sent the witchcraft to his patient. This is often done through divination (q.v.). To heal, a healer must have a good knowledge of herbs and their combination. He must also have a good knowledge of what we now know as psychology and psychiatry.

MELLANBY, DR. KENNETH. The first principal of Ibadan University College. Appointed in May 1947, he worked hard to settle the college in its permanent site within a short time and saw to the rapid academic and physical development of the institution. A hall of residence at the university was named in his honour. He left the institution in 1960.

MEMORANDUM ON EDUCATION POLICY IN BRITISH TROPICAL AFRICA. As a result of the 1922 Phelps-Stokes Commission (q.v.) Report entitled *Education in Africa,* the British government felt it had to do something about the criticisms levelled against colonial government education policy. The colonial office in London, therefore, set up an advisory committee on native education in the British tropical African dependencies in 1923 to advise the secretary of state on matters of native education. As a result of this, the government in 1925 issued its education policy contained in the *Memorandum on Education Policy in British Tropical Africa.* Requirements of the policy include the following: government would encourage voluntary educational efforts, but it reserved to itself the right to direct education policy and supervise educational institutions by inspection and other means; education should be adapted to the aptitudes, occupations and traditions of the people while conserving as far as possible all sound and healthy elements in the social life of the people; religious training and moral instruction should be related to the condition of life and the daily experience of the people; there should be set up in each dependency an advisory board on education to advise the government; voluntary agency schools which conform to the standard laid down should be grant-aided and teacher training institutions should be guided by the provision of the memorandum; and technical and vocational training should also be carried out with the help of government department and supervision.

The memorandum, in short, accepted the report of the Phelps-Stokes Commission and tried to adopt it.

METHODIST CHURCH. Methodist missionaries were the first to reach Badagry (q.v.) in 1842, setting up a mission house there. They were also the first to set up a western-type school by the name of Nursery of the Infant Church, after the slave trade (q.v.) had virtually wiped out the initial efforts of the Catholic Church (q.v.) in the kingdom of Benin (q.v.) in the early 16th century. From Badagry, Methodism spread all over the country.

MIDDLE-BELT PEOPLES PARTY. A splinter party from the Middle Zone League (MZL) (q.v.). The MBPP was formed in 1953 in opposition to the decision of the MZL to ally itself with the Northern People's Congress (q.v.), which was the ruling party in the north. The MBPP demanded the creation of a Middle Belt State in the Northern Region (q.v.). *See also* MIDDLE-BELT STATE MOVEMENT.

MIDDLE-BELT STATE MOVEMENT. In 1955 there was a movement, led by the late Joseph S. Tarka (q.v.), leader of United Middle Belt Congress, an ally of the Action Group Party (q.v.), demanding the creation of the Middle-Belt State out of the former Northern Region (q.v.). The state was to comprise all the minority groups of Northern Nigeria, an area which was made up of the Benue (q.v.), Plateau (q.v.) and Kwara states (q.v.). The Northern People's Congress (q.v.), which was in power in the north with the motto of "One north irrespective of tribes or religion," was opposed to this idea. But in 1967, during the military administration, their wish came true: the Benue Plateau Area was created as a state and so was Kwara Area. In 1976 Benue-Plateau State was further split into Benue State and Plateau State.

MIDDLE ZONE LEAGUE. A broad-based ethnic minority movement in the Northern Region (q.v.). It was formed in 1950 to fight for the creation of a separate region from the Northern Region (q.v.).

MID-WEST DEMOCRATIC FRONT. An alliance made up of the Mid-West People's Party, a branch of the Northern People's Congress (NPC) (q.v.), the regional branches of the United People's Party (q.v.) and the Action Group Party (q.v.). The MDF can be regarded as containing all the elements in the newly created region who were opposed to the National Council of Nigerian Citizens (NCNC) (q.v.) and struggling for political life.

In the 1964 Mid-Western election, the parties did not field common candidates. By fielding separate candidates, each of the parties became very weak, and they all lost badly to the NCNC, winning 11 out of the 65 seats. In the realignment for the 1964 federal elections, the Front joined the Nigerian National Alliance (NNA) (q.v.), made up of the NPC and the Nigerian National Democratic Party (NNDP) (q.v.) of Chief S.A. Akintola (q.v.) in the Western Region (q.v.). In April 1965, almost all the members of the MDF crossed to the NCNC, the government party in the region, and the leader of the carpet-crossers (q.v.) announced the formal dissolution of the MDF.

In 1966, after the military takeover of government, the party was banned along with all other political parties.

MID-WESTERN REGION. The Mid-Western Region is the name given to the first region created after independence. The region was originally part of the Western Region (q.v.) and while the Action Group Party (q.v.) controlled the politics of the region, the National Council of Nigerian Citizens (NCNC) had a lot of support in the Mid-west. The people of the Mid-west, being minorities in the Western Region had always made their intentions known to regional and federal governments that they wanted a region of their own, but it was not until the Action Group crisis of 1962 (q.v.) that they had their opportunity to get their own government. On August 9, 1963, the region was created. In 1967 when the 12-state structure came into being, the state became Mid-Western State and in 1976 when seven new states were created, it became the Bendel State, with minor boundary adjustments. In 1991 Bendel State was divided into two states—Edo and Delta States (qq.v.).

The Mid-Western Region had an area of about 15,244 square kilometres with a 1961 census of about 2,536,000 people. The regional capital was Benin City with a population well over 200,000 people in 1961. Benin (q.v.) is well known for its bronze, brass and ivory works of art which visitors can always see in museums (q.v.) all over the world.

The Mid-Western Region produced most of Nigeria's lump and crepe rubber (q.v.) and supplied much of the country's timber. What is more, it supplies about 40 percent of Nigeria's crude oil (q.v.). The Mid-west area is fairly well endowed with natural resources including natural gas and limestone. The region is made up of five main ethnic groups: the Edo (q.v.), the Ishan (q.v.), the Urhobo (q.v.), the Igbo (q.v.) and the Itsekiri (q.v.). *See also* BENDEL STATE.

MID-WESTERN STATE. *See* BENDEL STATE.

MID-WEST PEOPLE'S CONGRESS. A political party formed in 1963. It was a branch of the Northern People's Congress (NPC) (q.v.) in the Mid-Western Region (q.v.). After cracks in the coalition between the NPC and the National Council of Nigerian Citizens (q.v.) began to show, the NPC, in an effort to establish itself as a national party and extend its political support, decided to establish branches in the other regions of the country. The MPC was led by Apostle John Edokpolo who was then the commissioner of trade and industries in the Mid-western interim government.

MID-WEST STATE MOVEMENT. An ethnic minority movement formed in 1956 under the leadership of Chief Dennis Osadebay (q.v.), the leader of opposition in the Western House of Assembly (q.v.), its aim was to see that the Mid-Western Region (q.v.) was created. Being led by members of the National Council of Nigeria and the Cameroons (NCNC) (q.v.), it soon became a part of the NCNC and was later absorbed by it. The Mid-Western Region was eventually created in 1963.

MIGRATION. Population migration is the movement of people in and out of a country within a specific period of time. Within the country there is the usual rural-urban migration. Because of wage-earning employment and availability of many social services in the cities, people—young and old—do move from the rural areas of the country to the urban centres. Some of them look for employment, while others start small trading businesses. This type of migration accounts for the rapid growth rate of cities like Lagos (q.v.), Ibadan (q.v.), Kaduna (q.v.), Port Harcourt (q.v.) and Enugu (q.v.).

Migration outside the country rose in the 1950s when some Nigerians emigrated to Ghana (q.v.) to work in the gold mines. Because of Ghana's prosperity at the time, migration between Nigeria and Ghana was one way. Also some Nigerians went to Equatorial Guinea to work, and many became successful there. However, most of the citizens of West African countries living and working in Ghana in 1969 were ordered out of the country in that year during the rule of Dr. Kofi Busia.

In the latter part of the 1970s, the trend in migration changed. As a result of the oil boom in Nigeria and following the Economic Community of West African States (ECOWAS) (q.v.) Treaty, which eliminated the need to obtain a visa before a citizen of a member country could travel to another member country, many immigrants from neighbouring countries came to Nigeria in search of work—in construction companies, schools (as teachers) and in many other establishments. In 1982 the Federal Government (q.v.) saw the need to stem the tide, and it ordered illegal aliens to leave the country. Most of them left, but many of them, taking advantage of the ECOWAS Treaty and corrupt custom officials, returned.

MILITARY COUP. *See* COUP D'ETAT.

MILVERTON, LORD (SIR ARTHUR RICHARDS). A distinguished public servant and governor of Nigeria from 1943 to 1947. Born on February 21, 1885, in England, he served in many posts in the Federated Malay States before he became governor of Borneo in 1930. He also served as governor of the Gambia (1933–36), governor of Fiji and high commissioner for the Western Pacific (1936–38) and governor of Jamaica (1938–44). He became governor of Nigeria in 1943.

As governor of Nigeria, he succeeded Sir Bernard Bourdillon (q.v.), who, before his retirement, had laid the groundwork for the review of the 1922 constitution (q.v.) and had tried to persuade the people in the north to begin to take an active part in the affairs of the country. Sir Arthur Richards built upon the work of his predecessor by redrafting his constitution. In 1944 Richards's constitutional proposals were submitted to the secretary of state for the colonies, Colonel Oliver Stanley, without consulting public opinion or letting people know what he was planning. His objective was to draw up a constitution that would promote the unity of Nigeria, provide adequately for the diverse elements within the country and secure greater participation by Africans in the discussion of their own affairs. He recommended that the constitution remain in force for nine years subject to a limited review every three years.

The constitution went into effect in 1947. For the first time it provided for an unofficial majority in the Legislative Council (q.v.) and set up three regional councils for each of the three regions—the northern, eastern, and western provinces (q.v.)—each also having a majority of unofficial members.

The constitution, though an advance over previous ones, provoked much criticism. Sir Arthur Richards retired in 1947 to be succeeded by Sir John Macpherson (q.v.), who immediately upon arrival began measures to review the Richards Constitution.

MINERAL RESOURCES. Nigeria is rich in such mineral resources as limestone, tin, columbite, iron ore, lead, zinc, gold, marble, coal, petroleum, natural gas and uranium. Some of these are mined and are fairly well developed, but some others, like uranium, have still not been developed.

MINISTRY OF OVERSEAS DEVELOPMENT. The Ministry of Overseas Development was a ministerial department in the British government. The ministry, on behalf of the British government, was one of the overseas agencies that helped the Nigerian universities during the first six years of independence.

The ministry, through the London University, supplied a number of lecturers in the main branches of science, physics, chemistry, zoology, botany and biology. The program was called VISTA (Visiting Scientists Teaching Abroad).

MINORITIES COMMISSION. *See* MINORITIES PROBLEM.

MINORITIES PROBLEM. Each of the three former regions of Nigeria had its own share of ethnic minorities. The minorities in each region formed themselves into movements, agitating for constitutional safeguards against oppression from the larger ethnic groups that dominated the affairs of each region. For example, the Edo (q.v.), Urhobo (q.v.) and the Western Igbo (q.v.) agitated for the creation of the Mid-Western State (q.v.) from the Western Region (q.v.), while the peoples of the Calabar (q.v.), Ogoja and Rivers area asked for Calabar-Ogoja-Rivers State (COR State) (q.v.) to be created from the Eastern Region (q.v.). In the Northern Region (q.v.), the peoples of the Middle Belt made up of Niger, Ilorin, Kabba and Plateau provinces, with parts of Adamawa (q.v.) and Zaria (q.v.) provinces, also asked for a separate existence from the Northern Region.

The minorities problem became a major political problem when it became clear that Nigeria was going to adopt a federal system of government. Since each region was dominated by one ethnic group which in turn controlled the dominant party in that region, the minorities began to feel that if they were to avoid oppression they had better ask for their own separate existence. The issue became very important between 1954, when Nigeria became a federation (q.v.), and the 1957 Constitutional Conference (q.v.) in London. The conference devoted much attention to the problem and finally agreed on setting up a commission of inquiry to ascertain the facts about the fears of minorities in any part of the country and to propose means of allaying those fears as to whether or not they were well founded. However, the British government made it clear that recommendations for the creation of new states before independence should be seen as a last resort. Accordingly, on September 26, 1957, the Minorities Commission was set up and it later held hearings throughout the country.

Reactions to minorities demands were mixed in the regions. The north refused any fragmentation or adjustment of any boundaries. While the west supported the creation of the Mid-Western State, it contended that such an exercise could be carried out if other regions would comply. The east was opposed to any dismemberment as a sacrifice either for the sake of national unity or for administrative convenience. The commission's report was published in July 1958. It did not recommend the creation of new states, but recommended some palliative measures to allay the fears which it found really existed in many places. For example, it recommended that certain councils should be set up for minority areas of Calabar and Benin (q.v.) and that the Niger Delta Development Board (q.v.) be established for the area. It also recommended the inclusion of fundamental human rights (q.v.) in the federal constitution to protect and safeguard the interests of both the minorities and the majorities.

Even though the commission did not recommend the creation of any state, in 1963 the people of Benin and the Delta provinces succeeded in securing their own region called the Mid-Western region (q.v.). In 1967 the administration of General Yakubu Gowon (q.v.) decided in an effort: (1) to resolve the minorities problem, (2) to allay the fear of northern domination of the rest of the country and (3) to weaken the Eastern Region—should that region declare a secession from the rest of the country—to divide the country into 12 states. However, the 1967 state creation (q.v.) did not end all minorities' agitation for their own states, and in 1976 Nigeria became a federation (q.v.) of 19 states under the regime of General Murtala R. Muhammed (q.v.). In spite of this, agitation for more states continued. In 1991 Nigeria, under the administration of General Ibrahim B. Babangida (q.v.) became a federation of 30 states. In 1996, the Abacha regime increased the number to 36 states. From the foregoing, it is clear that state creation is not an adequate solution to the minorities problem. Until justice, fair play and an accountable government that will distribute the nation's resources equitably among the over 250 ethnic groups, minorities problem will continue to plague Nigeria.

These problems are especially acute in the area of the Niger Delta, where indigenous groups have become increasingly active in the 1990s, demanding a larger share of the oil revenues derived from their region.

MONGUNO, SHETTIMA ALI. Born in Monguno, Borno State (q.v.), in 1926, he attended Monguno Elementary School, Borno Middle School and Bauchi Teacher Training College. He also attended Katsina Higher College and the Nigerian College of Arts, Science and Technology (q.v.) in Zaria (q.v.). In 1958 he went to the College of Education, Moray House, Edinburgh and to Edinburgh University.

On his return to Nigeria he became education secretary to the Borno Local Authority. He later became chairman of the education committee of Borno Local Education Authority. In 1959 he became a member of Parliament (q.v.) in Lagos (q.v.) and a member of the Northern People's Congress (q.v.). He was appointed minister of state for the air force (q.v.) in 1965 and later became minister for internal affairs in 1965.

When the military came to power and began to appoint civil commissioners (q.v.) in 1967, he was appointed commissioner for industry and commissioner for trade in the same year and of mines and power in 1971 until 1975. He was a member of the Constituent Assembly (q.v.) from 1977 to 1978.

MOREL, EDMUND DERE. A journalist, born in 1873 in Paris, France. He later became interested in West Africa, read about it and later wrote about it. In 1911 he wrote a book, *Nigeria, Its Peoples and Its Problems,* in which he proposed what he called "an unauthorized scheme of amalgamation" of the northern and the southern protectorates (q.v.). He proposed that the country should be divided into provinces corresponding as far as possible with natural geographical boundaries and existing political conditions. He, therefore, suggested that the country should be divided into four provinces. According to him, the Niger (q.v.) and Benue (q.v.) Rivers were to be the natural boundaries of the Western and Eastern provinces from a third province, which roughly corresponded to the old Middle Belt and which he called Central Province. The remaining part of the country was to be the Northern Province. Each province was to be headed by a lieutenant governor. His objective was to put an end to the north-south dichotomy and open the landlocked north to the sea through the two rivers. His proposals were not accepted, but they certainly gave an impetus to the demand for a separate region for the Middle-Belt Area in the 1950s.

MOREMI. Said by Ife tradition to be the saviour of her people against the incessant attack by the Igbo (q.v.). When Ife Kingdom was being harassed and attacked, Moremi allowed herself to be captured by the Igbo people. Being a very beautiful woman, she became a favorite of the Igbo ruler who, in an unguarded moment, revealed the secret of his warriors against Ile-Ife (q.v.). According to him, the warriors were ordinary men disguised in raffia. Moremi later escaped and told her people the secret. When next they were attacked, the Ife set fire to their raffia clothing and burned them up. Moremi later sacrificed her son to the gods for her success. There is a festival in honour of Moremi in Ile-Ife, and many places are named after her.

MORGAN COMMISSION OF INQUIRY. The Morgan Commission, headed by Justice Adeyinka Morgan, was set up in 1963 as a result of an industrial strike embarked upon by Nigerian workers on September 27, 1963, agitating for a general upward revision of wages and salaries of junior civil servants as well as junior employees in private establishments. The commission was asked to investigate the existing wage structure, remuneration and conditions of service in wage-earning employments in the country and to make recommendations concerning a suitable new structure, as well as adequate machinery for a wage review on a continuing basis. It was also to examine the need for a general upward revision of salaries and wages of junior employees in both government and private establishments, the abolition of the daily wage system, the introduction of a national minimum wage and to make recommendations on all these problems.

Because of the government's delay in releasing the report, workers staged a demonstration in Lagos (q.v.) on June 1, 1964, followed by a general strike on the second day. On June 3, 1964, the government released the report and the government white paper on it. The commission recommended that the workers be paid a living wage, that is, wages high enough to enable them to support themselves and their families. The commission then divided the country into four zones and recommended a minimum wage for each one. The government accepted the recommendations with some modifications.

MOVEMENT FOR THE SURVIVAL OF THE OGONI PEOPLE (MOSOP). Founded in 1992 under the leadership of Ken Saro-Wiwa (q.v.), an author of international acclaim, MOSOP's aim was to turn government attention to the plight of the Ogoni people. Most of their land had badly deteriorated, and their water and air were polluted due to Shell Oil Company's exploration and exploitation of Nigerian oil (q.v.). The organisation campaigned for a greater share of federal revenue and greater autonomy and control over their affairs, including cultural, religious and environmental matters. In 1993 the organisation targeted its campaign on the Shell Oil Company, asking the company to compensate them for the environmental pollution caused in their land during a period of about four decades. After this, Ken Saro-Wiwa and the organisation came under continual military harassment, and in the same year, the military government moved forcefully against their protests. The government soon succeeded in dividing the organisation into those it regarded as willing to negotiate and those who were not. The division soon led to violent confrontations, exemplified by the killing of four of their leaders regarded as pro-government. Ken Saro-Wiwa and eight other leaders were arrested for murder, secretly tried by a military tribunal, found guilty and sentenced to death by hanging. The execution was carried out in November 1995 and was condemned nationally and internationally, leading to the suspension of Nigeria from the Commonwealth (q.v.) and the imposition of sanctions on the Nigerian military by the United States, Canada, several European countries, South Africa and many other nations. After the killing of Saro-Wiwa and his colleagues, it became clear that MOSOP could no longer operate freely under such oppressive control.

MUHAMMED, GEN. MURTALA RAMAT. Former Head of State, born on November 8, 1938, in Kano (q.v.), Murtala Muhammed was educated at Gidan Makama Primary School in Kano and at the Government College in Zaria (q.v.). He enlisted in the Nigerian Army in 1957 and was later sent to Sandhurst Royal Military Academy in Britain for training. He returned to Nigeria in 1961 as a commissioned second lieutenant and was posted to the Army Signals. He later served with the United Nations Peacekeeping forces in the Congo. On his return in 1962, he was appointed aide-de-camp to the administrator of Western Nigeria (q.v.) during the period of emergency in that region. In 1963 he was made officer-in-charge of the First Brigade Signal Troop in Kaduna (q.v.) and went to the School of Signals in Catterick, England for a course on advanced telecommunications techniques. In 1964 he was promoted to major, and in 1965 he became acting chief signals officer of the army. When the military took over in 1966, and under General Aguiyi-Ironsi (q.v.) he became a lieutenant colonel. He took active part in the 1966 July coup (q.v.) that brought General Yakubu Gowon (q.v.) to power.

In August 1967, when the Biafrans came within 70 miles of Lagos (q.v.), the Federal Government (q.v.) hastily raised a new second division and appointed him as its commanding officer. He pushed the Biafrans back toward the east and retook Benin on September 20. Here he broadcast his message of liberation of the Mid-West State (q.v.), appointing Major Samuel Ogbemudia the military administrator. He captured Asaba on the Niger River (q.v.) but was blocked by the retreating Biafrans who blew up the Niger bridge. After three costly attempts to cross the river by boat, he turned north, crossed at Lokoja (q.v.), which was firmly in federal hands, and began to advance down the river on the Biafran side, capturing Onitsha (q.v.) in March 1968.

He was appointed inspector of the Nigerian Army Signals in April 1968 and came down to Lagos to assume the new office. He was promoted to brigadier in October 1971 and became the federal commissioner (q.v.) for communications in August 1974.

Following the coup that ousted General Yakubu Gowon on July 29, 1975, Muhammed became the Head of State and Commander-in-Chief of the Nigerian armed forces (q.v.). As the new Head of State, he said that the nation for too long had been groping in the dark and the situation would lead to chaos and bloodshed if not arrested. He accused the Gowon administration of indecision and indiscipline. He instituted mass retirement and dismissal of about 10,000 public officials, including people in the armed forces, civil service, parastatals, universities and even the judiciary (q.v.), for incompetence, old age and corruption. He outlined a political program to hand over power to an elected civilian government. This included the creation of seven more states in February 1976, the drafting of a new constitution (q.v.) and the reform of local governments (q.v.) and the organisation of national elections to pave the way for a civilian administration in 1979. He decided on moving the capital of the country from Lagos to Abuja (q.v.), which is more central to the people of the nation. On the international plane, he recognized the MPLA government of Angola, and stated that Nigeria would no longer take orders from any country, no matter how powerful.

He was a simple man, beloved by most people, though not all, for he was ambushed and assassinated on February 13, 1976, during the abortive coup organised by Lt. Col. Dimka (q.v.). Today he is one of the Nigerian heroes. In order to immortalise his name, many places and institutions are named after him, including the International Airport at Ikeja (q.v.), Lagos. His portrait is also placed on Nigeria's 20 naira currency (q.v.) note. He was succeeded by General Olusegun Obasanjo (q.v.).

MUSA, ALHAJI ABUBAKAR BALARABE. A chartered accountant, politician and ex-governor of Kaduna State (q.v.), he was the first governor under the 1979 constitution (q.v.) to be successfully impeached. Born on August 21, 1936, in Kaya, Kaduna State he was educated at Zaria Middle School, the Institute of Administration in Zaria (q.v.) and at various colleges in London. In 1978 he joined the People's Redemption Party (q.v.) and was elected governor of Kaduna State. With the National Party of Nigeria (q.v.) controlling more than two-thirds of the majority in the state Legislative Assembly (q.v.), disagreement between him and the house on ideology and policy soon arose, but because of his uncompromising attitude, various charges were proferred against him in the house, and he was later, in 1981, impeached. He was succeeded by the deputy governor Alhaji M.A. Rimi (q.v.). In the country's march to the Third Republic (q.v.), Alhaji Musa joined the Social Democratic (q.v.) Party, one of the two parties the Babangida (q.v.) administration founded in 1989.

MUSEUMS. Established in 1957 and situated in Lagos (q.v.), the National Museum contains some of the finest collections of Nigerian art anywhere in the world. Other museums established by the Department of Antiquity include: the Ife Museum, established in 1954; Owo and Esie museums, opened in 1945; the Jos Museum, opened in 1952; Oron Museum, opened in 1958; Kano Museum, opened in 1960; Kaduna Museum, established in 1972 and the Benin Museum, opened in 1973. There is also the Museum of Natural History at the University of Ife (q.v.) (now Obafemi Awolowo University). All these museums, perhaps the richest in sculptural art and tradition, offer great attraction to tourists visiting the country.

MUSIC, HIGHLIFE. The saying that music as an art knows no territorial boundaries is very true of the highlife music that came to Nigeria through E.T. Mensah, a Ghanaian who worked hard to popularise it. The music itself is a merger of local African music, Black American dance music, Christian hymns and regimental band music. In Nigeria in the 1950s and 1960s, it was popularised by many artists like the late Paul Isamada, Eric Onugha, Eddie Okonta, Victor Olaiya and Roy Chicago (John Akintola)—who introduced Yoruba talking drum into the highlife music—and many others. Highlife music has been played in various ceremonies including marriage festivals, funerals and chieftaincy and coronation ceremonies.

MUSIC, JUJU. The origin of Juju music is not clear, but it is generally agreed that it comes from Western Nigeria and most probably from the Lagos (q.v.) area. Juju music is basically Yoruba (q.v.), which, starting with a small band of musical instruments, has grown into high-tech international music today. Some have said that Juju music was popularised by Tunde Nightingale in the early 1940s, but it was I.K. Dairo, popularly regarded as the Father of Juju music, who in the 1950s brought Juju music into its present modern form. Today famous and notable Juju musicians are Ebenezer Obey, Sunny Ade and Segun Adewale.

MUSLIMS. *See* ISLAM.

MUSTAPHA, ALHAJI MUHAMMED. Leader of the People's Redemption Party (PRP) (q.v.) in the House of Representatives (q.v.) under the second Republican Constitution (q.v.). Born in 1939 at Zanguza Village, Kano (q.v.), he had his early education at Islamiya Primary School in Zaria (q.v.) from 1949 to 1955 and his secondary education at West African Collegiate School in Freetown (q.v.) Sierra Leone (q.v.), from 1955 to 1961. He then went to Durham University in England where he obtained a B.Sc. in economics in 1964. He also attended Fourah Bay College (q.v.) from 1968 to 1971, where he received a diploma in public administration. He served later as assistant registrar at the Ado Bayero University in Kano (q.v.). In 1977 he resigned to set up an economic consultancy company in Kano. He later joined the PRP and was elected to the House of Representatives (q.v.) and became the leader of the party in the house.

-N-

NASIR COMMISSION. After the creation of seven new states from the existing 12 on February 3, 1976, the government on February 12, 1976, set up a six-man boundary adjustment commission (q.v.) under Supreme Court (q.v.) justice Muhammadu Nasir. The commission examined the boundary adjustment problems identified by the Irikefe (q.v.) on the creation of states, specified which areas of Andoni and Nkoro in Opobo Division of the Cross River State (q.v.) should be in the Rivers State (q.v.) and which areas of Ndoni should form part of the Rivers State or the Imo State (q.v.). It identified and defined the boundaries of any other area, district or division that might be brought to the Commission, defined interstate boundaries (especially in cases where there were intergovernmental disputes) and made recommendations.

NASSARAWA STATE. Created out of Plateau State by the Abacha regime on October 1, 1996. Its capital is Lafia.

NATIONAL AFRICAN COMPANY. Formed in 1882, the NAC took over the assets of the United African Company (UAC) (q.v.) and carried out its work. Two years later, the company had signed many so-called treaties with traditional rulers on both banks of the Niger River (q.v.) up to Lokoja (q.v.). During the 1884–85 Berlin Conference (q.v.), the areas under the control of the NAC were recognised as under the British government. In 1886 the NAC was granted a charter and renamed the Royal Niger Company. *See also* ROYAL NIGER COMPANY.

NATIONAL ANTHEM. Within two decades of Nigeria's independence, the country had adopted two different national anthems.

The first one, composed by a British citizen, was adopted October 1, 1960, but it ceased to be in use in 1978. A verse of the former anthem reads thus:

Nigeria we hail thee,
Our own dear native land.
Though tribe and tongue may differ,
In brotherhood we stand,
Nigerians all are proud to serve,
Our sovereign motherland.

In 1977 the then-military government announced their intention to change the anthem, and a committee was appointed to look for ways of composing the new anthem. The committee came out with a competition open to all Nigerians to send in entries for the anthem lyrics. The committee selected five of the entries and synthesised them into the present anthem. The music departments of the universities of Lagos, Zaria and Nsukka were invited together with some renowned classical musicians to give suitable music to the anthem. The anthem goes thusly:

Arise, O compatriots,
Nigeria's call obey
To serve our fatherland
With love and strength and faith
The labor of our heroes past
Shall never be in vain
To serve with heart and might
One nation bound in freedom,
Peace and unity.
Oh God of creation,
Direct our noble cause
Guide our leaders right
Help our youth the truth to know
In love and honesty to grow
And living just and true
Great lofty heights attain

To build a nation where peace
And justice shall reign.

NATIONAL ASSEMBLY. The official name for the legislature in the Second Republic (1979–83), Third Republic, and the Fourth Republic (1999–). In the Second Republic (q.v.) it consisted of a Senate with 95 members, and a House of Representatives with 449 members. In the Third Republic (q.v.), a National Assembly was elected in 1992, but never allowed to exercise its constitutional powers due to the failure of the military to surrender power. It consisted of a Senate of 91 seats and a House of Representatives with 593 members. It was dissolved in November 1993. In the Fourth Republic, it consists of a Senate with 109 members and a House of Representatives with 360 members.

NATIONAL ASSOCIATION OF NIGERIAN STUDENTS. *See* NATIONAL UNION OF NIGERIAN STUDENTS.

NATIONAL BANK OF NIGERIA. Established in 1933 by Chief Akinola Maja (q.v.), T.A. Doherty and H.A. Subair to make loans more readily available to Nigerians than expatriate banks, which discriminated against Nigerians. By 1951 the bank had been officially recognised, and it was appointed an authorised dealer under the Exchange Control Regulation. It became the banker to the Cocoa Marketing Board (q.v.). In 1961, owing to the bank's financial difficulties, it was converted to an official bank of the Western Region (q.v.).

In 1976, when the Western State (q.v.) was divided into three states, the National Bank became a subsidiary of the Odu'a Investment Company, a holding company jointly owned by the three new states. The bank had branches in many parts of Nigeria with its headquarters in Lagos (q.v.). As a result of gross mismanagement, the bank became distressed toward the end of the 1980s and stopped functioning in the early 1990s.

NATIONAL CHURCH OF NIGERIA. Established in 1948, it likened Dr. Nnamdi Azikiwe (q.v.) to Christ. It was the religious wing of the Zikist Movement (q.v.), and membership of both were almost completely the same. But while the Zikist Movement expressed protest against the political aspects of colonial rule, the church expressed protest against white-dominated churches. The church was one of the nationalist instruments to awaken racial and national consciousness in the minds of Nigerians.

NATIONAL COMMISSION FOR REHABILITATION. Established in 1969 by the federal military government, it had the function of supplying food, clothing, drugs and other essentials to needy persons in areas affected by the Civil War (q.v.) and its aftermath. It was empowered to: determine priority for all emergency relief operations and rehabilitation work in all parts of the Federation (q.v.); coordinate the activities of voluntary agencies engaged in emergency relief operations and rehabilitation work; coordinate the activities of the states in the administration of properties abandoned by displaced persons in the Federation; collect food and drugs and other humane gifts from foreign governments and receive financial and technical aid through appropriate federal ministries. The commission was composed of the federal commissioner (q.v.) for rehabilitation, one member from each state, a member to represent each of the ministries of finance, economic development, health and labour and not more than six other members.

NATIONAL CONCILIATION COMMITTEE. After the September 1966 massacre of the Igbo (q.v.) in Northern Nigeria (q.v.) and the return of the people of Eastern Nigerian (q.v.) origin to the Eastern Region (q.v.) the gap between the Federal Government (q.v.), headed by General Yakubu Gowon (q.v.) (a leader unacceptable to Lt. Col. C.O. Ojukwu), and the Eastern Nigerian government, headed by Ojukwu began to widen. Ojukwu's government was moving inexorably to the secession of the east from the rest of the country, while the Gowon administration was determined to keep Nigeria united. Some people, including Chief Obafemi Awolowo (q.v.), Sir Adetokunbo A. Ademola (q.v.) (the then-chief justice of the federation [q.v.]), Chief S.J. Mariere (q.v.) the former governor of the Mid-west and the then-advisor to the military governor of the Mid-west), Professor Samuel Aluko, Sir Kashim Ibrahim (q.v.), Zana Bukar Suloma Dipcharima, Godfrey Amachree and some others, disheartened by events, decided to form a committee that would work to bring the two sides together again and look into the demands of all the regions with a view to making them work together in the same federation. At the first meeting of the committee, known later as the National Reconciliation Committee, things could not go very far because the Eastern Region was not represented. A committee, later known as the National Conciliation Committee, led by Chief Awolowo, was sent in May 1967 to Enugu (q.v.) for talks with Lt. Col. Odumegwu Ojukwu (q.v.) to persuade him to send delegates to the National Reconciliation Committee but it failed. The National Conciliation Committee was well received, however.

NATIONAL CONGRESS OF BRITISH WEST AFRICA. The National Congress of British West Africa was founded in 1917 in the Gold Coast (q.v.) by Caseley Hayford, a Gold Coast lawyer. It was composed mainly of Gold Coast intellectuals, but it had branches in all the British West African countries—Nigeria, Sierra Leone (q.v.), and the Gambia. Its main aim was to unite the four British West African colonies into a kind of a federation and put pressure on the British government to grant the colonies the right of self-determination. Its branch in Nigeria was critical of the composition and role of the Nigerian Council (q.v.), set up by Lord Lugard (q.v.) after the 1914 Amalgamation of Nigeria (q.v.).

At the inaugural conference of the congress, members adopted a number of resolutions which were subsequently embodied in their memorandum submitted to the secretary of state for the colonies in 1920. Among other things, the Congress asked for a Legislative Council (q.v.) in each territory, half of whose members would be elected and the other half nominated; a House of Assembly (q.v.) composed of members of the Legislative Council together with six other representatives elected by the people to control taxation, revenue and expenditure; separation of the judiciary (q.v.) from the legislative branch of the government and the appointment of Africans to judicial offices; appointment and deposition of Chiefs (q.v.) by their own people; abolition of racial discrimination in the civil services; development of municipal governments; repeal of certain "obnoxious" ordinances; regulation of immigration of Syrians and other non-Africans and the establishment of a university in West Africa.

Secretary of State Lord Milner, having received unfavorable reports on the delegation from the governments of the British West African colonies, rejected their demands. But owing to continuous pressure in Nigeria, the colonial secretary agreed to the Clifford Constitution (q.v.) of 1922, which abolished the Nigerian Council and which introduced for the first time in British West Africa, the elective principle into the Nigerian constitutional development, whereby Lagos City (q.v.) elected three representatives and Calabar (q.v.) elected one representative to the Legislative Council.

NATIONAL CONVENTION OF NIGERIAN CITIZENS. The NCNC was the new name given to the National Council of Nigeria and the Cameroons, which was founded in 1944. This new name was given to the NCNC in 1961, after the plebiscite in which the people of Southern Cameroon (q.v.) declared their intention to join the Cameroon (q.v.) Republic. The NCNC leader was Dr. Michael I. Okpara (q.v.), Dr. Nnamdi Azikiwe having quit partisan politics sometime before his appointment as governor-general (q.v.) in October 1960. The party was in firm control of both the Eastern (q.v.) and the Mid-Western Regions (q.v.) during the First Republic (q.v.). It was, however, dissolved in 1966 when the military took over the government. *See also* NATIONAL COUNCIL OF NIGERIA AND THE CAMEROONS.

NATIONAL COUNCIL OF NIGERIA AND THE CAMEROONS. In 1944 a conference was called in Lagos (q.v.) for the purpose of organising a national council which would bring the diverse peoples of Nigeria together. Accordingly, on August 26, 1944, the inaugural meeting of the conference was held in the Glover Memorial Hall in Lagos. It was attended by various organisations—trade unions, political parties, professional associations, clubs and tribal unions.

Because the Cameroonian associations in Lagos wanted to affiliate with the Council, its name was changed to National Council of Nigeria and the Cameroons. At the conference Herbert Macaulay (q.v.), who was leader of the Nigerian National Democratic Party (NNDP) (q.v.), and whose party was represented at the conference, was elected president of the council while Dr. Nnamdi Azikiwe (q.v.) became the general secretary.

Until 1951, membership in the party was restricted to organisations, trade unions, political parties, clubs and tribal unions, among which was the Ibo Federal Union (q.v.). However, in 1951 individuals became members. The party's main aims were to extend democratic principles and advance the interests of the people of Nigeria and the Cameroons, to educate the people with a view to achieving self-government and to provide its members with a means of political expression so that they might be able to secure their political freedom, economic security and social and religious tolerance in Nigeria and the Cameroons. When the party was being formed, Dr. Nnamdi Azikiwe was seen as a dynamic educated young nationalist who brought to bear on Nigerian politics the experiences and the education he had received in the United States. He was, therefore, a popular person, not only in his home region but in Lagos and the Western Region (q.v.). But even though the party got much support from Lagos and the west, its base of support, especially after the election of 1951 in the Western Region when the Action Group Party (AG) (q.v.) outmaneuvered the NCNC in the west, was in the Eastern Region (q.v.), which was predominately Igbo (q.v.). It began to be seen more as a regional party. After the 1959 federal elections (q.v.), the NCNC formed a coalition with the NPC to rule Nigeria. This coalition broke down in the 1963–64 census crises.

After the plebiscite that determined that Southern Cameroon (q.v.) would be separated from Nigeria in 1961, the name of the party was changed to the National Convention of Nigerian Citizens. The party was one of those banned in 1966 when the military came to power.

NATIONAL COUNCIL OF TRADE UNIONS OF NIGERIA. With the breakup of the All-Nigerian Trade Union Federation (ANTUF) (q.v.) in 1957, the NCTUN was formed. Its principal officers were N.A. Cole, president, and Lawrence L. Bortha, general secretary. Its aims, among others, were to provide an effective central trade union body, independent of ideological influences, and to promote the interest of the working people in the country. It would encourage workers to organise free and democratic labour unions, aid in the establishment of trade unions in all industries, promote and foster legislation in the interest of the working class and cooperate with free and democratic international trade union federations whose aims were acceptable to the Council. In 1957 the NCTUN applied for affiliation to the International Confederation of Free Trade Unions (ICFTU), just as the ANTUF had done. But in 1958, since the ICFTU could accept only one application and no reconciliation between the ANTUF and the NCTUN was possible, the ICFTU accepted the application of the NCTUN. In 1958 a National Labour Peace Committee was formed to try to bring about a reconciliation between the two unions. In January 1959, the two came together under the umbrella of the Trade Union Congress of Nigeria (q.v.).

NATIONAL COUNCIL OF WOMEN'S SOCIETIES. Formed in 1958 in Ibadan (q.v.) when three women's volunteer organisations—Women's Movement of Nigeria, which later became the Nigerian Council of Women, the Women's Improvement Society and the Ibadan Progressive Union (Women's Section)—were merged. Since its founding, NCWS has been involved in many aspects of life that pertain to women—the celebration of Nigeria Women's Day, adult education awards and scholarships, child welfare programs, establishment of day-care centres, promotion of women's handicrafts, community development activities to improve the status of women and all activities that would promote the interest of Nigerian women. Some of the organisations affiliated with NCWS are Zonta International Club of Lagos, Medical Women's Society, Planned Parenthood Federation of Nigeria, International Federation of Lawyers, Diocesan Council of Catholic Women, Association of University Women, Army Officers' Wives, Muslim Mothers Association and Market Women Association. The NCWS has branches in all 30 states of the Federation (q.v.). The headquarters of the organisation is at Victoria Island in Lagos (q.v.).

NATIONAL DEFENCE AND SECURITY COUNCIL. In his effort to postpone the handing over of government to an elected government on January 1993, and to mollify passion against the postponement, President Ibrahim B. Babangida (q.v.) set up two bodies to rule the country. These were the Transitional Council (q.v.) and the National Defence and Security Council (NDSC), which replaced the Armed Forces Ruling Council (q.v.) as the highest policy-making body in the nation. The NDSC consisted of 14 members, nine of whom were military men while the remaining four were civilians, including Chief Ernest Shonekan (q.v.), the chairman of the Transitional Council, the attorney general and the inspector general of police. While the official role of the NDSC was to make major decisions for the nation, the truth that later emerged was that General Babangida was the real decision-maker. The NDSC rubber-stamped Babangida's decisions.

NATIONAL DEMOCRATIC COALITION (NDC). An umbrella organisation set up in May 1994 after it became clear that General Sani Abacha (q.v.), who came to power in November 1993 and who promised that his stay in power was going to be brief, was entrenching himself firmly in power. The organisation was to coordinate the activities of all other organisations in the country, struggling to see that the military would go back to the barracks and stay there. When the organisation saw that the national constitutional conference General Abacha promised was not going to have the power to seriously address the problems facing the country (q.v.), NADECO campaigned against the election to the national constitutional conference, and asked that it be boycotted. The campaign was fairly successful for, out of about 40 million registered voters, only about 300,000 went to vote. The Abacha government closely monitored NADECO leaders, and many of them were arrested and detained for months, including Chief Anthony Enahoro (q.v.). In May 1996, Chief Enahoro joined many of his colleagues in exile when it became clear that his life was in danger.

NATIONAL DIRECTORATE OF EMPLOYMENT. As a result of the worldwide depression and past government mismanagement in the early 1980s, industrial output in Nigeria shrank, leading to the high unemployment rate of over 10 percent for high school and university graduates. On March 26, 1986, President Ibrahim B. Babangida (q.v.) appointed a committee known as the Chukwuma Committee to deliberate on strategies for dealing with the mass unemployment. The report of the committee was submitted and later approved by government in October 1986. Based on the recommendation of the committee, the National Directorate of Employment (NDE) was established on November 22, 1986, and its core programmes were launched in January 1987.

The aim of the NDE was to create employment with emphasis on self-reliance and entrepreneurship. It was to concentrate its efforts on the reactivation of public works, promotion of direct labour, promotion of self-employment, the organisation of artisans into cooperatives and the encouragement of a culture of maintenance and repairs. The board of directors consist of a representation of a cross-section of the interest groups involved, i.e., from industry, commerce, agriculture, finance, employers, labour and government. The four programs of the directorate are the National Youth Employment and Vocational Skills Development Programme, Small-Scale Industries and Graduate Employment Programme, Agricultural Sector Employment Programme and Special Public Works Programme.

NATIONAL ECONOMIC COUNCIL. After the country became a federation (q.v.) of three regions and following the recommendation of the International Bank for Reconstruction and Development in 1954, the agreement was reached that there should be a body in which representatives of the regions would meet and discuss common economic problems. The result was the creation of the National Economic Council (NEC). It consisted of the prime minister, premier of the regional governments and all the ministers of finance and economic development. One of the tasks of the NEC was reaching agreements about the locations of new projects and the distribution of foreign aid. For effective programming of the work of the council, the NEC set up the joint planning committee, manned by the permanent secretaries from the several ministries of finance and economic development. The council also formulated and reviewed the progress of the development plan embarked upon by the government. During the military era, the National Economic Council was one of the forums in which all the state governors and the Head of State conferred on the economic development of Nigeria. Under the 1979 constitution (q.v.), the NEC became entrenched, and it was then made up of the vice president as chairman, the governors of the states and the governor of the Central Bank of Nigeria (q.v.). The constitution gave it power to advise the president on economic affairs of the Federation and, in particular, on measures necessary for the coordination of the economic planning efforts of all the various governments (q.v.) in the Federation.

NATIONAL ECONOMIC RECONSTRUCTION FUND (NERFUND). Established in February 1989 to provide a fund for financing small- and medium-scale enterprises up to an upper limit of N10 million. The chances of such entrepreneurs securing the loan depended on the viability of their projects and their ability to follow healthy financial procedures that would ensure that the funds released would be utilised for the right purpose and that the funded ventures would be in a position to contribute to the nation's economic development and repay the loans at the generous interest rates offered by NERFUND.

To launch and support this program, the World Bank provided $270 million, the African Development Bank about $230 million, the government of Czechoslovakia $50 million and Nigeria's federal military government provided an initial sum of N300 million.

NATIONAL ELECTORAL COMMISSION (NEC). Created in September 1987 by the administration of General Ibrahim B. Babangida (q.v.), it consisted of a chief national electoral commissioner who was the chairman, and eight other members appointed by the president. They were to be men of proven integrity and not known to have been actively involved in partisan politics. Their tenure was five years, and they might be reappointed for another term of five years.

The NEC were organized, conducted and supervised all elections and matters pertaining to elections into all the elective offices provided for in the constitution of the Federal Republic (q.v.) of Nigeria; provided clear guidelines, rules and regulations for the emergence, recognition and registration of two political parties; registered two political parties and determined their eligibility to sponsor candidates for any of the elections referred to above; monitored the organisation, conduct, campaign and financing of political parties, and provided rules and regulations which would govern the parties. The Commission also had the function of dividing areas of the states into constituents and preparing and maintaining the register of voters for the purpose of elections.

The Commission had a state electoral commission in each state of the federation to organise, undertake and supervise all elections to local government councils within the state and perform other duties that the NEC might delegate to them from time to time.

The commission's role as an impartial electoral body was tragically compromised after the June 12, 1993, presidential election (q.v.) when, after officially declaring the electoral returns from 14 states out of 30, it yielded to federal military government pressure not to declare the results from the remaining states, thereby denying the winning candidate Chief M.K.O. Abiola (q.v.) the fruit of his labour. The commission was later dissolved when General Sani Abacha (q.v.) came to power in November 1993, and in 1996 the government initiated the National Electoral Commission of Nigeria.

NATIONAL ELECTORAL COMMISSION OF NIGERIA (NECON). The body created by the Abacha regime in 1996 to supervise elections as part of its democratic transition program. NECON, however, never established significant credibility or integrity. Rather than being impartial, it is widely believed that NECON was used to manipulate the transition process in support of Abacha's personal political agenda. NECON was dissolved by the incoming Abubakar regime in 1998, and replaced by the Independent National Electoral Commission (INEC).

NATIONAL ELECTRIC POWER AUTHORITY (NEPA). A public corporation established under Decree No. 24 of 1972. It was empowered to develop and maintain an efficient, coordinated and economical supply of electricity for all parts of the federation. It replaced the Electricity Corporation of Nigeria and inherited all its assets and liabilities. NEPA is one of the government parastatals that have been commercialised. Beginning in 1996, the Abacha (q.v.) government decided to encourage and permit private sector enterprises to complement the services of NEPA.

NATIONAL EMERGENCY COMMITTEE. The National Emergency Committee was formed in November 1949 by leaders of the National Council of Nigeria and the Cameroons (NCNC) (q.v.) and the Nigerian Youth Movement (NYM) (q.v.), as a result of the shooting of coal miners at Enugu (q.v.) by the police during their go-slow strike action in which the government ordered the removal of the explosives from the mines in order to prevent the workers from causing trouble with the explosives. During the riots, 21 miners were killed. The committee protested vigorously against the shooting, and they demanded that the European assistant superintendent of police who ordered the shooting, F.S. Phillip, should be punished for recklessly wounding and taking the lives of harmless miners. The committee was disbanded in September 1950 because of rivalry among its leaders.

NATIONAL EXECUTIVE COUNCIL. With the promulgation of the Unification Decree No. 34 of 1966, the Federal Executive Council (q.v.) was changed to the National Executive Council because Nigeria ceased to be a federation (q.v.) from that date. The composition of the National Executive Council was: the head of the national military government who was the president; the head of the Nigerian Army; the head of the Nigerian navy; the head of the Nigerian air force; the chief of staff of the armed forces (q.v.); the chief of staff of the Nigerian army; the attorney general of the republic (q.v.); and the inspector general and the deputy inspector general of the Nigerian police.

With the change of government in July 1966, and the promulgation later of the decree reestablishing the federal system of government, the National Executive Council reverted to its former name, the Federal Executive Council.

NATIONAL FLAG. Designed by Taiwo Akinkunmi, a Nigerian student in London, the flag is divided vertically into three equal parts, green, white and green. The green outer parts represent the agricultural wealth of the country and the central white part represents unity and peace.

NATIONAL INDEPENDENCE PARTY. On February 23, 1953, during the Eastern Regional Government Crisis (q.v.), the National Independence Party was formed and led by Professor Eyo Ita (q.v.), who was previously the leader of the Eastern Regional government but expelled from the National Convention of Nigeria and the Cameroons (NCNC) (q.v.). The initial members of the party were the federal ministers, expelled from the party for their intransigence, regional ministers who supported them and others from outside the two legislative houses in the center and in the Eastern Region (q.v.).

The party, with the aid of Alvan A. Ikoku's (q.v.) United National Party, formed the opposition to the NCNC government in the region. The NIP did not take sides in the "self-government in 1956" motion crisis (q.v.), but acted rather as a bridge between the Northern Peoples Congress (NPC) (q.v.) in the north and the Action Group Party (AG) (q.v.) in the south. The party was represented at the 1953 Constitutional Conference (q.v.) in London in spite of the objection of the NCNC and AG parties which had formed a hurried alliance after the "self-government in 1956" issue. The party was regarded as a group of imperialist stooges. At the conference, the party warned against the dangers of strong regional governments and a weak center, which the AG and the NPC favoured.

The name of the party was later changed into the United Nigeria Independent Party (q.v.) and became an ally of the AG in the 1954 federal elections (q.v.).

NATIONALISATION OF BRITISH PETROLEUM COMPANY LTD. In 1979, nearly two years after the second phase of indigenisation in Nigeria, the British Petroleum Company Ltd. (BP) was nationalised. It was a measure taken by the federal military government outside the Nigerian Enterprises Promotion Decree of 1977 (q.v.). Apparently incensed by the indirect supply of oil (q.v.) to South Africa by BP, in contravention of the directive from the Organization of African Unity (q.v.), the federal military government took over all the assets of BP in Nigeria by the Acquisition of Assets (of British Petroleum Company Limited) Decree of 1979. It was the first nationalisation ever in the history of Nigeria since the attainment of sovereignty.

Nigeria nationalised in deference to the OAU directive concerning oil companies dealing with South Africa. Previously, Nigeria was an ardent adherent to the O.A.U. principles. The company was renamed the African Petroleum Company Ltd.

NATIONAL MANPOWER BOARD. Following the recommendations of the Ashby Commission's (q.v.) report on postschool certificate and higher education (q.v.) in the country, the National Manpower Board was set up in 1964. It was charged with the duty of analyzing the quality and the distribution of available manpower resources so that policies for a balanced development might be formulated. It was also to indicate areas in which additional training of essential manpower was needed from time to time and to coordinate the work of all the ministries concerned with manpower development. The board was directly responsible to the National Economic Council (q.v.), but it could also make recommendations to the ministries concerned with manpower development, like the ministries of Labour, of Education and of Economic Planning. The scholarship policy of the federal Ministry of Education generally took cognizance of the board's annual recommendations. To help the board in its work in the regions, regional manpower committees were set up to liase between the board and regional governments.

NATIONAL MILITARY GOVERNMENT. The national military government came into being on May 24, 1966, following the promulgation of Unification Decree No. 34 of 1966 (q.v.), which abolished the existing federal structure of government. On that day Nigeria ceased to be a federation (q.v.) and became the Republic of Nigeria (q.v.) with a unitary government. As such, the federal military government became known as the national military government. The idea of the national military government only featured prominently during the later months of General Aguiyi-Ironsi's regime (q.v.). General Yakubu Gowon (q.v.), who succeeded him in August 1966, issued Decree No. 59 of 1966, which returned the country to a federation.

NATIONAL ORIENTATION COLLEGE. During the Civil War (q.v.), the novelist Chinua Achebe (q.v.) and some intellectuals formed what they called the Political Orientation Committee to work on the future structure of Biafran society after the war. On June 1, 1969, Lt. Col. Odumegwu Ojukwu (q.v.) came up with the Ahiara Declaration (q.v.), which launched what he called the "Biafran Revolution." The Ahiara Declaration set up a National Orientation College, which was given the responsibility of politicising and reconstructing the army and the administration.

NATIONAL PARTY OF NIGERIA. Formed in 1978, the NPN was the third political party to emerge after the ban on politics was lifted in September of the same year. Its main aims were: to bring about social justice and social welfare; guarantee equality of opportunities for all, fundamental rights (q.v.) and freedom and a free electoral system; promote self-respect and self-reliance and bring about the unity of Nigeria. Realising that the country was still regionally divided, it adopted a zoning system of selecting party officials on a rotational basis. Party leaders then resolved that the presidential candidate of the party should come from the northern zone, while the vice presidential candidate was to come from the east and the chairman of the party from the west. At the 1979 national elections, Alhaji Shehu Shagari (q.v.) from Sokoto State (q.v.) was elected the first executive president, while Dr. Alex Ekwueme from the east became his vice president. The party also won the gubernatorial election in seven of the 19 states and won 36 out of the 95 seats in the Senate (q.v.) and 168 out of the 450 in the House of Representatives (q.v.). However, since it could not win a majority of the seats in both houses, an accord with the Nigerian People's Party (NPP) (q.v.) was reached under which the country would be governed. This accord was reminiscent of the 1959 coalition between the Northern People's Congress (q.v.) and the National Council of Nigerian Citizens (q.v.). The NPN-NPP accord broke down in 1981. In the 1983 general elections, which were characterised by massive rigging (q.v.) at different levels, the party won the presidential election and 13 out of the 19 gubernatorial elections, while it considerably improved its strength in the federal and state legislative houses. However, its victory was short-lived, for on December 31, 1983, the Nigerian Army again seized power in a bloodless coup. The party, like all the others, was later banned.

NATIONAL PROVIDENT FUND. Established by an act of Parliament in 1961, it is governed by that act, the Amendment Act of 1964 and Decree No. 40 of 1967. The National Provident Fund is a compulsory savings scheme to which non-pensionable workers and their employers are required to contribute equal proportions on a monthly basis for the overall benefit of the workers.

Members who can receive benefit payments are those who have reached the retirement age of 55, those who are physically or mentally declared to be medically invalid, dependents of a deceased member, or non-Nigerian members who are emigrating from the country.

All employers of labour, both public and private, employing not less than 10 workers are required to be registered under the scheme. To enforce this rule, the National Provident Fund has branches in all the states, manned by compliance inspectors who have power to enter premises or places where workers are employed.

NATIONAL RECONCILIATION COMMITTEE. *See* NATIONAL CONCILIATION COMMITTEE.

NATIONAL RECONSTRUCTION AND DEVELOPMENT SAVINGS FUND. Established in January 1968 by the federal military government to finance reconstruction and development programmes of the Federal Government (q.v.) from sources other than from the general revenue of the Federation (q.v.). It is a special fund that consists of contributions made from the incomes of workers. Thus, an employer is liable to contribute to the fund with respect to any worker employed by him. The amount was five percent per annum of the wages of each worker.

NATIONAL RECONSTRUCTION COMMITTEE. The National Reconstruction Committee was formed in October 1961 by Chief Obafemi Awolowo (q.v.). Membership included many university lecturers and professors, some of them not actually members of his Action Group Party (q.v.) but sympathizers. The Committee presented a number of working papers to the federal Executive Council (q.v.) in December 1961 on the case for austerity measures in government, the implication of the party's commitment to democratic socialism (q.v.), economic planning and on Pan-Africanism (q.v.).

NATIONAL REPUBLICAN CONVENTION. One of the two parties founded and funded by the federal military government of President Ibrahim B. Babangida (q.v.). When the ban on political activities was lifted in 1989,

13 political associations applied to the National Electoral Commission (NEC) (q.v.) for recognition as one of the two parties that the Third Republic's (q.v.) constitution (q.v.) would provide. The NEC recommended six of them for possible recognition to the Armed Forces Ruling Council (AFRC) (q.v.), but all of them were said to be ill prepared. The AFRC then proscribed the associations and founded two parties, one a little to the left and the other a little to the right. The National Republican Convention was supposed to be a little to the right of the centre. The government wrote its constitution and manifesto and built its party offices in each of the 589 local government (q.v.) headquarters in Nigeria. The NRC had most of its support among the conservative members of the citizenry, especially those who trace their roots to the banned National Party of Nigeria (q.v.) and the Nigerian People's Congress (q.v.) in the north, some members of the former National Convention of Nigeria Citizens (q.v.) and some minority ethnic groups. In the June 12, 1993, presidential election (q.v.) with Alhaji Bashir Tofa (q.v.) as the flag bearer, the party fared badly and was happy to support the annulment of the result of the election, which it clearly lost to the Social Democratic Party (q.v.), and gladly supported the Interim National Government (ING) (q.v.). When General Sani Abacha (q.v.) overthrew the ING, he banned the NRC.

NATIONAL UNION OF NIGERIAN STUDENTS. A federal union made up of all student unions in Nigeria and abroad. It was affiliated with the International Union of Students. It had no official ideology, and each branch was free to take any position on issues without reference to the central body. It was also supposed to maintain a neutral position on partisan issues. In the early 1960s, it was outspoken on a number of issues like the Defence Pact (q.v.) between Britain and Nigeria and the Preventive Detention Act (q.v.). In 1977 the organisation was represented on the Constituent Assembly (q.v.), which put finishing touches to the 1979 constitution (q.v.). In 1978 during the "Ali-Must-Go" crisis over the issue of democratisation of education in the country against the then-elitist educational system, it clashed with the federal military government and was proscribed. It, however, reorganised in 1980 under a new name, the National Association of Nigerian Students (NANS), which still consists of all students in the Nigerian universities, colleges of technology, polytechnical schools and colleges of education.

NATIONAL UNIVERSITIES COMMISSION. The National Universities Commission (NUC) was set up in 1962 as an administrative body after the government had agreed to implement most of the recommendations of the Ashby Commission's (q.v.) Report on higher education (q.v.) in Nigeria. Its responsibilities are mainly to inquire into and advise the Federal Government (q.v.) on the financial needs of universities; assist in planning a balanced and coordinated development of universities; receive annually a block grant from the federal government and disburse it on criteria the commission thinks appropriate; serve as an agency for channelling all external aids to the universities and conduct investigations relating to higher education in Nigeria and publish information relating to university finances and education at home and abroad, making recommendations to the government or the universities as the commission may consider to be in the nation's interest. When the commission was set up, there were only five universities in the country, the University of Ibadan (q.v.) and the University of Lagos were federally owned, while the remaining three in Ife (q.v.), Nsukka (q.v.) and Zaria (q.v.) were owned by the three regional governments. However, during the regime of Gen. Murtala Murtala and Gen. Olusegun Obasanjo (qq.v.), all nonfederally owned universities in Nigeria were taken over by the federal government and new universities were later created, including state-owned universities.

Since the takeover of the universities, the fortune of each of them began to deteriorate. The spirit of healthy rivalry in academic programmes, which characterised relations between the universities, has waned. The NUC, obeying government directives, embarked upon efforts to rationalise programmes and departments within and between the universities. What is more, it prescribed a minimum programme for accreditation for all universities, and it continues to serve as a conduit for federal funds to the universities. As the economic well-being of the nation grew worse in recent years, so also has the fortune of the universities, leading to brain drain, strikes and closures.

NATIONAL YOUTH EMPLOYMENT AND VOCATIONAL SKILLS DEVELOPMENT PROGRAMME. *See* NATIONAL DIRECTORATE OF EMPLOYMENT.

NATIONAL YOUTH SERVICE CORPS. Established under Decree No. 24 of 1973, the NYSC seeks to: inculcate discipline in Nigerian youth; raise their moral tone; develop common ties (and by so doing, promote national unity); encourage individual youth to seek employment in states other than their own and so promote mobility of labour and to induce employers to employ Nigerians regardless of their state of origin and finally to enable them to acquire a spirit of self-reliance. The idea of a Youth Corps was first mentioned in the second national Development Plan (q.v.) in which the federal military government planned for the establishment of a youth corps organisation. On October 1, 1972, the 12th Independence Anniversary, the Head of State, General Yakubu Gowon (q.v.) announced that the proposed NYSC was meant to transcend political, social, state and ethnic loyalties and that it would form one of the bases of fostering loyalty to the nation. The scheme was finally launched on June 4, 1973, by the Head of State and the first groups of students to be inducted in July 1973 were university graduates. The NYSC scheme was entrenched into the 1979 constitution (q.v.).

At present, graduates from the universities and polytechnical schools at home or from abroad are required to serve the nation for one year in a state other than their own. An exception to this rule is the case of married women who are allowed to serve in the states where their husbands live. As such, the scheme offers young men and women an opportunity to know the country and understand some of the problems of the various peoples. However, some youth corpers in many states complain of underemployment where they are posted, and that even though some would want to work where they served, they were not offered jobs. Employers require evidence of having served and being duly discharged before a graduate is employed.

NATIVE ADMINISTRATION. The system of local administration established by the colonial authorities through which they ruled the indigenous population. A native administration had a treasury and was under the authority of the Paramount Chief (q.v.), or Emir (q.v.) and his councils. Each was empowered to provide a variety of services from road building and maintenance to provision of health care and education to their citizens. Native authority revenues came largely from poll tax, community tax (q.v.) or cattle tax. Each native authority had its native court (q.v.), its police force and its prison. In the south, the system gave way to the British type of local administration in the early 1950s while it continued to the period after independence in the north. *See also* INDIRECT RULE.

NATIVE AUTHORITY. *See* NATIVE ADMINISTRATION; INDIRECT RULE.

NATIVE LAND ACQUISITION PROCLAMATION. A law enacted in 1900 for the Protectorate (q.v.) of Southern Nigeria for the purpose of preventing the exploitation of native landowners by expatriate aliens, and, thus, controlling the activities of such aliens in the protectorate.

NATIVE LAW AND CUSTOM. Native law and custom is a term used by the colonial authorities to distinguish local customary law (q.v.) from the imposed British statutory and common law. It is the law that has its origin in the custom of the people. It is the "common law" of the people of the area. Native law and custom are enforced by the local authorities and customary courts (q.v.). They deal mainly with succession, marriage and divorce. In the early 1950s, the word "native" was replaced by "customary" and so native law and custom became customary law.

NATIVE TREASURIES. By the Native Revenue Proclamation of 1906, the colonial government in the northern provinces tried to rationalise the various forms of tax assessment and collection that were in existence. But more important, the government laid down the principle of sharing the tax so collected between the government and its native authorities. By the Native Authority Proclamation of 1907, the government conferred upon some recognised Chiefs (q.v.) responsibilities for law and order in their areas. Subsequent to this, the government began to prepare the ground for the establishment of a native treasury into which tax would be diverted from the taxes that the Chiefs collected. Such money was to be used for the benefit of the new administration under the Chief, and be properly accounted for. In 1911 the first native treasuries were established, and they were gradually extended to the rest of the country, especially after the 1914 Amalgamation of Nigeria (q.v.).

NAVY, NIGERIAN. *See* ARMED FORCES.

NIGER COAST CONSTABULARY. In 1891 parts of the present Bendel (q.v.), Rivers (q.v.) and Cross River (q.v.) States were declared as the Oil Rivers Protectorate (q.v.) with its headquarters in Calabar (q.v.) where an armed constabulary was formed. In 1893 the area was proclaimed the Niger Coast Protectorate, and in 1894, the existing armed constabulary was reconstituted as the Niger Coast Constabulary.

NIGER COAST PROTECTORATE. The Niger Coast Protectorate was established in 1893 when the Oil Rivers Protectorate (q.v.), established after the 1885 Berlin Conference (q.v.) and covering mainly the coastal districts, was extended over the hinterland. The new Niger Coast Protectorate covered the former Oil Rivers Protectorate and the hinterland. It extended from the delta to Calabar (q.v.) and up to Benin City (q.v.). The protectorate maintained a force called the "Niger Coast Constabulary" (q.v.), which was used against any aggression or hostility on the part of the indigenous population, like the Akassa Massacre (q.v.) of 1895 and the Benin Massacre of 1897. In 1900, when the charter of the Royal Niger Company (q.v.) was revoked, the Niger Coast Protectorate became the Protectorate of Southern Nigeria (q.v.).

NIGER DELTA. The wetlands at the mouth of the Niger and Benue rivers. It is located on the coast of Nigeria between southeastern and southwestern Nigeria, and covers parts of Delta, Bayelsa, Akwa Ibom and Rivers states. The area of the Niger Delta is over 20,000 square kilometres and it includes four ecological zones: coastal barrier islands, mangroves, fresh water swamps and lowland rain forests. A large number of ethnic groups inhabit the Niger Delta, but by far the largest are the Ijaw (q.v.), who number as many as eight million (making them the fourth-largest ethnic group in the country). Important smaller groups include the Ogoni, Urhobo (qq.v.), Isoko and Itsekiri (q.v.), among others.

Traditionally, the peoples of the Niger Delta have made their living through farming and fishing. They have an additional economic importance, however, owing to the fact that most of the country's oil originates from the Niger Delta. According to Nigerian law, this oil is the property of the Federal Government (q.v.). In recent years, the indigenous communities of the Niger Delta have become increasingly vocal in demanding a larger share of these oil revenues. Some have argued that the environmental damage caused by oil production has disrupted or destroyed traditional fishing and farming practices. As these communities have been more assertive in their demands, they have been subject to repression and human rights abuses on the part of the Federal Government.

The most famous example of this was the Movement for the Survival of the Ogoni People (MOSOP) formed in 1988 and led by Ken Saro-Wiwa (q.v.). As MOSOP became increasingly assertive in demanding reparations from the oil companies for environmental damage and lost revenues, the government responded with a series of brutal crackdowns. These culminated in the execution of Saro-Wiwa by the Abacha regime on November 10, 1995.

By the late 1990s, the situation had become even more explosive. Youths from local communities began to sabotage and attack oil installations in their areas. The most prominent were the Ijaws, some of whom issued the Kaiama Declaration on December 11, 1998. The Kaiama Declaration demanded, among other things, the immediate departure of the military from oil producing areas, a halt to further oil exploration and production, and the abrogation of the 1978 Land Use Decree, which vested control of mineral resources in the Federal Government. Concurrent with this activism, violent interethnic conflicts began to increase as well, most notably between the Ijaws and the Itsekiris in Warri, Bayelsa State.

The government has made several attempts to address the concerns of oil-producing areas. In 1992, the Babangida regime created the Oil Mineral Producing Area Development Commission (OMPADEC) to promote development in the region. Later, the 1999 constitution promised to return 13 percent of all federal revenues derived from natural resources (including oil) to their state of origin. It is too soon to assess the success of these initiatives, but it is clear that Nigeria's economic and political future depends in no small measure on the government's ability to address the concerns of groups in the Niger Delta.

NIGER DELTA CONGRESS. The Niger Delta Congress (NDC) was an outgrowth of the Chiefs and Peoples Conference in the Rivers Area. It was primarily an Ijaw (q.v.) party, which was led by Chief Biriye and M.O. Ikolo. During the campaign for the 1959 federal elections (q.v.), NDC, allied with the Northern Peoples Congress (NPC), said that its aim was to make the

Niger Delta (q.v.) a federal territory. It won one seat in the federal House of Representatives (q.v.). In preparation for the 1964 elections, new alignments were brought about, and the NDC allied with the NPC, Nigerian National Democratic Party (q.v.) and Mid-West Democratic Front (q.v.) to form the Nigerian National Alliance (NNA) (q.v.). The party later broke up, and the two leaders Biriye and Ikolo were expelled for aligning with the NNA. The party was banned in 1966 together with all other parties when the military took over the government.

NIGER DELTA DEVELOPMENT BOARD. Following the recommendation of the Minorities Commission (q.v.) of 1957, the 1958 Constitutional Conference (q.v.) in London agreed to establish the Niger Delta Development Board to look after the physical development of the area and allay the fears and complaints of the Ijaw (q.v.) people. Thus, the board was to survey the area to: ascertain what was needed for land improvement and drainage, the improvement of communications and to investigate questions of agriculture, fisheries, land tenure and forestry; draw up schemes of development based on the findings of the survey and estimate the costs; conduct an initial survey and produce annual reports on its progress in implementing its proposals and present these to the federal and regional legislative houses; and finally to advise the government concerned how to plan and achieve the desired development of the area. The board was to exist for an initial period of 10 years, after which the federal and regional governments concerned would review the progress so far made. The board was to consist of a full-time chairman, appointed by the Federal Government (q.v.), one representative of each regional government and other representatives of the people of the area. The secretary was also to be a full-time member. The funds to execute its duties were to be provided by the Federal Government.

NIGERIA ADVANCE PARTY. Launched on September 28, 1978, by Tunji Braithwaite, a Lagos (q.v.) lawyer, the Nigeria Advance Party told the people of the country that their destiny was in their own hands. The symbol of the party was the map of Nigeria in a globe carried with both hands. Its flag was made up of white, orange, green and black. The party, if elected into power, promised to revolutionise the educational system and make it really practical. It promised to take over agricultural lands and compensate the owners and evolve a communal system whereby everyone would be involved. The party would see to the production of food so that the country could export the surpluses. The party did not meet the conditions of the Federal Electoral Commission (FEDECO) in 1979 and so it could not be registered for the 1979 elections and could not take part in it. However, in 1982 it obtained FEDECO's recognition and so it became the sixth recognised party in the Second Republic (q.v.) and a contestant in the 1983 elections. The party did not win any seat in the national elections, and when the military took over power in December 1983, it was one of the parties banned.

NIGERIA DEPOSIT INSURANCE CORPORATION. The corporation was established by Decree No. 22 of 1988, which became operational in March 1989. Its primary responsibility is to insure the deposit liabilities of all licenced banks when in financial difficulty. The corporation is also expected to assist monetary authorities in the formulation and implementation of banking policies. And since its prime objective is the protection of bank depositors, ensuring stability in the banking industry, encouraging healthy competition among banks and fostering informed risk-taking by licenced banks, some measures of confidence have been brought to the banking system by the readiness of the corporation to assist banks in financial distress and in the event of a bank failure, pay off a depositor up to a limit of N50,000.

NIGERIAN AGRICULTURAL BANK. Established in 1973, the Nigerian Agricultural Bank was set up with the objective of improving the rural life and economy of the country. To this end, it provides credit and loans for agricultural development and so helps to raise production and productivity of the rural population. Loans are, therefore, available, all conditions satisfied, for development of poultry, farming, fisheries and animal husbandry and also for storage, distribution and marketing of such projects.

NIGERIAN AGRICULTURAL COOPERATIVE MARKETING ORGANISATION. Established in 1982 as the apex cooperative organisation that would be responsible for the coordination of agricultural cooperative trade in food commodities in Nigeria. It was also set up to encourage and promote the development of fully integrated multipurpose cooperatives for food production, storage, processing, marketing and distribution. Other functions include working closely, at the primary level, with existing cooperative group farming societies, multipurpose cooperatives, produce marketing cooperatives, women cooperatives, the River Basin Development Authorities (q.v.) and the Agricultural Development Projects. It also provides transport facilities for evacuating farm supplies and food products, and can set up research, information and statistics departments for the promotion of agricultural cooperative marketing.

NIGERIAN ATOMIC ENERGY COMMISSION. The Nigerian Atomic Energy Commission was established by the federal military government in August 1976. The commission is charged with the responsibility of promoting the development of atomic energy and for all matters relating to the peaceful uses of atomic energy in the nation. The commission is to prospect for and mine radioactive minerals, construct and maintain nuclear installations for the purpose of generating electricity. It is also to produce, use and dispose of atomic energy as well as carry out research into matters connected with the peaceful uses of atomic energy.

NIGERIAN BANK FOR COMMERCE AND INDUSTRY. Established in April 1973 by the federal military government, to provide equity and loan capital to indigenous businessmen and women who are interested in setting up or expanding small-, medium- and large-scale commercial and industrial ventures. It also provides other services like opening of letters of credit, discounting of bills and acceptance of documentary bills for collection. It is a multipurpose bank to advance the rapid industrialisation of the country by giving assistance to genuine indigenous entrepreneurs.

NIGERIAN BROADCASTING CORPORATION. *See* FEDERAL RADIO CORPORATION OF NIGERIA.

NIGERIAN CHRONICLE. The *Nigerian Chronicle* was established in 1908 as the first newspaper that used Nigeria as its prefix. It was established by Christopher Kumolu Johnson, but it became defunct in 1915.

NIGERIAN COLLEGE OF ARTS, SCIENCE AND TECHNOLOGY. The establishment of the Nigerian College of Arts, Science and Technology came as a result of the Thorp and Harlow Commission (q.v.) report of 1949. The college was established on a tripartite basis, one branch to be in each of the three regions that made up the Federation (q.v.). The college was to have a principal, three assistant principals—one in each branch—heads of departments and lecturers. The constitution of the college also provided for a council or board of trustees made up of 15 members. The first branch of the college was opened in Zaria (q.v.), in the Northern Region (q.v.) in 1952. It offered courses in civil engineering, architecture, local government and secretarial work. The second branch was opened at Ibadan (q.v.), Western Nigeria (q.v.), in 1954. Courses offered included agriculture, forestry, bookkeeping and accountancy, education, arts, sciences and engineering. The third branch was opened in 1955 in Enugu (q.v.), Eastern Nigeria (q.v.), and offered courses in mining, surveying, science and arts. The college, however, was closed down in 1962, 10 years after its first branch came into existence, and its assets were taken over by the three regional universities of Ahmadu Bello in Zaria, Ife and Nsukka.

NIGERIAN COUNCIL. The Nigerian Council was created by Lord Lugard (q.v.) after the Amalgamation (q.v.) of the Northern Protectorate (q.v.) with the Southern Protectorate in 1914. Because it was designed to advise the governor on a nationwide basis, it was composed of representatives from all parts of the country. Its 36 members included the governor, members of his Executive Council (q.v.), residents, political secretaries, and seven unofficial Europeans and six unofficial Nigerians to represent various interests. There were also six traditional rulers and a member each to represent the Lagos (q.v.), Calabar (q.v.) and Benin (q.v.)/Warri (q.v.) areas. Because of the little interest the traditional rulers had in its proceedings—as shown by their not attending its meetings—and owing to the fact that it was not popular, it had to be abandoned in 1922 when the Clifford Constitution (q.v.) replaced it with a Legislative Council (q.v.) to legislate for Lagos and the southern provinces of Nigeria.

NIGERIAN COUNCIL FOR MEDICAL RESEARCH. Established by the federal military government in 1966, it consisted of 15 members and had the function of coordinating medical research in the country as well as initiating and carrying out research. It was also to support other persons' efforts to carry out research, train medical research workers, collect and disseminate information relating to medical science and to encourage and promote collaboration between those engaged in medical research in Nigeria and other countries.

NIGERIAN COUNCIL FOR SCIENCE AND TECHNOLOGY. Established in 1970 with the objective of determining priorities for scientific activities in the Federation (q.v.) in relation to the economic and social policies of the country and its international commitments; advising the federal military government on a national science policy, including general planning and the assessment of the requisite financial resources, and ensuring the application of the results of scientific activities to the development of agriculture (q.v.), industry (q.v.) and social welfare. The council consists of eleven ex-officio members—permanent ministers of federal ministries—and 24 appointed members, 12 of whom represented the states, with the remaining 12 representing fields of scientific knowledge like agriculture, industry, medicine, environmental sciences, social sciences and the natural sciences.

NIGERIAN COUNCIL FOR SCIENTIFIC AND INDUSTRIAL RESEARCH, THE. Established in 1966 by the federal military government with the following general functions: encourage, support and coordinate scientific and industrial research of all kinds in Nigeria; advise the government of the Federation (q.v.) and through it those of the regions on national policy relating to the application of science and technology to the development of the national economy (q.v.); and encourage and coordinate the survey and appraisal of the natural resources of the nation and develop such resources through applied research designed to develop the national economy and finally to encourage the study of all sciences and technology.

NIGERIAN COUNCIL OF WOMEN. *See* NATIONAL COUNCIL OF WOMEN'S SOCIETIES.

NIGERIAN DEFENCE ACADEMY. The Nigerian Defence Academy (NDA), established in 1964, is situated at Kaduna (q.v.) in Kaduna State (q.v.). It is the premier institution for the training of officer cadets in the country. Its history can be traced to the establishment of the Royal Nigerian Military Training College in April 1960 with the aim to conduct preliminary six-month training for officer cadets before they were sent overseas for further training. At independence, the authorities felt that the defence needs of the nation and the training of its officers were too sensitive to be left almost completely to overseas countries. Thus, in 1964, the Nigerian Military Training College changed its role from that of merely preparing suitable Nigerians for further training abroad to that of producing full-fledged military officers. Consequently, the college was transformed into the Nigerian Defence Academy to train regular officer cadets of the armed forces (q.v.) of Nigeria. In 1985 it was upgraded to a degree-awarding institution. Before 1979 a regular course lasted for a period of 30 months—18 months for academic study and 12 months for purely military training. In 1979 the course duration was increased to three years: two years of academic work and one year of military training. The academic curriculum then was designed to enable officers to obtain the Nigerian Defence Academy Certificate of Education (NDACE), which was then moderated by the University of Ibadan (q.v.). With the introduction of a degree program in 1985, the NDACE was gradually phased out. The degree program now lasts for five years, the first four years are devoted to academic study with light military training, while the fifth year is devoted mainly to military training.

NIGERIAN EDUCATIONAL RESEARCH COUNCIL. Established in 1972, it is charged with the function of encouraging, promoting and coordinating educational research programmes carried out in Nigeria. It is to identify educational problems on a periodic basis and to establish an order of research priority. It commissions and cooperates in financing research projects and compiles and publishes the results of educational research, particularly in relation to Nigerian problems. It also sponsors national and international conferences, maintains relationships with corresponding educational research bodies in and outside Nigeria, and assembles, maintains and extends collections of books and publications in libraries and other reading facilities.

NIGERIAN ENTERPRISES PROMOTION BOARD. The Nigerian Enterprises Promotion Board was established by the federal military government in 1972 for the purpose of developing and promoting enterprises in which

Nigerian citizens would participate fully and play a dominant role. The board advises the federal minister of industries on guidelines to promote Nigerian enterprises and on any other related matter that the minister may refer to it. The board is assisted by Nigerian Enterprises Promotion Committees established in all the states.

NIGERIAN ENTERPRISES PROMOTION DECREES, 1972 AND 1977. The first Nigerian Enterprises Decree was promulgated in 1972, the first serious attempt to enable Nigerian citizens to own and manage industrial and commercial business enterprises in Nigeria. It has its roots in one of the industrial objectives set by the first national Development Plan (q.v.), 1962–68, which was to create and stimulate an industrial climate that would enable Nigerians to participate to an ever-increasing extent in the ownership, direction and management of Nigerian industry (q.v.) and trade (q.v.). This objective could not be translated into reality until during the second national Development Plan, 1970–74.

The policy was given legal effect in the Nigerian Enterprises Promotion Decree of 1972, otherwise known as the "Indigenisation Decree." The decree represents a major landmark in Nigeria's progress toward economic emancipation. It classified enterprises into three schedules. The first schedule consisted of enterprises not involving much capital and technical skill. Foreigners were barred from the control and management of these, and they were to be wholly owned by Nigerians. In the second category were those enterprises that were more sophisticated than the first, requiring heavier capital outlay and superior technology and management. These could be jointly owned by Nigerians and foreigners, with foreigners allowed to own up to 40 percent of the enterprise. The third schedule comprised the most technically sophisticated enterprises. Foreigners were allowed 60 percent ownership of these.

The Nigerian Bank for Commerce and Industry (q.v.) was established to provide equity capital and funds for Nigerians to invest in industry and commerce. An Agricultural Bank with an authorised capital of N12 million was also set up to provide finances for businessmen and women who wished to invest in agriculture (q.v.) One provision that greatly enhanced Nigeria's relations with African neighbours was the concession to indigenes of the Organization of African Unity (q.v.) member states. They were not to be regarded as "aliens" for the purpose of the decree.

That the decree of 1972 did not quite achieve its objectives is an understatement. Various devices were worked out by foreigners in collusion with Nigerians to circumvent its provisions. Because of these abuses, the federal military government felt committed to review the implementation of the 1972 decree and to tighten any identified loopholes. The government embarked on the second phase of indigenisation by promulgating the Nigerian Enterprises Promotion Decree of 1977, which was more embracing than the first. In spite of this, it cannot be said that the 1977 measure was very successful. Apart from the wrath of the capital exporting countries of the West, which has been incurred by Nigeria, at home the Nigerian Enterprises Promotion measures have, in some instances, made the rich richer and the poor poorer.

As the deteriorating economic condition of the nation, following the unresolved crisis emanating from the annulment of the June 1993 presidential election (q.v.) continued, leading to capital flight from Nigeria, the military government of General Sani Abacha (q.v.), in his 1995 Independence Anniversary address, announced that he had repealed the Nigerian Enterprises Promotion Decree and issued the Investment Promotion Decree to attract foreign investment into the country.

NIGERIAN HOUSING DEVELOPMENT SOCIETY LIMITED. Incorporated in 1956, the Nigerian Housing Development Society, otherwise known as the Nigerian Building Society, commenced business in 1957. Its main objective is to help as many Nigerians as possible to own their own houses. As such, it promotes thriftiness and savings among members. It is wholly owned by the Federal Government (q.v.) and the former Eastern Nigeria (q.v.) government. The society has now been turned into a mortgage bank known as the Nigerian Mortgage Bank.

NIGERIAN INSTITUTE OF INTERNATIONAL AFFAIRS. Established in 1963 as an independent nonprofit research institution to encourage and facilitate the understanding of international affairs, especially the factors and the circumstances that condition the attitude and behaviour of other countries and their people. It also provides information on international problems and promotes the study of such problems by organising conferences, lectures, discussion and publication of their study. Furthermore the NIIA provides facilities for the training of diplomats and personnel for the foreign office.

NIGERIAN INSTITUTE OF SOCIAL AND ECONOMIC RESEARCH (NISER). Established at the University of Ibadan (q.v.) in 1962 under the 1962 University of Ibadan Act, the NISER replaced the old West African Institute of Social and Economic Research (q.v.). In 1977 the institute was taken over by the Federal Government (q.v.) under Decree No. 77 of 1977. According to the decree, the institute is to provide consultancy services to the federal and state governments, and their agencies in the field of economic and social development. It is to conduct research into the economic and social problems of the country with a view to the application of the results, to organise seminars and conferences on economic and social problems of the country and to cooperate with Nigerian universities, other research institutes and institutions so as to mobilise all of the country's research potential for the task of national development and disseminate research findings for the use of policy makers. The decree also established the NISER Council to take care of the management of the institute.

NIGERIANISATION. Nigerianisation was the policy of the colonial government that suitable Nigerians should be appointed to the senior service in the government as fast as possible. By this policy, government was committed to set up a body that would determine the suitability of the candidates. Furthermore, if government was to have suitable candidates, it had to provide scholarship and training opportunities to interested persons. This policy led to the setting up in 1948 of the Foot Commission (q.v.), charged with making recommendations on the steps government had to take to execute this policy. The commission laid down the principle that only where no Nigerians had relevant qualifications for a post should a non-Nigerian be considered for it.

Before the Nigerianisation policy was adopted in 1949, Nigerians in the senior service constituted about 10 percent, while the rest were Europeans. In 1952 the figures for Nigerians had risen to about 19 percent.

NIGERIANISATION COMMISSION. Set up in 1948 to inquire into the best and quickest methods of recruiting substantial numbers of Nigerians into the senior service. The commission was made up of 10 members: a European chairman, two other European civil servants, four Nigerian unofficial members of the Legislative Council (q.v.), two Nigerian trade union representatives and a woman representative.

In August, the Commission submitted its recommendations: (1) that no non-Nigerian should be recruited for any government post except when no suitable and qualified Nigerian was available; (2) all senior posts should be advertised only when there were no suitable Nigerian candidates already available for promotion within the civil service; (3) there should be no discrimination with regard to promotion against Nigerians and non-Nigerians already in the service; (4) an independent body, like a civil service commission should be set up to select candidates for senior posts; (5) junior service personnel should be reviewed annually with a view to selecting promising young people for special training and accelerated promotion; and (6) 385 scholarship and training scheme awards should be made for the initial period of three years during the policy implementation (i.e., 1949–51). These awards were to be distributed as follows: 100 in education and general degrees; 108 for professional courses in engineering, agriculture, medicine and forestry; 127 in technical courses; 30 in courses reserved exclusively for women and 20 "nongovernment" scholarships. Other scholarship awards were recommended to assist impoverished students in high schools and the University of Ibadan (q.v.). The government accepted the recommendations, appointed a civil service commission, a public service commission (q.v.), four public service boards—one for the national government and three for the emerging three regions—and many other departmental boards and promotion committees.

NIGERIAN LABOUR CONGRESS (NLC). The current Nigerian Labour Congress is the peak organisation representing labour in Nigeria. Its origins date back to 1975, when the leaders of the country's four most powerful unions agreed to form an umbrella organisation, the Nigerian Labour Congress (NLC). The military regime of Murtala Muhammedu found the initiative to be threatening and immediately intervened to halt the plan. The government then imposed its own restructuring of the country's unions. More than 1,000 independent unions were combined into 42 officially recognised unions (later reduced to 29), all affiliated with a reconstituted Nigerian Labour Congress, which was inaugurated in 1978.

While this corporatist reorganisation was apparently intended to subdue the labour movement, the government has often struggled to exercise its control over the NLC. In 1988, protests against the government's Structural Adjustment Programme (SAP) prompted it to dissolve the NLC executive and appoint new leaders. Similarly, in 1994 anti-government strikes once again prompted a removal of the union's leadership. From 1994 until January 1999, the NLC was led by a caretaker committee imposed by the military. In January 1999, a new leadership was elected by the members. Longtime member Adams Oshiomhole was elected president.

The first Nigerian Labour Congress was inaugurated on May 26, 1950, as a result of the reconciliatory move between the Trade Union Congress of Nigeria (TUC) (q.v.) and the Nigerian National Federation of Labour (NNFL) (q.v.). The principal officers of the union were M.A.O. Imoudu (q.v.) as the president and Nduka Eze as the general secretary. The organisation entered into difficulties almost immediately, leading to its disintegration. It sponsored the Mercantile Workers' strike in December 1950, which was a failure, and many affiliated unions decided to quit the congress. Worse still, in 1951 the congress opposed the visit of the delegation of the International Confederation of Free Trade Unions (ICFTU) (q.v.) to Nigeria, leading to the ICFTU choosing Accra, Ghana (q.v.) as the base for its operation in West Africa. That put an end to the NLC.

NIGERIAN LABOUR PARTY. Formed in 1964, by Chief Michael Imoudu (q.v.), it was intended to bring together all the Nigerian workers into a political party. The party met with great opposition from other labour leaders like Alhaji H.P. Adebola of the United Labour Congress (q.v.), Wahab Goodluck and S.U. Bassey of the Nigerian Trade Union Congress (q.v.). The party was short-lived.

NIGERIAN NATIONAL ALLIANCE (NNA). As the 1964 general election to the federal House of Assembly (q.v.) approached, the major political parties began to seek alliances with other parties to ensure victory. The NNA was one of the two major alliances formed before the election. It was made up of the Northern People's Congress (NPC) (q.v.), Mid-West Democratic Front (q.v.), the Nigerian National Democratic Party (q.v.) and the Niger Delta Congress (q.v.). The leader of the alliance was Sir Ahmadu Bello (q.v.), the Sardauna of Sokoto (q.v.) and the leader of the NPC.

At the close of nominations on December 19, 1964, 60 NNA candidates had been returned unopposed. The NNA won 36 out of the 57 seats in the west and 162 seats out of the 167 seats in the north. The NNA had a comfortable majority in the House of Representatives (q.v.). The alliance's leader in the house, Alhaji Tafawa Balewa (q.v.), was called to form the government, and he was made the prime minister in 1965.

NIGERIAN NATIONAL CONGRESS. A political party launched on September 26, 1978, in Lagos (q.v.) by Alhaji Mohammed Idirisu. The party, referred to as "the new breed," was to be run in complete exclusion of old politicians (people who participated in the premilitary government), but it set no age limits to its membership. It intended to correct the ills and blunders that led to the fall of the First Republic (q.v.). The party would build a new national economy (q.v.) and social order geared to the needs of the people by fighting for the economic emancipation of Nigeria from foreign domination. It would build a society where no man would be oppressed, a society free of hate, avarice, greed and exploitation. It would bring the benefit of modern civilisation to the rural and urban poor in forms of pipe-borne water, free health services, electricity, modern housing and recreational facilities. It would pursue a positive agrarian policy to guarantee abundant food for all Nigerians. There would also be freedom for the people: freedom of the press, movement, religion and conscience.

NIGERIAN NATIONAL DEMOCRATIC PARTY (NNDP). The Nigerian National Democratic Party was founded by Herbert Macaulay (q.v.), an engineer turned politician and nationalist after the introduction of the elective principle by the 1922 constitution (q.v.). The party was the most powerful of all those formed at the time, for not only did it win all three Lagos (q.v.) seats in the Legislative Council (q.v.) in 1923, 1928 and 1933, it also won the elections into the Lagos City Council during that period. One of the weaknesses of the party was that it was a Lagos party, that is, based in Lagos and concerned for the most part with the affairs of Lagos, especially the restoration of the ruling house of Dosunmu (q.v.), and, therefore, could not attract much following outside the city. In 1944 the NNDP became one of the organisations that made up the National Council of Nigeria and the Cameroons (NCNC) (q.v.), and Herbert Macaulay became the president of the new party.

Twenty years later, in March 1964 after the Action Group crisis of 1962 (q.v.), and during the political instability in Western Nigeria (q.v.), the United People's Party (UPP) (q.v.), led by Chief S.L. Akintola (q.v.), a faction of the NCNC in the Western Region, led by Chief R.A. Fani-Kayode (q.v.) and Chief Richard Akinjide (q.v.), and the Southern People's Congress formed a new party by the same name, the Nigerian National Democratic Party, with Chief S.L. Akintola as chairman. Its symbol was the hand. They claimed later that their membership in all other parties had been renounced. Their purpose was to put an end to the disunity and political unrest in Western Nigeria brought about by the Action Group crisis of 1962.

It was believed then that the emergence of the new party was brought about by the disagreement over the 1961 census by the UPP and NCNC. UPP accepted the figures, while the NCNC government rejected them.

During the political realignment of 1964, before the December federal elections (q.v.), the NNDP joined with the Northern People's Congress (q.v.) to form the Nigerian National Alliance (q.v.). The party was banned in 1966 after the military came into power.

NIGERIAN NATIONAL FEDERATION OF LABOUR. As a result of the decision of the general council of the Trade Union Congress of Nigeria (TUC) (q.v.) to affiliate with the National Council of Nigeria and the Cameroons (NCNC) (q.v.) in 1947 a crisis in the central trade union movement (q.v.) emerged. At the Sixth Annual Delegates Conference of the TUC in December 1948, the motion for affiliation was debated and defeated. As a result of this, a large number of affiliated unions that supported affiliation pulled out of the TUC. In March 1949, these splinter unions met to form the Nigerian National Federation of Labour (NNFL). Its aims were to assist member unions to attain their objectives, to foster a spirit of working-class consciousness among workers, fight for the realisation of the social and economic security of workers and advance their educational aspirations. It was also to press for the socialisation of many important industries with a view to realising a socialist government, and to cooperate with democratic federations of trade unions all over the world.

The leaders of the NNFL were M.A.O. Imoudu (q.v.) as president and Nduka Eze as general secretary. The union launched a weekly newspaper in 1950, the *Labour Champion,* its official organ. In the same year, as a result of the effort to reconcile the TUC and the NNFL, a merger was agreed upon and both formed the Nigerian Labour Congress (q.v.).

NIGERIAN NATIONAL OIL CORPORATION. A public corporation established in April 1971, it is directed by a board of directors made up of the permanent secretary to the federal ministry of Mines and Powers who was the chairman, and eight members, some of whom were government officials, and others with necessary ability, experience or special knowledge of the oil industry. The corporation has the job of exploring and prospecting for petroleum (q.v.) and possessing and disposing of petroleum. It could purchase petroleum and its by-products and market it. The corporation is managed by a general manager. In 1972, the corporation became the sole beneficiary of all oil concessions, though it could use private companies as contractors or minority partners. In 1977 it was amalgamated with the Ministry of Petroleum to form the Nigerian National Petroleum Corporation.

NIGERIAN NATIONAL PETROLEUM CORPORATION. In 1977 the Nigerian National Oil Corporation and the federal Ministry of Petroleum Resources were merged to form the Nigerian National Petroleum Corporation (NNPC). The corporation is empowered to engage in all commercial activities relating to petroleum industries. Recently, the NNPC was involved with three multinational oil companies—Shell, Agip and Elf—in the effort to acquire and ensure a growing share of the international gas market for Nigeria's abundant gas resources. It has secured markets for Nigerian gas in Europe and America, and it is hoped that by 1999, liquified natural gas would begin to be shipped to these continents. The business of the corporation is under the direction of a seven-man board of directors with the minister for petroleum as its chairman. It also has an independent department, known as the petroleum inspectorate, which enforces the regulatory measures relating to the general control of petroleum product.

NIGERIAN NATIONAL SUPPLY COMPANY, THE. The Nigerian National Supply Company was established by the federal military government in 1972 for the purpose of making bulk purchases of scarce commodities and selling these to government ministries, corporations and institutions. It also served as an instrument of price control and stabilisation.

NIGERIAN PEOPLE'S PARTY. The Nigerian People's Party (NPP) was formed in September 1978 after the ban on politics was lifted. Its major aims included efforts to promote the unity of the country and uphold its territorial integrity, work for the integration and equality of all the peoples of the country, full employment and equal opportunity, promote equitable distribution of the nation's resources, work for free and high quality of education, and a secular state which would uphold democracy and the rule of law.

Among the foundation members of the party were Alhaji Waziri Ibrahim (q.v.), Dr. Ben Nzeribe, Chief T.O.S. Benson (q.v.), Paul Unongo, Chief Kola Balogun (q.v.), Alhaji Ado Ibrahim, Chief Samuel Onitiri and Chief A. Ogunsanya (q.v.). During the struggle to choose the presidential candidate, a dispute arose on whether or not the position of party chairman should also be combined with presidential candidate. As a result, Alhaji Waziri Ibrahim, at the time the chairman and the party's main financial supporter, wanted to keep the chairmanship while he ran for the presidency. Because many other important members disagreed with him, he pulled out of the party to form the Great Nigerian People's Party (GNPP) (q.v.). After Waziri's exit, the party leaders invited Dr. Nnamdi Azikiwe (q.v.) to be its presidential candidate, a position which Dr. Azikiwe accepted. Chief Olu Akinfosile (q.v.) was then elected as party chairman at the party's first convention.

The party was one of the five registered parties for the 1979 general elections. It lost the presidency but won the gubernatorial elections in three states—Plateau (q.v.), Imo (q.v.) and Anambra (q.v.)—the last two being made up mainly of the Igbo (q.v.) people. During postelection politicking, the party and the National Party of Nigeria (NPN) (q.v.) came to an accord at the federal level to work together and share the spoils of office. At the 1980 party convention, Chief Ogunsanya was elected chairman, while Dr. Azikiwe was elected party leader. Some people saw the accord between the NPP and NPN as reminiscent of the coalition between the National Council of Nigeria and the Cameroons (NCNC) (q.v.) and the Northern Peoples Congress (NPC) (q.v.) after the 1959 federal elections. The NPP-NPN accord broke down in 1981. In the realignment effort to prepare for the 1983 elections and wrest power away from the NPN, the NPP joined the Unity Party of Nigeria (q.v.), together with a faction of the GNPP and the Imoudu faction of the People's Redemption Party (q.v.) to form the Progressive Parties Alliance (q.v.). However, since the alliance could not present common candidates for the elections, not even for the presidential election, the NPP, just like other parties, fielded its own candidates and was badly defeated in many places, including at the centre. The party was banned after the December 1983 coup d'état (q.v.).

NIGERIAN PIONEER. The *Nigerian Pioneer* was launched in 1914 as a newspaper by Sir Kitoyi Ajasa (q.v.). However, the paper never saw the grateful eyes of the Nigerian nationalists. This was because, unlike the *Lagos Weekly Record* (q.v.), owned by John Payne Jackson (q.v.), the *Nigerian Pioneer* was actively in support of the colonial government's policies. It was widely regarded as "His Master's Voice." Some people used to think that it was a government paper because of its pro-government posture. In reply to the allegation of the *Pioneer*'s collusion with the government, Sir Kitoyi said that the paper existed in order to interpret thoroughly and accurately the government to the people and the people to the government.

NIGERIAN PORTS AUTHORITY. An autonomous public corporation created by the Ports Act of 1954. The authority commenced operation on April 1, 1955, when it assumed the responsibility for the ports and harbours previously under eight different government departments.

The statutory duties of the authorities include: responsibility for the provision and operation of cargo handling and quay facilities, maintaining, improving and regulating the harbours in all ports in Nigeria, dredging to desired depths and providing and maintaining pilotage services, lighting lighthouses, buoys and navigational aids in all Nigerian ports. It is also responsible for identifying and satisfying demands for port facilities and services at minimum costs to the nation, and to use net revenues from previous years for new project developments and rate stabilisation.

The governing body is a board composed of a chairman and nine other members appointed by the Federal Government (q.v.). It formulates the policy of the authority, though the federal minister of transport can issue to it directives of a general character on matters affecting public interests and specific directives for the purpose of remedying particular defects. The day-to-day administration is under the supervision of the general manager, who is also the chief executive of the authority.

Due to the oil (q.v.) boom and an improved economic situation between 1975 and 1980, there was a sharp increase in Nigerian international trade. During the 1975–76 period, about 9.3 million tonnes of cargo passed through the various ports. They were designed for only 4.1 million tonnes. Hence, there was much port congestion. At its height there were over 450 vessels waiting to berth at the Lagos Port alone. Because of this, the third national Development Plan (q.v.) of 1975–80 provided for port development programmes consisting of short-term and long-term measures. By 1980 most of these developmental measures had been accomplished and ships no longer had to wait beyond the normal maximum international period of 10 days.

NIGERIAN PRESS COUNCIL. The effort by government to regulate the profession of journalism has a long history. In 1978 General Olusegun Obasanjo's (q.v.) regime promulgated the Nigerian Press Council decree, but it was rejected by journalists because of obnoxious provisions. In 1988 the regime of General Ibrahim B. Babangida (q.v.) issued the Nigerian Media Council Decree No. 59, which was also rejected. After a long and serious negotiation, in December 1992, a new decree devoid of the so-called obnoxious provisions was promulgated.

The council is headed by a board whose functions include making enquiries into public complaints about the conduct of the press or any person or organisation toward the press; researching into contemporary press development; engaging in updating press documentation; fostering the achievement and maintenance of high professional standards; reviewing developments that are likely to restrict the supply of information through the press or that are likely to prevent press access to remedy such developments and ensuring the protection of the rights and privileges of journalists in the lawful pursuance of their professional duties.

NIGERIAN RAILWAY CORPORATION. Railway construction began in 1898 and was, from then on, operated and managed as a government department until October 1955, when it was established as a public corporation. The corporation, with headquarters in Lagos (q.v.) is headed by a chairman appointed by the Federal Government (q.v.) and is in its day-to-day operation under the management of a general manager. The corporation is charged with the function of providing technically competent transportation services to the nation. The corporation maintains two main lines linking the two major ocean ports, Lagos and Port Harcourt (q.v.) with the states' headquarters and commercial centers all over the nation. The two lines from Lagos and Port Harcourt meet in Kaduna (q.v.), from where one line runs to Kano (q.v.) and then to Nguru near the border with the Niger Republic. The other branch from Kuru on the Kafanchan-Jos line runs through Bauchi to Maiduguri, the capital of the Borno State (q.v.) near the border with the Chad Republic. The railway system still remains single tracked and consists of two main routes. However, decisions were reached to construct standard-gauge railway track in three phases, linking some parts of the country, especially Sokoto (q.v.) through Kaura Namoda. The first phase will link Apapa to Lagos in Lagos State (q.v.), followed by the Kaduna to Kafanchan and finally from Kafanchan to the Port Harcourt lines.

For many years now, the Nigerian Railway Corporation has exhibited poor management, lack of patronage, aging facilities, and corrupt practices.

NIGERIAN SECURITIES AND EXCHANGE COMMISSION. The commission was established on April 1, 1978, as the apex institution of the Nigerian Capital Market. The functions of the commission include determining the price at which shares or debentures of a company are to be sold, the timing and the amount of sale, and, in the case of a company whose securities have been quoted on any recognised stock exchange, the price, timing and amount of any supplementary offers for sale.

The board of the commission is made up of 12 members with a representative from the Central Bank of Nigeria (q.v.) as chairman, one representative of the Nigerian stock exchange, one representative of the Nigerian Enterprises Promotion Board (q.v.), one representative each of the Ministries of Finance, Trade, and Industries, the executive director of the commission and five private members who are appointed by reasons of their ability, experience and specialised knowledge of the Nigerian Capital Market or because of business or professional attainment.

NIGERIAN SOCIALIST GROUP. Based in Enugu (q.v.), Enugu State (q.v.), the Nigerian Socialist Group was founded in 1960 as a nonpolitical organisation, drawing its members from various political parties and many others. The group favored a militant form of Pan-Africanism (q.v.) and believed that the fight against Western imperialism could only be won by the united efforts of all African states. The group directed most of its effort to foreign policy (q.v.). Believing that the sufferings of the African people everywhere were caused by the West, it advocated a policy of nonalignment for Nigeria so that Nigeria could be free to deal with both East and West without any discrimination. The group was one of those banned in 1966 when the military came to power.

NIGERIAN STOCK EXCHANGE. Established in January 1978 to replace the Lagos Stock Exchange as a limited liability company. Its functions include making rules and regulations for stockbrokers in their day-to-day activities, and granting quotations and listing for securities. It also has the responsibility to protect the interest of the investing public and to consider complaints about, and among, members of the stock exchange business.

NIGERIAN SUPREME COUNCIL FOR ISLAMIC AFFAIRS. The Nigerian Supreme Council for Islamic Affairs (NSCIA) was formed in 1973 to serve as an umbrella organisation for all Muslims throughout the country. Hitherto, there had existed a gulf between the Muslims in the southern parts of the country and their fellow Muslims from the northern part.

The council is under the leadership of the Sultan (q.v.) of Sokoto (q.v.) who is also regarded in official circles as the spiritual head of all Nigeria Muslims. It has an executive council comprising eight officers and representatives from each state. It is the main channel of contact to the government of Nigeria on Islamic affairs.

NIGERIAN TRADE UNION CONGRESS. Formed in April 1960 as a result of the suspension of Chief Michael Imoudu (q.v.) from the Trade Union Congress of Nigeria (TUCN) (q.v.), with Michael Imoudu as its president and Gogo Nzeribe as its secretary. There were a series of attempts to reconcile the NTUC and TUCN, including the intervention of the prime minister of the Federation (q.v.) Alhaji Tafawa Balewa (q.v.), but all to no avail. In 1961 further attempts were made. In 1962 the NTUC and the TUCN agreed to merge into the United Labour Congress (q.v.), and, in May 1962, both organisations stood dissolved.

NIGERIAN UNION OF STUDENTS (NUS). A nationalist organisation, founded in 1939 at the Abeokuta Grammar School and led by secondary-school graduates and young educated Nigerians. Its purpose was to spearhead the drive toward self-government for the country. In November 1943, it sponsored a youth rally at Ojokoro, at which members were addressed by prominent Nigerians like Bode Thomas (q.v.), Rotimi William (q.v.), H.O. Davies (q.v.) and Dr. Nnamdi Azikiwe (q.v.). The rally passed a resolution affirming the need for the formation of a national front. The occasion for the formation of such a front came in the spring of 1944, when students at King's College (q.v.) resorted to a strike action in protest against the continued use of their dormitories by soldiers during the Second World War, while they were made to live in the town in disagreeable lodging places. As a result of the protest, 75 of the student leaders were expelled while eight of them were drafted into the Nigerian Army.

In August 1944, prominent members of the NUS met Dr. Azikiwe and complained to him that the youth of the country were ready to be led but there was no leader. They later called a meeting of various organisations at the Glover Memorial Hall in Lagos (q.v.) for the purpose of forming a national council that would weld together all the heterogeneous masses of Nigeria into a solid block. The conference of the various organisations met on August 26, 1944, and they formed the National Council of Nigeria with Herbert Macaulay (q.v.) as president and Dr. Azikiwe as its general secretary. Thus came into being a political party later known as the National Council of Nigeria and the Cameroons (NCNC) (q.v.), which played a prominent role in Nigeria's political development before and after independence.

NIGERIAN UNION OF TEACHERS. The Nigerian Union of Teachers (NUT) was formed in 1931 for the purpose of fighting for the betterment of its members. Originally, it was made up of teachers from government and mission schools all over the country, but now its membership includes all grades of teachers from grade II teachers to university graduates. Its membership, however, does not include university teachers or lecturers, who have their own separate union.

NIGERIAN YOUTH CHARTER. The Nigerian Youth Charter embodied the official programme of the Nigerian Youth Movement (NYM) (q.v.). According to the charter, the aim of the NYM was the development of a united Nigerian nation out of the conglomeration of peoples that inhabit Nigeria, to encourage forces that would serve to promote understanding and a sense of common nationalism among the different elements that made up the country, to be a critic of the government as it was then constituted, working for the removal of inequality of economic opportunities and correcting abuses that militated against the cultural progress of the people.

The charter was divided into three sections—the political, the economic and the cultural. The political charter was aimed at complete autonomy within the British Empire and equal partnership with other member states of the British Commonwealth (q.v.) of nations, abolition of property or income qualifications for the exercise of the franchise and the substitution of universal suffrage. It also aimed at the separation of the administration of the judiciary (q.v.) from the executive.

The economic charter demanded for Nigerians economic opportunities equal to those enjoyed by foreigners. The movement would encourage and support all forms of local industry (q.v.), work for the amelioration of the welfare of the people, better pay for Africans in the civil service, the appointment of Africans into executive posts within the civil service and more Africans in the administrative branch of the civil service.

The cultural and social charter expressed its belief that mass education should be the pivot of the government's education policy. The NYM would urge government to make education progressively free and compulsory.

The NYM pursued these objectives vigorously. It fought for the Africanisation of the civil service—for the abolition of the discriminatory practices of regarding some posts as European posts. It demanded a minimum wage for workers and stimulated the organisation of labor unions.

NIGERIAN YOUTH CONGRESS. Established in 1960 as a nonpolitical movement, the congress drew its membership from young Nigerian intellectuals, educated elites and the major political parties. It was ideologically socialist and anti-West. It campaigned against what it regarded as neocolonialist powers, which members saw as subverting Nigeria's independence. Thus, in November 1960, the Congress criticised the defence agreement entered into between Nigeria and Britain, contending that the government was trying to bring Nigeria into the Western bloc. In December the Congress organised demonstrations against the agreement, leading to the arrest of some of its members. It also organised demonstrations in support of Patrice Lumumba in the Congo, putting pressure on the government to support his cause. In 1963 it campaigned against the introduction of the Preventive Detention Act (q.v.) in Nigeria. The demonstration often became violent and the National Council of Nigerian Citizens and the Action Group (qq.v.) parties asked their supporters to resign from the NYC. The president of the Congress was a Lagos (q.v.) medical practitioner, Dr. Tunji Otegbeve (q.v.). The congress was one of the organisations banned in 1966 when the military came to power.

NIGERIAN YOUTH MOVEMENT. In 1934 four Nigerians—Samuel Akinsanya (q.v.), Ernest Ikoli (q.v.), H.O. Davies (q.v.) and Dr. J.C. Vaughan (q.v.)—formed the Lagos Youth Movement (q.v.) to oppose the government's education policy with regard to the alleged deficiencies of Yaba Higher College (q.v.). In 1936, to make the organisation truly national, the name was changed to Nigerian Youth Movement (NYM). Its aim was "the development of a united nation out of the conglomeration of the people who inhabit Nigeria." It endeavoured to bring about understanding and a sense of common nationality among the different peoples of the country, and by 1937 the NYM had come to the forefront of the nationalist struggle for self-government in the country. In 1938, Dr. Nnamdi Azikiwe (q.v.) became a member, and the organisation became so popular in the capital city of Lagos (q.v.) that it won all the elections to the Lagos Town Council and the three Lagos seats on the Legislative Council (q.v.). However, in 1941 the movement had a nerve-racking crisis from which it never recovered. When Dr. K.A. Abayomi (q.v.), the president resigned from the Legislative Council (q.v.), Ikoli, an Ijaw (q.v.), and Akinsanya, an Ijebu (q.v.) Yoruba (q.v.), vied for the vacant seat. Dr. Azikiwe supported Akinsanya but others supported Ikoli, who finally won. Azikiwe felt hurt and disappointed and so withdrew from the organisation, accusing the leadership of tribal prejudice against his candidate. As a result of this, the organisation became moribund, and its leaders later left it, one by one, to engage in other affairs.

NIGER RIVER. The Niger rises in the Guinea Highlands and flows through the Republics of Mali and Niger before it enters Nigeria from the west and then runs southeasterly to Lokoja (q.v.), where it joins its main tributary, the Benue River (q.v.). From Lokoja, the Niger flows southwards, to the Niger Delta (q.v.) where it splits up into numerous creeks and channels before emptying itself into the Atlantic Ocean. The Niger is about 4,169 kilometres in length.

For many centuries the Niger was a mysterious river to Europeans who often confused it with the Senegal River or even the Nile. In 1788 the African Association (q.v.) was formed in Britain for the purpose of exploring Africa, but, more particularly, for finding out the course of the Niger. In 1795 Mungo Park (q.v.) offered his services to the association and started his first expedition, beginning from the Gambia. In July 1796, he caught sight of the Niger and saw that it flowed east. He followed the course of the river but had to turn back after having lost his men. In 1806 his next expedition took him to the rapids of Bussa (q.v.), where he and his men died. In 1830 Richard Lander (q.v.) and his brother John Lander sailed down the Niger from Bussa and showed that the Oil Rivers (q.v.) were the outlets of the Niger to the Gulf of Guinea.

NIGER STATE. Niger State was created in 1976 by the administration of General Murtala R. Muhammed (q.v.). In 1991 it merged with the Borgu and Agwara local government areas, which were excised from Kwara State (q.v.). It is located within latitudes 8°20′ and 11°30′N, and longitudes 3°30′ and 7°20′E and has a land area of 76,000 square kilometres, thus becoming the largest state in the country with nine percent of the country's land area. The state is bounded in the north by Kebbi State (q.v.), in the east by Kaduna State (q.v.) and the Federal Capital Territory (q.v.), in the south by Kogi (q.v.) and Kwara States and in the west by the Republic of Benin (q.v.). The state's lowlands within the Niger River (q.v.) basin are about 300 metres above sea level, while it is about 600 metres upland. It has two main seasons—rainy and dry. The rainy season begins in April and ends in October; the dry season is between November and March. About November the dry, cold and dusty northeasterly wind called the harmattan (q.v.) from the Sahara comes, ending about February, and lasting just a few days each time it comes. The hottest part of the year is generally between March and April, just before the rains begin to fall. The daily maximum temperature is about 32°C but drops during the rainy season. The vegetation falls within southern savannah forests, characterised by grasslands and short woodland. But, as one moves closer to the Niger, the vegetation becomes more tropical even to the extent that oil palms (q.v.) grow well. The state's mineral resources are gold, clay, silica, kyanite, marble, kaolinite, cassiterite, columbite and tantalite. The state is divided into 19 local government (q.v.) areas.

The population of the state in 1991 was 2,482,367 with a density of only 33 persons per square kilometres, making it the lowest densely populated state in the Federation (q.v.). The major ethnic groups in the state are Nupe (q.v.), Gwarri (q.v.), Hausa (q.v.) and Fulani (q.v.), but there are many others like Rafi, Magama, Rijau and Mariga. More than 18 different indigenous groups are found in the state, not counting migrants from other states. There are eight emirates, and all Emirs (q.v.) are members of the Niger State Council of Chiefs (q.v.), which is an advisory body to the government on certain matters. About 90 percent of the population are rural residents cultivating only about 25 percent of the arable land. As in many other northern states, a high proportion of the population is literate in the Arabic language (q.v.), but only about 30 percent are literate in the Western sense. In spite of this, the government is working hard to educate all its citizens. Even though Islam (q.v.) is firmly rooted in the state, Christianity (q.v.) is also growing, and there are other traditional religious (q.v.) groups in the state. The major population centers are Minna (the capital), Suleja, Bida, Mokwa, Kutiwenji, Tegina and Kontagora.

NJOKU, PROF. ENI. Born on November 6, 1917, in Ebem, Ohafia in Imo State (q.v.), he attended Ebem Primary School and Hope Waddell Training Institute in Calabar (q.v.) from 1933 to 1936. He then proceeded to Yaba Higher College, Lagos (q.v.). Later on, he went to the University of Manchester in England to study botany, where he graduated with first-class honours in 1947. In 1948 he received his M.A. degree there, and in 1954 he obtained a Ph.D. degree from the University of London. Dr. Njoku was appointed chairman of the Electricity Corporation of Nigeria, now the National Electric Power Authority (q.v.). In 1962 he became the first vice chancellor of the University of Lagos. He resigned in 1965, following a crisis over his proposed reappointment, and went to Michigan State University in the United States as a visiting professor. In 1966 he was appointed the vice chancellor of the University of Nigeria, Nsukka (q.v.). During the Civil War (q.v.) of 1967–70, he supported the Biafran cause. After the war, he returned to teach botany at the University of Nigeria, Nsukka.

Professor Njoku was not only an academician, he also took part in politics. He was elected to the Eastern House of Assembly (q.v.) in 1952 and from there to the federal House of Representatives (q.v.) in Lagos where he became the minister of mines and power from 1952 to 1953. He was, therefore, intimately involved in the Eastern Regional Crisis of 1953 (q.v.). He also became a member of the Senate (q.v.) in 1960.

Professor Njoku received honorary degrees of doctor of science from the University of Nigeria, 1964, and from the University of Lagos in 1973. Michigan State University also conferred on him an honorary degree of doctor of law. He also served on the boards of the Commonwealth Scientific Committee, on the United Nations Advisory Committee on the Application of Science and Technology, on the UNESCO Advisory Committee on Natural Sciences and on the Councils of the Universities of Zambia and Zaïre. He died in London on December 22, 1974.

NJOKU, RAYMOND AMANZE. A lawyer and a politician, Raymond A. Njoku was born in August 1915 in Emekuku in Owerri Division of Imo State (q.v.). He attended Our Lady's School in his hometown and from there Ahiara Catholic Secondary School from 1929 to 1936. He then went to St. Charles College at Onitsha (q.v.) to train as a teacher. He taught at the same school in 1939 but left in 1943 for St. Gregory's College in Lagos (q.v.). In the same year he left Nigeria to study law at the University of London. He was called to the bar at the Middle Temple in 1947.

Upon return to Nigeria in 1947, he set up a private legal practice in Aba and also became interested in politics. He later joined the National Council of Nigeria and the Cameroons (NCNC) (q.v.) and was chairman of the party's Eastern Region (q.v.) working committee. He tried to get elected to the Eastern House of Assembly (q.v.) in 1951 and failed. In the 1954 federal elections (q.v.), however, he was elected to the Nigerian Legislative Council (q.v.) in Lagos where he became minister of commerce and industry in the federal Council of Ministers (q.v.). In 1955 he became federal minister of trade and industry, and, in October 1955, he had become the second national vice president of the NCNC. In the federal elections of 1959, he was also elected and he became minister of transport in the coalition government of the Northern People's Congress (q.v.) and the NCNC under Prime Minister Alhaji Tafawa Balewa (q.v.). In 1964 he became minister of communications and aviation. When the military took over in 1966, he went into private practice.

He was chairman of the National Catholic Laity Council of Nigeria and was knighted by Pope John XXIII with the Knight Grand Cross of the Order of St. Gregory the Great. His services to the country were also duly recognised when he became the recipient of the national honour of the commander of the Federal Republic of Nigeria (q.v.). He died September 21, 1977.

NKRUMAH, DR. KWAME. A Ghanaian nationalist, a Pan-Africanist, the first premier of independent Ghana and its first president. Born in 1909, he was educated in the United States, and, upon his return to Ghana (q.v.), he became a politician. He later founded his own party, the Convention People's Party (CPP), which fought for Ghana's independence from the British, which was realized in 1957. From then on, Ghana's independence became a symbol for all of Africa. But Nkrumah's Pan-Africanism (q.v.) was more militant than that of Nigerian leaders.

In 1960 Nigeria became independent with Sir Abubakar Tafawa Balewa (q.v.), a moderate Pan-Africanist, as the prime minister and Chief Obafemi Awolowo (q.v.), leader of the Action Group Party (AG) (q.v.), as the leader of opposition. Nkrumah began to court the support of the opposition party in Nigeria to support his African position. In June 1961, Chief Awolowo visited Ghana for discussion with the Ghanaian president, and, upon his return, Chief Awolowo's criticism of Nigerian foreign policy (q.v.) became much louder and showed that he was leaning toward Nkrumah's Pan-Africanism. After the visit many AG members went to Ghana for one kind of training or another: some went to train in party organization, while others went to train in the use of firearms. Furthermore, when Chief Anthony Enahoro (q.v.), an AG leader, escaped from Nigeria when he was to be arrested for treasonable felony, he went first to Ghana before proceeding to London, and Sam Ikoku (q.v.), another AG leader, took refuge in Ghana under Nkrumah.

Dr. Nkrumah was removed from power on January 24, 1966, by the military, just over a week after the Nigerian coup (q.v.) of January 15, 1966. He died later in Côte d'Ivoire (Ivory Coast).

NOK. The name given to the culture of the people who lived in what are now called the northern and central parts of Nigeria about 900 B.C. Remains of the culture were first found as a result of mining the Jos Plateau, and similar objects have been found in the middle valley of the Benue River (q.v.). Archaeological findings suggest a settled people, flourishing in the area between 900 B.C. and A.D. 200. Some artifacts found there include stone axes, terra-cotta (q.v.) figurines and other iron materials, all suggesting a fairly well-developed culture in employing the technique of iron smelting. They were the first people known in Nigeria to have used iron tools. The Nok culture is said to have a common element in its figurines: human heads were usually portrayed with triangular eyes and perforations for the pupils, nostrils and the mouth.

NORTH-CENTRAL STATE. One of the six states created in Northern Nigeria (q.v.) in May 1967, North-Central State occupied the same land area as the present Kaduna and Katsina States (qq.v.), and its name was changed into Kaduna State in 1976 when the country became a federation (q.v.) of 19 states. It was then the policy of the federal military government not to designate any state with its geographical location of north, west or east. The capital of the state was Kaduna (q.v.).

NORTH-EASTERN STATE. The largest of the six states created in the Northern Region (q.v.) in 1967, it was made up of the Bornu, Bauchi, Adamawa and Sardauna provinces. It had an area of about 271, 950 square kilometres and a population of about 7.9 million people, according to the 1961 census. In 1976 the state was divided virtually into three states—Borno, Gongola and Bauchi States (qq.v.). The capital of the state was Maiduguri.

NORTHERN CAMEROON. *See* CAMEROON.

NORTHERN ELEMENT PROGRESSIVE ASSOCIATION. Formed in Kano (q.v.) in 1945 by Mallam H.R. Abdallah, the Northern Element Progressive Association was a northern extension of Dr. Nnamdi Azikiwe's (q.v.) nationalist struggle. In fact, the same Mallam Abdallah organised the branch of the Zikist Movement (q.v.) in Kano and became its national president. The Kano authorities were opposed to NEPA, and it was, therefore, short-lived.

NORTHERN ELEMENTS PROGRESSIVE UNION (NEPU). A political party formed in 1950 by Mallam Aminu Kano (q.v.), previously a member of the Northern People's Congress (NPC) (q.v.). Being dissatisfied with the moderate attitude of the NPC toward traditional rulers and many of the ordinary people in the country, he broke away to found the NEPU. As a political party, it allied itself with the masses against the authority of the Emirs (q.v.), traditional rulers whose authority is exercised through the Native Authority (q.v.). As such, NEPU leaders saw a class struggle between the masses and the Native Authorities, and their interest was to organise the masses for the conquest of the powers of government. Though based in the north, its programme aimed at a united Nigeria, which was patently different from the regional separatism of the NPC. It allied itself with the National Council of Nigeria and the Cameroons (NCNC) (q.v.), based in the south, which opened it to the charges that it was an agent of southern domination. The party's support came mainly from Kano Province and neighbouring areas and it was no match for the NPC, which effectively controlled political power in the north. The party was banned in 1966 after the military takeover.

NORTHERN HOUSE OF ASSEMBLY. The Richards Constitution (q.v.) of 1946 created the Northern Regional Council, consisting of two chambers: the House of Chiefs (q.v.) and the House of Assembly. The House of Assembly consisted of the senior resident as president, 18 other official members and 20–24 unofficial members, 14–18 of whom were selected by the Native Authorities (q.v.) and six to be appointed by the governor to represent interests and communities inadequately represented. In 1951 the house consisted of the president, four official members, 90 elected members and not more than 10 special members. In 1966, after the military takeover, the house ceased to exist.

NORTHERN HOUSE OF CHIEFS. The Northern House of Chiefs was created under the Richards Constitution (q.v.) of 1946 as the second chamber of the then-Northern Regional Council. The House of Chiefs consisted of the chief commissioner (q.v.) as president, all first-class Chiefs (q.v.) and not less than ten second-class Chiefs selected by the Chiefs themselves in accordance with the rules laid down by the Chiefs. In the Macpherson Constitution (q.v.) of 1951, the House consisted of the lieutenant governor as president, three official members, all first-class Chiefs, 37 other Chiefs and an adviser on Islamic law (q.v.). The house ceased to exist in January 1966 when the military took over power.

NORTHERNISATION POLICY. After Northern Nigeria (q.v.) became self-governing in internal affairs in 1959, it embarked on a northernisation policy. This was basically a recruitment policy designed to create a modern northern Nigerian elite. Expatriates were often engaged, though at great cost, in preference to Nigerians of non-Northern origin. Any non-Northerners recruited, be they expatriates or Nigerians, were recruited on a contract basis, that is, the contract would not be renewed if persons of Northern Nigerian origin became available.

NORTHERN NIGERIA. *See* NORTHERN REGION.

NORTHERN NIGERIA MARKETING BOARD. Established in 1954 as a corporate body, the Northern Nigeria Marketing Board was charged with the function of securing the most favourable arrangements for the purchase and exportation of produce, and by so doing, promote the development of the producing industries concerned for the benefit of the producers. It was given power to fix prices to be paid to producers and to appoint licensed buying and storage agents. It also had power to undertake investment projects. The board was, however, dissolved in 1977 after the establishment of the Commodity Boards (q.v.). The most important crops handled by the board were groundnuts (peanuts) (q.v.) and cotton.

NORTHERN NIGERIA POLICE FORCE. In 1900 the British government revoked the charter of the Royal Niger Company (q.v.) and proclaimed the area under the administration of the Protectorate (q.v.) of Northern Nigeria. The Royal Niger Constabulary (q.v.) was split into two: the Northern Nigeria Police Force and the Northern Nigeria Regiment.

NORTHERN PEOPLE'S CONGRESS. Following the pattern of ethnic group organisational activities going on in the south as seen by the establishment of a Pan-Ibo Federal Union in 1944 and Egbe Omo Odudua (q.v.), a Yoruba (q.v.) cultural group, first in London in 1945 and later on in Nigeria in 1948, people in the north too began to think of a Pan-Northern Nigerian cultural organisation. The organisation was formed in 1949 and was called Jam'iyyar Mutanen Arewa (q.v.), which means Northern People's Congress (NPC). The leaders of the organisation included the three leaders of the Bauchi General Improvement Union (q.v.). Mallam Sa'ad Zungur (q.v.), the first Northern Nigerian to attend Yaba Higher College (q.v.), Mallam Aminu Kano (q.v.), a Fulani (q.v.) schoolteacher who returned from London in 1947, Mallam Abubakar Tafawa Balewa (q.v.), the headmaster of Bauchi Middle School, together with Dr. R.A.B. Dikko (q.v.) and Mallam Yahaya Gusau. The aims of the organisation were clearly innocuous: it wanted to unite the peoples of the north into one organisation to preserve northern regional autonomy within a united Nigeria; it did not intend to usurp the authority of the traditional rulers. In fact, it intended to enhance it whenever possible. It believed that the north could be saved only by the northerners, but it still wanted to be friendly with the other peoples of Nigeria.

Because of this conservative attitude of the organisation and their deference to the Emirs (q.v.) and to the status quo, some more radical elements broke away. They felt they did not want an organisation that would unite the north against the feared domination of the south, but rather an organisation to which other people from other regions could join, and which would aim first and foremost at Nigerian unity. It was led by Mallam Aminu Kano, and they all formed another organisation known as the Northern Element Progressive Union (NEPU). Because of the successes of NEPU in the Kano (q.v.) area, a party which was allied with the National Council of Nigeria and the Cameroons (NCNC) (q.v.) and which the NPC saw as a symbol of southern domination, the Jam'iyya, which had appeared to be in limbo, began to regroup to fight NEPU in the forthcoming election to usher in the Macpherson Constitution (q.v.) in 1951. The remaining leaders of the organization together with Sir Ahmadu Bello (q.v.) the Sardauna of Sokoto (q.v.), renamed it the Northern People's Congress and decided to contest the elections under its platform. Alhaji Sir Ahmadu Bello was elected leader of the party, while Mallam Abubakar Tafawa Balewa became deputy leader of the party.

The party's aims were imbued with the fear of southern domination, which the people saw as a great threat. The aims included regional autonomy within a united Nigeria, local government (q.v.) reforms without doing much violence to the traditional emirate system (q.v.), initiating a drive for education (q.v.) throughout the region, while at the same time preserving and increasing the cultural influence on the people, retention of the traditional system of appointing the Emirs but with a wider representation on the electoral committee, inculcation in the northerners of a genuine love for their region, with the motto "One North, One People," regardless of religion, tribe or rank to fight for eventual self-government for Nigeria and to seek the cooperation of any organisation in or out of the Northern Region whose aims and aspirations coincided with those of the party.

The party became very powerful and overbearing. It not only effectively controlled the whole of Northern Nigeria, but it was the major coalition partner in the Federal Government (q.v.) until 1966, when the military came into power and disbanded all political parties.

NORTHERN PROGRESSIVE FRONT. The Northern Progressive Front (NPF) was formed in 1963 as an alliance between the Northern Element Progressive Union (q.v.) and the United Middle-Belt Congress (q.v.). They agreed on a single list of candidates and a common programme. The leader of the NPF was Mallam Aminu Kano (q.v.). For the 1964 general elections, the NPF joined the United Progressive Grand Alliance (q.v.), made up principally of the National Convention of Nigerian Citizens and the Action Group Party (q.v.).

NORTHERN PROVINCES LAW SCHOOL. A Muslim school set up by Abdullahi Bayero (q.v.), the former Emir (q.v.) of Kano (q.v.) after his return from Mecca in 1934. It was to train the alkalis in Islamic common law (q.v.) known as the Shari'a (q.v.). In 1947 it became the School for Arabic Studies and came under government control. The school then trained teachers in Arabic and Islamic subjects as well as English (q.v.), arithmetic and other subjects.

NORTHERN REGION. The Northern Region, made up of the old Protectorate (q.v.) of Northern Nigeria, consisted of over three-quarters of the total land area of the country and, according to the 1991 census, more than half the population. Though culturally heterogenous, it had the integrative bond of Islam (q.v.) and the former Fulani empire (q.v.) gave much of the area some feeling of identity. The Hausa language (q.v.), which became the lingua franca of the people in the region, also gave the area further identity. This was why people from the north, in spite of their ethnic differences, were generally referred to in the south as Hausa (q.v.). Though Islamic religion is strong in the north, all of the region did not accept Islam. There is the non-Muslim area of the Middle Belt, which escaped the Fulani conquest of the 19th century and has, therefore, been open to greater influence from the Christian (q.v.) missionaries and Western education. These people have only been partially integrated into the dominant culture, and they have been famous for their struggle for political freedom from the Hausa-Fulani hegemony. These people included the Tiv (q.v.), Gwari (q.v.) and the Nupe (q.v.). The major towns in the region were Kano (q.v.), Sokoto (q.v.), Ilorin (q.v.), Zaria (q.v.), Guasau, Katsina (q.v.), Yola (q.v.), Borno (q.v.), Jos (q.v.), Minna and Kaduna (q.v.), which was the capital city. The administrative capital of the region was Kaduna.

Because of the preponderance of the Northern Region in the federation (q.v.) as seen by its land area and its population, and because of the fact that only one party, the Northern People's Congress (NPC) (q.v.), effectively controlled the region before and after independence, fears began to be felt and expressed that for the foreseeable future, the north would dominate the politics of the whole federation. As such, demands began to be made that the north should be divided into more regions or states, but nothing was done about this by the colonial, postindependence, and the first republican governments until after the military took over power in January 1966. In 1967, before the outbreak of the Civil War (q.v.), General Yakubu Gowon (q.v.) divided the nation into 12 states—six in the south and six in the north. The six northern states were Benue-Plateau, Kwara, North-Western, North-Eastern, North-Central and Kano States (qq.v.). In 1976 these six states were further subdivided into ten states: Kano, Sokoto (q.v.), Kaduna, Borno (q.v.), Gongola (q.v.), Bauchi (q.v.), Kwara (q.v.), Niger (q.v.), Plateau (q.v.) and Benue (q.v.) States. In 1991 the 10 states were further divided into 16 states, and in 1996, the number increased to 19 states.

The leader of the NPC was Sir Ahmadu Bello (q.v.) the Sardauna of Sokoto (q.v.), and the first and only premier of the region. In 1961 the region established the Ahmadu Bello University in Zaria. The Northern Region falls within the savannah, which has made it a suitable place for animal husbandry (cattle, sheep and goats). A large percentage of the population engage in cattle rearing and the keeping of other livestock. A good number of the others are farmers or traders. Among the most important food crops in the north are groundnuts (peanuts) (q.v.), millet, rice, guinea-corn, beans and maize.

NORTHERN REGION DEVELOPMENT CORPORATION. This corporation was established in 1955 and, like its counterparts in the east and west, its purpose was to speed up the economic development of the region. To this end, it made most of its funds available for agricultural land settlement, agricultural production development, water supplies, irrigation and communications and the control of animal pests like the tsetse fly. The corporation also granted loans to Native Authorities (q.v.) for the development of markets, motor parks and abattoirs. Businessmen also benefitted from its loans.

NORTHERN TEACHERS' ASSOCIATION. Established in London in 1947 by Mallam Aminu Kano (q.v.), who later became the leader of the Northern Element Progressive Union (q.v.). In 1948 Mallam Aminu Kano convened the first meeting of the association in Nigeria. It was the first northern labour union in Nigerian history.

NORTH-WESTERN STATE. One of the 12 states created in May 1967, North-Western State shared common borders in the north with the Republic of Niger, in the south with Kwara (q.v.) and Benue-Plateau (q.v.) States and in the east with the North-Central State (q.v.). It had an area of about 168,770 square kilometres and a population of about 5.7 million people, according to the 1961 census. In 1976 the state was divided into Sokoto (q.v.) and Niger (q.v.) States. The capital of the state was Sokoto (q.v.).

NPN-NPP ACCORD. When National Party of Nigeria (NPN) (q.v.) candidate Alhaji Shehu Shagari's (q.v.) election as president had been confirmed by the Supreme Court (q.v.) in September 1979, the president-elect invited the leaders of the other four political parties to join him in a broad-based government, and asked them to allow their party members to accept any positions that he might offer them in his government. Only the Nigerian People's Party (NPP) (q.v.) agreed to join in his government. The two parties drew up an agreement, which was later known as the NPN-NPP Accord.

According to the accord, a special development agency would be set up to ensure the rapid economic development of those states whose social and economic development were lagging behind the other states or had suffered serious setback arising from natural disasters, war or the difficult nature of their terrain. They would also set up a constitution study and review committee, as a matter of urgency in order to ensure permanent stability by removing likely causes of friction arising from various types of ambiguities and conflicts in the new constitution (q.v.). The committee would, among other things, examine state creation (q.v.), the Land Use Decree (q.v.), the issue of adequate compensation for properties compulsorily acquired, and local government (q.v.). It would also initiate a workable program based on the manifestoes of the cooperating parties within the first 90 days of the new administration and recommend same for adoption by the Federal Government (q.v.). The two parties also agreed on their conduct of foreign affairs and their approach to religious issues: to abide by the 1979 constitutional provisions that forbid adoption of state religion and that guarantee freedom of thought, conscience and religion, and freedom from discrimination. Because the two parties were lacking in agreement on common economic and social programmes, the accord broke down in July 1981.

NUPE. Living mainly in Niger State (q.v.), the Nupe are divided into many subgroups like Batau, Beni, Kyedye, Eghagi, Ebe, Benu and many others. However, they speak related Nupe languages. Their main towns are Bida, Mokwa and Jebba. They are famous for their glass, silver, bronze and brass works, and their craftspeople are organised into societies and guilds, according to their work. Many others are farmers, growing such crops as rice, guinea corn, millet and yams (q.v.).

Nupe State was said to have been founded in the 15th century by Tsoede, the son of the Ata of Igala, whose capital was Idah. The state became very powerful between the 16th and the 18th centuries, during which it waged successful wars against the Oyo empire (q.v.). The Fulani (q.v.) jihad (q.v.) of the early 19th century had great difficulty in getting a foothold in the state through one Mallam Dendo, who became effective ruler of the state, and his successors, taking the title of Etsu Nupe (Chief of Nupe), who established themselves in Bida and ruled from there. At the end of the century, British rule was established through the activities of the Royal Niger Company (q.v.).

NWAFOR-ORIZU, DR. AKWEKE ABYSSINIA. Born in July 1920, he attended St. Thomas Central School and Onitsha Central School between 1924 and 1931. By taking private lessons, he passed the Junior Cambridge in 1937. In 1938 he secured a scholarship to study at Achimota College in Ghana (q.v.), and in 1939 he went to Lincoln University in Pennsylvania in the United States, where he met Dr. Kwame Nkrumah (q.v.) of Ghana. He later transferred to Howard University in Washington, D.C., where he studied political science.

In 1940 he became a member of the Marcus Garvey Movement in New York City, and in 1941, he, together with people like John Karefe-Smart of Sierra Leone (q.v.), Dr. K.O. Mbadiwe (q.v.) and Mazi Mbonu Ojike (q.v.), founded the African Students' Association of the United States and Canada (q.v.) under the International Students Union of the university. In 1944 he obtained his M.A. degree in public law and government from Columbia University in New York. He was editor of the *Negro Digest* and contributing editor to the *Pittsburgh Courier.* With Dr. Nkrumah as the president of the African Students Association of the United States and Canada, he was elected vice president, and he later became its president. In 1944 he published his book, *Without Bitterness*.Back in Nigeria in 1949, he championed the cause of the Nigerian mine workers during the Enugu (q.v.) massacre of 21 miners and was placed under house arrest for 14 days by the colonial government. In 1951 he became a member of the Eastern House of Assembly (q.v.), from which he was elected to the membership of the federal legislative house in Lagos (q.v.). Before independence, he, at different periods, occupied many political posts, including that of the chief whip of the National Council of Nigeria and the Cameroons (q.v.) Party in both regional and national legislative houses. In 1960 he was appointed the first senator to represent Onitsha Province in the Senate (q.v.). In 1964 he became the president of the Senate, a position he was holding when the military intervened in politics in January 1966, a fact which explained why it was he who was responsible for handing over federal power to the federal military government during the coup (q.v.) of January 1966. After the Civil War (q.v.), he became a private person. When party politics began again in 1978, he joined the National Party of Nigeria (q.v.) but was not a very active member. He died in March 1999.

NWANKWO, DR. ARTHUR AGWUNCHA. Born on August 19, 1942, in Jalli in the Eastern Region (q.v.). He is one of the most prominent social critics and political activists in the country. Dr. Nwankwo received his B.A.

from Eastern Mennonite College in Virginia in 1966 and his M.A. from Duquesne University, both in the United States, in 1967. He first came to national attention when he worked in the Propaganda Directorate of the breakaway Republic of Biafra (q.v.), editing the *Biafra Newsletter* (1967–69). In the Second Republic (1979–83) (q.v.), he was a governorship candidate (unsuccessful) for the socialist People's Redemption Party in Anambra State. After the annulment of the June 12, 1993, presidential election (q.v.) Nwankwo emerged as one of the most vocal defenders of M.K.O. Abiola's (q.v.) mandate in the Southeast, and was briefly imprisoned in the final days of the Abacha regime. He is a leader of the Eastern Mandate Union and the National Democratic Coalition (q.v.). Nwankwo is a prolific writer, and among his books are *The Military Option for Democracy* (1987) and *Civilianised Soldiers* (1984).

NWOBODO, JIM. Born May 9, 1940 in Lafia in the Northern Region. He is one of the most prominent and controversial politicians of eastern Nigeria. He graduated from the University of Ibadan in 1964, after which he taught briefly at King's College in Lagos and worked for Shell BP. In the 1970s he ran a number of businesses including Link Group International Limited and Universal Insurance Company Limited. In 1979 he was elected governor of Anambra State on the platform of the Nigerian People's Party (NPP). In his bid for re-election in 1983, however, he was defeated by the National Party of Nigeria candidate (C.C. Onoh). After the military came to power in 1984, he was imprisoned on charges of corruption, and was not released until October 1988 when he was pardoned by the Babangida regime. Although officially banned from politics during Babangida's transition program, Nwobodo was active in his support of the Social Democratic Party, resulting in his being briefly detained in 1991. Nwobodo was a representative to the National Constitutional Conference (1994–95) and served as Minister of Youth and Sports during the Abacha regime. During the Abacha transition program he competed unsuccessfully to be elected to the Senate. During Abubakar's democratic transition (1998–99) Nwobodo was an unsuccessful candidate for the presidential nomination of the People's Democratic Party (PDP). His candidacy was controversial among many Igbos, however, who feared that he would draw votes away from the favored eastern candidate, Alex Ekwueme. These feelings became more pronounced after Ekwueme lost the nomination to Olusegun Obasanjo in February 1999. After failing to win the presidential nomination, Nwobodo prevailed upon the Senator-elect from Anambra South to step down, allowing Nwobodo to contest for and win his senate seat in a bye-election.

NWOKEDI COMMISSION. The Nwokedi Commission was the one-man commission under F.C. Nwokedi appointed in March 1966 by the then-Head of State General Aguiyi-Ironsi (q.v.) who took over after the January 1966 coup (q.v.). The commission was to look into the problem of unifying the civil services of the Federation (q.v.) and make recommendations. As a result of its proposals, Unification Decree (q.v.) No. 34 of 1966 came into being.

NWOSU, PROF. HUMPHREY NWOBU. A political scientist, born on October 2, 1941, at Ajalli Aguta, Anambra State (q.v.), he was educated in Ajalli, Enugu (q.v.), Abakaliki and later at the University of Nigeria, Nsukka (q.v.) from 1963 to 1966, and afterwards at the University of California in Berkeley, California, U.S.A. He was later appointed to many political offices, the most important to the historical development of Nigeria was as chairman of the National Electoral Commission from 1989 to 1993. It has been said that Nwosu conducted the freest and fairest state, national and presidential elections in the history of Nigeria. However, working under a military administration, he was far from free. It was, therefore, a great shock to the nation when he was ordered to stop the announcement of the results of the June 12, 1993, presidential election (q.v.) after the results of 14 states and the Federal Capital Territory (q.v.) had been declared to the public. As the declared results showed, Chief Moshood Abiola (q.v.) was winning. On June 23, 1993, the results of the presidential election were annulled, creating the greatest political crisis since the end of the Civil War (q.v.) in 1970.

NZEOGWU, MAJ. PATRICK CHUKWUMA KADUNA. Leader of the first Nigerian coup d'état (q.v.) of January 15, 1966, Major Nzeogwu was born in 1937 in Kaduna (q.v.), in the Northern Region (q.v.) where his parents, both Igbos from Eastern Nigeria (q.v.), lived. He attended St. John's College in Kaduna from 1950 to 1955. He later joined the Nigerian Army as a cadet and was sent to Sandhurst where he became a commissioned officer. By January 1966, he had risen to the position of a major.

The plot to overthrow the government of Alhaji Sir Abubakar Tafawa Balewa (q.v.) was hatched in 1965 by Major Nzeogwu, Major Emmanuel Ifeajuna, Major D.O. Okafor and Captain E.N. Nwobosi. The plot became effective on January 15, 1966. Nzeogwu, the leader of the plot, was in charge of the Kaduna operation, that is, eliminating leading figures in the Northern People's Congress (NPC) (q.v.), which, at the time, dominated not only the politics of the Northern Region but also of the Federation (q.v.). As such, it was he who led his forces to the leader of the party, Sir Ahmadu Bello (q.v.), the Sardauna of Sokoto (q.v.) and premier of the Northern Region. The premier was killed, and on January 15, Nzeogwu broadcast a message to the nation that no citizen needed to fear so long as he was law abiding. The type of people his "Supreme Council of the Revolution" was after, he said, were political profiteers, swindlers, the men who received bribes and demanded 10 percent of contracts awarded, the tribalists and the nepotists.

The main aim of the coup, he said, was to establish a strong united and progressive nation, free from corruption and internal strife.

Unfortunately for his revolution, many of the people entrusted with operations in the other parts of the country did not creditably discharge their duties. They were able to get to the prime minister in Lagos (q.v.), and they killed him. They killed the premier of Western Nigeria (q.v.), Chief S.L. Akintola (q.v.) and they also killed Chief Festus S. Okotie-Eboh (q.v.) the federal minister of finance, together with other senior military officers. They did not get General Johnson T.U. Aguiyi-Ironsi (q.v.), and in the Eastern Region, the operation was a complete failure. Not being in complete control, he and his men had to surrender to General Aguiyi-Ironsi, to whom the federal cabinet had submitted power. On January 19, 1966, Nzeogwu went to Lagos to submit but he was detained first in Lagos and then later in Eastern Nigeria. Colonel Chukwuemeka Odumegwu Ojukwu (q.v.) released him in March 1967 before the Eastern Region declared its secession—as Biafra (q.v.)—from the rest of the country. Though he disagreed with Colonel Ojukwu on secession, he fought on the side of Biafra and was killed in action on July 26, 1967. The federal troops discovered his body, and it was buried with full military honours in Kaduna.

NZERIBE, CHIEF FRANCIS ARTHUR. An industrialist, philanthropist and politician, born in Oguta, Imo State (q.v.), on November 2, 1938. He was educated at Holy Ghost College, Owerri (q.v.), Portsmouth College of Technology and Manchester University in the United Kingdom. He founded many companies and became very wealthy. In 1983 he became a senator in the Federal Republic of Nigeria (q.v.). In 1989, when the ban on political activity was lifted, he became a member of the Social Democratic Party (SDP) (q.v.), one of the two government-founded, -funded, and -imposed parties that contested in the 1992 primaries for the presidency. The primary elections were nullified. After that, Nzeribe began to actively campaign for President Ibrahim B. Babangida (q.v.), the military Head of State, to continue in power rather than hand over power to an elected candidate. To achieve his objective, he founded the Association for Better Nigeria (q.v.), which became notorious in the role it played to scuttle the June 12, 1993, presidential election (q.v.) and to have it finally annulled by the president who had to "step aside" when he could no longer continue under the pressure to quit. The association—as revealed by member Chief Abimbola Davies who later defected—engaged in many shady deals to keep President Babangida in power for many more years after his promised hand-over. Nzeribe participated in the Abubakar transition program (1998–99) as a member of the All People's Party and was elected a Senator from Imo State.

-O-

OBA. Oba is the term for "king" among the Yoruba (q.v.) people and the title of the ruler of the Edo-speaking kingdom of Benin (q.v.). The Oba of each Yoruba kingdom is known by a specific title like the "Alaafin of Oyo" or the "Ooni of Ife," and so on. All the principal Obas in Yorubaland, including the Oba of Benin claim their descent from Oduduwa (q.v.), the ancestor of the Yoruba. Both the Benin and the Yoruba Obas were "divine" kings who, in the past, exercised great spiritual and political powers in their kingdoms, but whose authority was nonetheless checked by Councils of Chiefs (q.v.) or some secret societies like the Ogboni Society, composed of traditional religious and political leaders.

OBASANJO, GEN. OLUSEGUN. Former Head of State, head of the federal military government and Commander-in-Chief of the armed forces (q.v.) from 1976 to 1979, General Olusegun Obasanjo was born on March 5, 1937, at Abeokuta (q.v.) in Ogun State (q.v.). After his primary education, he went to Abeokuta Baptist High School. He enlisted in the Nigerian Army in 1958 and was later sent to Mons Officer Cadets' School in England. He returned to Nigeria and was commissioned in 1959. He was promoted to full lieutenant in 1960 and later served with the United Nations forces in the Congo. He later joined the engineering unit of the Nigerian Army and was promoted to captain in 1963 and commander of the Royal Engineers. He was sent to the royal engineering young officers course at Shrivenham in England and in January 1965 he was promoted to major. In the same year he attended the Indian Staff College, and was later on attachment to the Indian Army Engineering School at Kirkee. In 1967 he was promoted to lieutenant colonel and was commander of the second area command of the Nigerian Army, commander of the second division (Rear), Ibadan (q.v.), and commander of the Ibadan garrison from 1967 to 1969. He was promoted to colonel in 1969 and later commanded the third marine commando division operating on the southeastern front of Biafra (q.v.) during the Civil War (q.v.). He accepted the surrender of the Biafran forces in January 1970. In the same year he was appointed commander of the engineering corps. In 1972 he was promoted brigadier, and he later went on to further studies at the Royal College of Defence Studies in London from 1973 to 1974. He was appointed commissioner (q.v.) for works and housing from January to July 1975. Following the coup d'état (q.v.) of July 29, 1975, he became chief of staff supreme headquarters under the late General Murtala R. Muhammed (q.v.). After the attempted coup of February 13, 1976, staged by Lt. Col. B.S. Dimka (q.v.), in which General Muhammed was assassinated, he was appointed Head of State and Commander-in-Chief of the armed forces and chairman of the

Supreme Military Council (q.v.). He faithfully carried out the military program of disengagement and handed over power to Alhaji Shehu Shagari (q.v.), the newly elected president of Nigeria in 1979. He retired from the army in 1979 to become a farmer.

Because of his voluntary retirement from the military and his handing over of power to a civilian administration, General Obasanjo's image nationally and internationally rose. On the international scene, he played a leading role in the international monitoring of African rulers, and was a member of the Transparency International, an anticorruption organisation. He was a member of the United Nations Educational, Scientific and Cultural Organization Commission for Peace in the Minds of Men from 1981 to 1986, a member of the Independent Commission on Disarmament and Security Issues in 1983, a member of the World Health Organization Committee of Experts on the Effects of Nuclear Weapons and a member and cochairman of the Commonwealth Eminent Persons Group of South Africa in 1985. Nationally, he was seen as a man who stood by his words. His criticism of the administrations after him, especially that of General Ibrahim B. Babangida (q.v.), seemed to portray him as a man against corruption and a man who cared much for the ordinary people. However, the events following the annulment of the June 12, 1993 presidential election (q.v.), by the military administration of General Babangida dented his image as a born-again democrat. Rather than support the apparent winner, he began to campaign for an Interim National Government (q.v.) to succeed the military.

In March 1995, General Obasanjo was one of the retired military officers arrested for what the Abacha regime called plotting a coup to overthrow the government. He and about 40 others, military and civilian, were tried by a secret military tribunal and sentenced to varying terms of imprisonment. Obasanjo was sentenced to 25 years. This was after representatives by many world leaders had pleaded with the government to spare his life and those of his so-called coup plotters.

Following the death of Sani Abacha in June 1998, Obasanjo was released from prison. In October 1998 he declared his intention to contest for the presidency under the People's Democratic Party (PDP). Obasanjo enjoyed the support of a variety of different groups, including northern conservatives, retired military officers and the political machine of the late Shehu Yar'Adua. In February he was elected to the presidency, and on May 29, 1999 was sworn in as Nigeria's head of state once again, this time as a civilian.

General Obasanjo was honoured in 1980 with the title of Grand Commander of the Order of the Federal Republic of Nigeria and has received many honorary doctorate degrees. He has written many books, among which are *My Command: An Account of the Nigerian Civil War 1967–70* (1980), *Nzeogwu* (1987) and *Not My Will* (1990).

OBI, PROF. CHIKE. A mathematician and a politician. Born on April 7, 1921, in Zaria (q.v.), he was educated in Zaria, Onitsha (q.v.) and at Yaba Higher College, Lagos (q.v.). He later went to Britain for further studies. Upon his return to Nigeria, he lectured in mathematics at the University of Ibadan (q.v.) in 1951. In 1971 he was appointed professor of mathematics at the University of Lagos. Professor Obi was the founder and the leader of the defunct Dynamic Party of Nigeria.

ODEBIYI, CHIEF JONATHAN AKINREMI OLAWOLE. Leader of the Unity Party of Nigeria (UPN) (q.v.) in the Senate (q.v.) from 1979 to 1983. He was born in 1923 at Ipaja, Lagos State (q.v.), attended St. Andrew's School, Ipaja, Christian Missionary Society Grammar School, Lagos (q.v.), and in 1944 proceeded to Fourah Bay College (q.v.) in Freetown (q.v.), Sierra Leone (q.v.) to study arts, and received a B.A. degree from the University of Durham in Britain.

In 1951 he was elected Action Group Party (AG) (q.v.) member of the Western House of Assembly (q.v.), and in 1956 he became minister of education under Chief Obafemi Awolowo (q.v.) who was premier, and later was the minister of finance and leader of the House until the AG crisis of 1962 (q.v.), in which he took a prominent part. It was when he was about to move the first business motion of the day that E.O. Oke, member for the Ogbomosho South West constituency, raised an alarm and started to fling a chair across the floor of the House. In 1978, when the ban on political activity was lifted, he became a member of the UPN Unity Party of Nigeria and was elected a senator for the Egbado North/South Senatorial District.

ODUDUWA. There are two stories as to the origin of Oduduwa. According to the Yoruba (q.v.) creation myth, Oduduwa, the son of Olorun, the Supreme God, was sent down from heaven with a handful of earth, a cockerel and a palm nut. Upon arrival on the water-covered earth, he scattered the earth he brought with him over the water, the cockerel scratched it and the palm nut grew into a palm tree. The very place where the earth was created is called Ile-Ife (q.v.), from where the Yoruba people migrated to other parts of the world. The second story says that Oduduwa was a prince from Mecca, the son of a king named Lamurudu. He was driven out for his idolatrous worship and, after wandering for a long time, settled at Ile-Ife. He had many children and grandchildren who spread out to other parts, where they established their own kingdoms. These two stories go on to explain the Yoruba belief that Oduduwa was their ancestor. It is also important to note that all the Yoruba Obas (q.v.) and the Oba of Benin like to trace their ancestral line to Oduduwa. It is also believed that Oduduwa brought the Ifa religion to Ile-Ife, established it there, and also founded the Ogboni cult, devoted to the worship of the earth, to protect the ancient customs and institutions of his people. There is today a shrine in Ile-Ife, devoted to the worship of Oduduwa, and many institutions and places have been named after him, e.g., Oduduwa College in Ile-Ife and Oduduwa Hall at the University of Ife in Ile-Ife, now called the Obafemi Awolowo University, Ile-Ife.

ODUTOLA, ALHAJI JIMO AKINTUNDE. A pioneer industrialist who spent over 70 years as a business entrepreneur. Born about 1905, he never had any formal schooling but learned to read, write and speak fluent English (q.v.) on his own. At 11, he was apprenticed to a cousin to learn trading and later started to trade in palm oil and palm kernel. At 22 he had bought his first truck to go into the transport business. He later went into produce buying, buying cocoa and palm kernel, and selling them to foreign companies. In 1944 he went into gold mining and became the only licensed indigenous company in that business in Nigeria. Alhaji Odutola is said not to have forgotten the advice he once received at an Italian exhibition in Milan when a man asked him for his line of business and he told him he was trading in textiles. The man was reported to have told him "Every fool can buy and sell; not every fool can produce." With this always on his mind, he began to search for what he could produce for Nigeria. He settled on tire retreading and set up a retreading company in Ibadan (q.v.), Oyo State (q.v.) and in Aba in the former Eastern Nigeria (q.v.). In 1958 he set up a foam rubber manufacturing company, the Nigerian Foam Rubber Company, Ltd. in Ibadan (q.v.) and in 1960 added the J.A. Odutola Plastic Foam Company. In all these ventures, he was the first in Nigeria. He later went into the real estate business in large cities like Lagos (q.v.), Ibadan, Aba, Benin (q.v.) and Onitsha (q.v.). He died in 1995.

OGONI. The Ogoni are made up of about 500,000 people in the Niger Delta (q.v.), on land which covers an area of about 650 square kilometres. The people traditionally were farmers and fishers, but after the discovery of oil in their area in the 1950s, their life-style changed, constantly being threatened by the exploration and exploitation of oil (q.v.), and the attendant pollution to their land by Shell Oil Company. The Shell Oil Company's operations affect the lives of people in some 12 major ethnic groups divided into hundreds of communities. The Ogoni, being the most outspoken, cried out that, in spite of the revenue they received from the petroleum oil from their land, not much came back to the area to compensate them for their loss in income, pollution and other inconveniences. What was more, their standard of living continued to deteriorate.

In Nigeria, mineral rights are held by the Federal Government (q.v.), but the Ogoni, being a small minority, have never had any effective say in the politics of Nigeria. Under the administration of General Ibrahim B. Babangida (q.v.), the situation worsened, so much so that they began to organise themselves for a positive action of protest against the government and the Shell Oil Company, with the hope of attracting government and international attention to their plight. In 1990 they, under the leadership of Ken Saro-Wiwa (q.v.), presented what they called the Ogoni Bill of Rights, demanding a greater share of the federal revenue and greater autonomy and control over their own affairs, including cultural, religious and environmental matters. Between 1991 and 1993, their campaign began to ask for compensation for environmental pollution and degradation of their land and rivers. Specially targeted was the Shell Oil Company in a bid to raise the international profile of their problem. The military government began to harass their leaders and to use divide-and-rule tactics. Their organisation, Movement for the Survival of the Ogoni People (MOSOP) (q.v.), broke into factions, some preferring negotiation with the military government while the other continued to put pressure on the government and Shell. The division led to violent confrontations among the leaders, leading to the death of four pro-government leaders. Ken Saro-Wiwa and some other leaders were arrested and charged with murder. They were secretly tried by a military tribunal, which found Ken Saro-Wiwa and eight others guilty and sentenced them to be executed by hanging. Many world leaders appealed to the Federal Government for clemency, but the government was anxious to get rid of Ken Saro-Wiwa with the hope that his death would restore things to normal. The precipitate speed with which the execution was carried out in November 1995 created a loud furor nationally and internationally, leading to the suspension of Nigeria from the Commonwealth (q.v.) and the imposition of some sanctions on the Nigerian military by the United States, some European countries and many other countries.

OGUNDE, CHIEF HUBERT ADEDEJI. A playwright and dramatist, and a pioneer in the development of Nigerian theatre, born July 10, 1916, at Ososa in Ijebu-Ode, Ogun State (q.v.), he was educated in Ososa, Lagos (q.v.), and Ijebu-Ode before joining the Nigerian police force in 1941. In 1946 he established the Ogunde Theatre Company and Ogunde Record Company, and in 1966 he established Ogunde Dance Company. He represented Nigeria at the EXPO '67 in Montreal, Canada, in 1967. He was founder of the Ogunde Film Company, African Music Research Party and a founding member of the Association of Nigerian Theatre Practitioners. He was also leader of the Nigerian National Troupe. He wrote over 50 plays, one of the best known being *Yoruba Ronu* (Yoruba should think), written and performed in Yoruba in 1964, depicting the political situation among the Yoruba (q.v.) of Western Nigeria (q.v.) at the time. He was nationally honoured with the membership of the Order of the Federal Republic and received an honorary doctorate degree from the University of Ife (q.v.), now called the Obafemi Awolowo University. He died in 1990.

OGUNDIPE, BRIG. BABAFEMI OLATUNDE. Brigadier Babafemi Olatunde Ogundipe was the number-two man at the Supreme Headquarters as chief of staff in January 1966 when the military took over power. His senior, General J.T.U. Aguiyi-Ironsi (q.v.) became Head of State after the military takeover.

Brigadier Ogundipe was born on September 6, 1924. He attended the Wesley and Banham Memorial School in Port Harcourt (q.v.), and in 1943 he enlisted in the army and was posted to India and Burma, where he served the British during the Second World War. He had training in England and was commissioned in 1953. He served with the British forces in Germany before coming to Nigeria, and later served in the United Nations Peacekeeping Forces in the Congo from 1960 to 1963. Upon his return to Nigeria, he became Commander of the Second Brigade of the Nigerian Army. He was later sent to London as military adviser to the Nigerian High Commissioner.

The second military coup (q.v.) of July 1966, in which General Aguiyi-Ironsi was killed, left Brigadier Ogundipe as the most senior officer in the army. In normal circumstances, he should have succeeded the late Head of State, but things were not normal. The new coup-makers preferred Colonel Yakubu Gowon (q.v.) as Head of State. One of the reasons why Lt. Colonel Odumegwu Ojukwu (q.v.) refused to accept General Gowon as Head of State and Supreme Commander was that a more senior officer was still available and it was he who should have assumed the post. He was, however, posted by Gowon to London as Nigeria's High Commissioner, where he served during the Civil War (q.v.). After the war, he was replaced, but he died in London on November 20, 1971, and was buried in Nigeria.

OGUNMOLA, H. KOLAWOLE. An actor and a composer of Yoruba (q.v.) musical plays and entertainments, born in 1925, he used Yoruba tradition, history and mythology in modern popular entertainment. He wrote *Aqbara j'aqbara* (The mighty of the mighty), and, among other plays, the Yoruba version of *The Palmwine Drinkard* by Amos Tutuola (q.v.). He died in 1973.

OGUNSANYA, CHIEF ADENIRAN. A lawyer and a politician, Chief Adeniran Ogunsanya was born on January 31, 1918, at Ikorodu, Lagos State (q.v.). After his primary education, he went to the Lagos Government School and King's College, Lagos (q.v.). He later proceeded to the University of Manchester in England in 1945 and Gray's Inn School of Law in London where he was called to the bar.

Between 1956 and 1959, Chief Ogunsanya was the chairman of the Federal Government's (q.v.) industrial board. In 1959 he became a member of Parliament and was later appointed the secretary of the federal Parliamentary Party of the National Council of Nigeria and the Cameroons (q.v.) and federal minister of housing and surveys in 1965. In 1968 he was appointed attorney-general and commissioner (q.v.) for justice in Lagos State and was later made a commissioner for education in the same state. In the wake of political activities in 1978, he became a foundation member of the Nigerian People's Party (NPP) (q.v.) and ran for the governorship of Lagos State in 1979, but lost to Alhaji Lateef K. Jakande (q.v.). He later became chairman of NPP. He died November 22, 1996.

OGUNSOLA, ISHOLA. An artist, also known as "I SHOW PEPPER," Ogunsola was born in 1942 in Abeokuta (q.v.), Ogun State (q.v.). Ishola Ogunsola had his elementary education in Abeokuta and later joined Chief Ogunole's theatre group in 1959 where he trained until 1965 when he left to form a partnership with Afolayan, popularly known as "Jagua." Their new company, Afolayan Ogunsola Theatre group, lasted only two years when the two men decided to go their different ways. Ogunsola later formed his own theatre group in 1968. He produced many plays, including *Igbo Aginju* (1968), *Won Ro Pe Were Ni* (1969), *Oluwa lo m'ejo da.* He was also the author of the play *Efunsetan Aniwura,* which was about the reign of an Iyalode of Ibadan. He died in December 1992.

OGUN STATE. Created in 1976 from the old Western State (q.v.), it comprises two provinces (q.v.) of Abeokuta and Ijebu and it has survived all the state creation exercises that have come after it. The land area is 16,762 square kilometres and is bounded in the north by Oyo (q.v.) and Osun (q.v.) States, in the east by Ondo State (q.v.), in the south by Lagos State (q.v.) and the Atlantic Ocean, and in the west by the Republic of Benin (q.v.). The state has a humid tropical climate with high rainfall, high evaporation, high relative humidity and long sunshine hours. The vegetation is tropical forest including fresh water swamps and lowland rain forest. The state is divided into 15 local government (q.v.) areas. Its mineral resources include limestone kaolinite, shade, brick clays, sandstone, gravel and sand.

The population of the state in 1991 was 2,338,570 people, 51.04 percent of whom were women. Ethnically, it is mainly Yoruba (q.v.), but there are subdivisions or subethnic groups like the Egba (q.v.), the Ijebu (q.v.), Egbado, Remo, Awori, and some others. The area the state occupies first came in contact with Christian (q.v.) missionaries in the 19th century and, therefore, is one of the most educationally advanced and advantaged in the Federation (q.v.). In 1990 it had 1,297 primary schools, 244 secondary schools, two universities and many colleges of education and polytechnical colleges.

The population centers in the state include Abeokuta (the capital), Ijebu-ode, Ilaro and Shagamu. The state is popularly known as the gateway to Nigeria and to the outside world because of its porous borders with the Republic of Benin at Idi-Iroko, though which thousands of foreigners come into the country by land and through which many Nigerians, including politicians and political activists escape to the rest of the world. In the state, Christians and Muslims (q.v.) live peacefully together, even though members of the same family or extended family may adhere to different religious tenets, including those of traditional religions (q.v.).

Ogun State has many places of attraction for tourists like the Olumo Rock in Abeokuta, which served as a refuge for the early Egba settlers, the Oba's (q.v.) palace, built in 1854 with many antiquities and relics and Centenary Hall.

OIL. *See* PETROLEUM.

OIL MINERAL PRODUCING AREAS DEVELOPMENT COMMISSION. Created by decree in 1992 as the federal government agency for the development of the oil-producing areas, the OMPADEC receives monthly sums of money from the Federation Account (q.v.) for the development of oil mineral producing areas. It is responsible for the development of projects for the areas. Its goals include providing electricity for all the peoples of the area, all-season networks of roads, potable water, health services, canals to reduce distances between the various communities, education, communication facilities and markets. In 1992 the national government set aside three per cent of the oil revenue for OMPADEC.

In 1995, the Abacha regime produced a draft constitution promising to return 13 percent of the federal revenue derived from natural mineral to the communities from which those resources were derived. This was not implemented, however, until the promulgation of the 1999 constitution. In its early years, the performance of OMPADEC was disappointing, owing to a combination of corruption and insufficient resources.

OIL PALM. One of the world's sources of edible vegetable oil and soap-making oil. It is said to yield more oil per year than any oil-bearing plant. Most of the world's supply used to come from West African countries, most especially Nigeria, Ghana (q.v.), Liberia and Sierra Leone (q.v.). However, Malaysia, which first obtained its seedlings from Nigeria, is today the greatest palm oil exporting country.

The tree may grow to about 20 metres in height, and at the top there are a group of large branches with leaves. It begins to bear fruits at about the fourth or fifth year and may continue for many years after. The fruits grow in large bunches containing hundreds of fruits and a tree may produce up to 10 bunches a year. The color of the fruits can be yellow, brown, orange, red or black depending on maturity. Each fruit has an outer skin beneath which there is a pulp that is rich in palm oil. Inside the pulp is the seed called palm nut, which is covered by a very hard shell, and an inner kernel called palm kernel, also very rich in oil called palm kernel oil.

Palm oil is red, yellow or orange in color and contains carotene which the human body converts into vitamin A. Palm oil is used in many kinds of cooking in Nigeria. It is also used for soap, margarine, candles and industrial purposes. Palm kernel oil is also used for making soap, cooking fat and margarine. What is left of palm kernel when the oil has been extracted is used to feed livestock. Oil palm tree is also the source of a local alcoholic drink, palm wine, which is made by tapping the tree by palm wine tappers. Beautiful baskets and traditional brooms are also made from the palm leaves and the palm kernel shells are used as fuel. In fact, the oil palm has been of great importance in the economy and in the historical development of Nigeria. When the British were looking for legitimate trades (q.v.) to take the place of the slave trade (q.v.), the first they found was the products of oil palm: palm oil and palm kernel. Thus, these agricultural products became the oldest legitimate exports of Nigeria and perhaps the first indigenous agricultural export crop. It is this oil that gave the area from which it was first obtained for export its name, Oil Rivers (q.v.). In 1992 over 32 tons of palm oil and as many tons of palm kernel were exported.

OIL REVENUES, OFFSHORE. From April 1, 1971, the ownership of and the title to the territorial waters and the continental shelf was vested in the Federal Government (q.v.). Further, all royalties, rents and other revenues derived from oil (q.v.) accrue to the Federal Government.

OIL RIVERS. Oil Rivers was the name given by British merchants to the delta region of the Niger River (q.v.) and its surroundings. This area extended from the Benin River to the Cameroon (q.v.). The area got its name from the fact that there was an abundant supply of palm oil, which was needed in the soap factories in Liverpool. Trading in palm oil started very early. By 1806 about 150 tonnes of palm oil were shipped to Liverpool, and the figures rapidly increased as palm oil and palm kernel began to take prominence over the slave trade. In 1884 the British entered into treaties with the Chiefs (q.v.) of the area who feared that the treaties might undermine their middleman role. But in the end, they yielded. In 1885 the British proclaimed the area to be under their protection and called it the Oil Rivers Protectorate (q.v.). In 1886 the British also gave a charter to the National African Company (q.v.), later known as the Royal Niger Company (q.v.), a trading company in the area to ensure the smooth running and administration of the Oil Rivers. In 1893 the Oil Rivers Protectorate became the Niger Coast Protectorate (q.v.).

OIL RIVERS PROTECTORATE. The area previously known as the Oil Rivers (q.v.) came under British protection in 1885 and was known as the Oil

Rivers Protectorate. In 1893 the same area became the Niger Coast Protectorate (q.v.).

OJIGI. Ruler of Oyo when the Oyo empire (q.v.) flourished, Ojigi ruled from about 1724 to 1735. During his time, he made Dahomey (q.v.) (now Republic of Benin [q.v.]) pay tribute to Oyo, and the Oyo empire extended from the Atlantic coast north along the Niger River (q.v.).

OJIKE, MAZI MBONU. A politician and a cultural nationalist, Mbonu Ojike was born in 1912 in Akeme in Arochukwu in Eastern Nigeria (q.v.). He attended Arochukwu Primary School, and, after leaving the school, he took a teaching appointment in 1926. He entered college in 1929 and trained as a teacher at the CMS Training College, Awka. He left college in 1931 and became a teacher at the Central School in Abagana. In 1933 he joined Dennis Memorial Grammar School in Onitsha (q.v.) as a teacher. In 1938 Ojike met Dr. Nnamdi Azikiwe (q.v.), and they became friends. In the same year he left for the United States to study at Lincoln University in Pennsylvania. While in the States, he met people like Dr. Kwame Nkrumah (q.v.), and together they formed the African Students' Association of America and Canada (q.v.) in 1941. The association campaigned against colonialism in Africa and for justice for the black people. Ojike became its president. When Ojike came back to Nigeria, he became a member of the National Council of Nigeria and the Cameroons (NCNC) (q.v.) and began to write in the *West African Pilot* (q.v.), which had become the organ of the NCNC in its fight for independence. Ojike was a member of the 1953 Constitutional Conference (q.v.) in London, and in 1954 he became minister of finance in the NCNC-controlled Eastern House of Assembly (q.v.). He published his book, *My Africa,* in which his philosophy was carefully enunciated. He encouraged Africans to use their traditional names and dresses. He was the author of the slogan "Boycott all Boycottables." His campaign for cultural pride and awareness bore much fruit, but he died in 1956, just a few years before Nigeria became independent. In his honor, there is now Ojike Memorial Medical Center at Arondizuogu in Imo State (q.v.).

OJUKWU, CHIEF CHUKWUEMEKA ODUMEGWU. Leader of the Biafran secession, he was born on November 4, 1933, at Zungeru (q.v.) in Northern Nigeria (q.v.). He was educated in Lagos (q.v.), finishing at King's College (q.v.), before going to Epsom College Surrey, Lincoln College, and the University of Oxford in England where he studied history.

Returning to Eastern Nigeria (q.v.) in 1955, he became an administrative officer, and in 1957, he joined the Nigerian Army. He did a two-year officer training course at Eaton Hall, Chester, in England and returned to join the Fifth Battalion in 1958. He was promoted to major in 1961 and was among the Nigerian contingents in the United Nations Peacekeeping Force in the Congo. He became lieutenant-colonel in January 1963, and was put in command of the Fifth Battalion in Kano (q.v.). He did not participate in the January 1966 coup (q.v.) and was rewarded by being made the military governor of the Eastern Region by General Aguiyi-Ironsi (q.v.).

After the second coup of July 29, 1966, staged mainly by northern soldiers, which brought General Yakubu Gowon (q.v.) to power, Ojukwu refused to accept the leadership of Gowon because he was not the most senior officer available at the time. According to him, Ogundipe (q.v.) should have succeeded to Aguiyi-Ironsi, who was killed during the coup.

After the October 1966 massacre of the Igbo (q.v.) people in the north, and the great exodus of the Igbos from the north to the east, Ojukwu asked Gowon to remove Northern troops from Eastern Nigeria, and he began to train his own troops and to arm them. In January 1967, he met General Gowon and other top military leaders at Aburi (q.v.) in Ghana (q.v.) in an effort to find an amicable solution to the problems between the east and the Federal Government (q.v.). The Aburi Agreement was drawn up, but owing to different interpretations of the agreement, the problems remained. On May 27, Ojukwu was mandated by the Consultative Committee called at his behest to declare Eastern Nigeria a sovereign state by the name of Biafra. On the same day, General Gowon declared a state of emergency throughout the Federation and divided the country into 12 states with Eastern Nigeria being divided into three states, two of which were for the minority areas, while the third, the East-Central State (q.v.), consisted mainly of Igbo people. Two days later, Ojukwu declared Eastern Nigeria the sovereign Republic of Biafra (q.v.). A month later, war broke out, which lasted until January 1970 when Ojukwu left Biafra to go into exile, "in search of peace," and Biafran soldiers surrendered to the federal military government in Lagos. Ojukwu was granted political asylum in Côte d'Ivoire. He remained in exile until 1982 when he was pardoned by President Alhaji Shehu Shagari (q.v.), and he returned home. He later became a member of the National Party of Nigeria, under the banner of which he contested for the post of a senator in Anambra State (q.v.), but he lost. After the December 1983 coup d'état, he was put in detention for security reasons. He was released in October 1984.

In 1994 he was a member of the national Constitutional Conference (q.v.) set up by General Sani Abacha (q.v.) to review and rewrite the Nigerian constitution before the military would hand over power.

OJUKWU, SIR LOUIS ODUMEGWU. A businessman, politician and father of Lt. Col. Chukwuemeka Odumegwu Ojukwu (q.v.), military governor of Eastern Nigeria, who later declared the secession of that region from the rest of Nigeria as the Republic of Biafra (q.v.). Born in 1909 in Nnewi in

Anambra State (q.v.), he became a produce examiner in 1928 after leaving school. He joined the John Holt Company as a clerk. It was here that he developed his business interest. He resigned from the John Holt Company in 1934 and started a transport business that grew into a multimillion dollar business all over Nigeria.

In 1951 he joined the National Council of Nigeria and the Cameroons (NCNC) (q.v.) under the leadership of Dr. Nnamdi Azikiwe (q.v.). He was later elected to the federal House of Representatives (q.v.), but he resigned in 1956 to become chairman of the Eastern Nigerian Development Corporation. From this time on, he was at the head of many business concerns like the Eastern Nigerian Marketing Board, the Nigerian Cement Company and the African Continental Bank (q.v.). He was honored at home and abroad for his contributions to Nigerian development. He received an honorary degree of doctor of law from the University of Nigeria, Nsukka (q.v.), was awarded the Queen Elizabeth II Coronation Medal in 1953 and was knighted in 1960. He died on September 13, 1966, while his son, Lt. Col. Ojukwu wrestled with the problems created by the influx of refugees from other parts of the nation, following the massacre of many Igbo (q.v.) people in the north after the second military coup (q.v.) of July 1966.

OKEZIE, DR. JOSIAH ONYEBUCHI JOHNSON. A physician and politician born on November 24, 1926, at Umuahia Ibeku, Imo State (q.v.), he was educated at Yaba Higher College (q.v.), Achimota College, Ghana (q.v.), Yaba College of Medicine and University College, Ibadan (q.v.). He served in many important positions as a medical officer from 1950 to 1961. From 1961 to 1966 he was a member of the Eastern Nigeria House of Assembly (q.v.) and was the leader and the founder of the Republican Party (q.v.) in August 1964, a time when political parties were realigning themselves for the upcoming federal elections (q.v.) of 1964. He was a member of the Nigerian Medical Council from 1965 to 1968. He represented the East-Central State (q.v.) at the Federal Executive Council (q.v.) in 1970 and was federal commissioner (q.v.) for health from 1970 to 1971 and federal commissioner for agriculture and natural resources from 1972 to 1975.

OKIGBO COMMISSION. President A. Shehu Shagari (q.v.), keeping to his election promises, rejected the Aboyade Technical Committee's (q.v.) report on revenue allocation (q.v.), which he described as too technical to be applied and out of tune with the present political realities. In November 1979, he appointed a six-man Revenue Allocation Commission headed by Dr. Pius Okigbo, a former economic adviser to the government during the First Republic (q.v.) and the chairman of the Constitution Drafting Committee's (CDC) (q.v.) subcommittee on the economy, finance and division of powers, who also was a member of the Constituent Assembly (q.v.) in that capacity. Other members of the commission were Professor Dotun Phillips of the department of economics, University of Ibadan (q.v.), Alhaji Talib, Alhaji Balarabe Ismaila, Alhaji Muhammed Bello (q.v.) and Dr. W. Uzoagaa.

The commission was asked to examine the formula for revenue allocation with regard to such factors as the national interest, derivation, population, even development, equitable distribution and equality of states. The commission was to recommend new proposals considered necessary for revenue allocation between the federal, state and local governments. It was also to offer broad guidelines on the distribution of revenue among local governments (q.v.) within the states, and finally to make any other recommendations on any related matter as may be found necessary.

The commission recommended that the Federal Government (q.v.) should have a share of 55 percent of the national revenue, the states 30 percent, the local governments, eight percent and seven percent to go into a special fund. In January 1982 President A. Shehu Shagari signed into law a new revenue allocation bill, giving the Federal Government 55 percent, the states 35 percent and the local governments 10 percent.

OKIGBO, DR. PIUS NWABUFO CHARLES. An economist and administrator, born in 1924 at Ojoto, Idemili, Anambra State (q.v.), he was educated at Christ the King College, Onitsha (q.v.), Higher College, Yaba (q.v.), Achimola College, Ghana (q.v.), University of London, England, Nuffield College, University of Oxford, England, Northwestern University, Evanston, Illinois, U.S.A. He came back to Nigeria and was adviser to the Eastern Nigerian (q.v.) Government at Enugu (q.v.) in 1960, economic adviser to the Federal Government (q.v.) in 1962 and was Nigeria's ambassador to the European Economic Community in 1963. During the Civil War (q.v.), he was economic adviser to the Biafran (q.v.) government.

He is a renowned economist who has served on many national and international bodies, including many of the agencies of the United Nations. In 1994 he was appointed by the Abacha government to head an eight-member panel to enquire into the operations of the Central Bank of Nigeria (CBN) (q.v.). The panel submitted its report in September 1994 and found as a fact that out of the $12.4 billion of the Gulf-War windfall in oil revenue that went to the Dedicated Account set up by President Ibrahim B. Babangida (q.v.), $12.2 billion could not be accounted for by the previous military government (of which General Sani Abacha (q.v.) was a prominent member), or the CBN. The money was spent on what could "neither be adjudged genuine high priority nor truly regenerative investment." Worse still, Babangida and Abdulkadir Ahmed, the former governor of the CBN, accounted to no one for these massive extrabudgetary expenditures, clandestinely taken and of which there was no record. And, as the panel concluded, this represented "a gross abuse of public trust." The report exposed how profligate the Babangida administration had been with public money.

Pius Okigbo is nationally honoured as Commander of the Order of the Niger and is a recipient of the National Merit Award. He has many honorary degrees and has published many books among which are *Nigerian National Account, 1950–1957* (1960), *Nigerian Public Finance* (1965), *Africa and the Common Market* (1967), *Nigeria's Financial System: Structure and Growth* (1981) and *Essays in the Public Philosophy of Development,* Vol. 1 (1987).

OKOGIE, ARCHBISHOP ANTHONY OLUBUNMI. The Catholic Archbishop of Lagos (q.v.), he was born in June 1936 in Lagos. He first went to St. Gregory's College in Lagos before deciding to become a priest. He entered St. Theresa's Seminary in Oke Are, Ibadan (q.v.), and later entered the Major Seminary (SS Peter and Paul's) Bodija in Ibadan. From there he proceeded to the Urban University, Rome, where he studied theology and graduated with a bachelor of divinity licentiate in theology. He was later ordained a priest and was an auxiliary bishop of Oyo Diocese in 1971. In 1973 he became the archbishop of Lagos.

From his student days in St. Gregory's College, to the present, Okogie has been known as a person who would not hesitate to challenge his superiors when he believed he was right. And today, Archbishop Okogie has not been known to keep silent when things are going wrong. He criticised the compulsory takeover of voluntary agency schools by the Lagos State government in the Second Republic (q.v.), 1979–83, as being unjust. When the military government in 1984 imposed the death sentence for drug pushing, illegal bunkering and electric cable theft, he said it was too harsh. He stood up resolutely against the Babangida regime's surreptitiously making Nigeria a member of the Organization of the Islamic Conference (q.v.) and any move of government to derogate from the secularity of the Nigerian nation. The celebrated swindle of Nigeria to the tune of N6.2 billion through the Johnson Mathey Bank of London was loudly criticised, and he called for immediate investigation of the fraud. Archbishop Okogie has been aptly described as a "rebel with a cause."

OKO JUMBO. A former slave who rose to become the leading member of the Manilla Pepple House, one of the two major trading houses in Bonny (q.v.) in the 1860s. The other trading house, Anna Pepple House, headed by Jaja (q.v.) was more successful than Manilla Pepple House.

When Manilla Pepple House under Oko Jumbo attacked Anna Pepple House in 1868, Jaja, rather than fight, left Bonny (q.v.) to found Opobo (q.v.).

OKOTIE-EBOH, CHIEF FESTUS SAMUEL. A businessman and a politician, born in Jakpa, Benin River, Delta State (q.v.) in July 1912, Chief Okotie-Eboh was educated at the Baptist School in Sapele and later served as an assistant clerk in the Sapele Township Office from 1930 to 1931. He taught from 1931 to 1935 when he joined the Bata Shoe Company as a clerk, and through private studies he rose to the position of accountant and chief clerk at the Lagos Office in 1942. He later became the deputy manager of the Sapele branch of the company, which sent him to Czechoslovakia where he obtained a diploma in business administration and chiropody.

Upon his return to Nigeria, he decided to start out on his own. He became a timber and rubber (q.v.) merchant and opened up many schools and enterprises. Through all these, he became a very wealthy man.

Chief Festus Okotie-Ebor was the first secretary of the Warri National Union and secretary general of the Itsekiri National Society. He became interested in politics and was elected to the Western Regional House of Assembly (q.v.) in 1951. In 1954 he won the Warri Division seat to the federal House of Representatives (q.v.) and was made the national treasurer of his party, the National Council of Nigeria and the Cameroons (NCNC) (q.v.).

In the House, he became the federal minister of labour in 1958 and later the finance minister and leader of the NCNC parliamentary party. He continued as minister of finance until January 15, 1966, when the military forcefully seized power and killed him together with some other leading politicians and military officers.

OKPARA, DR. MICHAEL IBEONUKARA. A politician born in December 1920, he was educated at Yaba Higher College (q.v.) in Lagos (q.v.) and later proceeded to the Nigerian School of Medicine, where he qualified as a doctor. He worked as a medical officer in Lagos and Maiduguri before setting up a private practice at Umuahia.

He entered politics in 1950 and was elected to the Eastern Regional House of Assembly (q.v.) under the banner of the National Council of Nigeria and the Cameroons (NCNC) (q.v.) in 1953. He later became minister without portfolio. From then on, he moved up very rapidly and when Dr. Nnamdi Azikiwe (q.v.) decided to go to the federal House of Representatives (q.v.) as leader of the NCNC in 1959, Dr. Okpara was elected leader of the party in the Eastern Regional House of Assembly and consequently became the premier of the region. In 1960, when Dr. Azikiwe withdrew from party politics in preparation for his appointment as the governor-general (q.v.) of Nigeria, Okpara became the national president of the NCNC.

During the Action Group crisis of 1962 (q.v.) the NCNC, under Dr. Okpara, supported the Akintola (q.v.) faction. But after the breakdown of the Northern People's Congress (q.v.) and the NCNC coalition government in

1964, Dr. Okpara, in the realignment effort to prepare for the 1964 federal elections, allied his party with the remnants of the Action Group in the west to form the Southern Progressive Front, which in turn allied with the Northern Progressive Front, to form the United Progressive Grand Alliance (q.v.). In December 1964, he led a delegation to the president, Dr. Nnamdi Azikiwe, to ask for a postponement of the December 30th elections because of alleged irregularities, but the postponement was not granted, leading to a boycott of the elections in the Eastern Region controlled by his party, the NCNC.

During the Civil War (q.v.) (1967–70), Dr. Michael Okpara supported the Biafran cause, but he came back after the war. He later joined the National Party of Nigeria (q.v.). He died in December 1984.

OKUNNU, LATEEF OLUFEMI. A lawyer born in February 1933 in Lagos (q.v.), he started his education at the Ansar-Ud-deen School, Alakoro, in 1947 and later went to King's College (q.v.), Lagos. He went to the University of London, where he studied law and graduated with an LL.B. degree in 1958. While in Britain, he was the president of the Nigerian Union of Great Britain in 1959, and in 1960 he was the publicity secretary of the Committee of African Organisations, which often demonstrated on events in Rhodesia. He returned to Nigeria in 1960 and joined the Nigerian Youth Congress (q.v.) where he agitated against the Anglo-Nigerian Defence Pact (q.v.) and the Detention Act. He became editor of the *Nigeria Bar Journal* from 1964 to 1968 and a member of the executive committee of the Nigerian Bar Association. In 1967 he was made federal commissioner (q.v.) for works and housing and was one of the leaders of the Nigerian delegation to the peace talks in Niamey, Addis-Ababa and Monrovia during the Civil War (q.v.). He was also a member of the Constitution Draft Committee (q.v.) in 1975.

OLAUDAH EQUIANO. Born in 1745, he was captured from his village in Igboland at the age of 11 and was sold to British slavers. He was then taken to Virginia in the United States where a British naval officer bought him and took him to England. He served his master in the Anglo-French Seven Years' War of 1756–1763. At the end of the war he was sold to a slave trader in the West Indies. Under his new owner, he was able to save enough money to buy his freedom. In 1769 he returned to England where he worked as a barber. In the 1790s he joined the political movement in England to ban the slave trade (q.v.), and became one of its leaders. He became involved in the expedition that founded Freetown (q.v.) in Sierra Leone (q.v.) as a colony for freed slaves from Britain and America. In 1789 he published his memoirs as *The Interesting Narrative of Olaudah Equiano*.

OLDMAN COMMISSION. Set up in 1961 by the Northern Regional government to look into the financial and administrative problems that would arise if the Northern Region (q.v.) should embark on universal primary education (q.v.). The commission was to look into the form which local contribution to the cost of primary education should take, whether the control of primary education should be delegated to local education authorities, amendment to the education law and the grants-in-aid regulations, if necessary, and the future development of primary school inspectorate and the administrative machinery that would be required by universal primary education.

The commission recommended that a system of primary education should be developed in partnership among the government, native authorities (q.v.) and voluntary agencies. It recommended the establishment of local education authorities and local education committees, transfer of voluntary agency primary schools to local authorities, while the voluntary agencies would retain the right to inspect religious teaching and approve the names of teachers proposed for appointment, training courses for education officers, amendment to the education law to give effect to the recommendations, an inspectorate organisation for primary schools run by the government and the appointment in each province of a provincial education secretary. These recommendations were accepted and embodied in the 1962 Education Law.

OLOMU, CHIEF NANA. A successful and powerful Itsekiri (q.v.) trader and leader, he was born in 1858 at Jakpa in the Delta State (q.v.). Nana Olumu was the son of Olomu, founder of Ebrohimi and a traditional ruler. His father was a wealthy trader and a member of the house of Ologbotsere who ruled for only four years before Nana succeeded to the throne. Nana, as a young man, began to work for his father, and, because of his intelligence and ability, he soon became his father's right-hand man. When his father died in 1883, Nana, at the age of 31, succeeded him not only as the head of his family but also as governor of the Benin River. As governor, he, in 1884, signed a treaty with the British consul, Hewett, bringing Benin River, Warri (q.v.) and other parts of Western Ijo under British protection. These treaties gave the British exclusive rights to trade in the area. In 1891 problems between him and the British began to arise when the British decided to extend the control of the Oil Rivers Protectorate (q.v.) to the Itsekiri area under him. The British, interested in free trade in the area, did not want to accept the monopoly that Nana had created there. Nana was, therefore, accused of strangling trade on the Benin River and of defying the British authority in slave trading. He denied the accusations and, remembering the infidelity of the British to Jaja (q.v.) of Opobo (q.v.), refused to go to the British authorities to answer to those charges. The British, allied with his enemies among the Itsekiris, forbade the use of the river to his boats. Nana placed an iron barricade across the creek entrance. The British decided to blow it up, and war broke out. Nana's men fought gallantly but were defeated. Nana escaped to

Lagos (q.v.) where he surrendered to the British who deported him to Accra, Ghana (q.v.). While in Ghana, he sent numerous petitions to the British government asking that he be returned home. In 1906 he was allowed to return home. He settled down as an ordinary man in Koko where he designed and built for himself and family what is now known as Nana's Palace.

Nana was no doubt a great man. He opened up many palm oil markets, employing thousands of people. He stood up and fought against the British for his rights and those of his people, and he was able to offer serious resistance to the British who were all too anxious to extend their power over his area. He died in Koko on July 3, 1916.

OLORUN-NIMBE, DR. ABUBAKAR IBIYINKA. Born in Lagos (q.v.) in 1908, he attended Tinubu Methodist School and Aroloya Government Moslem School. He then proceeded to the CMS Grammar School and King's College (q.v.) in Lagos from which he graduated in 1928. He later went to the University of Glasgow to study medicine and received his degree in 1937. Upon his return to Nigeria he joined Government Medical Services.

Dr. Olurun-Nimbe became active in politics. He joined Herbert Macaulay's (q.v.) Nigerian National Democratic Party (NNDP) (q.v.), which later became an affiliate of the National Council of Nigeria and the Cameroons (NCNC) (q.v.) in 1944. He was elected to the Legislative Council (q.v.) in Lagos in 1947, and the same year he was a member of the NCNC delegation to London. In 1950 the NCNC-NNDP alliance in the city of Lagos won 18 out of the 24 seats on the Lagos Town Council and Dr. Olorun-Nimbe became the mayor of Lagos. In 1951, while still the mayor, he contested one of the five seats to the Western House of Assembly (q.v.) (Lagos was then in the Western Region), and he won. Out of the five members including Dr. Nnamdi Azikiwe (q.v.), NCNC party leader, two were to be selected by the Western House of Assembly to represent Lagos in the Central Legislative House. Dr. Azikiwe was interested, so were two other members—Adeleke Adedoyin (q.v.) and Dr. Olorun-Nimbe. Neither of these two men agreed to step down for Dr. Azikiwe. For his unyielding attitude, Dr. Olorun-Nimbe was expelled from the NCNC. From then on, things were not the same with him. He was at odds with his colleagues on the City Council and was the subject of opposition criticism. His administration of the Lagos Town Council was accused of malpractices and organised corruption. An inquiry conducted by Bernard Storey, town clerk for Norwich, England, was instituted to look into the allegations. It reported in 1953 that there was corruption along with other irregularities in the administration of the council. The council was later dissolved, but before the election took place, a new law had been passed, abolishing the position of mayor and making the Oba (q.v.) of Lagos the president of the council. Dr. Olorun-Nimbe later retired from active politics. He died on February 5, 1975, in Lagos.

OLUFOSOYE, MOST REV. TIMOTHY OMOTAYO. The archbishop of the Church of Nigeria, Anglican Communion, born in Ondo, Ondo State (q.v.), he began his pastoral work as a trainee in St. Andrew's College, Oyo, in 1940. In 1946 he was ordained deacon. In 1947 he was ordained priest by Archbishop L.G. Vining. He was consecrated bishop in 1965 and has served in various capacities not only in Nigeria but also in the Gambia, Senegal and the Republic of Guinea. He was vice president of the World Council of Christian Education, vice president of the All-African Conference of Churches and vice president of the Conference of Anglican Primates of Africa. He retired from active church administration in 1988 when he was 70 to devote himself mainly to pastoral and episcopal duties.

OLUNLOYO, DR. VICTOR OMOLOLU SOWEMIMO. Mathematician and politician, born on April 14, 1935, in Ibadan (q.v.), Oyo State (q.v.). He was a very bright student, even from his primary school days, for, in 1946 and 1947, he took the first position in examinations held for pupils in standards IV and V in all the schools in Ibadan Province. He entered the Government College in Ibadan with a scholarship and came out in the first division. He attended University College of Ibadan from 1953 to 1955 and the University of St. Andrews in Scotland from 1955 to 1961 and obtained a B.Sc. first-class honours degree in mechanical engineering and mathematics in 1958 and a Ph. D. in applied mathematics in 1961. He was a five-time medalist in mathematics and mechanical engineering. He was assistant lecturer at the University of Ibadan in 1961 but moved the same year to the University of Ife (q.v.) as a lecturer. He became senior lecturer in mathematics at the University of Ibadan in 1965.

In 1962 during the emergency administration (q.v.) in the Western Region (q.v.), he was appointed commissioner for economic planning and community development, and in 1967 he became a civil commissioner (q.v.) for special duties and chairman of the board of directors for the Western Nigeria Development Corporation. In November of the same year, he was appointed commissioner for education (1967–70 and 1971). Between 1970 and 1971, he was commissioner for local government and chieftaincy affairs. He later went back to teaching at the University of Lagos. When the ban on political activities was lifted in 1978, he joined the National Party of Nigeria (q.v.) and became a gubernatorial candidate for Oyo State in the 1983 elections. He won against the incumbent, Governor Bola Ige (q.v.). His administration, however, was short-lived, for the army took over the government of the country when he had been only three months in office.

During his short tenure in office, he took positive steps to resolve some long-festering problems like conflicts between the traditional rulers in Oyo State as to the chairmanship of the Council of Obas (q.v.), and the Ife-Modakeke dispute, which led to the loss of many lives and property during the communal disturbances of April 1981.

OLUWASANMI, PROF. HEZEKIAH ADEDUNMOLA. An agricultural economist and former vice chancellor of the University of Ife (q.v.) who worked very hard to build the newly established university both intellectually and physically so that today the university, now known as Obafemi Awolowo University, is one of the best academic institutions in Africa—and a very beautiful one. Born on November 12, 1919, at Ipetu-Ijesha, he was educated at St. Paul's School, Ipetu Ijesa, Ilesha Grammar School, Ilesha, Abeokuta Grammar School, Abeokuta (q.v.), and later went to Morehouse College, Atlanta (1941–51) and Harvard University, Cambridge, Massachusetts (1951–55) in the United States. Upon his return to Nigeria, he became a lecturer in the department of agricultural economics at the University of Ibadan, where he rose to the position of professor and head of the department and later dean of the faculty of agriculture. In 1966 he was appointed vice chancellor of the University of Ife, a post he occupied until 1975. He lived to see himself honoured by the naming of the University of Ife Library, Hezekiah Oluwasanmi Library, in 1980. He died in 1983.

ONABAMIRO, PROF. SANYA. Born May 24, 1916, at Ago Iwoye, Ogun State (q.v.), he went to Wesley College in Ibadan (q.v.), then to Yaba Higher College (q.v.), later to the University of Manchester, England, and the University of Oxford, England, where he studied chemistry and biology. He was a member of the Western House of Assembly (q.v.) for Ijebu North and later became minister of education of the Western Region. He then left to become a senior research fellow in parasitology at the University College, Ibadan (q.v.). He was later appointed professor of parasitology, University of Njala, Sierra Leone (q.v.).

Onabamiro was a member of the Action Group Party (AG) (q.v.) and the federal scholarship board, chairman of the land utilisation committee, Ministry of Agriculture and Natural Resources and a member of the federal higher education (q.v.) committee.

In 1960 he was appointed—as a member of AG—minister of education for Western Nigeria. In 1962 he resigned from the AG. He was one of those who gave evidence for the government in the treasonable felony case, saying that Chief A. Awolowo (q.v.) had formed a tactical committee, and he himself had attended some of its meetings. Chief Awolowo later denied that Dr. Onabamiro had been a member of the tactical committee. In 1963 he became minister of agriculture in Western Nigeria under the government of Chief S.L. Akintola (q.v.). *See* TREASON TRIAL.

ONABANJO, CHIEF VICTOR OLABISI. A journalist and politician, born on February 12, 1927, in Lagos (q.v.), he was educated at Baptist Academy in Lagos. From 1950 to 1951, he studied journalism at the Regent Street Polytechnic School of Modern Languages in London, where he earned a diploma. From 1951 until 1959, he held a number of editorial positions, which included the *Nigerian Citizen* in Zaria (q.v.), the *Radio Times* of Nigeria and deputy editor-in-chief of the Nigerian Broadcasting Service. In 1960 he became the editorial director of the Express Group of Newspapers. At this time he was most known and remembered by his pen name "Aiyekoto," meaning "the world hates the truth". Under this pen name, he made important contributions in his uncompromising attitude to what he believed was the truth. He was brutally frank and straightforward. His writings were terminated when he decided to go into politics in 1964. He was a member of the Action Group Party (q.v.) and entered Parliament where he remained until 1966 when the military seized power. In 1967 he was appointed a civil commissioner (q.v.) for home affairs and information, and later for lands and economic planning. He was in the Western State Executive Council (q.v.) until 1970. In 1977 he was a member of the Constituent Assembly (q.v.), and when the ban on political activities was lifted in 1978 he joined the Unity Party of Nigeria (UPN) (q.v.) and was elected governor of Ogun State (q.v.) under its banner. After the December 1983 second military takeover, he was detained and accused, together with Governor Bola Ige (q.v.) of Oyo State and Governor Michael Ajasin (q.v.) of Ondo State of illegally enriching the UPN by accepting a kickback of N2.8 million on a contract and passing it to the party. He was found guilty, while the other two accused governors were acquitted. He was sentenced to 22 years' imprisonment. He was, however, released in 1987 by the Babangida (q.v.) regime. He died in April 1990.

ONABOLU, CHIEF AINA. Born in 1882, Chief Onobolu was a painter who taught himself to paint. When he grew up, he was employed first as a customs officer. He later resigned and arranged in Lagos (q.v.) in 1920 the first exhibition of paintings in all of West Africa. He later studied painting in London and Paris and came back home to teach art in many schools. It has been said that, through his effort, art was introduced as a school subject in Nigerian schools.

ONDO STATE. Created in 1976 out of the old Western State (q.v.), Ondo State covers the old Ondo province (q.v.) created in 1915 with Akure as its headquarters, which today is the capital of the state. With a land area of 21,114 square kilometres, it lies within latitudes 5°45′ and 8°05′N, and longitudes

4°20′ and 6°E. It is bounded in the north by Kware (q.v.) and Kogi (q.v.) States, in the east by Edo (q.v.) and Delta (q.v.) States, in the south by the Atlantic Ocean and in the west by Ogun (q.v.) and Osun (q.v.) States. The land rises from about 15 metres to about 250 metres above sea level. The area is generally regarded as lowland tropical rain forest with wet and dry seasons. In the south, rain falls almost all year round even though it may be a little drier between November and January, but in the north the rainy season is between March and October. The annual rainfall is about 2,000 millimetres in the south, while in the north it is about 1,800 millimetres. The temperature is between 27°C and 30°C with relative humidity about 75 percent. The vegetation also varies from the coastal swamp forest to areas of hardwood timber forests and to a woody savannah forest in the north. The State's mineral resources include petroleum oil, tar, sand, kaolin, iron ore, granite, coal, columbite and marble. The state is divided into 26 local government (q.v.) areas, and its population centres are Akure (the capital), Ore, Owo, Okitipupa Ado-Ekiti, Ikare, Emure and Irun.

The population of the state in 1991 was 3,884,485. The people are mainly Yoruba (q.v.), but there are subgroups like the Akoko, Akure, Ekiti, Ijaw (q.v.), Ikale, Ilaje, Ondo and Owo. Even though there are many urban centres in the state, a good proportion still live in rural areas. Basically, the state is agricultural, with about 70 percent of residents in agriculture and agriculture contributing about 75 percent of the state's gross domestic product. Revenue-yielding crops and trees common in the state are cocoa (q.v.), oil palm (q.v.), and a variety of timber. Food crops include rice, maize, cassava (q.v.), yams (q.v.), plantain and bananas (q.v.).

The people take education very seriously. Building on the free primary education begun in the Western Region (q.v.) in 1955, the state now has about 1,560 primary schools, 360 secondary schools and two universities.

Christians and Muslims are peacefully coexisting with traditional religious worshippers. It is also a state with such beautiful scenery as the historical Idanre Hills, the Ikogosi Warm Springs and many beautiful waterfalls.

On October 1, 1996, the Abacha (q.v.) regime created Ekiti State out of part of Ondo State.

ONITSHA. A major commercial center in Anambra State (q.v.) and a town on the east bank of the Niger River (q.v.). Tradition says it was founded during the migration from Benin (q.v.) in the 18th century. Among the people who left Benin, some settled at Agbor, while some others settled at Onitsha. This can be seen from the similarities in political structures of Benin, Agbor and Onitsha. Onitsha, like Benin, has a king (Obi), which most Igbo (q.v.) societies do not have. In 1856 Macgregor Laird (q.v.) established a trading station at Onitsha and Rev. J. Taylor and Samuel Ajayi Crowther (q.v.) started a Church Missionary Society (CMS) (q.v.) station there. In 1885 the Roman Catholic (q.v.) Mission also started in Onitsha, and by 1906, government had opened two schools in the place, one for boys and the other for girls.

At present, the town is famous for its many educational institutions, which is a result of the early arrival of the CMS through Crowther's work, who later became the Bishop of the Niger. Onitsha produced the first CMS bishop, the first Catholic bishop and is the hometown of Dr. Nnamdi Azikiwe (q.v.), the first Nigerian governor-general (q.v.) and first Nigerian president. Onitsha Igbo in fact, regard themselves as superior to all other Igbo.

Onitsha is also a commercial center and is famous for its multimillion dollar market. A bridge across the Niger River links the town to Asaba in Delta State (q.v.) on the western side of the river. From Onitsha a good system of roads connects the town to other major population centres in the country.

ONWU, DR. SIMON EZIEVUO. Born in 1908 in Affa, Anambra State (q.v.), Dr. Onwu attended the Government School in Udi, St. Mary's School in Onitsha (q.v.), Wesley Boy's High School and King's College (q.v.) in Lagos. He later entered Edinburgh University Medical School and became a doctor in 1932; the first medical doctor from the Igbo (q.v.) ethnic group. Upon his return in 1933, he joined the government service and was posted to Port Harcourt (q.v.). He was given a most enthusiastic welcome by the people there. The reception was so successful that the reception committee was transformed into Igbo Union, embracing all Igbo elements in Port Harcourt. The Igbo Union provided an incentive to the Igbo people in other towns to form such cultural organisations, all of which in later years became the Federal Union (q.v.).

As a medical doctor, Dr. Onwu worked in many parts of the country and was appointed to a number of public agencies, including the Eastern Nigerian Housing Corporation. In 1953 he was awarded the Queen Elizabeth II Coronation Medal, and in 1954 the Queen conferred upon him the Order of the British Empire. In 1956 he became a Member of the Royal Victorian Order. Pope Paul VI also conferred upon him the Order of the Knight of Saint Sylvester in 1965. In 1968 his name became enrolled in the Papal Scroll of Honour. Dr. Onwu died on June 4, 1969.

OPERATION BIAFRAN BABY. The name given to the raids on the airfields of Port Harcourt (q.v.), Benin (q.v.) and Enugu (q.v.), under federal hands in May 1969 during the Civil War (q.v.). It was led by Carl Gustaf Von Rosen, a Swedish pilot who was once a relief pilot but later became a fighter pilot on the Biafran side.

OPERATION DO OR DIE. After the general elections of December 1964, the Action Group (q.v.) met and decided to launch Operation Do or Die, aimed to unseat Chief S.L. Akintola's (q.v.) government in Western Nigeria (q.v.) in the forthcoming Western Regional election. Akintola's Nigerian National Democratic Party (NNDP) (q.v.) was declared the winner in the 1965 October election to the Western House of Assembly (q.v.). Most people became so frustrated that they later took the law into their own hands. The chaos continued until the military put an end to it in January 1966.

OPERATION FEED THE NATION. OFN was a national campaign launched in May 1976 by General Olusegun Obasanjo (q.v.), former Nigerian Military Head of State, to make the country self-sufficient in its basic food needs. It was also to encourage general pride in agriculture (q.v.), especially backyard gardening and poultry. The government was to make artificial fertilizers, improved planting materials, insecticide and other materials available to farmers at subsidised prices and to persuade them to use them. However, government effort at persuasion was greatly hampered by the scarcity of sufficient numbers of agricultural extension officers. What is more, the effort was also hampered by various shortcomings in the distribution of fertilizers and other imputs, which often did not reach the farmers or reached them very late.

On February 1, 1980, the Shagari (q.v.) administration abolished the scheme and replaced it with the National Council on Green Revolution, which coordinated the activities of all the ministries and organisations dealing with agricultural production, processing, marketing and research.

Before the scheme was abolished, however, many people responded positively to the call by taking to gardening and small backyard poultry to supply family needs.

OPOBO. A trading settlement at the mouth of the Opobo River in the Niger Delta (q.v.), founded by Jaja (q.v.) in 1869 after he had left Bonny (q.v.) during the war between the Anna Pepple and Manilla Pepple trading houses in Bonny. Jaja established many plantations and built ports in Opobo (q.v.), which grew as a trading centre through which palm oil and palm kernel passed to the European traders.

OPTION A4. An electoral system used to nominate presidential candidates of each party during the 1993 presidential primaries. Option A4 was said to combine the advantages of direct and indirect election of party flag bearers. At the ward level, the process involved direct elections of ward congressmen and women and every registered party member could participate. The ward congress elected a presidential aspirant at the ward, 10 delegates to the party's local government congress and three delegates to the state congress.

At the ward level, if there were more than one candidate, the congress in open secret ballot (q.v.) elected presidential aspirants. The candidate with the highest number of votes cast was declared the winner and would proceed to the next stage, i.e., the local government (q.v.) level, at which ward delegates would vote for presidential candidates. They would also elect five of them as delegates to the party's national convention. The process then moved to the state level and finally to the national convention.

As experience during the 1993 presidential primaries showed, Option A4 provided ample room for money bags to buy delegates' votes and therefore to win in the long run. It was, therefore, riddled with bribery and corruption.

ORACLE. Oracles are usually objects that, even though they cannot speak, can indicate an answer to certain questions that people cannot normally answer. Many people in Nigeria still believe in oracles which provide them answers to difficult questions. One of the most famous oracles in Nigeria is the Oracle of Aro Chukwu among the Igbo (q.v.) of Eastern Nigeria (q.v.). People travel long distances to consult it.

ORAL TRADITION. In many societies that had no written languages before the arrival of the British, there were certain members in each community whose duty was to remember by heart the history of the community or their rulers and the events that had taken place during their reign. For example, among the Yoruba (q.v.), many Obas (q.v.) retained professional oral historians who gathered their information from various sources such as titles and names, poetry, genealogical lists, tales and commentaries. There are difficulties, however, in accepting and interpreting such tradition. The stories were open to distortion because of the desire to please the reigning Oba and to the weaknesses of memory.

ORANMIYAN. Son of Oduduwa (q.v.), who is regarded as father of all Yoruba (q.v.) Obas (q.v.). Yoruba tradition says he was the founder of Oyo, which later developed into Oyo empire (q.v.). The date he founded Oyo is not certain, but it is supposed to be between A.D. 10 and the 14th century. Furthermore, Oranmiyan was also said to be the first ruler of the Second Benin Kingdom (q.v.). Benin tradition says, during his reign, he had a son by a Bini woman, and abdicated in favour of his son before going to found Oyo.

ORDINANCE FOR THE PROMOTION AND ASSISTANCE OF EDUCATION FOR THE GOLD COAST COLONY (1882). The first government law passed in the Gold Coast (q.v.) to affect Lagos (q.v.), for at the time (1882) Lagos Colony was still administered jointly with the Gold Coast Colony. It provided for a general board of education, which had the power to establish local boards to advise the general board on the opening of new government schools, freedom of parents as to religious instruction for their children, grants-in-aid to schools for buildings and for teachers' salaries, conditions of grants-in-aid to private schools, granting of teachers' certificates, admission of children to government schools and the establishment of an inspectorate of education to cover the four British colonies of Lagos, Gold Coast, Sierra Leone (q.v.) and the Gambia. In 1886, when Lagos was separated from the Gold Coast and became the Colony and Protectorate of Lagos, a new law was made in 1887 that amended the 1882 law and which applied specifically to Nigeria.

ORGANIZATION OF AFRICAN UNITY (OAU). As the countries of Africa became independent in the late 1950s and early 1960s, there were debates as to how best to forge African unity, protect the independence of Africa and keep colonialism at bay. Two schools of thought emerged: one known as the Casablanca Group and the other the Monrovia Group. The Casablanca Group, made up of Ghana (q.v.), Guinea, Mali, the United Arab Republic and Morocco, believed in political union as a first step. They believed that a Union Government of Africa, which would have authority over all the member states, with its own civil service, an African High Command and a court of justice should be set up. The Monrovia Group, made up of Nigeria, Cameroon (q.v.), the Central African Republic, Chad, the Congo, Dahomey (q.v.), Ethiopia, Niger, Gabon, Ivory Coast, Liberia, Malagasy, Senegal, Mauritania, Sierra Leone (q.v.), Somalia, Togo and Tunisia, together with the French-speaking African countries known as the Brazzaville Twelve, believed that political union of Africa should be gradual. They argued that because of poor communication and language barriers on the continent of Africa, they should start first on regional economic, social and cultural cooperation, which in the long run would bring about a political unity of Africa. In May 1963, at the invitation of Emperor Haile Selassie of Ethiopia, heads of 32 independent African states met in Addis Ababa to discuss how best to bring about a single political organisation for the whole of Africa. Countries from the Casablanca Group, the Monrovia Group and the Brazzaville Twelve were in attendance. The view of the Monrovia Group prevailed, and on May 25, 1963, the Organization of African Unity (OAU) was born in Addis Ababa. Other independent African states have since joined the organisation.

According to Article II of the OAU Charter, the aims of the organisation are to promote the unity and solidarity of African States, to coordinate and intensify that cooperation and efforts to achieve a better life for their people, to defend their sovereignty, their territorial integrity and independence, to eradicate all forms of colonialism from Africa, and to promote international cooperation, having regard to the Charter of the United Nations and the Universal Declaration of Human Rights. To accomplish these aims, the organisation set up four organs for effectively running its affairs: the Assembly of Heads of State and Government, which is the supreme organ of the organisation, the Council of Ministers, responsible for preparing the agenda for the conference of the Assembly, the Secretariat, and the various commissions on major problem areas.

During the Nigerian Civil War (q.v.), the organisation tried to find a peaceful solution to the crisis. It held various peace talks in Kampala (q.v.), Uganda, in May 1968 and in Addis Ababa in August 1968. After the war, Nigeria continued to play a leading role in the organisation, especially in the struggle for the independence of Zimbabwe, Angola, Namibia, and up to the end of the white minority rule in South Africa. However, as a result of the political crisis in Nigeria beginning from 1993 and the economic adversity plaguing the country in the late 1990s, its role in the OAU has been markedly affected.

ORGANIZATION OF THE ISLAMIC CONFERENCE (OIC). An association of Muslim states dedicated to the promotion of Islamic solidarity and promoting Islamic issues. It was officially inaugurated in 1972 and eventually acquired 45 members. In 1975 Nigeria was granted observer status in the organisation, which persisted until 1985, when it is alleged that the regime of General Ibrahim Babangida (q.v.) secretly had Nigeria admitted to full membership status, apparently without the knowledge of Christian members of his administration. When news of this action became public in 1986, it triggered a significant religious furor. Christian groups felt that the decision reflected their political marginalisation by the Muslims, as well as a creeping "Islamisation" of the country. The government's evasive comments on the reported membership led to a significant amount of uncertainty regarding Nigeria's exact status in the organisation. The controversy was one of a number of factors together with the 1978 constitutional debate over the Shari'a, and the 1987 Kafancan riots that contributed to a marked increase in Muslim/Christian tensions in the country.

ORGANIZATION OF PETROLEUM EXPORTING COUNTRIES. Formed in 1960 at a meeting in Baghdad of representatives of the large oil-exporting countries—Iran, Iraq, Kuwait, Saudi Arabia and Venezuela. The objectives of the organisation include efforts to unify the oil policies of member countries and lay down the best means for safeguarding their interests, individually and collectively, as well as to stabilise prices with due consideration for the interests of both the producing and consuming nations. It also seeks to secure a steady income for the producing countries, a regular supply to the consumers, and a fair return on capital invested in the petroleum (q.v.) industry. Besides the five original members, other countries that have joined the organisation are Qatar, Indonesia, Libya, United Arab Emirates, Algeria, Nigeria, Ecuador and Gabon. The headquarters of the organisation is in Vienna, Austria.

ORIZU, DR. NWAFOR. *See* AFRICAN EDUCATION INCORPORATED.

ORR, SIR CHARLES WILLIAM JAMES. A military officer and an administrator in Northern Nigeria (q.v.). A British citizen, born in 1870, he was commissioned into the Royal Artillery at the age of 19. He was later sent to India, and in 1900 he was in China, engaged in the China War of 1900–01. In 1903 he was posted to Zaria (q.v.), Nigeria, as an assistant resident where he later became resident (q.v.). He wrote *The Making of Northern Nigeria* (1911).

OSADEBAY, DENNIS CHUKADEBE. A lawyer and politician, the first premier of Mid-Western Nigeria, born on June 29, 1911, at Asaba in Delta State (q.v.), he was educated at the Government School in Asaba and at Hope Waddell Training Institute in Calabar (q.v.). In 1942 he was a supervisor of customs, and in 1946 he proceeded to the University of London in England where he was called to the bar at Lincoln's Inn in 1949.

Coming back home, he became a private legal practitioner in 1949, and in 1951 he was elected to the Western House of Assembly (q.v.) as a member of the National Council of Nigeria and the Cameroons (NCNC) (q.v.) and in 1952 he was a member of the House of Representatives (q.v.) in Lagos (q.v.). In 1954 he was leader of the NCNC opposition in the Western House of Assembly and became the deputy speaker of the house in 1956.

In 1960 he was president of the Senate (q.v.), and in 1961 he acted as governor-general (q.v.) of Nigeria. When the Mid-Western Region (q.v.) was created in 1963, he was appointed administrator of the region, and in 1964, he became the first premier of the region, a position he held when the military seized power. In the same year, he was chosen as the national vice president of the NCNC. After the military suspended the office of premier, he went back to his private legal practice.

Chief Osadebay has been awarded many honors and traditional titles. He is the Ojiba of Asaba, the Odoguwu of Ashara, the Grand Commander of the Order of the Niger and Commander of the Order of Senegal. He was also awarded an honorary doctor of law (LL.D.) degree at the University of Nigeria, Nsukka (q.v.). He died on December 26, 1994.

OSHIOMHOLE, ADAMS ALIYU. Elected the president of the Nigerian Labour Congress (NLC) in January 1999. He was born in Edo State (q.v.) on April 4, 1953. From 1971 to 1977, he held a number of positions in the National Union of Tailoring, Garment and Textile Workers' Union. From

1977 to 1979 he attended Ruskin College in Oxford, England. Upon his return, he resumed his union activities and eventually established himself as an influential member of the NLC. From 1996 to 1997, he was a union representative in the Vision 2010 panel set up by the Abacha (q.v.) regime to formulate a development strategy for the country. Some activists criticised the decision to participate in the panel on the grounds that it served to legitimate Abacha's rule. Oshiomhole maintained his credibility as a union leader, however, and many observers expected his election to presage a period of greater activism and independence on the part of the NLC.

OSIFEKUNDE (JOAQUIM). Born toward the end of the 18th century in Ijebuland in southwestern Nigeria, not too far from the coast and Lagos (q.v.), he was captured in the lagoons by slave runners about 1810 when he was about 20 years of age, and sold into slavery. He was taken to Brazil where he lived about 20 years. His master later took him to France. He lived for many years in Paris where he met Marie Armand Pascal d'Avezac-Macaya, who was then the vice president of the Société Ethnologique. When Marie knew he was from the Ijebu (q.v.) kingdom on the Guinea Coast, he became interested in him and had numerous discussions with him about his people, his homeland and the Ijebu kingdom from which he had been so violently uprooted. Marie went so far as to arrange for him to return to Sierra Leone (q.v.), a place newly settled for freed slaves on the west coast of Africa. But Osifekunde, seeing that Sierra Leone was still far away from his homeland in Ijebu kingdom, declined, preferring to go back to Brazil and live with his children.

OSUN STATE. One of the nine states created in 1991, Osun State was until then part of Oyo State (q.v.) with the capital at Ibadan (q.v.). The capital of the state is Osogbo. It is bounded in the north by Oyo and Kwara States (qq.v.), in the east by Ondo State (q.v.), in the south by Ogun State (q.v.) and in the west by Oyo State. The state is about 150 metres to 450 metres above sea level. It has two main seasons—rainy and dry. The rainy season starts in March and ends in October. The vegetation falls within the tropical rain forest zone, but the area has been greatly affected by traditional farming, fuel-wood production, road construction, and clay, latrite and sand quarrying, together with cocoa (q.v.) and oil palm (q.v.) plantations. The state has 23 local government (q.v.) areas. The population was 2,203,016 in 1991, and the people are mainly Yoruba (q.v.) with subgroups like Osun, Ife, Ijesa and Igbomina. Although an agricultural area, the state has many large cities: Iwo, Osogbo, Ilesa and Ile-Ife (q.v.). The state has one university, many colleges of education and polytechnical and technical schools. Important places of interest include the Erin-Ijesa Waterfalls, the Osun Shrine in

Osogbo, the Ife Museum and the Natural History Museum in the Obafemi Awolowo University in Ile-Ife.

OTEGBEYE, DR. OLATUNJI. A medical practitioner and a politician. Born on June 4, 1929, at Ilaro in Ogun State (q.v.), he was educated at Government College, Ibadan, University of Ibadan (q.v.), and at Middlesex Hospital Medical School in London. While in London he was the secretary-general and president of the Nigerian Union of Great Britain and Ireland. And when he came back home he became president of the Nigerian Youth Congress (q.v.). He was also appointed secretary-general of the Socialist Workers and Farmers Party of Nigeria (q.v.). He is in private medical practice, and a member of the Council of Nigerian Medical Association.

OVIE-WHISKEY, JUSTICE VICTOR EREREKO. A jurist, born on April 6, 1924, at Ikiwewu, Agbarho, in Bendel State (q.v.), he was educated at Yaba Higher College, Lagos (q.v.), University of Ibadan and at the University of London in England. He was called to the bar at the Middle Temple in London in 1958. Upon his return to Nigeria, he served in many roles as magistrate, commissioner (q.v.) of customary courts (q.v.), director of public prosecution, judge of the Federal High Court (q.v.) and later the chief justice of the High Court in Bendel State. In 1980 he was appointed chairman of the Federal Electoral Commission (q.v.), charged with responsibility for organising and supervising the 1983 elections. The elections were so badly rigged that the military used the rigging as one of the reasons for staging another coup on December 31, 1983. Ovie-Whiskey is a Grand Knight of the Order of St. Gregory the Great.

OVONRAMWEN. The last Oba (q.v.) of the Kingdom of Benin (q.v.) before the British declared Southern Nigeria (q.v.) the Protectorate (q.v.) of Southern Nigeria. He became Oba in December 1888 with the ambition to put all the Chiefs (q.v.) under him in their places and to extend the Benin empire to its previous dimension, if possible. But at the time he was pursuing this twin objective, the British became interested in the exploitation of the wild rubber forest in his domain, and he resisted. In 1892 the British were able to persuade him to sign a treaty to place Benin under British protection, abolish human sacrifice and slave trade (q.v.) in his kingdom and open up trade. But the treaty did not last long. In 1897 acting consul General Phillips decided to visit the king and, without waiting for a reply, he set off on his journey with many of his officials, together with an escort of about 200 men. The time was inappropriate, for the Beni were celebrating a festival during which the Oba must not see someone who was not a Beni. Phillips was met by the Oba's messengers. Fighting broke out in which Phillips and most of his men were killed. The British then sent a punitive expedition to Benin which conquered Benin and set the town on fire. Oba Ovonramwen fled but was later delivered up to the British who tried him, deposed and deported him to Calabar (q.v.), where he died in January 1914. Thus, with the fall of Benin came the end of any major resistance to the British occupation of Southern Nigeria.

OYELAMI, MURAINA. A painter who once worked for the Duro Ladipo's (q.v.) theatre company and travelled with it to Europe and America. In 1964 he began to paint, basing his paintings on people whom he knew or on personal experience. He has helped in the setting up of the museum at Osogbo. He also has a musical group.

OYO EMPIRE. The Oyo empire was founded about the 13th century by Oranmiyan, who, tradition says, was an Ife prince, one of the sons of Oduduwa (q.v.), the acclaimed ancestor of the Yoruba (q.v.) Obas (q.v.). The capital of the empire was Oyo, a town situated in the savannah region, south of the Niger River (q.v.). The traditional ruler of the empire was the Alaafin (q.v.), who ruled with the assistance of a Council of Chiefs (q.v.) called Oyo Mesi. These chiefs were, and still are, the king makers of Oyo.

Oyo was strategically placed—it had close connections with Nupe and Borgu (q.v.) States, as well as prosperous trade with the kingdoms in the south. During the 14th century, Oyo became a powerful kingdom, and in the 17th century the Alaafin of Oyo became powerful in all Yorubaland and beyond, though his authority did not include the kingdom of Benin. In the 18th century, the Oyo empire extended to Dahomey (q.v.), the present Republic of Benin (q.v.), Nupe in Niger State (q.v.) and down to the coast, through Egba and Egbado kingdoms. In the same century, Oyo had a lucrative trade with the Europeans at the coast in slaves captured by its armies.

The empire was ruled by the Alaafin from Oyo, the capital city, while he allowed the conquered kingdoms to govern themselves, but they had to pay annual tributes or royalty to him. The empire had a standing army under the leadership of the Are-Ona-Kakanfo. It was a rule that the army leader should not live in the capital city with the Alaafin. He was, therefore, sent to a neighbouring town to stay as the governor of the place. This was one of the factors that led to the total collapse of the empire in the early 19th century, when Afonja (q.v.), Alaafin's army commander in Ilorin (q.v.) set himself up with the assistance of the Fulani (q.v.) as the independent ruler of Ilorin. The capital itself fell and Oyo town had to be resettled a little south of the old capital. Before this time, however, the empire had been declining. In the eighteenth century, Alaafin's army was defeated by the Bariba of Borgu in 1783 and by the Nupe (q.v.) in 1791. The Egba (q.v.), who were Yoruba, south of Oyo before this time, had gained their independence and Dahomey had refused to pay the annual tribute. Afonja's rebellion came in 1817–18, and in 1818, Dahomey declared itself independent. This chaotic situation encouraged other kingdoms to revolt, and the empire totally collapsed.

OYO STATE. The name, Oyo State, is reminiscent of the old Oyo empire (q.v.), which, before the advent of the British colonial authorities, extended far and wide in Yorubaland, including part of the present-day Republic of Benin (q.v.). The empire collapsed as a result of revolts and rebellions together with the efforts of the Fulani (q.v.) Jihadists to push the Fulani empire south of the Niger River (q.v.). Oyo State, before and after independence, was a part of the old Western Region (q.v.) with its headquarters at Ibadan (q.v.). In 1963, the Mid-Western Region (q.v.) was carved out of it, and in 1967 when the 12-state structure came into being, what remained of the Western Region (q.v.) was renamed Western State (q.v.). In 1976 the Western State was broken into three new states: Ondo (q.v.), Ogun (q.v.) and Oyo States, and in 1991 Osun State (q.v.) was carved out of the then Oyo State. Thus, the present Oyo State is the inheritor of the political headquarters of the colonial administration of the Western Provinces, post-colonial administration of the Western Region, Western State and the former Oyo State. The state is presently divided into 25 local government (q.v.) areas.

Oyo State is bounded in the north and northeast by Kwara State (q.v.), in the east by Osun State, in the south by Ogun State and in the west by the Republic of Benin. The rainy season begins in March and ends in October. The annual rainfall varies from 1,270 millimetres in the south to 1,170 millimetres in the north. The temperature is generally high ranging from 28°C to 34°C during the dry season especially in February and March. The vegetation is semitropical rain forest in the south and savannah forest in the north. Much of this, however, has been altered by traditional farming methods, fuel-wood production, erosion, and cocoa (q.v.) and oil palm (q.v.) tree plantations. The state's mineral resources include marble, talc, limestone, amphibiolites, granite, red clay and sand.

The population of Oyo State in 1991 was 3,488,789. The area is highly urbanised and densely populated. Ibadan (q.v.), the capital, is reputed to be the largest indigenous city in all of West Africa, with a population of about 1,829,187 in 1991. Ethnically, the people are Yoruba (q.v.), but like other Yoruba States, there are other subgroups—Ibadan, Ibarapa, Oyo and Oke-Ogun. There are also various peoples from the states of the federation and expatriates. Islam (q.v.) and Christianity (q.v.) have a high level of support and their adherents live amicably with those of other religions. The state's population centers, other than Ibadan, are Oyo, Shaki, Ogbomosho, Okeho, Iseyin and Igbeti.

Oyo State is rich in cultural artifacts like cloth-weaving and dyeing, calabash carving, and traditional Yoruba talking drums (q.v.). It also abounds with many festivals: the Egungun, Oro, Orisa Ogiyan, Sango, Obalufon, Ogun, Yemoja, Oke-Ibadan, Olofin, Gelede and Igunnu. The state has two universities and many colleges of education and technical and polytechnical colleges. There are about 114 adult education centers and four nomadic schools. In 1992 the pupils in primary schools were about 710,000, and 243,000 in secondary schools.

OZOLUA. Ruler of the kingdom of Benin, he was the third son of Ewuare (q.v.), the Oba (q.v.) of Benin. He succeeded to the throne of Benin in 1480, after the short reigns of his elder brothers. In 1485 the Portuguese explorer João Alfonso d'Aveiro (q.v.) visited Benin. Ozolua sent a Benin Chief back to Portugal with d'Aveiro and opened up diplomatic relations with Portugal. He also agreed to allow missionaries to come and teach his people. When the Benin Chief, accompanied by d'Aveiro, returned, he brought with him from the king of Portugal presents to the Oba, together with many priests, with orders to Christianise the people, set up factories in Benin and open up trade with the people. Tradition says he allowed one of his sons to be baptised. He even built a church for the Portuguese priests. He died in 1520.

-P-

PAGANS. A term used by Europeans to describe Africans who follow African traditional religions (q.v.). Before the coming of the Europeans in Nigeria, most Nigerians were believers in God, whom they generally worshipped through intermediaries. For example, the Yoruba (q.v.) believed in Orisas, whom they regarded as their intermediary or spokesman with the Supreme God whom they called Olorun.

Upon their arrival, the Europeans began to encourage Africans to abandon their religion in favor of their own Christian religion. Those who refused to embrace this new religion were initially regarded as pagans, i.e., people who did not believe in God. The word pagan began to be used pejoratively to mean nonbelievers in the Christian religion.

However, it must be stated that Nigerians of traditional belief do believe in a Supreme Being just like Christians and Muslims do; and like Christianity (q.v.)—which has Jesus as a kind of intermediary with God—traditional religions have other intermediaries with God.

PAM, HON. JOHN WASH. Deputy president of the Senate (q.v.) in the Second Republic (q.v.), Pam was born in 1940 in Foron, Barakin Ladi Local

Government area of Plateau State (q.v.). After his primary education, he went to Gindiri Boys' Secondary School from 1956 to 1960 and then to King's College (q.v.), Lagos (q.v.) and later to Ahmadu Bello University (q.v.) in Zaria (q.v.), where he obtained a B.A. degree in international affairs in 1966. Mr. Pam worked as a clerical officer in the prime minister's office in Lagos before entering the university in 1963 and as assistant secretary for political affairs in the military governor's office in Kaduna (q.v.), from 1966 to 1977. In 1968 he was sent to Freetown (q.v.), Sierra Leone (q.v.), as a member of the diplomatic corps, and in 1969 he returned to the Ministry of External Affairs in Lagos.

He also worked in many other capacities in the government service. He was in the Ministry of Transport (1970–71), served on the Statutory Corporations' Service Commission in Lagos (1971–72), the Ministry of Mines and Power (1972) and the Nigerian Industrial Development Bank in Lagos (1972–75). When local government councils were reformed and created in 1976, he became a member of the Barakin Ladi Local Government Council in Plateau State from 1976 to 1979, from where he was chosen to go to the Constituent Assembly (q.v.) in Lagos from 1977 to 1978. In 1979 he was elected to the Senate and became the deputy president of the Senate in 1979. He wrote *Customary Land Tenure System in Northern Nigeria*.

PAN-AFRICANISM. The belief entertained by some Africans and people of African descent that the whole continent of Africa is a national homeland. They, therefore, aspire to put an end to the colonial fragmentation of Africa by seeing it united and independent under African leadership. They also want to direct their activities toward the spreading of that belief. Early Pan-Africanists, like W.E.B. Du Bois and Marcus Garvey, had great influence on many Nigerian nationalists like Ladipo Solanke (q.v.) and Dr. Nnamdi Azikiwe (q.v.).

PARAMOUNT CHIEFS. A term applied by the colonial authorities to the traditional ruler of a town, a city-state, a division or a kingdom in contradistinction to the more appropriate word "king," which they did not want to use for the subjugated African kings.

PARK, MUNGO. Mungo Park was a young Scottish doctor, who, in 1796, became the first European to discover the easterly course of the Niger River (q.v.) and to take news back to Europe about this fact. In 1788 the African Association (q.v.) was formed in Britain for the purpose of the exploration of Africa and, more particularly, for discovering the route of the Niger River. Mungo Park offered his services to the association, and in 1795 he started his first expedition beginning from the Gambia. On July 20, 1796, he caught sight of the Niger and noted that it flowed east. He followed the river some distance and having lost his men—and being short of food—he turned back and reported what he had discovered. Later, the British government became interested, and in January 1805, Mungo Park was entrusted with another expedition. He then sailed to Gorce to organize the expedition which started in April 1805 with over 40 Europeans, including himself, his brother-in-law, Anderson, a priest and a guide. In August they reached the Niger, but by then, most of his men had died, leaving only Park, Anderson and eight other Europeans. By the time he actually started down the stream of the Niger River, he himself wrote that of the 44 Europeans that left the Gambia, only five were then alive. On November 19, 1806, his boat started down the stream and was never heard of again. He died with his men at the rapids of Bussa (q.v.).

PARTICIPATION IN POLITICS AND ELECTION DECREE. In October 1987, the government issued a decree, "Participation in Politics and Elections (Prohibition) Decree, No 25," disqualifying categories of persons from participating in politics for life, or during the transition from military rule to civilian rule. In the first category were such people who held political offices from October 1, 1960, the day of independence to January 15, 1966, when the military first came to power in a coup d'état (q.v.), and from October 1, 1979, the beginning of the Second Republic (q.v.), when the military handed over power voluntarily, to December 30, 1983, when the military again overthrew the Second Republic and who were subsequently indicted and found guilty of offences or misdeeds by any tribunal, special investigation panel, judicial commission or administrative inquiry. It also included public officers who had been found guilty from the time of independence to the end of the transition period and also military or police personnel in public offices from the first military coup d'état to the end of the transition who had been found guilty and removed from office.

In the second category were civilian officeholders: presidents, prime ministers, vice presidents, governors, state administrators and important officers of the Legislative Assemblies and military officers who had held comparable posts during military administrations. The power to declare a person disqualified rested solely with the National Electoral Commission (q.v.). However, an aggrieved person could appeal to the election tribunal whose decision was final.

PAYNE, JOHN AUGUSTUS OTUNBA. Born in August 1839 in Sierra Leone (q.v.), the son of a freed slave resettled in that country, he was originally a Nigerian from Ijebu Ode, now in Ogun State (q.v.). He attended the Church Missionary Society Grammar School in Freetown (q.v.) and came to Lagos (q.v.) about 1862. In that year he entered government service as a police clerk. He became commissioner in petty debt court and later registrar of births and deaths from 1866 to 1869. In 1869 he became chief registrar and taxing master of the Supreme Court (q.v.) in Lagos. In 1881 he was commissioned to take a census of Lagos. From 1874 he began to produce Payne's *Lagos and West African Dairy and Almanack,* published annually until a year after his death. In 1890 he organised the visit of Edward Wilmot Blyden (q.v.), who stayed with him. He retired in 1899 and died in 1906.

PENTECOSTAL CHURCHES. The pentecostal movement is said to have originated from the revival movement among Black Americans at the beginning of this century. In recent times pentecostalism was greatly influenced by the teaching of people like Oral Roberts through his television messages, the healing campaigns of T.L. Osborn and through organisations like the Full Gospel Business Men's Fellowship. From America the movement spread to other parts of the world, including Nigeria.

The cornerstone of the pentecostal teaching in Nigeria is that a person must be "born again," which makes people call the pentecostals "Born-Again Christians." To be born again, a person must accept Jesus as his Lord and Saviour and he must receive the baptism of the spirit, which is recognised by the initial sign of "speaking in tongues." Of great importance among the pentecostal churches are hymns, speaking in tongues, dreams and spontaneous forms of worship as a means of communication. In Nigeria today, some of the pentecostal churches are the Apostolic Faith, the New Covenant Church, The Assemblies of God, the Deep Life Church and the Church of God Mission. Even in the Catholic Church (q.v.), pentecostalism is growing as seen in the Catholic Charismatic Movement.

PEOPLE'S BANK OF NIGERIA. This is a "social bank" established by the Federal Government (q.v.) in May 1989 to provide low-income, self-employed groups, such as craftsmen, artisans, mechanics, carpenters and petty traders, with access to bank credit. These low-income self-employed people belong to poor socioeconomic groups who otherwise have no access to credit from the existing conventional banks due to their inability to provide the necessary collateral.

The People's Bank is expected to solve the venture capital needs of these low-income groups. The impact of the Peoples' Bank, therefore, includes increased capital formation at the level of the masses, more employment and enhanced confidence by the poor in the ability of the economy and government to cater for them.

However, as the 1994 report of the Central Bank of Nigeria (q.v.) stated, the activities of the bank showed mixed developments as reflected in its key performance indicators. The number of the branches of the bank rose only slightly from 271 in 1993 to 275 in 1994 and its total assets/liabilities of N928.3 million rose only by N86.2 million, or 10.2 per cent over the preceding year. The bank's reserves continued to be negative, worsening from N32.7 million in 1993 to N48.9 million in 1994. The Federal Government continued to be the major source of funds which were utilised largely to meet deposit withdrawals and defray operation expenses.

PEOPLE'S DEMOCRATIC PARTY (PDP). The dominant party to emerge during the Abubakar transition program (1998–99). It was formed in August 1998 as an outgrowth of the Group of 34 (q.v.), the collection of prominent politicians opposed to the Abacha regime. It included the most regionally encompassing collection of political personalities and networks in the history of Nigeria. Prominent factions within the PDP included the Northern conservatives (led by Adamu Ciroma and Bamanga Tukur), Northern radicals (led Abubakar Rimi and Sule Lamido), Eastern politicians (led by Alex Ekwueme [q.v.]), and progressive middle belt politicians (led by Solomon Lar, Iyorchia Ayu and Jerry Gana). But the most prominent faction to eventually emerge within the party was the national political network created by Shehu Yar'Adua (q.v.) and represented by such figures as Abubakar Atiku, Lawal Kaita and Ango Abdullahi. Solomon Lar, a driving force within the Group of 34 was selected as the first chairman of the party.

The PDP used its impressive networks to dominate the elections leading up to the Fourth Republic. In the December 5, 1998, local government elections the PDP won in slightly over 50 percent of the local government areas. It subsequently won 21 of 36 governorships, and nearly 60 percent of the seats in the National Assembly.

Immediately after the formation of the party, it appeared that former Vice President Alex Ekwueme would be chosen as the party's presidential nominee. This all changed, however, when former head of state Olusegun Obasanjo (q.v.) announced his own candidacy in October 1998. Drawing on the support of retired military officers (such as Ibrahim Babangida and Theophilus Danjuma) and the political network of the late Shehu Yar'Adua, Obasanjo won the party's presidential nomination at their convention in February at Jos (q.v.). In presidential elections held February 27, 1999, he emerged victorious over Olu Falae.

Given the wide variety of politicians within the PDP, lacked a strong ideology or program. Its initial goal was to unify the political class, and ensure a peaceful transition to civilian rule. Beyond this, the actual programme of the PDP was very ambiguous.

PEOPLE'S REDEMPTION PARTY. A political party formed after the ban on political activities was lifted in 1978. The party leader was Alhaji Aminu

Kano (q.v.), the former leader of the Northern Elements Progressive Union (NEPU) (q.v.). Ideologically, the party was a collection of radical leftist elements who could not find places in the other major parties. Their analysis of Nigerian society was based on class conflict, and they saw the country as moving toward a major social transformation. According to them, there were two major types of forces struggling for survival and ascendancy in the country: the forces of privilege, which were resolved to protect their interests under the existing social order, and the forces of the people, which were determined to replace the existing social order and which they saw themselves as representing.

The PRP contested the 1979 general elections. It failed to win the presidency, but it controlled two state houses, Kano (q.v.) and Kaduna (q.v.) States. However, the party did not win a majority of the seats in the Kaduna State House of Assembly (q.v.).

Not long after the elections, fissiparous tendencies began to manifest themselves within the party. Party leaders disagreed on whether or not the party should join in a national government which the president-elect was asking for. They also disagreed on whether or not the two PRP governors should be attending the periodic Nine Progressive Governors meeting, organised by the Unity Party of Nigeria (UPN) (q.v.) and consisting of the five UPN governors, two PRP governors and two Great Nigerian People's Party (q.v.) governors. The party had to break up into two major factions, one led by the party leader, Alhaji Aminu Kano (q.v.) and the other led by Chief Michael Imoudu (q.v.), the veteran labour unionist. The rift was later patched up. However, in the 1983 general elections, the party could win the gubernatorial elections only in Kano State. In January 1984, after the military had taken over power on December 31, 1983, the party, like all others, was banned.

PEPPLE, GEORGE. Ruler of Bonny (q.v.), he succeeded his father William Dappa Pepple (q.v.) who died in 1866. Before succeeding his father, he had been educated in England and had become a Christian, a change which did not go well with his people. He was regarded as a weak ruler, having allowed Bonny to be controlled by Oko Jumbo (q.v.), the head of the Manilla Pepple House, one of the rival trading houses in the state. Warfare later ensued, and Jaja (q.v.), who was head of the second house, Anna Pepple House, decided to quit and found Opobo (q.v.), which soon became more prosperous as a trading center than Bonny.

PEPPLE, OPOBO. Ruler of the Niger Delta (q.v.) trading state of Bonny (q.v.) from 1792 to 1830. It was during his rule that Bonny changed its role as a post for slaves for that of palm oil. When the king saw that the British would not relent in their efforts to put an end to the slave trade (q.v.), he linked up with the hinterland for the supply of palm oil and ensued for Bonny the position of a middleman. He died in 1830, succeeded by his son William Dappa Pepple (q.v.).

PEPPLE, KING WILLIAM DAPPA. Born in 1817 in Bonny (q.v.), a trading post in the Niger Delta (q.v.), now the Rivers State (q.v.). King William Dappa Pepple, who died in 1830, succeeded to his father's throne in 1837. Because he was a young prince at the time of his father's death, there was a period of regency. The regent not only refused to relinquish his claim to the throne but also supported the Spanish slavers against the British Anti-Slavery Patrol. In 1837 William Dappa Pepple, supported by the British, declared war on the regent, had him deposed and Pepple became king of Bonny.

In 1839 the new king signed a treaty abolishing the slave trade (q.v.) and giving the British more trading concessions in Bonny. But the treaty was never ratified. The British believed that, if they paid the compensation agreed upon, it would be used to finance the slave trade. In 1841 another treaty was negotiated, abolishing the slave trade and with a proviso that if Britain should permit the slave trade to be carried on, King Pepple was also free to do the same. The treaty was never ratified because the British never paid him the compensation agreed upon. The British patrol on the mouth of the Bonny River prevented the king from carrying on the trade openly and so he and his people rerouted their exports through the State of Brass (q.v.), which exported slaves to the West Indies. By 1844 King Pepple was becoming tired of the British, his erstwhile friends and supporters. Tension later rose in Bonny and some European traders were attacked, at which time they lost much property. The British, believing that the king engineered the attacks, retaliated. King William Pepple himself was tried in the Court of Equity (q.v.), presided over by the Consul John Beecroft (q.v.) and was found guilty. He was dethroned and exiled in 1854, first to Fernando Póo (q.v.) and finally to London. This was the beginning of the British intervention in the politics of the Niger Delta area. He was later allowed to return home from exile in 1861 but he died in 1865.

PETROLEUM. The story of oil in Nigeria dates back to 1937 when the first search for oil began. The first show of oil was announced in 1953, and the first export of crude oil was made in 1958.

Large deposits of crude petroleum have been discovered in Nigeria, both on land and offshore. In 1972 Nigeria exported almost 700 million barrels of oil. Today, Nigeria is the sixth-largest oil producing country in the world and the second in Africa after Libya.

Since 1958, several oil fields have been discovered in the Niger Delta (q.v.) areas of the country and offshore. In 1972 about 15 companies prospected for oil in the country. A N21 million refinery, the first in the country was built at Elesa-Eleme, near Port Harcourt (q.v.) in the Rivers State (q.v.), and was commissioned in 1965. This refinery, with just a capacity for 60,000 barrels per stream day, has been further expanded. Other oil refineries have been built in Warri (q.v.) and Kaduna (q.v.). The crude petroleum oil is converted at the refinery into gasoline, diesel, fuel, jet fuel, kerosene, lubricating oils, asphalt and petrochemicals.

The average oil production per day is about two million barrels, but in 1994, Nigeria produced on an average of 1.91 million barrels per day. The fall in that year was largely due to the protracted industrial action by the oil workers' unions, the National Union of Petroleum and Natural Gas Workers (NUPENG) (q.v.) and the Petroleum and Natural Gas Senior Staff Association of Nigeria (PENGASSAN). Domestic consumption is about 250,000 barrels per day. The production of associated natural gas in 1994 also declined by 3.5 percent to 32,699.8 million cubic metres. The fall again was due to the industrial action during that year. Gas flaring totalled 25,955 million cubic metres, thus accounting for 79.4 percent of all production.

The consumption of petroleum products in the country was also characterised by shortages in 1994 and decline since then. The shortages were due mainly to the industrial unrest in that year, but the cause of the decline was the sharp rise in the prices of petroleum products. Premium motor oil rose overnight from N3.25 to N11.00 per litre in 1994, kerosene from N2.75 to N6.00 per litre, and diesel oil from N3.00 to N9.00 per litre. The net effect of this is that the price of food and transportation rose astronomically, and many car owners who could not afford to fuel their cars or service them, as the price of motor parts shot up, had to park them. The increase in the price of oil locally led to unprecedented inflationary spiral from 57 percent in 1994 to over 75 percent in 1995.

How much revenue Nigeria gets from oil is governed by a Memorandum of Understanding between the Federal Government (q.v.) and the oil companies. According to the memorandum, if the price of oil per barrel is between $12.50 and $23.00, operating cost makes up $2.00 per barrel while $3.00 goes to provide the funds for investment, regeneration of the business and profit for the shareholders, while the rest goes to the Federal Government. In recent years, the general instability in the international oil market has greatly affected the nation's revenue. In 1994 the world crude oil prices were characterised by general instability, attributed largely to oversupply while demand was falling. In that year, the price of oil ranged between $14.28 and $17.85 a barrel, making average price to be $16.17. In 1995 the average selling price of crude oil was $17.25 per barrel, but because of price instability in the oil market, the 1996 federal budget was based on a conservative price of $16 per barrel.

PETROLEUM TRUST FUND. A development agency created during the regime of Sani Abacha (q.v.). In October 1994 Sani Abacha raised the price of gasoline by 400 percent. In order to address concerns that the revenues generated by the price increase would be squandered by the government he promised that the gains would be committed to a newly created agency, the Petroleum Trust Fund (PTF). The PTF was to address a number of pressing needs in the country, including infrastructural decline, educational problems and poverty. The PTF was inaugurated on March 21, 1995, and was initially headed by General Muhammadu Buhari, a former head of state with a reputation for honesty and discipline. By the end of 1997, its resources exceeded N100 billion.

During the 1999 presidential election the continued existence of the PTF became the subject of controversy. Supporters argued that it had done an impressive job of addressing a number of the country's development problems. Others accused it of being biased toward projects in the northern part of the country and criticised it as an "alternative government." In keeping with his campaign pledge, newly elected president Olusegun Obasanjo (q.v.) announced the dissolution of the PTF in June 1999.

PHELPS-STOKES COMMISSION. Set up on the initiative of the American Baptist Foreign Missionary Society to study the needs and resources of West, South and Equatorial Africa with special reference to the quality and quantity of education provided. The commission was funded by the Phelps-Stokes Funds, which was a voluntary philanthropic organization with interest in the education of black people in Africa and the United States. The Commission was to look into the educational work done in the areas under consideration, to investigate the educational needs of the people with reference to religious, social, hygienic and economic conditions, to ascertain the extent to which these needs were met and to make a full report of its study. The commission was headed by Dr. Thomas Jesse Jones, a sociologist from Hampton Institute in Virginia.

The report of the commission, entitled *Education in Africa,* came out in 1922. The commission criticised the colonial government education system and said that, even though missionaries had played an important role in the education of Africa, they did not completely realise the full significance of education in the development of the people of Africa. It urged the adaptation of education to meet the needs of the people and the conditions of their environment, and it claimed that many of the failures in the educational systems were due to poor organisation and supervision. Governments and missions in Africa had failed to apply sound principles of administration to the work of education.

PHILLIPSON-ADEBO COMMISSION. After the Nigerianisation (q.v.) Policy had been in effect for three years, the government, in 1952, decided that it was necessary to review the policy and the machinery for implementing it. In April 1952, the government appointed two civil servants to do this, one a Nigerian and the other a European. They formed the Phillipson-Adebo Commission.

The commission submitted its report in April 1953, but it was not immediately made public. Among its recommendations were that the qualifications or standards already prescribed for appointment to the senior service should not be lowered, that where vacancies occurred and no Nigerian was immediately qualified for promotion to them, such vacancies should be advertised for Nigerians at home and abroad and their applications should be considered before non-Nigerians were recruited, and non-Nigerians thus recruited should be on contract renewable until there were suitable Nigerians.

In 1954 the government released the report to the public, but the government made it clear that the report had been overtaken by political development which that year was to usher in a federal system of government.

PHILLIPSON COMMISSION. With the concept of regionalism written into the 1946 constitution, the problem of how the services to each of the regions would be financed arose. To look into this problem the Sidney Phillipson Commission was set up. The commission recommended the principle of derivation and even progress as a way of dealing with this problem. Under this principle central government grants to the regions would be related to the contribution by each of the regions to the government revenue. To obviate the natural effects of this by making the richer regions grow richer and the poorer, poorer, the commission recommended that the principle of derivation be tempered by that of even progress. According to this, relatively poor regions would receive a little more than would be due to them under the first principle. Revenue allocation (q.v.) to the three regions was based on this recommendation during the period of 1948 to 1951.

PLATEAU STATE. Plateau State derives its name from the Jos Plateau. In 1967, when Nigeria became a federation of 12 states, the old Benue and Plateau provinces of the then-Northern Region (q.v.) were merged to form Benue-Plateau State (q.v.), but in 1976 when seven more states were created out of the 12, Plateau province became Plateau State, and was divided in 1991 into 23 local government (q.v.) areas. The state is 53,585 square kilometres in area and is bounded in the north by Bauchi State (q.v.), in the east by Taraba State (q.v.) in the south by Benue (q.v.) and Kogi (q.v.) States and in the west and northwest by the Federal Capital Territory (q.v.) and

Kaduna State (q.v.). It rises from 200 metres above sea level from the plains around the Benue River (q.v.) in the south to 1,200 metres on the Jos Plateau. The Shore Hills extinct volcanoes and crater lakes on the Jos Plateau are said to be about 1,830 metres above sea level. The Jos Plateau is thus characterised by a near-temperate climate and a hot and humid climate in its lower parts. From April to October, during the rainy season, the weather is warm but cold during the harmattan (q.v.) period, December to February. The temperature varies from 20°C to 25°C, and the annual rainfall also varies from 1,317 millimetres to 1,460 millimetres on the Jos Plateau. The vegetation falls within the savannah forest zone with short trees and grasses. The state's mineral resources include columbite, zinc, gold and tin (q.v.).

The population of the state in 1991 was 3,283,704 people with a density of 61 persons per kilometre, thus, being one of the sparsely populated areas of the country with an average population of 96 persons per square kilometres. Important population centers include Jos (q.v.), the capital, Pankshin, Shendam, Wamba, Keffi, Akwanga, Lafia and Nassarawa. Ethnically, there are over 70 different groups, but none of them is so large that it can be described as the majority ethnic group. Among the various peoples are Birom, Angas, Gwandara, Gwari (q.v.), Afo, Amo, Bada, Alago, Mada, Mama, Ebirra, Mushere, Tiv (q.v.), Buji, Mupum and Rindire. As a result of the multiethnic nature of the state, there are many cultural forms and many cultural festivals like the Pusdung, Pus, Ka'at, Umaisha and Pandam fishing festivals. In the state both Islam (q.v.) and Christianity (q.v.) have substantial adherents among the population, but adherents of traditional religious (q.v.) beliefs are still many. A high proportion of the population engage in farming, growing such "exotic" crops as Irish potatoes, apples, grapes, wheat, barley and vegetables. The state produces about 300,000 tons of Irish potatoes every year.

On October 1, 1996, the Abacha regime created Nassarawa State out of a part of Plateau State.

PLEASS, SIR CLEMENT. Born in 1901 in England, he joined the Colonial Administrative Service in 1924 and was sent to Nigeria the same year. He moved up to become lieutenant governor for Eastern Nigeria (q.v.) in 1951. In 1953 he was faced with the Eastern Regional Government Crisis (q.v.), in which the National Council of Nigeria and the Cameroons (q.v.) turned its majority in the Eastern House of Representatives House into an opposition to defeat every bill that was bought before the House for debate, even the appropriation bill. The Lieutenant Governor had to use his reserve powers to decree an appropriation for the running of the government. In 1954 he became the governor of Eastern Nigeria, a constituent part of the new Federation (q.v.) of Nigeria. He remained there until 1957 when he retired.

***PLEIAD*, THE.** The *Pleiad* was a steamer built by MacGregor Laird (q.v.), a Liverpool merchant, with the purpose of opening up the Niger River (q.v.) to trade. The expedition started under Dr. R.N. Baikie (q.v.) in 1854. Dr. Baikie carefully prepared for the voyage, with a good dose of quinine (q.v.) for the crewmen. The *Pleiad* ascended the Niger up to Lokoja (q.v.) where the Benue River joined it, about 250 miles from the coast. It returned to England after four months in the Niger Delta (q.v.) without any loss of life. This was cogent proof that trade with the interior was a possibility and that it could be carried on without undue loss of life. Furthermore, with good precautionary preparations and the use of quinine, the interior of Nigeria could no longer be regarded as the "white man's grave."

POLICE FORCE, LOCAL AUTHORITY. During the colonial period, until the First Republic (q.v.), Local Authority Police forces operated side by side with the Nigeria Police Force, but their jurisdiction was limited to their local authority areas. These forces were merged with the Nigeria Police Force during the military era.

POLICE FORCE, NIGERIA. The Nigeria Police Force is headed by an inspector-general of police who is supported by a deputy inspector-general of police and commissioners in each state. The inspector-general is appointed and can be dismissed by the president after due consultation with the Police Service commission (q.v.), and police commissioners can be dismissed by the commission. State governors and commissioners (ministers) acting for them can issue lawful directives to police commissioners, but a police commissioner may ask that the directives be referred to the president. At present, the total strength of the police is about 100,000 men and women in over 1,300 stations. There is the Nigeria Police Council, which has the responsibility for policy, organisation and administration of the police force, including establishment and financial matters. For appointment, promotion and discipline there is the Police Service Commission, members of which are appointed by the president subject to the approval of the Senate (q.v.).

POLICE SERVICE COMMISSION. The 1963 Republican Constitution (q.v.) provided for the establishment of the Police Service Commission to see to the appointment, promotion and discipline of senior police officers. The members of the commission were appointed by the president on the advice of the prime minister.

Under the 1979 constitution, the Police Service Commission advises the president on the appointment of the inspector-general of police, and appoints persons to offices in the Nigerian Police Force (q.v.). It also has power to discipline and, if necessary, to remove such officers.

POLITICAL ORIENTATION COMMITTEE. During the Nigerian Civil War (q.v.), a group of intellectuals including the famous Nigerian novelist, Chinua Achebe (q.v.) in Biafra (q.v.) set up what was called the Political Orientation Committee. It was organised to work on the future structure of Biafran society and its institutions after the war.

POLITICAL PARTIES. Following the introduction of the elective principle into the choice of members of the Legislative Council (q.v.) by the Clifford Constitution of 1922 (q.v.), political parties began to be formed. The first party in Nigeria was the Nigerian National Democratic Party, founded in Lagos (q.v.) in 1923 by Herbert Macaulay (q.v.). The party did much in awakening national consciousness.

In 1934 a group of educated young men founded the Lagos Youth Movement (q.v.), which in 1936 became the Nigerian Youth Movement (q.v.), which sometimes later was divided by personal and ethnic feuds. Nnamdi Azikiwe (q.v.) broke away from it in 1941, and in 1944 he, in cooperation with Herbert Macaulay, founded the National Council of Nigeria and the Cameroons (q.v.), which began as a congress-type party with student groups, other associational groups and unions as members, together with individual affiliation.

In 1945 Obafemi Awolowo (q.v.) founded in London a Yoruba Cultural Group known as Egbe Omo Oduduwa (q.v.). In 1951 the Egbe became the nucleus of the Action Group Party (q.v.) in preparation for the 1951 regional elections as provided by the Macpherson Constitution (q.v.). Following the pattern of group organisation in the south, a pan-Northern Nigerian cultural organisation was founded in 1948 known as Jam'iyyar Mutanen Arewa (Northern Peoples' Congress). Its membership became the core of the political party known as the Northern Peoples' Congress (q.v.). There were other parties before Nigeria became independent, but these three were the most significant. After independence in 1960, there were alliances but they did not become solidified before the military struck in January 1966. It is to be noted that political parties during the colonial days and immediately after independence grew to be regional parties. None could claim to have a national base.

The next round in party politics began in 1978 when the ban on politics was lifted by the military government of General Olusegun Obasanjo (q.v.). To ensure that parties would be national as against regional parties of the First Republic, the 1979 constitution made elaborate provisions with regard to their organisation and representation and stipulated that their headquarters should be in the capital. Only five parties were recognised to run for elections in 1979. These were the National Party of Nigeria (NPN) (q.v.), the Unity Party of Nigeria (q.v.), the Nigerian Peoples' Party (q.v.), the Great

Nigerian People's Party (q.v.) and the People's Redemption Party (q.v.). In terms of representation, only the NPN could be said to be somewhat national, having won elections in the north, east and west of the country.

The third round was during President Ibrahim B. Babangida's (q.v.) transition to civilian rule. The 1989 constitution, which was to lead to the Third Republic (q.v.) provided for only two political parties. Thirteen political associations applied for recognition, but none was found fit for recognition by the government. The government, therefore, decided to found two parties, the Social Democratic Party (q.v.) and the National Republican Convention (q.v.). It funded them and built them offices in all local government areas. The two parties under strong manipulation by the Babangida administration failed woefully to stand up for democracy after the June 12, 1993, presidential election (q.v.). In November 1993, the new military administration of General Sani Abacha (q.v.) disbanded them.

As part of the Abacha regime's transition program, five political parties were allowed to register in 1996: the Congress for National Consensus (CNC), the Democratic Party of Nigeria (DPN), the Grassroots Democratic Movement (GDM), the National Center Party of Nigeria (NCPN), and the United Nigeria Congress Party (UNCP). All five appeared to be under the control of the military regime, leading to the frequent observation that they were "five fingers of the same leprous hand." This assessment appears to have been confirmed in early 1998 when each of the five picked Sani Abacha as their presidential candidate.

Following Abacha's death in June 1998, the Abubakar regime (1998–99) dissolved the existing political parties and initiated a fresh transition programme. Eventually three political parties emerged. The People's Democratic Party (PDP) boasted the most powerful and ethnically diverse collection of politicians of any party in the country's history. It was all backed by powerful retired military officers. The All People's Party (APP) consisted of an ethnically diverse collection of nationally known politicians, but many were tainted by their association with the Abacha regime. The Alliance for Democracy (AD) enjoyed strong support among the Yoruba (q.v.) of the southwest and "June 12" activists. In elections held between December 1998 and February 1999, the PDP eventually emerged victorious, producing President Olusegun Obasanjo (q.v.).

Throughout its history, Nigeria's political parties have been weak. They have usually lacked a strong ideology, they have not had deep grass-roots support in the society, and they have generally been dominated by powerful individuals. This has contributed to instability and a corrupt, personalistic style of politics. On the other hand, the history of political parties demonstrates a movement toward multiethnic and truly national parties. These trends are likely to be critical in the success and stability of the democratic Fourth Republic (1999–).

POLYGAMY. A union of one man with several wives at the same time (called polygyny) or one woman with several husbands simultaneously (called polyandry). Polygyny is the most common practice in Nigeria, but most people call it polygamy. In traditional society, multiple marriage or a plurality of wives with the attendant number of children who would help on the farm enhanced a man's power and his wealth. Among the Muslims, a man can marry as many as four wives as long as he has the means to care for them. But in spite of the Christian teaching of one man one wife, many Nigerian Christians still have several wives. After his first wife, a man generally marries women much younger than he. Today, as a result of the economic situation of the country with the cost of taking care of children becoming very high, together with improvement in health care leading to lower infant mortality, the attraction that the practice of polygamy has enjoyed is fast waning.

POPULATION. The population of Nigeria at anytime has always been a subject of controversy. In fact, no one can say with any degree of accuracy how many people live in Nigeria. Nigerians have never been able to count themselves accurately. The 1952–53 census put Nigerians at 30,403,305 people but there were reports that many people were not counted or refused to be counted. The 1963–64 census figures put Nigerians at 55,653,821. This figure engendered a lot of controversy but was finally accepted. The figure declared from the 1973 census generated so much debate and criticism that it was cancelled. Thus, for planning and administrative purposes, the government used the projections based on the 1963 population figure of 55,653,821 until 1992 when the results of the 1991 census were announced. According to those results, the population of Nigeria stood at 88.5 million in 1991. The figures have been published on a state and local government basis, not yet on a city, town or village basis. Many states, believing that figures for their areas were inaccurate, petitioned against them. *See* CENSUS.

PORT HARCOURT. The capital of Rivers State (q.v.) and the second largest seaport in the country, the city is situated on the Bonny River and is about 60 kilometres from the Atlantic Ocean. It is one of the new towns, the construction of which began in 1913 when the colonial authorities decided to build a railway line from there to Northern Nigeria through the Enugu coalfields. As a result of the railway construction, many people went to the place to work and settle. Today Port Harcourt is one of the growing industrial cities especially since the establishment of oil refinery and other petro-

allied industries. It has sheetmetal, cigarettes, tire and aluminum factories. The city is well connected by air, land and sea and it is the southern terminus of the North-South-East Railway Line. The University of Port Harcourt is named after the city.

PORTO NOVO. A major center for trade contacts between the Europeans and Africans in the precolonial period. Located in what would later become the country of Benin, Porto Novo was particularly infamous for its role in the slave trade, and was the site of embarkation for many of the slaves captured by the rulers of the Oyo empire.

PORTS. As Nigeria became exposed to the outside world in the Gulf of Guinea, the need to open up ports became felt and the people rose up to satisfy the needs. During the period of the slave trade (q.v.), there were ports in Badagry (q.v.), Lagos (q.v.), Bonny (q.v.), Brass (q.v.), Calabar (q.v.) and some other places through which slaves were transferred into European ships and manufactured goods were brought on land. When the British took over the government of the country, their aim was to develop two major ports, Lagos and Port Harcourt (q.v.) through which agricultural and other raw materials could be exported and manufactured goods brought in. In 1955 the government created the Nigerian Ports Authority (q.v.), and from 1958 to 1967, when the Civil War (q.v.) broke out, the Apapa port in Lagos had recorded a throughput of 32,319,728 metric tonnes while the Port Harcourt port recorded 7,298,001 metric tonnes. Also during the same period a total of 37,527 vessels had used the existing port facilities.

During the Civil War, when Port Harcourt wharf was closed, there was great pressure on the Apapa port facilities. After the war ended in 1970, there was a need for reconstruction. Facilitated by the oil boom of the early 1970s, congestions began to develop at the ports and the government faced the problem by building new ports and developing existing ones. Thus, in 1977 the multipurpose Tin Can Island port was completed. In 1979 Apapa Wharf extension also became a reality. The new Warri (q.v.) and Calabar ports also became operational. In 1981 new developments in Port Harcourt and Sapele ports were completed.

After all this development had been completed, the oil glut of the 1980s set in. Government policy of import restriction reduced the use of the ports' facilities and the increase in the export sector could not adequately compensate for the loss. The number of ships calling at the ports dropped from 6,569 in 1981 to 2,824 in 1987. The Nigerian Ports Authority is one of those government parastatals that have been commercialised. It now must reorganise itself and make profit to survive.

PRESIDENTIAL LIAISON OFFICERS. Appointed early in 1980, Presidential Liaison Officers were special assistants to the president, who were to serve as liaison officers between the president, the state governments and the federal institutions in the states. They supervised various Federal Government projects in the state and reported directly to the president. They were not an intermediary between the state governors and the president.

PRESIDENT OF NIGERIA. In 1963 when Nigeria became a republic, it adopted a constitutional presidential system in which the president was only the Head of State but not the Head of Government. This system worked until 1966 when the military came into power and suspended the office of the president of Nigeria. However experience during the military era showed that Nigeria might do better under an executive presidential system. As such, the 1979 constitution provided for an executive president who must be popularly elected. To win this election, where there were more than two candidates (as happened in 1979), a candidate must not only have the highest number of votes cast at the election but must also have not less than one-quarter of the votes cast at the election in each of at least two-thirds of all the states in the Federation. If there was no clear winner, a second election was to be conducted between the candidate with the highest number of votes and another candidate who had a majority of votes in the highest number of states. This runoff election was to be held in each House of the National and State Assemblies. In the first election conducted under these provisions a serious controversy emerged as to the interpretation of one-quarter of the votes cast at the election in each of at least two-thirds of all the 19 states in the Federation. According to the Federal Electoral Commission (FEDECO) (q.v.) one-quarter of two-thirds of 19 states meant 12 states plus one-quarter of the two-thirds of the votes cast in the 13th state. The interpretation was challenged by Chief Obafemi Awolowo (q.v.) the second-best candidate who had put his hope for winning in the second ballot, first before the Electoral Tribunal and finally on appeal to the Supreme Court which accepted FEDECO's interpretation and confirmed Alhaji Shehu Shagari, (q.v.) who had the highest number of votes cast and one-quarter of two-thirds of the votes cast in Kano State (q.v.) which was the 13th state as the winner.

Before the military withdrew into the barracks, they amended that corruption-prone section of the constitution, providing for a runoff election in the State and National Legislative Houses, and substituted in its place a general election between the two leading candidates by the people of the country within seven days of the first one.

Under the military administration which took over in December 1983, the office of the president was suspended. However, the new military government that succeeded the Buhari administration in August 1985 decided that the new military Head of State, Major-General Ibrahim Babangida (q.v.), would be called President. In May 1999, Olusegun Obasanjo (q.v.) was inaugurated as the first president of the democratic Fourth Republic. Thus, the presidents of Nigeria have been Dr. Nnamdi Azikiwe (1963–66), Alhaji Shehu Sagari (1979–83), General Ibrahim B. Babangida (1985–93), and Olusegun Obasanjo (1999–).

PREST, CHIEF ARTHUR EDWARD. Born in March 1906 in Warri, Delta State (q.v.) he was educated at Warri Government School and later at King's College in Lagos. After graduating in 1926, he joined the police force and rose to the rank of chief inspector of police. He resigned in 1943 to go to London University to study law, and was in 1946 called to the bar at the Middle Temple Inn.

Back in Nigeria he set up a private practice but he was soon attracted to politics and he became a member of the Action Group (AG) (q.v.) Party, the ruling party in the then Western Nigeria which included the present Delta State. He was elected to the Western House of Assembly and later to the federal House of Representatives in Lagos and there he was made the minister of communications, being the first Nigerian politician to occupy that post. In the federal elections of 1954, he was defeated in his constituency by Chief Festus Okotie-Eboh (q.v.) but he was later appointed to the Public Service Commission with his base in London. He later became the Agent-General of Western Nigeria in London. After the creation of the Mid-Western Region (q.v.) in 1963, he became a judge of the region's High Court. In 1966, when the military came to power, he went back to his private practice in Warri. He died on September 11, 1976.

PREVENTIVE DETENTION ACT. At the All-Party Constitutional Conference of July 1963, a proposal was tabled to empower Parliament, if and when it deemed fit, to enact a law curtailing personal liberty in certain circumstances. This proposal was generally referred to as the Preventive Detention Act. It generated a lot of controversy, both in Parliament and in the pages of newspapers.

The proponents of the act, mainly the leaders of the Northern People's Congress (NPC) (q.v.), the National Council of Nigerian Citizens (NCNC) (q.v.) and the United People's Party (UPP) (q.v.) which broke away from the Action Group (AG) (q.v.) Party, argued that the act was a necessary evil, designed to be an insurance policy against subversion, which they said many African nations and in fact many nations all over the world were making use of. The opposition against the act was great and massive. The *West African Pilot,* joined by other newspapers, led a fierce opposition to the act. Opposition to the act also included student and professional organisations, especially the Bar Association, which described it as a measure to starve out liberal democracy in Nigeria. The opposition party in the House of Representatives condemned the proposal as a move to curb the fundamental human rights guaranteed by the constitution.

Because of the nationwide opposition to it, the prime minister was persuaded to drop it and so the proposed bill never came up for debate in the House of Representatives.

PRICE CONTROL. Owing to the nationwide inflation following the end of the Civil War (q.v.), the government enacted Decree Number 33 of 1970, establishing a Price Control Board. The board was empowered to fix the prices of certain commodities like textiles and clothing, cement, beer and soft drinks, salt, motor vehicles etc. Price control inspectors were appointed throughout the Federation to see to the strict observance of the prices as fixed. Persons who contravened the law were punished by fines and forfeiture of the commodities which could be disposed of by the board as it saw fit. In spite of its efforts, however, it was ineffective and therefore it was abolished in 1980 because the government saw that in a situation of acute shortage, it could not work.

PRIME MINISTER OF THE FEDERATION. Before the 1957 Constitutional Conference in London, there was no provision in the Nigerian constitution for the office of the prime minister. However agreements were reached at the conference for the creation of the office of the prime minister for the Federation. The prime minister was to be the Head of Government but not the Head of State, the Governor-General was to appoint a person who appeared to him to command the support of a majority of the members in the House of Representatives. He in turn was to recommend to the Governor-General members of the House of Representatives and Senate whom he wanted as ministers in his cabinet. The ministers were to serve at his discretion. On September 2, 1957, Alhaji Abubakar Tafawa Balewa (q.v.), deputy leader of the Northern People's Congress (NPC) (q.v.) and Minister of Transport in the federal Council of Ministers, was appointed the first prime minister of the Nigerian Federation. In 1966 when the army took over government, the post of the prime minister was suspended. The 1979 constitution, however, has no provision for the post of the prime minister.

PRIVATISATION AND COMMERCIALISATION PROGRAMMES. Privatisation and Commercialisation Decree No. 25 of 1988 was promulgated in July 1988, and by 1989 the programme had been successfully launched. Under the decree privatisation takes place where formerly owned government corporations or firms are sold to interested members of the public who are now expected to manage the organisation more efficiently in order to raise a profit for the owners. Commercialisation is a reorganisation of an enterprise wholly or partly owned by the government so that such enterprise can now operate as a profit-making commercial venture without subventions from the government. Commercialised companies are not, therefore, sold to the public like the privatised ones. The reason for privatisation and commercialisation was that with the downturn in economic well-being of both government and people, it was no longer advisable to continue to put precious resources in unviable companies.

The job of privatising and commercialising was given to the Technical Committee on Privatisation and Commercialisation (TCPC). By 1992, 65 companies had been privatised. These included insurance and manufacturing companies, hotels and banks. Among the commercialised companies are the Nigerian National Petroleum Corporation (q.v.), National Electric Power Authority (q.v.), and the Nigerian Airport Authority. By privatising and commercialising these companies, government would, in normal circumstances, be in a position to allocate its resources more rationally to areas of pressing needs. In 1994 the TCPC was replaced by a new body known as the Bureau for Public Enterprises.

PRIVY COUNCIL. *See* JUDICIAL COMMITTEE OF THE PRIVY COUNCIL.

PROGRESSIVE GOVERNORS' MEETING. After the victory of the National Party of Nigeria (NPN) (q.v.) in the presidential elections of 1979 and the signing of the accord between the NPN and the Nigerian People's Party (NPP) (q.v.) the leadership of the Unity Party of Nigeria (UPN) (q.v.) began to organise the nine state governors—five from the UPN, two from the People's Redemption Party (PRP) (q.v.) and two from the Great Nigerian People's Party (GNPP) (q.v.)—into a kind of opposition group to the Federal Government as part of its strategy to win the 1983 presidential elections. The nine governors met regularly to discuss matters of common and national importance. In July 1981, when the NPN/NPP accord broke down, the three NPP governors also joined the nine governors, and they all formed an unofficial opposition to the Federal Government.

PROGRESSIVE PARTIES ALLIANCE. After the breakdown of the accord between the National Party of Nigeria (NPN) (q.v.) and the Nigerian People's Party (NPP) (q.v.) in July 1981, the three NPP governors began to attend the Progressive Governors' Meetings (q.v.), which, before then were attended only by the five governors of the Unity Party of Nigeria (UPN) (q.v.) two governors of the People's Redemption Party (PRP) (q.v.) and two governors of the Great Nigerian People's Party (GNPP) (q.v.). Talks then began about a realignment of the UPN, GNPP, NPP and the Imoudu Faction of the PRP (q.v.). In March 1982, at the summit meeting of the leaders of the four parties at Maiduguri, Borno State (q.v.), agreement was reached to form the Progressive Parties Alliance (PPA) in an effort to win the 1983 elections against the National Party of Nigeria (NPN). The Alliance, in May 1982, decided to present a common list of candidates for the five elections to be held in 1983, but it later could not agree on a common list for any of the elections, not even for the presidential elections. The two major leaders of the alliance, Chief Obafemi Awolowo (q.v.) and Dr. Nnamdi Azikiwe (q.v.) could not agree to step down, one for the other, as each of them became a candidate for the election. They both lost to the incumbent president, Alhaji Shehu Shagari (q.v.) of the National Party of Nigeria. The Alliance failed to agree on a presidential candidate because of personal ambition and animosity, together with personal and ethnic rivalry.

PROGRESSIVE PEOPLE'S PARTY. A proposed reunion of the Nigerian People's Party (NPP) (q.v.) and the Great Nigerian People's Party (GNPP) (q.v.). In 1978 after the ban on politics was lifted, the Nigerian People's Party (NPP) was formed, but it soon broke into two factions, one retaining the old name and the other, led by Alhaji Waziri Ibrahim (q.v.) becoming the Great Nigerian People's Party (GNPP). These two parties were among the four that formed the Progressive Parties Alliance (q.v.) in March 1982. But soon after, disillusionment set in, and a new alliance was proposed, the Progressive People's Party (PPP), which was to be a union of the NPP and the GNPP. The PPP applied to the Federal Electoral Commission (FEDECO) (q.v.) for recognition as a political party, but its application was rejected.

PROTECTORATE. In 1861, Lagos became a British Crown colony, and from there, British officials extended their influence into the interior of Nigeria. They began to enter into "treaties" with the local chiefs, granting them trade privileges with their people, opening up trade routes from the interior to the coast and guaranteeing the chiefs British protection against foreign influence or attack from neighbouring people. The competition between Britain, Germany and France for colonies in Africa led to the Berlin Conference (q.v.) of 1885, at which the areas around the Niger (q.v.) where the British had made treaties with the local chiefs were conceded to be under their influence. In 1887 the British proclaimed its zones of influence in the coastal districts in the Niger Delta and the Oil Rivers Protectorate (q.v.). In 1893, the protectorate was extended into the interior and was renamed the Niger Coast Protectorate (q.v.). In 1900, when the charter of the Royal Niger Company (q.v.) was revoked, the company's territories became the Protectorate of Southern Nigeria while the territory north of Idah became the Protectorate of Northern Nigeria, each under the administration of a High Commissioner. In 1906 the Colony of Lagos was merged with the Protectorate of Southern Nigeria to become the Colony and Protectorate of Southern Nigeria. In 1914 the Protectorate of Southern Nigeria was merged with the Protectorate of Northern Nigeria to form the Colony and Protectorate of Nigeria.

PROTECTORATE OF SOUTHERN NIGERIA. *See* PROTECTORATE.

PROVINCES. A province was an administrative subdivision of the country under the colonial administration. These subdivisions were, in most cases, based upon the territorial boundaries of the indigenous political units. In areas where this was not feasible, colonial authorities resorted to administrative convenience. Each province was divided into divisions and districts. The administrative head of a province was the resident (q.v.) while that of a division was a district officer (D.O.) (q.v.).

PROVINCIAL ADMINISTRATION. For the purposes of administration, the colonial authorities divided the whole country into provinces—13 in the Northern Region, (q.v.) 12 in the Eastern Region (q.v.) and eight in the Western Region (q.v.). Each province was further subdivided into a number of divisions and each division into districts. In charge of each province during the colonial era was the resident (q.v.) and in charge of the division or the district was a divisional or district officer (q.v.). When the British system of local government was adopted, provincial commissioners who were political appointees with a cabinet rank were put in charge of the provinces. They were assisted by the provincial secretary, who was an administrative officer. Some of the functions of the provincial secretary included the supervision of local governments and local government treasuries in his province.

PROVINCIAL COURTS. Set up by the colonial administration in each of the provinces during the early years of the Protectorate (q.v.) they were presided over by the residents (q.v.) who were the administrative heads of the provinces.

PROVISIONAL RULING COUNCIL. The highest policy-making body under General Sani Abacha's (q.v.) military administration. When General Muhammadu Buhari (q.v.) overthrew Alhaji Shehu Sharagi's (q.v.) civilian administration in December 1993, the highest decision-making body under him was the Supreme Military Council (SMC) (q.v.), which was a carry-over from previous military administrations. In 1985 when General Ibrahim B. Babangida (q.v.) overthrew the Buhari administration, the highest decision-making body was renamed the Armed Forces Ruling Council (q.v.), which under General Abacha became the Provisional Ruling Council. These are all names signifying very little because the council has never had real power but rather it is the Head of State who has power to make and unmake the council.

PUBLIC ACCOUNTS COMMITTEE. One of the parliamentary committees in the Federal Legislatures, it was introduced under the Lyttelton Constitution (q.v.) of 1954. The committee was established to allow the Parliament to control government finances. The committee looked into the finances of the government and reported any irregularities to the Parliament. For instance in 1958–59, it was revealed that £7.5 million was spent without the authority of a warrant from the Ministry of Finance. Although this system of examining public accounts did not give the legislature any control over public finances in the true sense that it could punish or dismiss any head of department who had misused funds, it nonetheless deterred them from careless use of funds in that no head of department would want to be criticised publicly in the Public Account Committee Reports.

PUBLIC COMPANIES. Apart from public corporations, which are set up primarily to serve the public in their economic and social lives and which are financed by the government if they are unable to make ends meet, there are also public companies. These companies were set up by the government to operate on a purely commercial basis, partly to break the monopoly of foreign companies and partly to meet the needs which are not being sufficiently met by private financial arrangements. These companies include the Commodity Board, the Nigerian National Shipping Lines, the National Insurance Corporation of Nigeria, the Nigerian External Telecommunications Limited, the Industrial Development Bank, the Bank for Commerce and Industry, the Nigerian Agricultural Bank, the Nigerian Mortgage Bank, the National Supply Company and the Nigerian Re-Insurance Corporation. Many of these public companies have now been privatised.

PUBLIC COMPLAINTS COMMISSION. Because of the delay of the judicial process in redressing abuse or misuse of power by government officials, the need for a public agency, free of government control has been felt even in some mature democracies. In others where such agencies have not been set up, the citizens' access to their representatives is well recognised and protected. Under a military administration, the need becomes more visibly felt. Thus, after the Civil War (q.v.) in the early 1970s, many people began to ask for an ombudsmanlike agency to check official abuses, and some daily newspapers began to open up columns for people to air their grievances against some government officials.

In 1975 during the administration of General Murtala R. Muhammed (q.v.), the Public Complaints Commission was born with branches in all the states. The commission is made up of a chief commissioner and one commissioner for each state of the Federation (q.v.) and the Federal Capital Territory (q.v.). The chief commissioner and the other commissioners are expected to be persons of unquestionable integrity who should not have been involved in party politics. The chief commissioner coordinates the work of all other commissioners and a commissioner has power either on his own initiative or following complaints lodged before the commission to investigate any administrative action taken by any department or ministry of the federal or state government or any department of any local government (q.v.). The commission also has power to investigate complaints against any statutory corporation or any public institution or any servant or officer of any of the above-named agencies. A commissioner has the power to compel the attendance of any person to give evidence, supply information or produce documents. However, before a person can take his complaint to the commission, he must have exhausted his administrative remedies and he must have personal interest in the matter.

PUBLIC CORPORATIONS. Public corporations, both at the federal and state levels, are statutory bodies established and financed by the government that creates them to operate certain public utilities. These corporations (or boards as some of them are called) have their own staff distinct from the civil service and are independent in their day-to-day activities of the government officials. However, they are accountable to certain ministries on a number of issues like policy matters. While most of them are expected to operate along commercial lines, their major duty is service to the people: they are to function effectively in the overall interest of the economy and the social needs of the people. However some of them, like the National Electric Power Authority, are better known for their gross inefficiency as demonstrated by incessant power failures and complete blackouts for days and weeks in some parts of a city. Federal public corporations include the Nigerian Railway Corporation, the Federal Radio Corporation of Nigeria, the Nigerian Ports Authority, the Nigerian Airways, the Nigerian Coal Corporation, the National Electric Power Authority, the Nigerian Steel Development Authority, the National Mining Corporation, the Nigerian National Petroleum Corporation, the Nigerian Television Authority, the Nigerian Airport Authority and the Federal Housing Authority. In 1989 the federal military government decided to privatise some of its companies while it commercialised many others. Many of these corporations have now been fully or partially commercialised.

PUBLIC LAND ACQUISITION ACT. Promulgated in 1917, the law empowered the government of Nigeria to acquire land compulsorily for public use but subject to the payment of compensation to the person expropriated of his land. Such lands became "crown" or "state lands."

PUBLIC ORDER DECREE NUMBER 34 OF 1966. Issued on May 24, 1966 it dissolved all the 81 existing political parties and 26 tribal unions and cultural organisations. It also prohibited the formation of all such parties, associations or organisations. The decree also banned party slogans and gave power to the police to enter buildings or places where political meetings were suspected to be taking place and arrest persons found in such places. The police were also given power to disperse unlawful processions. This ban was lifted in September 1978 in preparation for elections to usher in the Second Republic (q.v.).

In addition, Nigeria, under the decree, ceased to be a federation and became simply the Republic of Nigeria. *See also* UNIFICATION DECREE.

PUBLIC SERVICE COMMISSION. Set up in 1952, the Public Service Commission evolved from the Lagos Civil Service Commission of 1948. In 1954 the commission was decentralized as a result of the adoption of a new federal constitution. Each region in the Federation had its own Public Service Commission with the power of appointments and promotions in the respective services. Each commission is expected to be politically independent of the executive and well insulated from politics. Under the 1979 constitution, members of the commission must be approved by the Senate (in case of the federal) or the State Legislature (in case of the state).

-Q-

QADIRIYYA. One of the two main Islamic brotherhoods (or Sufi orders) in Nigeria. Qadiriyya is reputed to have been established in Kano (q.v.) in 1610 (although exposure to its ideas date back to at least the 15th century). The Qadiriyya did not become dominant, however, until the victory of Usman Dan Fodio's (q.v.) jihad (q.v.) in the early 19th century. The leaders of the jihad were Qadiriyya, and as a consequence allegiance to it came to characterise the ruling elite during the period of the Sokoto (q.v.) Caliphate.

While the Qadiriyya generally retained its position as the brotherhood of the establishment, it was increasingly challenged in the last half of the 20th century. In the 1950s and 1960s, the growth of a rival brotherhood, the Tijaniyya led to a number of violent clashes necessitating the mediating efforts of political and religious leaders. In the late 1970s, the Izala movement challenged the Islamic orthodoxy of the Sufi brotherhoods, including the Qadiriyya. This led to a series of conflicts, some violent, that lasted into the 1980s.

QUININE. A malaria drug obtained from the bark of several species of the cinchona tree. The tree is evergreen with a hard and thick gray bark. The tree grows in areas of high temperatures and an annual average rainfall of about 1,500 millimetres. The tree can be grown from seeds. Cinchona tree grows in parts of Nigeria, and traditionally, its leaves are squashed in water. People who have an attack of malaria (q.v.) drink the water, which is usually very bitter. The discovery of quinine in 1854 helped a great deal in checking deaths due to malaria among Nigerians and European explorers of Nigeria and West Africa.

-R-

RAILWAY WORKERS UNION (RWU). Founded in 1931 by Michael Imoudu (q.v.) in opposition to the introduction of hourly payments of the railway employees, the union was inaugurated in 1932 with Messrs. Babington A. Macaulay as president and E.T.Z. Macaulay as secretary. As the union grew in strength, the railway management tried to weaken it by transferring Babington Macaulay to Zaria (q.v.) and E.T.Z. Macaulay to Kafanchan in 1939. In 1940, after the death of Babington, Michael Imoudu was elected president of the union. The same year, following the promulgation of the Trade Union Ordinance, the RWU was recognised, and was granted some concessions, including paying workers for the loss they had sustained by the 1931 conversion into hourly payment. In October 1941, the hourly rate was abolished.

RAISMAN COMMISSION. A fiscal review commission appointed after the London Constitutional Conference of 1957 by the secretary of state for the colonies, Mr. Alan Lennox-Boyd, to examine the division of powers to levy taxation and the system of revenue allocation. The commission, headed by Sir Jeremy Raisman, was to consider the country's experience with the existing system, the allocation of functions between the regional and federal governments, the desirability of each government collecting the maximum proportion of its income, the allocation of funds from the Federal Government to the regions, the special taxation problems of Lagos (q.v.), fiscal arrangements for the Southern Cameroons, which were still part of the Federation, and the adequacy of the government's loan policy on government borrowing and capital issues.

The commission combined the operation of independent revenues, derived revenues, and allocation from the Distributable Pool to come out with the distribution of revenue that would assist in bringing about balanced development of all the parts of the Federation. In making its recommendation it sought to see that the financial stability of the Federal Government would be guaranteed so that it could readily come to the aid of needy regions.

The commission therefore recommended that the constitution should provide for the Federal Government, after consultation with the regional governments, to appoint, from time to time, a Fiscal Review Commission in light of the general revenue situation of the country. Since the north was not getting its fair share of revenue from import duties, the Federal Government should pay a bulk sum of money to it from the 1958–59 year. The constitution should ensure complete freedom of internal trade throughout the Federation. The general power of the Federal Government to control the tax imports should remain and the Federal Government should retain jurisdiction over export and excise duties, and jurisdiction to impose sales tax should be federal. The Federal Government should have full power to levy taxes on beer, wines and spirits and the principle of derivation in this regard should be discontinued. The regions should retain jurisdiction over personal income taxes, and jurisdiction over mining royalties and rents should be exclusively federal and the proceeds from them should be shared between the regions of origin, the Federal Government and all the regions in the proportion of 50 percent to the regions of origin, 20 percent to the Federal Government and 30 percent to all the regions by way of the Distributable Pool (q.v.) and the proportion of 40 percent to the north, 24 percent to the west, 31 percent to the east and 5 percent to the Southern Cameroons.

Finally the commission recommended that external borrowing should be in the federal exclusive list and funds to service the loans on behalf of regions should be deducted from the proceeds of revenues which it collected on their behalf and which were to be paid to them.

RAMADAN. Ramadan is the month in which Muslims have their yearly 30-day fast. In Nigeria the fast is observed by having a meal before dawn. There is no food or water taken during the day until sunset.

RANSOME-KUTI, DR. BEKOLARI. A physician and human rights activist, popularly known as Beko, Ransome-Kuti was born on August 2, 1940, and educated at Mrs. Kuti's Class, Abeokuta (q.v.), from 1945 to 1950, Abeokuta Grammar School from 1951 to 1956, Coventry Technical College, England, from 1957 to 1958 and the University of Manchester in England 1958 to 1963. He was appointed a physician at the Massey Street Children's Hospital in Lagos (q.v.) in 1964. From then on, he served in various capacities as a medical doctor in Lagos. In 1977 he became chairman of the Nigerian Medical Association, Lagos State Chapter. In 1984 he was national first vice president of the Nigerian Medical Association and a member of the management board of the Lagos University Teaching Hospital (LUTH) in 1986. He later became chairman of the committee for the defence of human rights in Nigeria and was appointed member of the Eminent Person Advisory groups on Human Rights in the Commonwealth (q.v.) in 1989. And in 1993 he was the chairman of the Campaign for Democracy (CD) (q.v.), an umbrella organisation for many democratic organisations in the nation. Because of his committment to the defence of the rights of the Nigerian citizens, his criticisms of the military government and his activities as cochairman, he became a victim of frequent arrests and detention. In 1995 he was arrested and detained many times. He was imprisoned incommunicado for his exposing to the world the Nigerian government's sentencing prisoners of conscience to death or imprisonment by secret military trials. He was later charged with being accessory to treason and was sentenced to life imprisonment, which was later commuted to 15 years.

He was released from prison in 1998 after the death of Sani Abacha (q.v.).

RANSOME-KUTI, REV. CANON JOSIAH. A clergyman, born in 1855 at Igbein in Western Nigeria, he attended the CMS Training Institution in Abeokuta (q.v.) and later in Lagos (q.v.). In 1876 he became a teacher at St. Peter's School in Ake, Abeokuta. He later went to the CMS Girls' School in Lagos as a teacher. In 1891 he became a catechist at the Gbagura Church Parsonage at Abeokuta. In 1895, he became a deacon and in 1896 he was transferred to Sunren-Ifo District. In 1897 he was ordained a priest. In 1903 he became the superintendent of the Abeokuta Church Mission. By 1906, he had seen to the establishment of many churches and schools in the Sunren-Ifo District. In 1911 he became pastor of St. Peter's Church in Ake. When in 1914, the Egba State lost its independence and became a part of the amalgamated North/South protectorates under British rule, Reverend Ransome-Kuti played a major role in mediating between opponents of the change, and in 1918, when there was an uprising against British rule, he was also called upon to mediate. In 1922 he visited the Holy Land and in the same year he became a canon of the Lagos Cathedral Church of Christ. He died in 1930.

RANSOME-KUTI, PROF. OLIKOYE. A paediatrician and administrator, born on December 30, 1927, at Ijebu Ode, Ogun State (q.v.), he attended Mrs. Ransome-Kuti's Class from 1932 to 1935, Abeokuta Grammar School from 1935 to 1944 and Yaba Higher College (q.v.) from 1946 to 1947. He then went to the University College Ibadan (q.v.) (now University of Ibadan) in 1948 and moved from there to Trinity College, University of Dublin, Ireland, from 1948 to 1954. He obtained his postgraduate degree in medical education in London in 1962 and obtained many other qualifications.

He came back to Nigeria in 1955 and since then has held many important positions. He became professor and head of the department of paediatrics, College of Medicine in the University of Lagos in 1970 and retired from the university in 1988. Before his retirement he had been appointed federal minister of health in 1985, a position he held until 1992. In his career he has served on various national and international committees and commissions as an expert or consultant to WHO, UNESCO and many others. He wrote many books, including *Patent Vitello—Intestinal Duct with Illeal Prolapse* (1965), *Intestinal Absorption of Lactose in Nigerian Ethnic Groups* (1971), *The Development of Family Planning Service Strategy at an MCH-FP Clinic in Lagos Nigeria* (1978) and *Oral Therapy of Infant Diarhoea* (1978).

RANSOME-KUTI, CHIEF OLUFUNMILAYO. A politician and a fighter for women's rights, Mrs. Olufunmilayo Ransome-Kuti was born on October 20, 1900, in Abeokuta and attended the Anglican Church Primary School and later the Abeokuta Girls' Grammar School. She proceeded to Wincham Hall College, Manchester, England, to study music and domestic science in 1920. Returning later to Nigeria, she became a teacher at the Abeokuta Girls' Grammar School and there she married Reverend Israel Ransome-Kuti, the son of Reverend Josiah Ransome Kuti (q.v.). After her marriage, she joined her husband, who was the principal of Ijebu-Ode Grammar School in Ijebu-Ode. Later on Reverend Ransome Kuti came back to Abeokuta with his wife, where he became principal of Abeokuta Grammar School.

Back in Abeokuta, Mrs. Kuti began to organise the women of the town. She founded a Ladies' Club and another club for market women. Adult education for market women was also started. Later, the two clubs were merged to form the Egba Women's Union.

In 1948, the Egba Women's Union became a very powerful force in Abeokuta, so powerful that their campaign against the Alake of Abeokuta, Oba Ademola II (q.v.), who was the Sole Native Authority (q.v.) in the area, had to lead to the temporary exile of the Oba. The women complained of the hardship created by the Oba's enforcement of the British food trade regulations during the Second World War, which they claimed made market women in the town suffer a great deal. They accused the Oba of abuse of powers. They criticised the imposition of the poll tax on women without any regard for their ability to pay and they complained of discriminatory pay for women in employment and they asked for women's right to vote. On July 29, 1948, the British, in their effort to maintain peace, had to temporarily deport the Alake to Oshogbo after which some major reforms were initiated in the taxation policy of the Egba Native Authority.

Ransome-Kuti was also a party activist. Early in the founding of the National Council of Nigeria and the Cameroons (NCNC) (q.v.), she joined the party and was the only woman in the party's delegation to London in 1947 to protest against the Richards Constitution (q.v.). She later held important party posts such as treasurer of the party in the Egba Division and was also a member of the national executive.

Ransome-Kuti travelled far and wide, not only in Africa, but in Europe and North America, representing women's interests in various international conferences. For her contribution, she was honoured with many awards: the Order of the Niger in 1963, Doctor of Laws by University of Ibadan in 1968, Lenin Peace Prize in 1968 and was later awarded an honorary chieftaincy title. She died on April 13, 1978, leaving four famous children behind, among whom are Fela Anikulapo-Kuti (q.v.) one of Nigeria's renowned musicians, and two medical doctors, the younger of which, Beko Ransome-Kuti (q.v.) is a civil rights activist who for his belief has been many times detained in police cells and prisons all over the country.

RED CROSS. *See* INTERNATIONAL COMMITTEE OF THE RED CROSS.

REGIONALISATION OF THE CIVIL SERVICE. Until 1954, when Nigeria became a federation of three regions, there was a national civil service system in accordance with the unitary system of government then in operation. However under the Lyttelton Constitution (q.v.) of 1954, which ushered in a federal system of government, each regional legislature was given power to provide for new posts in the regional civil service and fix their salaries, allowances and conditions of service. Furthermore, the recruitment, transfer and discipline of civil servants were to be under the control of the regional Governor, who was to be advised by the regional Public Service Commission. The effect of this was that many capable senior civil servants in the previous unitary public service transferred their services to their regions of origin, thereby leaving the federal civil service in a poorer situation than before.

RELIGIONS, TRADITIONAL. Before the coming of Islam (q.v.) and Christianity (q.v.), all ethnic groups in Nigeria believed in a Supreme Being and some lesser gods whom they worshipped. God, to them, knows all things and has full responsibility for all that happens on earth. As such, the individual person feels dependent upon God for all that happens to him and, therefore, seeks God's guidance and protection against all evil. He fears God's anger. Important events in life, such as birth, marriage, planting, harvesting and death are linked with God and his worship. When there is failure or a major problem in any of these areas, the individual goes to the priests and diviners who are the interpreters of the intention and the will of God. To appease God, they may employ various means, including offering sacrifices.

With the coming of Christianity and Islam, these new religions coexist with traditional religions. What is interesting is that many adherents of these universal religions still defer to the practitioners of traditional religions by consulting them when in difficulties and asking for their protection against evil. It is, therefore, not uncommon for a Christian or even a church pastor or a Muslim or an Alhaji (someone who has gone on pilgrimage to Mecca) to consult a traditional religious practitioner. The reason for this is not far-fetched. In the traditional society of many Nigerian peoples, religion permeate every aspect of the life of the society. Every group has its own religious system which exercises a lot of influence on the thinking and living of the people. Thus, when one embraces Christianity or Islam, it is not always the case that the new religion embraces one's thought pattern, philosophical outlook, social relations and fears. When a person encounters a serious problem, neither of the new religions is able to allay one's fears and one relapses into the religious practices of one's people. He or she goes to the practitioners of the traditional religions to look into the future, perform some rituals to ward off evil or, when necessary, may be asked to carry amulets, charms or some fetish materials or even offer sacrifices.

Traditional religions have priests, but they have no missionaries to propagate them. Since they are not universal, each religion is limited to the people among whom it evolved. But traditional religious ideas, beliefs and practices have spread to other regions and peoples through migration, marriage or conquest, but efforts to propagate them or make other people accept them is lacking. Finally, traditional religions believe in spirits and life after death as seen in the masquerade (q.v.) festivals in many societies. They also believe in the supernatural power of medicine, a concoction of many material objects together with incantation to reorder events on earth.

REPUBLICAN PARTY. The Republican Party was formed in 1963 by Dr. Josiah Onyebuchi Johnson Okezie (q.v.), who was a former member of the National Council of Nigerian Citizens (q.v.). It had its foothold in the former Eastern Region (q.v.). During the 1964 alliance formation, the party joined the Nigerian National Alliance (q.v.). In the Little Election (q.v.) of 1965, it competed in 13 constituencies and was badly beaten. It was banned, along with others, in 1966 after the military took over power.

RESIDENT. The resident was the most important of the subordinate officials in the groups of provinces in Nigeria during the colonial era. He was in charge of the various activities in a province. Under him were district officers and other minor administrative officers. He had responsibility for a number of things. He was responsible for law and order, he was required to keep the account of the province and he was expected to supervise government construction of roads and buildings. He directed the postal system in his area, collected revenue and compiled statistics with respect to population, crime and trade, and he was to write reports on native organizations, tribal customs, languages and taxation. He also served as judge, counsellor and adviser to Chiefs (q.v.). He was said to be the "backbone" of the colonial administration.

REVENUE ALLOCATION. From 1946 to 1979, the government of Nigeria had set up eight different revenue allocation commissions—Phillipson (1946), Hick-Phillipson (1951), Chick (1953), Raisman (1958), Binns (1964), Dina (1968), Aboyade (1978) and Okigbo (1979)—to look into the problem of revenue sharing among the constituent parts of the country and the national government. The problem of revenue allocation arose from the fact that even though regional and later state governments had independent sources of revenue, they were not commensurate with their constitutional responsibilities and the national government controlled most of the important revenue sources like import and export duties, excise taxes, mining rents and royalties from offshore oil production.

The major principles that have figured prominently in revenue sharing in the country as recommended by the various commissions were equality of status among the regions or states, derivation, needs, national interest, even development and geographical peculiarities. However the most important of these was the principle of derivation which was subject to a more precise measurement. According to this principle, each region and later state would share in the distributable revenues put in the distributable pool account in accordance with the proceeds derived from the relevant taxed transactions within its borders.

Under the 1979 constitution, there was a distributable pool account called the Federation Account into which almost all revenues collected by the Federal Government were paid, and it was to be shared between the federal, state and local governments on the terms that the National Assembly prescribed. Until December 1983, the Federal Government (q.v.) got 55 percent, all state governments got 35 percent and local governments got 10 percent. In 1992, all the states statutorily got 24 percent, while local governments got 20 percent of all federally collected revenue in the Federation account (q.v.). In 1994 a new source of revenue for the three levels of government was added in terms of the Value-Added Tax (VAT), which began in January of the year. In 1994 the revenue from VAT was N8.6 billion. This increased almost by 250 percent to N21.0 billion in 1995. Government in the 1996 budget decided on a formula for the sharing of the revenue: 35 percent goes to the Federal Government, 40 percent to the state governments and Abuja (q.v.), the federal capital, and 25 percent to the local governments. Another significant development was the decision of the Abacha (q.v.) government to increase the percentage set aside for the oil mineral producing areas from 3 percent to 13 percent of the revenue accruing to the Federation account from natural resources.

RIBADU, ALHAJI MUHAMMADU (1910–1965). Born in 1910 at Balala, Adamawa State, Alhaji Muhammadu Ribadu was educated at Yola Middle School after which he taught for some time at the school. In 1931 he joined the Yola Native Administration as an accountant. In 1936 he was made district head of Balala and the treasurer of Adamawa Native Authority Treasury. In 1946 he was sent on a local government training course to Britain.

Back in Nigeria, he became interested in politics. Following the coming into effect of the Richards Constitution (q.v.) he entered the Northern House of Assembly in Kaduna (q.v.) in 1947. When the Northern People's Congress (NPC) (q.v.), originally a cultural organisation, became a political party in 1951, he became prominent in it and rose very rapidly. In the 1951 elections to usher in the Macpherson Constitution (q.v.), Alhaji Ribadu was elected to the Northern House of Assembly and later to the federal House of Representatives, where he was appointed minister of natural resources. In 1954, after Nigeria became a federation, he was appointed federal minister of land, mines and power. In 1957 he was made minister for Lagos affairs (Lagos [q.v.] then had ceased to be part of Western Nigeria and had become a federal territory). In 1960, he was appointed federal minister of defence.

Alhaji Ribadu was an influential leader in the NPC, which dominated the politics of Nigeria before the military took over in 1966. He was second vice president of that party and a powerful person in the Federal Government of Alhaji Sir Abubakar Tafawa Balewa (q.v.). In fact, he was so powerful that he was later described by a former colleague as the only person in the NPC who could face the party leader and premier of the Northern Region, the Sardauna of Sokoto (q.v.), Sir Ahmadu Bello (q.v.) squarely, tell him off and get away with it. For some time Ribadu was the recognised link between Sardauna and the prime minister in Lagos. He died in May 1965.

RICHARDS CONSTITUTION. The Richards Constitution came into being in 1946. Its aim was to promote the unity of the country, provide adequately within that unity for the diverse elements in the country and to secure for the Africans greater participation in the discussion of their own affairs. As such, the constitution set up a Legislative Council (q.v.) of 45 members, 28 of whom were Nigerians, four of whom were elected from Lagos (q.v.) and Calabar (q.v.) while the remaining 24 were nominated. The constitution set up a Regional Council for each of the three regions made up of only one chamber in the Eastern and the Western regions, and two chambers in the Northern Region, the House of Chiefs and the House of Assembly. The regional Legislative Assemblies were to consider and advise the governor on matters referred to them, or introduced by a member in accordance with the constitution. Thus the regional councils did not have legislative powers. With regard to the Executive Council, the constitution provided no changes in representation. This constitution brought for the first time representatives of the northern provinces into the Legislative Council which had the power to make law for the whole country, unlike in the past when the governor made laws for the north by proclamations. Furthermore the constitution, for the first time in Nigeria, provided for unofficial members of the Legislative Council to be in the majority.

However the constitution did not differ from the Crown colony type of government that had previously been in existence. Effective power still resided in the governor, the Executive Council and the administrative staff who were mainly British officials. Because of the shortcomings of this constitution, the National Council of Nigeria and the Cameroons (NCNC) bitterly attacked it and sent a delegation to the secretary of state for the colonies in London in 1947. According to the NCNC, once regions were created, they would help to crystallise the disintegrative tendencies in the country. The party also complained that the constitution was the work of one man without the consent of the millions of people who were to live under it. The new constitution, they said, should not only seek to secure greater participation by Africans in the discussion of their own affairs, but it should enable Africans to secure greater participation in the management of their affairs. Finally, the party objected to the continued practice of nominated members and suggested that it should be replaced by popular representation based on adult suffrage. *See also* LORD MILVERTON.

RIGGING, ELECTION. Rigging is a popular term used in Nigeria to describe election malpractices such as buying ballot papers and stuffing them illegally into the ballot boxes of party candidates and manipulating election figures in favour of one party. While many allegations can be substantiated and have been substantiated, even in court, many others cannot be so substantiated. It is common for the loser to allege that the elections were rigged, even in areas where they have little or no support. *See also* ELECTORAL MALPRACTICES.

RIGHT OF OCCUPANCY. The right of an individual to use and occupy a piece of land. This could be statutory or customary. A statutory right of occupancy is one granted by the governor or his delegate under powers conferred upon him by the Land Use Act (q.v.). This statutory right can be granted to natives of the state as well as to nonnatives. A customary right of occupancy used to be one derived by force of customary law. Under the

Land Use Act, local government is enpowered, with respect to land in rural areas, to grant customary rights of occupancy to any person or organization for agricultural, residential or other purposes.

RIMI, ALHAJI MOHAMMED ABUBAKAR. The first executive governor of Kano State (q.v.) in the Second Republic (q.v.), born in 1940 in the Wudil Local Government Area in Kano State, he was educated at Sumaila Junior Primary School, Birnin Kudu Senior Primary School, Clerical Training Centre in Sokoto (q.v.), the Institute of Administration in Zaria (q.v.) from 1961 to 1962 and the University of London and the University of Sussex, Brighton, from 1972 to 1975.

He worked in many capacities before entering politics in 1978. He was an instructor at the Institute of Administration in Zaria, and at the Clerical Training Center in Sokoto in 1962. He also worked at the Kano local government in 1965 and at the federal Ministry of Information in Lagos from 1966 to 1970. He was the cultural attaché at the Nigerian Embassy in Cairo from 1970 to 1972, and in 1976 he worked at the Nigerian Institute of International Affairs (q.v.).

He was a member of the Constituent Assembly (q.v.) in 1977, and when the ban on politics was lifted, he was elected the People's Redemption Party's (q.v.) governor for Kano State in 1979.

In the party realignment for the 1983 elections, he joined the Nigerian People's Party (q.v.). He was, however, not elected into power in 1983. After the military government of President Ibrahim B. Babangida (q.v.) had created two parties for the country in 1989, the Social Democratic Party (SDP) (q.v.) and the National Republican Convention (q.v.) he joined the SDP, and worked very hard for the party's victory in Kano State.

Rimi angered a number of his supporters among Nigerian progressives when he accepted the post of minister of communication in General Sani Abacha's (q.v.) first cabinet. He served from November 1993 until being dismissed in February 1995. He was later able to redeem some of his radical credentials when he joined the Group of 18 (q.v.) in February 1998, which was a coalition of northern politicians opposed to Sani Abacha's efforts to remain in power. For this, he was briefly imprisoned, not being released until after Abacha's death in June 1998. Rimi emerged as one of the kingpins of the newly formed People's Democratic Party in 1998, and made an unsuccessful bid for the party's presidential nomination in 1999, losing out to Olusegun Obasanjo (q.v.).

RITUAL. A religious ceremony that generally celebrates special events in the life of a society. Rituals are actions which may consist of recitations of prayers, dancing and singing. Sacrifices often accompany rituals in many religious groups in Nigeria.

There are many kinds of rituals. Birth rituals are performed after the birth of a child in thanksgiving to God. This is done very often on the eighth day in Nigeria in what is known as naming ceremonies. Funeral rituals are those that are performed when a person dies to show the transition of a person from this life to another. Different rituals traditionally exist among the Yoruba (q.v.) of the west depending on a person's form of worship when alive. There are also initiation rituals, which are held when some people are taking up a new position. When a person takes a new chieftaincy title, there are rituals which are performed. Marriage rituals are also common in Nigeria like washing of the feet of a new bride before entering her husband's house or rituals relating to betrothal of a woman to a man. Other rituals include those at the beginning and end of an agricultural season. Rituals in Nigeria are not limited to traditional societies. They also exist even in Christian churches like those connected with the sacrifice of the Mass in the Catholic Church (q.v.).

RIVER BASIN AUTHORITIES. There are 11 statutory River Basin Development Authorities, created by the Federal Government for the purpose of using the major rivers in the country for agriculture through irrigation for year-round cultivation. These authorities are at Sokoto-Rima, Hadejia Jama'are, Chad Basin, Upper Benue, Lower Benue, Cross River, Anambra-Imo, Niger Delta, Niger River, Ogun-Oshun, and Benin River. They undertake comprehensive development of underground water resources, control of floods and erosion, water-shed management, and construction and maintenance of dams, dykes, wells, boreholes, irrigation and drainage systems. They also develop irrigation for crops and lease irrigated land to farmers.

RIVERS STATE. The agitation for the creation of the Rivers State began in the early 1950s when plans were on the way to give Nigeria its first federal constitution (q.v.). As such, minorities in each of the regions began to express fear of domination, oppression and victimisation. In 1953, the peoples of the present Cross River (q.v.), Akwa Ibom (q.v.) and Rivers States joined together to form the Calabar-Ogoja-Rivers (COR) State Movement (q.v.) in Uyo, the present capital of Akwa Ibom. In 1954 the Rivers Chiefs and Peoples Conference submitted a memorandum for the Nigerian Constitutional Conference (q.v.) for their felt need for a separate state. Also, in 1957, the people of the area submitted memoranda to the Minorities Commission (q.v.), set up to inquire into the fears of the minorities and the means of allaying them. As a result of the report of the commission, the Niger Delta Development Board (q.v.) was set up in 1961 to monitor and incorporate the development of the area now known as the Rivers State. In 1967, when General Yakubu Gowon's (q.v.) administration decided to create new states in the former regions, the Rivers State was carved out of the former Eastern Region (q.v.) with Port Harcourt (q.v.) as its capital.

The state is located in the Niger Delta (q.v.) area of Nigeria and is linked by many rivers and many tributaries. The area used to be known as the "Oil Rivers" because of the palm oil which was plentiful all across the rivers. Today it is, in a more important sense, the Oil Rivers, for much of Nigeria's crude oil comes from there.

It is bounded in the north by the Delta (q.v.) and Anambra (q.v.) States, in the northeast by Imo State (q.v.), in the east by Abia (q.v.) and Akwa Ibom States, and in the south by the Atlantic Ocean. The land area is 28,000 square kilometres but only about 25 percent of this is upland, while the rest is covered by rivers entering the ocean, creeks, lakes and lagoons. The riverine of the delta area is a lowland, a few metres above sea level. The rainfall is almost all year round, and the annual rainfall in the south is about 4,700 millimetres while it decreases to 1,700 millimetres in the north. Monthly temperature varies from 25°C to 28°C. The state is divided into 22 local government (q.v.) areas.

The population was 3,983,857 in 1991 and the inhabitants are made up of the Abua, Andoni, Degema, Ebana, Egbema, Epie, Gokana, Igbo (q.v.), Ijo, Eleme, Okrika, Ikwerre, Kalabari and others. Their major towns are Port Harcourt (the capital), Membe, Elele, Okrika, Omoku, Yenagoa, Ahoada, Bori, Opobo (q.v.), Bonny (q.v.) and Brass (q.v.). Small as the state is, it contains ancient kingdoms and autonomous communities such as the kingdoms of Bonny, Kalabari, Nembe, Ogbakiri, Opobo, Andoni, Okrika, Abua, Amassom and Ikwerre. The people of the state are farmers and fishers. They produce palm oil, rubber, rice, coconut (q.v.) and cassava (q.v.).

Educationally, the peoples of the Rivers State, especially the coastal peoples, came in contact with the Europeans in the 15th century but Western education started only in 1864 when the first missionary schools were established in Bonny. The first secondary school in the state was the Bonny High School in 1890 sponsored by the Anglican Mission. It later became government college in 1927. The state now has about 1,110 primary schools, 248 secondary schools and two universities. Christianity (q.v.) is fairly well established in the area, but there are adherents of other religious beliefs peacefully co-existing. Communication and transportation in the state is not easy. Because of the peculiar nature of the terrain, the development of rural transportation has been difficult, making communication between the riverine and the mainland people difficult. Rail and air transportation serve mostly interstate, rather than intrastate areas.

On October 1, 1996, the Sbacha regime created Bayelsa State out of part of Rivers State.

ROADS. Roads are the primary means through which goods and services are transported in Nigeria. Roads are essential for the economic development of the country for it is through them that most agricultural and industrial goods are brought to the market for the people who will buy them, process them or consume them. Road building has, therefore, been one of the major areas of government investment. Roads in Nigeria are divided into three categories: Trunk "A" roads which are built and maintained by the Federal Government (q.v.) cut across state boundaries; Trunk "B" roads are built and maintained by the state government, and they link major towns in the state; and Trunk "C" roads, composed of urban and rural roads, are maintained by local governments in their areas of jurisdiction.

ROBERTSON, SIR JAMES. First governor-general of independent Nigeria, born on October 27, 1899, he was educated in Edinburgh and at Oxford. In 1922 he entered the Sudan public service and held such important posts as governor of various provinces. In 1955 he was appointed Governor-General of the Federation of Nigeria, a post he occupied until November 1960, two months after Nigeria became independent. It was therefore his lot to pilot the young Federation to independence. He was succeeded in office by Dr. Nnamdi Azikiwe (q.v.), the first Nigerian to become Governor-General of the Federation. He died in 1983.

ROSIJI, CHIEF AYOTUNDE. A foundation member of the Action Group Party (AG) (q.v.), he was born in January 1917 in Abeokuta. He attended Ibadan Grammar School and Ibadan Government College. He later went to Yaba Higher College where he studied civil engineering. He then went to London to study law from 1944 to 1947. As a member of the Action Group, he held many important positions, including being a member of the Western Region Education Advisory Board and the Electricity Corporation Advisory Board in 1953. In 1954 he was appointed the General Secretary of the party and its legal advisor. He was also elected to the federal House of Representatives the same year. In 1957 he was appointed minister of health in the national government formed by the Prime Minister Sir Abubakar Tafawa Balewa (q.v.). After the 1959 general elections, the Action Group became the Opposition Party and Chief Rosiji became a member of the Opposition Shadow Cabinet. During the Action Group crisis (q.v.) of 1962, he supported Chief S.L. Akintola's faction. He spoke in the federal Parliament in favor of the declaration of the state of emergency in the Western Region and in 1963 he became the deputy leader of the United People's Party (q.v.). In 1964 after the federal elections, he became the minister for information.

ROTIMI, PROF. OLA EMMANUEL GLADSTONE. A playwright and a university teacher born April 13, 1938, at Sapele, Delta State (q.v.), he was educated at St. Cyprian's School in Port Harcourt (q.v.) from 1945 to 1949, St. Jude's School in Lagos (q.v.) and Methodist Boys High School in Lagos from 1952 to 1956. He later went to the United States to attend Boston University from 1959 to 1963 and Yale University from 1963 to 1966. He became a research fellow at the Institute of African Studies at the University of Ife (q.v.) (now Obafemi Awolowo University) in 1966. He later moved to the University of Port Harcourt. He has written many books and plays, including *The Gods Are Not To Blame* (1971), *Kurumi* (1972) and *Our Husband Has Gone Mad Again* (1976).

ROYAL EXCHANGE INSURANCE (NIGERIA) LIMITED. A subsidiary of the Royal Exchange Assurance Limited of London. Founded in Nigeria on February 28, 1921, when Mr. C.C. Alldridge, the first full-time insurance official in West Africa, reported his arrival in Lagos (q.v.) to the general manager of the home company in London. This also was the beginning of the insurance industry in West Africa. The company has grown, with branches all over the nation. At present, the federal and state governments own a majority of the shares, even though the company still retains a link with the parent company, which is allowed to retain a minority shareholding in the name of their successor, Guardian Royal Exchange Assurance Limited of London. In the company's history, the first Nigerian to become its chief executive was Mr. K.A. Onalaja, who was appointed in 1980, but who joined the company in 1949.

ROYAL NIGER COMPANY (RNC). In 1886, the British government granted the National African Company (NAC) (q.v.) the charter it had long sought and it was renamed the Royal Niger Company. The company was authorised to hold and retain the benefit of the several treaties already signed and to administer the areas and preserve public order; it was to interfere as little as possible in the affairs of native Chiefs (q.v.). The company made regulations for the area which was known then as the Oil Rivers Protectorate (q.v.) and established an armed constabulary of three British officers and about 150 local people. The company moved ahead, acquiring more territories, and in 1893 the Oil Rivers Protectorate was renamed the Niger Coast Protectorate. The company met with local resistance as it extended its influence over the rest of the country, and strong competition from the French, who were established on the frontiers of the company's area of interest. In 1898, the British government sent Captain Frederick Lugard (q.v.), who later became Lord Lugard, to the country to raise troops to help to uphold its authority. He raised a force which later became West African Frontier Force (q.v.), which was independent of the Royal Niger Company. On December 31, 1889, the British government revoked the charter of the company and all the areas under it came under British protection on January 1, 1900. The administration of the Niger Coast Protectorate was merged with the area south of Idah under the company's control and was named the Protectorate of Southern Nigeria, while the area north of Idah, under the company, became the Protectorate of Northern Nigeria, with Captain Lugard as its High Commissioner. Thus the Royal Niger Company reverted to its private role after laying the foundation for a united Nigeria. *See also* PROTECTORATE.

ROYAL NIGER CONSTABULARY. After the British government granted the Royal Niger Company (q.v.) a charter to administer the northern parts of the country in 1886, the company set up the Royal Niger Constabulary in 1888 with its headquarters at Lokoja (q.v.), the confluence of the Niger River and the Benue River. The Royal Niger Constabulary was modelled on the Hausa Constabulary but emphasis was placed more on their military role.

RUBBER. In the southern part of Nigeria, varieties of plants produce natural rubber, which is obtained in the form of latex, a milky fluid that flows from the bark of the tree. The fluid is collected by cutting an opening in the tree's bark. After collection, latex can be shipped for processing either as liquid or coagulated by mixing in acid and rolling it into sheets. It can then be treated to make foam rubber, sponge rubber, tires and inner tubes. From 1989 to 1991, Nigeria produced about 180 tonnes of natural rubber annually and exported about 105 tonnes every year.

RUMFA, MUHAMMAD. The King of Kano from 1463–99. He is associated with a number of important changes in the development of the kingdom. Most important of these was his role in promoting religion. It was during his reign that Islam (q.v.) became Kano's official religion, and it emerged as a center for Muslim scholars. In addition, Rumfa extended the city walls of Kano (q.v.) and established the famous Kurmi Market. In terms of governance, Rumfa is the king who first used eunuchs and slaves in official positions, and introduced the important nine member executive council, "tarata-Kano."

RURAL DEVELOPMENT. For a long time after independence in 1960, and even though the rural areas of the country continued to supply the bulk of the food needs and the foreign exchange earnings from crops such as cocoa (q.v.), cotton, groundnuts (q.v.), palm produce, timber and rubber (q.v.), most of the country's development projects were concentrated in the urban areas. Even with the oil boom of the 1970s, the urban areas benefitted most from the oil wealth.

However, things began to change somewhat in 1975 when the World Bank-assisted Agricultural Development Projects (ADPs) introduced the idea of rural integrated development with the construction of roads and water projects and many other infrastructal facilities in the rural areas. The ADP became a nationwide project. In 1976 the Federal Government (q.v.) also initiated Operation Feed the Nation (q.v.), the River Basin Development Projects in 1976, and the Green Revolution (q.v.) in 1979, all designed to improve life in the rural areas. Between 1979 and 1983, various other agricultural schemes were introduced.

The greatest push came between 1985 and 1990, when the government decided to concentrate more of its development projects in rural areas and stem the tide of migration from the rural areas to the overcrowded cities. In 1986 the Directorate for Food, Roads, and Rural Infrastructure (q.v.), was established. Its purpose was to provide rural feeder roads, potable water, rural electrification, and rural health and housing schemes. Through its activities, over 5,000 communities have benefitted, and many rural areas have been connected to the national electricity system. This effort was followed in 1987 by the Better Life for Rural Women Programme.

-S-

SABON-GARI. Literally means "new town," Sabon-Gari is the area set aside in the Muslim north for Nigerians who were regarded as strangers or "aliens." These people generally were of southern origin (east and west). In the south, especially in the Yoruba (q.v.) towns, there are such residential areas set aside for the "Hausa" people.

SALEM, ALHAJI KAM. Inspector General of Police in General Gowon's administration, born in 1924 in Dikwa Borno State, he was educated at Dikwa and Bornu Middle School in Maiduguri. He joined the Police Force in 1942 and from there rose fairly rapidly. In 1962 he became commissioner of the Northern Region and in 1965 he was deputy inspector general of police. After January 1966, and the retirement of the then inspector general of police, Mr. Louis Edet for health reasons, he was promoted to inspector general of police with a place in the Federal Executive Council and in 1967 became the federal commissioner for internal affairs. In 1975, after the July coup which brought Brigadier Murtala Muhammed (q.v.) to power, he was retired, succeeded by Alhaji M.D. Yusuf. When the ban on politics was lifted in 1978, he became a foundation member of the National Party of Nigeria (NPN) (q.v.).

SARAKI, HON. (DR.) ABUBAKAR SOLA. Physician, politician and leader of the National Party of Nigeria (NPN) in the Senate (q.v.) during the first term in the Second Republic (q.v.). Born in 1933, he attended Edward Blyden Memorial School and Eko Boys High School in Lagos (q.v.). He later went to the College of Technology, Chatham University College and St. George's Hospital Medical School in London. In 1962 he was a House Surgeon in St. George's Hospital, but returned home in 1963 to the General Hospital in Lagos and then went on to the Creek Hospital in Lagos in 1964. He was a member of the Constituent Assembly (q.v.) from 1977 to 1978, became a NPN (q.v.) senator in 1979 and was chosen as NPN leader in the Senate. He was a national vice chairman of the party in Kwara State (q.v.). After the military ousted the Shagari (q.v.) administration in December 1983, he, like many other politicians, was arrested and detained. In August 1985 the Babangida (q.v.) administration released him. In the march to the Third Republic (q.v.), he joined the Social Democratic Party (q.v.). He was a member of the 1994 Constitutional Conference (q.v.) in Abuja (q.v.).

Saraki was considered a presidential candidate under the Abacha transition programme, but withdrew when it became clear that the head of state intended to manipulate the elections to secure his own election. Under the Abubakar regime, Saraki was a leading member of the All People's Party (APP). When he felt that he was unfairly denied the opportunity to pursue the party's presidential nomination, he briefly switched his allegiance to the rival People's Democratic Party (PDP). This move resulted in the PDP winning the 1999 presidential elections in Kwara State, which had previously been an APP stronghold. In the aftermath of the elections, Saraki's disaffection continued to be a major problem undermining the stability of the APP.

SARKI. The Hausa word for "king" or "chief" (sarakuna pl.). It is most commonly used to refer to the leaders of various kingdoms (thus the Emir of Kano is referred to as Sarkin Kano [note: the "n" is a linker]). Traditionally, the Sarki would be appointed by a council of kingmakers, who would choose a successor from a restricted group of eligible candidates. In the exercise of his authority, the Sarki would be assisted by a number of advisors and officials such as the Galadima, the Madawaki, the Ajiya and the Makama. Different professions were represented by guild leaders, and local areas under the control of the Sarki often had their own representatives, as did ethnic minorities. While the power of the Sarki was in principle absolute, in practice these leaders often deferred to the views of these other leaders, as well as to the expectations generated by custom and religion.

SARO-WIWA, KENULE BEESON. A writer, businessman, publisher and political activist, born in 1941 at Bori in Rivers State (q.v.), was educated at the Government College in Umuahia from 1954 to 1961, University of Ibadan, Ibadan, from 1962 to 1966, and joined the University of Nigeria,

Nsukka (q.v.), in 1967. In 1968 he was appointed Rivers State commissioner (q.v.) for works, land and transport, and later commissioner of education. He was executive director of the National Directorate for Social Mobilisation (q.v.) in 1987 but resigned the following year. He was the president of the Movement for the Survival of the Ogoni People, an organisation seeking that the rights of the Ogoni people be duly recognised. In May 1994, Saro-Wiwa and many members of his organisation were arrested for the murder of four Ogoni leaders and was, for many months, detained before being charged to court. He and eight others were secretly tried by a military tribunal and found guilty. They were sentenced to death by hanging. His appeal to the Provisional Ruling Council (q.v.) was denied. Later, appeals for clemency began to pour in from world leaders all over the world, including Commonwealth (q.v.) leaders in Auckland. But the government turned a deaf ear and hurriedly ordered his execution and that of his colleagues. He was killed on November 10, 1995. His execution was seen as a slap in the face of the Commonwealth and other world leaders, leading to the suspension of Nigeria's membership in the Commonwealth and the imposition of ineffective sanctions on the military by the United States and members of the European Union. Saro-Wiwa wrote many books, including *Tambari* (1973), *Sozaboy* (1985), *In A Time of War* (1985), *A Forest of Flowers* (1986) and *Prisoners of Jebs* (1988).

SCHOOLS. Schools are places where young people are taught. Even though much learning occurs outside the school, for example, between parent and child at home, within communities as a child grows up, at work sites as an adult, schools provide children with formal education at many levels. In Nigeria there are mainly two types of schools: Islamic religious schools and formal Western schools. Islamic religious schools teach Arabic education to children so that they can read the Koran and pray in Arabic (q.v.). Sometimes they are constituted in the house of the Arabic teacher, or Mallam, or under a tree or in the vicinity of a mosque. Western schools require buildings and are formally organised. At the beginning are primary schools for children about five or six years of age; it lasts for six years. The secondary school, known as high schools or college education, lasts for six years. The third level is postsecondary school such as universities, polytechnical and technical schools and so on. The present government policy on education is based on what is called the 6-3-3-4 education system. The first six years are spent in the primary school. The next three years are spent in junior secondary school, and the second three years are spent in the senior secondary school. The next level is university education, which is expected to last for four years. Besides these, many remedial institutions prepare candidates for qualifications of choice.

SCHOOLS, KORANIC. Koranic Schools are schools where the Holy Koran—the Muslim holy book—is learned, usually by young boys and girls. At the school they learn the Arabic (q.v.) alphabets and they can read the Koran in Arabic and interpret it. They are also trained in the correct method of worship and the basic rules of social conduct. In the past in many Muslim places, this was the only school that Muslim children were sent to. Today children go to secular schools and take lessons in the Holy Koran as well as in other subjects. This, however, does not mean the end of Koranic schools. They still exist, but their hours are now fixed for the evenings after the children would have come back home from the secular schools and also in the mornings during the weekends.

SCHOOLS, SECONDARY MODERN. The Secondary Modern School, introduced in the former Western Region (q.v.) of Nigeria in 1955, was a three-to-four year course. Its objective was to provide a means whereby primary school graduates who could not be admitted into grammar schools could be prepared for vocational and professional training. In the school, students took a good number of courses. Those who offered commercial subjects spent four years while those who offered basic courses took three years. Products of these schools were generally admitted into three-year grade II teacher training colleges and to trade centres. Some graduates also found their way into grammar schools. In 1978 government began to phase them out and by the beginning of the 1980–81 academic year, none of them was still in existence. Most of them had been converted into full-fledged secondary grammar schools and others into primary schools. It must be noted that the experiment existed only in the former Western Region of Nigeria and the states created from it.

SCIENCE AND TECHNOLOGY. Before independence in October 1960, Nigeria had some research institutes, most serving the agricultural sector of the economy (q.v.). Such institutes included the Nigerian Institute for Oil Palm Research and the Federal Department of Forest Research. In 1962 the government set up the Cocoa Research Institute of Nigeria in Ibadan (q.v.) to take over research projects carried on outside the country by the West African Cocoa Research Institute. Other research projects in industry and medicine were coordinated by various ministries. After the Civil War (q.v.), various research coordinating councils were set up covering agriculture (q.v.) in 1971, industry (q.v.) and medicine in 1972 and natural science in 1973. These councils advised on scientific and technological development of the of the country. Their activities were coordinated by the National Council for Science and Technology. Later, the council was dissolved, replaced by the National Science and Technology Development Agency in 1977. In 1979 the government set up the Ministry of Science and Technology to coordinate, promote, and formulate policies and supervise and fund scientific and technological development in the country. Today there are over 20 research institutes concerned with agriculture, industrial plant, engineering design and fabrication, food science and technology, food processing, medicine and pharmaceutical matters. Many products of the research institutes, especially in farm implements, have been commercialised. For example, the Project Development Agency in Enugu (q.v.) has come up with a locally fabricated car and aircraft known as the 'Air Beetle.'

SEASONS. Generally, Nigeria has two main seasons, the rainy season and the dry season. The rainy season begins in March in the south (May in the north) and lasts until October or November. The dry season starts in November and ends in March. In the south, the prevailing wind during the rainy season is from the southwest and with it comes the rain, which is generally heavy along the coast and progressively decreases as it travels inland and north. The annual rainfall varies from place to place. In the southwest the average annual rainfall is about 177.8 cm. while in the southeast, it is about 431.8 cm. In the central part of Northern Nigeria it is about 127 cm. while it is about 50.8 cm. in the far north. Lightning and thunder often accompany rains in April, May, September and October.

SECESSION THREATS. The three major regions of Nigeria—Northern, Eastern and Western—have each made secession threats at one time or another, but it was the Eastern Region (q.v.) that carried out its threat. Following the independence-in-1956 Constitutional Crisis (q.v.) of 1953, the Northern Region (q.v.) put forth an Eight-Point Programme (q.v.), which, if accepted, was tantamount to a demand for secession. At the London Conference of 1953, the north accepted a compromise on a federal system and gave up its Eight-Point Programme. However, the west was angry over the Lagos issue (q.v.). The Action Group Party (AG) (q.v.), which controlled the west, wanted Lagos (q.v.), the capital of Nigeria, to be a territorial part of the Western Region (the slogan then was "Lagos belongs to the West" as it was under the 1951 Macpherson Constitution [q.v.]), but the Northern People's Congress (NPC) (q.v.) and the National Council of Nigeria and the Cameroons (NCNC) (q.v.) wanted a neutral capital, as is the case in many federal countries. When the AG could not get what it wanted, it declared that if the north had to lay down conditions before joining the Federation (q.v.), the west would like to be counted out of the Federation.

Again, after the 1963–64 census, and the Supreme Court's (q.v.) decision disallowing the appeal of Eastern Nigeria, it was alleged that the east was contemplating secession. This was not proved, but events in 1966 led to a real threat of secession. After the second coup (q.v.) in July 1966 and the mass killing of the Igbo (q.v.) in the north, many Igbo leaders began to think and believe that no part of the Federation was safe for them. All people of Eastern Nigeria origin went back to the east, and in May 1967, Col. Odumegwu Ojukwu (q.v.) declared the secession of the east and a proclamation of the Republic of Biafra (q.v.). This led to a thirty-month Civil War (q.v.), which finally reunited all the peoples of the country again.

Following the annulment of the June 12, 1993, elections, sentiments in favor of secession began to surface in the Western part of the country. The west was the home region to the probable winner of those elections, M.K.O. Abiola (q.v.). Over time, those sentiments began to dissipate.

SECOND NATIONAL DEVELOPMENT PLAN, 1970–74. This plan was launched shortly after the Civil War (q.v.) as a means to reconstruct the facilities destroyed during the war, and to promote the economic and social development of the country. The plan aimed to spend over N3 billion during the four years. This amount was distributed between public and private sectors. The average growth rate expected throughout the plan period was 7 percent per annum.

There were a number of important achievements during the plan. Agricultural farms abandoned during the Civil War—especially in the East-Central and South-Eastern States—were rehabilitated and brought back into production. Government distributed fertilisers to farmers and brought more acres of land into cultivation. In industrial development, a number of manufacturing establishments, damaged during the war, were reactivated and new ones were set up. In transportation, over 3,000 kilometres of roads were built while work was progressing over 2,000 kilometres more. Airports were built and damaged ports were reconstructed. In education the story is very much the same. Enrollment in primary schools went up from 3.5 million in 1970 to 4.5 million in 1973. In secondary schools, enrollment nearly doubled from 343,000 in 1970 to 649,000 in 1973. Many higher institutions were also built, all geared to the technological development of the country.

SECOND REPUBLIC. The struggle to capture governmental power during the Second Republic started in earnest in September 1978, when the ban on political activities had been lifted and the Republican Constitution, which was to take effect on October 1, 1979, had been approved by the Supreme Military Council. Political parties began to emerge and out of about 50 such parties, only five of them satisfied the criteria laid down by the Federal Electoral Commission (FEDECO) (q.v.) for recognition. Thus the major parties that juggled for power during the Second Republic were the National Party of Nigeria (NPN) (q.v.), the Unity Party of Nigeria (UPN) (q.v.), the Nigerian People's Party (NPP) (q.v.), the Great Nigerian People's Party (GNPP) (q.v.) and the People's Redemption Party (PRP) (q.v.).

The Second Republican Constitution was modelled on the American presidential system, which laid down a system of checks and balances. The president was nationally elected and was given power to execute the law of the land. The National Assembly was given power to make laws and the judiciary was to enforce and interpret the law.

Elections to national and state offices took place between July and August 1979. The election returns favored the NPN, in that that party, by judicial interpretation, won the presidential elections, and won seven out of the 19 state gubernatorial elections. It also had more seats in the national assembly than any one of the other four parties. The President-elect, in an effort to promote national unity, called all the other parties to join him in forming a national government, but it was only the NPP that acceded to his call by coming into an accord to work together without any party losing its identity. The other parties began to get together, and they formed a kind of an unofficial opposition.

The politicians of the Second Republic were more concerned about their personal interests than the interest of the generality of the people. At the national level, corruption was rampant and the president was too weak to moderate it. At the state level the story was not much different except that state officials had less access to public money and so they misappropriated less than their national counterparts. Politicians and public officials got bribes and kickbacks in millions of naira, which they carefully syphoned away to Europe and America. The economy was in a terrible state of affairs and the government had to resort to austerity measures to keep the country afloat.

Added to this economic malaise was the farce of election processes that the country went through in 1983. Because the stakes were high, i.e., because the opportunity to loot the public treasury was wide open to government functionaries, the struggle for power was desperate and vicious; people killed and maimed opposition members and destroyed their property with great zest, and the major parties heavily rigged the elections in a way unparalleled in the history of the country. Again, the governing NPN party, which had full control of the police, won not only the presidency but it also improved its position in the states, winning 13 out of the 19 state elections and having an overwhelming majority in the National Assembly.

The president and the governors that had been declared winners were sworn in on October 1, 1983, but just four months after, on December 31, 1983, a coup d'etat (q.v.) put an end to the Shagari (q.v.) administration and suspended many parts of the Second Republican Constitution.

SECRETARY OF STATE FOR THE COLONIES. The secretary of state for the colonies was a minister of cabinet rank in the British government. It was he who was in charge of the colonial office in London and oversaw the various activities and developments in the colonies and overseas territories. However, his power was limited by the circumstances in which a particular territory had been acquired or by the constitutional arrangements reached by his predecessors. Governors of the colonial territories were responsible to him and they kept him constantly informed. In the history of Nigeria's constitutional development, various secretaries of state for the colonies played important roles. In 1920, a delegation of the National Congress of British West Africa (q.v.) went to London to see the Secretary of State Lord Milner on the need for increased participation of Africans in their own affairs, and even though the demands were rejected, two years later, the government yielded to the demand for elected members on the Legislative Council (q.v.). In 1947, the National Council of Nigeria and the Cameroons (NCNC) (q.v.) delegation to London had a meeting with the Secretary of State Lord Arthur Creech Jones on the revision of the Richards Constitution (q.v.). When Sir John Macpherson (q.v.) in 1948 succeeded Richards, he promised a review of the constitution in 1950. The secretary of state held constitutional conferences with the Nigerian leaders from 1953 to 1960 on the issue of Nigeria's self-government and independence.

SEFUWA DYNASTY. The regime in control of the empire of Bornu during its period of greatest strength. The Sefuwa dynasty was originally established in the kingdom of Kanem north of Lake Chad at the end of the 11th century. This empire expanded to incorporate the kingdom of Bornu to the southwest of Lake Chad in the 13th century. At the end of the 14th century, the collapse of order in Kanem forced the leaders of Sefuwa dynasty to flee to Bornu, which they made the centre of a new state. Bornu prospered under Sefuwa leadership, becoming one of the great powers of the region. After a long period of turmoil in the 19th century, the Sefuwa dynasty was supplanted by the Al-Kanemi dynasty in 1846.

SEGREGATION. The white man in Nigeria lived segregated from the people he came to rule, carving out a separate residential area for himself and a few Africans of the same standing. These areas were referred to as "government reservations" and could be found in all the capital cities. The reason the white man generally gave for this was the incidence of malaria (q.v.), which he said was prevalent among the indigenous population. The practice was highly resented and has long been abandoned.

SELF-GOVERNMENT MOTION CRISIS. In March 1953, an Action Group Party (AG) (q.v.) member, Chief Anthony Enahoro (q.v.) tabled a private member's motion in the Central Legislature for self-government in 1956. This was resented by Northern representatives, even though it resulted in a temporary alliance between the Action Group Party, which controlled the west and the National Council of Nigeria and the Cameroons (NCNC) (q.v.), which controlled the east. The Northern Delegation, believing that 1956 was too early, moved a counter motion with the phrase "as soon as possible" instead of "in 1956." Because of failure to agree on a motion, the Action Group members and the NCNC members walked out of the House. This was the death blow to the Macpherson Constitution (q.v.). The north later presented its Eight-Point Program (q.v.) which, if carried out, would have amounted to a virtual secession from the rest of the country. In the Constitutional Conference of 1954, the British government helped to resolve the crisis by agreeing to give self-government to those regions, constituent members of the federal system of government that was to be set up, which desired it. At the Constitutional Conference held in London in 1957, arrangements were completed for the Eastern and Western regions to become self-governing later in the same year. In 1958 there was another Constitutional Conference in London at which agreements were reached that the Northern Region should also become self-governing in 1959. Her Majesty's Government also agreed that if a resolution asking for independence was passed by the federal Parliament which would come into being in early 1960, Her Majesty's Government would agree to that resolution and would introduce a bill in Parliament in London to make Nigeria a fully independent country on October 1, 1960.

SENATE. Even though Nigeria became a federation in 1954, it did not have a second Legislative House until after the 1957 Constitutional Conference, at which a decision was reached to establish a second chamber at the federal level. The first set of Nigerian senators were appointed toward the end of 1959 and the first sitting of the Senate took place in January 1960. According to the Independence Constitution of 1960, each region was to be represented by 12 senators selected at a joint sitting of the Legislative Houses of each region. In addition, four senators were appointed to represent the federal territory of Lagos (q.v.) and four others were appointed by the governor on the advice of the prime minister. The power of the Senate was very limited, much like the British House of Lords. It could not amend money bills unless the House of Representatives agreed, and it could not delay money bills for more than one month and other bills for more than six months. During the Second Republic (q.v.) 1979–83, the constitution, following American practice, gave greater powers to the Senate. In the first place, members of the Senate were elected, five from each state. The Senate's consent was required on all legislation and it had other constitutional powers to give or refuse its consent to certain presidential appointments like those of cabinet ministers, ambassadors and members of certain commissions. The constitutional provision for the Senate was suspended after the December 1983 coup d'etat.

SENIOR ADVOCATE OF NIGERIA. The highest honour available to a legal practitioner in Nigeria, this status is conferred on a person who has practiced for not less than 10 years and who has achieved high distinction in the legal profession. The rank may also be conferred, in exceptional circumstances, on academic members of the legal profession who have distinguished themselves through teaching and/or publishing of works that have made substantial contributions in the field of law and jurisprudence. They should also be people of good character, good reputation, honesty, integrity, ability, sound knowledge of the law and who respect the code of conduct and etiquette at the bar. A senior advocate of Nigeria has the exclusive right to sit in the Inner Bar, or where there is no Inner Bar, on the front row of the seats available for legal practitioners. Furthermore, he has the right to mention any motion in which he is appearing—or any other cause which is on the list for mention and not otherwise listed—for hearing out of its turn on the cause list.

SETTLEMENT. A term made popular in 1992 by General Olusegun Obasanjo (q.v.) in his memorandum to President Ibrahim B. Babangida (q.v.) to describe Babangida's method of purchasing people's silence. By assisting people in times of need or adversity, Babangida was able to keep many people, including critics of his administration, quiet about the shortcomings of his administration. Presently, the term applies to all kinds of bribes in cash or in kind and to all good turns done by a person to keep the receiver quiet about the doer's shortcomings and make him abandon his independence of thought.

SHANGO. Shango was the son of Oranmiyan (q.v.), who was the son of Oduduwa (q.v.) the traditional ancestor of the Yoruba (q.v.). Shango was the fourth king of Oyo. He was famous for his magical powers. He had the habit of emitting fire and smoke out of his mouth, a feat which greatly increased the dread his subjects had for him. He reigned in Yorubaland for seven years, during which he fought many battles. Shango was reputed to have the power to attract lightning. One day, having made the charm, he ascended a hill with some relations and tested his charm on his own palace. Very soon a storm gathered and before the king and his followers could get back to the palace, the palace had been struck by lightning and was set on fire, in which many of his wives and children died. Shango was filled with remorse. He abdicated the throne and decided to retire to the court of his maternal grandfather, Elempe, the King of the Nupes (q.v.). On the way, his followers deserted him and because he could not proceed alone or for shame, he returned home, climbed a tree and hanged himself. Shango was later deified and is worshipped today in Yorubaland and in some parts of South America as the god of thunder and lightning.

SHARI'A. Shari'a is the law of Islam (q.v.) which applies to all human activities. In Northern Nigeria, it deals mostly with civil cases, but it is in the area of family law and succession that it is strongest and most important. Shari'a law is recognised by the Nigerian constitution as a law which is applicable to Muslims.

The Shari'a is said to have four main sources: the Koran, which is considered as the ultimate source of the Shari'a; the Sunna or the tradition which deals with the precepts and customs of the Prophet Muhammed himself and which are used to explain and interpret the Koran; the Kiyas or analogical deductions, from established principles in the Koran or the Sunna, and Ijma or the consensus of Muslim jurists.

The law in Northern Nigeria is administered by Shari'a Courts. Under the 1979 Constitution, appeals lie from the Shari'a Court of Appeal to the Federal Court of Appeal in any civil proceedings with respect to any question of Islamic law.

SHARI'A COURT OF APPEAL. *See* ISLAMIC LAW.

SHATA, ALHAJI MAMMAN. The most famous Hausa (q.v.) musician of the 20th century. Shata was born around 1912–16 (exact date unknown) in Musawa in the Northern Region. As a teenager, Shata made a living hawking kola nuts until his musical talents became evident. Shata built upon a tradition of Hausa praise singing, in which a performer, accompanied by kalangu drums, sings in honour of an event of esteemed person. The form requires not only musicianship, but clever word play as well. In recognition of his artistry, Shata received honorary degrees from Ahmadu Bello University, Zaria (q.v.), and the University of California, Los Angeles, in 1976. In his later years, Shata became interested in politics and was elected a local government councillor. Mamman Shata died in Kano on June 18, 1999.

SHELL PETROLEUM DEVELOPMENT COMPANY OF NIGERIA. The Shell Oil Company started exploration for crude oil in Nigeria as early as 1937, and production started in 1958, two years before Nigeria became independent. Shell is the largest oil company in Nigeria with more than 90 oil fields and a 6,200-kilometre network of pipelines spread over more than 31,000 square kilometres of the Niger Delta (q.v.). There are over 80 production stations. Its operations are mainly land based and affect the lives of people in some 12 major ethnic groups divided into about 800 communities. These operations have destroyed most of the land and water in the area. The company records an average of 221 spills every year, much of which is due to aging facilities. As a result of this, there is deforestation, leading to rapid erosion and infertility of the soil.

The communities in the area have always complained that Shell operations have destroyed their land and water and deprived them of the sources of their livelihood. In spite of the huge oil revenue to the Federal Government (q.v.), they have not had a compensating share. One of the peoples that have been seriously affected by its operations are the Ogoni (q.v.) who were traditionally farmers and fishers. But Shell Company claimed that the standard applied by some countries may be an inappropriate and unwarranted economic and social cost to other countries, in particular, to developing countries like Nigeria.

Not only were its activities destroying the land and the rivers in the area, the flaring of gas 24 hours a day pollutes the atmosphere. The people who suffered most from these activities protested, but the company and the government paid little attention. Their discontent, therefore, led to agitation, disturbances and, at times, violence. The Ogoni people's frustration led to the formation of the Movement for the Survival of the Ogoni People (q.v.), which was led by Ken Saro-Wiwa (q.v.) who was executed together with eight other Ogoni leaders after a secret military trial in November 1995 on the pretext that they were responsible for killing four other Ogoni leaders. There were allegations that Shell colluded with the government to get rid of Ken Saro-Wiwa, and that the company was importing arms into Nigeria.

SHINKAFI, ALHAJI UMARU. A lawyer by profession, a businessman, an administrator and a presidential candidate in the 1992 primaries. Born January 19, 1937, in Kaura-Namoda in Zamfara State (q.v.), he attended Shinkafi Elementary School, Sokoto Middle School (1946–52) and Barewa College, Zaria (q.v.) (1952–58).

He later went to the University of Lagos to study law. He started his public service career as a police officer and rose to the rank of commissioner (q.v.) in 1978. Under the Murtala R. Muhammed (q.v.) and O. Obasanjo (q.v.) administration, he served as federal minister of internal affairs (1975–78). In 1979 he was appointed the director-general of the Nigerian Security Organisation (q.v.) (now the State Security Services [q.v.]), from which he retired in 1983.

As a public officer, he was a member of the national committee to reconcile and rehabilitate the Igbo (q.v.) after the Civil War (q.v.). He also served as chairman of the Organization of African Unity (q.v.) Refugee Committee and as chairman of its Arbitration and Conciliation Committee at different times. In 1978 the Federal Government (q.v.) honoured him with the title of the Commander of the Order of the Niger. He also holds the traditional prestigious title of Marafan Sokoto. In 1992 he ran in the presidential primary for the National Republican Convention (q.v.), but the primary elections were cancelled for alleged irregularities.

During the Abubakar transition program Shinkafi played an active role in establishing the All People's Party (APP). He played an important role in negotiating an agreement with the Alliance for Democracy (AD) to field a common presidential candidate. After it was decided that Olu Falae would be the joint candidate of the parties, Shinkafi was picked to be the vice-presidential candidate. In the February elections, Falae and Shinkafi lost to Olusegun Obasanjo and Abubakar Atiku. Nevertheless, Shinkafi was able to use his clout to win several states in the northwestern part of the country for the alliance.

SHONEKAN, CHIEF ERNEST ADEGUNLE OLADEINDE. A lawyer, administrator and industrialist, born May 9, 1936, in Lagos (q.v.), Shonekan was educated at the Church Missionary Society (q.v.) Grammar School in Lagos before he went to the University of London to study law. He was called to the bar in 1962. In 1964 he joined the United African Company (UAC) (q.v.) as a legal assistant in conveyancing. In 1967 he became assistant legal adviser. In 1978 he was made general manager of the UAC's Bordpak Premier Packaging Division where he distinguished himself as a good manager. In 1980 he became chairman of the UAC Group of Companies, thus presiding over the largest commercial, industrial and technical company in the country with a turnover then of about N600 million.

In January 1993, Chief Shonekan was made the chairman of a makeshift government known as the Transitional Council (q.v.), which President I.B. Babangida (q.v.) set up as a palliative to assuage the nerves of people who were tired of military rule and wanted him to quit power in January 1993. On August 26 when Babangida left office, Shonekan became the Head of the Interim National Government (q.v.). But before he was three months in office, his government was declared illegal, and on November 17, General Sani Abacha (q.v.) overthrew it.

In 1996, Chief Shonekan was picked to head the high-profile Vision 2010 panel to formulate a long-range economic plan to develop the Nigerian economy. In September 1997, the panel submitted its recommendations, which included a liberalisation of the economy, deregulation, and the privatisation of public utilities and the oil sector.

SHUGABA, ALHAJI ABDURAHMAN DARMAN. Majority Leader in Borno State House of Assembly and a member of the Great Nigerian People's

Party (GNPP) (q.v.). On January 29, 1980, the federal Cabinet Office stated that President Shuhu Shagari (q.v.) had approved the deportation of Alhaji Abdurahman Shugaba because he was not a Nigerian and was a security risk. The government also stated that it had set up a judicial inquiry to determine whether or not the deportee was a Nigerian, and Mr. Justice Tunji Adeyemi of the Oyo State High Court was appointed the sole commissioner. The deportation order aroused great concern and outcry. The new government was seen as beginning to eliminate its opponents in a most crude way, without a hearing. Shugaba himself challenged the order in court. Many lawyers, especially from the Unity Party of Nigeria (UPN), offered their services.

Justice Oye Adefila declared in his judgement that Shugaba was a Nigerian. The deportation order was ultra vires and so void. The order was a violation of Shugaba's constitutional rights to personal liberty, privacy and freedom of movement. It awarded damages of N350,000.

SICKLE CELL ANAEMIA. A hereditary disorder occurring in Africa and many parts of the world, which causes sickle-shaped red cells in the blood instead of the normal disk-shaped cells. The disorder is caused by the presence of an abnormal hemoglobin in the red blood cells. When a person inherits the sickle-cell gene from both parents, he or she will most likely have the disease. The disease is characterised by anaemia, shortness of breath and periodic episodes, called crisis, marked by fever with severe pains in the abdomen, bones and muscles. Because there is no cure yet for the disease, many young people in Nigeria die of it.

SIERRA LEONE. Founded in 1787 as a colony for black Africans then living in England or set free from slavery by the British antislavery squadron on the Atlantic Sea. Later on, more people from the West Indies joined them. In 1808 Sierra Leone became a Crown colony (q.v.) and a naval base for the antislavery patrol. By 1850 more than 70,000 freed slaves had settled there, among whom were many Nigerians, such as Bishop Ajayi Crowther (q.v.), who later came back to Nigeria as missionaries, teachers and traders. From 1866 until 1888, the Crown colony of Lagos (q.v.) was placed under the British administration in Sierra Leone, even though, Lagos still retained its own separate Legislative Council (q.v.) and its own administrator, and was responsible for its own affairs. Before the founding of universities in Nigeria, Fourah Bay College (q.v.) in Freetown (q.v.), capital of Sierra Leone, provided opportunities for many Nigerians to have a university education. The country became independent in 1961.

In 1997, when a democratically elected regime was overthrown by a military coup in Sierra Leone, Nigerian troops, leading the ECOMOG (q.v.) forces, intervened to secure the restoration of the previous government. In February 1998, the democratically elected regime was successfully returned to power. The victory proved short-lived, however, as Sierra Leone disintegrated into a bitter civil war shortly thereafter.

SLAVE TRADE. The first slaves from Africa landed in Lisbon, Portugal, in 1441 and by 1472, the Portuguese, in their effort to open up trade with people on the coast of West Africa, had reached the Bight of Benin and their vessels had safely anchored in the Niger Delta (q.v.). In 1482, they built a fort at Elmina on the Gold Coast (q.v.) now Ghana, and in 1485, João Alfonso d'Aveiro (q.v.) had visited Benin City and opened up trade in ivory and pepper in exchange for European goods. Other nations soon joined in opening up trade with the West African countries. By 1553 the first English ships had reached the Benin River.

The first slaves acquired by Portugal were used on São Tomé, but with the discovery of America and the establishment of Spanish colonies in the West Indies, there were great demands for African slaves to replace the aborigine Indians who were unable to cope with the hard work demanded in Spanish mines and plantations. The Portuguese served then as their main suppliers since the Spaniards themselves, in deference to the Papal Bull of 1493, which divided the undeveloped parts of the earth between Spain and Portugal and assigned the greater part of Africa to Portugal, could not go to Africa for their slave supplies. But the British soon entered into the trade and in 1562 Sir John Hawkins, said to be the first Englishman to engage in slave trade, was reported to have taken 300 slaves from Sierra Leone to Haiti. British, Dutch, French and Portuguese nationals, encouraged by their governments, entered into keen competition to secure a monopoly of the trade. Thus, by the 18th century the Nigerian coastlines were strewn with slave trading posts—Lagos (q.v.), Brass (q.v.), New Calabar (Kalabari), Bonny (q.v.) and Old Calabar—all which became thriving centres of the slave trade. Trade routes from these centres extended to the hinterland, even to the Hausa states of the north. The trade led to a lot of intertribal warfare in an effort to secure the trade routes to the coast, and by destroying the able-bodied young men and women either through fruitless wars or by being sold into slavery it contributed immensely to the political and economic underdevelopment of the area. However, opinions in Britain against the slave trade were gradually growing. In 1727, the Quakers denounced it and in 1787, the Society for the Abolition of the Slave Trade (q.v.) was formed in London but bills presented to Parliament between 1788 and 1796 to stop the trade were all defeated. As the 19th century began, opinions were changing in many nations against the trade. In 1802 the Danish government declared it illegal. In 1804 the importation of slaves into the United States was prohibited, even though slaves were still getting in until the American Civil War. In 1807 an

Act of the British Parliament prohibited British ships from carrying slaves or other ships from landing slaves in British colonies from March 1, 1808.

In spite of all these efforts on the parts of various governments, the trade still continued, not only because Europeans derived great profit from it but also because many Africans had become dependent on the trade. It was therefore not an easy task for British merchants in Nigeria, who were turning their efforts to what they called legitimate trade in palm oil, gold and other goods to persuade many Nigerians and their Chiefs (q.v.) to give up their lucrative trade.

The effects of slavery on the development of the West African countries are many. It drained the population of a considerable number of able-bodied men and women, in their prime of life, leaving behind old men and women. It destroyed many villages and flourishing towns and created distrust and hatred between various ethnic groups and even within the same ethnic groups, especially as seen by the Yoruba (q.v.) civil wars. Still important is the fact that it diverted West African efforts away from agriculture and industry. And finally the suppression of the slave trade gave the European empire builders a good opportunity to intervene in local African affairs—to support one group against the other and finally to subjugate all of them.

SLESSOR, MARY MITCHELL. A Scot, born in 1848, she was a Presbyterian missionary who in 1876 joined the Calabar Mission to Nigeria. She devoted much of her life and time to putting an end to human sacrifices, ritual killings, the killing of twins, the outlawing of their mothers and the ill-treatment of widows. Reportedly she rarely had in her little house less than a dozen twin babies who were rescued from parents who would have killed them due to their superstitions. She saved the lives of hundreds of twins in this way. Mary Slessor spoke Efik (q.v.) with great ease, moved among the people freely and ate with them. Wherever she went, she was at home with the people. Her work among them was highly appreciated. She was loved and admired all over the area; the people used to call her "Mother of All the People." In 1890 she was appointed vice-consul for Okoyong among the people whom she had worked so hard to change and serve. She died at Itu on January 13, 1915.

SMALL-SCALE INDUSTRIES AND GRADUATE EMPLOYMENT PROGRAMME. *See* NATIONAL DIRECTORATE OF EMPLOYMENT.

SMUGGLING. Smuggling is not strange to any nation, but across Nigeria's porous borders, it has become a very lucrative business, carried out almost in spite of government. The increasing incidence of smuggling across the borders is evidence that something is very wrong in the country's socioeconomic and political decision-making process. For example, the incidence of smuggling increases when people consider government bans on certain goods to be too extreme or unnecessary, especially when there are no substitutes or alternatives, or when the substitute is of inferior quality to what the people want. The ban on rice importation is a case in point. The locally produced rice is not always free of sand and small stones while the imported and smuggled rice is sand-free.

The sudden devaluation of the naira has also accentuated the incidence of smuggling. The deregulation of the naira in 1992, which made the price of the naira fall by more than 100 percent together with the fixed price of premium motor spirit, encouraged smuggling of Nigerian refined oil across the borders. Added to this is the fact that Nigeria is a consumer-oriented country, and many people are prepared to pay for what they need, even at exorbitant prices.

Still more important is the nature of the Nigerian society. Business persons want to make quick money. Government officials want their share of the money made. Customs officials who are given the duty to patrol the borders most often prefer personal gratification to enforcing the law. They protect smugglers and collaborate with them for their personal monetary interest. Sometimes the government wants to give the impression of doing something about smuggling by drafting security personnel to border posts, but they too are easily persuaded to seek their personal interest rather than the nation's interest. The government's effort to curb smuggling has, therefore, been ineffective. Until government decision makers begin to tackle the conditions that encourage smuggling, smuggling will continue unabated.

SOCIAL DEMOCRATIC PARTY. One of the two political parties founded and funded by the federal military government of President Ibrahim B. Babangida (q.v.). When the ban on political activities was lifted in 1989, 13 political associations applied to the National Electoral Commission (NEC) (q.v.) for recognition as one of the two parties that the Third Republic's (q.v.) constitution (q.v.) would permit. The NEC recommended six of them to the Armed Forces Ruling Council (AFRC) (q.v.), but the AFRC found none prepared to be recognised as political parties. The AFRC then proscribed all 13 associations and set up its own two parties, one a little to the right and the other a little to the left. The Social Democratic Party was supposed to be a little to the left. The government wrote its constitution and manifesto, and built a party office for the SDP in each of the 589 local government (q.v.) areas.

In spite of the people's general unhappiness at government imposition of two parties on the nation, many people agreed to work within the system and change it to a more democratic system. Much of its support came from the old Western Region (q.v.) progressive Northern states like Kano (q.v.), Kaduna (q.v.), Plateau (q.v.) Kwara, Borno and many others and some states in the east.

In 1993, the SDP's candidate, M.K.O. Abiola (q.v.), won presidential elections staged by the military. When these elections were annulled, the SDP initially demanded that Abiola be installed as president. Several weeks after the annulment, however, the leadership of the party reversed themselves and agreed to a compromise proposal that would allow the Babangida regime to surrender power to an Interim National Government (ING) rather than Abiola. This agreement was a serious blow to Abiola's campaign to have his election recognised, and was bitterly resented by his supporters. When General Sani Abacha (q.v.) overthrew the ING on November 17, 1993, the SDP, along with other democratic structures, was disbanded.

SOCIALIST WORKERS AND FARMERS PARTY. The Socialist Workers and Farmers Party (SWAFP) was launched under the leadership of Dr. Tunji Otegbeye (q.v.) a medical practitioner in 1963 at Enugu, capital of Enugu (q.v.) State. The aim of the party was to mobilise the support of the workers and the farmers to improve their welfare. The party had official support from almost all the major trade unions, but this support was not translated into votes in the 1964 federal elections, for it won no seats. In 1966, after the military takeover, the party was banned with all the other parties.

SOCIETY FOR THE ABOLITION OF THE SLAVE TRADE. Formed in London in 1787 to fight against the slave trade in which many European countries were engaged. Granville Sharp, the chairman, and Thomas Clarkson were the most active members of the organisation. They saw to it that many bills were presented to Parliament on the issue, but success did not crown their effort until they had sufficiently educated the people and until Parliament, in 1807, 20 years after the foundation of the society, passed a bill for an act prohibiting the slave trade. The act took effect from March 1, 1808.

SOKOTO. Before the start of the jihad (q.v.) of Usman Dan Fodio (q.v.) in 1804, Sokoto was a small town. In 1809 Muhammad Bello (q.v.), the son of Usman Dan Fodio, realising the natural advantages of Sokoto as the headquarters of his new empire, decided to build a wall around it, as he had done three years previously in Gwandu (q.v.). After the wall was built, Dan Fodio went to live there. But before he died, Dan Fodio had divided the empire into two, between Abdullahi, his brother, and Bello. Abdullahi was to look after the affairs of the empire to the west of Gwandu, while Bello was to look after the affairs of the empire to the east of Gwandu. And even though the two caliphates (q.v.) existed until the British occupation of Northern Nigeria (q.v.), the authority of Sokoto was accepted as supreme. However, after the death of Bello, Sokoto gradually declined. When the British arrived in 1903, Attahiru (q.v.), the reigning Sultan (q.v.) fled, and Sir Frederick Lugard (q.v.) installed Muhammadu Attahiru II (q.v.), son of Ali Babba as Sultan. Today Sokoto is still a very significant center of political and religious power in Nigeria.

SOKOTO CALIPHATE. Founded by Usman Dan Fodio (q.v.), the leader of the Islamic holy war (jihad) (q.v.) begun in 1804, which swept through the Hausa States (q.v.). By 1808 most of the Hausa States had been brought under the Fulani (q.v.) rulers including Kano (q.v.), Katsina (q.v.), and Zaria (q.v.). The empire was divided into two—the Western Sector with headquarters at Gwandu (q.v.) came under the administration of Abdullahi (q.v.) who was the brother of Usman Dan Fodio, and the Eastern Sector with headquarters at Sokoto (q.v.) came under Muhammad Bello (q.v.), son of Usman Dan Fodio, who became the Sultan of Sokoto, the town which Usman himself had made his home, and which today gives Sokoto a focal point of Islamic religion in Nigeria.

The empire extended all the way to Ilorin (q.v.), south of the Niger River (q.v.)—a Yoruba (q.v.) town, Lokoja (q.v.), Yola, Gombe but was checked by the Al-Kanemi (q.v.) and the forces of the Mai of Bornu (q.v.). By 1830 most of the area, later known as the Protectorate (q.v.) of Northern Nigeria (q.v.), with the exception of Bornu, the Tiv (q.v.) area and some part of Jos Plateau had fallen to the Fulani (q.v.). The empire gave unity to the whole of Northern Nigeria, which for long had been torn asunder by local wars; it also set up a uniform system of government in the area, and made for easy flow of commerce in the empire.

The empire lasted for 100 years. In 1903 Lord Lugard (q.v.) told the conquered Fulani in Sokoto that he, the British High Commissioner, was acquiring in the name of Britian the right of Usman Dan Fodio to rule all of the empire. However, Sokoto still retains its role as the Muslim religious center.

SOKOTO STATE. Sokoto State is located at the center of the old Sokoto Caliphate (q.v.) founded in 1804 by people led by Usman Dan Fodio (q.v.) who sought to establish a political system based upon Islamic teaching in Northern Nigeria (q.v.). His effort succeeded to a great extent when his Fulani (q.v.) lieutenants became installed as the Emirs (q.v.) of their respective territories. Today Emirs in Northern Nigeria trace their ancestry to these original Emirs. The caliphate flourished until the British conquest of northern Nigeria in 1903 under Lord Frederick Lugard (q.v.). After the conquest, the Sokoto Caliphate was broken up into provinces (q.v.) consisting of one or more emirates and the provinces formed the then-Northern-Region (q.v.). In 1967 the Northern Region was broken into six separate states, among which was North-Western State (q.v.) made up of Sokoto and Niger Provinces. In 1976 North-Western State was split into Niger (q.v.) and Sokoto States. In 1991 Sokoto State was further divided into Kebbi (q.v.) and Sokoto States with the capital at Sokoto, the seat of the old caliphate.

The state is located at the extreme northwest of the country, it lies between latitudes 10° and 14°N, and longitudes 3° and 9°E. It shares a common border with the Niger Republic in the north, Katsina State (q.v.) in the east, Kaduna State (q.v.) in the southeast and Kebbi State in the south and west. The land area is 56,000 square kilometres. The state can be said to have two main seasons—rainy and dry. The rainy season is between April and September, while the dry season is between October and March. During the dry season, between November and February, comes a cold, dry and dusty wind from the Sahara Desert, which is known as the harmattan (q.v.). The vegetation is savannah forest, grassy with short scattered trees, which become dry during the dry season, making bush fires a common occurrence during this period.

The population of the state in 1991 was 4,392,390 and the density varies from place to place. Ethnically, it is predominantly Hausa (q.v.) and Fulani, but there are others who have migrated to the state, like the Yoruba (q.v.), Igbo (q.v.), Tiv (q.v.) and Idoma. The state is also predominately Muslim even though Christianity (q.v.) and other religions have a foothold. Sokoto State, with many medium-sized towns, has two major towns, Sokoto and Gusau, and the whole state is divided into 28 local government (q.v.) areas. Educationally, it has over 1,800 primary schools and about 52 secondary schools, a federal university and many colleges of education and polytechnical and technical schools. About 80 percent of the people engage in agriculture, planting millet, guinea corn, sugar cane, beans and cereals. It is also high in animal production.

On October 1, 1996, the Abacha regime created Zamfara State out of part of Sokoto State.

SOLANKE, OLADIPO. A lawyer and founder of the West African Student Union (WASU) (q.v.) in Britain, Mr. Solanke was born in Abeokuta (q.v.) in 1884. He attended Ake Primary School in Abeokuta and after his high school education went to Fourah Bay College in Sierra Leone (q.v.) where he obtained a B.A. degree from Durham University in England. In 1917 he taught at Leopold Educational Institution in Freetown. In 1922 he went to Britain to study law. In 1924 he founded the Nigerian Progress Union, but the Union was replaced in 1925 by WASU, also founded by him and to which he devoted most of his active life.

Solanke in 1927 wrote his book, *United West Africa at the Bar of the Family of Nations,* in which he attributed the decline of West Africa to the slave trade. He saw a conflict between British imperialism and African nationalism. He encouraged Africans to drop foreign names. He asked the British political officers not to think that educated Africans were enemies—they were copartners in the guardianship of Africa and sooner or later educated Africans and the traditional rulers would join together and fight the white man. Solanke died on September 2, 1958, in London and was buried there.

SOLE NATIVE AUTHORITIES. Under the indirect rule system (q.v.), the British governed the local population through their traditional rulers called Chiefs (q.v.) or Emirs (q.v.) or Obis. In some local government areas each such Chief or any other person was constituted into a Sole Native Authority. This meant that the decision of the Chief was supreme in his area, although in most cases he was advised by a traditional council.

SOUTHERN ALLIANCE. An alliance between the two major parties, the National Council of Nigeria and the Cameroons (NCNC) (q.v.) and the Action Group Party (AG) (q.v.) in the south in 1953. It was hurriedly formed during the 1953 crisis on "Self Government in 1956" motion (q.v.). In the preparation for the Constitutional Conference in London in 1953, the Alliance agreed on common proposals to be put before the Conference. These included:

1. the exclusion of special members from the central and regional legislatures;
2. uniform electoral laws for election to the federal legislature based on universal adult suffrage; and
3. delimiting the boundaries of the regions into practically equal units so as to avoid the fear of domination by one region over others.

Both parties, however, agreed on a federal type of constitution and they also agreed that the issue of Lagos would not be raised at the Conference, but when the Northern People's Congress (NPC) (q.v.) asked for the neutralisation of Lagos as a federal territory, the NCNC supported the NPC. As a result the Alliance broke down immediately. Dr. Nnamdi Azikiwe (q.v.) later accused the Action Group of "overt acts which stultified the freedom of Nigeria" and the Action Group countered by saying that the NCNC had stabbed them in the back.

SOUTHERN CAMEROON. *See* CAMEROON.

SOUTHERN NIGERIA. Emerged as the result of the amalgamation of a number of protectorates in 1900: Protectorate of Lagos, Oil Rivers Protectorate, and the Niger Coast Protectorate. These, together with some of the territories controlled by the Royal Niger Company, were brought together to form the Protectorate of Southern Nigeria. This unit existed until the Richards Constitution of 1946 divided Southern Nigeria into the Eastern Region and the Western Region (qq.v.). Today, the territory that once comprised the protectorate of Southern Nigeria consists of 17 of Nigeria's 36 states.

SOUTHERN NIGERIAN CIVIL SERVICE UNION. Inaugurated on August 18, 1912, it was the first trade union in Nigeria. In 1914, after the amalgamation of the Southern and Northern protectorates, it changed its name to the Nigerian Civil Service Union.

SOUTHERN NIGERIA POLICE FORCE. In 1900 when the Protectorate of Southern Nigeria was proclaimed, the Lagos Police Force and part of the Niger Coast Constabulary (q.v.) became the Southern Nigeria Police Force, while the remaining part became the Southern Nigeria Regiment.

SOUTHERN PROGRESSIVE FRONT (SPF). This was an alliance signed in Ibadan (q.v.) on June 3, 1964, by Dr. Michael Okpara (q.v.) leader of the National Council of Nigerian Citizens (NCNC) (q.v.) with the Action Group Party (AG) (q.v.). It was a reaction to the formation of the Nigerian National Democratic Party (NNDP) (q.v.) of Chief S.L. Akintola (q.v.) made up of the breakaway faction of the Action Group known then as the United People's Party (UPP) (q.v.) and another faction of the NCNC led by Chief R.A. Fani-Kayode (q.v.). Since the NNDP was effectively in power, the remnants of the AG and NCNC in opposition had no choice but to come closer together to form a kind of an alliance. Okpara's signature on June 3, 1964, only formalised this informal arrangement. The alliance decided to present a common list in the forthcoming federal elections. This alliance came to be known as the United Progressive Grand Alliance (UPGA) (q.v.).

SOYINKA, PROF. AKINWANDE OLUWOLE. A playwright, poet, actor, teacher, social critic and political activist, and a Nobel Laureate, born July 13, 1934, at Isara, Ijebu-Remo, near Abeokuta (q.v.) in Ogun State (q.v.), Soyinka was educated at St. Peters' School, Ake in Abeokuta, Abeokuta Grammar School and Government College, Ibadan (q.v.) from 1946 to 1950. In 1952 he entered the University College Ibadan (q.v.) (now University of Ibadan) and in 1954 proceeded to the University of Leeds, England. When he was there, he worked at the Royal Court Theatre in London in 1957. In 1960 he was a research fellow in drama at the University of Ibadan. In 1962 he was a lecturer at the newly established University of Ife (q.v.) (now Obafemi Awolowo University). In 1967 he went back to the University of Ibadan as director of the school of drama.

He was arrested in 1967 during the Civil War (q.v.), begun by the General Yakubu Gowon (q.v.) administration. Soyinka was detained until October 1969. Between 1971 and 1975, he was in exile in Britain and Ghana (q.v.). He returned to Nigeria in 1976 and was appointed professor of comparative literature at the University of Ife. In 1980 he was chairman of the Oyo State Safety Corps, and in 1988 he became chairman of the Federal Road Safety Corps.

Professor Soyinka is well known all over the world for his literary works for which he received the Nobel Prize in Literature in 1986. He has also received many other national and international awards and honorary degrees.

During the political crisis emanating from the annulment of the June 12, 1993, presidential election (q.v.), Wole Soyinka stood firm with the undeclared winner. After General Sani Abacha (q.v.) came to power, and because of Soyinka's outspokenness, he became a man to watch. Not long after, his passport and other travelling documents were seized, and he quietly escaped into exile where he continued his campaign for a democratic government for Nigeria.

Among his many publications are *A Dance of the Forest* (1963), *The Lion and the Jewel* (1963), *The Trials of Brother Jero* (1964), *The Strong Breed* (1965), *The Swamp Dwellers* (1965), *Kongi's Harvest* (1967), *Madman and Specialist* (1971), *Before the Black-Out* (1971), *Death and the King's Horsemen* (1975), *Opera Wonyosi* (1978), *Season of Anomy* (1974), *The Man Died* (1972), *Ake, The Years of Childhood* (1981), *Myths, Literature and the African World* (1976), *Idanre and Other Poems* (1967), *A Shuttle in the Crypt* (1972) and *Poems from Black Africa* (1975).

In 1997 the Nigerian government charged Soyinka with treason in connection with a series of bombings in the country. The charges did not appear to have much credibility and were dropped after the end of the Abacha regime in 1998.

SPECIAL PUBLIC WORKS PROGRAMME. *See* NATIONAL DIRECTORATE OF EMPLOYMENT.

STATE BOUNDARIES DELIMITATION COMMISSION. Appointed after the creation of the 12 states in 1967, its job was to adjust, where necessary, the boundaries of states with regard to districts, provinces or ethnic groups as the case might be.

STATE CREATION. The demand for the creation of states in Nigeria appears to be a perennial one. It arose in the 1950s when the regions were being given self-government and the minorities in each region, fearing discrimination and oppression began to agitate for their own states. The areas that were much affected were the Middle-Belt (q.v.) in the Northern Region (q.v.), the Mid-West (q.v.) in the Western Region (q.v.) and the Calabar-Ogoja-Rivers (q.v.) areas in the east. Furthermore, because of the population of the Northern Region (q.v.), which was said to be slightly more than that of the south, and because of the land area of the north being about three-quarters of the land area of the whole country, many people believed that the Federation was too lopsided, for a constituent part, if united could dictate the political tune of the nation for the foreseeable future. The north, under the Northern People's Congress (NPC) (q.v.), was fairly united and it was not easy for southern parties to penetrate it.

The Action Group Party (AG) (q.v.) got most of its support in the Middle-Belt because of its support for their aspiration for their own state. The National Council of Nigeria and the Cameroons (NCNC) (q.v.) went into an alliance with the Northern Element Progressive Union (NEPU) (q.v.) a Northern party, but the NPC controlled the government not only at the regional level but also at the local level. As such the north appeared impregnable, and so the demand was loud in the south for breaking up the north.

These demands led to the setting up of the Minorities Commission (q.v.) in 1957 by the British government. But the British had already told the nation and the commission the kind of recommendation that the British were willing to hear: state creation should be a last resort, for if new states or regions were created, then independence might not be possible in 1960. The commission therefore did not recommend creation of more states but rather some amendment to the constitution which would protect minorities' interests. But these amendments amounted to little more than cosmetic changes.

Two years after independence, during the Action Group crisis (q.v.) of 1962, the NCNC, thinking that it would have a second region under its control, and the NPC (the major coalition partner at the federal level), believing that the opportunity had offered itself to clip the wings of the Action Group in the Mid-West (which was predominantly NCNC), decided to accede to the demand of the people of the area for their own region in the Federation. The reinstated Akintola (q.v.) government in the west, which owed its existence to the NCNC NPC coalition at the center, also supported the move and the Mid-Western Region (q.v.) was created in 1963. This event spurred on the agitation of other areas for their own states and the need to create more states in the north to have a more balanced federation. This demand was not met until 1967, during the crisis between the former Eastern Region, headed by Lt. Colonel Odumegwu Ojukwu (q.v.) and the Federal Government, headed by General Yakubu Gowon (q.v.). The crisis was inescapably leading to a Civil War (q.v.) and partly in an effort to create disaffection in the support Ojukwu was getting in all of the Eastern Region, the Federal Government decided to create 12 states in the country. Three of these were in the east, two of which gave the minorities what they wanted while the majority Igbo (q.v.) were confined to the East-Central State (q.v.). The north was divided into six states while the Lagos (q.v.) State was created from the Western Region.

This move was very popular but it did not satisfy the demands of people who saw state creation not only as a means to satisfy genuine minorities demands or the fear of domination but, more important, as a means of "regional" and local development and as a means of sharing effectively in the sudden surge in oil revenues. Their demands were again acceded to in February 1976, when out of the 12 existing states, seven others were created, making the total 19. The hope then was that these 19 states would do it: there would be no more agitation that would be worth anybody's consideration. But the cry went on. In 1983, the House of Representatives and the Senate were thinking of whether or not Nigeria should not be broken up into as many as 40 states.

During the military administration of General Ibrahim Babangida (q.v.) 1985–93, 11 more states were created out of the existing 19 states, making the number of states 30 in 1991. In 1996, the regime of General Sani Abacha (q.v.) created six more states, bringing the total to 36. Notwithstanding this proliferation of states, agitation for more states is unabated.

STATE ELECTORAL COMMISSION. A State Electoral Commission, set up by the 1979 constitution, was composed of a Chairman and five to seven members. It had the power to organise, undertake and supervise all elections to local government councils within the state and to tender advice to the Federal Electoral Commission (FEDECO) (q.v.) on the compilation of the register of voters insofar as the register was applicable to local government elections in the state.

STATE JUDICIAL SERVICE COMMISSION. This is the state counterpart of the Federal Judicial Service Commission. Under the 1979 constitution it is responsible in each state to advise the governor of the state on the appointment of judges to the High Court of a state but the appointment needs the approval of a simple majority vote in the State House of Assembly. The Commission also can recommend removal of judges for inability to discharge duties or for misconduct or contravention of the Code of Conduct.

STATE SECURITY (DETENTION OF PERSONS) DECREE. The State Security (Detention of Persons) Decree was enacted in January 1966. This decree dealt with the detention of certain specified persons in the interest of the security of the country for a period not exceeding six months in places where the head of the National Military Government (q.v.) might, from time to time, direct. Persons so detained were entitled to make representations in writing to the national military government which might, if it thought fit, constitute a tribunal for that purpose under conditions laid down in the decree. Furthermore the decree suspended Chapter III of the Republican Constitution of 1963, which dealt with fundamental human rights (q.v.).

STATUTORY REVENUE ALLOCATION TO STATE AND LOCAL GOVERNMENTS. *See* REVENUE ALLOCATION.

STATUTORY RIGHT OF OCCUPANCY. *See* RIGHT OF OCCUPANCY.

STRUCTURAL ADJUSTMENT PROGRAMME. The Structural Adjustment Programme (SAP) was introduced by the Babangida (q.v.) administration in 1986 to rectify the structural imbalance in the Nigerian economy (q.v.). Before July 1986 when the program came into operation, the country was regarded as no longer creditworthy. Its foreign reserve could sustain imports for only about two months and many foreign financial institutions, especially banks, refused to honour letters of credit for imports bound for Nigeria. Many of these banks wanted the International Monetary Fund (IMF) to guarantee that whatever they sold to the country would be paid for when due. There then arose a debate whether or not Nigeria should take an IMF loan. Many people believed that the loan should not be taken because of the IMF conditionalities. Hence, SAP became unavoidable.

The objectives of establishing SAP were to stabilise the economy by ensuring external balance and fiscal viability, and to restructure the country's production and expenditure pattern. The programme was also to redress the fiscal imbalances and structural distortions in the economy with a view to propel the country toward self-sustaining growth. Specifically, SAP was to restructure and diversify the productive base of the economy in order to reduce the country's dependence on the oil sector and on imports; achieve fiscal balance and ensure balance of payments viability; lay the basis for a sustainable and noninflationary growth; enhance efficiency of the public sector operations as well as lessen the dominance of unproductive investments in the public sector, and to intensify the growth potential of the private sector.

To achieve all these objectives, the government had to take many unpopular decisions, including the flotation of the naira in the exchange market, the abrogation of import licensing, abolition of commodity boards, reduction of tariffs on imported machinery, privatisation and commercialisation of public enterprises and the rationalisation of the public service. As a result, the economy did record some sectoral growth. For example, agricultural output was said to have increased at an average annual rate of 5 percent between 1986 and 1991 compared to average annual growth rate of 1.0 percent between 1980 and 1985. And in the industrial sector, the average annual growth rate was said to be 8 percent between 1987 and 1992. More still, SAP forced Nigerians to begin to think about how they could maintain what they have.

On the other hand, SAP has brought untold hardship to most Nigerians. The naira which was worth about $1.50 in 1977, by early 1993 was worth in the Bureaux de Change (q.v.) and black market about $0.04, and it continued to fall. As a result, inflation skyrocketed, leading to uncontrollable strikes by workers of all categories. Interest rates became prohibitive for businesses, leading inevitably to a cutdown in production and unemployment of young high school and university graduates, not to talk about others who had to be retrenched. The manufacturing sector, as the 1993 Federal Government budget put it, had groaned "under the yoke of problems including high cost of funds, high naira cost of forex, depressed demand and low capacity utilisation."

The weaknesses of SAP were inadequate attention to its social dimension, its effects on education, health and the family, and also its obsession with monetary and fiscal balances without due consideration for their impact on the productive sectors. But even then the Babangida administration became profligate, unresponsible and unaccountable, and engaged freely in extra-budgetary expenses. Under SAP, most Nigerians, including even the most educated or skilled, could no longer buy new cars or equipment. Nigeria became a dumping ground for used equipment like motor vehicles, engines, motor parts, motorcycles, used refrigerators, air conditioners and their parts; in short, all kinds of goods, known popularly as "Tokunbo" (fairly used from abroad), were dumped in Nigeria.

SUDAN. *See* WESTERN SUDAN.

SUDAN INTERIOR MISSION. Canadian missionaries were permitted by Lord Lugard (q.v.) to set up in Northern Nigeria (q.v.) about the end of the 19th century. The mission's initial aim was to introduce industrial education in the area. As such they set up farms at Pategi, Bida and other places.

SULE, ALHAJI YUSUF MAITAMA. Former diplomat and politician, born in Kano (q.v.), Kano State (q.v.), in 1929, he went to Shahuri Elementary School in Kano, Kano Middle School and later to Kaduna College (now Barewa College [q.v.]). In 1947 he attended Special Higher Elementary Teachers' Course in Zaria (q.v.) and became a teacher in Kano Middle School and Kano Provincial Secondary School. In 1954 he became a member of the House of Representatives (q.v.) and in 1955 the chief party whip in the House. In 1959 he was the federal minister of mines and power until the military came to power in 1966. During the military administration, he held many political appointments in Kano State.

Alhaji Sule has represented Nigeria at many international conferences, including the Conference of Independent African States in Addis Ababa, Ethiopia, in 1960, which proposed resolutions that led to the creation of the Organization of African Unity (q.v.). He was also a member of the first Nigerian delegation to the United Nations after Nigeria's independence in

1960, and in 1980 he was Nigeria's permanent representative to the United Nations.

Politically, he was a member of the Northern People's Congress (q.v.) from 1954 to 1966 and later a member of the National Party of Nigeria (q.v.). Alhaji Sule has always been well regarded, not only in the north of the country but also in the south. However, his image nationally has been adversely affected by the publication of an address he was said to have given in 1993 at the launching of a book, *Power of Knowledge,* edited by Alhaji Kaita. In the address he explained how the merit principle of recruitment into the military and other offices was assaulted by the ruling oligarchy during the premiership of Sir Ahmadu Bello (q.v.), the Sardauna of Sokoto. But more important was his statement that God had endowed the northerners with leadership qualities (to rule the country), while the Yoruba (q.v.) were endowed with diplomatic qualities and the Igbo (q.v.) with commercial, innovative and technological abilities.

SULTAN. An Islamic (q.v.) term used to designate a sovereign ruler. The Islamic ruler of the Sokoto Caliphate (q.v.) is the Sultan of Sokoto.

SUPREME COUNCIL OF THE REVOLUTION OF THE NIGERIAN ARMED FORCES. On Saturday January 16, 1966, when Major Chukwumah Nzeogu (q.v.) seized power in the Northern Region (q.v.) he went on the air to announce the coup in the name of the "Supreme Council of the Revolution of the Nigerian Armed Forces." The aim of the Council was to establish a strong, united and prosperous nation which would be free from corruption and internal strife. The name was coined by the coupmakers, but unfortunately they were not allowed to carry out their revolution since the coup in the south was not very successful. General Aguiyi-Ironsi (q.v.), quickly reacting to the coup, took over the rein of affairs after the rump of civilian government had handed over power to him and he ordered the detention of the coupmakers in prison.

SUPREME COURT. Following the abolition of appeals to the Judicial Committee of the Privy Council in London (q.v.) under the 1963 Republican Constitution, the Supreme Court, composed of the Chief Justice and not more than 15 justices with five or in special cases seven, of them forming a quorum has been made the highest court of the land. Its jurisdictions are both original and appellate. The original jurisdiction covers cases of dispute between a state and the Federal Government or between one state and another. In addition, the House of Assembly could confer further original jurisdiction on it provided it is not with respect to criminal matters. Its appellate jurisdiction includes appeals from the decision of the Federal Court of Appeal, either as of right or with leave of the Federal Court of Appeal. Being the final interpreter of the law and the constitution for the nation, the Supreme Court carries a lot of responsibility for maintaining the integrity of the Federation.

SUPREME MILITARY COUNCIL (SMC). Established by Decree Number 1 of 1966. The council was the highest policy-making body in the nation. It consisted of the head of the federal military government who was the president of the Supreme Military Council, the heads of the Nigerian Army, Navy and Air Force, the two chiefs of staff of the Armed Forces and of the Nigerian Army, the military governors of the four regions that made up the Federation and the attorney general of the Federation. In 1967, the secretary to the federal military government and other appropriate officials of the federal and state governments could attend its meetings in an advisory capacity. But in 1975, after the third military coup which overthrew General Gowon's (q.v.) administration, military governors were no longer members of the Council and government officials could no longer attend its meetings. After the 1983 coup d'état the Supreme Military Council consisted of 19 members, made up of the Head of State, heads of various military units, other military members, the inspector general of police and his deputy, the director general of the Nigerian Security Organisation and his deputy, and the secretary to the federal military government, who was also the head of the civil service. The SMC became the Armed Forces Ruling Council (AFRC) (q.v.) in August 1985 after Major-General Babangida (q.v.) came to power. In 1993 when General Sani Abacha (q.v.) became Head of State, it became the Provisional Ruling Council.

-T-

TACTICAL COMMITTEE. After the federal election of 1959 at which the Action Group Party (AG) (q.v.) won only 75 out of the 312 seats Chief Obafemi Awolowo (q.v.) became the leader of the opposition rather than the prime minister in the federal House of Assembly. Fearing that the Federal Government after independence in 1960 might want to use its powers to declare a state of emergency in the Western Region (q.v.) (which was the stronghold of the Action Group Party) and impose a caretaker administration to replace that of the Action Group, the Federal Executive Council of the party in September 1960 decided to set up what it called the Tactical Committee.

Chief Awolowo was given power to be solely responsible for the functioning of the committee and its members were to remain secret. As the treason trials (q.v.) showed, Chief Awolowo appointed three members: Chief

Anthony Enahoro (q.v.), who was then a federal vice-president of the party and chairman of the party's regional organisation in the Mid-West; Chief Ayo Rosiji (q.v.), the party's federal secretary and Chief S.L. Akintola (q.v.), deputy leader of the party and premier of the Western Region. But as Professor Sanya D. Onabamiro (q.v.) testified at the treason trial, rather than Chief Akintola and Chief Rosiji being members, it was he himself and Sam Ikoku (q.v.) who were members.

The purpose of the committee was to devise ways and means of protecting the party base in the Western Region and to forestall any Federal Government plan to assail democracy and the rule of law. This the committee planned to do in the following ways:

1. To ensure that the party's field organisation in the Western Region was maintained in a state of constant preparedness to deal with any attempt by the National Council of Nigerian Citizens (NCNC) (q.v.) to provoke acts of lawlessness which might be used as a pretext for a takeover.
2. To conduct publicity in Nigeria and abroad so as to discredit any attempt by the Federal Government to take over Western Regional government by any means other than elections.
3. To make overtures to the NCNC with a view to cooperating on a nationwide basis in order to enhance the security of the Action Group in the Western Region and the likelihood of success of the progressive elements in the future federal elections.
4. To intensify organisational efforts in the Northern and Eastern regions so as to extend Action Group popular support and at the same time relieve pressure on the Western Region.

In March 1962, after Chief Awolowo had alleged at the peace meeting of party elders that S.L. Akintola had been spreading the rumor that he was planning to overthrow the Federal Government by means of a coup d'état (q.v.), Chief Awolowo asked the Federal Executive Council to dissolve the committee because its work and its purposes were being misrepresented.

TALKING DRUM. Drumming is the art of playing music on drums. Although one drum can be played by itself, it is generally accompanied by two or three or more different sizes of drums. The talking drum is specially built. There is first a round and hollow piece of wood which may be one to two feet long. The wood is carved so it tapers toward the middle from both ends. The two ends are then covered with leather specially tanned for it. And from the leather coverings are strings of pure leather, again specially made for that purpose. On both ends are metal jingles, and there is a decorated strap with which to hang the drum on the shoulder.

The playing of a talking drum is a very skilled art because a drum can produce a variety of sounds depending on the way it is hit and the tension created by the leather strings with the second hand or elbow. Furthermore, the part of the top of the drum that is struck will affect the sounds it makes. In this way a skillful drummer can manipulate the drum to say things, send messages, identify a person among many guests and so on. The drum can also be used to say both complimentary and noncomplimentary things about a person or family and, as such, may be used to create rivalry or conflict in society. The talking drum, when accompanied, may produce rhythmic music for people to dance.

TARABA STATE. Created in 1991, it comprises the pre-1976 divisions of Muri, Mambila and Wukari. The land area is 54,428 square kilometres, and it lies within latitudes 6°25′ and 9°30′N, and longitudes 9°30′ and 11°45′E. It is bounded in the north by Bauchi State (q.v.), in the northeast by Adamawa State (q.v.), in the east and south by the Republic of Cameroon (q.v.), in the southwest by Benue State (q.v.) and in the west by Plateau State (q.v.). It is divided into 12 local government (q.v.) areas. The topography may be divided into the swampy areas around the Benue River (q.v.), which passes through the western part of the state. This area is thinly settled and virtually left uncultivated. The lowland area is about 350 metres above sea level, and the Mambilla Plateau, which has many of Nigeria's highest mountains with peaks reaching between 1,840 metres and 2,000 metres above sea level. There are two main seasons—rainy and dry. The rainy season is between April and October, and the annual rainfall is about 1,058 millimetres in the north and over 1,300 in the south. The dry season is between November and March, and the average annual temperature is about 28°C. The vegetation is grassland, but there are mountain forests on the Mambilla Plateau. The main mineral resources are marble, graphite, gelano, barytes, salt, lead and iron ore.

The population in 1991 was 1,480,590, and is ethnically heterogeneous, with over 70 different groups speaking different languages in the state. The major ones among them include Fulani (q.v.), Mumuye, Jukun (q.v.), Jonjo, Kuteb, Chamba and Mambilla. As such, the culture of the people in the state varies from place to place and so do their festivals. There is the Nwunyo fishing festival, the Purma of the Chamba, Puje of the Jukum, the Sharo of the Fulani and the Kati of the Mambilla. The major population centers are Jalingo, the capital, Mutum, Wukari and Donga. About 70 percent of the population are peasant farmers, planting crops like oil palm (q.v.), cocoa (q.v.), coffee tea, coconut, citrus, cotton, millet, sweet potatoes, yams (q.v.), beniseed and cassava (q.v.). Many people are also engaged in fishing and fish-smoking. The state has about 665 primary schools with about 255,509 pupils and 62 secondary schools with about 35,700 students.

TARKA, JOSEPH SARWUAN. Born on July 10, 1932, at Igbor in the Tiv Division of Benue State, he attended Gboko Primary School, the Katsina-Ala Middle Secondary School and Bauchi Teachers' Training College.

Being interested in politics early in his life, he formed the United Middle Belt Congress (UMBC) (q.v.) and became its president. The aim of the party was to campaign for the Middle-Belt Region (q.v.). In 1954, he won a seat in the federal House of Representatives for the UMBC. While in the federal Parliament, he allied his party with the Action Group Party (AG) (q.v.) of Chief Obafemi Awolowo (q.v.). Both parties presented a coordinated opposition to the government of Alhaji Tafawa Balewa (q.v.).

Tarka led his party's delegation to the constitutional conferences of 1957 and 1958 in London. After the federal elections of 1959, Tarka acted as the shadow cabinet for commerce and industry. In 1962 he was arrested with prominent Action Group members, including Chief Awolowo, charged with plotting to overthrow the Federal Government, but was later discharged for want of sufficient evidence. In 1964, his party joined the so-called Southern Progressive Parties and, under the alliance known as the United Progressive Grand Alliance (UPGA) (q.v.) he fought the elections. The UPGA lost, but he continued his campaign for a separate Middle-Belt State. On May 27, 1967, his wishes came true when General Gowon's administration created the Benue Plateau State as one of the 12 states created out of the former four regions.

In 1966, after the military came to power, Tarka was appointed member of the northern delegation to the All-Nigeria Constitutional Conference. In June 1967 he became a member of the Federal Executive Council, where he served first as commissioner for transport and later, in 1971, as commissioner for communications in the regime of General Yakubu Gowon (q.v.). In 1974, he had to resign following allegations of corruption and abuse of office. He then went into private business. In 1978, when the ban on politics was lifted, Tarka went back into politics and became a member of the National Party of Nigeria (NPN) (q.v.). He was elected vice chairman of the party and later won a seat in the Senate on the party's ticket. He died in London on March 30, 1980, and was buried in his hometown.

TECHNICAL AID CORPS. Set up in 1987 by the administration of President Ibrahim B. Babangida (q.v.) to systematise and institutionalise Nigeria's technical assistance to other countries in Africa and the diaspora. It was also meant to facilitate meaningful contact between young Nigerians and young people of other countries. As of 1993, there were TAC volunteers in over 20 countries from various fields, including doctors, nurses and teachers.

TELECOMMUNICATIONS. Communication is central to the social, economic and political development of any nation and a necessary ingredient of international cooperation. In an effort to improve communication within and outside the country, the government, especially in the 1970s after the Civil War (q.v.), began to invest heavily in telephone and other electronic communications. In 1985 the government separated telecommunication services from the postal services, both of which used to be known as the Post and Telegraph Department of the Ministry of Communication. The postal services became the Nigerian Postal Services while the communication services became the Nigerian Telecommunications (NITEL). NITEL in 1990 had a total installed capacity of almost half a million telephone lines and about 13,000 telex lines. The organisation has also invested heavily in satellite communication to make it easy for various parts of the country to be connected. Still more important, and perhaps revolutionary, was the government decision in 1992 to break its own monopoly over telecommunication. In November of that year, it promulgated a decree empowering the Nigerian Communications Commission to accredit individuals and corporate bodies to compete with NITEL in providing telecommunication services, which until then was provided only by NITEL.

TELEVISION BROADCASTING. Television broadcasting in Nigeria started in October 1959 when the Western Nigerian Television Service (WNTV) was launched. It was the first television service in the whole of Africa and WNTV proudly described itself as "First in Africa." A year later the Eastern Nigeria Television Service (ENTV) came into operation and in 1962 the Northern Region Television Service (NRTV) joined them. It was not until 1963 that the Nigerian Television Service (NTV) began operation. In 1978 television broadcasting in the country was placed under the Nigerian Television Authority (NTA) by the military administration. Thus NTA took over all the television stations in the country, but each station in the states was allowed to draw up its own programmes. However it was required to relay the national network programmes.

With the return of the civilian administration, states began to set up new state television stations. The state television operates on UHF while NTA stations are allocated channels on VHA.

TERRA-COTTA SCULPTURE. Terra-cotta sculptures are made from clay which is shaped and baked to be hard like a pot. Terra-cotta sculptures were made by the Nok (q.v.) people in the Jos Plateau area of Nigeria as far back as the fifth century B.C. The sculptures include beautiful heads of people and animals. In Ile-Ife (q.v.), Osun State (q.v.), terra-cotta sculptures date back to A.D. sixth century. Most of these were human heads, and some of them are preserved in the Museum in Ile-Ife.

THIRD REPUBLIC. The name of the regime that was to result from the democratic transition of the Babangida (q.v.) regime (1985–93). Despite the fact that preparations for the Third Republic were the most expensive and drawn out in the history of the country, it was not allowed to come into existence. Preparations began in 1986, a constitution was released in 1989, local government elections were held in 1989, gubernatorial elections were held in 1991 and National Assembly elections were held in 1992. All of these elected officials were already in place when presidential elections were held on June 12, 1993. Although these elections were held relatively peacefully, they were annulled by the military government on June 23, 1993. This led to a protracted period of political crisis that persisted until the Abacha (q.v.) regime came to power on November 17, 1993, and immediately dissolved all the political structures of the stillborn Third Republic. The failure of the Third Republic remains one of the defining events of modern Nigerian history.

THOMAS, CHIEF BODE. A lawyer and a politician, born in 1919 in Oyo, Oyo State. He was a foundation member of the Action Group Party (AG) (q.v.), whose ideas that the country should be organised on a regional basis, both for government and party purposes, greatly influenced government and party development in the country. Before his death in 1953 he was the deputy leader of the Action Group, and the minister of transport in the central government in Lagos (q.v.). He was also awarded the chieftaincy title of Balogun of Oyo.

THORP AND HARLOW COMMISSION. The commission, consisting of F.J. Harlow, principal of Chelsea Polytechnic in London and W.H. Thorp, Nigerian deputy director of technical education, was appointed to look into the possibilities of setting up technical institutions in Nigeria. The commission submitted its report in April 1949. It recommended that technical colleges should be set up, which would cater to the needs of secondary school leavers for additional education. The commission recommended that a Nigerian College of Arts, Science and Technology be set up on a tripartite basis with a branch of the college in each of the three regions into which the country was divided. Government accepted the report and by 1952 the first branch of the college had been set up in Zaria (q.v.) in Northern Nigeria.

THUGGERY. An important feature of Nigerian politics in 1964, 1965 and 1983 was thuggery. Each political party operating in Nigeria between 1964 and 1966 had a quasi-military corps called "thugs." These thugs went about, especially during electioneering campaigns, molesting innocent citizens and their party opponents. There were situations where thugs of different political parties clashed. Thuggery became more pronounced in the west in 1965, at the approach of the Western Regional election. They disrupted the campaigns of opposing parties and engaged in acts of vandalism, wanton destruction of property and lives. After the announcement of the Western Regional election results of 1965, thugs of opposing parties engaged in open battles. They began "Operation Wet E," that is, "operation wet it," in which petrol was sprayed on opponents and they were set on fire. It is important to note that the 1979 constitution banned the operation or inclusion of any quasi- or para-military corps or institution in any political party. In spite of this, thugs operated during the 1983 elections, particularly in the western part of the country.

TIJANIYYA. One of the two major Islamic brotherhoods (or Sufi orders) in Nigeria. While the dominant brotherhood, the Qadiriyya had been in existence in Hausaland for 500 years, Tijaniyya was not introduced until the 19th century. Despite the controversial allegation that Sultan Muhammad Bello had been secretly initiated into the Tijaniyya in the 1830s, it was not until the 20th century that the Tijaniyya began to seriously challenge the Qadiriyya. Shortly after the First World War, Emir (q.v.) Abbas of Kano affiliated himself with the Tijaniyya, a sign of both the growing strength of the brotherhood in Kano (particularly among traders), and his desire to demonstrate his independence from the Qadiriyya dominated Sokoto Caliphate. In the 1950s and 1960s, growing conflicts between the Qadiriyya and the Tijaniyya led to violent clashes that prompted the mediating efforts of religious and political leaders.

TIN MINING. Tin mining had long been one of the indigenous industries in Northern Nigeria. However in 1900, when the Royal Niger Company (q.v.) gave up its charter to administer Northern Nigeria, it was allowed to keep a share of the mineral rights in the area lying north of the Niger (q.v.) and Benue (q.v.) Rivers. The company, having discovered long before then that the tin the Hausas used for their brassware was being mined in the Bauchi Plateau, sponsored expeditions to locate tin in commercial quantity in the area. In 1906, the company began tin mining operations on a commercial basis, and other companies soon joined in. By 1913, investment by individual non-Nigerians and companies had exceeded £4 million. To facilitate transportation of the tin ore to the sea, some of the companies agreed to invest in building roads to link the centers of production with the major roads and with the railway line. In 1914 the railway was extended to the Bauchi Plateau and so it aided in the expansion of the mines. Nigeria later became the fourth-largest tin-producing nation in the world. At present tin is Nigeria's most important mineral export after oil. However, it earns very little, compared to other export products. In 1978 it earned only N22 million. The tin was managed by the Nigerian Mining Corporation (NMC), which engages in direct exploration and joint ventures with mining companies.

TINUBU, MADAM. A 19th-century prominent businesswoman, born in Abeokuta (q.v.) in Ogun State (q.v.). She served as a business apprentice to her mother, after which she went to Badagry (q.v.), near Lagos (q.v.), to set up her trading business in tobacco and salt. She came in contact with the European slave dealers and served as a middle woman.

In 1846, when King Akintoye (q.v.) of Lagos was deposed, he went to Badagry seeking Madam Tinubu to use her influence to organise support for Akintoye to regain his throne. In 1851 Akintoye regained his throne in Lagos and Madam Tinubu was asked to come to Lagos. She later transferred her trading business to Lagos, serving, as before, as an intermediary between the Europeans and the Nigerians of the interior. In Lagos, she soon became a prominent and powerful woman, so powerful that people believed that she was the power behind the throne, a situation which led to rebellion among some chiefs. In 1853, Akintoye died and was succeeded by his son Dosunmu (q.v.). During the reign of Dosunmu, whom historians described as a weak king, the influence of Madam Tinubu grew. In 1855 she organised a campaign against wealthy immigrants who were from Brazil and Sierra Leone, using their wealth and power against the king. She accused them of an attempt to destroy the tradition and custom of the people of Lagos. The immigrants did not fold their arms; they struck back and Tinubu together with her supporters had to be expelled from Lagos and she went to Abeokuta where her business enterprises grew. In Abeokuta she became a prominent and powerful woman. In recognition of her contribution to the peace and progress of Abeokuta, she was made Iyalode of Abeokuta by the Alake of Abeokuta in 1864. She died in 1887. A monument was created in her name in Abeokuta and in memory of her patriotism, Tinubu Square, which is the focal point of the city of Lagos, is named after her.

TIV, THE. The Tiv are one of the largest ethnic groups in the former Northern Nigeria (q.v.). They live in the middle Benue valley. According to local tradition, they descended from an ancestor many generations ago and each group traces its origin from this ancestor through his son. The smallest effective group in their traditional organisation is the *tar,* made up of people descended from an ancestor about three or four generations from the present elders. A Tiv has the right to farm a land, which a *tar* controls. The Tiv traditionally did not have a centralised government. When the Tiv appointed a Chief, they never wanted him to usurp their authority to manage their own affairs. This was one of the reasons why they had not much respect for the Chiefs (q.v.) who the colonial authorities, for administrative purposes, imposed upon them. The present traditional leader is the Tor Tiv. They were the last groups to be "pacified" by the British. Furthermore, they were never conquered by the Fulani (q.v.) during the Jihad (q.v.).

TIV RIOTS. The Tiv (q.v.) are an ethnic group with a tradition of common decent living in an area south of the Benue River (q.v.) in the present Benue State (q.v.). They constituted an important group in the former Northern Nigeria (q.v.). They were never conquered by the Fulani (q.v.) during the jihad (q.v.).

The Tiv riots occurred in March 1960 as a result of the people's dissatisfaction with the Native Authority System (q.v.). The riot also had a political overtone in that the Tiv were mainly members of the United Middle-Belt Congress (UMBC) (q.v.), which opposed the rule of the native authorities, which supported the Northern People's Congress (NPC) (q.v.), the ruling party in the Northern Region. The riots were precipitated by the speech made by a clan chief, which was regarded as an anti-Action Group Party (AG) (q.v.) member. The UMBC was in an alliance with the AG. The riots started in Yander and, a week later, moved to other places in the area lasting until October 1960. The UMBC Party supporters went out in a rampage and burnt the houses of NPC supporters, including those local chiefs who supported the NPC. The police opened fire, and many people were injured or killed. The resident (q.v.) in the area appealed to the leader of the two parties, J. Tarka for UMBC and Mr. Anja, NPC local leader, to assist in putting an end to the violence. They agreed to tour the area in an effort to appeal for peace and calm. The resident later met with the Northern Regional Cabinet, where it was resolved that the native authorities in the area should be dissolved, and their powers were temporarily vested in district officers (q.v.).

In February 1964, another uprising was started in the Tiv Division in which not less than 11 people were killed. The situation became so grave that the maintenance of law and order was handed over to the Nigerian Army.

TOWNSEND, REV. HENRY. A lay minister of the Church Missionary Society (CMS) (q.v.) sent to Abeokuta (q.v.), Ogun State (q.v.), on January 4, 1842, accompanied by two freed Egba (q.v.) slaves from Sierra Leone (q.v.), to explore the possibility of establishing a mission in Abeokuta. He saw to the opening of mission stations and schools in Badagry (q.v.) and Abeokuta.

TRADE, FOREIGN. Structurally, the foreign trade of Nigeria is made up of exports and imports, and these comprise basic commodities, manufactured goods, minerals and capital goods. The imports are food items, drinks and tobacco, textile and footwear products, iron, steel and cement products, automobiles, petroleum oil and petrochemical goods together with industrial machinery, tools, implements, generators and electrical equipment. The main export goods are agricultural products like cocoa (q.v.), palm oil and kernel, groundnut (q.v.) and benniseed, minerals like columbite, tin (q.v.), coal and petroleum (q.v.) products, fibre and wood products, and animal products.

From early colonial times to 1969, the traditional export goods earned the bulk of the country's foreign exchange. In other words, Nigeria depended, to a large extent, on export products, such as cocoa, groundnut, cotton, palm produce and rubber (q.v.) to finance its imports of manufactured goods. This situation drastically changed in the 1970s when oil displaced the traditional export goods. Since then, oil has been the main source of revenue for Nigeria and continues to be the major source of financing for its economic and social development. *See also* TRADE, EXPORT. For example, in 1991 the oil export fetched the Federal Government (q.v.) N116,856.5 m, while the non-oil exports only fetched N4,677.2 m. Non-oil imports in 1991 cost N81,716.0 m, while oil sector imports cost only N7,772.2 m. In 1990, 56.0 per cent of Nigeria's oil was bought by the United States, dropping to 39.0 per cent in 1992. Western Europe bought 35.7 per cent in 1990, while it bought 46.9 per cent in 1992.

Between 1986 and 1993, during the Babangida (q.v.) administration, great effort was made through the International Monetary Fund's inspired structural adjustment programme (q.v.), designed to reduce Nigeria's dependence on oil, to diversify its non-oil exports and reduce its dependence on imports. But due to bad implementation of policy, extrabudgetary expenses and lack of accountability within the administration, the policy woefully failed, leading to much inflation and hardship for the majority of the people. *See also* EXPORT TRADE.

TRADE, LEGITIMATE. Owing to the many pressures put on the British government by many organisations and individuals to put an end to slave trading, Parliament in London abolished the slave trade in 1807 and efforts from then on were directed at finding suitable substitutes, then called legitimate commerce; that is, trade in tropical produce like palm oil instead of the abolished slave trade. The desire to get such products made people in Britain want to penetrate into the hinterland and led to the exploration of the Niger River (q.v.) by people like Mungo Park (q.v.), a Scottish doctor, and Richard Lander (q.v.) and his brother John. By 1830, it had become clear that the Niger emptied into the Atlantic through the delta from which Europeans had been obtaining their slaves. This discovery encouraged the British government to sponsor trading expeditions to the lower Niger. The first of these failed in 1841 because of the high mortality among the men on the ship as a result of malaria fever (q.v.). However, when quinine was discovered, another expedition was launched in 1856, with no lives lost, thanks to the use of the new drug, entrepreneurs like Macgregor Laird (q.v.), a Liverpool businessman, began the pioneering search for legitimate trade on the lower Niger. This they initially found in palm oil.

TRADE, TRANS-SAHARAN. Trade between the Sudan (q.v.) and North Africa across the Sahara Desert started long before A.D. 1000. Gold was one of the main commodities from the south of the desert to the north of it. But other precious stones, ivory and slaves exchanged hands. Agricultural products were also exchanged. The people of the south exchanged these for salt, clothes, brass goods, pottery and later, weapons. The city of Kano (q.v.) and the Kanem-Bornu empire (q.v.) were prominent centers of trans-Saharan trade in Nigeria. The history of the Sudan can be said to be the history of various groups trying to control trade routes. The routes were also important in the spread of ideas, civilisation and Islam (q.v.) in the area including Northern Nigeria.

TRADES UNION CONGRESS OF NIGERIA. (TUCN) Formed in 1943, its aims, among other things, were to unite all trade unions into one organised body, deal with general labour problems affecting workers in Nigeria, protect the rights of trade union organisations and see to the proper organization of trade unions. The TUC was accorded recognition by the government soon after its formation. The organisation became very successful soon after its formation, influencing labour legislation and showing great interest in worker's education.

Problems, however, arose in 1947 over the decision by the General Council to affiliate with the National Council of Nigeria and the Cameroons (NCNC) (q.v.), a political party. At the Sixth Annual Delegates Conference of December 1948, the decision was put to a motion and was defeated. As a result of this disaffiliation vote, many affiliated unions withdrew their membership, leading in March 1949 to the formation of the Nigerian National Federation of Labour (NNFL) (q.v.). In May 1950 the TUC and the NNFL agreed to merge into a central union, the Nigerian Labour Congress (NLC) (q.v.). Not much was heard again of the TUC until 1959, when the All-Nigerian Trade Union Federation (ANTUF) (q.v.) and the National Council of Trade Unions of Nigeria (NCTUN) (q.v.) agreed to unite under the umbrella of the Trade Union Congress of Nigeria. However, the merger did not last long. In 1960 the organisation split again over the suspension of Michael Imoudu (q.v.), who called a conference to form the Nigerian Trade Union Congress. However, the two organisations agreed in 1962 to merge together again under the United Labour Congress (q.v.).

TRADE UNION MOVEMENT. In pursuance of the British government policy to encourage the growth of labour union organisations in its colonies, the colonial government helped in no small way to foster the development of trade unionism in Nigeria. The government, even before the Second World War, had passed legislation dealing with the registration of unions. The first trade union in Nigeria, the Southern Nigeria Civil Service Union (q.v.), was formed in 1912. In 1914, after the amalgamation (q.v.) of the Northern and the Southern protectorates, its name was changed to the Nigerian Civil Service Union. In 1931, the first effort to organise workers in the private sector was that of the Nigerian Union of Teachers (NUT) (q.v.), which was composed of teachers in voluntary agency schools as well as some government schools. The same year the Railway Workers Union was founded. In 1936 the Marine Daily Paid Workers' Union was formed—its name was changed in 1937 to Nigerian Marine African Workers' Union. In 1941 the existing trade unions in the public services merged into the African Civil Servants and Technical Workers' Union (ACSTWU), with the aim of protecting the interests of African technical workers and establishing better understanding between them and the government. In 1942 another attempt was made to establish a central labour movement. This gave birth to the Federated Trade Unions of Nigeria, but its name was changed in 1943 to the Trade Union Congress of Nigeria (q.v.), which the government recognised as the legitimate representative of the workers' interests. Among the main objectives of the congress was to unite all trade unions into one organised body, protect the rights of trade unions and their members and establish a newspaper which they called the *Nigerian Worker*. In 1949 a group of members became disaffected. They broke away and formed the Nigerian National Federation of Labour (NNFL), led by Chief Michael Imoudu (q.v.), who became president, and Nduka Eze, who was the general secretary. Following this rift, other trade union organisations emerged: All-Nigeria Trade Union Federation (ANTUF) in 1953 and National Council of Trade Unions of Nigeria (NCTUN) in 1957. These two merged in 1959 into the Trade Union Congress of Nigeria (TUCN) (q.v.). In 1960 Nigerian Trade Union Congress (NTUC) was formed and in 1962 United Labour Congress (ULC) was formed. On the same day that the ULC was formed, Imoudu's supporters formed the Independent United Labour Congress (IULC). This division continued even when the military took over power and it was not until 1978 when, through the efforts of the federal military government, major differences were reconciled and a restructuring of the existing labour unions was carried out. At present there is a central labour organisation, The Nigerian Labour Congress, to which labor unions affiliate. Some of the reasons responsible for past instability in the movement were problems of ideology, personal ambition and political alignment.

TRADE UNION ORDINANCE. As a follow-up to the directive of September 1930 issued by the secretary of state for the colonies, Lord Passfield (formerly Sidney Webb) asking colonial governments in British dependencies to take steps to smooth the passage of labour union organisations into constitutional channels rather than allowing them to be taken over and dominated by disaffected persons, the 1939 Trade Union Ordinance, was proclaimed. Under the ordinance, a union, in order to engage in collective bargaining with its employer, must first be registered.

TRANSITIONAL COUNCIL. As a result of election rigging (q.v.), massive use of money and other election malpractices that accompanied the presidential primary elections in September 1992, the primary election results were cancelled. On November 17, 1992, in a nationwide address President I.B. Babangida (q.v.) postponed his handover of government to an elected president from January 2, 1993, to August 27, 1993, the anniversary of his seizing power in 1985. To assuage tension arising from his failure to hand over in January 1993, he set up two bodies, the Defence and Security Council and the Transitional Council, which were to replace the former federal council of ministers (q.v.) (cabinet) with the responsibility to conduct the presidential election and revive an economy (q.v.) on the verge of collapse.

The Transitional Council was made up of 27 members with Chief Ernest Sonekan (q.v.) as chairman and Head of Government. Four of the former members of the council of ministers were retained, including General Sani Abacha (q.v.) as defence secretary and Air Vice Marshal Nuru Iman, for power and steel.

The Transitional Council had no real power to effect any change in the economy or oversee the June 12, 1993, presidential election (q.v.), and its annulment on June 23, 1993, which led to a serious political crisis. Real power resided in the National Defence and Security Council with Babangida as chairman. The Transitional Council metamorphosed into the Interim National Government (ING) (q.v.) on August 26, 1993, when President Babangida, seeing that he no longer had the support of the army and the national assembly members to pass a vote to enable him to remain as ING head quickly retired from the army and, as he said, "stepped aside" from the government.

The eight-month period of the council was a dismal failure as Chief Shonekan, its chairman, confessed. The economy was in a more perilous situation than when he assumed office and it was during this period that the greatest political crisis since the Civil War (q.v.) was created by the annulment of the presidential election won by Chief Mosheod K.O. Abiola (q.v.).

TRANSPORTATION. The transportation sector has for many years been a major area of government investment. In the Third National Development Plan it was second to industries, attracting the highest investment with a total of N7.3 billion. This represented 24.3 percent of the total investments for the plan period.

Transportation in Nigeria is basically through four means—road, air, water and rail. The roads in Nigeria are divided into three categories: Trunk "A" roads, which are maintained by the Federal Government, cut across state boundaries; Trunk "B" roads, maintained by the state government, link the towns in the state; and Trunk "C" roads, composed of urban and rural roads, are maintained by local government in their areas.

The second means of transportation in Nigeria is by rail. The railway system comprises a total of 3,505 kilometres route of 1,067 millimetres (3 ft. 6 in.) gauge and runs through many states of Nigeria. The railway is single-tracked and consists of two main routes, linking the two major ocean ports of Lagos (q.v.) and Port Harcourt (q.v.) with the state capitals and with industrial and commercial centres in the country.

The third means of transportation in Nigeria is by water or sea. The transportation by sea is controlled by the Nigerian Ports Authority (q.v.), which established harbours at Lagos, Port Harcourt (two major ports), Calabar (q.v.), Akassa, Bonny, Warri, Sapele, Burutu and Degema. Ships from Nigeria and other countries load and off-load at these harbours. There are inland waterways, which is made possible by the use of the Niger River (q.v.).

The last and the latest means of transport in Nigeria is air travel. Flights in Nigeria are operated both locally and internationally. The Nigerian Airport Authority has built airports in some major towns in Nigeria and has plans to connect all state capitals by air. There are two main international airports—Kano (q.v.) and Ikeja—with a number of ports in others. The management of these ports are under the control of Nigeria Airport Authority.

TRANSPORTATION, WATER. Waterways are important means of transportation in Nigeria. But like roads, they are subject to physical changes and natural obstructions. A major physical problem is the sharp division between the dry and the rainy seasons, and the resultant fluctuations in the water level, which in turn hinders the movement of canoes and other vessels. During the dry season, some rivers dry up or are so low that boats and canoes cannot safely move around. Among the natural obstructions are rocks, rapids, creeping weeds, water hyacinth, stumps and overhanging bushes.

Nigeria has many rivers, but the most important ones are the Niger River (q.v.), entering the country from the west and the Benue River (q.v.), entering it from the east. Both meet at Lokoja (q.v.) before they move south to the Atlantic Ocean where they form numerous creeks and swamps. In addition to this are lakes such as Lake Chad (q.v.) and coastal lagoons, all which serve rafts, canoes and boats of different kinds and sizes together with other vessels. In 1970 six of the then-existing 12 states in Nigeria—Benue-Plateau,

East-Central, Mid-West, Kwara, North-Western and North-Eastern States (qq.v.)—formed the Central Water Transportation Company (CWTC) with its base in Onitsha (q.v.). The CWTC operated river transportation with a fleet of tugs and barges from Warri (q.v.) and Burutu ports in the then-Bendel State, and Port Harcourt (q.v.) in the Rivers State (q.v.) to river ports on the Niger and Benue rivers. The company also offered ferry and passenger services along the rivers. In the riverine areas of the country where road construction is difficult, water transportation of goods and services through boats and canoes is still the most common.

TREASON TRIAL. On October 1, 1962, the Prime Minister, Alhaji Sir Abubakar Tafawa Balewa (q.v.) announced to the nation that the government was aware of the intention of some people in the country to violently overthrow the government. The police, in September, had searched a house in Mushin, Lagos, and found a large quantity of firearms, including submachine guns, automatic pistols, revolvers and plenty of ammunition. Later, on October 5, 1962, the police reported that they had found three stores of arms during their search of the homes of some Action Group Party (q.v.) leaders. On November 2, 1962 Chief Obafemi Awolowo (q.v.) was charged, along with 26 other persons, with conspiring to overthrow the Federal Government. The prosecution alleged that the accused had, between December 1960 and September 1962 in Lagos (q.v.) and in many other places in Nigeria, formed an intention to levy war against the Queen within Nigeria in order to compel the Queen to change her measures or her counsels and had manifested such intention by overt act, treasonable felony. Similar charges were made against Anthony Enaboro (q.v.) and Samuel Ikoku, (q.v.), both of whom had fled the country and were wanted persons.

Among the accused were Dr. Oladipo Maja, Alahaji Lateef Jakande, Mr. Olabisi Onabanjo, J.S. Tarka, Mr. Josiah Olawoyin and Mr. Michael Omisade. Charges against Oladipo were later withdrawn for lack of evidence, but he later gave evidence for the prosecution. Chief Awolowo's counsel, Mr. E.F.N. Gratiaen from the United Kingdom, was refused permission to enter Nigeria to defend him and so he had to defend himself. On December 6, 1962, a bill was passed forbidding non-Nigerians to enter Nigeria to practise any profession without the written consent of the Minister for Internal Affairs. The law was supported by the Nigerian Bar Association, for on November 10, it had called on the government to pass laws against expatriate lawyers practising in Nigeria. But the Association did not support the government action with regard to Mr. Gratiaen, Q.C., since he was a lawyer enrolled to practise in Nigeria. Chief Awolowo challenged the Federal Government for refusing to allow his lawyer to enter Nigeria, but he lost.

Chief Awolowo and 17 other accused persons were found guilty and were sentenced to varying years of imprisonment: Awolowo to 10 years, Jakande and Omisade to seven years each.

TRIBALISM. A term used to denote doing something to favor one's ethnic group or giving apparently undue privilege to people from one's own ethnic group.

Nigeria, as a country, was the creation of the British. It is made up of many ethnic or "tribal" groups who are geographically located and whose languages are quite different from one another. A few of these language groups are those of the Hausa, Fulani, Kanuri, Tiv, Yoruba, Nupe, Edo, Ibo, Urhobo, Ibibio (qq.v.), Anang, Ijaw (q.v.), Tikar and many other minority groups scattered in geographical locations all over the country. Most people, even the highly educated ones in the universities, government and business, still feel stronger loyalties and sympathy to their local or ethnic group than to the nation as a whole.

This ethnic or tribal feeling has been often exploited by politicians when campaigning. For example Dr. Nnamdi Azikiwe (q.v.), one of the architects of modern Nigeria and a presidential candidate campaigning in 1979 said concerning his tax problem with the Federal Electoral Commission (FEDECO) (q.v.), that his tribulations came as a result of the fact that he was an Igbo (q.v.).

The term also has become a convenient word for many Nigerians when they are penalised for certain action, especially when the person in charge is of a different ethnic group from the one who is penalised. It is also used in a scapegoat fashion over failure to secure a post when another person of a different ethnic origin gets the post.

TRIBAL MARKS. Tribal marks were used as a means of identification, especially during the period of intertribal wars and slavery. Thus, in the past, members of most ethnic groups and their subdivisions had facial marks made during infancy by incision or tattooing. The incisions, while being treated, were deliberately kept open so that the scars would remain permanent. Even though some traditionally oriented families, especially in Yorubaland (q.v.), still continue with this practice, most people have long put an end to it since the need for it is no longer present.

TRIBE. A derogatory term generally applied by Europeans to any nationality or ethnic group of non-European origin in colonial territories of Africa, irrespective of population and sociocultural development. Thus the Yoruba (q.v.), and the Hausa-Fulani, each numbering many millions of people when the British colonial authorities arrived in Nigeria, were described as tribes. In spite of the inappropriateness of the term, it lingers on, especially in its derivative of tribalism. Today words like nation, ethnic group, group or race are used.

TRIPLE A. *See* ALHAJI, ABUBAKAR ALHAJI.

TSETSE FLY. A fly that causes sleeping sickness. The parasites that cause the disease are transmitted through a bite by the tsetse fly by injecting them directly into the victims through the process of blood sucking. The parasites then multiply under the skin within a short time, and are then transmitted into the blood vessels, from where they move to the central nervous system, thus leaving the victim open to various attacks, including mental illness and paralysis of the limbs. The most common sign of the disease is that the patient sleeps involuntarily, and at odd times. The disease attacks both humans and animals and can be transmitted through a fly that acts as a carrier or through unsterilised needles used to inject healthy people after injecting a sleeping sickness patient. It has been said that one of the reasons for the concentration of cattle in the Jos Plateau of Northern Nigeria (q.v.) is the absence of this fly as compared to many other places.

TUAREG. The Tuareg people live mainly in the Western Sudan (q.v.). They are scattered all over the area. Many of them are in Northern Nigeria (q.v.) and in many cities like Kano (q.v.), Zaria (q.v.) and Kaduna (q.v.). Most Tuaregs depend entirely on their flocks of animals, but some of them grow vegetables and many other crops. The Tuareg in the past raided neighbouring peoples and for centuries controlled the salt trade across the Sahara Desert. As they follow their flocks, they usually wear a veil across their nose and mouth to protect them against the dust. Others who have settled engage in trade in metal ornaments, leatherwork and weapons for local markets. Many Tuaregs are Muslims, but a substantial number still believe in traditional religions (q.v.).

TUDOR DAVIES COMMISSION. The Tudor Davies Commission was set up in October 1945, following the June 1945 General Strike (q.v.) which lasted for about two months. The commission, consisting of W. Tudor Davies as commissioner and F.W. Dalley and G.P.W. Lamb as assessors, was to consider: the government representation with regard to government and native authority employees, an increase in the cost of living allowance for Nigerian workers and make recommendations as to what government should do. The commission started sitting in November 1945 and continued until March 1946. The commission recommended that the cost of living allowance existing in July 1945 be increased by 50 percent and that the 50 percent award should apply not only to Africans earning £220 per annum or less but also to the special allowances paid since October 1944 to African employees whose salaries were over £220, except for those receiving local allowances because they held superior posts. It also recommended that the award should remain in force until a new wage structure was set up by a team of statistical officers and nutritionists, which should be set up within two years from the date of the report.

TUTUOLA, AMOS. A writer, and perhaps the first Nigerian to achieve international fame, born in 1920 in Abeokuta (q.v.), Ogun State (q.v.), he was educated at Lagos High School in 1934, and the Anglican Central School in Abeokuta from 1938 to 1939. He later became an apprentice blacksmith in Lagos (q.v.) in 1940 and later joined the Royal Air Force in Lagos during the Second World War. After the war, he worked in the Ministry of Labour in Lagos and later became the storekeeper and clerk for the Nigerian Broadcasting Corporation. He was a visiting fellow at the University of Ife (q.v.), Ile-Ife. His first publication *The Palmwine Drinkard* (1952) brought him international fame and recognition. Some of his other publications are *My Life in the Bush of Ghosts* (1954), *Feather Woman of the Jungle* (1962), *Ajayi and His Inherited Poverty* (1967), *The Witch Herbalist of the Remote Town* (1980) and *Pauper, Brawler and Slanderer* (1987). He died on June 8, 1997.

-U-

UDOJI COMMISSION. The Public Service Review Commission, popularly known as the Udoji Commission, was set up in September 1972 under the chairmanship of Chief Jerome Oputa Udoji, a distinguished public servant. The commission was to carry out a review of the organisation, structure and management of the Nigerian public services, including recruitment, career and staff development, pensions and superannuations as well as the grading system. The sectors of the public services covered in the exercise were the federal and state civil services, the public corporations and enterprises, universities, the judiciary, the police, teaching services and the local government administration.

The commission submitted its report in September 1974 and the government made the report public in January 1975. In its report, the commission, among other things, called for a new style public service in the country which would be production- or result-oriented, and which would concentrate attention and resources on the purposes for which an institution was set up. With regard to the structure of the public services, the commission recommended the abolition of the former division into classes which was a source of great conflicts, and asked that a unified grading structure be introduced which would embrace all posts in the civil service from the lowest to the highest and provide equal opportunity for every person to advance to the highest post in the service irrespective of his discipline. The commission recommended a grading level from 1 to 17 and suggested the salary appropriate to each level to make public servants' salaries commensurate with their responsibilities and comparable to the private sector so as to stem the movement from the public to the private sector.

The government accepted most of its recommendations. It was the time of the oil boom and rather than space out the payment of the salary areas as the commission had recommended, the government paid all of it at once, leading to skyrocketing inflation.

UKIWE, COMMODORE EBITU. Chief of general staff and number-two man in the Babangida administration for about a year, Ukiwe was born at Abriba, Imo State (q.v.). He was a member of the Supreme Military Council (q.v.) in 1975 and was military governor of the Niger State (q.v.) in 1977. In 1978, when the military was preparing to hand over power, he was posted to Lagos State (q.v.) as military administrator of the state and commanding officer of the NNS *Beecroft*. In 1979, when the civilian administration came to power, he returned to regular naval duties. In 1980 he was at War College, Rhode Island, in the United States, and in 1981, he became the head of the naval faculty at the Command Staff College in Jaji. In 1984 he became a member of the Supreme Military Council under Major-General Muhammadu Buhari (q.v.), and, when General Buhari was removed from power in 1985, he was appointed chief of general staff to take care of the general administration of the Federal Government (q.v.), but without having responsibility for the military as was the case of the chief of staff Supreme Headquarters under the previous military regime. He retired from the Navy in December 1986 and went into private business. After the annulment of the June 12, 1993 elections Ukiwe was a vocal supporter of M.K.O. Abiola. He was among the most prominent non-Yoruba members of NADECO (the National Democratic Coalition).

UMAR, COL. ABUBAKAR DANGIWA. Born September 21, 1949, to an aristocratic family in Birnin Kebbi, Northern Region. Colonel Umar was the military governor of Kaduna State from 1985–88, but he is best known in Nigeria for his support for democracy. Abubakar Umar joined the army in 1967 and rose steadily up the ranks. Col. Umar was appointed to serve as a military governor of Kaduna State from 1985–88. Even after being removed from office, he was a strong supporter of the regime, and was identified with a group of young officers known as the "Babangida boys." Col. Umar's strong opposition to the military's annulment of the June 12, 1993, election led to his retiring from the service that summer. Umar's principled stance on this issue was unusual both for a military man and a member of the conservative northern aristocracy. Col. Umar made news again in 1998, when he was a member of the Group of 18, and the Group of 34 (qq.v.), coalitions of prominent public figures opposed to the plan of Gen. Sani Abacha (q.v.) to extend his tenure in office.

UMAR IBN IDRIS. Ruler of the Kanem-Bornu empire between 1384 and 1398, it was during his reign that the center of the empire was moved from Kanem to Bornu in 1389. Dunama Dibalemi (q.v.) had a serious conflict with the Bulala (q.v.) nomads who were the descendants of an earlier Kanemi king. The conflict continued for many years, such that it was said that five predecessors of Umar had been killed in wars with the Bulala people. Perhaps not wanting to get killed like his predecessors, Umar moved his kingdom to Bornu (q.v.). He died in 1398.

UMAR IBN MUHAMMAD AL-AMIN AL-KANEMI. Ruler of Bornu from 1837 to 1881, he succeeded his father Al-Kanemi (q.v.) who had overthrown the Sefawa dynasty (q.v.) of Bornu (q.v.). While he ruled, he, like his father, allowed the Sefawa kings to remain as titular rulers. But, in 1846, when Ibrahim, the last of the Sefawa kings, tried to regain real power by allying with the king of Wadai, Umar had him and his son killed, thus ending the Sefawa dynasty.

In spite of this, Umar was said to be a weak ruler who relied too much on his chief adviser. His Chiefs (q.v.) planned a coup against him and installed his brother, Abdurrahman in power in 1853.

Abdurrahman became tyrannical and people withdrew their support from him and went back again to Umar who in 1854 was reinstated. Abdurrahman died later. Because Umar's adviser had died, he chose a new adviser, Laminu Njitiya, said to be formerly a bandit but who became the most powerful person then in Bornu. Laminu died in 1871. Before Umar died in 1881, the power of the nobles in Bornu considerably increased. His son Bukar succeeded him.

UMARU. Ruler of the Sokoto (q.v.) caliphate (q.v.) from 1881 to 1891, and a grandson of Usman Dan Fodio (q.v.). Umaru, seeing that the jihad (q.v.) war had lost focus, in raiding neighbouring states, instead of extending the empire's boundaries, decided to discontinue the wars. Having lost the revenue that the wars brought, he concentrated more on raising revenue internally and from the various Emirates in the caliphate. This policy of peace was accepted by his people, and trade expanded. He died in 1891, succeeded by Abdurrahman.

UNEMPLOYMENT. Unemployed people in Nigeria can be regarded as those willing and able to work but who cannot find employment at the prevailing wage rate. Before the oil boom of the 1970s, unemployment was not a common phenomenon in the country, for agriculture (q.v.) was able to absorb most of the labour force while the rest found employment in industry (q.v.), commerce, administration and teaching. In the 1970s with the wealth coming from oil, many young people left the rural areas for the fast-growing cities. But since they were not skilled, it was not easy to become employed. In 1992 unemployment among this group was about 15.1 per cent. Unemployment among primary school leavers was about 19.9 per cent in the same year. The worst hit group were the secondary school leavers. Because secondary school education is still based on reading, writing and arithmetic, most students upon graduation find themselves without any specific skill. It has been, therefore, difficult to absorb this class of people into the workforce and unemployment was said to be at 62.3 per cent, while university graduate unemployment was 2.7 per cent.

To improve the employment situation, government therefore set up the National Directorate of Employment (NDE) (q.v.) in 1986 to create employment opportunities with emphasis on self-reliance and entrepreneurship. The NDE has trained more than 200,000 people by 1992 for its National Open Apprenticeship Scheme at different trade centres all over the country, and about 50,000 people have also been trained under its School-On-Wheel programme in 44 different units of well-equipped mobile training workshops.

UNIFICATION DECREE. When General Aguiyi-Ironsi (q.v.) assumed power in January 1966, he set up three important commissions, one of which was the Nwokedi Commission (q.v.) under Mr. F. Nwokedi, who was the sole commissioner. His responsibility was to put forward proposals for the unification of the regional and federal public services. The military government accepted the recommendations and issued Decree Number 34, which Ironsi said was intended to remove the last vestiges of the excessive regionalism of the recent past and to produce a cohesion in the governmental structure which was necessary to achieve and maintain the paramount objective of national unity. According to the decree, Nigeria ceased to be a federation and it was known as the Republic of Nigeria. The former four regions of the country were to be known as the Northern, Eastern, Western and the Mid-Western groups of provinces. The federal territory of Lagos became the capital territory. The federal military government became the national military government and the Federal Executive Council became the Executive Council. The federal and regional public services became unified under a National Public Service Commission. The decrees also dissolved the 81 existing political parties and ethnic associations all over the country. The unification decree was seen as a threat to the less developed Northern Region, and helped prompt the July 1966 coup of northern officers that overthrew the Ironsi

Regime. The part of the decree setting up a unitary form of government was later revoked by General Yakubu Gowon (q.v.) after the second coup in Decree Number 59 of 1966.

UNION BANK OF NIGERIA LIMITED. One of the leading banks in Nigeria, formerly known as the Barclays Bank DCO (Nigeria) Limited, was formed in 1925 as Barclays Bank Dominion Colonial and Overseas (DCO) and took over the activities of some other banks. The bank has branches all over the country. At present, the Federal Government together with Nigerian citizens hold 80 percent of its share capital while the Barclays Bank International (BBI) holds the remaining 20 percent. The Federal Government then terminated the subsidiary relations of the bank to the BBI, and to reflect this changed relationship, its name was changed in 1979 to the Union Bank of Nigeria Limited. The bank still maintains correspondent relationship with the BBI.

UNITED AFRICAN COMPANY (UAC). Formed in 1879 by Mr. George Dashwood Goldie Taubman, later knighted as Sir Taubman Goldie (q.v.) by the amalgamation of four British firms in the Niger Delta. The firms were West African Company, Central African Company, Miller Brothers and James Pinnock, each competing against the other in the area. Before the merger, the French and the Germans had begun to look for ways to expand their interest in the Niger Delta (q.v.) and the hinterland, and Goldie designed the merger to forestall this. He persuaded the companies that the only cure for overcompetition among them was for all of them to amalgamate.

In 1882 the UAC changed its name to National African Company (q.v.) and applied to the British government for a charter, which was then refused. By this time, two French companies had formed on the Niger and when they refused to join the National African Company, a price war was started which pushed the two French companies off the market. After the Berlin Conference (q.v.) of 1885, which recognised the area around the Niger as being under British protection, Britain in 1886 finally granted the company the charter it had long sought for and was renamed the Royal Niger Company. Under the terms of the charter, the company was given political authority over the areas. The company set up a governing council subject to the control of the Foreign Office in London. In July 1899 the bill divesting the Royal Niger Company of its administrative functions was passed and the company then became a private concern. Since then, the UAC has exercised a prominent role in the country's economy. In the 1930s it controlled more than 40 percent of the country's import-export trade and by 1949 it handled about 34 percent of commercial merchandise imported into Nigeria. The UAC was a member of the Association of West African Merchants (AWAM) (q.v.), through which members made import agreements and allocated export quotas. Today the UAC is indigenised, with most of its shares owned by Nigerians and its management in the hands of Nigerians. The company has remained one of the biggest commercial firms in Nigeria.

UNITED AFRICAN METHODIST CHURCH. *See* WESLEYAN CHURCH.

UNITED FREE CHURCH. Founded in 1846 by Rev. Hope Waddell who had been doing missionary work in Jamaica, together with some other missionaries including his son George. These missionaries were sent by the United Secession Church of Scotland and the Scottish Missionary Society. They first landed in Calabar (q.v.), escorted on shore by Consul John Beecroft (q.v.). Later on, the church missionaries moved to Ogoja (q.v.) and other provinces (q.v.).

UNITED LABOUR CONGRESS (ULC). The United Labour Congress (ULC) came into being as the result of a merger of the Trade Union Congress of Nigeria (TUCN) (q.v.) and the Nigerian Trade Union Congress (NTUC) (q.v.) in 1962 during the joint conference of the two factions. But disagreements at the conference over the international affiliation of the congress led to another split: one faction led by Chief Michael Imoudu (q.v.) who, together with his supporters, formed the Independent United Labour Congress (IULC) (q.v.) while others continued with the conference. At the conference, Alhaji Adebola (q.v.) was elected the president of the Congress.

UNITED MIDDLE BELT CONGRESS (UMBC). The United Middle Belt Congress was founded in 1955 as a result of a merger between two previously formed organisations, the Middle Zone League (q.v.), founded in 1950 and the Middle Belt Peoples Party (MBPP) (q.v.), founded in 1953. The UMBC later split into two, one part joined with the Northern People's Congress (NPC) (q.v.) while the other, under the leadership of Mr. Joseph S. Tarka (q.v.), retained the organisation and went into an alliance with the Action Group Party (q.v.). The party advocated the creation of a Middle-Belt Region for the area and constantly agitated against the NPC government of the north. The party, together with all other political parties, was banned in 1966 when the military came to power. But in 1967, the people of the Middle-Belt got the state they had been asking for, the Benue/Plateau State.

UNITED NATIONAL INDEPENDENCE PARTY (UNIP). The United National Independence Party (UNIP) was formerly known as National Independence Party (NIP) (q.v.), a breakaway party from the National Council of Nigeria and the Cameroons (NCNC) (q.v.) and formed in 1953 by three federal ministers dismissed from the NCNC as a result of the 1953 Eastern Regional Crisis (q.v.). The party, led by Professor Eyo Ita (q.v.), joined the Action Group Party (AG) (q.v.) in an alliance with which they both jointly won seven seats in the 1954 federal elections in the Eastern Region (q.v.). The main stronghold of UNIP were the areas known as COR areas, that is, Calabar-Ogoja and Rivers areas. The party advocated for the creation of separate states for the areas. The party was dissolved along with others in 1966 but in 1967 the areas got their states, known as the South-Eastern and Rivers (q.v.) States.

UNITED NATIVE AFRICAN CHURCH. The church originated as a protest to the white-dominated Christian churches. The United Native African Church seceded in 1891 from the Anglican Church because the founders believed that Africa was to be evangelised by Africans, since such circumstances as climate and other such influences made it difficult for the Europeans to do so. Furthermore they wanted a purely Native African church that would evangelise the people and be governed by Africans. The group that founded the church was much influenced by the writings of Dr. Edward Blyden (q.v.) and his visit to Lagos (q.v.) in 1890 when he urged African Christians to establish native churches patterned on the black churches in the United States. By 1892, branches were opened in Ilaro and Ijebu, and Ebute Metta in 1893.

UNITED PEOPLE'S PARTY (UPP). The United People's Party was formed after the Action Group crisis (q.v.) of 1962 by Chief S.L. Akintola (q.v.), who, together with 23 members of the Western House of Assembly who supported him, formed its nucleus. The UPP formed a coalition with the National Council of Nigerian Citizens (NCNC) (q.v.) to run the government of the Western Region after the state of emergency was lifted in 1963 in the region. Chief S.L. Akintola then became the premier and the leader of the NCNC coalition partner Chief Fani-Kayode (q.v.) became the deputy premier. In 1964 members of the UPP and a faction of the NCNC in the west, led by Chief Fani-Kayode and Chief Richard Akinjide (q.v.) formed the NNDP, Nigerian National Democratic Party with Chief S.L. Akintola as Chairman. During the political realignment of 1964 before the December federal elections, NNDP joined with the NPC (Northern People's Congress) to form the Nigerian National Alliance (NNA) (q.v.).

UNITED PROGRESSIVE FRONT. An alliance of four parties—the Great Nigerian People's Party (GNPP) (q.v.), Nigerian People's Party (NPP) (q.v.), Unity Party of Nigeria (UPN) (q.v.) and People's Redemption Party (PRP) (q.v.)—proposed during the 1979 general elections to stop the National Party of Nigeria (NPN) (q.v.), the leading party, from winning. The alliance helped the PRP to win the gubernatorial elections in Kaduna State (q.v.) which had its legislative house controlled by the NPN with more than two-thirds majority. The alliance did not hold for the presidential elections, which the NPN won.

UNITED PROGRESSIVE GRAND ALLIANCE (UPGA). Formed at Ibadan (q.v.) in June 1964 by the Action Group Party (AG) (q.v.) together with its northern ally, the United Middle Belt Congress (UMBC) and the National Council of Nigerian Citizens (NCNC) (q.v.), together with its ally in the north, the Northern Element Progressive Union (NEPU) (q.v.) which, together with UMBC (q.v.) had formed the Northern Progressive Front while the NCNC and the AG had formed themselves into the Southern Progressive Front. Thus UPGA was an alliance of the Southern and Northern Progressive fronts.

The purpose of the Alliance of the two erstwhile rival parties was to enable them to win the 1964 federal election. The Alliance ran into difficulties in the west over the nomination of candidates. Both the Action Group and the National Council of Nigerian Citizens wanted to field their candidates on the platform of the Alliance. They finally reached a compromise in which 37 out of the 57 seats in the region were to be contested by the Action Group while the rest went to the National Council of Nigerian Citizens. A few days before the election, the UPGA leaders led a delegation to the president of the Federation asking him to postpone the election because of election malpractices in various parts of the Federation. They also said that if their request was not granted they would boycott the election. When all efforts to postpone the election had failed, they decided to boycott the election and their decision was broadcast on December 29, 1964, just a day before the election. The boycott succeeded only in the east, while elections were held in the other three regions. When the result of the election was announced, the National Democratic Party (NDP) (q.v.) which was in alliance with the Northern People's Congress (NPC) (q.v.) to form the Nigerian National Alliance (NNA) (q.v.), won 36 of the 57 seats in the west and an overwhelming victory in the north. Because of the election boycott of the UPGA, another election, called the Little Election (q.v.), was held in March 1965 in the Eastern Region (q.v.) and the NCNC won the majority of the seats. But overall, UPGA came out the loser. The UPGA was dissolved and banned in 1966 when the army took over.

UNITY PARTY OF NIGERIA. Launched on September 22, 1978, it was the first political party to be formed at the wake of political activities. At the formation of the party, Chief Obafemi Awolowo (q.v.), who was the leader of the party, highlighted the UPN's four cardinal programs:

1. free education at all levels for all, effective October 1, 1979.
2. integrated rural development which would be aimed at boosting food production and feeding the people of the nation
3. the provision of free health facilities for all citizens
4. full employment for all

The party was formed out of the National Committee of Friends, an association formed by Chief Awolowo in anticipation of civilian rule.

At the party's convention, Chief Obafemi Awolowo was selected as the presidential candidate of the party and Chief Philip E. Umeadi was chosen as his vice-presidential running mate. The party submitted its registration forms to the Federal Electoral Commission (FEDECO) in December 1978 and was subsequently registered along with four others. Owing to the personality of the founder, Chief Awolowo, and the programmes of the party, many people saw the UPN as a rebirth of the former Action Group Party (q.v.), disbanded in 1966 when the military seized power.

The UPN contested the 1979 elections. It won 28 senatorial seats out of 95 and 110 seats in the National House of Assembly. The party won overwhelming support in the old Western Region (q.v.) (now Lagos Ogun, Oyo, Ondo and Bendel states), and it controlled both the state executive and legislative branches in those states.

The party's presidential candidate, Chief Obafemi Awolowo, lost to the National Party of Nigeria's candidate Alhaji Shehu Shagari (q.v.). Although he challenged the Federal Electoral Commission's verdict at both the electoral tribunal and at the Supreme Court of Nigeria, both judicial bodies upheld the interpretation of FEDECO that the constitutional requirement that the winner should have the highest number of votes at the election and must have at least one-quarter of the votes cast at the election in each of at least two-thirds of the states of the Federation.

In preparation for the 1983 elections, because the party did not appear to have enough support in the other, older regions (north and east), to win the presidential election, it was in the forefront of the effort to ally with the other minority parties to defeat the National Party of Nigeria. Thus the UPN, the Nigerian People's Party (NPP) (q.v.), the Imoudu faction of the People's Redemption Party (PRP) (q.v.) and the Mahmud faction of the Great Nigerian People's Party (GNPP) (q.v.) formed themselves into a kind of an alliance, the PPA (Progressive Parties Alliance) (q.v.).

However, the PPA was unable to agree on a common list for the 1983 elections, not even on the presidential candidate, and each party went it alone in all the states. The UPN lost the presidential race to the NPN and lost two of the states it controlled in 1979, Oyo and Bendel (qq.v.), but won the Kwara State (q.v.) gubernatorial election. The party was with all other parties proscribed after the December 1983 coup which toppled the government of Alhaji Shehu Shagari.

UNIVERSAL PRIMARY EDUCATION (UPE). In 1955, the government of Western Nigeria (q.v.), under the Action Group Party (q.v.), launched its Universal Free Primary Education plan in the region. Two years later the east followed suit but, in 1958, owing to financial constraints, the Eastern Region (q.v.) reimposed fees from primary III upward. In the west, the scheme continued until 1976, when the federal military government, under the leadership of General Olusegun Obasanjo (q.v.), launched the nationwide Universal (Free) Primary Education plan in Nigeria. The scheme was launched to correct the imbalance between educational development in the south and the north. For example, in 1972 while about 70 percent of the school-age children were in school in the south, only about 10 percent were in school in the north. In 1974 General Yakubu Gowon (q.v.), the Head of State and a northerner, announced in the North-Western State that the government had planned to introduce free compulsory primary education throughout the country. But before he could launch the programme he had been overthrown and it was the lot of General Olusegun Obasanjo, the then Head of State in 1976, who launched the programme of Universal Free (not compulsory) Primary Education all over the nation. As the Head of State said, education in Nigeria was no longer a privilege but a right of every citizen. By the late 1990s, as a result of the economic downturn, many states were considering re-introducing school fees and tuition.

UNIVERSITIES, FINANCING OF. All universities in Nigeria are either federally owned or state owned. They all derive most of their income from the federal or state governments. The University of Ibadan, the first University in Nigeria, was jointly financed by the British government and the Nigerian government between 1948 and 1952. The full responsibility of the institution fell on the Federal Government after 1959. The University of Lagos, established by the Federal Government, was fully financed by the Federal Government right from its inception in 1962. The regional University of Nigeria, Nsukka, University of Ife, and Ahmadu Bello University were fully financed by their regions for some years before the National Universities Commission took over part of the financial responsibility on behalf of the Federal Government. In 1964, the Federal Government assumed 100 percent financial responsibility for the Universities of Ibadan and Lagos, while it agreed to finance 30 percent of recurrent and 50 percent of capital expenditure for Nsukka and Ife and assumed 50 percent of both recurrent and capital expenditure for Ahmadu Bello. There were other changes in 1967 but the big change came in August 1972 when the federal military government assumed full responsibility for all the then existing universities, and in 1976 the Federal Government declared that all the Nigerian universities were federally owned and no longer under state control. However, with the coming of politicians in 1979, not only was the Federal Government establishing new universities in the states that had none in 1979, but many state governments embarked upon setting up state universities, and each government had to look for money to finance them. It is to be remembered that under the 1979 constitution, university, technological and post-primary education is on the concurrent list.

However, in the early 1990s all the nation's universities were suffering from the economic malaise that came upon the country, leading to strikes in the universities, brain drain and educational instability.

UNIVERSITY COLLEGE OF IBADAN. The University College of Ibadan was established in January 1947 following the recommendations of the Elliot Commission on Higher Education (q.v.) in 1945 in the then British colonies of which Nigeria was one.

The college opened in January 1948 and the students of the old Yaba College started as undergraduates of the new institution. The standard of academic instruction was based upon what was obtained at London University and students retained London University degrees. In 1953, work began on the building of the University College Hospital as a university teaching hospital. In 1962 the University College of Ibadan became a full-fledged university, the University of Ibadan.

UNIVERSITY OF IBADAN. *See* UNIVERSITY COLLEGE OF IBADAN.

UNIVERSITY OF IFE. Founded by the Western Regional government in 1961, it was temporarily located on the site of the Ibadan branch of the Nigerian College of Arts, Science and Technology when it was formally opened in October 1962 with 244 foundation students.

Its staff came from the incorporated college while others were from the University College of Ibadan. It was therefore greatly influenced by Ibadan University, which itself was influenced by the British. The university was taken over in August 1975 by the Federal Government.

UNIVERSITY OF NIGERIA, NSUKKA. Formerly opened on October 7, 1960 by Her Royal Highness Princess Alexandra, who represented Her Majesty Queen Elizabeth II at the independence celebration, the University of Nigeria became the second university to be opened in Nigeria. In the 1961–62 session, the Enugu branch of the Nigerian College of Arts, Science and Technology was incorporated into the university and was designated as the Enugu Campus of the university. The university was different from its predecessor, University of Ibadan, in certain ways: it was not completely residential and so could admit a much larger number of candidates, its admission requirements were not as demanding as those of Ibadan University, the range of courses offered were much wider and examination schemes were based on course work similar to that in the United States, and finally, it awarded its own degrees from the very start without being affiliated with any university. The university was regionally owned until it was taken over by the Federal Government in April 1973.

UNIVERSITY STUDENT FINANCING. Until 1977, tuition fees were paid in the Nigerian universities, and other levies included accommodation, boarding, examination, caution and teaching practice (education students) fees. In 1978 tuition fees were removed from among all these fees for Nigerian students while foreign students still had to pay the tuition fees. Various state governments assist their indigenes by way of bursaries and scholarships and the Federal Government has scholarship schemes for students in Nigerian universities and those abroad. In spite of all this, much of the burden of the cost of higher education is still borne by parents and relatives.

URHOBO. An Edo-speaking minority ethnic group, the Urhobo live in the Delta State (q.v.). They are divided into many smaller groups, each with its own traditional Chief (q.v.) or Ovie. Their main occupation is farming, growing crops like cassava and yams. They also fish and produce and market oil palm (q.v.) products. Some of their old villages, like Sapele and Ughelli, have become large towns and centres of oil and timber industries.

USMAN DAN FODIO. A Fulani (q.v.) Islamic (q.v.) scholar, leader and revolutionary. He was among a number of religious leaders who waged jihads to purify the practice of Islam in 19th century West Africa. Born in 1754 at Marata in Gobir, he was educated in Islamic religion and law. After his education, he became a preacher, preaching religious and social reforms among the people of Gobir. Toward the end of the 18th century, he became a teacher and preacher of so great distinction that the king of Gobir entrusted the education of his son Yunfa to him. When the king died, Yunfa, with the support of his old teacher, Dan Fodio, became king of Gobir. But relations between him and the king soon became strained. As Dan Fodio's popularity grew in the kingdom, the king became apprehensive of the threat posed by Islam to traditional authorities. In an effort to prevent the Muslims in his state from developing into a separate group, Yunfa decided to put an end to the efforts of his reformist teacher. An attempt was made on Usman's life, but it failed. As Yunfa's persecution of the Muslims continued, they decided it was time for them to have their own government. Usman was, therefore, elected caliph and leader of the revolt against the king of Gobir. He and his followers then withdrew to Gudu, a place fairly far from Gobir, but people still followed him there. Yunfa decided to attack Usman in 1804, thus precipitating the jihad (q.v.), seen as a holy war. In 1808 Gobir was taken by the Fulani Jihadists after killing Sarkin Gobir Yunfa and his chiefs. The jihad removed most Hausa (q.v.) kings from their thrones and replaced them with Fulani Emirs. This marked the beginning of the Sokoto Caliphate.

The empire grew far and wide, even to Ilorin (q.v.), a Yoruba (q.v.) town in the south and Adamawa (q.v.) in the east. But it could not encompass Bornu (q.v.) and some other areas in the Middle Belt. In 1812 Usman Dan Fodio divided the conquered territories into two between his brother Abdullahi (q.v.) and his son Muhammad Bello (q.v.). He later established himself in Sokoto (q.v.) and handed over active military and administrative duties to Abdullahi and Bello. He died in 1817.

-V-

VILLAGE HEADS. Under the Native Authority (q.v.) system in Northern Nigeria, a village was a part of a district and the village was under the authority and leadership of the village head, who had the responsibility for collecting taxes and other forms of revenue. In places where taxes were levied on villages as units, it was the task of the village head to determine how much each taxpayer was to pay. Village heads were members of the district council.

VINCENT, DAVID BROWN. *See* AGBEBI, DR. MOJOLA.

VISION 2010. A panel that was set up by the Abacha regime in 1996 to formulate a long-range strategy for the development of the country. It is modeled upon Malaysia's Vision 2020 panel. The panel was chaired by former head of state Ernest Shonekan, and consisted of 172 members. This membership was a formidable collection of traditional rulers, retired military officers, academics, businesspeople and former administrators. The final report of the panel was submitted in September 1997, and called for a liberalisation of the economy, including deregulation and an accelerated programme of privatisation.

VON ROSEN, CARL GUSTAF. A Swedish pilot who, during the Civil War (q.v.) flew relief materials for the Scandinavian churches (NORD CHURCHAID). He later joined the Biafrans and led the air raid on the Port Harcourt (q.v.) airfield in May 1969. His men also raided Benin and Enugu airfields, when occupied by federal troops, and destroyed many aircraft on the ground.

-W-

WACHUKWU, JAJA ANUCHA. Lawyer and politician, born in 1918 at Mbawsi Ngwa Imo State, he was educated at St. George's School, Mbawsi,

Government School Afikpo, Government College, Umuahia, Yaba Higher College, Lagos and at the Trinity College, University of Dublin in Ireland. He was called to the bar in Dublin and he returned to Nigeria in 1947, and from 1949 to 1952 he was a member of the Ngwa Native Authority Council. In 1951, he was elected into the Eastern House of Assembly and in 1952 to the House of Representatives in Lagos and became the Nigerian Speaker of the federal House of Representatives in 1960, but in October 1960, he was appointed federal Minister for Economic Development. In 1962 he was minister for foreign affairs and Commonwealth relations and in 1965 he was appointed minister of aviation. When the military took over power in 1966, he became managing director of the Jawach Properties and Development Corporation. He also went back into private legal practice in 1966. In 1978 he joined the Nigerian People's Party (NPP) (q.v.) and was elected senator for Imo State (q.v.). He later became the NPP leader in the Senate. He has an honorary LL.D. from the University of Dublin.

WADDELL, REV. HOPE MASTERTON. A Presbyterian missionary sent, in 1846, to Calabar (q.v.) in Eastern Nigeria. He and his party of Jamaican Christians landed at Duke Town, Calabar. They set up mission houses and built schools. They worked hard to put an end to some of the traditional practices like the killing of slaves to accompany a dead chief on his way to eternity and twin murder.

WALLACE-JOHNSON, ISAAC THEOPHILUS AKUNNA. A Sierra Leonian resident in Lagos (q.v.), Wallace-Johnson was born in 1894 at Wilberforce Village in Sierra Leone. In the late 1920s he came to Lagos and worked on the *Daily Times*. In 1931 he saw to the organisation of the African Workers Union, the first Nigerian labour organisation and became its general secretary while at the same time acting as editor of the *Nigerian Daily Telegraph* and contributing to the *Negro Worker*. He soon became unpopular with the colonial authorities and he moved to Accra, Ghana, and joined Dr. Nnamdi Azikiwe (q.v.) in the publication of a new nationalist paper, the *African Morning Post*. In 1938 he returned to Sierra Leone, his native country, where he continued the nationalist struggle. He died in May 1965.

WAR AGAINST INDISCIPLINE (WAI). One of the major problems militating against Nigeria's social, political, and economic development is lack of discipline among many of its people. This lack of discipline is seen in all aspects of life—in the rush and push to board a bus or plane when there are more than enough seats for everyone, in ostentatious living, in election rigging and other malpractices, and generally in various aspects of its economic life. General Olusegun Obasanjo (q.v.) the former Head of State, in his 1977 Jaji Address clearly identified this problem and called for greater discipline in the nation's private and public life. However, the civilian administration that succeeded him was perhaps the most undisciplined that the nation had ever had. The administration provided the atmosphere of free-for-all, leading to the collapse of the national economy and the Second Republic (q.v.).

The military administration that succeeded the Shagari administration, which regarded itself as the offshoot of the Murtala/Obasanjo administration of 1975 to 1979, decided to combat this evil. On March 20, 1984, the chief of staff, Supreme Headquarters, Brigadier Tunde Idiagbon (q.v.) launched a nationwide campaign against indiscipline known as War Against Indiscipline (WAI). The campaign was to bring sanity to the society by replacing indiscipline with discipline in all facets of the nation's life. It involved the propagation of the ideals of national consciousness and patriotism, and it tried to demonstrate the significance of nationhood and national unity by instilling respect for such national symbols as the flag, the anthem, and the pledge. The government intended to use for the campaign the mass media, government information services, community leaders, trade unions, traditional rulers, religious leaders, and many other organisations including youth organisations, that were interested in the objectives of the campaign. The mass media were especially enjoined to set a good example and help instill in the minds of the people the noble ideals of national consciousness and patriotism and to remold and redirect national values and destiny, a task greatly impeded by the Public Officers Protection Against False Accusation Decree Number Four of 1984 which protected public servants against false accusation and the government from embarrassment.

The campaign had limited success. It established what may be called the queueing culture. People began to queue in some public places and they began to conform to the work ethics. The streets also began to be clean. However, the WAI Campaign soon existed more in words than in deeds. Rules and regulations were being circumvented by many people, including even some who carried the WAI badges, and the campaign turned more and more to symbolic events, like competition by states or local government areas for monetary reward for being the cleanest state or local government area in the country. The military administration that succeeded the Buhari administration in August 1985 was aware of this perversion of the campaign. As the new military president, Major-General Ibrahim Babangida (q.v.) said on assuming power: "The War Against Indiscipline shall continue but this time in the minds and conduct of Nigerians, and not by way of symbolism or money-consuming campaigns. This government on its part will ensure that the leadership exhibits proper example." During Babangida's eight-year administration, discipline in many facets of life completely broke down.

In 1993 when General Sani Abacha (q.v.) became head of state after a bloodless coup which overthrew the Interim National Government (ING) (q.v.) of Chief Ernest Shonekan (q.v.), he inaugurated War Against Indiscipline and Corruption (WAI-C). But many Nigerians did not take him too seriously and asked that he declare first and foremost his assets and explain how he became so stupendously wealthy. The belief was that if he could not justify his wealth, he could not wage any war against indiscipline and corruption.

WARRANT CHIEFS. These were chiefs created in the former Eastern Region (q.v.) by warrants issued to them by the colonial government. Many Igbo (q.v.) communities in the region did not have the kind of centralised administration that was characteristic of the emirates of Northern Nigeria and the chiefdoms of Western Nigeria. Since the system of Native Administration (q.v.) being extended to the south after the 1914 amalgamation (q.v.) was based on ruling through the indigenous chiefs, the government resorted to creating such chiefs who were given a cap of office and a warrant of authority; hence they were called "Warrant Chiefs." These chiefs were unpopular because in choosing them the colonial authorities (the district commissioners) did not take into consideration the social and the cultural milieu of the people from which they were being chosen. In some places local traditional rulers were not even considered and therefore, rather than securing the loyalty and confidence of the people, the creation of Warrant Chiefs made for suspicion of British intentions and rule. This suspicion, together with the fact that the Native Courts in which the Chiefs (q.v.) sat were corrupt and the fear that women were to be asked to pay taxes, led to the Aba Riot (q.v.) of 1929, in which many people died and much property was destroyed.

WARRI. Founded in the 15th century by an ousted Benin prince together with his followers, Warri is the chief town of the Itsekiri (q.v.) people. Warri was, for long, the centre of trade, including slave trade in the area. Today Warri has become the centre of administration of many of the oil-producing companies.

WAYAS, DR. JOSEPH. President of the Senate in the Second Republic. He was born on May 21, 1941 in Basang, Obudu, Cross River State (q.v.). He attended Central School, Sankwala Obudu, St. Charles School, Obudu, the Central Commercial Academy, Enugu and the Dennis Memorial Grammar School in Onitsha. He later went to Tottenham Technical College, London, West Bromwich College of Commerce, Science and Technology and Birmingham and Aston Universities in Birmingham. He has a diploma in business administration, a higher diploma in business finance and a diploma in industrial relations. He also has an honorary doctorate degree in law and human letters. He was commissioner for transport in the former South-Eastern State and was appointed later to the Constituent Assembly. Until his election to the Senate, he was director and managing director of many companies.

The December 31, 1983, coup d'état (q.v.), which removed the government of Alhaji Shehu Shagari (q.v.) from power, found Dr. Wayas safely in the United States, where he preferred to remain for some time. Dr. Wayas has authored *Nigeria's Leadership Role in Africa.*

WESLEYAN MISSION. The first Protestant mission to start work in Nigeria. Many of the freed slaves in Sierra Leone (q.v.) who were members of the Wesleyan Church (q.v.) appealed to their London office to send a mission to Nigeria. Rev. T.B. Freeman (q.v.) was sent and arrived first in Badagry (q.v.) in 1842. Rev. Freeman was also the first missionary to reach Abeokuta (q.v.) in the same year. From there the mission spread to Ijebuland and other parts of Nigeria. In 1917 the United African Methodist Church (q.v.) seceded from the Wesleyan Church, and has now spread all over the country.

WEST AFRICAN AIRWAYS CORPORATION (WAAC). The West African Airways Corporation was an Interterritorial statutory corporation which was established in 1946 to serve Nigeria, Ghana (Gold Coast), the Gambia and Sierra Leone on air transportation. The governing body which controlled the activities of the corporation and which formulated its general policies was the West African Air Transport Authority. Members of the authority consisted of representatives of the governments of Nigeria, the Gold Coast, Sierra Leone and the Gambia. West African Airways Corporation operated internal services in Nigeria and the Gold Coast and an intercontinental service from Lagos to Dakar. With this corporation, the air transportation in Nigeria became developed. The corporation developed 28 airports and landing grounds in Nigeria, including the international airports of Lagos and Kano. The activities of the West African Airways Corporation in Nigeria were taken over by the Nigerian Airways when it was established in 1958.

WEST AFRICAN CURRENCY BOARD. The West African Currency Board was established in 1912 with the functions of providing and controlling the supply of currency issued to the West African colonies and protectorates of Nigeria, the Gold Coast, the Gambia and Sierra Leone. It was also to make arrangements to withdraw notes from circulation so that they could be destroyed when necessary, and finally to make arrangements to mint coins for circulation. The activities of the board were wound up in Nigeria with the establishment of the Central Bank of Nigeria in 1958.

WEST AFRICAN EXAMINATION COUNCIL. Established in 1952 by the British colonial authorities, it had the responsibility of determining and conducting examinations, and awarding appropriate certificates in the English-speaking countries of Nigeria, the Gold Coast (q.v.) (now Ghana), Sierra Leone (q.v.) and the Gambia. Liberia, which was not then a member, became a member in 1974.

From its modest beginning of conducting examinations for about 4,000 candidates in 1953, the number of candidates in 1992 rose to many millions. The council took over many examinations which were formerly handled by expatriate bodies such as Cambridge University and the University of London. Among the many examinations that the council conducts, the most popular are the General Certificate Examination and the Senior Secondary Certificate Examination, all which are available for high school graduating students, and are necessary for admission into institutions.

WEST AFRICAN FRONTIER FORCE. After the Royal Niger Company (q.v.) had received its charter in 1885, it organised a small constabulary force made up of five British and two African officers and about 400 rank and file, most of whom were drawn from the Gold Coast (q.v.), now Ghana. But with the French pressure on the company's territory between 1894 and 1897, the British decided to send Sir Frederick Lugard (q.v.) to Africa to raise and command a local force. By 1900, it had become a very disciplined force which helped the British in their campaign in the Ashanti.

In 1901, all the colonial military forces in West Africa were constituted into the West African Frontier Force (WAFF), but each territory was responsible for the maintenance of its own force. In Nigeria the force initially consisted of the Northern Nigerian Regiment, the Lagos Battalion and the Southern Regiment, made up of the Niger Coast Protectorate Force and the Niger Company Constabulary. When Lagos and Southern Nigeria were amalgamated in 1906, the Lagos Battalion became the Second Battalion of the Southern Nigeria Regiment. In 1914 when the Northern and Southern protectorates were amalgamated, the two regiments became known as the Nigerian Regiment.

WEST AFRICAN INSTITUTE OF SOCIAL AND ECONOMIC RESEARCH. Set up in 1950, it was meant to be an institute of social and economic research with no teaching commitments. Its job was to coordinate the social and economic research being carried on in all the British West African territories and to cooperate with other such bodies working on African affairs outside the area. In 1951 the name was changed to the Institute of Social and Economic Research. This was later converted into the Nigerian Institute of Social and Economic Research (NISER) (q.v.), located in Ibadan (q.v.).

WEST AFRICAN PILOT. The *West African Pilot,* a daily newspaper, was set up in 1937 by Dr. Nnamdi Azikiwe (q.v.) who, between 1934 and 1937, was the editor of the *African Morning Post* in Accra, Ghana. The *Pilot* was the first Nigerian newspaper whose editor and proprietor was a Nigerian, who held a diploma in journalism and a graduate degree in political science and anthropology. With the arrival of the *Pilot* on the scene, the general trend among the existing papers changed considerably: they became more nationalist and harped on the evils of colonial rule in the country.

WEST AFRICAN STUDENT UNION (WASU). West African Student Union was founded in London in 1925. It replaced the Nigerian Progress Union, founded previously by Oladipo Solanke (q.v.) a law student from Abeokuta, the capital of the present Ogun State (q.v.). The organisation was of great importance to Nigerian students in the United Kingdom, for it was the social and political center for them. Its objectives, among others, were: to act as a center for information and research on African history, culture and institutions; to promote good will and understanding between Africans and other races, fostering a spirit of national consciousness and racial pride among its members; to provide and maintain accommodation in London for students from West Africa; and to publish a monthly magazine called *WASU*. The organisation served as a pressure group against alien rule in Africa, but its main achievement was in stimulating among its members political and racial consciousness.

WESTERN HOUSE OF ASSEMBLY. Established under the Richards Constitution (q.v.) in 1947, the Western House of Assembly consisted of the chief commissioner as president, 13 other official members and 15–19 unofficial provincial members, 7–11 of whom were to be selected by the native authorities while five were nominated by the governor to represent interests and communities inadequately represented. In addition, three Head Chiefs were nominated by the governor after consultation with the Head Chiefs in the region. In 1951, there was added a House of Chiefs with the lieutenant governor as president, three official members and not more than 50 Chiefs. The House of Assembly consisted of a president, four official members, 80 elected members and not more than three special members. Under the federal constitution of 1954, the bicameral legislative system was retained but the House of Assembly was presided over by a speaker. The House was dissolved in 1966 when the military seized power.

WESTERN HOUSE OF CHIEFS. The Western House of Chiefs was established following the adoption of the Macpherson Constitution (q.v.) of 1951. According to the constitution, the membership of the House of Chiefs comprised the lieutenant governor as president, three official members appointed by him and not more than 50 Chiefs and Head Chiefs. The House exercised legislative power similar to the House of Assembly and apart from the finance bill, the House could initiate any bill. The 1954 constitution removed the lt. governor from the presidency of the House of Chiefs. The Chiefs were then empowered to appoint a president from among themselves. The first president of the Western House of Chiefs was Oba Adesoji Aderemi (q.v.) the Ooni of Ife. Ministers were also appointed from the members of the House of Chiefs. The House of Chiefs was dissolved following the military takeover in 1966. The 1979 constitution did not make any provision for the House of Chiefs.

WESTERN NIGERIA. *See* WESTERN REGION.

WESTERN NIGERIA GOVERNMENT BROADCASTING CORPORATION. The corporation was established in 1959. In partnership with the Overseas Rediffusion (Service), it formed the Western Nigeria Radiovision Service Limited. However the company later became fully owned by the Western Regional government. The corporation had two broadcasting services: the Western Nigeria Broadcasting Service (WNBS) and the Western Nigeria Television Service (WNTV), which was the first television service in black Africa and is popularly called "First in Africa." The WNTV made its first broadcast on October 31, 1959, while the WNBS commenced its commercial broadcasting in May 1960.

The corporation has ceased to function since 1976, when the former Western State was divided into three states, with each state having its own radio station and the Federal Government taking over the WNTV.

WESTERN NIGERIA MARKETING BOARD. The Western Nigeria Marketing Board was established in 1954 to secure the most favorable arrangements for the purchases and exports of Western Nigeria agricultural products. It bought and exported major cash crops like cocoa (q.v.), found in the region. It also invested in cocoa industries and in office complexes like the Cocoa House in Ibadan (q.v.). The board ceased to function with the promulgation of Decree Number 29 of 1977, which established the Commodity Board. The decree vested the functions of the Marketing Board with the Commodity Board.

WESTERN REGION. The Western Region came into being with the adoption of the Richards Constitution (q.v.) of 1946, which provided for regional councils. The region was comprised of the former Ondo, Oyo, Ibadan, Abeokuta, Ijebu colony, Benin and Delta provinces. The region was estimated at 6,085,065 in population in the 1952–53 census but during the 1963–64 census, the region was estimated to be 12,811,837 in population. The people of the region were predominantly Yoruba (q.v.). Other ethnic groups in the region were the Edo, the Ijaw, the Urhobo, and the Itsekiri (qq.v.). Because the Yoruba, the predominant ethnic group, were noted for their high degree of urbanisation, the region contained some of the largest towns in the country like Ibadan (q.v.), Ogbomoso, Osogbo, Ife, Iwo, Abeokuta (q.v.), Ilesha, Benin city (q.v.), Oyo and Iseyin.

The religion of the inhabitants varied from people to people. But Christianity (q.v.) and Islam (q.v.) had strong adherents while adherents of traditional religions still abound. In fact, the region was singular in that adherents of Christian, Islamic and traditional religions might live in the same household without any religious friction.

The region was an agricultural region and proceeds from the export crops in the region used to form a great share of the government external earnings. These crops included cocoa (q.v.), rubber (q.v.), palm produce, yams and many others. The region was also blessed with thick forests providing timber for use in both furniture and house building and also for export.

The seat of the regional government was Ibadan. The first regional government was formed in 1951 by the Action Group Party (q.v.) led by Chief Obafemi Awolowo (q.v.) under whom the region became noted as the initiator of many development programmes in the country. For instance, the free primary education started successfully in the region in 1955—other regions were not able to execute theirs until 1976 when the federal military government stepped in. Furthermore, the first television station in the whole of black Africa was established in the region in 1959 and the premiere stadium in Nigeria, the Liberty Stadium in Ibadan, was opened in 1960. Even before the Action Group Party came into power, the colonial government in 1948 had made Ibadan the seat of the first university in Nigeria, the University of Ibadan (q.v.). Also in 1961 the Action Group government in the region established a regional university in Ile-Ife, the University of Ife (q.v.).

However in 1962, things began to fall apart when an intraparty crisis erupted in the Action Group Party. The resultant effect of the crisis was the state of emergency declared in the region in May 1962. The crisis led to the split in the Action Group—one faction led by Chief Awolowo and another faction led by the premier, Chief S.L. Akintola (q.v.). Chief Akintola was removed from office as premier but at long last he was declared victorious and he continued his premiership until the military took over power in January 1966. During the period of emergency, Dr. Majekodunmi (q.v.) was the administrator of the region.

In 1963, a region was carved out of the Western Region, that is, the Mid-Western Region (q.v.) made up of the former Benin and the Delta provinces. In 1965, trouble started again in the region after the Western Regional election. There were allegations of gross election malpractices. The people swiftly reacted to the election result, which gave victory to the Nigerian National Democratic Party (NNDP) (q.v.) instead of giving it to the Action Group. The people took the law into their hands and began to commit arson, looting and rioting that led to many deaths. The crisis continued until January 1966, when it became obvious that the government had lost control of the region. This and many other factors led to the army takeover of 1966. The region was changed to the Western State with some minor boundary adjustments (e.g., the Lagos colony became Lagos State) in May 1967 and the state was in turn divided into Oyo, Ogun and Ondo (qq.v.) States in 1976. In 1991, Osun State was created from part of Oyo State. In 1996, Ekiti State was created from part of Ondo State.

WESTERN STATE. Created in May 1967, the Western State was bounded on the north by Kwara State (q.v.), on the east by Bendel State (q.v.), in the south by Lagos State (q.v.) and the Atlantic Ocean and in the west by the Republic of Benin (previously known as Dahomey) (q.v.). It was about 29,100 square miles in area and had a population of about 9.5 million people. In May 1967, the Western State was one of the three states created out of the old Western Region—the other two were the Mid-Western State (q.v.) which was originally created in 1963, during the Action Group crisis (q.v.) and the Lagos State.

The state abounded in a wide variety of natural resources: fertile agricultural land, mineral deposits and ocean fishing. The state was a large producer of cocoa (q.v.) and timber, and it exported also rubber, palm oil, coffee and large quantities of citrus.

The state was blessed with two good universities, the University of Ibadan and the University of Ife. The capital of the state was Ibadan (q.v.), traditionally the largest town in West Africa.

The people of the state are predominantly Yorubas, the most urbanised people in all of Nigeria. As such there are, in addition to Ibadan—many large cities like Ogbomoso, Abeokuta, Oshogbo, Iwo, Ile-Ife, Ilesa, Oyo and Iseyin. In 1976, the state was split up into three: Oyo, Ogun and Ondo States (qq.v.).

WESTERN SUDAN. Sudan is a general term applied to the area lying between the Sahara Desert and the tropical rain forest, stretching from the Atlantic Ocean in the west to the Red Sea coast. The Western Sudan covers roughly half of Sudan from the Atlantic Ocean in the west to the area around Lake Chad (q.v.), and is made up in part or in whole of the following states: Senegal, Mauritania, Mali, Upper Volta, Niger, Northern Nigeria, Chad and Sudan. Two major rivers, Senegal and Niger, run through the area and have greatly contributed to the economic development of the area by providing an easy means of communication and encouraging people to settle down. Much of the area can be described as an open country, making it possible for the people to make contact with one another and encouraging the passage of goods and ideas from place to place, thus promoting trade between the Western Sudan and North Africa through many of the trans-Saharan (q.v.)

routes. As a result of this, many empires like Ghana, Mali and Songhai arose, but, because the territories covered by these empires were large and more easily acquired than they could be protected, they soon disintegrated as a result of attacks from neighbouring states.

The original inhabitants of the area were mainly Negroid, but there were non-Negroid elements from the north and northeast. As far back as the medieval period, the Arabs (q.v.), Berbers and Tuaregs (q.v.) had made their way there.

WEY, JOSEPH EDET AKINWALE (VICE-ADMIRAL). A naval officer and marine engineer, born on March 7, 1918, in Calabar (q.v.), Cross River State (q.v.), he went to Holy Cross School, Lagos, Methodist School, Ikot Ekpene and St. Patrick's College, Calabar. In 1939 he joined the Marine Department as a trainee technical apprentice, becoming a junior engineer at the end of his training and in 1949 he attended the London County School of Technology for Marine Engineers. In 1950 he became a marine engineer second class and in 1956 he became a sublieutenant and engineer for the navy. In 1960 he was made lieutenant commander and fleet engineer officer and commander in charge of the Apapa Naval Base in Lagos (q.v.). In 1963 he served in India as captain on Commonwealth exercises. He returned in March 1964 to become commodore and head of the Nigerian Navy. In 1966 he was appointed to the Supreme Military Council. He attended the Aburi Conference (q.v.) in January 1977 between Yakubu Gowon (q.v.) and Odumegwu Ojukwu (q.v.) in an attempt to ward off any future hostilities. When the Civil War (q.v.) started, the Nigerian Navy under him effectively blockaded the Biafran ports throughout the war. On July 27, 1967, the navy captured Bonny and blocked Biafra's route to sea.

He was promoted to rear admiral on January 2, 1967 and in 1971 he became commissioner for establishments. He also acted as commissioner for labour in 1971 and was appointed vice-admiral in the same year. In 1973 he was appointed chief of staff, Supreme Headquarters and was also the chairman of the Administrative Committee of the Nigerian Defence Academy and responsible to the Commander-in-Chief of the Armed Forces. He retired in 1975.

WHITLEY COUNCIL. Following the Cowan Report (q.v.) of 1948, asking the government to provide facilities for consultation and negotiation between the government, its departments and trade unions, government set up Whitley Councils with the function of determining the general principles governing conditions of service such as recruitment, remunerations, hours of work, promotion, discipline and tenure. Decisions were to be taken by agreement and not by voting, but such decisions required the approval of the governor.

WILLIAMS, CHIEF FREDERICK ROTIMI ALADE. A constitutional lawyer who has had great influence on the constitutional development of the country since the 1950s. Born on December 16, 1920, in Lagos (q.v.), he was educated at CMS Grammar School in Lagos and at the University of Cambridge in England and was later called to the bar. Returning to Nigeria, he served in many important positions in the former Western Regional government, including those of the attorney general and minister of justice. In 1975 he was appointed chairman of the Constitution Drafting Committee, which drafted the Second Republican Constitution of 1979. He is in private legal practice and a member of the Senior Advocates of Nigeria (SAN).

WILLINK COMMISSION. As a result of the ethnic minorities' demands for separate regional identity to remove the fear of domination by the ethnic majorities in each of the three regions that made up the Federation, the British government agreed to set up in 1957 a Minorities Commission to look into the fears of ethnic minorities in all parts of the country and to propose means of allaying the fears whether or not they were well founded. The commission was chaired by Sir Henry Willink, a lawyer and former member of Parliament in London, and it is sometimes called the Willink Commission. The commission reported in July 1958, but did not recommend the creation of new regions as a means to allay those fears. Rather it, among other things, recommended the inclusion of fundamental human rights (q.v.) in the federal constitution. *See also* MINORITIES PROBLEM.

WOMEN'S IMPROVEMENT SOCIETY. *See* NATIONAL COUNCIL OF WOMEN'S SOCIETIES.

WOMEN'S MOVEMENT OF NIGERIA. *See* NATIONAL COUNCIL OF WOMEN'S SOCIETIES.

WOMEN'S RIOT OF 1929. *See* ABA RIOT.

WOOD SCULPTURE. Wood sculpture is common in many parts of Nigeria, but because wood does not last too long, no one can say for certain when it first developed. Generally, good, durable wood is used and is in one piece. Some wood sculptures have been used to represent ancestors like the sculpture made by Fakeye (q.v.) to represent Oduduwa (q.v.), the ancestor of the Yoruba (q.v.) Obas (q.v.), now in Odudua Hall, Obafemi Awolowo University, in Ile-Ife. In some places, the wooden sculpture represents the power of spirits like the *Ikenga* figures among the Igbo (q.v.). Some represent gods in traditional religions like Shango (q.v.) or Obatala in Yorubaland. The Yoruba have also traditionally made wooden figures called *Ibeji,* which are connected with the birth of twins, and if one of the twins died, the figure used to be specially cared for. There are other wooden sculptures that have no religious or traditional beliefs attached to them. These are works of art that people buy simply for art appreciation and decoration.

-Y-

YABA HIGHER COLLEGE. Yaba Higher College was opened in Lagos in 1934 with only 18 students. The college was to provide the manpower needed to fill the government technical departments. Unlike the Fourah Bay College (q.v.) in Sierra Leone, Yaba College was not affiliated with any English university; hence the college awarded its own diplomas and certificates. Thus examination standards were Nigerian and educated Nigerians resented that it was only a Nigerian diploma recognised in Nigeria that would be obtained from the college. This and other deficiencies in the institution led to the formation of the Nigerian Youth Movement (q.v.) in 1934.

Besides the medical school, opened in 1930, Yaba Higher College was the first postsecondary institution in Nigeria. The products of the college were among the early nationalists in Nigeria. The name of the college was changed in 1969 to Yaba College of Technology. The college offers courses leading to the award of both Ordinary National Diploma (OND) and Higher National Diploma (HND).

YAMS. A very important food crop in Nigeria, yams are planted by cutting its tuber into seed yams and planting them either toward the end of the raining season or as the new rains begin. Generally, heaps or mounds of earth are made for them to plant them in. Yams are climbing plants and need some stakes or other support to climb upon. They have a large storage tuber that contains a lot of carbohydrate but very little protein. The tuber can be boiled or roasted and eaten, and it can be pounded into what is known as pounded yam, and it can be made into flours for another kind of food called Amala in Western Nigeria. There are many varieties of yams. There is the water yam, the white yam, the yellow yam and also potato yam. They all need an annual rainfall of 1,000 millimetres to 1,200 millimetres.

YAR'ADUA, MAJ. GEN. SHEHU MUSA. Born in 1943 in Katsina (q.v.), Katsina State (q.v.), Major General Shehu Musa Yar'Adua attended the Government Secondary School in Katsina, then the Nigerian Military Training College in Zaria (q.v.), the Royal Military College, Sandhurst, and the Command and Staff College in England. He was a platoon commander between 1964 and 1965, a battalion adjutant from 1965 to 1967, assistant adjutant general, Second Division in 1967 and commander, Sixth Infantry Brigade in the Second Infantry Division in 1968 and became commander, Ninth Infantry Brigade in 1969. After the 1976 abortive coup (q.v.), during which the Head of State, General Murtala R. Muhammed (q.v.) was killed, Yar'Adua was, for geopolitical considerations, catapulted from relative obscurity as a lieutenant colonel to the rank of a brigadier and became chief of staff Supreme Headquarters and also the vice chairman of the Supreme Military Council (q.v.), posts which he occupied until his retirement when the military in October 1979 handed over power to an elected president. After his retirement, he went into business, ranging from banking, farming, manufacturing, shipping and publishing.

When the bans on political activities were lifted in 1989, Yar'Adua was the prime mover and the financier of the Peoples' Front of Nigeria (q.v.), one of the 13 organisations which applied to the National Electoral Commission (q.v.) for recognition as political parties, and later became a major faction of the Social Democratic Party (SDP) (q.v.), one of the two parties formed and funded by the military government in 1989. Yar'Adua, in his ambition to be president of the Third Republic (q.v.) used his money and organisational ability to gain control of the SDP. And when his ambition was scuttled in 1992 by the military government cancelling all the primary elections which he was poised to win, he kept a firm grip on the party machine, unmatched, even by Chief M.K.O. Abiola (q.v.), the party's flagbearer.

When the result of the presidential election of June 12, 1993 (q.v.), which Chief Abiola won, was annulled, Yar'Adua, seeing an opportunity to begin a new struggle for the presidency, supported the annulment and began afresh to put his political machine in order. He was a member of the 1994 Constitutional Conference (q.v.), set up to fashion a new constitution for the country, an opportunity he adroitly used to begin to organise a new political party.

In March 1995, Yar'Adua was arrested with his Commander-in-Chief, General Olusegun Obasanjo (q.v.) for, as the Abacha government put it, plotting a coup to overthrow the government. He, together with Obasanjo and about 40 other persons, military and civilians, were secretly tried by a military tribunal and he was sentenced to life imprisonment. Many people did not believe that Yar'Adua—who was planning for a presidential campaign when the military government would lift the ban on political activity—would interest himself in a coup that would prolong the realisation of his presidential ambition.

On December 8, 1997, Yar'Adua died in prison. While officials claimed that he died of natural causes, the suspicion was widespread that he was killed for his opposition to the Abacha regime. Ironically, even in death Yar'Adua remained one of the country's most powerful politicians. His political network remained intact, and it played a critical role in securing the election of Olusegun Obasanjo as president in 1999. The continuing vitality of Yar'Adua's political network also reflects the eclipse of the older northern politicians by the younger "Kaduna mafia." Yar'Adua held the traditional title, Tafidan Katsina.

YELLOW FEVER. A disease caused by a virus transmitted by a small dark-coloured mosquito known as Aedes aegypti. It is characterized by chills, severe headache, backache, blood in the stool and general weakness. The temperature may rise up to 40°C and the pulse rate to about 100 per minute. There may be upper abdominal pain, nausea and vomiting. After about three days, the patient becomes depressed and lethargic. The headache may diminish, but jaundice develops. If not properly treated, the patient may become delirious before dying. However, proper care will lead to complete recovery and relapses do not occur. In Nigeria, epidemics of yellow fever occurred in 1946, 1954, and 1969. The disease can be prevented by not allowing infected mosquitoes access to human beings and, most important, through immunisation.

YERO, BUBA. Buba Yero was born in about 1762 near Mada in what is now known as Numan District. He was of Fulani descent and during his youth, he was a student under Shehu Usman Dan Fodio (q.v.) at Gobir. He later became a mallam and a preacher. On hearing about Shehu's Jihad (q.v.) in 1804, he came to Gobir, where Usman was staying. It was there he received a flag from Shehu Usman Dan Fodio as one of the 14 flag bearers he sent to conquer the Hausa States (q.v.). He was asked to go to Gombe and became the first Emir of Gombe in 1804. During the Jihad, he conquered the Muri people and the areas in the valleys of the Gongola and Kilengi rivers. He died in 1841 and was succeeded by his son, Sule, who died just three years later.

YOLA. The capital of Adamawa State (q.v.), Yola's history dates back to the conquest of Modibbo Adama, the Fulani (q.v.) lieutenant of Usman Dan Fodio (q.v.) in the Upper Benue region of Nigeria, who made Yola the headquarters of the ruling family. During the colonial era, it was the headquarters of the Adamawa province, and when Gongola State (q.v.) was created in 1976, Yola was its capital. Yola is also a commercial centre that attracts a high rate of rural-urban migration as young people throng to the major cities in search of jobs.

One of the important festivals in Yola is the fishing festival called "Njuwa," which is celebrated annually and attracts many tourists. The town has a number of higher educational institutions such as the Federal Advanced Teachers College and the College of Preliminary Studies. There is also the Federal University in Yola.

YORUBA. The Yoruba are one of the three largest groups of people in Nigeria, and they live concentrated in Lagos, Ogun, Oyo, Osun, Ondo and Kwara States (qq.v.). Some of them also live in the Repubilc of Benin (q.v.).

They constitute an ethnic group, but there are subethnic groups like the Oyo, Ekiti, Owo, Ijebu (q.v.) and Egba (q.v.), all of whom speak different dialects of the same language. As a result of the slave trade (q.v.) through which many Yoruba people were taken to the Americas, there are also groups of Yoruba people in Brazil and in other places.

The origin of the Yoruba is not clearly known, but tradition has it that they are descendants of Oduduwa (q.v.) who migrated from the east probably from Upper Egypt or Nubia, and settled in Ile-Ife (q.v.). This appears to be confirmed by the similarities observed between the Egyptian sculpture and the Ife marbles seen in Ile-Ife. According to tradition, Oduduwa, had seven children from whom grew the various "tribes" that made up the Yoruba Nation. These were Owu, Ketu, Benin, Ila, Sabe, Olupopo of Popo and Oranmiyan (q.v.) who settled in Oyo.

During the 17th century, the leading Yoruba State was Oyo, which developed an empire extending to Borgu (q.v.) in the north, and in the south and southwest to Egbaland, and all the way to Dahomey (q.v.), now the Republic of Benin. The empire collapsed as a result of the rise of other states in Yorubaland to the south of Oyo town, rebellion and attacks from the Fulani (q.v.) Jihadists of Usman Dan Fodio (q.v.) in the early 19th century. This caused the Yoruba in Oyo and its surrounding areas to move south and settle in the present-day Oyo. In the 19th century, as a result of intense competition for trade with the Europeans especially in slaves and weapons, internecine wars ravaged the area, leading to the emergence of towns like Ibadan (q.v.) and Abeokuta (q.v.). Yoruba wars were fought between states like Ibadan, Abeokuta, Ijaye and Ekiti, and peace only came when the British took steps to pacify the area. By 1896 Yorubaland had been pacified and brought under British protection from Lagos.

Traditionally, Yoruba people were farmers growing crops like yams (q.v.), maize, cassava (q.v.), cocoa (q.v.), oil palm (q.v.) and vegetables. They usually lived in large towns and travelled to their farms in the surrounding areas, or some of them came home to the town only at the weekends or monthends. Because of the large size of their towns and cities, trade became important, and they had many large markets where local and foreign goods were exchanged.

In Yorubaland, the family is not only nuclear; it also extends to cousins, uncles, nieces, nephews and aunts of many generations. Traditionally, Yoruba houses were built around a square yard. It was here that the head of the family lived with all his relations in an extended family system. Inheritance was through the father and so was succession to titles. Women have always played important roles in the social, religious and economic life of the area. In Yorubaland Christianity (q.v.), Islam (q.v.) and traditional religions (q.v.) coexist most amicably.

The Yoruba have rich tradition in drama, masquerades (q.v.), language and poetry. The terra-cotta and bronze sculptures of Ife, which date back to the 13th century, are among the finest in the world. They also have a long tradition of wood carving, which today is continued by many artists like Lamidi Fakeye (q.v.) of Obafemi Awolowo University, Ile-Ife.

Before the arrival of the British, the Yoruba had developed fairly large political organisations and traditional constitutional monarchy. Of all the peoples of Nigeria, the Yoruba are the most urbanised. They have been exposed to more intensive westernisation than any other part of the country.

YORUBA LANGUAGE. Yoruba language is spoken by over 18 million people. It is generally classified as one of the Kwa branch of the Niger-Congo family. There are regional and local dialects, but there is the standard Yoruba language which is taught in all schools and universities.

Yoruba language has a rich poetry which, though was not written down until recently, was passed down orally from generation to generation. These are generally found in *Ewi*, which used to be sung at traditional festivals and were usually comments on events and people; *Odu*, which are learnt and recited by Ifa priests and people learned in the *Ifa* system; *Oriki*, which are praise songs of families reminding a person of his ancestors: where they came from and their past feats (The talking drum (q.v.) beautifully performs this function.); *Ijala*, which hunters and worshippers of Ogun, Egungun (Masquerades [q.v.]) are specialists in, and *Rara*, which are generally recited by women during festivals.

YORUBA TOWNS. Most Yoruba towns, according to Samuel Johnson's *History of the Yoruba* have certain identifiable features. They each have a founder who first settled there and attracted others to settle with him. The towns were either farmsteads or rest places where people could have some refreshments and, if it was a popular place or a crossroad, a market could spring up. When houses were built, and what might be called a village or small town was formed, the original founder was made the Baale (father of the land). The Baale then appointed his Chiefs (q.v.) like Otun, right-hand man, Osi, left-hand man and Balogun, the War Chief. In most Yoruba towns, the principal marketplace is in the centre of the town and in front of the Oba's or King's palace. For defensive purposes, many Yoruba towns had walls around them—this was a ditch or moat dug around the towns.

YUNFA. Ruler of Gobir from 1801 to 1808 during which time the jihad (q.v.) of Usman Dan Fodio (q.v.) began and swept through the Hausaland. As a young man, he was tutored by Dan Fodio (q.v.), a Muslim scholar and preacher, who was then resident at Gobir. Upon his father's death, Dan Fodio supported his ascendancy to the throne against his rival cousins. But relations between Usman and Yunfa soon became strained. As Usman became popular in the kingdom, Yunfa became apprehensive of the threat posed by Islam (q.v.) to traditional authorities. Yunfa made some attempts at assassinating Dan Fodio but failed. Usman and his followers then withdrew to Gudu a place fairly far from Gobir. But Usman still attracted many followers to Gudu, which added to his perceived threat. Yunfa decided to attack Usman in 1804, precipitating the jihad. He was killed during the war at Alkalawa by the forces of Muhammad Bello (q.v.), the son of Usman Dan Fodio.

YUSUF, BELLO MAITAM. Minister for commerce in the Shehu Shagari (q.v.) administration during the Second Republic (q.v.). Born on April 22, 1945, in Gwaram, Kano State (q.v.), he received an LL.B. degree from Ahmadu Bello University in Zaria (q.v.) in 1973 and was called to the bar in 1974. In 1979 he was appointed minister for internal affairs, and while in that office, he ordered the deportation of Alhaji Abdurahman Shugaba (q.v.), the Great Nigeria People's Party (GNPP) (q.v.) majority leader in the Borno State House of Assembly because he was said not to be a Nigerian, and was therefore a security risk.

Yusuf remained active in politics, and was briefly imprisoned in December 1991 (along with 11 other political notables) for violating Decree No. 25 of 1987, which prohibited "old breed" politicians from participating in politics.

-Z-

ZAMFARA STATE. Created out of Sokoto State by the Abacha regime on October 1, 1996. Its capital is Gusau.

AL-ZAKZAKY, SHEIKH MU'ALLIM IBRAHIM. Born in May 1953 in Zaria (q.v.) in the Northern Region. He is a prominent Islamic activist. Sheikh Al-Zakzaky studied economics at Ahmadu Bello University (ABU) in Zaria, completing his studies in 1979. While at ABU Al-Zakzaky was active in the Muslim Students' Society, and helped organise a number of violent protests, including a 1978 attack on a drinking club, and a 1979 attack on the vice-chancellor's house. In 1980 he led demonstrations in the city, calling for a second jihad (q.v.) and the implementation of Shari'a law nationally leading to Al-Zakzaky's imprisonment from 1981–84.

Since that time, Al-Zakzaky's aggressive opposition to the government, and his calls for the establishment of an Islamic regime have attracted an increasing number of followers, particularly in the north. He has been in and out of prison on charges of inciting violence in a number of incidents. He was incarcerated from 1987–89 on charges of contributing to the Kafancan riots and from 1996–98 in connection with a conflict at Kaduna Polytechnic. Violent clashes between Al-Zakzaky's followers and the police have become regular in northern Nigeria.

ZANGON-KATAF. A town inhabited by the Kataf and Hausa (q.v.) peoples in the Kaduna State (q.v.) of Northern Nigeria (q.v.). The town came into the limelight in 1992 as a result of the ethnic and religious (Christian [q.v.] versus Muslim [q.v.]) riots which took place there during the year and the Okadigbo tribunal set up by the Federal Government (q.v.) to try all the accused. The Katafs, the indigenous people of Zango-Kataf, had always resented the dominance of the Hausa people over the affairs of their area. There had been before then farmland disputes and disputes over location of marketplaces. The first led to a wave of violence in February 1992, and, before the Commission of Inquiry set up to look into the crisis could submit its report, another disturbance started on May 15, extending to May 16, 1992, before it was brought under control. The disturbance spread to the state capital, Kaduna (q.v.), leading to the loss of many lives and property.

As a result of the disturbances, six of the seven accused persons—all Christians, including a retired Major-General, Zamani Lekwot, a former governor of Rivers State (q.v.) and a former ambassador to Senegal and Mauritania—were found guilty. The tribunal which tried them was alleged to be biased in its composition with five Muslims, three of whom were Hausa of Zango background and two Christians, one of whom was the chairman of the tribunal, Mr. Justice Benedict Okadigbo and the other Mr. Godwin Graham-Douglas, a Senior Advocate of Nigeria (SAN) who resigned from the tribunal, as he said, on issues of principle because of the many irregularities. The tribunal had no Kataf member on it. To complicate matters, the federal military government issued Decree 55 of 1992, which made the decisions of the tribunal unassailable in any court of law. There could be no appeal from its decisions. The provisions of this decree compelled the defence lawyers, led by Chief G.O.K. Ajayi, to withdraw from the case in anger and frustration for it was clear to them that the seven accused persons, all Katafs, could not have justice. Justice Okadigbo was undaunted and returned a verdict of death by hanging for six of the accused, including Zamani

Lekwot, while the seventh person was discharged and acquitted. There was a great uproar against the conviction, both nationally and internationally. In October 1995, Zamani Lekwot and others convicted with him were set free.

ZARIA. The capital of Zazzau, one of the original seven Hausa States (q.v.). The *Zaria Chronicle* gave a list of 60 rulers of Zaria before the Fulani (q.v.) conquest in the early 19th century. The 22nd ruler known as Bakua Turuku was said to have had two daughters, Amina (q.v.) and Zaria. Amina, the elder daughter was said to have travelled extensively and to have built a camp wherever she halted. She was famous in war, conquering many neighbouring states, including Kano (q.v.) and Katsina (q.v.) and all the way to Nupeland and Kwararafa. Her younger daughter, Zaria, gave her name to the capital city of Zazzau, Zaria, which was founded about 1536.

When the news of the Fulani uprising in Gobir in 1804 came to Zaria, Mallam Musa, a Fulani who had been a preacher in Zaria, went to Gobir and received a flag from Usman Dan Fodio (q.v.). On getting back to Zaria, the ruler, King Makau fled with many of his people and settled in Abuja (q.v.). In 1901 the Emir (q.v.) of Zaria requested that a company of British soldiers be stationed in Zaria as a protection against Kontagora, and by 1903 the city was under the control of the British troops. Zaria is now a big manufacturing and educational centre, the seat of Ahmadu Bello University (q.v.).

ZIKIST MOVEMENT. In 1945, Dr. Nnamdi Azikiwe (q.v.) announced that there was a plot to assassinate him. Many people were critical of this so-called plot and in February 1946 three young admirers of his (Mr. Kolawole Balogun, Mr. M.C.K. Ajuluchuku and Abiodun Aloba) began to form the Zikist Movement to defend their hero. The movement had a philosophy which they called Zikism, which aimed at redeeming Africa from political servitude and economic weakness. Because of its militancy against and uncompromising attitude toward colonial rule, the government saw it as an organisation whose purposes and methods were dangerous to the good of the colonial government and it was thus banned in 1950 after a Zikist member had made an unsuccessful attempt on the life of the government's chief secretary, Mr. Foot. But soon after, its members regrouped to form themselves into another organisation, the Freedom Movement (q.v.).

"ZIK MUST GO." A call by 31 members of the National Council of Nigerian Citizens (NCNC) (q.v.) on Dr. Nnamdi Azikiwe (Zik) (q.v.) to resign as the Eastern Regional premier and party president. The leaders of this call were Dr. K.O. Mbadiwe, who was then federal Minister of Commerce and Chief Kolawole Balogun, federal Minister of Information. They accused Zik of splitting the party asunder and of losing interest in the party. Rather than

Zik going, it was these leaders and some others who were expelled by the National Executive Committee of the NCNC Party.

ZONING. According to the constitution of the National Party of Nigeria (NPN) (q.v.), zoning refers to the convention to recognise the need for adequate geographical spread in the allocation of offices within the party. The country was divided into four zones, Northern, Western, Eastern and Minority. In 1978, the presidency went to the Northern Zone, the vice presidency to the Eastern Zone, the chairmanship of the party to the Western Zone and the presidency of the Senate to the Minority Zone. By this means, all the major ethnic groups were brought together at the top-most level of decision making in a kind of consensus. In fact, zoning is the NPN's practical interpretation of the constitutional requirement of the federal character in the governing body of political parties. The offices that are zoned at the national level are those of the national Chairman, the President, Vice President, President and Deputy President of the Senate, National Secretary, Speaker and Deputy Speaker of the House of Representatives, the Senate Leader and Majority Leader of the House of Representatives. The idea is that these offices will rotate periodically among the zones.

ZUNGERU. A town on the Kaduna River, chosen in 1902 as the headquarters of the Northern Provinces of Nigeria. In 1917, the colonial authorities moved the headquarters from there to Kaduna (q.v.), leaving the town practically abandoned.

ZUNGUR, SA'ADU. One of the first nationalist leaders from northern Nigeria. Born in 1915 to the imam of Bauchi, he studied at Yaba College in Lagos in the 1930s, where he was introduced to nationalist politics. From 1938–48, he held a number of different teaching positions in Kano, Zaria and Bauchi. In the early 1940s, he helped form the Zaria Friendly Society with Abubakar Imam, and from 1943–46, he participated in the Bauchi discussion Group and Bauchi General Improvement Union, all three considered to be forerunners of the political parties that emerged several years later in the north.

In 1948, Sa'adu Zungur joined the National Council of Nigeria and the Cameroons (NCNC), which was led by Nnamdi Azikiwe. At the time, the participation of one of the north's most prominent politicians in what was considered to be an "Igbo" party was quite surprising. By the early 1950s, however, Zungur had come to feel that the NCNC was not sufficiently attuned to the problems of the north, and he left to briefly join the main conservative party of his home region, the Northern People's Congress (NPC). This affiliation proved to be short-lived, and in 1954 he joined the radical

Northern Elements Progressive Union (NEPU), of which he was an active member until his death from illness in 1958.

Despite his early death, Zungur's influence continues to be seen in the tradition of radical northern politics he helped establish. This tradition was best exemplified in Aminu Kano (q.v.), who was considered to be his protégé. Zungur's ideas combined Islam, nationalism and a radical opposition to tradition authority. He expressed many of these ideas in his poetry, which is still read in Northern Nigeria.

Bibliography

GENERAL

Abiola, M.K.O. *Legend of Our Time: The Thoughts of M.K.O. Abiola*. Lagos: Tanus Communications, 1993.

Adejuyigbe, Omolade. *Social Considerations in Political Territorial Organization of Society*. Ile-Ife: University Press, 1982.

Adesina, Lam. *Voice of a Patriot*. Ibadan: Teton Book Makers, 1992.

Afigbo, A.E. *Of Men and War: Women and History*. Enugu: Sandax Nigeria, 1992.

Afolayan, A.A., ed. *A Geography of Nigerian Development*. Ibadan: Heinemann, 1983.

Ajayi, J.F., and Michael Crowder, ed. *History of West Africa*. Vol. 2. New York: Columbia University Press, 1972.

Alubo, Sylvester Ogoh. *Beyond the Illusion of Primary Health Care in an African Society: The Political Economy of Health Care and Crisis*, 1995.

Amadi, Elechi. *Ethics in Nigerian Culture*. Ibadan: Heinemann, 1982.

Amadi, Kate. *The Sex War*. Enugu, Nigeria: Delta, 1992.

Ananaba, Wogu. *The Trade Union Movement in Africa: Promise and Performance*. London: C. Hurst, 1979.

Arikpo, Okoi. *The Development of Modern Nigeria*. Harmondsworth, England: Penguin Books, 1967.

Austin, Dennis. *West Africa and the Commonwealth*. London: Penguin Books, 1957.

Bamgbose, Ayo. "Nigeria's Choice." *UNESCO Courier* 47, no. 2 (Feb. 1994).

Barrett, David B. "Who's Who of African Independent Church Leaders." *Risk* 7, no. 3 (1971).

Boahen, A.A. *Topics in West African History*. London: Longman, 1965.

Bown, Lalage, and Michael Crowder, ed. *Proceedings of the First International Congress of Africanists*. London, 1964.

Buchanan, K.M., and J.C. Pugh. *Land and Peoples of Nigeria*. London: University of London Press, 1955.

Cary, Joyce. *Britain and West Africa*. London: Longmans, Green, 1940.

———. *The Case for African Freedom*. London: Secker and Warburg, 1941.

Cervanka, Zdenek. *The Organization of African Unity and Its Charter*. London: Hurst and Co., 1969.

Dambazau, Abdul-Rahman Bello. *Law and Criminality in Nigeria: An Analytical Discourse*. Ibadan: University Press, 1994.

Davidson, Basil. *The New West Africa*. London: G. Allen and Unwin, 1953.

Du Bois, Woe, Burghardt. *The World and Africa*. New York: Viking, 1947.

Duignam, Peter, and Lewis H. Gann, ed. *Colonialism in Africa, 1870–1960*. Vol. 2. Cambridge: Cambridge University Press, 1970.

Eades, J.S. *Strangers and Traders: Yoruba Migrants, Market and the State in Northern Ghana*. Edinburgh: Edinburgh University Press, 1995.

Echema, Austin. *Corporate Personality in Traditional Igbo Society and the Sacrament of Reconciliation*. New York: Peter Lang, 1995.

Fage, J.D. *An Introduction to the History of West Africa*. Cambridge: Cambridge University Press, 1955.

Flint, J.E. *Nigeria and Ghana*. Englewood Cliffs, N.J.: Prentice Hall, 1966.

Forde, D., and P. Kaberry. *West African Kingdom in the Nineteenth Century*. London: Oxford University Press, 1967.

Forrest, Tom. *Politics and Economic Development in Nigeria*. Boulder, Colo.: Westview Press, 1995.

Freville, Nicholas, and C. John Caldwell. *Let's Visit Nigeria*. New York: The John Day Co., 1970.

Garvey, Amy Jacques, ed. *Philosophy and Opinions of Marcus Garvey*. New York: Universal Publishing House, 1923.

Graf, W.D., ed. *Towards a Political Economy of Nigeria: Critical Essays*. Benin City: Koda Publishers, 1981.

Hailey, Lord. *An African Survey Revised*. London: Oxford University Press, 1938.

———. *Native Administration in British African Territories*. 5 vols. London: Her Majesty's Stationary Office, 1951.

Haives, C. Grove, ed. *Africa Today*. Baltimore: Johns Hopkins University Press, 1955.

Hancock, W.K. *Survey of British Commonwealth Affairs*. 2 vols. London: Oxford University Press, 1952.

Hargreaves, J.O. *Prelude to the Partition of West Africa*. London: Macmillan, 1963.

Hodgkin, Thomas. *Nationalism in Colonial Africa*. London: Frederick Muller, 1956.

Horton, James Africanus B. *West African Countries and Peoples and a Vindication of the African Race*. London: W.J. Johnson of 121 Fleet Street, 1868.

Hovet, Thomas Jr. *Africa in the United Nations*. Evanston, Ill.: Northwestern University Press, 1963.

Howard, C., and J. Plumb. *West African Explorers*. London: Oxford University Press, 1951.

Huntar, Oluwatoyin. *Traditional African Environments: The Science, the History, the Thought Processes*. Lagos: Touchi Ltd., 1992.

Jennings, W. Ivor. *The Approach of Self-Government*. Cambridge: Cambridge University Press, 1956.

Kirk-Green, A., and D. Rimmer. *Nigeria since 1970: A Political and Economic Outline*. London: Hodder and Stoughton, 1981.

Kogbe, C.A., ed. *Geology of Nigeria*. Lagos: Elizabethan, 1976.

Mair, L.P. *Native Policies in Africa*. London: Routledge, 1935.

Matory, James Lorand. *Sex and the Empire That Is No More: Gender and the Politics of Metaphor in Oyo Yoruba Religion*. Minneapolis: University of Minnesota Press, 1994.

McPhee, Allan. *The Economic Revolution in West Africa*. London, 1926.

Melson, R., and H. Wolpe, ed. *Nigeria Modernization and the Politics of Communalism*. East Lansing: Michigan State University Press, 1971.
Morel, E.D. *Nigeria: Its Peoples and Problems*. London: Frank Cass and Company Ltd., 1908.
———. *Trading Monopolies In West Africa*. Liverpool: Richardson and Sons, 1901.
Murdock, G.P. *Africa Its Peoples and Their Culture History*. New York: Dakar, 1961.
Novicki, Margaret A. "Interview: Adebayo Adedeji." *Africa Report* 38, no. 6 (Nov.-Dec. 1993).
Obasanjo, Olusegun. *Hope for Africa: Selected Speeches of Olusegun Obasanjo*. Abeokuta, Ogun State, Nigeria: ALF Publications, 1993.
Odemerho, F.O., and A. Arwunudiogba. "The Effects of Changing Cassava Management Practices on Soil Loss: A Nigerian Example." *The Geographical Journal* 159, no. 1 (March 1993): 63.
Ogundipe-Leslie, Molara. *Re-Creating Ourselves: African Women and Critical Transformations*. Trenton, N.J.: Africa World Press, 1994.
Oho, Fred. *With Their Boots On: The C-130 Tragedy. In Memory of the C-130 Air Crash Victims of September 26, 1962*. Lagos: Transcan Graphics, 1993.
Ojo, J. Afolabi. *The Cultural Dimension in Geography*. Ile-Ife: University Press, 1973.
———. *Yoruba Culture: A Geographical Analysis*. London: University of London Press, 1966.
Okonkwo, Rina. *Protest Movements in Lagos, 1908–1930*. Lewiston, N.Y.: E. Mellen Press, 1995.
Oluwole, Richard. *The Management of Solid Waste in Nigerian Cities*. New York: Garland Publications, 1992.
Osaghae, Eghosa. *Crippled Giant: Nigeria since Independence*. Bloomington: Indiana University Press, 1998.
Oseni, Kayode. *InsideOut: The Circumstance of Nigeria Police Force*. Victorial Island, Lagos: Raose, 1993.
Otegbetu, Junji. *Awo and the Politics of the 90s*. Yaba, Lagos: Macmillan, Nigeria, 1991.
Oyediran, ed. *Survey of Nigerian Affairs, 1975*. Lagos: OUP, 1978.
Padmore, George. *Africa: Britain's Third Empire*. London: Dobson, 1949.
———. *How Britain Governs Africa*. London: Dobson, 1936.
———. *Pan Africanism or Communism?* London: Dobson, 1956.
Pedlay, F.J. *West Africa*. London: Methuen, 1951.
Peil, Margaret. *Lagos: The City Is the People*. Boston, Mass.: G.K. Hall, 1991.
Perham, Margery. *Africans and British Rule*. Oxford: Oxford University Press, 1941.
Phelps-Stokes Fund. *The Atlantic Charter and Africa from American Standpoint*. New York: Committee on Africa, 1942.
Record, Wilson. *The Negro and the Communist Party*. Chapel Hill: University of North Carolina Press, 1949.
Robinson, K., and F. Madden, ed. *Essays in Imperial Government*. Oxford: Oxford University Press, 1963.
Royal Institute of International Affairs. *Nigeria: The Political and Economic Background*. London: Oxford University Press, 1960.
Senghor, Léopold, Sédar. *On African Socialism*. London and Durmow: Pall Mall Press, 1964.

Shagari, S. *My Vision of Nigeria*. London: Frank Cass, 1981.
Thompson, Sdewale. *Reminiscences at the Bar*. Ibadan: Bookcraft Ltd. and Associated Book Makers, Nig. Ltd., 1991.
Udo, Reuben, K. *Migrant Tenant Farmers of Nigeria: A Geographical Study of Rural Migrations*. Lagos: African University Press, 1975.
———. *The Human Geography of Tropical Africa*. Ibadan: Heinemann, 1982.
Umukoro, Simon Obikpeko. *Drama and Politics in Nigeria*. Ibadan: Kraft Books, 1994.
William, G., ed. "Nigerian Issue." *Review of African Political Economy* 13 (1979).
———. *State and Society in Nigeria*. Lagos: Afrographika, 1980.
William, G., and T. Turner. "Nigeria." *In West African States,* edited by J. Dunn, 132–72. Cambridge: Cambridge University Press, 1979.
Williams, Pat. *Religious Impact on the Nation State: The Nigerian Predicament*. Aldershot, England, and Brookfield, Vt: Avebury, 1995.
Wright, Stephen. *Nigeria: Struggle for Stability and Status*. Boulder, Colo.: Westview Press, 1998.

ECONOMICS

Abdullahi, Ango. *The Role of Agriculture in Reversing the Present Economic Crisis in Nigeria*. Ibadan: NISER, 1985.
Aboyade, O. *Foundations of an African Economy*. New York: Praeger, 1966.
———. *Some Missing Policy Link in Nigerian Agricultural Development*. Ibadan: IITA, 1990.
Adedeji, Adebayo. *Nigerian Federal Finance*. London: Hutchinson, 1969.
Adegboye, R.O. "Impact of Farm Settlement on Surrounding Farmers." *Nigerian Journal of Economic and Social Studies* 11, no. 2 (1969).
Adeoye, Tafa. *Agbe-Ko-Ya: Farmers against Oppression*. Lagos: Lagos International Press, 1970.
Aju, Akin. *Industrialisation and Technological Innovation in an African Economy*. Akoka: Regional Centre for Technology Management, 1994.
Akande, S. O. *Structural Adjustment Programme and Agrochemical Product Marketing in South-West Nigeria*. Ibadan: NISER, 1989.
Ake, Claude. *Political Economy of Nigeria*. London: Longman, 1985.
Akeredolu-Ale, E.O. *The Underdevelopment of Indigenous Entrepreneurship in Nigeria*. Ibadan: Ibadan University Press, 1975.
Akintunde, Ifedayo. *Technological Development through Self-Reliance: Selected Speeches*. Ibadan: Ife Akintunde, 1994.
Apeldoorn, G.J. *Perspectives on Drought and Famine in Nigeria*. London: Allen and Unwin, 1981.
Ayida, A.A. "Contractor Finance and Supplier Credit in Economic Growth." *Nigerian Journal of Economic and Social Studies* 7 (1965): 175–86.
Ayida, A.D., and H.M.A. Onitiri, ed. *Reconstruction and Development in Nigeria*. Ibadan: Oxford University Press, 1971.
Baldwin, K.D.S. *The Marketing of Cocoa in Western Nigeria*. New York: Oxford University Press, 1954.

Baldwin, K.D.S. *Nigerian Cocoa Farmers—An Economic Survey of Yoruba Cocoa Farming Families*. Oxford: Oxford University Press, 1956.

Bauer, P.T. *West African Trade—A Study of Competition, Oligopoly and Monopoly in a Changing Economy*. Cambridge: Cambridge University Press, 1954.

Berry, S.S. *Cocoa, Custom and Socioeconomic Change in Rural Western Nigeria*. Oxford: Oxford University Press, 1975.

Bienen, Henry, and Mark Gersovitz. *Nigeria: Absorbing the Oil Wealth*. London: Euromoney, 1982.

———. *Oil Revenue and Policy Choice in Nigeria*. Washington, D.C.: World Bank, 1983.

Bienen, H., and V.P. Diejomoah, ed. *The Political Economy of Income Distribution in Nigeria*. New York: Africana, 1981.

Biersteker, T.J. *Distortion or Development: Contending Perspectives on the Multinational Corporation*. Cambridge, Mass.: MIT Press, 1978.

Bohannan, Laura, and Paul Bohannan. *The Tin of Central Nigeria*. London: International African Institute, 1953.

Brautigam, Deborah. "Substituting for the State: Institutions and Industrial Development in Eastern Nigeria." *World Development*, Vol. 25, no. 7 (July 1997).

Brown, Charles V. *Government and Banking in Western Nigeria*. Ibadan: Oxford University Press, 1964.

Buxton, T.F. *The African Slave Trade and Its Remedy*. London: J. Murray, 1839.

Callaway, Achibald. "From Traditional Crafts to Modern Industries." *Odu* 2, no. 1 (July 1965): 62–79.

Callaway, B. and R. Harris, ed. "The Political Economy of Nigeria." In *The Political Economy of Africa*. 93–135. New York: Schenkman, 1973.

Central Bank of Nigeria. *Annual Report: Economic and Financial Review*. Lagos: CBN, 1975–95.

———. *Impact of Structural Adjustment Programme (SAP) on Nigerian Agriculture and Rural Life*. Lagos: CBN/NISER National Study, 1992.

———. *Annual Report and Statement of Accounts for the Year Ended 31st December, 1992*. Lagos: CBN, 1993.

Chubo, L.T. *Ibo Land Tenure*. 2d ed. Ibadan: Ibadan University Press, 1961.

Clough, P. "Farmers and Traders in Hausaland." *Development and Change* 12, no. 2 (1981).

Codesria. *Deadened to Nigerian Development: An Analysis of the Political Economy of Nigeria, 1979–1989* Dakar: Publisher, 1993.

Collins, Paul. "The Policy of Indigenization: An Overall View." *Quarterly Journal of Administration* 9, no. 2 (January 1975): 135–47.

———. "The Political Economy of Indigenization: The Case of the Nigerian Enterprises Promotion Decree." *The African Review* no. 4 (1976): 491–508.

———. "Public Policy and the Development of Indigenous Capitalism: The Nigerian Experience." *Journal of Commonwealth and Comparative Politics* 15, no. 2 (July 1977): 127–50.

Cook, Arthur N. *British Enterprise in Nigeria*. Philadelphia, Pa.: University of Pennsylvania Press, 1943.

Davies, F. *The Royal African Company*. London: Longman, 1957.

Dean, E. *Plan Implementation in Nigeria, 1962–66*. Ibadan: Oxford University Press, 1972.

Diejomoah, V.P. "The Economics of the Nigerian Conflict." In *Nigeria: Dilemma of Nationhood,* edited by J. Okpaku, 318–65. New York: Third Press, 1972.

———. "Industrial Relations in Nigeria." In *Industrial Relations in Africa,* edited by U.K. Damachi. London: Macmillan, 1979.

Dike, Enwere. *Economic Transformation in Nigeria: Growth, Accumulation, and Technology*. Zaria, Nigeria: Ahmadu Bello University Press, 1991.

Durotolu, Olusegun. *A Blueprint for Nigeria's Economic Survival and Some Essays on Commercial Law*. Osogbo: Jehova Lovelinks Press, 1993.

Economic Commission for Africa. *Multinational Corporations in Africa*. Addis Ababa, Ethiopia: ECA, 1979.

Eicher, C.K., and C. Leidholm, ed. *Growth and Development of the Nigerian Economy*. East Lansing: Michigan State University Press, 1970.

Ekundare, R.O. *The Economic History of Nigeria, 1860–1960*. London: Methuen, 1973.

Ezeala-Harrison, Fidel. "Structural Re-Adjustment in Nigeria: Diagnosis of a Severe Dutch Disease Syndrome." *The American Journal of Economy and Sociology* 53, no. 2 (April 1993): 193.

F.A.O. *Agricultural Development in Nigeria, 1965–1980*. Rome: F.A.D., 1966.

Falola, Toyin. *Development Planning and Decolonization in Nigeria*. Gainesville: University Press of Florida, 1996.

Famoriyo, Segun. *Land Tenure and Agricultural Development in Nigeria*. Ibadan: NISER, Ibadan University Press, 1979.

Fashoyin, T. *Industrial Relations in Nigeria*. London: Longman, 1981.

First Bank of Nigeria Limited. *First Bank of Nigeria: A Century of Banking*. Ibadan: Spectrum Books, 1994.

Forrest, Tom. *Political and Economic Development in Nigeria (Second Edition)*. Boulder, Colo.: Westview Press, 1995.

———. *The Advance of African Capital: the Growth of Nigerian Private Enterprise*. Charlottesville: University Press of Virginia, 1994.

Gbosi, Augustus N. *Monetary Economics and the Nigerian Financial System*. Port Harcourt, Nigeria: Pam Unique Publishers, 1993.

Guyer, Jane I. *An African Niche Economy: Farming to Feed Ibadan*. Edinburgh: Edinburgh University Press, 1997.

Guyer, Jane I., and Eric F. Lambin. "Land Use in an Urban Hinterland: Ethnography and Remote Sensing in the Study of African Intensification." *American Anthropologist* 95, no. 4 (December 1993).

Hawkins, E.K. "Marketing Boards and Economic Development in Nigeria and Ghana." *Review of Economic Studies* 26, no. 69 (October 1958).

Hazlewood, Arthur. *The Finances of Nigerian Federation*. London: Oxford University Press, 1956.

Helleiner, G.K. "The Eastern Nigeria Development Corporation: A Study in Sources and Uses of Public Development Funds, 1949–1962." *Nigerian Journal of Economic and Social Studies* 6, no. 1 (March 1964): 98–123.

———. "The Fiscal Role of the Marketing Boards in Nigerian Economic Development, 1947–61." *Economic Journal* 74, no. 295 (September 1964): 414–48.

———. "Marketing Boards and Domestic Stabilization In Nigeria." *Review of Economic and Statistics* 48, no. 1 (February 1961).
———. "The Northern Region Development Corporation: Wide-Ranging Development Institution, 1949–52." *Nigerian Journal of Economic and Social Studies* 6, no. 2 (July 1964).
———. *Peasant Agriculture, Government and Economic Growth in Nigeria*. Homewood, Ill.: R.D. Irwin, 1966.
Hill, P. *Population, Prosperity and Poverty: Rural Kano, 1900 and 1970*. Cambridge: Cambridge University Press, 1977.
———. *Rural Hausa*. Cambridge: Cambridge University Press, 1972.
Hodder, B.W. "Rural Periodic Day Markets in Parts of Yorubaland, Western Nigeria." *Transactions and Papers of the British Institute of Geographers* No. 29 (1961): 152.
Hopkins, A.G. *An Economic History of West Africa*. London: Longman, 1972.
Imade, U.O. *Directory of Management Development Programmes in Nigeria, 1982*. Lagos: Center for Management Development, 1982.
"Inching Forwards: Nigeria." *The Economist* 336, no. 7921 (July 1, 1995): 35.
International Bank for Reconstruction and Development. *The Economic Development of Nigeria*. Baltimore, Md.: Johns Hopkins University Press, 1955.
———. *Options for Long Term Development of Nigeria*. Washington, D.C.: I.B.R.D., 1976.
Lewis, Peter. "From Prebendalism to Predation: The Political Economy of Nigeria." *Journal of Modern African Studies*. Vol. 34, no. 1. 1996.
Lewis, P. and Stein, H. "Shifting Fortunes: the Political Economy of Financial Liberalization in Nigeria." *World Development*, Vol. 25, no. 1 (January 1997).
"Little Nigeria: A Big Country Diminished by Its Military Rulers." *The Economist*. (March 25, 1995).
MacDonald, Scott B. *New Tigers and Old Elephants: The Development Game in the 1990s and Beyond*. New Brunswick, N.J.: Transaction Publishers, 1995.
Mannix, Daniel P., and Malcolm Cowley. *Black Cargoes*. New York: Viking Press, 1962.
Martin, Ann. *The Oil Palm Economy of the Ibibio Farmer*. Ibadan: Ibadan University Press, 1956.
Meek, C.K. *Land Tenure and Administration in Nigeria and the Cameroons*. London: HMSO, 1957.
Morel, E.O. *Trading Monopolies in West Africa*. Liverpool: Richardson and Sons, 1901.
Mortimore, M. *Adapting to Drought: Farmers, Famine and Desertification in West Africa*, Cambridge: Cambridge University Press, 1989.
Naanen, Ben. "Economy within an Economy: The Manilla Currency, Exchange Rate Instability and Social Conditions in South Eastern Nigeria, 1900–48." *The Journal of African History* 34, no. 3 (August 1993).
Nafzinger, E.W. *African Capitalism: A Case Study in Nigerian Entrepreneurship*. Stanford, Calif.: Hoover, 1977.
Newlyn, W.T., and D.C. Rowan. *Money and Banking in British Colonial Africa*. Oxford: Clarendon Press, 1954.
Nigerian Economic Society. *Poverty in Nigeria*. Ibadan: NES. 1976.
———. *1994 Conference on African Debt Burden and Economic Development: Selected Papers*. Ibadan: NES, 1995.

Nigerian Institute of International Affairs. *The African Debt Crisis.* Lagos: NIIA, 1989.

———. *Structural Adjustment in West Africa.* Lagos: NIIA, 1994.

Nigerian Ports Authority. Lagos: Management Service Division, 1981.

Norman, D.W. *Technical Change and the Small Farmer in Hausaland.* East Lansing: Michigan State University, 1979.

Nwosu, A.C. *Structural Adjustment and Nigerian Agriculture.* Washington, D.C. U.S. Department of Agriculture, 1992.

Oculi, O. "Dependent Food Policy in Nigeria 1975–79." *Review of African Political Economy* 15/16 (1979).

Odife, Dennis O. *The Nigerian Securities Market.* Lagos: Malthouse Press, 1993.

Odigie, Stephen A. *State Intervention in Industrial Relations in Nigeria, 1861–1989.* Benin City: S.A. Odigie, 1993.

Ogunpola, G.A. "The Pattern of Organization in the Building Industry—A Western Nigeria Case Study." *Nigerian Journal of Economic and Social Studies* 10, no. 3 (1968): 339–60.

"Oiling the Big Wheels." *The Economist* 329, no. 7836 (Nov. 6, 1993).

Okediji, F. Olu. "Indigenization Decree and Income Distribution: The Social Implications." *Quarterly Journal of Administration* 9, no. 2 (January 1975).

Okigbo, Pius N. *African Common Market.* London: Longman, Green and Co. Ltd., 1967.

———. *Nigerian National Accounts, 1950–57.* Enugu, Nigeria: Government Printer, 1962.

———. *Planning the Nigerian Economy for Less Dependence on Oil.* Ibadan: NISER, 1983.

Okolo, Amechi, *Foreign Capital in Nigeria, 1900–1975: Roots of Underdevelopment.* Lagos: Heartland, 1987.

Olanrewaju, S.A. *External Financing and Nigeria's Economic Recovery Programme.* Ibadan: National Centre for Economic Management and Administration, 1993.

Olashore, Oladele. *Perspectives on Finance, Banking and Economic Policy in Nigeria.* Ibadan: Heinemann, 1988.

———. *The Challenges of Nigeria's Economic Reform.* Ibadan: Fountain Publications, 1991.

Olatunbosun, Dupe. *Nigeria's Neglected Rural Majority.* Ibadan: Oxford University Press, 1975.

Olayide, S.O., ed. *Economic Survey of Nigeria, 1960–75.* Ibadan: Aromolaran Publishing Co., 1976.

Olomola, Ade. *Agricultural Credit and Production Efficiency: A Case Study.* Ibadan: NISER, 1988.

Olukoshi, Adebayo O. *The Politics of Structural Adjustment in Nigeria.* London: James Currey, 1993.

Oluwasanmi, H.A. *Agriculture and Nigerian Economic Development.* Ibadan: Oxford University Press, 1966.

Oluwasanmi, H.A., and J.A. Alao. "The Role of Credit in the Transformation of Traditional Agriculture." *Nigerian Journal of Economic and Social Studies* 7, no. 1 (March 1965).

Omotola, J.A., ed. *The Land Use Decree: Report of a National Workshop.* Lagos: Lagos University Press, 1982.

Oni, Ola, and B. Onimode. *Economic Development of Nigeria—The Socialist Alternative*. Ibadan: Nigerian Academy of Arts, Sciences and Technology, 1975.
Onimode, B. "Imperialism and Multinational Corporations—A Case Study of Nigeria." In *Decolonization and Dependency—Problems of Development of African Society*, edited by Y. Yansane, 207–32. Westport, Ct.: Greenwood Press, 1980.
———. *Imperialism and Underdevelopment in Nigeria*. London: Macmillan, 1983.
Onitiri, H.M.A., and D. Olatubosun, ed. *The Marketing Board System*. Ibadan: NISER, 1974.
Onoh, J.K., ed. *The Foundation of Nigeria's Financial Infrastructure*. London: Croom Helm, 1980.
Onyemelukwe, C.C. *Problems of Industrial Planning and Management in Nigeria*. London: Longman, 1966.
Osemwota, Osa. *Regional Economic Disparity and Conflict in Nigeria, 1960–1967*. Benin City, Nigeria: Omega Publishers, 1994.
Oshikoya, Temetope Waheed. *The Nigerian Economy: A Macroeconometric and Input-Output Model*. New York: Praeger, 1990.
Owosekun, Akinola, Adeniyi. *Prospects of Nigeria's Major Export Commodities in the Expanded EEC*. Ibadan: NISER, 1980.
Oyejide, T.A. *Tariff Policy and Industrialization in Nigeria*. Ibadan: Ibadan University Press, 1975.
Panel on Nigeria since Independence History Project. *The Economy*. Edited by Kayode, M.O., and Y.B. Usman. Ibadan: Heinemann, 1989.
Pearson, S.R. *Petroleum and Nigerian Economy*. Stanford, Calif.: Stanford University Press, 1970.
Perham, M., ed. *Economics of a Tropical Dependency*. 2 vols. London: Faber, 1946.
———. *Mining, Commerce and Finance in Nigeria*. London: Faber, 1948.
———. *The Native Economies of Nigeria*. London: Faber, 1946.
Phillips, A.O. "Revenue Allocation in Nigeria, 1970–1980." *Nigerian Journal of Economic and Social Studies* (1976): 1–28.
Phillips, Adedotun. "Nigeria's Federal Financial Experience." *Journal of Modern African Studies* 9 (1971).
Prest, A.R., and I.A. Stewart. *The National Income of Nigeria*. London: H.M.S.O., 1953.
Sanda, Akinade O. *The Challenge of Nigeria's Indigenization*. Ibadan: NISER, 1982.
Schatz, L.H. *Petroleum in Nigeria*. Ibadan: Oxford University Press, 1969.
———. *Development Bank Lending in Nigeria—The Federal Loans Board*. Ibadan: Oxford University Press, 1964.
———. *Nigerian Capitalism*. Berkeley: University of California Press, 1977.
Schatz, Sayre P. "Under-Utilized Resources, Directed to Demand and Deficit Financing, Illustrated by Reference to Nigeria." *Quarterly Journal of Economics* 73, no. 4 (November 1959).
———. *Economics, Politics, and Administration in Government Lending: The Regional Loans Board of Nigeria*. Ibadan: NISER, 1970.
Schatzl, L.H. Industrialization in Nigeria—A Spatial Analysis. München, Germany: Weltforum Verlag, 1973.
———. *The Nigerian Tin Industry*. Ibadan: Oxford University Press, 1971.
———. *Petroleum in Nigeria*. Ibadan: Oxford University Press, 1969.

Smith, M.G. *The Economy of Hausa Communities of Zaria*. Colonial Research Studies No. 16. London: HMSO, 1955.

Smock, A.C. "Ethnicity and Attitudes toward Development in Eastern Nigeria." *Journal of Developing Areas* (1969).

Stolper, W. *Planning without Facts*. Cambridge, Mass.: Harvard University Press, 1966.

Teriba, O. "Nigerian Revenue Allocation Experience, 1952–65: A Study in Intergovernmental Fiscal and Financial Relationships." *Nigerian Journal of Economic and Social Studies* 8 (1966): 361–82.

Teriba, O., and M.O. Kayode, ed. *Industrial Development in Nigeria*. Ibadan: Ibadan University Press, 1977.

Tiffen, M. *The Enterprising Peasant: Economic Development in Gombe Emirate*. London: HMSO, 1976.

Uvieghara, E.E. *Trade Union Law in Nigeria*. Benin City: Ethiope Publishing, 1976.

Wallace, T. *Rural Development through Irrigation: Studies in a Town on the Kano River Project*. Zaria, Nigeria: ABU Center for Social and Economic Research, 1979.

Wells, J.C. *Agricultural Policy and Economic Growth in Nigeria, 1962–68*. Ibadan: Ibadan University Press, 1972.

Williams, G., ed. *Nigeria: Economy and Society*. London: Collins, 1976.

World Bank. *Nigeria: Options for Long-Term Development*. Baltimore, Md.: Johns Hopkins University Press, 1974.

———. *Adjustment in Africa: Lessons from Country Case Studies*. Washington, D.C.: World Bank, 1994.

Yesufu, T.M. *Industrial Relations in Nigeria*. Ibadan: Oxford University Press, 1962.

Zartman, I. William, ed. *The Political Economy of Nigeria*. New York: Praeger, 1983.

Zwingina, Jonathan Silas. *Capitalist Development in an African Economy*. Ibadan: University Press, 1992.

EDUCATION

Adelowo, Ayo. *Education in Ogbomoso: 1885 to the Founding of a University*. Ibadan: Irepo Printers, 1994.

Adeyinka, Augustus A. *A History of Secondary Grammar-School Education in Oyo, Ogun and Ondo States of Nigeria, 1909–1980*. Ilorin: Faculty of Education, Ilorin, 1993.

Alauja J. Bala. *"Koranic and Master Law Teaching in Hausa Land."* Nigeria 37 (1951).

Ashby, Eric. *Universities: British, Indian, African*. Cambridge, Mass.: Harvard University Press, 1966.

Asiwaju, A.I. "Ashby Revisited: A Review of Nigeria's Educational Growth, 1961–1971." *African Studies Review* 1005, no. 1 (April 1974).

Awokoya, S.O. "Curriculum Development in Nigeria." *West African Journal of Education* 8, no. 3 (October 1954).

Beckett, P., and J. O'Connell. *Education and Power in Nigeria: A Study of University Students*. London: Holder and Stoughton, 1977.

Burns, D.G. *African Education*. London: Oxford University Press, 1956.

Callaway, A., and A. Musone. *Financing of Education in Nigeria*. Paris: United Nations Economic Social and Cultural Organization, 1968.

Dudey, D. *An Introduction to the Sociology of Nigeria Education*. London: Macmillan, 1979.

Eze, Agon. *Economics of Education: The Nigerian Experience*. Owerri, Nigeria: New Africa Publishing Co., 1983.

Fafunwa, A.B. *The Growth and Development of Nigerian Universities*. Washington, D.C.: Overseas Liaison Committee, American Council on Education, 1974.

———. *History of Education in Nigeria*. London: Allen and Unwin, 1974.

———. *A History of Nigerian High Education*. Lagos: Macmillan, 1971.

———. *An Historical Analysis of the Development of Higher Education in Nigeria*. New York: New York University Press, 1955.

———. *New Perspective in African Education*. Lagos: Macmillan, Nigeria, 1967.

———. *Up and On: A Nigerian Teachers' Odyssey*. Lagos: West African Books, 1990.

Fajana, A. *Education Policy in Nigeria: A Century of Experiment*. Ile-Ife, Nigeria: University Press, 1982.

Gbadamosi, G.O. "The Establishment of Western Education among Muslims in Nigeria, 1896–1926." *Journal of the Historical Society of Nigeria* 4, no. 1 (February 1967).

Graham, Sonia F. *Government and Mission Education in Nigeria, 1900–1919*. Ibadan: Ibadan University Press, 1966.

Groves, C.P. *The Planting of Christianity in Africa*. 4 vols. London: Lutterworth Press, 1954.

Hilliard, F.H. *A Short History of Education in British West Africa*. Edinburgh, Scotland: Nelson, 1957.

Ikejiani, O., ed. *Nigerian Education*. Ikeja: Longman of Nigeria, 1964.

ILO. *Report to the Government of the Federation of Nigeria on Cooperative Education*. Geneva, Switzerland: ILO, 1963.

Kilby, P. "Technical Education in Nigeria." *Bulletin of the Oxford University Institute of Economics and Statistics* 26, no. 2 (1964).

Lewis, L.J., and A.J. Loveridge. *The Management of Education*. London: Pall Mall Press, 1951.

Mellanby, Kenneth. *The Birth of Nigeria's University*. London: Methuen, 1958.

Murray, A. Victor. *The School in the Bush*. London: Longman, 1929.

National Universities Commission. *Approved Minimum Academic Standards in Education for All Universities*. Lagos: NUC, 1989.

Nduka, O. *Western Education and the Nigerian Cultural Background*. Ibadan: Oxford University Press, 1964.

Nuffield Foundation and the Colonial Office. *African Education: A Study of Education Policy and Practice in British Tropical Africa*. London: Oxford University Press, 1953.

Nwangwa, M.A., and Maria J. Okure. "Perceived Health Needs of Secondary School Students in Uyo, Akwa Ibom State, Nigeria." *Journal of School Health* 63, no. 4 (April 1993).

Ogunsola, A.F. *Legislation and Education in Northern Nigeria*. Ibadan: Oxford University Press, 1975.

Ojo, J.D. *Students Unrest in Nigeria*. Ibadan: Spectrum Books, 1995.
Okafor, I. Ndukar. *The Development of Universities in Nigeria*. London: Longman, 1971.
Okeke, P.U. *Educational Reconstruction in an Independent Nigeria*. New York: New York University Press, 1956.
Okongwu, J.N. *History of Education in Nigeria, 1842–1942*. New York: New York University Press, 1946.
Ozikii, Albert O. *Education in Northern Nigeria*. London: Allen and Unwin, 1981.
Panel on Nigeria since Independence History Project. *Education*, edited by Tekena N. Tamuno and J.A. Atanda. Ibadan: Heinemann, 1989.
Phelps-Stokes Fund. *Education in Africa*. New York: Phelps-Stokes Fund, 1932.
———. *A Survey of African Students Studying in the United States*. New York: Phelps-Stokes Fund, 1949.
Phillipson, Sydney. *Grants in Aid of Education in Nigeria*. Lagos: Government Printer, 1948.
Read, Margaret. *Education and Social Change in Tropical Areas*. 2d ed. Edinburgh, Scotland: Nelson, 1956.
Smyke, Raymond J., and Denis C. Stover. *Nigeria Union of Teachers—An Official History*. Ibadan: Oxford University Press, 1974.
Solaru, T.T. *Teacher Training in Nigeria*. Ibadan: Ibadan University Press, 1964.
Stock, Eugene. *The History of the Church Missionary Society*. London: C.M.S., 1899.
Taiwo, C.O. "The Administration and Control of Education in Nigeria." *West African Journal of Education* 19, no. 1 (June 1972).
———. *Seventy Years in the Nigerian Education System*. Lagos: Nelson Publishers Ltd., 1992.
Taiwo, C.O., and Henry Carr. *An African Contribution to Education*. Ibadan: Oxford University Press, 1969.
———. *The Nigerian Education System, Past, Present and Future*. Nigeria: Thomas Nelson Ltd., 1980.
Taylor, O.W. "Reflections of an American Teacher after Seven Years in Nigeria." *West African Journal of Education* 6, no. 2 (June 1962).
Uchendu, Patrick K. *Politics and Education in Nigeria*. Enugu: Fourth Dimension, 1995.
Ukeje, B.O. *Education for Social Reconstruction*. London and Lagos: Macmillan, 1966.
Van Den Berghe, P.L. *Power and Privilege at an African University*. London: Routledge, 1973.
Wheeler, A.C.R. *The Organization of Educational Planning in Nigeria*. African Research Monographs, 1968.
Williams, D.H. *A Short Survey of Education in Northern Nigeria*. Kaduna, Nigeria: Ministry of Education, Northern Region of Nigeria, 1960.
Wise, Colins. *A History of Education in British West Africa*. London: Longman, 1956.

HISTORY

Abba, Isa Alkali. *Mahmudu Ribadu: A Statesman and Nigeria's First Minister of Defence*. Kaduna: Arewa House, Centre for Research and Historical Development, Ahmadu Bello University, 1993.

Abdulkadir, D. *The Poetry, Life and Opinions of Sa'adu Zungur*. Zaria, Nigeria: Northern Nigeria Publishing Corp., 1974.
Adeleye, R.A. *The Sokoto Caliphate*. Ibadan: Ibadan University Press, 1975.
African Encyclopedia. London: Oxford University Press, 1974.
African Journal Ltd. *Africa Who's Who*. London: African Books Ltd., 1981.
———. *Makers of Modern Africa: Profiles in History*. London: African Books Ltd., 1981.
Ajayi, J.F. Ade. "The British Occupation of Lagos 1851–1861." *Nigerian Magazine* no. 69 (August 1961).
———. "Nineteenth Century Origins of Nigerian Nationalism." *Journal of Historical Society of Nigeria* 2, no. 2 (1961): 196–210.
———. *Milestones in Nigerian History*. Ibadan: University College, 1962.
———. *Christian Missions in Nigeria, 1841–1891*. London: Longman, 1965.
———. *The Problems of National Integration in Nigeria: A Historical Perspective*. Ibadan: NISER, 1984.
Ajayi, J.F. Ade, and Ian Epie, ed. *A Thousand Years of West African History*. London: Nelson for Ibadan University Press, 1958.
Ajayi, J.F. Ade, and Robert Smith. *Yoruba Warfare in the Nineteenth Century*. London and Ibadan: Cambridge University Press, 1964.
Akinjogbin, I.A. "A Chronology of Yoruba History." *Odu* 2(2): 81–86.
———. "The Prelude to the Yoruba Civil Wars of the Nineteenth Century." *Odu* No. 2 (1965): 21–46.
———. "The Oyo Empire in the Nineteenth Century: A Reassessment." *JHSN* 3, no. 3 1966: 449–66.
———. *Dahomey and Its Neighbours*. Cambridge: Cambridge University Press, 1967.
Akinjogbin, I.A., and Segun Osoba, ed. *Topics on Nigerian Economic and Social History*. Ile-Ife, Nigeria: University Press, 1980.
Alagoa, Ebiegheri J. *The Small Brave City State—A History of Brass-Nembe in the Niger Delta*. Ibadan: Ibadan University Press, 1964.
———. *Jaja of Opobo: The Slave Who Became a King*. London: Longman, 1970.
———. *A History of the Niger Delta: A Historical Interpretation of Ijo Oral Traditions*. Ibadan: Ibadan University Press, 1972.
Ali, Sidi H. *Power of Powers: A Biography of the Late Alhaji Muh. Ribadu*. Zaria, Nigeria: Gaskiya Corporation, 1974.
Alimen, H. *The Prehistory of Africa*. London: Hutchinson, 1957.
Ananaba, Wogu. *The Trade Union Movement in Nigeria*. Benin City: Ethiope Publishing, 1969.
Anene, J.C. "The Southern Nigerian Protectorate and the Aros, 1900–1902." *Journal of Historical Society of Nigeria* 2, no. 1 (1960).
Arikpo, Okoi. *The Development of Modern Nigeria*. New York: Penguin Books, 1970.
Arnold, Guy. *Modern Nigeria*. London: Longman Group Ltd., 1977.
Aronson, D.R. *The City Is Our Farm: Seven Migrant Ijebu Yoruba Families*. Cambridge, Mass.: Shenkman, 1978.
Atanda, J.A. *The New Oyo Empire: Indirect Rule and Change in Western Nigeria, 1894–1934*. London: Longman, 1973.
Awolowo, Obafemi. *Awo: The Autobiography of Chief Obafemi Awolowo*. Cambridge: Cambridge University Press, 1960.

Ayandele, E.A. *African Historical Essays*. London: Frank Cass, 1979.

———. *Holy Johnson, Pioneer of African Nationalism, 1836–1917*. London: Frank Cass, 1970.

———. *The Missionary Impact on Modern Nigeria, 1842–1914*. London: Longman, 1966.

Azikiwe, N. *My Odyssey*. London: Hurst, 1970.

Balewa, Alhaji Sir Abubakar Tafawa. *Nigeria Speaks*. Cambridge: Cambridge University Press, 1962.

Balewa, Balarabe Abubakar Tafawa. *Governing Nigeria: History, Problems and Prospects*. Lagos: Malthouse Press, 1994.

Beier, Ulli. "Before Oduduwa." *Odu* 3 (1956): 25–32.

Beier, Ulli, and S.O. Biobaku. "The Use and Interpretation of Myths." *Odu* 1 (1955).

Bello, Alhaji Sir Ahmadu. *My Life*. Cambridge: Cambridge University Press, 1962.

Biobaku, S.O. *The Egba and Their Neighbours, 1832–1872*. Oxford: Clarendon Press, 1957.

———. "The Problem of Traditional History with Special Reference to Yoruba Traditions." *Journal of Historical Society of Nigeria* 1, no. 1 (1959).

———. *The Origin of the Yorubas*. Lagos: Federal Ministry of Information, 1955.

Boahen, Adu. *Britain, The Sahara and the West Sudan, 1788–1861*. London: Clarendon Press, 1964.

Bourdillon, Sir Bernard. *The Future of the Colonial Empire*. London: S.C.M. Press, 1945.

———. *Memorandum on the Future Political Development of Nigeria*. Lagos, 1939.

Bovill, E.W. *Caravans of the Old Sahara*. London: Oxford University Press, 1933.

Bowen, T.J. *Adventures and Missionary Labours in Several Countries in the Interior of Africa*. Charleston, S.C.: Southern Baptist Publication Society, 1857.

Bradbury, R.E. *The Benin Kingdom and the Edo-Speaking Peoples of South-Western Nigeria*. London: International African Institutes, 1957.

Bradbury, R.E., and Peter C. Lloyd. *The Benin People and Edo Speaking Peoples, etc., plus the Itsekiri*. London: International African Institutes, 1959.

Brenner, L. *The Shehu of Kukawa: A History of the Al-Kanemi Dynasty of Bornu*. Oxford: Clarendon Press, 1993.

Burdon, J.A. *Northern Nigeria Historical Notes on Certain Emirates and Tribes*. Farnborough: Gregg International Publishers Limited, 1972.

Burns, Alan. *History of Nigeria*. 4th ed. London: George Allen and Unwin, Ltd., 1948.

———. *In Defence of Colonies*. London: George Allen and Unwin, 1957.

Buxton, T.F. *The African Slave Trade and Its Remedy*. London: John Murray, 1839.

Callaway, Barbara. *The Heritage of Islam: Women, Religion, and Politics in West Africa*. Boulder, Colo.: Lynne Rienner, 1994.

Christelow, Allen. *Thus Ruled Emir Abbas: Selected Cases from the Records of the Emir of Kano's Judicial Council*. East Lansing: Michigan State University Press, 1994.

Clapperton, Hugh. *Journal of a Second Expedition into the Interior of Africa, etc*. Philadelphia: Carey, Lea and Carey, 1829.

Collis, Robert, J.M. *Nigeria in Conflict*. London: Secker and Warburg, 1970.

Crowder, M. *The Story of Nigeria*. London: Faber and Faber, 1973.

———. *West Africa under Colonial Rule*. London: Hutchinson, 1968.
Crowder, M., and O. Ikime, ed. *West African Chiefs: Their Changing Status under Colonial Rule and Independence*. Ile-Ife, Nigeria: University of Ife Press, 1970.
Crowther, S.A. *Journals of an Expedition up the Niger and Tshadda Rivers, etc*. London: Cass, 1970.
Daily Times. *Nigeria Year Book*. Lagos: Daily Times, 1973–1984.
———. *Who's Who in Nigeria*. Lagos: Daily Times, 1983.
Davidson, Basil. *Black Mother*. Boston: Little Brown, 1961.
———. *Old Africa Rediscovered*. London: Gollancz, 1959.
Davidson, Basil, and Adenekan Ademola, ed. *The New West Africa*. London: Allen and Unwin, 1953.
Davies, O. *West Africa before the Europeans*. London: Methuen, 1967.
Dickie, John, and Alan Rake. *Who's Who in Africa: The Political, Military and Business Leaders of Africa*. London: African Buyer and Trader, 1973.
Dike, K. Onwuka. *100 Years of British Rule in Nigeria, 1851–1951*. Lagos: Federal Information Service, 1957.
———. *Origins of the Niger Mission, 1841–1891*. Ibadan: Ibadan University Press, 1962.
———. *Trade and Politics in the Niger Delta, 1830–1885*. Oxford: Clarendon Press, 1956.
———. "John Beecroft, 1790–1854." *JHSN* 1, no. 1 (1956).
Eades, J.S. *The Yoruba Today*. Cambridge: Cambridge University Press, 1980.
Egbarevba, J.U. *A Short History of Benin*. Ibadan: Ibadan University Press, 1960.
Elegbede-Fernandez, Abiodun Dosumu. *Lagos: A Legacy of Honour: Dosumu (1861)—Babangida (1991)*. Ibadan: Spectrum Books, 1992.
Enahoro, Anthony. *Azikiwe—Saint or Sinner?* Lagos, 1946.
Enegwea, Gregory. *NYSC: Twenty Years of National Service*. Abuja, Nigeria: National Youth Service Corps, Directorate, 1993.
English, M.C. *An Outline of Nigerian History*. London: Longmans, 1959.
Ewelukwa, D.I.O. *Historical Introduction to Nigerian Constitution*. Awka, Nigeria: Meksling Publishers, 1993.
Fage, J.D. *An Introduction to the History of West Africa*. London: Cambridge University Press, 1955.
Falola, Toyin. *Development Planning and Decolonization in Nigeria*. Gainesville: University Presses of Florida, 1996.
Feinstein, A. *African Revolutionary: The Life and Times of Nigeria's Aminu Kano*. New York: Quadrangle, 1973.
Flint, J.E. *Sir George Goldie and the Making of Nigeria*. London: Oxford University Press, 1960.
———. "Mary Kingsley—A Reassessment." *JAH* 4, no. 1 (1963).
Forde, Daryll. *The Yoruba-Speaking Peoples of South-Western Nigeria*. London: International African Institute, 1951.
Forde, Daryll, and G.I. Jones. *The Ibo and Ibibio-Speaking Peoples of South-Eastern Nigeria*. London: International African Institute, 1950.
Forsyth, Frederick. *The Biafra Story*. Harmondsworth, England: Penguin, 1969.
Gunther, John. *Inside Africa*. New York: Harper's, 1955.

Hargreaves, J.D. *Prelude to the Partition of West Africa.* London: Macmillan, 1963.
Heussler, Robert. *The British in Northern Nigeria.* London: Oxford University Press, 1968.
Hinderer, Anna. *Seventeen Years in the Yoruba Country.* London: Seely, Jackson and Halliday, 1873.
Hodgkin, Thomas. "Uthman dan Fodio." In "Nigeria 1960," a special independence issue of *Nigeria Magazine* (October 1960).
———. *Nigerian Perspective: An Historical Anthology.* London: Oxford University Press, 1960.
Hogben, S.J. *The Muhammedan Emirates of Nigeria.* London: Oxford University Press, 1930.
Hogben, S.J., and A.H.M. Kirk-Greene. *The Emirates of Northern Nigeria.* London: Oxford University Press, 1966.
Howard, C., and J.H. Plumb. *West African Explorers.* London: Oxford University Press, 1952.
Hussey, E.R.J. *Tropical Africa, 1908–1944.* London: St. Catherine Press, 1959.
Igbafe, P.A. *Benin under British Administration, 1897–1938.* London: Longman, 1979.
Ikime, O. "Colonial Conquest and Resistance in Southern Nigeria." *Journal of Historical Society of Nigeria* 4, no. 3 (December 1972): 1–13.
———. *Merchant Prince of the Niger Delta: The Rise and Fall of Nana Olomu, Last Governor of the Benin River.* London: Heinemann, 1968.
———. *The Fall of Nigeria: The British Conquest.* London: Heinemann, 1977.
Ikpe, Eno Blankson. *Food and Society in Nigeria: A History of Food Customs, Food Economy and Cultural Change, 1900–1989.* Stuttgaut: Steiner, 1994.
The International Who's Who, 1981–1982. London: Europa Publications Ltd., 1981.
Isichei, Elizabeth. *A History of the Igbo People.* London: Macmillan, 1976.
Jaggar, Philip John. *The Blacksmiths of Kano City: A Study in Tradition, Innovation and Entrepreneurship in the Twentieth Century.* Cologne: Rudiger Koppe Verlag, 1994.
Jaja, S.O., E.O. Erim and B.W. Andah. *History and Culture of the Upper Cross River.* Enugu: Harris Publishers, 1990.
Johnson, Samuel. *The History of the Yorubas.* Lagos: Church Missionary Society Bookshop, 1937.
Jones, G.I. *The Trading States of the Oil Rivers.* Oxford: Oxford University Press, 1963.
Jones-Quartey, K.A.B. *A Life of Azikiwe.* Harmondsworth, England: Penguin, 1956.
Kanya-Forstner, A.S. and Lovejoy, Paul E. (eds.) *The Sokoto Caliphate and the European Powers, 1890–1907.* Frankfurt: Frobenius-Gesellschaft, 1994.
Kingsley, Mary H. *Travels in W. Africa.* London: Macmillan, 1900.
———. *West African Studies.* London: Macmillan, 1899.
Kirk-Greene, A.H.M. *Adamawa—Past and Present.* London: Oxford University Press, 1958.
———. *Barth's Travels in Nigeria.* London: Oxford University Press, 1962.
———. "Who Coined the Name Nigeria?" *West Africa* (December 22, 1956): 1035.
———. *Lugard and the Amalgamation of Nigeria.* London: Frank Cass, 1968.
Laird, Macgregor, and R.A.K. Oldfield. *Narrative of an Expedition to the Interior of Africa in 1832, 1833 and 1834.* 1837. Reprint, London: Frank Cass, 1971.

Laminu, Hamsatu Zanna. *Scholars and Scholarship in the History of Borno*. Zaria, Nigeria: Open Press, 1993.
Lander, Richard, and John Lander. *Journals of an Expedition to Explore the Course and Termination of the Niger*. New York: J. and J. Harper, 1832.
Legum, Colin, ed. *African Contemporary Record: Annual Survey and Documents, 1976–1977*. London: Rex Collings, 1977.
Lewis, L.J. *Henry Carr*. London: Oxford University Press, 1949.
Lipschutz, Mark R., and R. Kent Rasmussen. *Dictionary of African Historical Biography*. London: Heinemann, 1978.
Livingstone, W.P. *Mary Slessor of Calabar*. London: Hodder and Stoughton, 1929.
Lloyd, P.C. "Conflict Theory and Yoruba Kingdoms." In *History and Social Anthropology*, edited by I.M. Lewis, London: Tavistock Publications, 1968.
Lovejoy, Paul E. *Slow Death for Slavery: The Course of Abolition in Northern Nigeria, 197–1936*. Cambridge: Cambridge University Press, 1993.
Low, Victor N. *Three Nigerian Emirates: A Study in Oral History*. Evanston, Ill.: Northwestern University Press, 1972.
Low, Victor N., and A.F.C. Ryder. "Don Domingos, Prince of Warri—Portuguese Contact with the Itsekiri." *Odu* (1954).
Lugard, F.D. *The Dual Mandate in British Tropical Africa*. London: W. Blackwood and Sons, 1922.
———. *Political Memoranda*. 1919. Reprint, London: Frank Cass, 1970.
———. *Report on the Amalgamation of Northern and Southern Nigeria and Administration*. London: H.M.S.O., 1920.
Lumley, Frederick, ed. *Nigeria: The Land, Its Art and Its People*. London: Studio Vista, 1974.
MacCartney, William M. *Dr. Aggrey*. London: S.C.M. Press, 1949.
MacFarlane, Donald M. *Calabar and the Church of Scotland Mission, 1846–1946*. London, 1946.
Mair, Lucy P. *Native Policies in Africa*. London: George Routledge, 1936.
Makar, Tesemchi. *The History of Political Change among the Tiv in the 19th and 20th Centuries*. Enugu: Fourth Dimension, 1994.
Mannix, D.P., and M. Cowley. *Black Cargoes: A History of the Atlantic Slave Trade, 1518–1865*. New York: Viking Press, 1963.
Martins, E.C. *The British West African Settlements, 1750–1821*. London: Longman, 1927.
Maxwell, J. Houvif. *Nigeria: The Land, The People and Christian Progress*. London: World Dominion Press, 1931.
Meek, C.K. *The Northern Tribes of Nigeria*. London: Oxford University Press, 1925.
———. *A Sudanese Kingdom*. New York: Humanities Press, 1950.
Mefarlaw, Donald M. *Calabar*. Edinburgh, Scotland: Nelson, 1946.
Miles, William F.S. *Hausaland Divided: Colonialism and Independence in Nigeria and Niger*. Ithaca, N.Y.: Cornell University Press, 1994.
Miller, W.R.S. *Reflections of a Pioneer*. London: Church Missionary Society, 1936.
———. *Yesterday and Tomorrow in Northern Nigeria*. London: S.C.M., 1938.
Morel, E.D. *Nigeria: Its Peoples and Its Problems*. London: Smith, Elder, 1911.
Natalia, B. Kochakova. *Nigeria: Thirty Years of Independence*. S.I. Mockba, 1990.

Newbury, C.W. *The Western Slave Coast and its Rulers*. Oxford: Clarendon Press, 1961.

Nigeria Handbook. London: Crown Agents, 1954.

Niven, C.R. *A Short History of Nigeria*. London: Longman, Green and Co. Ltd., 1957.

———. *A Short History of the Yoruba Peoples*. London, Longmans, 1958.

Nwabara, S.N. *Iboland: A Century of Contact with Britain, 1860–1960*. London: Hodder and Stoughton, 1977.

Nwabughuogu, Anthony I. *Portrait of a Nation Builder: The Biography of Chief Dr. G.E. Okeke*. Ikoyi, Lagos, Nigeria: Vista Books, 1994.

Obafemi, Olu. *Nigerian Writers on the Nigerian Civil War*. Lagos: J. Olu Olatiregun, 1992.

Obi, Chike. *My Struggle*. Lagos, 1954.

———. *Our Struggle*. Ibadan, 1953.

Obiozor, George A. *The United States and the Nigerian Civil War: An American Dilemma in Africa, 1966–1970*. Lagos: Nigerian Institute of International Affairs, 1993.

Odebiyi, Oladapo, ed. *Builders of Modern Nigeria*. Lagos: VBO International, 1985.

Odogwu, Bernard. *No Place to Hide: Crises and Conflict inside Biafra*. Enugu, Nigeria: Fourth Dimension, 1985.

Ojiako, James Obioha. *First Four Years of Nigerian Executive Presidency: Success or Failure*. Lagos: Daily Times of Nigeria, 1983.

———. *Nigeria: Yesterday, Today and. . . .* Onitsha, Nigeria: African Educational Publishers, 1981.

———. *13 Years of Military Rule, 1966–1979*. Lagos: Daily Times, n.d.

Ojo, G.J.A. *Yoruba Palaces*. London: University of London Press, 1966.

Ojukwu, C.O. *Biafra*. 2 vols. New York: Harper and Row, 1969.

Okafor, Samuel O. *Indirect Rule: The Development of Central Legislature in Nigeria*. Watson on Thames, Surrey: Nelson Africa, 1981.

Okonjo, I.M. *British Administration in Nigeria, 1900–1950*. New York: Nok Publishers, 1974.

Olawoyin, J.S. *My Political Reminiscences: 1948–1983*. Ikeja, Nigeria: John West Publications, 1993.

Oliver, Roland. *Sir Harry Johnston and the Scramble for Africa*. London: Chatto and Windus, 1957.

Oliver, Roland, and J.D. Fage. *A Short History of Africa*. New York: New York University Press, 1963.

Oloidi, Sola. *Sir Olateru Olagbegi II KBE: The Legendary King*. Surulere, Lagos, Nigeria: Mednet Limited, 1994.

Oluleye, James J. *Military Leadership in Nigeria, 1966–1979*. Ibadan: University Press, 1985.

Onuorah, R.U. *Twenty-One Years of Independence: A Calendar of Major Political and Economic Events in Nigeria, 1960–1981*. Ibadan: NISER, 1981.

Orr, Charles. *The Making of Northern Nigeria*. London: Frank Cass, 1965.

Osayameh, Ralph Oluwole. *The Crusade for a Profession: A History of the Chartered Institute of Bankers of Nigeria, 1963–1993*. Lagos: CIBN, 1993.

Otite, O. *Autonomy and Independence: The Urhobo Kingdom of Okpe in Nigeria*. London: Hurst, 1973.

Oyediran, O., ed. *Survey of Nigerian Affairs, 1975*. Lagos: OUP, 1978.
Oyeweso, Siyan. *The Post-Gowon Nigerian Accounts of the Civil War, 1975–1990: A Preliminary Review*. Lagos: African Peace Research Institute, 1992.
Padmore, George. *Africa—Britain's Third Empire*. London: Dobson, 1949.
———. *How Britain Rules Africa*. London: Dobson, 1936.
———. *How Russia Transformed Her Colonial Empire*. London: Dobson, 1949.
——— *Pan Africanism or Communism*. London: Dobson, 1956.
Palmer, H.R. *The Bornu, Sahara and Sudan*. London: J. Murray, 1936.
———. *Sudanese Memoirs*. 3 vols. Lagos: Government, 1928.
Panel on Nigeria since Independence History Project. *The Civil War Years*, edited by Tekena N. Tamuno and Samson C. Ukpabi. Ibadan: Heinemann, 1989.
Park, Mungo. *Journal of a Mission to the Interior of Africa in the Year 1805*. London: J. Murray, 1815.
———. *Travels in the Interior Districts of Africa, in 1795, 1796 and 1797*. London: Bulmer and Co., 1799.
Parrinder, Geoffrey. *The Story of Ketu—An Ancient Yoruba Kingdom*. Ibadan: Ibadan University Press, 1956.
Pedrarza, H.J. *Borioboda-Gha: The Story of Lokoja: The First British Settlement in Nigeria*. London: Oxford University Press, 1960.
Perham, Margery. *Africans and British Rule*. London: Oxford University Press, 1941.
Robertson, James W. *The Last of the Proconsuls: Letters from Sir James W. Robertson KT, GCMG, GCVO, KBE, Order of the Nile*. London: Radcliffe Press, 1994.
Soyege, Solomon Adelanwa. *My Sojourn in Life: An Autobiography*. Ibadan: Y-Books, 1992.
Tinubu, S.A. *S.L. Akintola, His Politics and His Nation: The Reminiscence of One of His Associates*. Ibadan: African Digest Co., 1992.
Townsend, George. *Memoir of the Rev. Henry Townsend*. London: Marshall Brother, 1887.
Tremearne, A.J.N. *The Niger and the West Sudan*. London: Stoughton, 1900.
Trimingham, J.P. *The Christian Church and Islam in West Africa*. London: S.C.M. Press, 1955.
Trimingham, J. Spencer. *A History of Islam in West Africa*. London: Oxford University Press, 1962.
———. *Islam in West Africa*. London: Clarendon Press, 1959.
Tucker, Miss. *Abeokuta or Sunrise within the Tropics*. London: Nisbet, 1853.
Turaki, Yusufu. *The British Colonial Legacy in Northern Nigeria*. Jos: Challenge Press, 1993.
Ukpabi, Sam. C. *Strands in Nigerian Military History*. Zaria, Nigeria: Gaskiya, 1986.
Vaughan, James and Kirk-Greene, Anthony H.M. (eds.) *The Diary of Hamman Yaji: Chronicle of a West African Muslim Ruler*. Bloomington: Indiana University Press, 1995.
Venn, Henry III. *Memoir of the Rev. Henry Venn (II)*. London: William Knight, 1880.
Waddell, Hope M. *Twenty-Nine Years in the West Indies and Central Africa*. Edinburgh, Scotland: Nelson, 1863.
Walker, F.D. *A Hundred Years in Nigeria*. London: Cargate Press, 1942.
———. *The Romance of the Black River*. London: Church Missionary Society, 1931.

Wellesley, Dorothy. *Sir George Goldie*. London: Macmillan, 1934.
Westermann, Diedrich. *The African To-day*. London: Oxford University Press, 1934.
———. *The African To-day and To-morrow*. 3d ed. London: Oxford University Press, 1949.
Yaji, Hamman. *The Diary of Hamman Yaji: Chronicle of a West African Muslim Ruler*. Bloomington: Indiana University Press, 1995.
Yakubu, Alhaji Mahmood. *An Aristocracy in Political Crisis: The End of Indirect Rule and the Emergence of Party Politics in the Emirates of Northern Nigeria*. Aldershot: Avebury, 1996.
Yusuf, Jolly Tanko. *That We May Be One: The Autobiography of Nigerian Ambassador Jolly Tanko Yusuf*. Grand Rapids, Mich: W.B. Eerdmans, 1995.

MILITARY HISTORY

Courtesy of Thomas P. Ofcansky

Biafra War

Achizua, J.O.G. *Requiem Biafra*. Enugu, Nigeria: Fourth Dimension Publishing Company Ltd., 1986.
Amadi, Elechi. *Sunset in Biafra: A Civil War Diary*. London: Heinemann, 1973.
Amuta, Chidi. "The Nigerian Civil War and the Evolution of Nigerian Literature." *Canadian Journal of African Studies* 17, no. 1 (1983): 85–99.
Anafulu, Joseph C. "An African Experience: The Role of a Specialized Library in a War Situation." *Special Libraries* 62, no. 1 (1971): 32–40.
Anglin, Douglas G. "Zambia and the Recognition of Biafra." *African Review* 1, no. 2 (1971): 102–136.
Bach, Daniel. "Le General de Gaulle et la Guerre Civile au Nigeria." *Canadian Journal of African Studies* 14, no. 2 (1980): 259–272.
"Biafra: Gestorben für das Petroleum der Anderen." *Wiener Tagebuch*, no. 3 (1970): 15–17.
Biafra Ministry of Information. *Biafra Deserves Open World Support*. Enugu, Nigeria: Biafra Ministry of Information, 1968.
Bonneville, Floris de. *La Mort du Biafra!* Paris: Solar, 1968.
Christian Council of Nigeria. *Relief and Reconciliation in Nigerian Crisis*. Lagos: Christian Council of Nigeria, 1970.
Cronje, Suzanne. *The World and Nigeria: The Diplomatic History of the Biafran War, 1967–1970*. London: Sidgwick and Jackson, 1972.
D.O. "The Military and Politics: Some Reflections from the Nigerian Case." *Nigerian Opinion* (October 1967): 245–252.
Dent, Martin J. "Nigeria: After the War," *The World Today*, no. 3 (March 1970): 103–109.
———. "Nigeria: The Task of Conflict Resolution." *The World Today*, no. 7 (July 1968): 269–280.
Eastern Nigeria Ministry of Information. *Nigerian Crisis—1966*. Enugu, Nigeria: Eastern Nigeria Ministry of Information, 1966.

Ekwe-Ekwe, Herbert. *The Biafra War: Nigeria and the Aftermath*. New York: Edwin Mellen Press, 1990.

Etinger, Ia Ia. "Nigeriiskii Krizis 1967–1970 Godov," *Voprosy Istorii*, no. 4 (1976): 133–147.

Feuser, Wilfried F. "Anomy and Beyond: Nigeria's Civil War in Literature." *Présence Africaine*, nos. 1/2 (1986): 113–151. Previously published in *Cultures et Dévelopement* 16, nos. 3/4 (1984): 783–820.

Forsyth, Frederick. *The Biafra Story*. Baltimore, Md.: Penguin, 1969.

Gbulie, Ben. *The Fall of Biafra*. Emgu: Benlie, 1989.

Hooper, James. "Coverage of the Nigerian Civil War in Two Canadian Daily Newspapers." Master's thesis, McGill University, Montréal, Quebec, 1972.

Ibelema, Minabere. "Tribes and Prejudice: Coverage of the Nigerian Civil War." In *Africa's Media Image*, edited by Beverly G. Hawk, 77–93. New York: Praeger, 1992.

Ifejika, Samuel U. "Mobilizing Support for the Biafran Regime: The Politics of War and Propaganda." Ph.D. diss., York University, Toronto, 1979.

Ihonvbere, Julius. "The Role of Oil in the Nigerian Civil War, 1967–1970." *African Studies*, no. 10 (1986): 156–171.

———. "A Critical Evaluation of the Failed 1990 Coup in Nigeria." *Journal of Modern African Studies*. Vol. 29, no. 4 (1991).

Ikpuk, John Smith. *Militarisation of Politics and Neo-Colonialism: The Nigerian Experience 1966–90*. London: Janus Publishing Company, 1995.

Islam, M. Rafiqui. "Secessionist Self-Determination: Some Lessons from Katanga, Biafra and Bangladesh." *Journal of Peace Research* 22, no. 3 (1985): 211–221.

Jacobs, Dan. *The Brutality of Nations*. New York: Alfred A. Knopf, 1987.

Jervis, Steven. "From Nigeria to Biafra." *Michigan Quarterly Review* 10, no. 4 (1971): 275–286.

Kirk-Greene, A.H.M. *The Genesis of the Nigerian Civil War and the Theory of Fear*. Uppsala, Sweden: The Scandinavian Institute of African Studies, 1975.

Kwarteng, C. "'Babangidazation' after Babangida: The Nigerian Military and the Politics of Incumbency." *Round Table*. No. 338 (April 1996).

Madiebo, Alexander. *The Nigerian Revolution and the Biafran War*. Enugu, Nigeria: Fourth Dimension Publishing Company Ltd., 1980.

Nafziger, E. Wayne, and William L. Richter. "Biafra and Bangladesh: The Political Economy of Secessionist Conflict." *Journal of Peace Research* 13, no. 2 (1976): 91–109.

Nigerian Christian. *Christian Concern in the Nigerian Civil War: A Collection of Articles Which Have Appeared in Issues of* The Nigerian Christian *from April 1967 to April 1969*. Ibadan: Daystar Press, 1969.

Nixens, Sir Rex. *The War of Nigerian Unity*. London: Evans Brothers/Nigerian Publishers, 1970.

Nixon, Charles R. "Self-Determination: The Nigeria/Biafra Case." *World Politics* 24, no. 4 (1972): 473–497.

Njoku, H. *A Tragedy without Heroes: The Nigeria-Biafra War*. Enugu, Nigeria: Fourth Dimension Publishing Company Ltd., 1987.

Nkpa, Nwokocha K.U. "Rumors of Mass Poisoning in Biafra." *Public Opinion Quarterly* 41, no. 3 (1977): 332–346.

Nwankwo, Arthur A. *Nigeria: The Challenge of Biafra*. Enugu, Nigeria: Fourth Dimension Publishing Company Ltd., 1972.

Obasanjo, Olusegan. *My Command: An Account of the Nigerian Civil War, 1967–70*. London: Heinemann, 1980.

Obiozor, George A. *The United States and the Nigerian Civil War: An American Dilemma in Africa, 1966–1970*. Lagos: Nigerian Institute of International Affairs, 1993.

O'Brian, Daniel. "Biafra: Ein Jahr nach dem Ende." *Wort und Wahrheit* 26, no. 3 (1971): 256–262.

Ogbudinkpa, Nwabeze Reuben. *The Economics of the Nigerian Civil War and Its Prospects for National Development*. Enugu, Nigeria: Fourth Dimension Publishing Company Ltd., 1985.

Ogunbadejo, Oye. "Nigeria and the Great Powers: The Impact of the Civil War on Nigerian Foreign Relations." *African Affairs* 75, no. 298 (January 1976): 14–32.

Olawoyin, James A. "Historical Analysis of Nigeria-Biafra Conflict." LL.M. thesis, York University, Toronto, 1971.

Onu, Paul E. "The Nigerian Civil War in the Nigerian and World Press: A Study in International News Flow." Master's thesis, McGill University, Montréal, Quebec, 1973.

Orobator, S.E. "The Biafran Crisis and the Midwest." *African Affairs* 86, no. 344 (1987): 367–384.

———. "The Nigerian Civil War and the Invasion of Czechoslovakia." *African Affairs* 82, no. 327 (April 1983): 201–214.

Panter-Brick, S. Keith, ed. *Nigerian Politics and Military Rule: Prelude to the Civil War*. London: Athlone Press, 1970.

Perham, Margery. "The Nigerian Crisis and After." *Listener* 27 (January 1966): 121–123.

Peters, Jimi. *The Nigerian Military and the State*. London: Tauris, 1997.

———. "Nigeria's Civil War." In *Africa Contemporary Record,* edited by Colin Legum and John Drysdale, 1–12. New York: Africana Publishing, 1969.

———. "Reflections on the Nigerian Civil War." *International Affairs* (April 1970): 231–246.

———. "The War in Nigeria." *Listener* 19 (September 1968): 353–355.

Post, K.W.J. "The Crisis in Nigeria." *The World Today* (February 1966): 43–47.

———. "Is There a Case for Biafra?" *International Affairs* (January 1968): 26–39.

———. "Revolt in Nigeria." *The Round Table* (July 1966): 269–273.

Riemenschneider, D. "The Biafra War in Nigerian Literature." *Journal of Commonwealth Literature,* no. 1 (1983): 55–68.

Samuels, J.W. "Humanitarian Relief in Man-Made Disasters: The International Red Cross and the Nigerian Experience." *Behind the Headlines* 34, no. 3 (1975): 1–44.

Saro-Wiwa, Ken. *On a Darkling Plain: An Account of the Nigerian Civil War*. Lagos: Saros International Publishers, 1989.

Schwarz, Walter, "Civil War in Nigeria." *Venture* (December 1968); 5–6.

———. "Foreign Powers and the Nigerian War." *Africa Report,* no. 2 (February 1970): 12–14.

———. "Tribalism and Politics in Nigeria." *The World Today* (November 1966): 460–467.

St. Jorre, John de. *The Brothers' War: Biafra and Nigeria*. Boston, Mass.: Houghton Mifflin, 1972.

Stephan, Klaus. "Nigeria nach dem Krieg." *Europa-Archiv* 26, no. 17 (1971): 617–622.

Sterken, Jacob. "Nigerian Civil War: The Role of Humanitarians." Master's thesis. University of Waterloo, Ontario, 1973.

Strah, Michael Sherman. "An Ethical Analysis of United States Involvement in the Nigerian/Biafran Conflict." Ph.D. diss., Boston University, 1984.

Stremlau, John J. *The International Politics of the Nigerian Civil War, 1967–1970*. Princeton, N.J.: Princeton University Press, 1977.

Thompson, Joseph E. *American Policy and African Famine: The Nigeria-Biafra War, 1966–1970*. Westport, Conn.: Greenwood Press, 1990.

Ugokwe, J.B.C. "The Politics and Consequences of the Nigerian Biafra War." *African Scholar* (August 1968): 17–21.

Uwechue, R. *Reflections on the Nigerian Civil War: A Call for Realism*. New York: Africana Publishing, 1971.

Wiseberg, Laurie S. "The International Politics of Relief: A Case Study of the Relief Operations Mounted during the Nigerian Civil War, 1967–1970." Ph.D. diss., University of California at Los Angeles, 1973.

Wolf, Jean, and Claude Brovelli. *La Guerre des Rapaces: La Vérité sur la Guerre du Biafra*. Paris: Michel, 1969.

General

Ajaiyi, Daniel A. "Non-Military Educational Programs in the Nigerian Army, 1914–1981." Ph.D. diss., University of Pittsburgh, 1982.

Nigerian Army Education Corps and School. *History of the Nigerian Army, 1863–1992*. Lagos: Gabumo Publishing Company, 1992.

Precolonial Period

Achi, Bala. "Arms and Armour in the Warfare of Pre-Colonial Hausaland." *African Studies Monographs* 8, no. 3 (1988): 145–158.

Ajayi, J.F. Ade, and Robert Sydney Smith. *Yoruba Warfare in the Nineteenth Century*. London: Cambridge University Press, 1964.

Dantiye, Nasiru Ibrahim. "A Study of the Origins, Status and Defensive Role of Four Kano Frontier Strongholds Ribats in the Emirate Period, 1809–1903." Ph.D. diss., Indiana University Press, Bloomington, 1985.

Falola, Toyin, and Robin Law, ed. *Warfare and Diplomacy in Pre-Colonial Nigeria*. Madison: African Studies Program, University of Wisconsin, 1992.

Fischer, Humphrey J. "Leo Africanus and the Songhay Conquest of Hausaland." *International Journal of African Historical Studies* 11, no. 1 (1978): 86–112.

McCall, John C. "The Ohafia War Dance as Lived Experience: History and Identity in a Nigerian Community." Ph.D. diss., Indiana University, Bloomington, 1992.

Milsome, John. "The Growth of Power in Northern Nigeria." *Contemporary Review* 216, no. 1251 (1970): 189–193.

Oguntomisin, G.O. "The Ijaye-Egba Military Alliance, 1860–1862." *Odu: A Journal of West African Studies,* no. 30 (1986): 129–146.

Oriji, J.N. "The Slave Trade, Warfare and Aro Expansion in the Igbo Hinterland." *Transafrican Journal of History* 16 (1987): 151–166. Previously published in *Genève-Afrique* 24, no. 2 (1986): 101–118.

"La Pacification du Sahara: Nigeria Nord." *L'Afrique Française* (July/August 1917): 267–268.

Record of the Overseas Contingent, Nigeria Regiment, West African Frontier Force, Dec. 1916 to June 1917. Lagos: Government Printer, 1917.

Wilson, J. Leighton. *The British Squadron on the Coast of Africa.*

Colonial Period

Ahire, Philip Terdoo. *Imperial Policing: The Emergence and Role of the Police in Colonial Nigeria, 1860–1960.* London: Open University Press, 1991.

Allen, A.R. "Disaster at Satiru." *Journal of the Society for Army Historical Research* 50, no. 203 (1972): 169–176.

Amadi, Levi Onyemuche. "The Reactions and Contributions of Nigerians during the Second World War: Agents of Political Integration in Nigeria, 1939–1945." *Transafrican Journal of History* (1977/1978): 1–11.

Anyika, F. "Military Force and the Spread of the Gospel in Southern Nigeria: The 1901–2 Aro Expedition." *African Theological Journal* 20, no. 1 (1991): 28–41.

Atteridge, Andrew H. "Recent Expeditions in West Africa, 1894–1899." *The Journal of the Royal United Service Institution* 94 (February 1900): 111–136.

Blackwell, H.F. *The Occupation of Hausaland: 1900–1904.* Lagos: Government Printer, 1927.

Bourdillon, B.H. "Nigeria's War Effort." *Journal of the African Society* 39 (1940): 115–122.

Bowen, C.G. "Service in West Africa." *The Journal of the Royal United Service Institution* 93, no. 571 (August 1948): 414–416.

Braithwaite, W.C. *West African Warfare.* 1905.

British Colonial Office. *Report on the Health of the British Troops Serving with the West African Frontier Force.* London: British Colonial Office, n.d.

Brown, Spencer H. "Colonialism on the Cheap: A Tale of Two English Army Surgeons in Lagos—Samuel Rowe and Frank Simpson, 1862–1882." *The International Journal of African Historical Studies* 27, no. 3 (1994): 551–558.

Clarke, F.A.S. "The Military and Economic Importance of West Africa." *The Journal of the Royal United Service Institution* 93, no. 569 (February 1948): 109–116.

———. "The Development of the West African Forces in the Second World War." *The Army Quarterly* 55, no. 1 (October 1947): 58–73.

Crooks, J.J. *History Records of the Royal African Corps.* Dublin, Ireland: Browne and Nolan, 1925.

Crozier, Frank Percy. *Five Years Hard.* New York: Jonathan Cape and R. Ballou, 1932.

Denholm-Young, C.P.S. "R.W.A.F.F." *The Army Quarterly and Defence Journal* 105, no. 1 (January 1975): 60–66.

Dodd, Norman L. "The Nigerian Battery." *The Journal of the Royal Artillery* 88, no. 1 (1951): 20–25.

Downes, Walter Douglas. "The Apes at Sea." *Blackwood's Magazine* (April 1918): 20–31.

Dusgate, Richard H. *The Conquest of Northern Nigeria*. London: Frank Cass, 1985.

Ekechi, Felix. "The British Assault on Ogbunorie Oracle in Eastern Nigeria." *Journal of African Studies* 14, no. 2 (Summer 1987): 69–77.

Ekoko, A.E. "Borders in International Relations and Military Strategy: Focus on Nigeria's Western Boundary, 1989–1945." In *Borderlands in Africa: A Multidisciplinary and Comparative Focus on Nigeria and West Africa,* edited by A.I. Asiwaju and P.O. Adeniyi, 279–291. Lagos: University of Lagos Press, 1989.

———. "British Defence Policy in Western Africa, 1878–1914." Ph.D. diss., University of Aberdeen, Scotland, Great Britain, 1976.

Fika, Adamu Mohammed. *The Kano Civil War and British Over-Rule, 1882–1940*. Ibadan: Oxford University Press, 1978.

Gifford, George. "The Royal West African Frontier Force and Its Expansion for War." *The Army Quarterly* 50, no. 2 (July 1945): 190–196.

Gordon-Lennox, Lord Esmé Charles. *With the West African Frontier Force in Southern Nigeria*. London: H.J. Ryman, 1905.

Gore, Albert A. *A Contribution to the Medical History of Our West African Campaigns*. London, 1876.

Great Britain War Office. *Statistical Reports on the Sickness, Mortality, and Invaliding among the Troops in Western Africa, St. Helena, the Cape of Good Hope, and the Mauritius*. London: Great Britain War Office, 1840.

Hall, Herbert Colley. *Barracks and Bush in Northern Nigeria*. London: G. Allen and Unwin, 1923.

Harper, T. *Red Dust: Extracts from an Army Officer's Diary*. New York, 1990.

Haywood, A.H.W. *Sport and Service in Africa*. London: Seeley, Service and Company, 1926.

Heneker, W.C.G. *Bush Warfare*. London: Rees, 1907.

Hennessy, M.N. "The Nigerian Advance from Mogadiscio to Harrar." *The Army Quarterly* 57, no. 1 (October 1948): 65–71.

Ikime, Obaro. "The British 'Pacification' of the Tiv, 1900–1908." *Journal of the Historical Society of Nigeria* 7, no. 1 (1973): 103–109.

Lawson, Richard. *Strange Soldiering*. London: Hodder and Stoughton, 1963.

Matthews, James K. "Clock Towers for the Colonized: Demobilization of the Nigerian Military and the Readjustment of Its Veterans to Civilian Life, 1918–1925." *International Journal of African Historical Studies* 14, no. 2 (1981): 254–271.

Muffett, D.J.M. *Concerning Brave Captains*. London: Deutsch, 1964.

Nigeria. *Record of the Overseas Contingent—Nigerian Regiment W.A.F.F., December 1916—June 1917*. Lagos: Government Printer, 1917.

The Nigeria Regiment: Spearhead of Victory—Yan Jagaban Nasea. Lagos: 1944.

Noah, Monday Efiong. "The Establishment of British Rule among the Ibibio, 1885–1910." *Nigeria Magazine,* no. 148 (1984): 38–51; and no. 149 (1984): 24–34.

Nwaka, Geoffrey I. "Rebellion in Umuahia, 1950–1951: Ex-Servicemen and Anti-Colonial Protest in Eastern Nigeria." *Transafrican Journal of History* 16 (1987): 47–62.

Ohadike, Don C. *The Ekumeku Movement: Western Igbo Resistance to the British Conquest of Nigeria, 1883–1914*. Athens: Ohio University Press, 1991.

Osuntokun, Akinjide. "Disaffection and Revolts in Nigeria during the First World War, 1914–1918," *Canadian Journal of African Studies* 5, no. 2 (1971): 177–192.

———. "The EADC, 1917–20." *Lagos Notes and Records* 6 (1977): 1–9.

———. "Nigeria in the First World War." Ph.D. diss., Dalhousie University, Halifax, Nova Scotia, 1970.

———. *Nigeria in the First World War*. Ibadan: University of Ibadan Press, 1979. Also published with London: Longman Group Ltd., 1979; and Atlantic Highlands: Humanities Press, 1979.

———. "Nigeria's Colonial Government and the Islamic Insurgency in French West Africa, 1914–1918." *Cahiers d'Etudes Africaines* 57, no. 15 (1975): 85–92.

———. "Problems of Military Recruitment in Nigeria during the First World War." *Calabar Historical Journal* 1 (November 1976): 114–131.

———. "The Response of the British Colonial Government in Nigeria to the Islamic Insurgency in the French Sudan and the Sahara during the First World War." *Odu: A Journal of West African Studies* 10 (1974): 98–107. Also published in *Bulletin de l'Institute Fondamental d'Afrique Noire* 26, no. 1 (1974): 14–24.

Percival, A.E. "The West African Frontier Force." *The Army Quarterly* 15, no. 1 (October 1927): 91–99.

Plotnicov, Leonard. "An Early Nigerian Civil Disturbance: The 1945 Hausa-Ibo Riot in Jos." *Journal of Modern African Studies* 9, no. 2 (1971): 297–305.

Royal West African Frontier Force. *Our Regiment*. Lagos: Great Britain Army Public Relations Department, 1946.

Shaw, Jesse. *Special Force: A Chindit's Story*. London: Sutton, 1986.

Stronge, H.C.T. "Nigeria: A Soldier Looks Back." *The Army Quarterly and Defence Quarterly* 98, no. 2 (July 1969): 205–208.

Swynnerton, C.R.A. *Arakan: A Short History of the First West Africa Infantry Brigade, 1944–1945*. Lagos: Ife-Olu Printing Works, 1949.

———. "The 1st West African Infantry Brigade in the Arakan, 1944–1945." *The Army Quarterly* 52, no. 2 (July 1946): 189–201; and 53, no. 1 (October 1946): 48–60.

———. "West African Scene." *The Army Quarterly* 61, no. 2 (January 1951): 218–236.

Tamuno, Tekena N. *The Police in Modern Nigeria, 1861–1965: Origins, Development and Role*. Ibadan: University of Ibadan, 1970.

Taylor, A.S. *Short History of the Nigeria Regiment*. Lagos: West African Printing and Stationary Services, 1930.

Ukpabi, S.C. "British Colonial Wars in West Africa: Image and Reality." *Civilisations* 20, no. 3 (1970): 379–404.

———. "British Military Expeditions in West Africa Reexamined." *Pan-African Journal* 8, no. 1 (1975): 31–43.

———. "Recruiting for British Colonial Forces in West Africa in the Nineteenth Century." *Odu: A Journal of West African Studies*, no. 10 (July 1974): 79–97.

Ukpabi, Samson L. "The West African Frontier Force: An Instrument of Imperial Policy, 1897–1914." Master's thesis, Birmingham, Alabama, 1964.
Vaughan, C.P. *Record of Operations of the 7th Battalion, The Nigeria Regiment: Burma, April–July, 1944*. Lagos, 1954.

Independence

Aboaba, Doyinsola Abiola. "The Nigerian Press under Military Rule." Ph.D. diss., State University of New York, Buffalo, 1979.
Adamolekun, Ladipo, John Erero, and Basil Oshionebo. "'Federal Service' and Management of the Federal Civil Service and the Military." *Publius* 21, no. 4 (1991): 75–88.
Adejumobi, Said, and Abubakar Momoh. *The Political Economy of Nigeria under Military Rule: 1984–1993*. Harare: Southern Africa Printing and Publishing House, 1995.
Adekanye, J. Bayo. "Domestic Production of Arms and the Defence Industries Corporation of Nigeria." *Current Research on Peace and Violence* 4 (1983): 258–269.
———. "'Federal Character' Provisions of the 1979 Constitution and Composition of the Nigerian Armed Forces: The Old Quota Idea by New Name." *Plural Societies* 13, nos. 1–2 (1983): 66–78.
Adekson, J. Bayo. "The Brawn versus Brain Conflict in Contemporary African Civil-Military History and Thought." *Plural Societies* 10, nos. 3–4 (1979): 3–20.
Adeniran, Tunde. "Military Rule and Nation-Building: Praetorianism Revisited." *Journal of Economics and Social Studies* 27 (November 1985): 329–344.
Adepoju, Aderanti. "Military Rule and Population Issues in Nigeria." *African Affairs* 80, no. 318 (January 1981): 29–47.
Adewuyi, A.A. "Nigerian Population Policy during the Military Administration: A Critique of Socio-Economic Development Hypothesis." *Nigerian Behavorial Science Journal* nos. 1/2 (1980): 86–107.
Adisa, Jinmi. "Political Risk and Social Obligation: The Demobilization of the Nigerian Army, 1970–1979." *Plural Societies* 15, no. 2 (1984): 97–113.
Agambila, Gheysika A. "Militarization among the ex-British Colonies of West Africa." Ph.D. diss., New York University, 1993.
Agbakoba, Olisa. "In Defence of National Security: An Appraisal of the Nigerian Intelligence System." *Spectrum* (January/February 1984).
Agbese, Pita Ogaba. "The Military and the Privatization of Repression in Nigeria." *Conflict* 10, no. 3 (1990): 239–266.
———. "The Political Economy of Militarization in Nigeria." *Afrika-Spectrum* 25, no. 3 (1990): 293–312.
Ahanotu, Austin. "The Nigerian Military and the Issue of State Control of Mission Schools." *Church History* 52, no. 3 (1983): 333–344.
Ajayi, Daniel Ayoola. "Non-Military Educational Programs in the Nigerian Army." Ph.D. diss., University of Pittsburgh, 1982.
Akinsanya, A. "The Machinery of Government during the Military Regime in Nigeria." *Africa Quarterly* 16, no. 3 (1977): 28–41.
Akiwowo, Akinsola. "The Armed Forces in the Nigerian Economy: A Sociologist's Approach to Their Peaceful Use." *Politico* 37, no. 3 (1972): 562–581.

Akpan, Moses E. "The Nigerian Military and National Integration, 1966–1979." *Journal of African Studies* 15, nos. 1/2 (Spring/Summer 1988): 40–46.

Aminu, A.L. "Nigeria's Defence Preparedness and Planning." *Nigerian Journal of International Affairs* 12, nos. 1/2 (1986): 77–87.

Aminu, L. Salawu. *Nigeria's Weapons Procurement Process: Its Implications for Her Defence Policy.* Lagos: Nigerian Institute of International Affairs, 1993.

Auma-Osolo, Agola. "Objective African Military Control: A New Paradigm in Civil-Military Relations." *Journal of Peace Research* 17, no. 1 (1980): 29–46.

Baker, Pauline. "Nigeria: The Politics of Military Rule." *Africa Report* 16, no. 2 (February 1971): 18–21.

Bassey, Celestine O. "Defence Planning and the Nigerian Armed Forces Modernization Process, 1970–1991: An Institutional Analysis." *Armed Forces and Society* 19, no. 2 (Winter 1993): 253–277.

———. "The Military Instrument and Strategic Policy in a Democratic Order: A Theoretical Reconsideration of Some Unresolved Issues concerning Nigeria." *The Journal of Political Science* 13, nos. 1/2 (1990): 15–31.

———. "Nigeria, African Security and the Nuclear Option." *Bodija Journal* 1, no. 2 (1989): 61–70.

———. "Nigeria and Inter-African Peacekeeping Approach to Conflict Management." *Calabar Journal of Liberal Studies* 3, no. 2 (1991): 21–42.

———. "Nigeria's Defense Policy in a Future Continental Order." *Nigerian Journal of International Affairs* 13, no. 2 (1987): 83–105.

———. "Nigeria's Quest for a Military-Industrial Complex." *Nigerian Journal of International Studies* 12 (1988): 46–55.

———. "The Political Economy of Defence Expenditure in Nigeria: The 'Gun' or 'Gari' Controversy Revisited." In *Proceedings of the 15th Annual Conference of the Nigerian Political Science Association,* edited by Sonni Tyoden. Ibadan: University of Ibadan, 1988.

Bauder, Ingegerd. "Militarismen i Nigeria och Ethiopien." *Militarhistorisk Tidskrift* (1985): 85–129.

Beckman, Bjorn. "The Military as Revolutionary Vanguard: A Critique." *Review of African Political Economy,* (December 1986): 50–63.

Biaghere, Sunny. "Interview with Nigerian Navy Chief Rear-Admiral Nyako." *African Defence Journal,* no. 120 (August 1990): 33.

———. "Nigeria: Creating a National Defence Industry." *African Defence Journal.* no. 80 (April 1987): 64–65.

———. "Nigeria: Getting the Police Ready for the Third Republic." *African Defence Journal,* no. 105 (May 1989): 50–51.

———. "Nigeria: Why a Rapid Deployment Force?" *African Defence Journal,* no. 99 (November 1988): 48–49.

———. "Nigeria's Rapid Deployment Force: How Viable?" *African Defence Journal,* no. 112 (December 1989): 38–39.

———. "The Nigerian Air Force Celebrates Its Silver Jubilee." *African Defence Journal,* no. 106 (June 1989): 46–47.

———. "Nigerian Navy: 33 Years of Coastal Defence." *African Defence Journal,* no. 110 (October 1989): 48–49.

Bienen, Henry. "Military Rule and Political Process: Nigerian Examples." *Comparative Politics* 10, no. 29 (1978): 205–226.

Boam, T.A. "Nigeria's Staff College." *The Army Quarterly and Defence Journal* (July 1978).

Campbell, Horace. "The Lessons of the Military Coup in Nigeria." *Ufahamu* 13, nos. 2/3 (1984): 112–126.

Chazan, Naomi. "The Transformation of a Faltering Giant: Studies of Nigeria under Military Rule." *Asian and African Studies* 18, no. 2 (1984): 205–230.

Dare, L.O. "Military Withdrawal from Politics in Nigeria." *International Political Science Review,* no. 3 (1981): 351–362.

———. "On Leadership and Military Rule in Nigeria." *Odu: A Journal of West African Studies,* no. 16 (1977): 70–84.

Dilke, P. Chike. "Nigeria's New War Museum: An Overview." *Nigeria Magazine* 54, no. 3 (1986): 25–31.

Diya, Oladipo. "Nigeria Sets Up Africa's First National War College." *The Army Quarterly and Defence Journal* 123, no. 2 (April 1993): 204–207.

Dodd, Norman L. "The Armed Forces of Nigeria, Ghana and Kenya." *Asian Defence Journal,* no. 4, (April 1984): 78–79; 81–84; 86–88.

Ebigbola, J.A. "Population Statistics during Military Interregnum in Nigeria." *Nigerian Behavioral Science Journal,* nos. 1/2 (1980): 108–120.

Eke, Kenoye Kelvin. *Nigeria's Foreign Policy under Two Military Governments, 1966–1979: An Analysis of the Gowan and Muhammad/Obasanjo Regimes.* Lewiston, N.Y.: E. Mellen, 1990.

Ekoko, A.E., and M.A. Vogt, ed. *Nigerian Defense Policy: Issues and Problems.* Lagos: Malthouse Press, 1990.

Ekwelie, Sylvanus A. "The Nigerian Press under Military Rule." *Gazette* 25, no. 4 (1979): 219–232.

Fawole, W. Alade. "National Role Conceptions and Foreign Policy: Nigeria's African Diplomacy under Military Rule." Ph.D. diss., George Washington University, Washington, D.C., 1990.

Gbulie, B. *Nigeria's Five Majors: Coup d'Etat of 15th January 1966. First Inside Account.* Onitsha, Nigeria: Africana Educational Publishers, 1981.

Graf, William D. "The Nigerian New Year's Coup of December 31, 1983: A Class Analysis." *Journal of Black Studies* 16, no. 1 (1985): 21–45.

Hughes, Arnold. "The Army as 'Social Engineers' in Nigeria." *Contemporary Review* 231, no. 1343 (1977): 286–291.

Ihonvbere, Julius O. "Continuity and Change in Nigerian Foreign Policy under Military Rule, 1966–1979." *Asian and African Studies* 19, no. 2 (1985): 199–218.

Ikegwooha, Bernard-Thompson. *The Military Participation in the Politics and Government of Nigeria: A Socio-Political Review.* Rome: N. Domenici-Pecheur Press, 1988.

Ikoku, S.G. *Nigeria's Fourth Coup d'Etat.* Enugu, Nigeria: Fourth Dimension Publishing Company Ltd., 1985.

Imobighe, Thomas A. "Libyan Intervention in Chad: Security Implications for Nigeria." *Nigerian Journal of International Studies* 4, nos. 1/2 (January/June 1980).

———, ed. *Nigerian Defence and Security: Issues and Options for Policy.* Lagos: Macmillan, 1987.

Joseph, Richard A. "Democratization under Military Tutelage: Crisis and Consensus in the Nigerian 1979 Elections." *Comparative Politics* 14, no. 1 (1981): 75–100.

Kamanu, O. "Nigeria: Reflections on the Defence Posture for the 1980s." *Genève-Afrique* 6, no. 1 (1977/78): 27–42.

Khanin, V.E. "Grazhdanskie I Voennye Politiki V Nigerii: Konfrontatsiia lli Partnerstvo?" *Narody Azii i Afriki*, no. 4 (1986): 24–33.

Kraus, Jon. "From Military to Civilian Regimes in Ghana and Nigeria." *Current History* 76, no. 445 (1979): 122–126; 134–136; 138.

———. "Nigeria under Shagari." *Current History* 81, no. 473 (1982): 106–110, 136.

———. "The Return of Civilian Rule in Nigeria and Ghana." *Current History* 78, no. 455 (1980): 115–118; 128–129; 137–138; 144.

Lagos Correspondent. "Dispatch from Nigeria." *The Army Quarterly and Defence Journal* 113, no. 3 (July 1983): 305–306.

———. "Nigeria: The Army's Role." *The Army Quarterly and Defence Journal* 115, no. 2 (April 1985): 135–140.

Lawson, Richard. *Strange Soldiering*. London: Hodder and Stoughton, 1963.

Lawyers Committee for Human Rights. *The Nigerian Police Force: A Culture of Impunity*. New York: Lawyers Committee for Human Rights, 1992.

Luckham, A.R. "Institutional Transfer and Breakdown in a New Nation: The Nigerian Military." *Administrative Science Quarterly* 16, no. 4 (1971): 387–405.

Luckham, Robin. *The Nigerian Military: A Sociological Analysis of Authority and Revolt, 1960–1967*. Cambridge: Cambridge University Press, 1971.

Marenin, Otwin. "Policing Nigeria: Control and Autonomy in the Exercise of Coercion." *African Studies Review* 28, no. 1 (March 1985): 73–93.

Mays, Terry Maynard. "The White Helmets: Nigerian Foreign Policy and Multinational Peacekeeping." Ph.D. diss., University of South Carolina, Columbia, 1993.

"Meeting the Defense Needs of Nigeria." *The Nigerian Economist* (12–25 September 1990): 19–34.

Miners, N.J. *The Nigerian Army, 1956–1966*. London: Methuen, 1971.

Misawa, Buba. "The Consequences of Military Growth, Military Expenditures, and Military Political Dominance on Nigerian Foreign Policy, 1960–1990." Ph.D. diss., University of Pittsburgh, 1992.

Murray, David J. "Nigeria: The Experience of Military Rule." *Current History* 68, no. 405 (1975): 216–219.

Nigerian Army Education Corps and School. *History of the Nigerian Army, 1863–1992*. Lagos: Gabumo Publishing Company, 1992.

Nigerian Army Museum. *A Pictorial History of the Nigerian Army*. Kano, Nigeria: Directorate of Army Education, 1987.

Nigerian Army Public Relations Department. *The Nigerian Army*. Lagos: NAPRD, 1979.

Nwabueze, Ben O. *Military Rule and Constitutionalism in Nigeria*. Ibadan: Spectrum Books Ltd., 1992.

———. *Military Rule and Social Justice in Nigeria*. Ibadan: Spectrum Books Ltd., 1993.

Nwachuku, Levi A. "Nigeria: Why Gowon Fell." *Africa Report* 20, no. 5 (May 1975): 8–11.

Nwankwo, Arthur A. *Civilianised Soldiers: Military/Civilian Government in Nigeria.* Enugu, Nigeria: Fourth Dimension Publishing Company Ltd., 1985.

———. *The Military Option to Democracy: Class, Power and Violence in Nigerian Politics.* Enugu, Nigeria: Fourth Dimension Publishing Company Ltd., 1987.

———. *Retreat of Power: The Military in Nigeria's Third Republic.* Enugu, Nigeria: Fourth Dimension Publishing Company Ltd., 1990.

Nwuzor, Anene. "The Military and Education in Nigeria: An Experiment in Centralization in a Federal Context." *Journal of Education Administration and History* 15, no. 1 (January 1983): 50–55.

Nzimiro, I. "Militarization in Nigeria: Its Economic and Social Consequences." *International Social Science Journal* 35, no. 1 (1983): 138–154.

O'Ballance, Edgar. "Nigerian Armed Forces." *Armed Forces* 6 (December 1987): 558–561.

Obong, Sudany Isong. "A Study of Higher Education Policies and Their Implementation by the Nigerian Military Regimes, 1966–1978." Ph.D. diss., Atlanta University, Georgia, 1980.

Odetola, T.O. *Guns, Pens and Words: The Military, the Politicians and the Intelligentsia in the Process of Political Mobilisation.* Lagos: Obafemi Awolowo University Press, 1986.

———. *Military Politics in Nigeria: Economic Development and Political Stability.* New Brunswick, N.J.: Transaction Books, 1978.

Ogbondah, Chris W. *Military Regimes and the Press in Nigeria, 1966–1993: Human Rights and National Development.* Lanham, Md.: University Press of America, 1993.

———. "The Sword versus the Pen: A Study of Military-Press Relations in Chile, Greece, and Nigeria." *Gazette: International Journal for Mass Communication Studies* 44, no. 1 (1989): 1–26.

Ogunbadejo, Oye. "Nigeria's Foreign Policy under Military Rule, 1966–1979," *International Journal* 35, no. 4 (1980): 748–765.

Ohiorhenuan, John F.E. "The Political Economy of Military Rule in Nigeria," *Review of Radical Political Economics* 16, nos. 2–3 (1984): 1–27.

Okolo, Julius Emeka. "Nigeria's Military Capability." *Journal of Social, Political and Economic Studies* 9, no. 4 (1984): 413–436.

Oladimeji, Olutunde A. "Nigeria: On Becoming a Sea Power." *United States Naval Institute Proceedings* 115 (March 1989): 69–70.

———. "The Nigerian Navy and Maritime Security." *African Defence Journal,* no. 117 (May 1990): 34–36.

Oladoyin, O.O. "Management of Nigeria's Intelligence Community: An Alternative Option." *Defence Strategy Review* 11, no. 11 (4 November 1985).

Olomola, Isola. "The History of Nigeria Military Barracks." *Nigeria Magazine,* nos. 132/133 (1980): 112–119.

Olusanya, G.O. "The Role of Ex-Servicemen in Nigerian Politics." *Journal of Modern African Studies* 6, no. 2 (1968): 221–232.

Omu, Paul Ufuoma. "The Nigerian Command and Staff College Jaji: Ten Years of Development and Success." *The Army Quarterly and Defence Journal* 117, no. 2 (April 1987): 166–170.

Orok, Michael Etim. "An Exploratory Study of the Nigerian Agricultural Development under the Military Establishment, 1966–1980." Ph.D. diss., Atlanta University, Georgia, 1988.

Oyediran, Oyeleye. *Nigerian Government and Politics under Military Rule, 1966–1979*. London: Macmillan, 1979.

Panter-Brick, Keith, ed. *Soldiers and Oil: The Political Transformation of Nigeria*. London: Frank Cass, 1978.

Pardoe, G.R. "Nigeria's Return to Civilian Rule: An Assessment of Corrective Military Government." *Militaria* 10, no. 3 (1980): 28–39.

Peil, Margaret. "A Civilian Appraisal of Military Rule in Nigeria." *Armed Forces and Society* 2, no. 1 (1975): 34–45.

Peters, Jimi. "Intelligence: Its Role and Future in Nigeria's Foreign Policy: Reflections on Past Experience and a Note on the Future." *Nigerian Journal of International Affairs* 12, nos. 1/2 (1986): 151–162.

———. "Issues in Nigerian Defense Planning." *Nigerian Journal of International Affairs* 11, no. 2 (1985): 28–49.

———. "Nigeria's Intelligence System: An Analysis." *Afrika Spectrum* 22, no. 2 (1987): 181–191.

Peters, Jimi, and A.L. Amunu. "The Armed Forces and Nigeria's Foreign Policy: Reflections on Past Experience and a Note on the Future." *Nigerian Journal of International Affairs* 12, nos. 1/2 (1986): 88–99.

Peters, S.B. "National Security Management in Nigeria." *Nigerian Journal of International Affairs* 9, no. 2 (1983): 114–123.

Pradeep, P. Barua. "Ethnic Conflict in the Military of Developing Nations: A Comparative Analysis of India and Nigeria." *Armed Forces and Society* 19, no. 1 (Fall 1992): 123–137.

Pribytkovski, L.N. "Nigeriia V Period Voennykh Rezhimov," *Narody Azii i Afriki*, no. 6 (1980): 45–57.

———. "Nigeriia: Vozvraschenie Voennykh." *Aziia i Afrika Segodnia*, no. 6 (1984): 8–12.

———. "Ot Voennogo Pravleniia-K Grazhdanskomu." *Aziia i Afrika Segodnia*, no. 6 (1973): 4–8.

Seme, V. "Armee und Politik in Afrika." *Militärgeschichte* 26, no. 3 (1987): 202–208, 214.

Sheehan, Michael. "Nigeria and the ECOWAS Defence Pact." *The Army Quarterly and Defence Journal* 116, no. 1 (January 1986): 9–15.

Tijjani, Audu, and David William, ed. *Shehu Shagari*. London: Frank Cass, 1981.

Torimiro, Frederic Belle. "Civil-Military Relations in Mexico and Nigeria: A Comparative Analysis." Ph.D. diss., University of Missouri, Columbia, 1989.

Uko, Ndaeyo. *The Rock 'N' Rule Years: A Stairist's View of Nigeria's Military Presidency*. Lagos: Bookcraft, 1992.

Ukpabi, Samuel C. "The Military in Nigerian Politics, 1900–1970." *Nigeria Magazine*, nos. 132/133 (1980): 69–87.

———. *Strands in Nigerian Military History*. Zaria, Nigeria: Gaskiya Corporation, 1986.

Uphoff, Norman. "The Rise of Persistence of Nigeria's General Gowon." *Pan-African Journal* 5, no. 3 (1972): 347–355.

Utomi, Patrick. "Legitimacy and Governance: One More Year of Military Rule in Nigeria." *Issue: A Journal of Africanist Opinion* 14 (1985): 39–42.

Uwazurike, Chundi. "Nigeria: Soldiers, Intellectuals and Democratization." *TransAfrica Forum* 8, no. 1 (1991): 29–41.

Vaughan, Olufemi O. "The Impact of Party Politics and Military Rule on Traditional Chieftaincy in Western Nigeria, 1946–1988." Ph.D. diss., Oxford University, 1993.

Vlakhov, A.S. "Osobennosti Formirovaniia Nigeriiskoi Armii." *Narody Azii i Afriki,* no. 2 (1983): 35–45.

Vogt, Margaret A. "Approaches towards the Enhancement of the Security of Nigeria's International Borders." *Nigerian Journal of International Affairs* 12, nos. 1/2 (1986): 68–76.

———. "Nigeria's Defence Policy: A Framework for Analysis." In *Nigeria's External Relations,* edited by Gabriel O. Olusanya and Rafiu A. Akindele, 459–476. Ibadan: University of Ibadan Press, 1986.

Vogt, Margaret A., and A.E. Ekoko, ed. *Nigeria in International Peace-Keeping 1960–1992*. Lagos: Malthouse Press, 1993.

———. *Nigerian Defence Policy: Issues and Problems*. Lagos: Malthouse Press, 1990.

Welch, Claude E. "Civil-Military Agonies in Nigeria: Pains of an Unaccomplished Transition." *Armed Forces and Society* 21, no. 4 (Summer 1995): 593–614.

West Africa Correspondent. "Tragedy in Lagos." *Army Quarterly and Defense Journal* 122, no. 4 (October 1992): 391–397.

POLITICS

Abernethy, David B. "Nigeria Creates a New Region." *Africa Report* 9, no. 3 (March 1964): 8–10.

Adamolekun, Ladipo. *The Fall of the Second Republic*. Ibadan: Spectrum Books, 1985.

———. *Politics and Administration in Nigeria*. Ibadan: Spectrum Books, 1986.

Adamolekun, Lapido, and L. Rowlands, ed. *The New Local Government System in Nigeria*. Ibadan: Heinemann, 1979.

Adams, Paul. "Legacy of the General." *Africa Report* 38, no. 5 (September–October 1993).

Adamu, Haroun, and Alaba Ogusanwo. *Nigeria: The Making of the Presidential System, 1979 General Elections*. Kano, Nigeria: Triumph Publishing Co. Ltd., 1982.

Adebayo, A. *Principles and Practice of Public Administration in Nigeria*. Chichester, England: Wiley, 1981.

Adebayo, Augustus. *Power in Politics*. Ibadan: Spectrum Books Ltd., 1986.

Adebayo, A.G. *Embattled Federalism: History of Revenue Allocation in Nigeria, 1946–1990*. New York: P. Lang, 1993.

Adedeji, A. "The Finances of Nigeria's State Governments." *Administration* 2, no. 4 (July 1969): 269–88.

Adedeji, Adebayo, and Onigu Otite. *Nigeria: Renewal from the Roots—The Struggle for Democratic Development*. London: Zed Books, 1997.

———, ed. *Nigerian Administration and Its Political Setting.* London: Hutchinson Educational, 1968.

Ademoyega, A. *Why We Struck: The Story of the First Nigerian Coup.* Ibadan: Evans Brothers Nigeria Publishers, 1981.

Adeniran, Tunde. *The Politics of Wole Soyinka.* Ibadan: Fountain Publications, 1994.

Adu, A.L. *The Civil Service in Commonwealth Africa.* London: George Allen and Unwin, 1969.

Afigbo, A.E. *The Warrant Chiefs—Indirect Rule in South-Eastern Nigeria, 1891–1929.* London: Longman, 1972.

Africa Research Group. *The Other Side of Nigeria's Civil War.* Boston: Africa Research Group, 1970.

Aguwa, Jude C.U. *Religious Dichotomy in Nigerian Politics.* Enugu, Nigeria: Fourth Dimension Publishing Co., Ltd., 1993.

Ahmad Khan, Sarah. *Nigeria: The Political Economy of Oil.* Oxford: Oxford University Press, 1994.

Ake, Claude. "Explaining Political Instability in New States." *Journal of Modern African Studies* 11, no. 3 (September 1973): 347–60.

———. *Democratization of Disempowerment in Africa.* Lagos: Malthouse Press Ltd., 1994.

Akinola, Anthony Abioye. "The Concept of a Rotational Presidency in Nigeria." *Round Table,* no. 337 (January 1996): 13–24.

———. *The Search for a Nigerian Political System: Confederation, Diarchy, Zoning.* London: Afroworld, 1986.

Akinyemi, A.B. "Nigeria: What Should Follow Army Rule—and When?" *Africa Report* 16 (1971): 22–23.

———. *Foreign Policy and Nigerian Federation.* Ibadan: Ibadan University Press, 1975.

———, ed. *Nigeria and the World.* Ibadan: Oxford University Press, 1978.

———. *Foreign Policy and Constitution.* Lagos: NIIA, 1979.

Akiwowo, A. "The Performance of the Nigerian Military from 1966 to 1970." In *On Military Ideology,* edited by M. Janowitz and J. van Doorn. Rotterdam University Press, 1971.

Akpan, N. *The Struggle for Secession, 1966–70.* London: Frank Cass, 1971.

———. *Epitaph to Indirect Rule.* London: Cassell, 1956.

Alkali, Sa'idu Muhammed. *Nigeria and Cameroon in World Affairs: Crisis Management on International Borders.* Bauchi, Nigeria: Ramadan Press, 1990.

Aluko, Olajide. *Essays in Nigerian Foreign Policy.* London: Allen and Unwin, 1981.

———. *Ghana and Nigeria, 1956–70.* New York: Barnes and Noble, 1976.

———. *Options in Nigerian Foreign Policy.* Lagos: NIIA, 1978.

Anber, Paul. "Modernization and Political Disintegration: Nigeria and the Ibos." *The Journal of Modern African Studies* 5, no. 2 (September 1967): 163–79.

Andrae, Gunilla, and Bjorn Beckman. *Union Power in the Nigerian Textile Industry: Labour Regime and Adjustment.* Uppsala: Nordiska Afrikainstitutet, 1998.

Anglin, D.G. "Brinkmanship in Nigeria: The Federal Election of 1964–65." *International Journal* 20, no. 2 (Spring 1965): 173–88.

Anifowose, R. *Violence and Politics in Nigeria: The Tiv and Yoruba Experience, 1960–66*. Lagos: Nok, 1980.
Arnold, Guy. *Modern Nigeria*. London: Longman Group Ltd., 1977.
Atanda, J.A. *The New Oyo Empire: Indirect Rule and Change in Western Nigeria, 1894–1934*. London: Longman, 1973.
Awa, Eme O. *Federal Government in Nigeria*. Berkeley: University of California Press, 1964.
———. *National Integration in Nigeria: Problems and Prospects*. Ibadan: NISER, 1983.
Awolowo, Chief Obafemi. *The People's Republic*. Ibadan: Oxford University Press, 1968.
———. *Path to Nigerian Freedom*. London: Faber, 1947.
———. *Awo on the Nigerian Civil War*. Ikeja, Nigeria: John West Publications, 1981.
———. *Adventures in Power: My March through Prison*. Lagos: Macmillan, 1985.
———. *The Travails of Democracy and the Rule of Law*. Ibadan: Evans Brothers, 1987.
Azikiwe, Nnamdi. *Renascent Africa*. 1937. Reprint, London: Cass, 1968.
———. *Assassination Story: True or False?* Lagos: African Book Company, 1945.
———. *Political Blueprint of Nigeria*. Lagos: African Book Company, 1945.
———. *Economic Reconstruction of Nigeria*. Lagos: African Book Company, 1948.
———. *Dr. Zik's Famous Speeches*. Place of Publication: The Pacific Printers, 1961.
———. *Zik: A Selection from the Speeches of Nnamdi Azikiwe*. Cambridge: Cambridge University Press, 1961.
———. "Essentials for Nigerian Survival." *Foreign Affairs* 43, no. 3 (April 1965).
———. *Democracy with Military Vigilance*. Benin City, Nigeria: Midwest Newspapers Corporation, 1974.
Babangida, Ibrahim Badamosi. *For Their Tomorrow We Gave Our Today: Selected Speeches of IBB*. Ibadan: Safari Books, 1991.
———. *Portrait of a New Nigeria: Selected Speeches of IBB*. Ibadan: Precision Press, 1990.
"Babangida Yields to Interim Government." *Facts on File* 53, no. 2753 (Sep. 2, 1993).
Babatope, Ebenezer. *Awo's Great Life Battles*. Lagos: Friends Foundation, 1989.
Balogun, Fidelis Odun. *Adjusted Lives*. Trenton, N.J.: Africa World Press, 1995.
Barrett, Lindsay. *Agbada to Khaki; Reporting a Change of Government in Nigeria*. Enugu: Fourth Dimension Publishers, 1985.
Beckett, Paul A., Crawford Young. *Dilemmas of Democracy in Nigeria*. Rochester, N.Y.: University of Rochester Press, 1997.
Beer, C.E.F. *The Politics of Peasant Groups in Western Nigeria*. Ibadan: Ibadan University Press, 1976.
Bienen, Henry. *Political Conflict and Economic Change in Nigeria*. London: Cass, 1985.
Blitz, L.F., ed. *The Politics and Administration of Nigerian Government*. London: Sweet and Maxwell, 1964.
Bohannan, Laura. "Political Aspects of Tiv Social Organization." In *Tribes without Rulers*, edited by J. Middleton and D. Tait. London: Routledge and Kegan Paul, 1958.
Bolaji, S.L. *Shagari: President by Mathematics*. Ibadan: Automatic Printing Press, 1980.
Bretton, H.L. *Power and Stability in Nigeria: The Politics of Decolonization*. New York: Praeger, 1962.

Brown, Charles V. *Government and Banking in Western Nigeria.* Ibadan: Oxford University Press, 1964.

Bull, Mary. "Indirect Rule in Northern Nigeria, 1906–11." In *Essays in Imperial Government,* edited by Kenneth Robinson and Frederick Madden. Oxford: Publisher, 1963.

Cameron, Donald. *Principles of Native Administration and Their Application.* Lagos: Government Printer, 1934.

"Cameroon/Nigeria." *Africa Report* 39, no. 3 (May–June 1994).

Campbell, Ian. *Nigeria's Continuing Crisis: The Quest for a Democratic Order.* London: Research Institute for the Study of Conflict and Terrorism, 1995.

Campbell, M.J. *Law and Practice of Local Government in Northern Nigeria.* London: Maxwell, 1963.

Carter, G.M. *Politics in Africa: 7 Cases.* New York: Harcourt, 1966.

Centre For Democratic Studies. *Grassroots Democracy and the New Local Government System in Nigeria.* Bwari, Abuja: FTC, 1992.

Clarke, John Digby. *Yakubu Gowon; Faith in a United Nigeria.* London: Frank Cass, 1877.

Cohen, A. *Custom and Politics in Urban Africa.* London: Routledge, 1969.

Cohen, R. *Organized Labour in the Nigerian Political Process.* London: Heinemann, 1974.

Cole, M. *Modern and Traditional Elites in the Politics of Lagos.* Cambridge: Cambridge University Press, 1975.

Cole, R.T., and R.O. Tilman, ed. *The Nigerian Political Scene.* Durham, N.C.: Duke University Press, 1962.

Coleman, J.S. "Nationalism in Tropical Africa." *The American Political Science Review* 47, no. 2 (June 1954): 404–26.

———. "Emergence of African Political Parties." In *Africa Today,* edited by C. Girovehaines, 225–55. Baltimore, Md.: Johns Hopkins University Press, 1955.

———. *Nigeria: Background to Nationalism.* Berkeley and Los Angeles: University of California Press, 1958.

Coleman, J.S., and Carl G. Rosberg, ed. *Political Parties and National Integration in Tropical Africa.* Berkeley and Los Angeles: University of California Press, 1965.

Collins, P., ed. *Administration for Development in Nigeria.* Lagos: African Education Press, 1980.

———. "Public Policy and the Development of Indigenous Capitalism: The Nigerian Experience." *Journal of Commonwealth and Comparative Politics* 15, no. 2 (1977): 127–50.

Cowan, L. Gray. *Local Government in West Africa.* New York: Columbia University Press, 1958.

Crocker, W.R. *Nigeria: A Critique of British Colonial Administration.* London: George Allen and Unwin, 1936.

———. *Self-Government for the Colonies.* London: Allen and Unwin, 1949.

Cronje, S. *The World and Nigeria: The Diplomatic History of the Nigerian Civil War, 1967–70.* London: Sidgwick and Jackson, 1972.

Crowe, B.E. *The Berlin West African Conference, 1884–1885.* London: Longmans, 1942.

da Cosa, Peter. "The Politics of 'Settlement.'" *Africa Report* 38, no. 6 (November–December 1993).
Daily Times. The Constitution on Trial—Balarabe Musa vs. The Assembly. Lagos: Times Press, 1981.
———. *Elections 1983.* Lagos: Times Press, 1983.
———. *The Light and Darkness.* Lagos: Times Press, n.d.
Danbazau, Lawan. *Politics and Religion in Nigeria.* Kaduna: Vanguard Printers, 1991.
Davies, H.O. *Nigeria: The Prospect for Democracy.* London: Wendenfeld and Nicolson, 1961.
———. "Nigeria's New Constitution." *The West African Review* 16, no. 212 (May 1945).
Dent, M., and D. Austin, ed. *Implementing Civil Rule: The First Two Years.* Manchester, England: Manchester University Press, 1981.
De St. Jorre, J. *The Nigerian Civil War.* London: Hodder and Stoughton, 1972.
Diamond, Larry. *Class, Ethnicity and Democracy in Nigeria: The Failure of the First Republic.* London: Macmillan, 1988.
Diamond, Larry, Anthony Kirk-Greene, and Oyeleye Oyediran (eds.). *Transition without End: Nigerian Politics and Civil Society under Babangida.* Boulder: Lynne Rienner Publishers, 1997.
Dudley, B.J. "Federalism and the Balance of Political Power in Nigeria." *Journal of Commonwealth Political Studies* 5 (1966): 16–29.
———, ed. *Nigeria 1965: Crisis and Criticism.* Ibadan University Press, 1966.
———. *Parties and Politics in Northern Nigeria.* London: Frank Cass, 1968.
———. "The Military and Development" *Nigerian Journal of Economic and Social Studies,* 13, no. 2 (1971).
———. *Instability and Political Order: Politics and Crisis in Nigeria.* Ibaden: Ibadan University Press, 1973.
———. "The Political Theory of Awolowo and Azikiwe." In *Themes in African Social and Political Thought*, edited by O. Otite. New York: Africana Publishing Co., 1978.
———. *An Introduction to Nigerian Government and Politics.* London: Macmillan, 1982.
Duignam, Peter, and Lewis H. Gann, ed. *Colonialism in Africa, 1870–1960.* Vol. 2. Cambridge: Cambridge University Press, 1970.
Ekeh, P.P. "Citizenship and Political Conflict: A Sociological Interpretation of the Nigerian Crisis." In *Nigeria: Dilemma of Nationhood,* edited by J. Okpaku, P–P. New York: Third Press, 1972.
Ekwe-Ekwe, Herbert. *Issues in Nigerian Politics since the Fall of the Second Republic, 1994–1990.* Lewiston: E. Mellen Press, 1991.
"Election Turmoil Deepens." *Facts on File* 53, no. 2747 (July 22, 1993).
Elias, T.O. *Groundwork of Nigerian Law.* London, 1954.
———. *Local Government in the Western Provinces of Nigeria.* Ibadan, 1951.
———. *The Nigerian Legal System.* London: Routledge, 1963.
Enahoro, Chief Anthony. *Fugitive Offender: The Story of a Political Prisoner.* London: Cassell, 1965.
Enwerem, Iheanji M. *A Dangerous Awakening: The Politicization of Religion in Nigeria.* Ibadan: Institut Francais de Recherche en Afrique, 1995.

Ezera, Kalu. *Constitutional Developments in Nigeria*. Cambridge: Cambridge University Press, 1960.

Falola, Toyin, and Julius Ihonbere. *The Rise and Fall of Nigeria's Second Republic, 1979–1984*. London: Zed, 1985.

First, Ruth. *The Barrel of a Gun: Political Power in Africa and the Coup*. London: Penguin Books, 1969.

Forsyth, Frederick. *The Biafran Story*. London: Penguin, 1969.

Fortes, M., and E.E. Evans-Pritchard. *African Political Systems*. London: Oxford University Press, 1940.

Frank, L.P. "Ideological Competition in Nigeria: Urban Population v. Elite Nationalism." *Journal of Modern African Studies* 17, no. 3 (1979): 433–52.

French, Howard W. "In Nigeria, a Strongman Tightens the Vise." *New York Times* (March 31, 1995).

The Future of Local Government in Nigeria: The Report of the National Conference on Local Government Held at the University of Ife, 1969. Ile-Ife: University of Ife Press, 1969.

Gambari, I.A. *Party Politics and Foreign Policy: Nigeria during the First Republic*. Zaria, Nigeria: ABU Press, 1979.

———. *Theory and Reality on Foreign Policy Making: Nigeria after the Second Republic*. Atlantic Highlands, N.J.: Humanities Press International, 1989.

Gamer, Robert E. *Government and Politics in a Changing World*. Madison, Wis.: Brown and Benchmark, 1994.

Garba, Joseph. *Diplomatic Soldiering: Nigerian Foreign Policy, 1975–1979*. Ibadan: Spectrum Books, 1983.

———. *The Honor to Serve: Reflections on Nigeria's Presidency of the 44th U.N. General Assembly*. Ibadan: Heinemann Educational Books, 1993.

Gbulie, Ben. *Nigeria's Five Majors*. Onitsha, Nigeria: Africana Educational Publishers, 1981.

Geary, William N.M. *Nigeria under British Rule*. London: Methuen, 1927.

Graf, W.D. *Elections 1979: The Nigerian Citizens' Guide to Parties Politics and Issues*. Lagos: Daily Times, n.d.

———, ed. *Towards a Political Economy of Nigeria: Critical Essays*. Benin City, Nigeria: Koda Publishers, 1981.

Green, Fred. "Toward Understanding Military Coups." *Africa Report* 11, (1966).

Green, Harry A. "The Theory of Local Government and Managerial Effectiveness." *The Nigerian Journal of Public Affairs* 4, no. 1 (May 1976).

Gutteridge, F.F. *Military Regimes in Africa*. London: Methuen, 1976.

Hailey, Lord. *An African Survey*. London: Oxford University Press, 1938.

———. *An African Survey: Revised 1956*. London: Oxford University Press, 1957.

———. *Native Administration in the British African Territories*. 5 vols. London: H.M.S.O., 1951.

Harris, P.J. *Local Government in Southern Nigeria*. Cambridge: Cambridge University Press, 1957.

Harris, Richard L. "Nigeria: Crisis and Compromise." *Africa Report* 10, no. 3 (March 1965).

Hazelwood, A. *African Integration and Disintegration*. London: Oxford University Press, 1967.
Herskovits, Jean. *Nigeria: Power and Democracy in Africa*. New York: Foreign Policy Association, 1983.
Hunwick, John. "An African Case Study of Political Islam: Nigeria." *The Annals of the American Academy of Political and Social Science* 524 (November 1992): 143.
Ibo State Union. "Nigerian Disunity—The Guilty Ones." Pamphlet No. 1, Enugu, Nigeria, 1964.
Idang, Gordon J. "The Politics of Nigerian Foreign Policy: The Ratification and Renunciation of the Anglo-Nigerian Defence Agreement." *African Studies Review* 13, no. 2 (September 1970).
———. *Nigeria: Internal Politics and Foreign Policy, 1960–1966*. Ibadan: Ibadan University Press, 1973.
Idress, Aliyu Alhaji. *Domination and Reaction in Nupeland, Central Nigeria: The Kyadya Revolt, 1857–1905*. Lewiston: E. Mellen Press, 1966.
Ige, Bola. *People, Politics and Politicians of Nigeria (1940–1979)*. Lagos: Heinemann Educational Books, 1996.
Igwe, Agagor. *Nnamdi Azikiwe: The Philosopher of Our Time*. Enugu, Nigeria: Fourth Dimension Publishing Co., 1992.
Ihonvbere, Julius Omozuanvbo. *Nigeria: The Politics of Adjustment and Democracy*. New Brunswick, N.J.: Transaction Publishers, 1993.
Jemibewon, D.M. *A Combatant in Government*. Ibadan: Heinemann, 1978.
Jibo, Mvendaga. *Tiv Politics since 1959*. Katsina Ala, Nigeria: Mandate International Ltd., 1993.
Johnson, Segun. *Dimensions in Nigeria's Foreign Policy*. Lagos: Blada, 1990.
Joseph, Richard. "Nigeria: Inside the Dismal Tunnel." *Current History* 95, no. 601 (May 1996).
Keay, E.A. *The Native and Customary Courts of Nigeria*. London: Sweet and Maxwell, 1966.
Kingsley, Mary. *West African Studies*. London: Macmillan, 1901.
Kirk-Greene, A.H.M. *The Principles of Native Administration in Nigeria Selected Documents, 1900–1947*. London: Oxford University Press, 1965.
———, ed. *Crisis and Conflict in Nigeria: A Documentary Source Book, 1966–69*. 2 vols. London: Oxford University Press, 1971.
Kirk-Greene, A.H.M., and Douglas Rimmer. *Nigeria since 1970: A Political and Economic Outline*. London: Hodder and Stoughton, 1981.
Kochakova, Natalia B., ed. *Nigeria: Thirty Years of Independence*. Meckba, 1990.
Koehn, P. "The Nigerian Elections of 1979." *Africa Today* 28, no. 1 (1981).
Kukah, Matthew H. *Religion, Politics and Power in Northern Nigeria*, Ibadan: Spectrum Books Limited, 1993.
Kumu, S., and A. Aliyu, eds. *Issues in the Nigerian Draft Constitution*. Zaria, Nigeria: Institute of Administration, 1977.
Langa, Langa. *Up against It in Nigeria*. London: G. Allen and Unwin, 1992.
Lewis, Peter. "Endgame in Nigeria? The Politics of a Failed Democratic Transition." *African Affairs* 93, no. 372 (1994).

Lindley, M.F. *The Acquisition and Government of Backward Territory in International Law*. London: Longmans, Green, 1926.

Lloyd, Peter C. "Development of Political Parties in Western Nigeria." *The American Political Science Review* 49, no. 3 (September 1955): 693–707.

———. "The Traditional Political System of the Yoruba." *South-Western Journal of Anthropology* 10, no. 5 (Winter 1954): 366–84.

———. "Conflict Theory and Yoruba Kingdoms." In *History and Social Anthropology*, edited by I.M. Lewis. London: Tavistock Publications, 1968.

Loimeier, Roman. *Islamic Reform and Political Change in Northern Nigeria*. Evanston, Ill.: Northwestern University Press, 1997.

Luckham, R. *The Nigerian Army: A Sociological Analysis of Authority and Revolt, 1960–1967*. New York: Cambridge University Press, 1971.

Lugard, F.D. *Political Memoranda, 1913–1918*. Memo No. 4, para. 1. London: Waterlow, 1919.

———. *Report on the Amalgamation of Northern and Southern Nigeria and Administration*. London: H.M.S.O., 1920.

———. *The Dual Mandate on British Tropical Africa*. London: W. Blackwood, 1922.

Lugard, Lady A. *Tropical Dependency*. London: J. Nisbet and Co., 1905.

Mackintosh, J.P. "Electoral Trends and the Tendency to a One Party System in Nigeria." *Journal of Commonwealth Political Studies* 1 (November 1962): 194–210.

———. *Nigerian Government and Politics*. London: George Allen and Unwin, 1966.

———. "Politics in Nigeria: The Action Group Crisis of 1962." *Political Studies* 11 (June 2, 1963): 126–55.

Madeibo, A.A. *The Nigerian Revolution and the Biafran War*. Enugu, Nigeria: Fourth Dimension, 1980.

Madunagu, E. *Problems of Socialism: The Nigerian Challenge*. London: Zed, 1981.

Max, Conrad, and Benedict Brann. "Democratisation of Language Use in Public Domain in Nigeria. *The Journal of Modern African Studies* 31, no. 4 (December 1993): 639–656.

Melson, R., and H. Wolpe, ed. *Nigeria: Modernization and the Politics of Communalism*. East Lansing: Michigan State University Press, 1971.

Middleton, J., and D. Tait, ed. *Tribes without Rulers*. London: Routledge and Kegan Paul, 1958.

Milley, Walter R. *Have We Failed in Nigeria?* London: Butterworth Press, 1947.

———. *Success in Nigeria*. London: Butterworth Press, 1948.

Miners, N.J. *The Nigerian Army, 1956–1966*. London: Methuen, 1971.

Mockler-Ferryman, A.F. *British Nigeria*. London: Cassell and Co., 1902.

Murray, D.J. *The Work of Administration in Nigeria: Case Studies*. London: Hutchinson Educational, 1969.

Ndem, Eyo B.E. *Ibos in Contemporary Nigerian Politics*. Onitsha, Nigeria: Eludo Ltd., 1961.

Ngosu, H.N., ed. *Problems of Nigerian Administration: A Book of Readings*. Enugu, Nigeria: Fourth Dimension, 1980.

Nicholson, I.F. *The Administration of Nigeria, 1900–1960*. Oxford: Clarendon Press, 1969.

Niven, C.R. *How Nigeria Is Governed*. London: Longmans, 1950.

———. "Can There Be Unity in Nigeria?" *The New Commonwealth* 30, no. 2 (July 1955).
———. *Nigeria, Outline of a Colony,* 2d ed. London: T. Nelson and Sons, 1967.
Nnoli, Okwudiba. *Ethnic Politics in Nigeria*. Enugu, Nigeria: Fourth Dimension, 1978.
———. *Ethnicity and Development in Nigeria*. Aldershot: Avebury, 1995.
Nwabueze, B.O. *Constitutional Law of the Nigerian Republic*. London: Butterworth, 1964.
———. *A Constitutional History of Nigeria*. London: Hurst, 1982.
———. *Federation in Nigeria under the Presidential Constitution*. London: Sweet and Maxwell, 1983.
———. *Military Rule and Social Justice in Nigeria*. Ibadan: Spectrum Law Pub., 1993.
Nwagbo, Nduka. *The Vote*. Ibadan: Spectrum Books, 1992.
Nwankwo, A.A. *Nigeria: The Challenge of Biafra*. London: Rex Collings, 1972.
———. *Nigeria: The Political Transition and the Future of Democracy*. 1993.
Nwankwo, Uchenna. *Strategy for Political Stability*. Ikeja, Lagos: Pathway Communications, 1995.
Nwigwe, H.E. *Nigeria: The Fall of the First Republic*. London: Ebony Press, n.d.
Nwosu, Humphrey N. *Political Authority and the Nigerian Civil Service*. Enugu, Nigeria: Fourth Dimension, 1977.
Nzimiro, I. *Studies in Ibo Political Systems—Chieftaincy and Politics in Four Niger States*. Berkeley: University of California Press, 1972.
———. *The Babangida Men: The Making of Ministers*. Oguta, Nigeria: Zim Pan African Publishers, 1993.
Obasanjo, O. *My Command*. Ibadan: Heinemann, 1980.
Obiozor, George A. *The Politics of Precarious Balancing: An Analysis of Contending Issues in Nigerian Domestic and Foreign Policy*. Lagos: Nigerian Institute of International Affairs, 1994.
O'Connell, J. "Authority and Community in Nigeria." In *Nigeria: Modernization and the Politics of Communalism,* edited by R. Melson and H. Wolpe, 629–72. East Lansing: Michigan State University Press, 1971.
O'Connell, J., and P.A. Beckett. *Education and Power in Nigeria*. London: Hodder and Stoughton, 1977.
Oden, G.W.E., ed. *A New System of Local Government*. Enugu, Nigeria: Nwamife Press, 1977.
Odetola, O. *PRP Crisis Making and Unmaking the Key, Who Wins?* Ibadan: Sketch Publishers, 1981.
Odetola, T.O. *Military Politics in Nigeria: Economic Development and Political Stability*. New Brunswick, N.J.: Transaction Books, 1978.
Odumosu, Oluwole I. *The Nigerian Constitution: History and Development*. London: Sweet and Maxwell, 1963.
Ofonagoro, W.I., and A. Ojo, ed. *The Great Debate: Nigerian Viewpoints on the Draft Constitution, 1976/77*. Lagos: Daily Times, n.d.
Ogunbadejo, O. "Ideology and Pragmatism: The Soviet Role in Nigeria." *Orbis* 21, no. 4 (1978): 803–30.
Ogundowole, E. Kolawole. *Colonial Amalgam: Federalism and the National Question: A Philosophical Examination*. Lagos: Pumark Nigeria, 1994.

Ogunsanwo, G., ed. *The Great Debate*. Lagos: Daily Times, 1978.

Ojo, J.D. *The Development of the Executive under the Nigerian Constitution, 1960–1981*. Ibadan: University Press, 1985.

Ojo, Olatunde J.B. "Federal-State Relations 1967–1974." *Quarterly Journal of Administration* 10 (January 1976).

Okafor, Samuel, O. *Indirect Rule: The Development of Central Legislature in Nigeria*. Lagos: Nelson Africa, 1981.

Okonjo, I.M. *British Administration in Nigeria, 1900–1950*. New York: NOK Publishers, 1974.

Okpaku, J., ed. *Nigeria: Dilemma of Nationhood*. New York: Third Press, 1968.

Okpu, U. *Ethnic Minority Problem in Nigerian Politics, 1960–1965*. Stockholm: Libertryck A, 1977.

Oladosu, S.A. *Kaduna Essays in Local Government*. Kaduna, Nigeria: Dosu Publications, 1981.

Olagunju, Tunji. *Transition to Democracy in Nigeria, 1985–1993*. Ibadan: Safari Books, 1993.

Olowu, Dele, and Dele Ayo. *Managing the Nigerian Federal System; Issues and Policy Options*. Ile-Ife: University of Ife, 1985.

Olowu, Dele, Kayode Soremekun, and Adebayo William, (eds.). *Governance and Democratisation in Nigeria*. Ibadan: Spectrum Books, 1995.

Olusanya, G.O. "The Role of the Ex-servicemen in Nigerian Politics." *Journal of Modern African Studies* 6 (1968): 221–32.

———. *The Second World War and Politics in Nigeria, 1939–53*. London: Evans, 1973.

Omoruyi, Omo. *Mallam Aminu Kano and the Legacy of Grassroots Politics in Nigeria*. Bwari, Abuja: Centre for Democratic Studies, 1991.

Orizu, A. Nwafor. *Without Bitterness*. New York: Creative Age Press, 1944.

Osaghae, Eghasa E. *Ethnicity and Its Management in Africa: The Democratization Link*. Lagos: Malthouse Press Ltd., 1994.

———. *Trends in Migrant Political Organizations in Nigeria: The Igbo in Kano*. Ibadan: Institut Français de Recherche en Afrique, 1994.

Osoba, S.O. "The Nigerian Power Elite." *African Social Studies*, edited by P.C.W. Gutkind and P. Waterman, 368–82. London: Heinemann, 1976.

Ostheimer, J.M. *Nigerian Politics*. New York: Harper and Row, 1973.

Othman, Shehu. "Nigeria: Power for Profit—Class, Corporation and Factionalism in the Military." In *Contemporary West African States* edited by Donal B. Cruise O'Brien, John Dunn and Richard Rathbone. Cambridge: Cambridge University Press.

Otite, O. *Autonomy and Independence: The Urhobo Kingdom of Okpe in Modern Nigeria*. London: Hurst, 1973.

"Out You Go." *The Economist* (September 3, 1994).

Oyediran, O., ed. *Nigerian Government and Politics under Military Rule, 1968–79*. London: Macmillan, 1979.

———. *Survey of Nigerian Affairs, 1976–77*. London: Macmillan, 1981.

Oyewo, Alade Toriola. *The Application of the Presidential System into Nigerian Local Governments*. Ibadan: Jartor, 1991.

Oyinbo, J. *Nigeria: Crisis and Beyond*. London: Charles Knight and Co. Ltd., 1971.

Oyovbaire, Sam, and Tunji Olagunju, ed. *Foundations of a New Nigeria: The IBB Era.* Lagos: Precision Press, 1991.

Paden, John N. *Ahmadu Bello, Saradauna of Sokoto: Values and Leadership in Nigeria.* Zaria, Nigeria: Hudabuda, 1986 .

Panter-Brick, S.K., ed. *Nigerian Politics and Military Rule: Prelude to the Civil War.* London: Athlone Press, 1970.

———. *Soldiers and Oil: The Military and the Political Transformation of Nigeria.* London: Frank Cass, 1978.

Park, A.W.W. *The Sources of Nigerian Law.* London: Butterworth, 1963.

Peil, M. *Nigerian Politics: The People's View.* London: Cassell, 1976.

Perham, Margery. *Native Administration in Nigeria.* London: Oxford University Press, 1948.

———. *Lugard: The Years of Authority, 1899–1945.* London: Collins, 1960.

Perham, Margery, and Mary Bull. *The Diaries of Lord Lugard.* Evanston, Ill.: Northwestern University Press, 1963.

Phillips, A.O. "Three Decades of Intergovernmental Financial Relationships in Federation of Nigeria." *The Quarterly Journal of Administration* 14 (1980).

Phillips, Claude S., Jr. *The Development of Nigerian Foreign Policy.* Evanston, Ill.: Northwestern Univesity Press, 1964.

Phillipson, Sidney, and S.O. Adebo. *Nigerianization of the Civil Service.* Lagos: Government Printing Office, 1954.

Post, K.W.J. "Forming a Government in Nigeria." *Nigerian Journal of Economic and Social Studies* 2, no. 1 (1960): 1–11.

———. *The Nigerian Federal Election of 1959.* London: Oxford University Press, 1963.

———. "Is There a Case for Biafra?" *International Affairs* 44, no. 1 (January 1968): 26–39.

———. "Nigeria's Un-Election." *New Society,* no. 22 (January 1965): 24–25.

Post, K.W.J., and George O. Jenkins. *The Price of Liberty: Personality and Politics in Colonial Nigeria.* Cambridge: Cambridge University Press, 1973.

Post, K.W.J., and M. Vickers. *Structure and Conflict in Nigeria 1960–1965.* London: Heinemann, 1973.

Quinn-Young, C.T., and I. Herdman. *Geography of Nigeria.* London: Longman, 1954.

"Reign of the Generals." *Africa Report.* (November–December 1994).

Rothchild, Donald S. *Toward Unity in Africa: A Study of Federalism in British West Africa.* Washington, D.C.: Public Affairs Press, 1960.

Royal Institute of International Affairs. *Nigeria: The Political and Economic Background.* London: Oxford University Press, 1960.

Saro-Wiwa, Ken. *Genocide in Nigeria: The Ogoni Tragedy.* London: Saros International Publishers, 1992.

Schwarz, Walter. *Nigeria.* London: Pall Mall, 1968.

Schwarz, F.A.O., Jr. *Nigeria, The Tribes, the Nation or the Race—The Politics of Independence.* Cambridge, Mass.: M.I.T. Press, 1965.

Seibel, H.D. "Some Aspects of Inter-Ethnic Relation in Nigeria." *Nigerian Journal of Economic and Social Studies* 9, no. 2 (July 1967): 217–28.

Shagari, S. *My Vision of Nigeria.* London: Frank Cass, 1981.

Sklar, Richard L. *Nigerian Political Parties*. Princeton, N.J.: Princeton University Press, 1963.

———. "Contradictions in the Nigerian Political System." *Journal of Modern African Studies* 3, no. 2 (1965): 201–13.

———. "Nigerian Politics: The Ordeal of Chief Awolowo, 1960–65." In *Politics in Africa,* edited by Gwendolen M. Carter, 119–65. New York: Harcourt, Brace and World Inc., 1966.

———. *African Politics and Problems in Development*. Boulder, Colo.: L. Rienner, 1991.

Sklar, Richard L., and C.S. Whitaker Jr. "The Federal Republic of Nigeria." In *National Unity and Regionalism in Eight African States,* edited by Gwendolen M. Carter, 7–150. Ithaca, N.Y.: Cornell University Press, 1966.

———. "Nigeria." In *Political Parties and National Integration in Tropical Africa,* edited by James S. Coleman and Carl G. Rosberg Jr. Berkeley: University of California Press, 1964.

Smith, M.G. *Government in Zazzau*. London: Oxford University Press, 1960.

Smith, S. "Colonialism in Economic Theory: The Experience of Nigeria." *Journal of Development Studies* 15, no. 3 (1979).

Smock, A.C. *Ibo Politics: The Role of Ethnic Unions in Eastern Nigeria*. Cambridge, Mass.: Harvard University Press, 1971.

———. "NCNC and Ethnic Unions in Biafra." *Journal of Modern African Studies* 7 (1969): 21–34.

Soyinka, Kayode. *Diplomatic Baggage: MOSSAD and Nigeria, The Dikko Story*. Lagos: Newswatch Books, 1994.

Soyinka, Wole. *The Open Sore of a Continent: A Personal Narrative of the Nigerian Crisis*. New York: Oxford University Press, 1996.

Stremlau, J.J. *The International Politics of the Nigerian Civil War, 1967–70*. Princeton, N.J.: Princeton University Press, 1977.

Tamuno, T.N. *Nigeria and Elective Representation, 1923–1947*. London: Heinemann, 1966.

———. *The Police in Modern Nigeria, 1861–1965*. Ibadan: Ibadan University Press, 1970.

Taylor, J.V. *Christianity and Politics in Africa*. London: Penguin African Series, 1957.

Temple, Charles Lindsay, ed. *Native Races and Their Rulers: Sketches and Studies of Official Life and Administrative Problems in Nigeria*. 2d ed. London: Cass, 1968.

Tignor, Robert L. "Political Corruption in Nigeria before Independence." *The Journal of Modern African Studies* 31, no. 2 (June 1993): 175–202.

Tilman, R.O., and T. Cole, ed. *The Nigerian Political Scene*. Durham, N.C.: Duke University Press, 1962.

Tukur, M. "The Establishment of State Governments in Northern Nigeria." *Journal of Modern African Studies* 8 (1970): 128–33.

Turner, T. "Multinational Corporations and the Stability of the Nigerian State." *Review of African Political Economy* 5 (1976): 63–79.

———. "Nigeria: Imperialism, Oil Technology and the Comprador State." In *Oil and Class Struggle,* edited by P. Nore and T. Turner. London: Zed, 1980.

Usman, Y.B. *For the Liberation of Nigeria*. London: New Bacon Books, 1979.

Uwanaka, Charles U. *Awolowo and Akintola in Political Storm*. Lagos: Yaba, 1964.
Uwechue, R. *Reflections on the Nigerian Civil War*. London: O.I.T.H. International Publishers Ltd., 1969.
Waugh, Auberon, and Suzanne Cronje. *Biafra: Britains' Shame*. London: Michael Joseph, 1969.
Wheare, Joan. *The Nigerian Legislative Council*. London: Faber and Faber, 1950.
Whitaker, C.S. *The Politics of Tradition Continuity and Change in Northern Nigeria, 1946–66*. Princeton, N.J.: Princeton University Press, 1970.
———. "Three Perspectives on Hierarchy: Political Thought and Leadership in Northern Nigeria." *Journal of Commonwealth Political Studies* 3 (1 March 1965): 1–19.
Whiteman, K. "Enugu: The Psychology of Secession." In *Nigerian Politics and Military Rule*, edited by S.K. Panter-Brick, 111–27. London: Athlone Press, 1970.
Williams, B.A., and A.H. Walsh. *Urban Government for Metropolitan Lagos*. New York: Praeger, 1968.
Williams, G. "Political Consciousness among the Ibadan Poor." In *Sociology and Development*, edited by E. de Kadt and G. Williams. London: Tavistock Publications, 1974.
———, ed. "Nigeria Issue." *Review of African Political Economy* 13 (1979).
———. *State and Society in Nigeria*. Lagos: Afrographika, 1980.
Williams, Pat, and Toyin Falola. *Religious Impact on the Nation-State: The Nigerian Predicament*. Aldershot: Avebury, 1995.
Wolpe, H. "Port Harcourt: Ibo Politics in Microcosm." *Journal of Modern African Studies* 7 (1969): 469–93.
———. *Urban Politics in Nigeria: A Study of Port Harcourt*. Los Angeles: University of California Press, 1974.
Yahaya, A.D. *Native Authority System in Northern Nigeria*. Zaria, Nigeria: ABU Press, 1979.
———. *Contending Issues of the Moment: Essay in Public Policy Analysis*. Lagos: Administrative Staff College of Nigeria, 1992.
Yahya, Mahmoud. *Neo-Colonialism; France's Legacy to Africa*. Kaduna: Emwai Centre for Political and Economic Research, 1994.

SOCIETY

Abraham, R.C. *The Tiv People*. Lagos: Government Printer, 1933.
Achebe, Chinua. *Things Fall Apart*. London: Heinemann, 1958.
———. *No Longer at Ease*. London: Heinemann, 1960.
———. *Beware Soul Brother*. London: Heinemann, 1972.
———. *The Trouble with Nigeria*. Enugu, Nigeria: Fourth Dimension, 1983.
Adejare, Oluwole. *Language and Style in Soyinka: A Systemic Textlinguistic Study of a Literary Idiolect*. Ibadan: Heinemann Educational Books, 1992.
Adepegba, C.O. *Decorative Arts of the Fulani Nomads*. Ibadan: Ibadan University Press, 1986.
Afigbo, A.E., and S.I.O. Okita. *The Museum and Nation Building*. Owerri, Nigeria: New Africa Publishing Co., 1985.

Afonja and Tola Olu Pearce. *Social Change in Nigeria*. Ibadan: Longman Group Ltd., 1986.
Akinkugbe, O.O., ed. *Priorities in National Health Planning*. Ibadan: Caxton Press, 1973.
Akpabot, Samuel Okpe. *Foundation of Nigerian Traditional Music*. Ibadan: Spectrum, 1986.
———. *Ibibio Music in Nigerian Culture*. East Lansing: Michigan State University Press, 1975.
Aluko, T.M. *Conduct Unbecoming*. Ibadan: Heinemann, 1993.
Amadi, Elechi. *Ethics in Nigerian Culture*. Ibadan: Heinmann Educational Books, 1982.
Anderson, J.H.D. *Islamic Law in Africa*. London: H.M.S.O., 1955.
Arikpo, Okoi. *Who Are the Nigerians?* Lagos: Federal Information Service, 1958.
Babatunde, Emmanuel D. *A Critical Study of Bini and Yoruba Value Systems of Nigeria in Change: Culture, Religion, and the Self*. Lewiston: E. Mellen Press, 1992.
Bankole, Akinrinola. *The Role of Mass Media in Family Planning Promotion in Nigeria*. Calverton, Md.: Macro International, 1994.
Barton, F. *The Press of Africa*. London: Macmillan, 1979.
Bascom, William Russell. *Sixteen Cowries: Yoruba Divination from Africa to the New World*. Bloomington: Indiana University Press, 1980.
Beier, Ulli. *Art in Nigeria*. Cambridge: Cambridge University Press, 1960.
Ben-Amos, Paula. *The Art of Benin*. Washington, D.C.: Smithsonian Institution Press, 1995.
Bolaji, L. *Anatomy of Corruption in Nigeria*. Ibadan: Daystar Press, 1970.
Bolaji, S. Labanji. *The Golden Pen of Eselby: S.Labanji Bolaji, 1935–1989*. Ibadan: Primrose Communications, 1994.
Bradbury, R.E., and Peter C. Lloyd. *The Benin People and Edo Speaking Peoples, etc., Plus the Itsekin*. London: International African Institute, 1959.
Callaway, Barbara. *Muslim Hausa Women in Nigeria: Tradition and Change*. Syracuse, N.Y.: Syracuse University Press, 1987.
———. *The Heritage of Islam: Women, Religion, and Politics in West Africa*. Boulder, Colo.: Lynne Reinner, 1994.
Callaway, Helen. *Gender, Culture and Empire: European Women in Colonial Nigeria*. Houndmills: Macmillan, 1987.
Carroll, Kevin. *Architecture of Nigeria: Architectures of the Hausa and Yoruba Peoples and of the Many Peoples*. London: Lester Crook Academic Publishing, 1992.
Centre for Black and African Civilization. *Nigerian Studies in Religious Tolerance*. Ibadan: Centre for Black and African Civilization and National Association for Religious Tolerance, 1989.
Clarke, J.D. *Omu Aran: An African Experiment*. London: Longman, 1937.
Coker, Increase. *Seventy Years of the Nigerian Press*. Lagos: Times Press, 1952.
Collins, Harold. *Amos Tutuola*. New York: Twayne Publishers, 1969.
Comrie, Bernard, ed. *The World's Major Languages*. London: Croom Helm, 1989.
Cooksey, J.J., and A. McLeish. *Religion and Civilisation in West Africa*. London: World Dominion Press, 1931.
Daily Sketch. FESTAC 77. Ibadan: Sketch Publishing Company Ltd., 1977.

Daily Times. The Black of the World. Lagos: Times Press, n.d.

Drewal, Henry John. *Yoruba: Nine Centuries of African Art and Thought*. New York: Center for African Art in Association with H.N. Abrams, 1989.

Echeruo, M.J.C., and E.N. Obiechina. *Igbo Traditional Life, Culture and Literature*. Owerri, Nigeria: Conch Magazine Limited, 1971.

Egejuru, Phanuel Akebueze. *The Seed Yams Have Been Eaten*. Ibadan: Heinemann, 1992.

Elias, T.O. *Nigerian Land Law and Custom*. London: Routledge and K. Paul, 1950.

———, ed. *Law and Social Change in Nigeria*. Lagos: Evans Brothers, 1972.

Enahoro, P. *How to Be a Nigerian*. Ibadan: Caxton Press, 1966.

Fadipe, N.A. *The Sociology of the Yoruba*. Ibadan: Ibadan University Press, 1970.

Fagg, Angela. "Thoughts On Nok." *African Arts*. (July 1994).

Fagg, Bernard. "The Nok Culture." *West African Review* (December 1956).

Fagg, William. *The Living Arts of Nigeria*. London: Studio Vista, 1971.

Familusi, M.M. *Methodism in Nigeria, 1842–1992*. Ibadan: NPS Educational Publishers, 1992.

Fasuyi, T.A. *Cultural Policy in Nigeria*. Paris: UNESCO, 1973.

Folayan, Adekunle. *The Corrupt Kings*. Lagos: Crier Communications, 1993.

Forde, Daryll. *The Yoruba-Speaking Peoples of South-Western Nigeria*. London: International African Institute, 1951.

———, ed. *Efik Traders of Old Calabar*. London: Oxford University Press, 1956.

———. *Peoples of the Niger-Benue Confluence*. London, 1955.

Forde, Daryll, and G.I. Jones. *The Ibo and Ibibio-Speaking Peoples of South-Eastern Nigeria*. London: Oxford University Press, 1950.

Furnis, Graham. *Poetry, Prose and Popular Culture in Hausa*. Edinburgh: Edinburgh University Press, 1996.

Gefu, J.O. *Pastoralist Perspectives in Nigeria: The Fulbe of Udubo Grazing Reserve*. Uppsala: Scandinavian Institute of African Studies, 1992.

Gerson, Mary-Joan. *Why the Sky Is Far Away: A Folktale from Nigeria*. Boston: Little, Brown, 1992.

Green, M.M. *Ibo Village Affairs*. London: Sidgwick and Jackson, 1947.

Greenberg, Joseph H. *Studies in African Linguistic Classification*. New Haven, Conn.: Compass Publishing Company, 1955.

Gunn, Harold D. *Peoples of the Plateau Area of Northern Nigeria*. London: International African Institute, 1953.

Hambly, Wilfrid D. "Culture Areas of Nigeria." *Field Museum of Natural History Anthropological Series* 31, no. 3 (1953): 373–502.

Hassan, Salah M. *Art and Islamic Literacy among the Hausa of Northern Nigeria*. Lewiston, N.Y.: E. Mellen Press, 1992.

Ibitokun, Benedict M. *African Drama and the Yoruba World-view*. Ibadan: Ibadan University Press, 1995.

Idowu, E. Bolaji. *Olodumare—God in Yoruba Belief*. London: Publisher, 1962.

Isaacson, Alan. *Deeper Life*. London: Hodder and Stoughton, 1990.

Islam in Africa Conference. *Islam in Africa: Proceedings of the Islam in Africa Conference*. Ibadan: Spectrum Books, 1993.

Iyam, David Uru. *The Broken Hoe: Cultural Reconfiguration in Biase Southeast Nigeria.* Chicago: University of Chicago Press, 1992.

Iyam, David Uru. *The Broken Hoe: Cultural Reconfiguration in Biase, Southern Nigeria.* Chicago: University of Chicago Press, 1995.

Kalu, Ogbu U. *Divided People of God: Church Union Movement in Nigeria, 1875–1960.* New York: Nok Publishers, 1978.

Kasunmu, A.B., and J.W. Salacuse. *Nigerian Family Law.* London: Butterworth, 1960.

Kayode, Femi. *The Confused Society.* Ibadan: Evans Brothers, 1987.

Kuper, Leo, and M.G. Smith. *Pluralism in Africa.* Berkeley: University of California Press, 1969.

Lewis, Leonard John. *Society, Schools and Progress in Nigeria.* Oxford: Pengamon Press, 1965.

Lloyd, P.C. "Conflict Theory and Yoruba Kingdoms." In *History and Social Anthropology,* edited by I.M. Lewis. London: Tavistock Publications, 1968.

———, ed. *The New Elites of Tropical Africa.* London: Oxford University Press, 1966.

Lubeck, P. "Class Consciousness and Islamic Nationalism among Nigerian Workers." In *Research in the Sociology of Work* Vol. 1, edited by R.L. and I.H. Simpson. Greenwich, Conn.: JAI Press, 1980.

Mabogunje, A.L. *Urbanization in Nigeria.* London: University of London, 1968.

Maja-Pearce, Adewale. *A Mask Dancing: Nigerian Novelists of the Eighties.* London: Hans Zell Publishers, 1992.

Makinwa, P. Kofo. *Adolescent Reproductive Behaviour in Nigeria: A Study of Five Cities.* Ibadan: Nigerian Institute of Social and Economic Research, 1991.

Meek, C.K. *Law and Authority in a Nigerian Tribe.* London: Oxford University Press, 1937.

Michael Imoudu Institute for Labour Studies. *Michael Imoudu: A Study in Adventures in the Nigerian Labour Movement.* Ilorin, Nigeria: Michael Imoudu Institute for Labour Studies, 1992.

Ministry of Information. *Pictorial Nigeria.* Lagos: Federal Ministry of Information, 1973.

Moneke, Romanus Okey. *Art, Rebellion and Redemption: A Reading of the Novels of Chinua Achebe.* New York: Peter Lang, 1994.

Norborg, Eke. *The Musical Instruments of the Edo-Speaking People of South-Western Nigeria.* Stockholm: Musikmuseet, 1992.

Nwabara, S.N. *Iboland: A Century of Contact with Britain, 1860–1960.* London: Hodder and Stoughton, 1977.

Nwanunobi, D. Onyeka. *African Social Institutions.* Nsukka: University of Nigeria Press, 1992.

Nwapa, Flora. *Women Are Different.* Trenton, N.J.: 1st African World Press, 1992.

———. *Wives at War, and Other Stories.* Trenton, N.J.: Africa World Press, 1992.

Nwolise, O.B.C. "Blacks in Diaspora: A Case of Neglected Catalysts in Achievement of Nigeria's Foreign Policy Goals." *Journal of Black Studies* 23, no. 1 (September 1992).

Nzimiro, I. *The Nigerian Civil War: A Study in Class Conflict.* Enugu, Nigeria: Fourth Dimension, 1978.

Odetola, Theophilus Olatunde. *Guns, Pens and Words: The Military, the Politician and the Intelligentsia in the Process of Political Mobilization*. Ile-Ife: University Press, 1985.

Ogbaa, Kalu. *Gods, Oracles and Divination: Folkways in Chinua Achebe's Novels*. Trenton, N.J.: Africa World Press, 1992.

Ohonbamu, O. *The Psychology of the Nigerian Revolution*. Ilfracombe, England: Arthur H. Stockwell, 1969.

Ojaide, Niyi. *Midlife*. Ibadan: Heinemann, 1993.

Okiri, Ben. *Astonishing the Gods*. London: Phoenix House, 1995.

Okpara, Enoch Emejuaobi. *Perspectives in Settlement Processes in Igboland: The Case of Okwelle in Okigwe L.G.A., Imo State*. Owerri: Nobel Enterprises, 1990.

Olaleye, Isaac. *The Distant Talking Drum: Poems from Nigeria*. Honesdale, Pa.: Wordsong, 1995.

Olaniyan, Richard. *In the Service of God: The Catholic Church in Oyo Diocese, 1884–1994*. Ile-Ife: Obafemi Awolowo University Press, 1994.

Olorunnisola, Funmilola. *The Royal Eagle of Yoruba*. Ibadan: Bookcraft, 1992.

Omotoso, Kole. *Achebe or Soyinka?: A Study in Contrasts*. West Sussex, England: Hans Zell Publishers, 1996.

Omoyajowo, J. Akinyele. *Diversity in Unity: The Development and Expansion of the Cherubim and Seraphim Church in Nigeria*. Lanham, Md.: University Press of America, 1984.

Onwueme, Tess Akaeke. *Three Plays*. Detroit, Mich.: Wayne State University Press, 1993.

Osuchudwu, Peter. *The Spirit of Umunna and the Development of Small Christian Communities in Igboland*. New York: P. Lang, 1995.

Osundare, Niyi. *Selected Poems*. Oxford: Heinemann, 1992.

Oyeneye, O.Y., and M.O. Shoremi. *Nigerian Life and Culture: A Book of Readings*. Ago-Iwoye, Nigeria: Ogun State University, 1985.

Paden, J. *Religion and Political Culture in Kano*. Berkeley: University of California Press, 1973.

Panel on Nigeria since Independence History Project. *The Society*. Edited by Yusufu Bala Usman. Ibadan: Heinemann, 1989.

———. *Religion*. Edited by J.A. Atanda, Garba Ashiwaju and Yaya Abubakar. Ibadan: Heinemann, 1989.

———. *Culture*. Edited by Peter Ekeh and Garba Ashiwaju. Ibadan: Heinemann, 1989.

Parrinder, Geoffrey. *West African Religion*. London: Harvester Press, 1949.

Peace, A.J. *Choice, Class and Conflict*. Hassocks: Harvester Press, 1979.

Pearce, Tola Ulu, and Toyin Falola (eds.) *Child Health in Nigeria: The Impact of a Depressed Economy*. Aldershot: Avebury, 1994.

Peel, J.D.Y. *Aladura: A Religious Movement among the Yoruba*. London: Oxford University Press, 1968.

———. "Inequality and Action: The Forms of Ijesha Social Conflict." *Canadian Journal of African Studies* 14, no. 3 (1980): 473–502.

Pemberton, John, and S. Afolayan. *Yoruba Sacred Kingship: A Power Like That of the Gods*. Washington: Smithsonian Institution Press, 1996.

Rasmussen, Lissi. *Christian-Muslim Relations in Africa: The Case of Northern Nigeria and Tanzania Compared.* London: British Academic Press, 1983.
Roth, Henry L. *Great Benin: Its Customs, Art and Horrors.* Halifax, Nova Scotia: F. King, 1903.
Sawyerr, Harry. *God, Ancestor or Creator? Aspects of Traditional Belief in Ghana, Nigeria and Sierra Leone.* Harlow, England: Longman, 1970.
Segynola, A.A. *Women Involvement in Rural Small-Scale Food Processing and Distribution Industries in Bendel State.* Nigeria: *Research Report,* 1992.
Seibel, H. Dieter. "Some Aspects of Inter-Ethnic Relations in Nigeria." *The Nigerian Journal of Economics and Social Studies* 9, no. 2 (July 1967): 217–28.
Sieber, Roy. *Sculpture of Northern Nigeria.* New York: Museum of Primitive Art, 1961.
Smith, M.G. "Historical and Cultural Conditions of Political Corruption among the Hausa." *Comparative Studies in Society and History* 6 (1964).
Sodipo, Harold. *A Dynasty of Missioners: Memoirs and Perspectives* Ibadan: Spectrum Books, 1992.
Sofola, J.A. *African Culture and the African Personality (What Makes an African Person African).* Ibadan: African Resources Publisher, 1973.
Sola-Onifade, Bosede. *The Nigerian Woman.* Yaba, Lagos: Julia Virgo Enterprises, 1991.
Soyinka, Wole. *A Dance of the Forest.* London: Oxford University Press, 1963.
———. *Kongi's Harvest.* London: Oxford University Press, 1967.
———. *The Man Died.* London: Rex Collings, 1972.
———. *Season of Anomy.* London: Rex Collings, 1974.
———. *Ake: The Years of Childhood.* London: Rex Collings, 1981.
———. *Isara: A Voyage around Essay.* New York: Random House, 1989.
———. *From Zia, with Love and a Scourge of Hyacinths.* London: Methuen Drama, 1994.
St. Croix, F.N., de. *The Fulani of Northern Nigeria.* Lagos: Government Printer, 1944.
Stone, Robert Henry. *Yoruba Lore and the Universe.* Ibadan: University of Ibadan, 1965.
Sufstkasa, N. *Where Women Work: A Study of Yoruba Women in the Market Place and Home.* Ann Arbor: University of Michigan Press, 1973.
Talbot, P. Amaury. *The Peoples of Southern Nigeria.* 4 vols. London: Oxford University Press, 1926.
———. *Tribes of the Niger Delta.* London: Sheldon Press, 1932.
Tanko, Bauna Peter. *The Christian Association of Nigeria and the Challenge of the Ecumenical Imperative.* 1993.
Taylor, J.V. *Christianity and Politics in Africa.* London: Penguin African Series, 1957.
Temple, C.L. *Native Races and Their Rulers.* 2d ed. London: Frank Cass, 1968.
———, ed. *Notes on the Tribes, Provinces, Emirates and States of the Northern Provinces of Nigeria.* Lagos: Christian Missionary Society Bookshop, 1922.
Thomas, Northcote Whitridge. *Anthropological Report on Ibo-Speaking People of Nigeria.* 1914. Reprint, New York: Negro Universities Press, 1969.
Thomas, T. Ajayi. *History of Juju Music: A History of African Popular Music from Nigeria.* Jamaica, N.Y.: The Organization, 1992.
Tutuola, Amos. *The Palmwine Drinkard.* London: Faber and Faber, 1952.

———. *The Palm-Wine Drinkard; and My Life in the Bush of Ghosts.* New York: Grove Press, 1994.

Uchendu, V.C. *The Igbo of Southeast Nigeria.* New York: Holt, Rinehart and Winston, 1965.

Vaz, Kim Marie. *The Woman with the Artistic Brush: A Life History of Yoruba Batik Artist Nike Davies.* Armonk, N.Y.: M.E. Sharpe, 1995.

Westermann, Diedrich, and M.A. Bryan. *Languages of West Africa.* London: Oxford University Press, 1952.

Williams, G. *State and Society in Nigeria.* Lagos: Afrographika, 1980.

Wright, Derek. *Wole Soyinka Revisited.* New York: Twayne, 1993.

About the Authors

Anthony Oyewole is associate professor of political science at Bennett College in Greensboro, North Carolina. Dr. Oyewole has contributed to many books on Nigeria, including *Democratic Experiment in Nigeria* and *Nigeria since Independence*.

John Lucas is assistant professor at Pierce College in Washington. He received his Ph.D. in political science from Indiana University. His research deals with the political class in Nigeria and business–government relations.